Connecting with Emigrants

A GLOBAL PROFILE OF DIASPORAS

This work is published on the responsibility of the Secretary-General of the OECD. The opinions expressed and arguments employed herein do not necessarily reflect the official views of the Organisation or of the governments of its member countries.

This document and any map included herein are without prejudice to the status of or sovereignty over any territory, to the delimitation of international frontiers and boundaries and to the name of any territory, city or area.

Please cite this publication as:
OECD (2012), *Connecting with Emigrants: A Global Profile of Diasporas*, OECD Publishing.
http://dx.doi.org/10.1787/9789264177949-en

ISBN 978-92-64-17793-2 (print)
ISBN 978-92-64-17794-9 (PDF)

The statistical data for Israel are supplied by and under the responsibility of the relevant Israeli authorities. The use of such data by the OECD is without prejudice to the status of the Golan Heights, East Jerusalem and Israeli settlements in the West Bank under the terms of international law.

Photo credits: Cover © Cienpies Design/Shutterstock.com.

Foreword

The worldwide stock of international migrants has risen significantly in recent decades, from 77 million persons in 1960 to an estimated 214 million in 2010 – an increase of 177% – equivalent to just over 3% of the global population in 2010. In addition, the composition of migrant communities has also gone through major changes with more high-skilled migrants, more migrant women and a diversification of both countries of origin and destination. In the meantime, contacts with the origin countries have been greatly facilitated as a result of both recent advances in information and communication technology and decreasing transportation costs. In this context, the potential impact of diasporas on the development of origin countries has become a crucial issue for governments and development agencies.

The contribution of a diaspora to the economic and social development of its country of origin, however, depends on many factors, such as its size, average skill level, wealth, seniority and degree of organisation. It also depends on the prevailing conditions in the country of origin and on the institutional support the diaspora receives. Governments of both origin and destination countries can facilitate the involvement of diasporas, by supporting networks, by facilitating communications channels with the country of origin, by creating an enabling environment or – more directly – by easing skill mobility and use. In support of this objective, detailed knowledge about diasporas is crucial.

The lack of precise information on diasporas – whom they comprise, where they are, what they are doing and their aspirations for the future – has indeed been a significant impediment to understanding and promoting their role in the development of origin countries. This publication aims at filling that gap by gathering a broad range of statistical information on migrant populations and their children worldwide by origin country, which can help policy makers to tailor policies to the specific needs and circumstances of the population groups in question.

The concept of "diaspora" is relatively fuzzy and diasporas members cannot easily be counted in practice. In theory, it covers all people who maintain some form of attachment to a specific country of origin in relation to their migration background. These people can be migrants themselves or the children or grand-children of migrants. Some of them have the citizenship of the country in question, others have multiple nationalities or only the citizenship of their current country of residence. Ideally, members of the diaspora should be identified through population surveys by self-declaration. In practice, however, because of data limitations, quantitative analyses on diasporas are limited and usually restricted to the first generation of migrants. This publication takes one step further by also considering the children of immigrants and by paying a special attention to those who are not yet members of the diaspora but express the desire to emigrate.

Information presented in this publication gathers all available data sources on migrants by country of origin, building largely on the results of a longstanding co-operation between the Organisation for Economic Co-operation and Development (OECD) and the Agence Française de Développement (AFD) in compiling data on migrants from population censuses in OECD countries and beyond.

This publication contains 140 country notes summarising diaspora sizes, including the number of children of migrants born in the destination countries; the characteristics of emigrant populations (gender, age, education, labour market outcomes); the numbers and main destinations of international students; recent migrant flows to OECD countries; and information on the desire to emigrate among different population groups.

We hope that this publication will help to portray more accurately the migrant communities worldwide in order to facilitate the design of sound policies to better mobilise migrant skills for development in origin countries.

John Martin
Director for Employment, Labour and Social Affairs
OECD

Robert Peccoud
Head of the Research Department
Agence Française de Développement

Acknowledgements

This publication is the result of a joint effort by the OECD and the Research Department of the Agence Française de Développement.

The publication was edited by Jean-Christophe Dumont (OECD), Thomas Mélonio (AFD) and Sarah Widmaier (OECD). The first chapter benefitted from an important contribution from Neli Esipova and Julie Ray with the support of Gallup. Regional chapters were drafted by Jonathan Chaloff (Asia and Oceania); Jean-Baptiste Meyer (Latin America and the Caribbean); Sarah Widmaier (OECD countries); Natalia Buga (non-OECD Europe and Central Asia); Thomas Mélonio (Middle East and North Africa); and Flore Gubert and Jean-Noël Senne (Sub-Saharan Africa). Research and statistical assistance was provided by Philippe Hervé and Véronique Gindrey. Editorial assistance was provided by Nathalie Bienvenu, Marlène Mohier and Sylviane Yvron.

Table of contents

Figures

This book has...

StatLinks

A service that delivers Excel® files from the printed page!

Look for the *StatLinks* at the bottom right-hand corner of the tables or graphs in this book. To download the matching Excel® spreadsheet, just type the link into your Internet browser, starting with the *http://dx.doi.org* prefix.

If you're reading the PDF e-book edition, and your PC is connected to the Internet, simply click on the link. You'll find *StatLinks* appearing in more OECD books.

Acronyms and abbreviations

AFD	French Development Agency
ASEAN	Association of Southeast Asian Nations
CIDESAL	Création d'Incubateurs des Diasporas du Savoir pour l'Amérique Latine
CIS	Commonwealth of Independent States
CPS	US Current Population Survey
DIOC	OECD Database on Immigrants in OECD Countries
DIOC-E	OECD Database on Immigrants in OECD Countries, extended to non-OECD countries
DKN	Diaspora Knowledge Networks
EU-LFS	European Union Labour Force Survey
GDP	Gross domestic product
HDI	Human Development Index
HILDA	Household, Income and Labour Dynamics in Australia Survey
HTA	Hometown associations
ISCED	International Standard Classification of Education
LFS	Labour force survey
MENA	Middle East and North Africa
MICAL	Migration of Knowledge Workers of Latin America
MIDA	Migration for Development in Africa
PISA	Programme for International Student Assessment
PPP	Purchasing power parities
PPS	Personal Public Service
SANSA	South African Network of Skills Abroad
SAR	Special autonomous regions
TOKTEN	Transfer of Knowledge Through Expatriate Nationals
UNDP	United Nations Development Programme
UOE	UNESCO/OECD/Eurostat Education Database
USD	American dollar

Chapter 1

Diasporas – Definition, Data and Dynamics

The potential contribution of a diaspora to the economic and social development of its country of origin will depend on many factors, such as its size, average skill level, wealth, seniority and degree of organisation. This chapter presents a panorama of the diasporas, including children of immigrants, in OECD countries and discusses some of the main challenges and opportunities involved with channeling their economic potential to support the development of origin countries. Looking forward, the chapter also presents data on the desire to emigrate for different population groups, based on the results of the Gallup World Poll Survey.

International migration has risen significantly in recent decades, from 77 million persons in 1960 to 214 million in 2010 – an increase of 177%. Globalisation, technological progress and new means of communication have contributed to these trends by decreasing financial and personal migration costs. Given the size of migrant diasporas and the fact that contacts with the origin countries are greatly facilitated, the potential impact of diasporas on the development of origin countries has become a crucial issue for governments and development agencies.

The lack of precise information on diasporas (see Box 1.1), whom they comprise, where they are, what they are doing and their aspirations for the future – is a significant impediment to understanding and promoting their role in the development of origin countries. This publication aims at filling that gap by gathering a broad range of statistical information on migrant populations and their children worldwide by origin country, which can help policy makers to tailor policies to the population groups in question. The statistical information on which this volume is based was compiled from many different OECD databases as well as from other, non-OECD sources.

Box 1.1. **Diaspora defined**

Historically, the term diaspora has been associated with the notion of forced displacement. To date, there are many definitions of diaspora; some refer not only to the foreign-born or foreign population abroad but also to their descendants. Sheffer's (1986) includes the notion of a collective memory or sentimental link to the origin country, as does the definition proposed by the European Commission (2005, p. 23): "The diaspora from a given country therefore includes not only the nationals from that country living abroad, but also migrants who, living abroad, have acquired the citizenship of their country of residence (often losing their original citizenship in the process) and migrants' children born abroad, whatever their citizenship, as long as they retain some form of commitment to and/or interest in their country of origin or that of their parents. In some extreme cases, such as the Chinese diaspora, people may still feel part of country's diaspora even though their family has been living in another country for several generations".

Cohen (1997) includes in his definition different reasons for leaving the origin country initially; these often involve traumatic events or job seeking. He too raises the aspects of collective memory and myth about the homeland/idealisation of the supposed ancestral home.

The diasporas discussed is limited to both the foreign-born persons (15+) by country of birth and their children who were born in the destination country. Information on the latter group is, however, limited to headcounts, whereas the characteristics of the foreign-born population are much more detailed (see Annex A for more information on underlying data sources and definitions). As data refer mainly to persons living in the OECD, which implies that depending of the size of the migrant population which located outside the OECD area, the size of the diaspora may be more or less underestimated.

Data were culled from 140 country notes summarising diaspora sizes, including the number children of migrants born in the destination countries; the characteristics of emigrant populations (gender, age, education, labour market outcomes); the numbers and main destinations of international students; recent migrant flows to OECD countries; and information on the attitudes to emigrate of different population groups. The country note information is grouped into six regions: Asia and Oceania; Latin America and the Caribbean; OECD countries; Non-OECD Europe and Central Asia; Middle East and North Africa; and Sub-Saharan Africa. The situation in each region is introduced by a separate chapter, which looks at historical migration trends, the main characteristics of diasporas originating from the region, and likely future developments and challenges.

The potential of a diaspora as a source of economic and social development in origin countries and whether diasporas could help foster development depend on its characteristics, such as size, composition, skill levels and degree of concentration, but also on the degree of integration into the destination countries and the economic, political and social environment in origin countries. The first section of this chapter presents the panorama of the diasporas today; the second section discusses the financial and human capital potential resources of the diasporas and summarises some of the main challenges and opportunities involved with channelling these to assist the development of origin countries. The third section presents data on the desire to emigrate and potential emigration rates by origin countries and different population groups, based on the results of the Gallup World Poll Survey.

1. A profile of today's diasporas

Many diasporas are important and growing

The potential contribution of a diaspora to the economic and social development of its country of origin will depend on many factors, such as its size, average skill level, wealth, seniority and degree of organisation. It will also depend on the prevailing conditions in the country of origin and on the institutional support the diaspora receives. Governments of origin and destination countries can indeed facilitate the involvement of diasporas, by supporting networks, by facilitating communication channels with the country of origin, by creating an enabling environment, or – more directly – by easing skill mobility and use. In this regard, the capacity to characterise the profile of diasporas is instrumental.

The largest diasporas in the OECD area are from other OECD countries, Asian countries and North African countries

In 2005/06, 89 million migrants lived in the OECD area, representing approximately 46% of the total migrant population worldwide; this was a 23% increase over the 2000 figure (Widmaier and Dumont, 2011). The largest emigrant population in the OECD comes from other OECD countries (38 million) followed by Asia and Oceania (15 million), South and Central America (14 million) and European non-OECD countries and Central Asian countries (11 million) (Figure 1.1). Migrants from Sub-Saharan Africa, the Middle East and North Africa account only for 4.5% and 7.8% respectively of the total foreign-born population in the OECD area – significantly below their share in world population. However, Sub-Saharan African migrant communities register the fastest growth, with a 39% increase on average since 2000. In the meantime, emigration from the OECD area increased only by 13%.

The largest foreign-born populations in the OECD area are from Mexico (11 million), the United Kingdom (3.4 million), Germany (3 million) and Poland (2.8 million), followed by India and China, each with 2.7 million migrants in the OECD area (Figure 1.1 and Table 1.1).

Figure 1.1. **Number of emigrants by origin country, 2005/06**

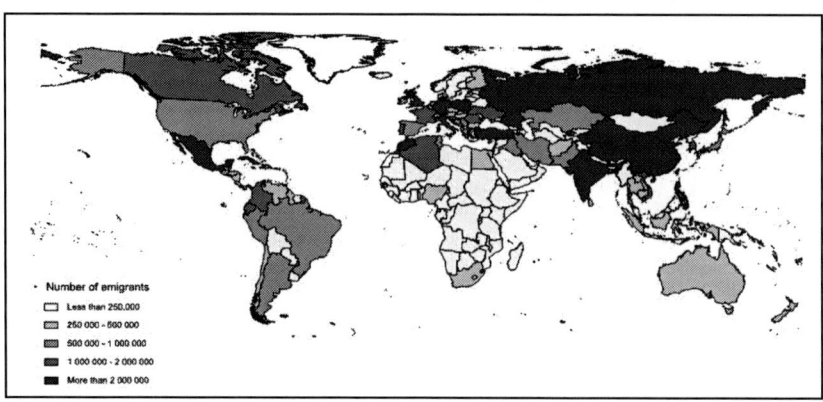

Source: OECD Database on Immigrants in OECD Countries (DIOC 2005-06).

Data on the number of migrants are complemented by data on the number of descendants born in the destination countries. By adding the numbers of children of migrants born in the destination countries disaggregated by their parents' country of origin,[1] the Mexican diaspora in the OECD area reaches about 20 million persons, followed by the Italian diaspora (5.2 million) and the German diaspora (4.1 million) (Figure 1.2, Table 1.1). The number of migrants and their children exceeds 1 million persons for 31 origin countries.

Figure 1.2. **Migrants and native-born children of migrants by origin in OECD countries, 15 years old and over, 2008**

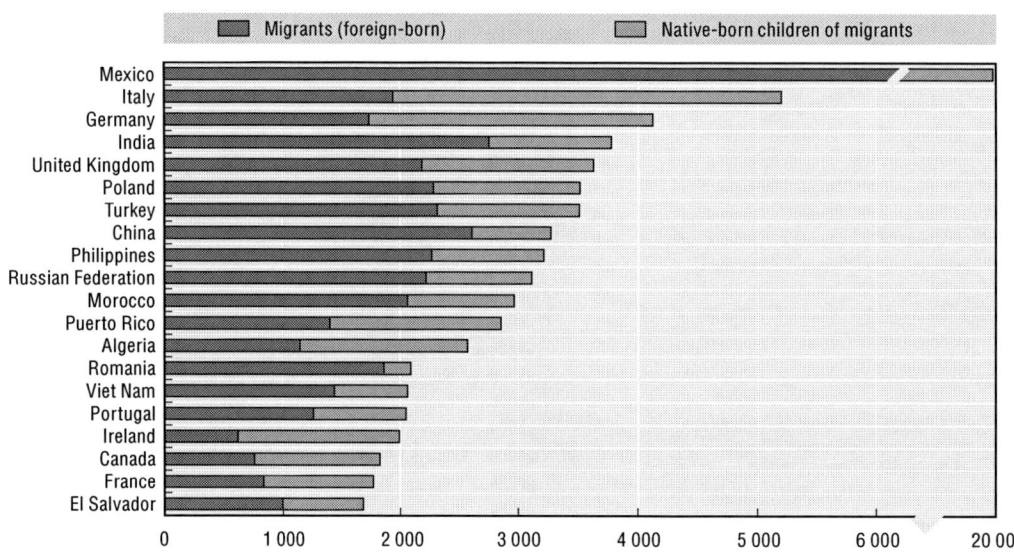

Note: OECD destination countries covered in this graph include all OECD European countries, the United States and Australia.
Source: European Union Labour Force Survey (EU-LFS) 2008; US Current Population Survey (CPS) 2008; Household, Income and Labour Dynamics in Australia (HILDA) Survey 2009.

StatLink ᴍᴤ᠊ᴤ *http://dx.doi.org/10.1787/888932671795*

Table 1.1. Key indicators on main migrant groups in OECD countries

	Migration flows to the OECD in 2010 (thousands)	Remittances received in 2010 (USD million)	Total number of international students in 2009 (thousands)	Diaspora[1] in 2008 (thousands)	Number of people aged 15 and over (thousands)	Growth rate since 2000 (%)	Women (%)	15-25 years old (%)	Highly educated (%)	Emigration rate[2] 2005/06 (%)	Emigration rate of the highly educated 2005/06 (%)
					Migrant population in 2005/06						
Total[3]	4 656	436 944	2 499[4]	124 886	90 519	24.2	51.0	14.9	32.8	1.9	5.0
OECD	1 614	132 301	701	59 784	39 545	15.6	50.2	9.4	33.5	3.8	3.8
Asia and Oceania	1 367	174 938	915	18 094	14 902	27.7	52.6	15.7	34.8	0.6	4.1
Latin America and the Caribbean	489	35 838	118	20 391	13 940	35.8	52.6	12.7	29.8	4.4	10.6
Non-OECD Europe and Central Asia	580	37 319	161	13 048	11 095	36.9	53.6	16.5	30.3	3.9	5.9
Middle East and North Africa	316	37 859	175	9 169	6 948	22.5	45.5	21.3	35.9	2.8	7.6
Sub-Saharan Africa	290	18 689	151	4 399	4 089	38.7	49.3	17.0	33.4	1.0	13.3
Mexico	157	22 048	25	20 194	10 784	29.4	44.2	16.6	7.4	13.0	7.2
United Kingdom	118	7 399	20	3 628	3 449	6.4	50.8	5.5	40.2	6.5	11.6
Germany	118	11 338	67	4 125	3 039	4.4	56.7	10.8	33.8	4.1	7.3
Poland	226	7 575	29	3 517	2 849	31.0	54.3	13.6	26.8	8.2	15.8
India	253	54 035	180	3 776	2 775	40.8	47.0	9.8	63.3	0.4	4.2
China	509	53 038	448	3 270	2 724	31.9	54.0	15.8	44.7	0.3	1.7
Turkey	64	993	28	3 510	2 627	24.3	47.6	10.3	8.3	4.8	5.2
Philippines	167	21 423	9	3 213	2 502	29.1	61.4	9.5	51.9	4.4	8.0
Russian Federation	69	5 264	27	3 112	2 472	40.2	56.4	17.7	31.2	2.0	4.7
Italy	78	6 803	26	5 200	2 361	0.0	46.5	3.0	15.6	4.5	7.2
Morocco	124	6 423	39	2 967	2 263	35.1	45.1	11.5	15.3	9.6	16.4
Viet Nam	88	8 260	36	2 060	1 758	16.0	51.4	8.4	27.7	2.9	15.4
Romania	289	3 952	22	2 089	1 694	75.5	53.5	14.5	23.6	8.5	19.9
Korea	76	8 708	119	208	1 653	14.3	56.6	14.8	45.1	0.6	0.8
Algeria	35	2 044	21	2 572	1 461	10.3	48.2	5.0	19.3	5.9	12.9
Ukraine	81	5 607	13	1 568	1 423	43.8	58.4	11.4	39.7	3.4	3.9
Portugal	44	3 540	11	2 048	1 382	9.6	49.6	6.5	8.6	13.5	11.6
France	92	15 629	50	1 766	1 298	13.4	55.4	8.5	39.4	2.5	5.0
Canada	42	..	44	1 825	1 122	5.0	55.1	9.3	47.1	4.1	6.9
El Salvador	23	3 449	2	1 683	1 107	32.5	47.2	12.3	10.6	20.1	22.7

StatLink http://dx.doi.org/10.1787/888932674911

1. Diaspora includes migrants and native-born children of migrants aged 15 and over. OECD destinations include OECD European countries, the United States and Australia.
2. OECD countries are all included in the OECD total but are excluded from the regional groupings.
3. The emigration rates are defined as the share of people born in one country who are currently living in OECD countries (other than their own country of birth).
4. Of which 277 000 students with unspecified country of origin.

Source: OECD *International Migration Database;* World Bank Remittances Data; UNESCO/OECD/Eurostat Education Database; European Union Labour Force Survey 2008; OECD *Database on Immigrants in OECD Countries (DIOC 2005/06).*

In only one of five migrant populations is the number of native-born children of migrants higher than the number of their parents. This pattern reflects the seniority of migration and is hence most pronounced for European countries. The number of migrants' descendants is much higher than the number of first generation migrants, for example in the case of Ireland (69%), Belgium (65%) and Italy (63%). The opposite is true for more recent migrant populations, such as Romania (11%) and Ecuador (15%), but also China (20%) and India (27%).

Often, children of migrants will keep a strong link with their parents' country of birth. They may return for short periods (diaspora tourism), may be engaged there in non-profit operations, or may utilise their skills and networks to develop specific business activities. A good number of these children may have the nationality of the country of birth of their parents, or have multiple citizenships. In any case, greater consideration should be given to the large and growing number of migrants' descendants in OECD countries when designing policies to support diasporas' engagement. The data presented in the country notes of this publication is a first step toward more properly identifying the size and the location of this group.[2]

Destinations have become more diverse between 2000 and 2005/06

About 42% of migrants in the OECD area are living in the United States, slightly fewer than in Europe (44%). Overall, migration to the OECD area seems slightly more dispersed in 2005/06 than in 2000; the importance of the five main destination countries (Figure 1.3) has decreased substantially in the overall stock of migrants from nearly all regions of origin. The exceptions, non-OECD European and Central Asian countries, are notably due to the increasing importance of Germany as the main destination country. Spain recorded an important increase of migrants from Latin America and the Caribbean, and to a lesser extent from non-OECD European and Central Asian countries. In 2005/06, the United Kingdom became the new main destination of migration from Sub-Saharan Africa, passing ahead of the United States. The picture by individual origin countries is even more diverse. Migrants from China, Romania and Poland, for instance, have travelled to a wider range of destinations, while migrants from India, the Russian Federation and Turkey seem to be more concentrated in 2005/06 than they were in 2000.

Countries in Latin America and the Caribbean have the highest total emigration rates

In 2005/06, about 2% of the total population 15 and over lives in the OECD area and no longer in its country of birth. The highest emigration rates[3] are observed for Latin America and the Caribbean (4.3%) and the lowest rates for Asia (0.6%) (Table 1.1) but total emigration rates vary largely across countries, even within the same region. The emigration rate for Morocco, for instance, is close to 9%, whereas corresponding figures for North Africa and Sub-Saharan Africa are, respectively, 2.2% and 0.9%.

The highest emigration rates are generally recorded for countries with smaller populations, notably small island states. In 2005/06, one-third of the persons born in Jamaica were living in OECD countries, and more than 20% of the population originating from Cape Verde, Trinidad and Tobago, Malta and Fiji were in the OECD area. In contrast, large countries – such as India, China, the United States, Indonesia, Brazil, Japan, Bangladesh, Pakistan and Nigeria – all had less than 0.1% of their population in the OECD area. Among all 35 larger countries (with a total population aged 15+ of over 20 million), Mexico is the only country with a double-digit emigration rate (13%).

Countries with a high population growth tend to show limited increases, or even decreases, in emigration rates between 2000 and 2005/06. For example, Eastern African

Figure 1.3. **Share of five main destination countries in the total stock of migrants aged 15 and over by region of origin, 2000 and 2005/06**

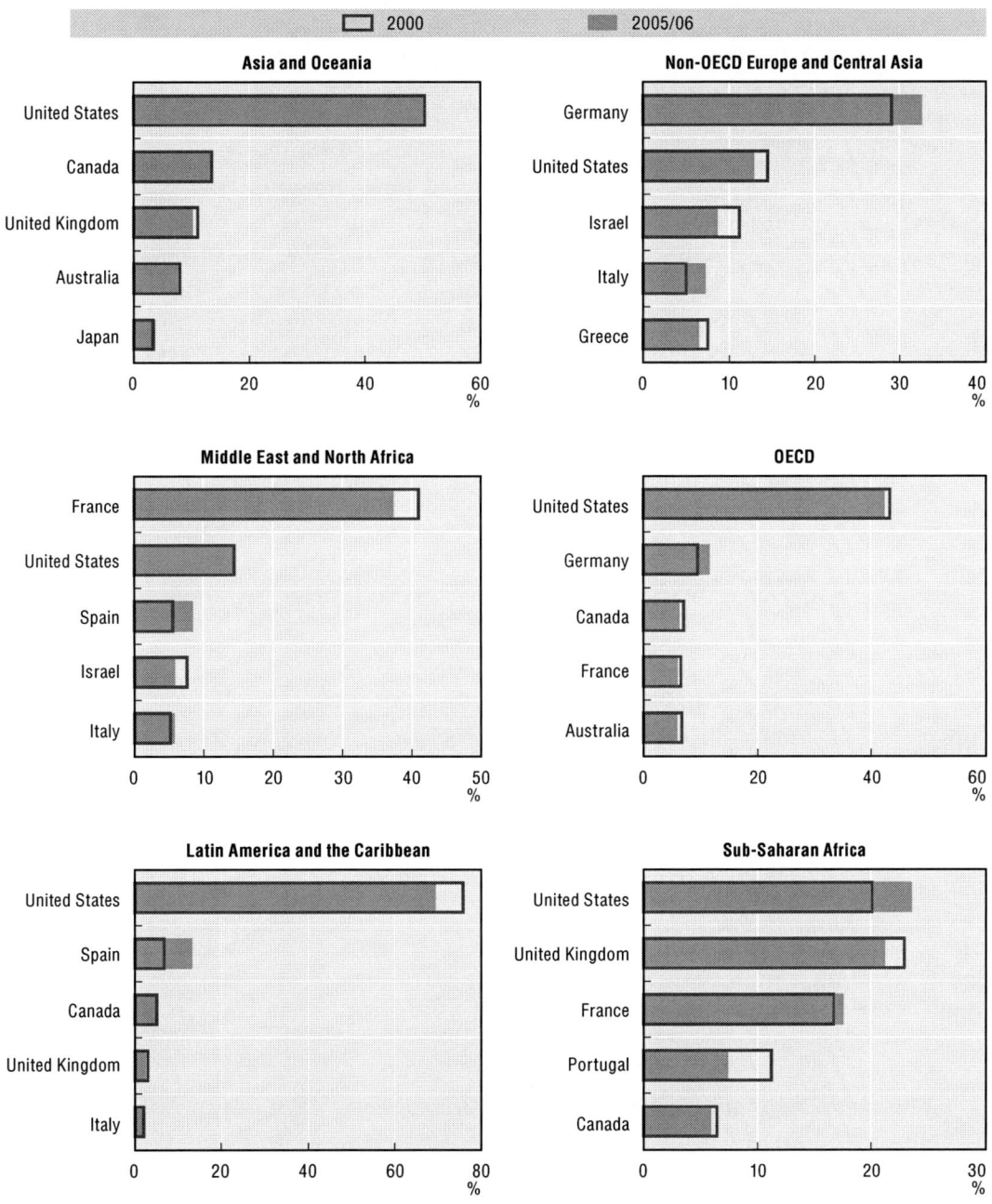

Source: OECD Database on Immigrants in OECD Countries (DIOC 2000 and 2005/06).

StatLink ⫘⫘ http://dx.doi.org/10.1787/888932671814

countries such as Rwanda, Burundi and Eritrea experienced particularly rapid increases in their populations between 2000 and 2005/06, but limited change in emigration rates. Similarly, populations in Syria, Jordan and Yemen grew by more than 18% over the period considered, but registered little change in total emigration. Paradoxically, the countries that have contributed most to the growth in immigration in the OECD area do not necessarily have strong demographic dynamics. This is the case, for instance, with the countries from Central and Eastern Europe, China and Mexico.

Largest migrant flows come from other OECD countries and China

In 2010, about 5 million persons relocated to the OECD area.[4] One out of three immigrants came from another OECD country – the largest inflow with 1.6 million persons, followed by migrants from Asia, with 1.3 million people. Migration flows from all regions increased post-2000, especially from other OECD countries and Asia (Figure 1.4). Flows from Latin America and the Caribbean peaked in 2006 and then decreased, returning to their 2000 level by 2010 because of the great recession, which hit hard the two main destination countries, the United States and Spain. Migration flows from non-OECD European and Central Asian countries increased sharply in 2007 following the accession of Bulgaria and Romania to the European Union, and then decreased to the level of 2000 in 2010. Although migrant flows from Sub-Saharan Africa and countries in the Middle East and North Africa are the smallest in absolute numbers, they almost doubled between 2000 and 2010. In 2010 China was the single most important country of origin (508 000), followed by Romania (277 000), India (228 000), Poland (221 000) and Mexico (180 000).

Figure 1.4. **Migration flows to the OECD by main region of origin, 2000-10**

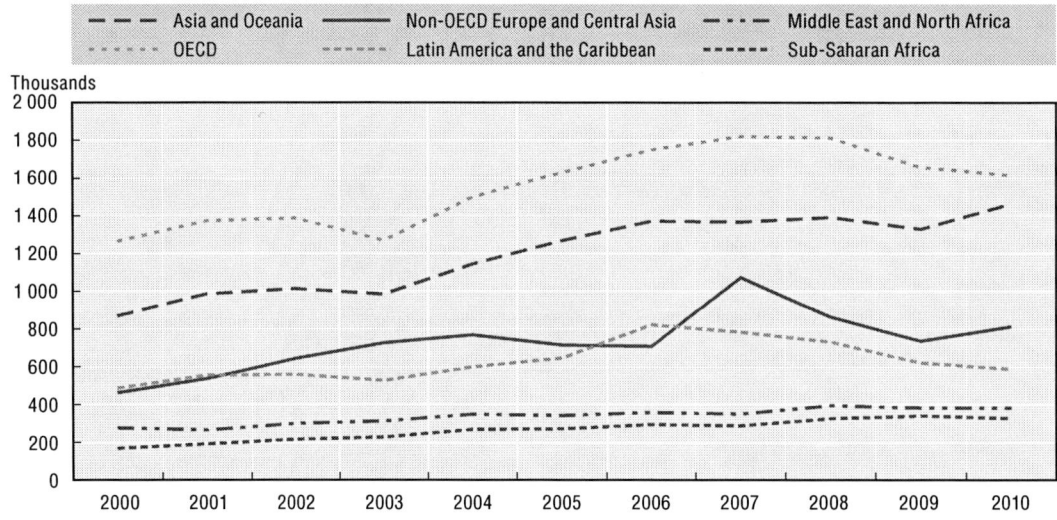

Note: This chart does not include data of intra-European migrant flows for France and Portugal.
Source: OECD International Migration Database.

StatLink ⧉ http://dx.doi.org/10.1787/888932671833

The main destination countries are the United States (20%), Germany (11%), Spain (9%), Italy (8%) and the United Kingdom (6%). Migrant flows from the OECD are more dispersed than flows from other regions. Migrant flows from Latin America and the Caribbean are for the most part concentrated, notably in the United States, Spain and (to a smaller extent) Italy.

Diasporas are mainly working age and active

Young persons are overrepresented in migrant communities from non-OECD European, Central Asian and Sub-Saharan African countries

Young migrants (foreign-born persons aged 15 to 24) represent only 12% of the total emigrant population 15 and over. However, they are overrepresented in migrant populations from non-OECD European and Central Asian countries (16%) and Sub-Saharan

Africa (15%). Among migrants from the Russian Federation, one out of five is between 15 and 24 years old. In contrast, migration from Italy and Algeria, which took place mainly in the 1960 and 1970s, is characterised by relatively small shares of youth (3% and 5%, respectively).

Migrants from Latin America and Sub-Saharan Africa have more favourable labour market outcomes

In the OECD area, the average employment-to-population ratio for migrants (15-64) reached 59% in 2005/06. However, labour market outcomes of immigrants vary significantly depending on the region and country of origin. The highest regional (weighted) average employment is observed for Latin American as well as Sub-Sahara African migrants, with 65% each. Migrant populations from Namibia, Zimbabwe, Mozambique and South Africa have among the highest employment in the OECD area, with rates of over 75%. The lowest employment rates are observed for diasporas from the Middle East and North Africa, notably Saudi Arabia, Qatar, Libya and Algeria each with less than 40%).

The pattern of unemployment rates is very much in line with these findings. On average, the highest unemployment rates for the foreign-born population aged 15 to 64 are observed for people from Middle East and North African origin countries (17%). The lowest unemployment rates are registered for migrants from Asia and Oceania (7%) and OECD countries (8%). The most heterogeneous region in this respect is Sub-Saharan Africa. Migrants from South Africa (4%), Tanzania and Mozambique (6% each) fare relatively well in OECD countries, but migrants from Comoros (30%), Rwanda (27%) and the Democratic Republic of the Congo (24%) face particularly high unemployment rates. Cross-country differences in terms of labour market outcomes largely reflect differences in the labour market conditions of the destination countries but are also related to the composition of migration by category of entry, duration of stay and key socioeconomic characteristics.

In many OECD countries, labour shortages and recruitment difficulties were increasing prior to the recent economic crisis, both for high-skilled occupations and for low-skilled occupations in agriculture, construction, industrial cleaning and domestic services. Some countries have registered significant inflows of labour migrants in these occupations, but foreign workers who took the jobs did not necessarily always have low education levels; this gave rise to the phenomenon of skill mismatch termed "overqualification". Highly educated migrant workers tend to be more exposed to this problem than their native-born counterparts. On average in the OECD area, 30% of immigrants holding a university degree were working in intermediate or low-skilled jobs compared with 21% of those native-born. The figure increased by more than 4 percentage points for the foreign-born between 2000 and 2005/06 and the gap with those native-born widened.

Comparisons of levels of overqualification should be formed with some caution, as these may be influenced by differences in national classification of education systems or occupations. Nonetheless, mismatches seem to be more of a problem for immigrants in Southern European countries, the United Kingdom and Ireland – countries where immigration flows are relatively recent. In the United Kingdom, the overqualification rate increased by more than 10 percentage points between 2000 and 2005/06, partly because of the importance of recent arrivals of highly educated workers from new EU member states in the context of the 2004 EU enlargement. The problem also holds for migrants from non-OECD European and Central Asian countries in the OECD area, with 49% of highly educated persons working in low- or medium-skilled jobs.

How to reinforce the impact of migrants on the home-country labour market

Well-integrated migrant populations in the destination countries increase the potential role of diasporas in origin countries through assets and savings, as well as job-specific skills acquired abroad. Personal or entrepreneurial investments in the origin countries based on the savings of migrants could be fostered by favourable investment conditions, good infrastructure and transparency of the legal processes, as well as better information on how to set up projects and businesses and where the opportunities are. This includes suspending restrictions on non-residents wishing to purchase property (as was done in India in 2003), introducing tax incentives for investment, helping returning migrants set up small enterprises, and creating employment or offering incentives for diaspora members to invest in former state-owned enterprises. Origin country governments could build personal investment schemes (*e.g.* for the purchase of a home) and offer technical assistance and information. More generally, it is important to improve the business environment and to build awareness of business opportunities for potential foreign resident investors, including emigrants.

Some of the diaspora may wish to return home permanently. To maximise the gain from returning migrants, reintegration programmes and counselling before and after return are crucial. This can include help in getting capital for investment, and assistance in finding adequate jobs enabling migrants to fully use their skills, notably those acquired abroad. India and China are examples where origin countries promoted returns and a large transfer of knowledge to the home country economy occurred. Skills and social capital acquired abroad can also help to foster research and technological development in the home country. However, major obstacles remain: lack of access to information on work opportunities; difficulties transferring rights accumulated in the host country, such as pensions; and concerns of the parents about integrating the children of migrants born and educated in the host country.

2. Diasporas as carriers of substantial financial and human resources

Many migrants are highly educated

While there may be a greater number of low-educated immigrants – more than 32 million persons in 2005/06 – still, about 26 million immigrants holding a university degree were living in the OECD area at that time. On average, one-third of the migrant population in that area is highly educated, *i.e.* holds at least a first-stage tertiary degree. Almost half of the Asian migrants are highly educated, as are about 36% of those originating from Sub-Saharan Africa, while only about one in four migrants from other regions holds a university diploma. The migrant communities with the highest share of university graduates come from Chinese Taipei (70%), India (63%), and Nigeria (61%). The least educated emigrant populations, with less than 10% university graduates, are from Mexico (7%), Turkey (8%) and Portugal (9%).

In absolute numbers, highly educated migrants are from India (1.7 million), the United Kingdom (1.3 million), the Philippines (1.3 million), China (1.2 million) and Germany (1 million) (Figure 1.5). These five largest highly educated migrant populations account for about 26% of all tertiary-educated migrants in the OECD area.

Since 2000, the number of tertiary-educated migrants in the OECD area has increased significantly. Among the largest emigrant populations, the growth rate of the highly educated represents over 60% for the Indian (67%), Mexican (69%), Polish (61%) and Romanian (63%) migrant communities. For about 15 rather diverse countries (*e.g.* Ecuador, Malawi, Afghanistan and Bulgaria), the number of highly educated emigrants even doubled between 2000 and 2005/06.

Figure 1.5. **Number and share of highly educated emigrants in the OECD area, by main origin country, 2000 and 2005/06**

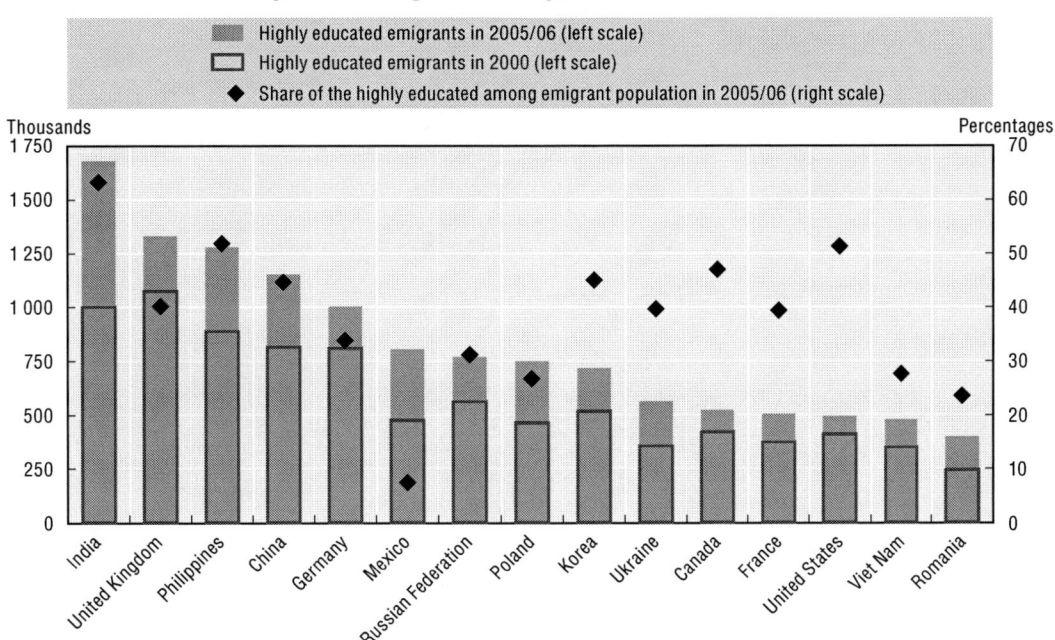

Note: Highly educated emigrants are defined as those holding a tertiary diploma.
Source: OECD Database on Immigrants in OECD Countries (DIOC 2000 and 2005/06).
StatLink ᵃ⁵ᵖ http://dx.doi.org/10.1787/888932671852

A large share of total international students come from China, India and Korea

Of the nearly 2.5 million international students in the OECD area in 2009, about 40% come from Asia and more than 30% from OECD countries. International students from other regions only account for between 5% and 8% of the total. The number of Chinese students in the OECD area is by far the largest – almost half a million – followed by India and Korea, with 180 000 and 119 000, respectively. The countries ranking next, Germany and France, respectively register 67 000 and 50 000 international students in other OECD countries. International students tend to prefer English-speaking OECD countries – notably the United States, the United Kingdom and Australia, which together host 56% of all international students in the OECD area.

The "brain drain"

In all regions of origin outside the OECD area, highly educated persons are more likely to emigrate to OECD member countries than total population. Emigration rates of the highly educated born within the OECD area are the lowest compared with other regions, and on a par with the emigration rate of total population from the OECD (3.8%) (Figure 1.6). Sub-Saharan Africa (13.3%) and Latin America and the Caribbean (10.6%) are the regions with the highest emigration rates of the highly educated. As for individual origin countries, more than 75% of the highly educated born in Barbados, Guyana, Haiti and Trinidad and Tobago live in the OECD area. The out-migration of the highly educated is especially problematic for some occupations, such as health professionals in small origin countries (Box 1.2).

Figure 1.6. **Emigration rates of the highly educated by origin country, 2005/06**

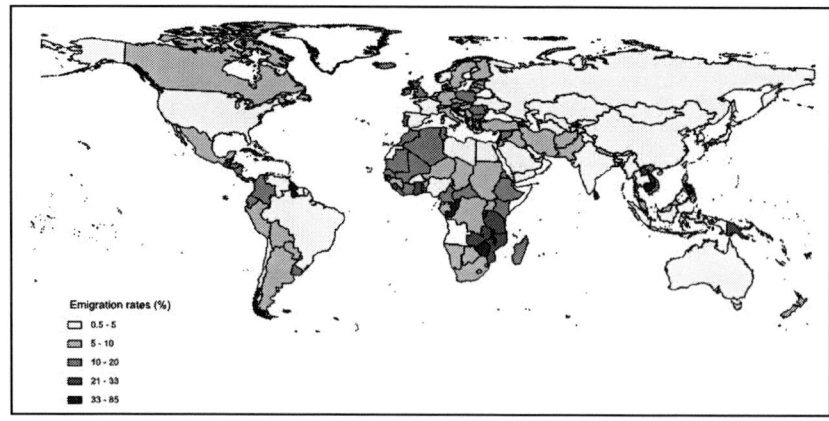

Source: OECD Database on Immigrants in OECD Countries (DIOC 2005/06); Barro, R. and J.-W. Lee (2010), "A New Data Set of Educational Attainment in the World, 1950-2010", NBER Working Paper No. 15902, Cambridge, MA.

Box 1.2. **The brain drain in the medical profession**

The number of foreign-born doctors in OECD countries is largest for Asian non-OECD countries, accounting for about 164 000 persons in 2000; the second largest is for OECD origin countries, with 105 000 foreign-born doctors working in other OECD countries (Annex C). As to the number of foreign-born nurses, OECD origin countries rank first, sending about 232 000 nurses to other OECD countries, while about 189 000 nurses born in Asian non-OECD countries work in OECD member countries. Filipino-born nurses (110 000) and Indian-born doctors (56 000) each represent about 15% of all immigrant nurses and doctors in the OECD area. The United Kingdom and Germany are the second and third most important origin countries for foreign-born nurses and doctors working in the OECD area. About half of all foreign-born doctors or nurses work in the United States, almost 40% in Europe and the remainder in Australia and Canada.

The emigration rates for doctors are particularly high for Caribbean countries and a number of African countries, such as Mozambique, Angola, Sierra Leone, Tanzania and Liberia, where more than half of the doctors worked in the OECD area in 2000. In some of these countries, the high emigration rate is combined with a small number of doctors in the home country, creating an alarming situation for the domestic health sector. On the other hand, for large origin countries such as India or China, the high number of health professionals working overseas does not seem to have particularly affected domestic density, at least at an aggregate level.

More recent data indicate a further increase of the number of foreign-born health professionals in the OECD area. Around 2005, taking into account only the two main destination countries – the United States and the United Kingdom – the number of Indian-trained doctors increased to about 75 000, and Pakistan and Canadian-trained doctors each reached 19 000.

Source: OECD (2008), The Looming Crisis in the Health Workforce. How Can OECD Countries Respond?, OECD Publishing, Paris, www.oecd.org/health/workforce.

Although educational attainment levels increased in most origin countries, the emigration rates of the highly educated also increased. This indicates a faster outflow of university graduates than the increase in their number in the origin country.[5] The emigration rate of the highly educated increased significantly in upper-middle-income countries, from 3.6% in 2000 to 5.2% in 2005/06 – but also in low-income countries, from 4.2% to 5.4%.

The largest increases in emigration rates of the highly educated are observed in Congo, Zimbabwe and Malawi, with all about 20 percentage points more in 2005/06 than in 2000. North Africa is the only region in which a slight decline in the emigration rates of highly educated is observed, primarily due to a decrease in Morocco. The rapid increase in the share of highly educated there has not been absorbed by the increase in overall out-migration and the selectivity of emigration.

Highly educated women have higher emigration rates than men

On average, 51% of the migrant population in OECD countries in 2005/06 are women. Women are overrepresented in European non-OECD migrant populations (54%), Asian migrant populations and South and Central American migrant populations (53% each). By contrast, men are more likely to migrate from the Middle East and North Africa (45%). The share of women is over 60% for three Asian countries – Thailand, Japan and the Philippines – but also for Finland. The share of women among emigrants may be explained by historical migration trends, with women being overrepresented in older and recent migration waves. In addition, the characteristics of migration policies (i.e. the possibility of family migration and reunification), but also the needs of the labour markets (i.e. in sectors or occupations in which employment of women is dominant, such as domestic services or the care sector), have in some countries encouraged more female than male migration.

In about two-thirds of origin countries, the emigration rate of highly educated women is higher than the emigration rate of highly educated men. Gender differences are largest in Sub-Saharan African countries, such as Malawi, Sierra Leone and Zimbabwe. Emigration of highly educated women is more pronounced in low-income countries, and increased further from 2000 to 2005/06 than the emigration of highly educated men. The reason may be that gender inequalities in poor countries tend to be larger, leading to greater incentives to migrate for better opportunities abroad and higher possible returns from emigration for women than for men.

Mobilising migrants' skills for development in home countries

Given the right conditions, the human capital of diasporas can be an important source of economic development in the origin country. Search networks and Diaspora Knowledge Networks (DKN) facilitate transfers of knowledge, skills and expertise, as well as the creation of business networks. In search networks, the main players are diaspora members who have become key executives in relevant companies and have important business networks and influence to promote diaspora entrepreneurship. The programmes offer networking, monitoring, training and investment, as well as venture capital and partnerships (Newland and Tanaka, 2010). The potential of these networks is illustrated by the successful search network Globalscot[6] implemented by Scottish Enterprise. This network consists of about 600 Scots all over the world, using their expertise, contacts and influence to help Scotland-based enterprises develop projects in that country. The network is interdisciplinary, identifies new projects, and brings together organisations (MacRae and Wright, 2006).

DKNs may help to benefit from highly educated expatriates through networks, in which the scientific diaspora engage as partner in the development of the origin country, i.e. research partnership programmes or investment in research projects (Wickramasekara, 2009). The South African Network of Skills Abroad (SANSA) – initiated by the University of Cape Town, the Institute for Research and Development and the French Development Agency (AFD) – is an example of a DKN, linking academics, researchers and other persons working in science and technology in South Africa and emigrants abroad (Marks, 2004). Diaspora networks usually need to be supported by origin country governments to develop and be sustainable. Further, sustained alliances with established development actors should be built, and collective development projects initiated or implemented by diaspora organisations and their members should be supported (de Haas, 2006).

Skills and knowledge can be transferred upon return to the origin country, even if the return is temporary. The Dutch IntEnt project for migrant entrepreneurs and the TOKTEN (Transfer of Knowledge Through Expatriate Nationals) Programme of the UNDP are interesting examples of such programmes to favour skill mobility without imposing return. They bring knowledge, expertise and experience of qualified emigrants back to the origin country through short-term consultancy missions. Another well-known initiative is the Migration for Development in Africa (MIDA) programme, which focuses on "brain circulation" and temporary return. An evaluation in 2008 of the MIDA Great Lakes programme revealed that diasporas had little interest in virtual skill transfer, and that capacity building by virtual volunteers was hampered because of limited access to computers or Internet. Such capacity-building projects actually need to be developed in co-operation with governments in the origin countries. Furthermore, more systematic evaluation of the impact of these programmes, which often remain limited in scope, is clearly necessary (Terrazas, 2010).

Diasporas have substantial financial resources

In 2010, most remittances worldwide were transferred to Asia and to OECD countries. These transfers are nine and seven times higher than remittances to Sub-Saharan Africa, and about four times higher compared with remittances sent to other regions.

The largest remittance flows are sent to India and China (USD 54 billion and USD 53 billion, respectively in 2010). These financial flows are only slightly lower than remittances sent to Latin America (USD 38 billion), non-OECD European and Central Asian countries (USD 37 billion), the Middle East and North Africa (USD 36 billion) and to Sub-Saharan Africa (USD 19 billion), taken together. In small and developing countries, remittances can contribute significantly to household incomes. Indeed, in about ten countries, remittances represent more than 20% of GDP per capita (i.e. 35% in Tajikistan, 24% in Lesotho, 23% in Nepal, 22% in Lebanon and 21% in Kyrgyzstan).

Remittance flows to all regions more than doubled between 2000 and 2010, with the highest increase in non-OECD European and Central Asian countries (+466%), Asia and Oceania (+428%) and Sub-Saharan Africa (+370%), and the smallest (though not negligible) increase in OECD countries (+131%) and Latin America and the Caribbean (+180%). However, all regions except Asia saw a decline in remittances following the financial crisis in 2008. The largest impact of the crisis is observed for remittance flows to OECD and to non-OECD European and Central Asian countries, which decreased most in absolute terms between 2008 and 2009 (by USD 13.3 billion and USD 10.2 billion, respectively). From 2009 to 2010 remittances to all regions increased again, albeit never reaching their pre-crisis level.

Mobilising remittances for development in origin countries

Remittances sent by migrants to their families back home represent one channel through which diasporas can have an impact in their countries of origin. Remittances represent one of the largest sources of foreign currency. But they are mainly private, intra-familial flows; they have positive direct effects on the socioeconomic conditions of the recipients, but less obvious macroeconomic impacts (OECD, 2005; Adams and Page,

2005; Torres and Kuznetsov, 2006; Fajnzylber and López, 2007). Furthermore, the potential positive impact of remittances on the community through short-term multiplier effects are expected to be limited, because remittances are largely used for basic consumption. Increasing evidence suggests, however, that remittances are also largely used for investing in education and health, notably for children, and so have a direct impact on human capital accumulation.

Community or hometown associations (HTAs) can have an important role in collecting remittances for the benefit of local communities. HTAs pool remittances based on an organised network of emigrants from the same village, state or region. Their use is flexible and can be targeted at specific investment purposes according to local needs. Although there are no systematic estimates of the flow of community remittances, it seems that they represent only a small share of total flows. However, even small they can still have a positive impact on local infrastructure and development as illustrated by the famous "tres por uno" Mexican programme. Sustainability of these projects is nonetheless an important challenge in many cases.

In order to foster remittance flows, diasporas should be better informed about transfer mechanisms and costs. Several OECD countries and international organisations have developed internal portals were migrants can easily compare the cost of transferring money, helping through these tools to increase competition between different providers.

3. Looking forward: the profile of prospective migrants[7]

To better illustrate emerging trends in possible diaspora formation and possible changes in global diasporas, Gallup collects data on the desire to emigrate by country of origin and different socio-demographic characteristics. This information allows identification of the origin countries that are mostly affected by emigration, the population groups that are most likely to emigrate, and how this evolution can change current diasporas' profiles. Results of these data are presented in the next section.

Who are the prospective migrants?

Gallup collected data on the desire to emigrate in 146 countries from 2008 to 2010. About 14% of world's adults – roughly 630 million persons aged 15 and over – would like to move to another country permanently if they had the opportunity to do so. However, less than one-tenth of them – about 48 million persons aged 15 and over – are planning to move in the following year, and less than half of those who are in the planning stages – about 19 million people – are already engaged in the necessary preparations for moving, such as applying for visas and purchasing tickets (Figure 1.7).

People are more likely to express their wish to migrate for temporary work than for permanent work

People are nearly twice as likely to say they would like to migrate for temporary work (26%) as to leave permanently (14%). Across the 119 countries and areas surveyed in 2009 and 2010, an estimated 1.1 billion people wish to migrate to work temporarily to another country. The profiles of those who would like to move temporarily and permanently are, however, similar. Potential temporary migrants tend to be young, have a secondary education or higher, and are usually underemployed. Overall, men are more inclined than women to say they would like to migrate for temporary work, but the gender gap closes among those currently in the workforce.

Figure 1.7. **Global desire to migrate permanently, plans and preparations to move, 2008-10**

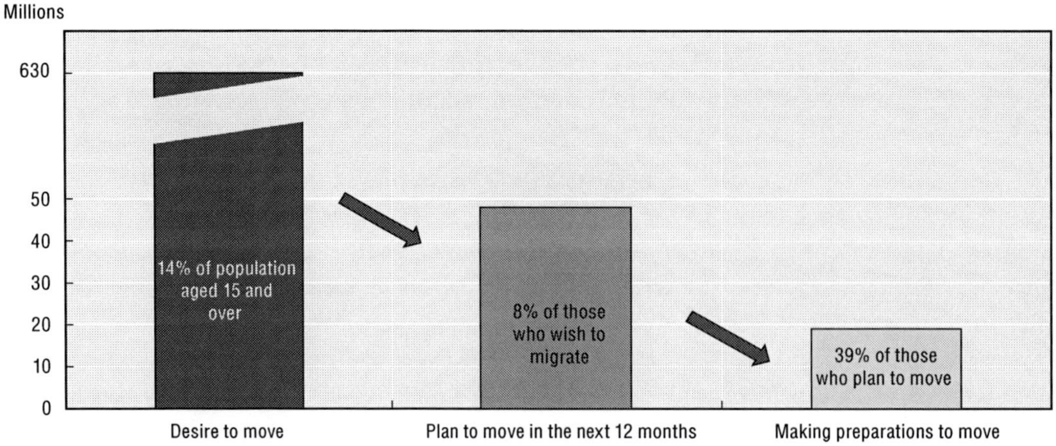

Millions

630
50
40
30
20
10
0

14% of population aged 15 and over

Desire to move

8% of those who wish to migrate

Plan to move in the next 12 months

39% of those who plan to move

Making preparations to move

Note: The Gallup World Poll Survey was conducted in 146 countries from 2008 to 2010.
Source: Gallup World Poll Survey 2008-10.　　　　　　StatLink ᴍᴤᴇ http://dx.doi.org/10.1787/888932671871

One in three Sub-Saharan Africans would like to emigrate permanently

One in three residents in the Sub-Saharan African countries surveyed expresses a desire to migrate permanently to another country. Although this proportion decreased by 5 percentage points from earlier readings, it still represents the highest percentage among all regions. The desire to leave to take up permanent residence elsewhere decreased slightly in South and Central America and in Southeast Asia between 2007 and 2010, and remained stable for persons living in other regions. One in five persons living in South and Central America, the Middle East and North Africa, as well as in European non-OECD and Central Asian countries, would like to migrate to another country.

As expected, the picture is more diverse across countries than across regions with regard to the desire to emigrate (Figure 1.8). About half of the population aged 15 and over in Haiti (54%), Sierra Leone (52%), the Dominican Republic (52%), Liberia (47%) and in the Democratic Republic of the Congo (46%) express their desire to move permanently to

Figure 1.8. **Proportion of persons who would like to move abroad permanently, 2008-10**

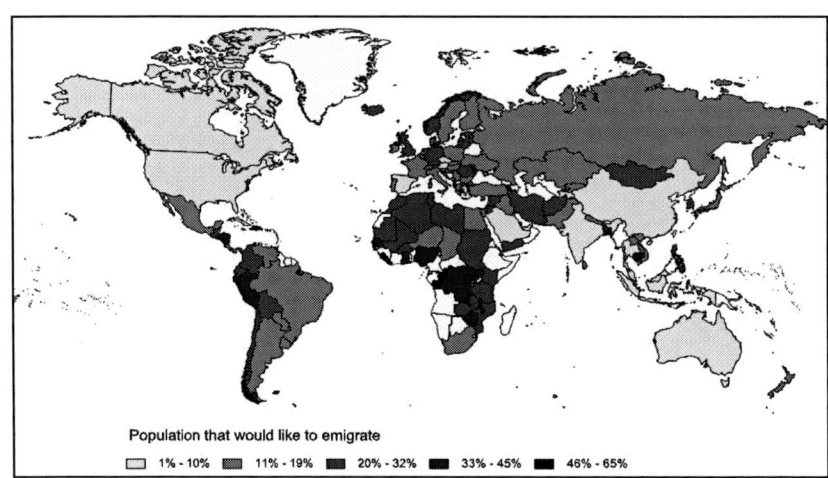

Population that would like to emigrate
☐ 1% - 10%　▨ 11% - 19%　▨ 20% - 32%　■ 33% - 45%　■ 46% - 65%

Source: Gallup World Poll Survey 2008-10.

another country. At the other end of the spectrum are mainly Asian and Gulf countries, from which only 5% or less of the resident population would like to emigrate: 5% in Bahrain, India and Malaysia, 4% in Thailand, and 3% in Indonesia.

Plans to migrate do not always materialise

One in five persons living in Sub-Saharan Africa would like to migrate and 16% of those living in the Middle East and North Africa plan to leave their country in the next 12 months (Table 1.2). In other regions, the share of those who plan to migrate is much

Table 1.2. **Desire to migrate permanently, plan and preparations to move by region of origin and socio-demographic characteristics, 2008-10**

Percentage

	Desire to migrate					Plan to move in the next 12 months	Preparations
	Women	Highly educated	15-24	Three main preferred destinations	Total	Total	Total
OECD	15	18	27	United States 16	16	6	39
				Canada 11			
				Australia 10			
Russian Federation	11	17	23	Germany 19	12	2	..
				United States 12			
				United Kingdom 5			
Other CIS countries	18	25	29	Russian Federation 28	19	6	..
				United States 11			
				Germany 11			
European countries not included above	23	23	44	Germany 14	23	10	..
				United States 12			
				Italy 10			
Middle East	15	26	27	Saudi Arabia 22	20	16	..
				United Arab Emirates 14			
				United States 7			
North Africa	19	27	35	France 18	24	24	52
				Saudi Arabia 16			
				United States 11			
West Africa	37	40	50	United States 38	40	18	34
				United Kingdom 16			
				Saudi Arabia 6			
South Africa	16	20	26	United States 41	17	12	..
				United Kingdom 22			
				Australia 6			
Other African countries	30	40	41	United States 28	33	26	..
				United Kingdom 14			
				South Africa 13			
India	3	13	9	United States 31	5	11	..
				United Kingdom 7			
				United Arab Emirates 4			
China	6	17	12	United States 32	7	5	..
				Korea 8			
				Canada 7			
Other Asian countries	11	21	20	United States 28	14	10	..
				Saudi Arabia 16			
				United Kingdom 8			
South and Central America and the Caribbean	20	25	35	United States 32	22	11	29
				Spain 17			
				Canada 5			

Source: Gallup World Poll Survey 2008-10.

StatLink ⏵ http://dx.doi.org/10.1787/888932674930

smaller. About one in ten potential migrants in South and Central America (11%) and in Asia (7%) and only 6% of OECD and 7% of European non-OECD potential migrants plan to move in the following year.

Wishing and planning to migrate do not necessarily lead to the actual move. A better indication of prospective migrants is whether the respondents have already made preparations for departure, such as purchasing tickets or applying for a visa. Worldwide, 39% of those persons who plan to move are already preparing their move. This share is highest in North Africa (52%) and lowest among potential migrants in South and Central America (29%).

A close look at the rate of the desire to migrate compared with the actual emigration rates of the total population and those of the highly educated reveals that the desire to migrate seems to be as pronounced for the total population as for the highly educated in most of the countries under review (Figure 1.9a). However, this is not the case with actual emigration rates (Figure 1.9b). In most of the countries, the observed emigration rate of the highly educated is greater than that of the total population. The gap between the desire to emigrate and the actual move seems to be larger for the total population than the gap for the highly educated.

However, certain data-related issues limit the scope of such comparisons. The actual emigration rate and the desire to migrate are measured at two different points in time, around 2005/06 and 2008/10, respectively. Therefore, the observed gaps could be due to differences over that time in home and destination country economies, as well as changes in migration policies over time. Moreover, the actual emigration rates reflect migration to OECD countries only, whereas the desire to emigrate refers to all possible destinations. Keeping these drawbacks in mind, this comparison supports the high selectivity of international migration to the OECD. The largest discrepancies between the wish and the actual move for the highly educated are observed in Yemen, Nigeria, Nicaragua and Sudan, where a difference of over 30 percentage points is observed.

Figure 1.9. **Observed emigration rates and desire to emigrate by skill level**

A. Desire to migrate for total and highly educated population aged 15 and over, 2008-10

B. Emigration rates to the OECD for total and highly educated population aged 15 and over, 2005/06

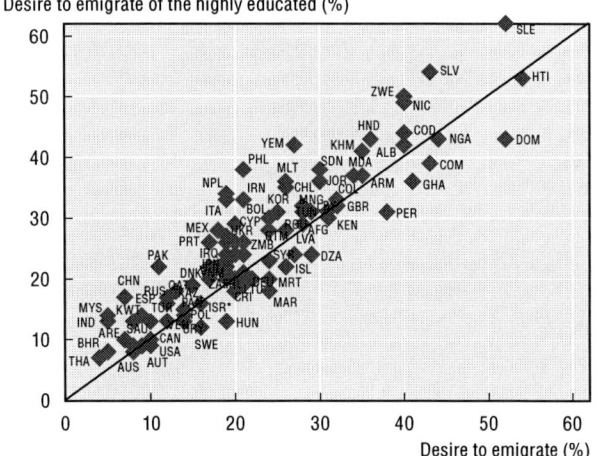
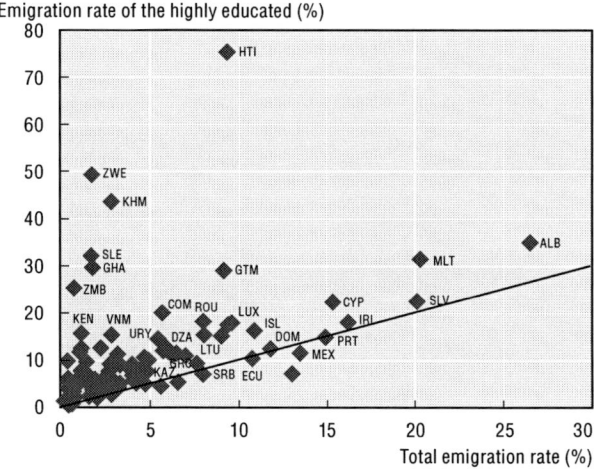

* Information on data for Israel: *http://dx.doi.org/10.1787/888932315602.*
Source: Gallup World Poll Survey 2008-2010, OECD Database on Immigrants in OECD Countries (DIOC 2005/06).

StatLink ᴹᴵˢᴾ *http://dx.doi.org/10.1787/888932671890*

About one in four potential migrants would like to migrate to the United States

Sixteen countries attract more than 70% of potential migrants worldwide, with North America and countries in the European Union appearing as the destination countries that appeal most. About 23% of potential migrants – 145 million adults worldwide – indicate the United States as their desired country of residence. This figure is close to the actual share of migrants living in the United States among the global migrant population, which was close to 20% in 2005 (Figure 1.10). Canada, the United Kingdom, France, Spain and Australia are the most desired destinations by at least 25 million adults. One out of five persons who would like to move to a country of the European Union already lives in the European Union.

Figure 1.10. **Most desired destination countries, 2008-10**

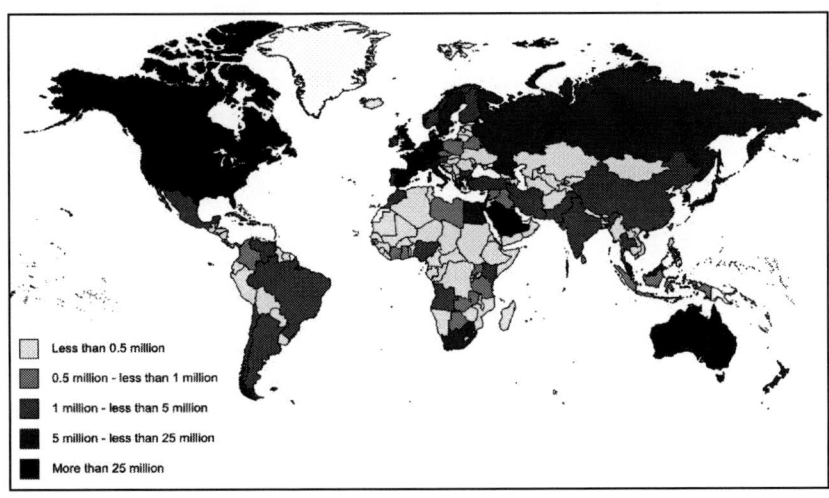

Less than 0.5 million

0.5 million - less than 1 million

1 million - less than 5 million

5 million - less than 25 million

More than 25 million

Source: Gallup World Poll Survey 2008-10.

The desired destinations by regions of residence reflect the main migration corridors worldwide (Table 1.2). Besides the United States, residents in OECD countries would like to move to the English-speaking countries Canada and Australia, while other Europeans and persons from countries of Central Asia prefer the Russian Federation and Germany. Residents of South and Central America wish to migrate also to Spain and Canada, and residents in the Middle East and North Africa would like to migrate permanently to Saudi Arabia and France. Asian and West African residents would like to migrate permanently to the United Kingdom and Saudi Arabia, while other Sub-Saharan residents prefer to move to South Africa rather than to Saudi Arabia.

Certain population groups are more likely to migrate than others

There is no single factor explaining why the desire of some people to migrate to another country does not necessarily translate into planning and preparation. Many factors can influence the situation, such as the potential migrants' individual characteristics and personal circumstances – their financial situation, their health status, their family situation and their job status. In addition, cultural and institutional characteristics such as administrative barriers and migration policies in the origin and the desired destination country either encourage migration by keeping costs of migration relatively low, or increase migration costs through for instance language training requirement, high legal barriers, etc.

Overall, women are almost as likely as men to express the desire to migrate permanently to another country and to plan to move, but the gender gap varies across regions of residence. The gender gap (male over female) is most pronounced in the Middle East and North Africa and to a lesser extent in Sub-Saharan Africa (Table 1.2). In the other regions, the share of women and the share of men who would like to migrate to another country are not significantly different.

Age and education also strongly affect people's desire to migrate worldwide. The youngest population group (15-24 years) is more likely to express their wish to migrate to another country if they could than persons who are 25 and older (Table 1.3). Overall, nearly one in four persons aged 15 to 24 would like to migrate, compared with 15% in the prime age group 25 to 44; 9% in the age group 45 to 64; and only 5% of persons aged 65 and over. The wish to migrate among the young population is particularly high in Sub-Saharan Africa – notably West Africa, where half of the young population would like to move away (Table 1.2). One in four young people living in the Middle East and North Africa and in South and Central America wish to migrate. The smallest rate is observed in Asia where, especially in India and Malaysia, less than 10% of youth would like to migrate to another country.

Table 1.3. **Persons who wish, plan and prepare to migrate among different population groups, 2008-10**

	Desire to migrate →	Plan to move in the next 12 months →	Preparation
Gender			
% among men	15	10	37
% among women	12	6	40
Marital status			
% among married	11	7	44
% among divorced	10	10	49
% among single	25	10	32
Age			
% among 15-24	23	9	30
% among 25-44	15	9	44
% among 45-64	9	5	38
% among 65+	5	6	30
Education			
% among low-educated	9	8	31
% among intermediate-educated	19	9	37
% among highly educated	19	9	60
Employment status			
% among employed at capacity	11	8	35
% among underemployed/unemployed	20	13	28
% among not in workforce	13	7	35
Employment			
% among professionals	17	9	54
% among others	13	8	34

Note: The population of reference is adult population aged 15 and above. Gallup classifies respondents as "employed at capacity" if they are employed full-time or are employed part-time but do not want to work full-time. Respondents are "underemployed" if they are employed part-time but want to work full-time.
Source: Gallup World Poll Survey 2008-10.

StatLink ⧉ http://dx.doi.org/10.1787/888932674949

Persons with a secondary degree have on average a higher desire to migrate than those with a lower education level (20% versus 9%, in Table 1.3). Again, the desire rates of highly educated potential migrants are particularly high in Sub-Saharan Africa, notably in West Africa where about 40% of the university graduates would like to migrate to another country (Table 1.2). In the Middle East and North Africa, as well as in South and Central America, one in four highly educated persons would like to emigrate, and in the other regions this percentage is only somewhat smaller, at 20%. The countries that could mainly be affected by this potential brain drain are Sierra Leone, El Salvador, Haiti, Zimbabwe and Nicaragua, where about half of the people with tertiary degrees would like to emigrate if they had the opportunity to do so. This rate is below 10% for some OECD countries (the United States, Austria and Australia), but also for Saudi Arabia, Bahrain and Thailand.[8]

Factors such as age and education are also strongly related to people's preparations for migration (Table 1.3). The likelihood that potential migrants are actively preparing their move increases with higher educational attainment. Six in ten highly educated adults who are planning to migrate in the next year are already making their preparations, while only one in three less-educated potential migrants are already doing so. More than four in ten persons aged 25-44 are preparing their move, while this is the case for only three in ten potential migrants in the youngest and the oldest age groups.

As expected, underemployed[9] adults in many parts of the world are often the most likely to say they would like to move to another country permanently if given the chance (Table 1.2). Worldwide, underemployed adults are more likely (20%) than those employed full time (13%) or not in the workforce (11%) to express their wish to migrate. In addition, they are most likely to plan to migrate in the following year. In the Middle East and North Africa, potential migrants who are underemployed are nearly three times as likely (33%) to say they are planning to migrate than those who are employed full time (13%) or those not in the workforce (12%). However, those who are working full time are the most likely to say they are making the necessary preparations to move (35%), whereas only 28% of the underemployed potential migrants are preparing their move – possibly because those employed full time have the means to finance such preparations and the actual move.

Regarding occupation, professionals are more likely to express their wish to migrate permanently than those working in other occupations (17% vs. 13%) (Table 1.3). More than half (54%) of potential migrants who are professionals say they are preparing to migrate, compared with a third of those working in other occupations.

Adults who are more likely to have the means to move – those in the fourth and fifth income quintiles that make up the richest 40% – have a higher desire to migrate and a higher probability of preparing their move than their relatively poorer counterparts (Table 1.4). Likewise, adults living in urban areas versus those in rural areas are more likely to say they would like to migrate and are more likely to already be engaged in preparations.

The presence of transnational social networks clearly plays a role in peoples' desire to migrate. Adults who can count on help from friends and family in other countries are almost three times as likely to express their desire to migrate (30%) as those who cannot rely on these kinds of networks (11%) (Table 1.4). Furthermore, 14% of potential migrants with networks abroad are planning to make this move in the following 12 months, compared with 6% of those without family or friends abroad. Almost half (47%) of those with family and friends abroad who plan to migrate are actively preparing to move, compared with one in four (26%) of those without such contacts abroad.

Table 1.4. **Persons who wish, plan and prepare to migrate among different population groups, 2008-10**

	Desire to migrate →	Plan to move in the next 12 months →	Preparation
Networks			
% among those who have someone to count on in another country	30	14	47
% among those who have no one to count on in another country	11	6	26
Remittances			
% among those who receive remittances	38	21	50
% among those who receive no remittances	12	7	34
Income			
% among the poorest 20%	11	7	29
% among the second 20%	12	9	36
% among the middle 20%	13	6	35
% among the fourth 20%	15	8	47
% among the richest 20%	17	11	42
Rural vs Urban			
% among rural residents	12	8	34
% among urban residents	17	9	42

Source: Gallup World Poll Survey 2008-10.

StatLink ⇱ http://dx.doi.org/10.1787/888932674968

The same pattern emerges for persons receiving help through remittances from abroad, an indication of the existence of networks abroad as well as a form of income to finance a potential move. Almost 40% of those whose household receives remittances from abroad would like to migrate permanently, while only 12% of people in households not receiving remittances wish to migrate. Likewise, half of the persons living in household receiving remittances and who plan to migrate are already actively preparing to move, but only one in three in a household without financial support from abroad but planning to migrate actively prepare to do so.

4. Conclusion

International migration will most likely intensify in the coming decades, because of the demographic pressure in developing countries and an increase in the demand for labour in developed countries, in turn due to population ageing.

In 2011, global population reached 7 billion persons, of which 5.7 billion live in developing countries. According to the UN World Population Prospects (2010 Revision) the population in developing countries will further increase by 40% until 2050, while the population in developed countries will remain stable. Keeping emigration rates constant at 2000 levels,[10] such population growth would triple the African diaspora in OECD countries by 2050. Furthermore, the persisting divergence of economic growth between developing and developed countries will continue to explain high levels of desire to emigrate, within traditional migration corridors but also increasingly to emerging economies, some of which are also rapidly ageing. In addition, climate change and its consequences, such as desertification, shoreline erosion and agricultural disruption, may increasingly force persons in these areas to relocate to other countries.

The possible impact of diasporas on the development of origin countries is already high and likely to grow further, with larger migrant communities easier to reach through improved means of communication and technology. Furthermore, new technologies have allowed for new ways of involvement of the diasporas in the home-country economic, social and political lives, making physical presence less necessary. However, the possibility of a complex and sustainable engagement of diasporas depends not only on the migrants' willingness and personal efforts but also on the institutional setting and political support in the origin country. Public policies in countries of origin and destination, notably when they are co-ordinated and aligned with the expectations of the people involved, can help to strengthen the links. To efficiently design these policies however, the capacity to accurately portray the profile of diasporas remains instrumental.

The rest of this publication provides an overview of the international migration statistics currently available for identifying and characterising diasporas; these can greatly facilitate the design of sound policies. Further monitoring of international migration by origin country and socio-demographic characteristics will be necessary in order to go beyond this level and build detailed databases – tools to better mobilise migrant skills for development in origin countries.

Notes

1. The figures on the descendants of migrants by origin are based solely on data of the European Union Labour Force Survey 2008; the US Current Population Survey, March Supplement 2008; and the Australian HILDA data 2008. Other OECD destination countries could not be taken into account, since no data detailing parents' country of birth were available.

2. Because of data limitations, however, this chapter refers mainly to foreign-born populations. The terms diasporas, migrant communities and emigrant populations are used interchangeably throughout the publication.

3. The emigration rate of a given origin country in a given year is defined as the share of the native population of that country residing abroad at that time (see Annex A for more information on definition and sources).

4. Migration flow data are derived from national administrative data sources that utilise different definitions of "flows"; these might refer, for example, to temporary and seasonal migration, or only permanent migration. The so-called "settlement countries" (Australia, Canada, New Zealand and the United States) consider as immigrants persons who have been granted the right of permanent residence. In contrast, other countries such as Germany also include temporary migrants, i.e. foreigners holding a residence permit and intending to stay for at least one week. This comparability issue must be kept in mind when comparing migration flows. For further information, see Lemaître (2005).

5. North Africa is the only region where a decline in the emigration rate of the highly educated is observed since 2000 (–1.2 percentage point), because of the rapid rise in the share of persons holding tertiary degrees in that region.

6. *www.globalscot.com.*

7. This section was prepared with the support of Gallup by Neli Esipova and Julie Ray.

8. These figures by origin country should be interpreted with caution, since sample sizes for the highly educated are small for some countries.

9. These results are based on interviews with 107 404 adults in 105 countries in 2009 and 2010. Gallup classifies respondents as "employed" if they are employed full time or are employed part time but do not want to work full time. Respondents are "underemployed" if they are employed part time but want to work full time or are unemployed. Those "not in the workforce" are not working and are not looking for and/or are not available for work. They may be full-time students, retired, disabled or home makers, though they may not fit any of these categories.

10. However, the largest emigrant population in OECD countries would still come from South and Central America (33 million), Asia (27 million) and Europe (26 million). These figures are based on population estimates of the UN World Population Prospects (2008 Revision) and emigration rates calculated with DIOC-E 2000.

Chapter 2

Asia and Oceania

This chapter looks at recent migration flows and diasporas from Asian countries to the OECD area. It shows that in 2010 almost 1.5 million new Asian migrants settled in OECD countries, accounting for about 30% of total immigration flows. In 2005/06 there were 14.9 million emigrants, 15 years old or older, from the region in OECD countries, of which 53% were women and 46% hold a tertiary diploma. Total emigration rate for those over 15 years of age reached 0.6% for the region as a whole. The emigration rate for the highly educated was 4.1%, but high rates prevailed for the small island nations. Future challenges relate notably to the management of labour migration within the region and the recent developments in international migration of women.

This chapter also contains 19 country notes for Afghanistan, Bangladesh, Cambodia, China (not including Hong Kong, China and Macao, China), Fiji, India, Indonesia, Laos, Malaysia, Myanmar, Nepal, Pakistan, Papua New Guinea, Philippines, Singapore, Sri Lanka, Thailand, Tonga and Viet Nam.

1. Historical migration patterns

The Asian and Pacific countries covered in this chapter,* with 3.6 billion inhabitants, represented 53% of the world's population in 2010 and 16.6% of world GDP. Since 1990, Asia has represented more than half (53%) of population growth and 22% of world economic growth; GDP in these countries increased by 680% over the two decades, compared with 155% for the rest of the world.

Nevertheless, there are significant economic, social, political and demographic differences among these countries that make it impossible to generalise about Asia as a whole. The region contains a number of countries that count significantly in the world population and economy – notably China, India and Indonesia, as well as some of the most developed non-OECD countries (Singapore, with a 2010 per capita GDP of USD 41 000, Chinese Taipei – USD 18 500, Hong Kong, China and Macao, China – USD 31 800 and 52 000 respectively) and an oil-rich outlier (Brunei Darussalam, with a 2010 per capita GDP of USD 31 000). Some Asian countries have seen enormous growth in the past decades, with Malaysia in particular joining the ranks of upper-middle income economies with a per capita GDP of USD 8 400 in 2010. Thailand is approaching that threshold with a per capita GDP of USD 4 600 in 2010. Others languish in poverty, notably Afghanistan, Cambodia, Laos and Nepal. The region also contains countries where the population is rapidly aging, due to low fertility rates (*e.g.* Japan) and those in which the youth population is rapidly expanding (*e.g.* Afghanistan).

These differences explain some of the variety of today's international migration patterns in Asia, along with past economic, cultural and geopolitical circumstances. Economic and cultural ties were forged during centuries of colonisation in South Asia and Southeast Asia especially. The Philippines was in the first half of the 20th century an unincorporated territory of the United States, which exempted Filipinos from restrictions on migration that were applied to the rest of Asia in the early 1900s and made them subject to military recruitment. Colonial ties, as well as rural poverty, were also responsible for the creation of a significant diaspora from India in other countries of the Commonwealth, in Africa, the Caribbean and within Asia to Malaysia and Oceania, principally Fiji. Most of these diasporas were formed initially through migration of indentured labourers, although some African countries received mostly traders. Even in the 19th century, education systems in colonised countries created linguistic and institutional ties with today's OECD countries. Tertiary education for the local elite often involved study in the colonising country. The predominance of English especially, but also French, as a second or administrative language in a large number of Asian countries has reinforced migration channels with other countries sharing these languages long after independence – primarily the United Kingdom, France and the United States, but also Australia, Canada and New Zealand.

* This chapter covers 37 countries, eight non-sovereign Pacific territories, and two special autonomous regions (SAR) of China, in Asia and Oceania. Detailed country notes are provided for 19 countries. The region excludes OECD member countries, former republics of the USSR in Central Asia and the Caucasus, Iran, and Arab countries in the Gulf and on the Arabian peninsula.

In the post-colonial period, especially following the Second World War, migration patterns developed along with political and cultural ties. The communist-bloc countries in Europe cultivated ties with Viet Nam, which sent students and workers to Eastern Europe at a time when those countries were relatively closed to migration from abroad, creating communities that continue to grow. The United States' involvement in Viet Nam also led to migration – especially after regime change in 1975, when a large number of South Vietnamese came to the United States; over 100 000 Vietnamese arrived in the United States in that year alone. Conflict in a number of these countries continued to produce flows of asylum seekers and refugees towards OECD countries; this is particularly true for Cambodia and Laos in the 1970s and 1980s, and more recently for Afghanistan. Today migration from the region continues, led by migration to traditional destination countries and to new OECD destination countries for study, employment and family formation.

Asia has become an increasingly important source country for international students, with growing numbers in Japan, Korea and Australia especially; some of these students stay on after finishing their studies. Canada's selection system for skilled migrants attracted increasing numbers of Asians over the past two decades, as did other programmes such as its long-term care and its investor schemes. Migration for family formation – or "marriage migration" – increased, towards Korea, Japan and some Scandinavian countries. Bilateral agreements for labour migration with Korea, and for recruitment in the Czech Republic, also created new channels from some Asian countries. Finally, conflict in Afghanistan led to an increase in humanitarian flows to certain European OECD countries.

In 2000, 52% of migrants from these countries were in OECD countries. There is, however, substantial intra-Asian migration. Only 1.2% of Asian migrants were in a non-OECD country outside the region, although this excludes the countries not covered in the Gulf, which host a large number of emigrants. Once this is taken into account, 47% of migrants from the region are in another country of the region. Some migration channels are consolidated, such as those between Bangladesh and India, Nepal and India, and Indonesia and Malaysia. Most migration within the region in the past decades has been for employment, followed by family formation rather than family reunification or humanitarian flows, although refugee flows from Afghanistan to Pakistan represent a notable exception.

Only a few Asian countries host proportionally large numbers of migrants, and these tend to be small countries serving as regional hubs. In 2010, this was the case for Macao, China (55% of its population born abroad), Hong Kong, China and Singapore (both 39%), although Singapore attracted more educated migrants than the two Chinese special administrative regions (22% of Singapore's immigrants were highly educated, compared to less than 11% in Macao, China and Hong Kong, China). The only other countries in the region with a relevant proportion of foreign-born were countries with large migrant worker stocks: Brunei Darussalam (37%) and Malaysia (8%). Singapore, Brunei Darussalam, Malaysia and Thailand all saw the proportion of immigrants rise between 2000 and 2010; in Thailand, which became a destination for migrant workers, the increase was 35%, to about 1.7% of the population according to official figures. However, most countries in the region have low levels of immigration relative to their total population.

Employment flows are both formalised – through contract worker schemes, generally with limits on stay and settlement – and irregular. While much of the migration to India occurs outside legal channels, irregular migration exists alongside legal migration to

Malaysia, with an estimated 2.4 million irregular migrants, and predominates in Thailand, with an estimated 2 million irregular migrants. The Philippines is a major sending country to Singapore and Hong Kong, China. In addition to intra-regional migration, Asia is a major sending region to the OECD and to non-OECD countries. The predominance of temporary contract work and of irregular migration helps explain why intra-regional migrants tend to be less educated. There is also a certain degree of mobility skilled workers have, especially within Chinese territories and towards Singapore, where opportunities for return to education may approach the conditions offered in OECD countries.

2. Current profile of emigrant populations

Flows and stocks

Total legal flows to OECD countries from the region, which had been climbing since 2003, declined slightly between 2008 and 2009, from 1.3 million (Figure 2.1). The decline in migration from the region was however much less marked than for other regions and it strongly rebounded in 2010 with almost 1.5 million new Asian migrants to the OECD area. Migrants from the region accounted for about 30% of migrants to the OECD area in 2010.

Flows to OECD countries in the period 2005-10 largely reflected prior migration patterns. China, India and the Philippines have been leading source countries for migrants to the OECD for the past decade, consistently ranking in the top ten, with China and India usually leading the list. Flows from China to the OECD area reached 500 000 in 2010. China accounted for about 10% of total flows to the OECD area in 2010. China is not among the top ten countries of inflows in only a handful of European countries (Austria, Belgium, Slovenia and Switzerland), as well as Turkey and Israel. These countries did not have a history of migration from Asia in general, and none had a large Asian-born population at the beginning of the 2000s.

Remittances to the Asian region have steadily increased in the past decade, although the sharp rate of growth slowed during the economic crisis in 2009 (Figure 2.1). Overall, many countries in the region rely on remittances. In 2010, five main Asian receiving countries account for almost half of total remittances to developing countries (India, USD 54 billion; China, USD 53 billion; Philippines, USD 21 billion; Bangladesh, USD 11 billion; Pakistan, more than USD 10 billion). In Nepal, they account for 22.3% of GDP, and more than 10% in the Philippines and Bangladesh. Other countries in the region dependent on remittances – in Sri Lanka they account for 8.3% of GDP, in Fiji 6% – also saw them stabilise in 2009.

Asia contains a number of giants of international migration, both in absolute terms and relative to their population. The stock of emigrants from China and India alone represented 3% each of migrants in OECD countries in 2005/06, and the Philippines accounted for 2.5%. Migrants from Asia and Oceania accounted for about 17% of all those born abroad living in the OECD area, and more in major receiving countries: 19% in the United States, 33% in Canada, 28% in Australia and 29% in the United Kingdom.

There were 14.9 million emigrants, 15 years old or older, from the region in OECD countries in 2005/06, of which 2.9 million had arrived in the previous five years (Figure 2.2). The percentage of recent emigrants from the region – those with less than five years' stay in the host country – was about 18% in 2000 and 20% in 2005/06. In 2005/06, about 28% of Indian and 24% of Chinese migrants to the OECD were recent arrivals.

Figure 2.1. **Migrant flows from Asia and Oceania to OECD countries and remittance flows, 2000-10**

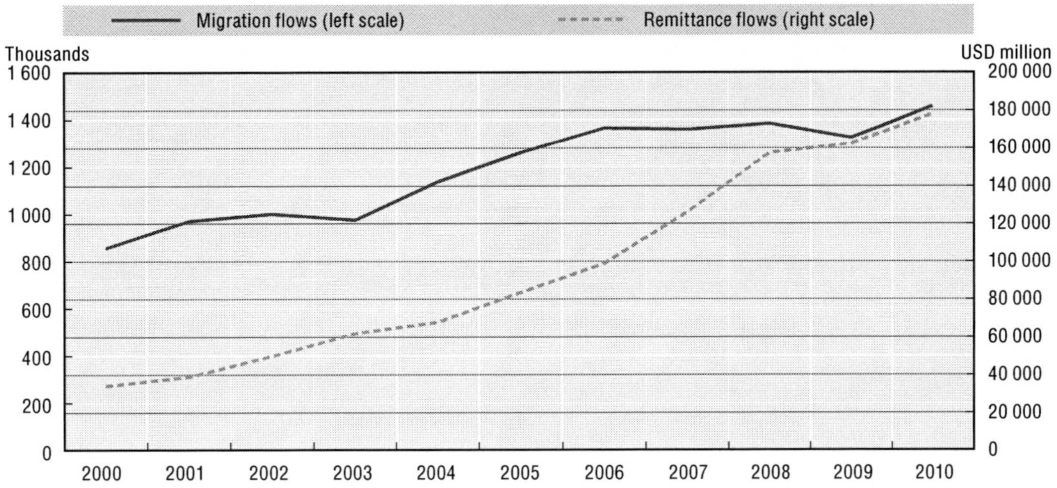

——— Migration flows (left scale)   - - - - - - Remittance flows (right scale)

Thousands | USD million

Source: OECD International Migration Database; World Bank.

StatLink ᝈ᠍ᢆ *http://dx.doi.org/10.1787/888932671909*

Twenty-two per cent of Bangladeshi and Pakistani migrants were recent arrivals. The figure was 17% for the Philippines and 9% for Viet Nam. The proportion of recent migrants was slightly higher among women overall, but for some countries much higher. The explanations for this differ. Thailand's case, for example, reflects the increasing feminisation of flows through family formation. For Nepal and Bangladesh, it also reflects the effect of family reunification through migration channels, where the migration pioneers were men.

Figure 2.2. **Total and highly educated emigrant population aged 15 and over from Asia and Oceania in the OECD area, 2005/06**

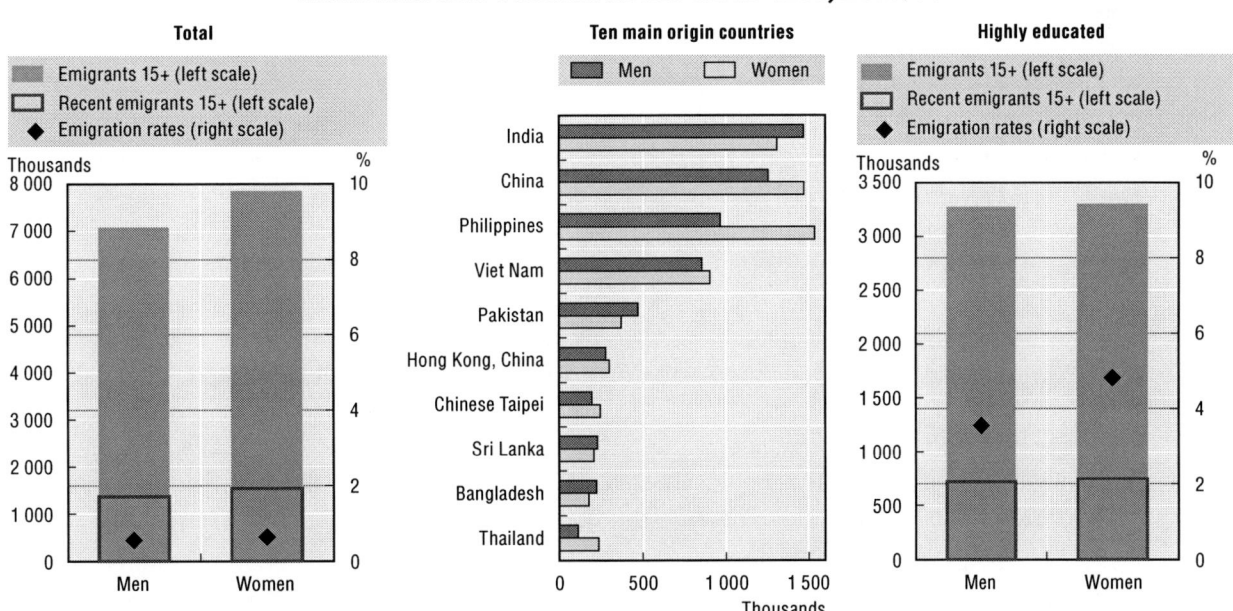

Source: Database on Immigrants in OECD Countries (DIOC 2005/06).

StatLink ᝈ᠍ᢆ *http://dx.doi.org/10.1787/888932671928*

International migration from the area to OECD countries is primarily directed to few destinations: the United States, to which half of all those born in the region and living in the OECD area in 2005/06 have migrated; Canada (14% of those in the OECD area); the United Kingdom (10%); and Australia (8%) (Figure 2.3). This reflects the economic and geopolitical factors mentioned above. From Pakistan and Bangladesh, for example, most emigrants in the OECD area are in the United Kingdom. From Indonesia, most are in the Netherlands. France is the second destination for emigrants from Cambodia and Laos, after the United States.

Figure 2.3. **Emigrant populations and migrant flows from Asia and Oceania to the five main destinations within the OECD area, population aged 15 and over**

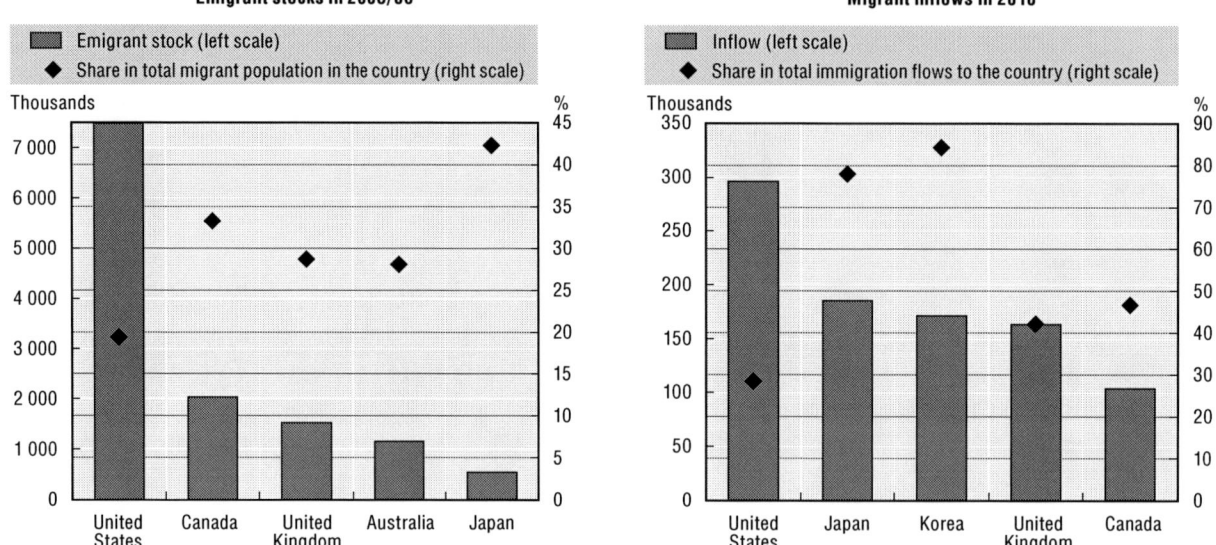

Source: *Database on Immigrants in OECD Countries (DIOC 2005/06); OECD International Migration Database.*

StatLink ⬛️ *http://dx.doi.org/10.1787/888932671947*

Characteristics of emigrant populations

Overall, migration from the region to the OECD area comprises more women (about 53% of the total) and some countries have substantially more female than male migrants: Thailand (67%), Philippines (61%), China (54%) and Indonesia (54%). The large number of Thai women abroad is related to the frequency of international marriages with men in OECD countries; this is particularly evident for some of the main destination countries – Australia, Japan and Sweden, for example. For the Philippines, labour demand and opportunities in disproportionately female occupations play a role. Many Filipinas move to the OECD to engage in domestic work, childcare and long-term care. The Philippines is the main sending country for Canada's live-in caretaker programme, for example. Other countries tend to have more male emigrants: Nepal (61%), Pakistan and Bangladesh (56%), India (53%). For Pakistan and Bangladesh, to some extent this reflects the large proportion of men among recent migrants to new destination countries (Italy and Spain, particularly).

Nearly half the migrants from Asia are highly educated (46%), and this proportion has in general been rising since 2000 (Table 2.1). However, there is significant variation with both country of origin and country of destination. To some extent, this reflects the education level in the country of origin and selectivity in the country of destination.

Table 2.1. **Characteristics of migrants from Asia and Oceania in the OECD area, by gender, 2005/06**

Percentage

	Unweighted averages			Weighted averages		
	Men	Women	Total	Men	Women	Total
15-24	16.5	15.3	15.7	13.0	11.6	12.3
25-64	75.6	75.8	75.8	76.9	77.2	77.0
65+	7.9	8.9	8.4	10.1	11.2	10.7
Low-educated	25.5	28.6	27.1	21.1	25.4	23.4
Highly educated	35.0	34.1	34.8	47.9	43.9	45.8
Total emigration rates	10.7	11.4	11.1	0.6	0.6	0.6
Emigration rates of the highly educated	13.7	17.6	15.3	3.6	4.8	4.1

Source: Database on Immigrants in OECD Countries (DIOC 2005/06).

StatLink ⟐ http://dx.doi.org/10.1787/888932674987

Australia, Canada and New Zealand all apply selective criteria for migrants, favouring highly skilled migration. The United States is also a destination for the highly skilled, although family migration is also an important channel to the United States from Asia and does not apply the same selection criteria. Recent countries of migration from Asia – especially those, such as Italy, where no selection was made on the basis of education, and initial entry or stay was often irregular – tend to attract migrants with proportionally lower education. A similar effect is observed for migration between countries with past colonial ties, where less educated immigrants may face fewer obstacles to enter. Still, selectivity and colonial ties are not the only explanatory factors. For example, less than 30% of Indonesians in the Netherlands are highly educated, compared with more than 50% of Indonesians in Canada and the United States. Partially this also reflects the generation of emigrants, since the Indonesians born in the Netherlands tend to be older.

The region is a major and growing source country for international students in OECD countries. From 2004 to 2009, the number of international students from the region studying in OECD countries increased from 525 000 to 818 000, an increase of 56%. Much of this increase was driven by China, which increased from 215 000 to 368 000, and India, which increased from 114 000 to 180 000. While the United States remains the main destination, with 303 000 international students from the region, other countries accept a proportionately larger number of students: there were 183 000 in Australia and 136 000 in the United Kingdom. International students represent an important target for universities in these countries, where education is a major export industry. Japan and Korea have recently started to attract students from Asia. Both countries have a policy of increasing the number of international students, but Japan has seen less increase in enrolment from Asia in the past five years; most of the increase occurred between 1999 and 2003. Korea, in contrast, has seen sharp growth in the number of its international students – especially from China, which accounted for 87% of its 45 000 international students in 2009.

In 2005/06, emigrants from the region had an employment rate of 62%, compared with 59% for all immigrants in OECD countries (Table 2.2). Their unemployment rate was lower than that of other immigrants as well, 7% compared with 9%. The employment rate for women, 54%, was 17 percentage points lower than for men. Women from certain countries had much lower employment rates: 29% for Pakistan, 31% for Bangladesh, and 35% for Afghanistan.

Table 2.2. **Labour market characteristics of migrants from Asia and Oceania in the OECD area, by gender, 2005/06**

	Unweighted averages			Weighted averages		
	Men	Women	Total	Men	Women	Total
Employment rate (%)	74.0	57.0	65.6	71.1	54.1	62.2
Unemployment rate (%)	7.9	9.5	8.3	6.4	7.7	7.0
Participation rate (%)	80.1	62.7	71.4	75.9	58.6	66.9
Total employed (thousands)	**4 681**	**3 860**	**8 542**			
Employment rate of the highly educated (%)	83.0	69.9	76.8	79.8	65.7	72.7
Unemployment rate of the highly educated (%)	5.7	7.0	6.1	4.4	6.0	5.1
Participation rate of the highly educated (%)	87.9	75.0	81.7	83.4	69.9	76.7
Highly educated employed (thousands)	**2 547**	**2 094**	**4 641**			
Persons with tertiary degrees in low- or medium-skilled jobs (%)	39.4	38.5	38.8	32.2	37.0	34.4

Source: Database on Immigrants in OECD Countries (DIOC 2005/06).

StatLink ⫶⫶⫶⫶ http://dx.doi.org/10.1787/888932675006

Emigrants from the region are employed in a wide range of occupations; one in four is in a high-skilled occupation (managers, professionals) and one in eight in elementary occupations. Men are more likely to be employed either in highly skilled occupations or in low-skilled manufacturing occupations, while women are more likely to work in mid-level service occupations. The occupational distribution varies by country of origin. Those born in China are more likely to work as professionals (19%) or in retail services (23%). Indians are overrepresented among professionals (19%) but also the manufacturing and elementary occupations (13% each). Indonesians are more likely to be professionals (22%) or associate professionals (17%).

One area of particular concern for many countries concerns health sector workers. The percentage of life science and health professionals among employed immigrants from the region in the OECD area was 3.6% in 2005/06, a slightly higher proportion than for migrants from other areas. Among the main sending countries, Malaysia had the highest concentration: 9.8% of Malaysians employed in the OECD area were in the field, and the emigration rate for Malaysian doctors was 22.5%. The Philippines is a well-known sending country for nurses, and is the leading country for nurses working abroad. There were 111 000 Filipino nurses working in the OECD area in 2000, representing an emigration rate of 46.5%, although many of these nurses trained with the desire of working abroad.

Examining the employment of immigrants from the region in the OECD area, the proportion of those highly educated proves significant: 35% are highly educated, compared with 24% for migrants from other regions. The participation rate for highly educated immigrants is higher than for immigrants in general: 77% compared with 67%. For immigrants from some countries, however, highly educated women have a much lower participation rate than highly educated men; this is true especially for educated women from South Asia, notably from Bangladesh, Pakistan and to a lesser extent India. For many East and Southeast Asian countries, the gap in participation rates between women and men is much smaller.

The proportion of those with tertiary degrees employed in low-skilled jobs is particularly high for immigrants from Bangladesh (51%), Thailand (50%), Pakistan (46%) and the Philippines (46%). A number of different factors are at work here, such as the willingness of educated migrants to accept employment for which they are overqualified; obstacles to recognition of qualifications, or non-equivalence of education; lack of assessed skills; and possible discrimination.

Emigration rates and the "brain drain"

The emigration rate from countries within the region to the OECD area for those over 15 years of age in 2005/06 varies significantly. The rate is 0.6% for the region as a whole, but high rates prevail for the small island nations (above 40% for Tonga and Samoa, and above 20% for Fiji) and much lower rates in large countries such as Indonesia (0.2%). Among populous countries, the highest emigration rate is for the Philippines, with 4.4% of its population in the OECD area, and 5.4% of its migrant female population over 15 years of age.

Across the region – as is generally the case around the world – the emigration rate to OECD countries is higher for the highly educated than for those without a tertiary degree. For the region as a whole, the emigration rate for the highly educated is 4.1%, although this conceals variations among countries. For some countries it is much higher, raising concern over possible brain drain. Some of the highest emigration rates for the tertiary educated are in poor countries such as Cambodia (44%), Laos (25%) and Papua New Guinea (22%). The island countries also have high rates. That may reflect the limited opportunities for tertiary education in these countries, since many of those born in the country that have a tertiary education will have studied and remained abroad. Emigration rates for highly educated women are even higher, at about 4.8%. Among the main countries sending immigrants to the OECD area, only Bangladesh had emigration rates for highly educated women lower than those for highly educated men.

Not all countries are concerned about the emigration of the highly skilled. Sri Lanka and Indonesia are two examples of countries with a stated objective of increasing skilled emigration. Another example is India, which specifically includes provisions for migration of its skilled professionals in its negotiation of Free Trade Agreements.

3. Future trends and challenges

The rapid development of many Asian countries has improved the number and quality of opportunities available, attracting some emigrants – particularly the educated – to return. For countries such as India, with its substantial recent emigrant community in the OECD area, or for Chinese Taipei, the return of entrepreneurs is well known. China too has seen opportunities multiply for those abroad, especially students who have finished their studies. For countries where development has been slower the question is what prospects are available to attract skills home again.

Migration flows are currently largely within the region and to the Gulf countries, due to the preponderance of low-skilled migration. Highly educated migrants have in the past headed mostly for OECD countries, but this may change in the near future as conditions in the region change, intra-regional international study increases, and a free movement area for professionals develops among ASEAN countries. Most traditional sending countries in the region still assign importance to intergovernmental bilateral agreements for the management of temporary migration. This model is not easily applicable to skilled migration and to migration to most OECD countries, which may represent a challenge to this type of migration management.

Among the OECD countries included in this region, a number are undergoing profound demographic transition, with fertility rates having fallen from high levels to close to or below replacement rate in less than two decades. At the same time, education levels for youth cohorts are increasing rapidly, which is expected to change the nature of labour market demand in upcoming decades. This is also true for China, although Thailand and Malaysia are also affected by the trend, with low-skill demand already increasingly met through migration from poorer neighbours. China and India are also affected by a sharp imbalance in the gender ratio among youth, with effects expected on the probability of young men marrying, and a possible expansion in the existing phenomenon of arranged intra-regional marriages.

Recent and young migrants from the region tend to be women. This is in part related to the role of family reunification and formation, but also to the changing labour demand in OECD countries, which favours occupations such as care sector jobs, nursing and domestic work that have been dominated by women. There is a substantial and growing literature on the impact of women's migration on home countries, including its influence on the use of remittances and on children who remain under the care of other family members. In a number of sending countries, the protection of migrants is given more emphasis when the migrants are women, and several countries in the region have imposed recruitment bans on domestic work for certain destination countries as a reaction to poor treatment of migrant women. Such bans, difficult to enforce, have generally been short-lived, but sending countries are expanding their pre-departure orientation and support networks for migrant women, especially those in the Gulf and inside the region.

The prevalence of intra-regional temporary migration raises the question of reintegration of returning migrants. Many sending countries face a persistent problem reintegrating returning migrants into productive activities, as there may not be opportunities – especially for the less skilled – and returnees may be unwilling to work for local wages after their experience abroad. The inclusion of reintegration in temporary work programmes, such as Korea's, is one means of attempting to improve the success of return.

Country Notes

Asia and Oceania

Total population 2010 (millions)	34.4	**Afghanistan compared to:**	**World**	**Region**
Population growth 2010 (%)	2.8	Human Development Index (HDI)	172/187	31/31
GDP per capita 2010 (current USD)	501	GDP per capita	172/194	32/33
GDP growth 2010 (%)	8.2	Emigration rate	129/203	21/38
Poverty rate 2010 (USD PPP 2 a day, in %)	..	Emigration rate of the highly educated	105/157	15/25

Age structure of the population 0+ (2010): "0-14": 20%; "15-24": 46%; "25-64": 31%; "65+": 2%.
Level of education of the population 15+ (2010): "Low": 68%; "Medium": 26%; "High": 7%.

Emigrant population living in OECD countries

Immigrant population

Emigrant population: persons born in Afghanistan living abroad

	2000						2005/06		
	All destinations			OECD destinations			OECD destinations		
Population 15+	Men	Women	Total	Men	Women	Total	Men	Women	Total
Emigrant population (thousands)	102.5	66.9	169.5	79.7	55.5	135.2	142.3	117.5	259.7
Recent emigrants (thousands)	..	..	..	15.6	13.5	29.1	29.7	29.5	59.1
15-24 (%)	24.7	20.7	23.1	26.5	20.2	23.9	27.3	25.0	26.2
25-64 (%)	71.2	73.3	72.0	68.8	73.2	70.6	69.3	70.2	69.7
65+ (%)	4.0	6.0	4.8	4.6	6.6	5.5	3.4	4.8	4.0
Low-educated (%)	43.0	53.5	47.1	43.8	50.5	46.5	40.6	48.6	44.2
Highly educated (%)	21.2	17.6	19.8	23.1	18.9	21.4	25.9	20.6	23.5
Total emigration rates (%)	1.8	1.3	1.5	1.4	1.0	1.2	2.0	1.8	1.9
Emigration rates of the highly educated (%)	3.3	8.2	4.2	2.8	7.4	3.6	4.5	12.6	6.0

Main destinations in 2005/06

	Total		Recent emigrants	Women	Highly educated	15-24	Total in 2000
Population 15+	Thousands	%	%	%	%	%	Thousands
Germany	58.2	22.4	–	42.9	14.3	26.7	29.9
United States	55.0	21.2	11.8	51.2	37.7	12.6	43.0
Canada	32.9	12.7	41.9	49.9	27.8	27.8	18.8
United Kingdom	32.3	12.4	35.9	37.4	–	36.9	11.8
Netherlands	29.2	11.2	17.0	44.5	18.6	31.2	–
Australia	14.1	5.4	39.9	45.6	23.2	29.1	9.6
Sweden	8.3	3.2	55.5	43.6	22.1	36.9	5.2
Denmark	7.4	2.8	24.4	46.4	20.4	35.8	4.6
Austria	6.2	2.4	29.4	38.5	–	–	–
Norway	3.7	1.4	89.4	36.1	8.8	36.6	3.1

Labour market indicators of persons born in Afghanistan living in OECD countries

Population 15-64	2000			2005/06		
	Men	Women	Total	Men	Women	Total
Employment-population ratio (%)	55.9	29.6	44.4	59.5	34.8	48.4
Unemployment rate (%)	12.4	14.6	13.0	16.0	17.5	16.5
Participation rate (%)	63.8	34.7	51.1	70.8	42.2	58.0
Total employed (thousands)	**34.0**	**14.0**	**47.9**	**74.2**	**35.5**	**109.6**
Employment rates of the highly educated (%)	65.9	53.9	61.3	84.5	62.9	76.3
Unemployment rates of the highly educated (%)	12.4	11.8	12.2	11.5	12.7	11.9
Highly educated in low- and medium-skilled jobs (%)	51.1	53.3	51.8	50.2	51.5	50.6
Highly educated employed (thousands)	**10.1**	**5.0**	**15.2**	**22.9**	**10.4**	**33.4**
Legislators, senior officials and managers	9.4	5.8	8.3	12.0	3.3	9.5
Professionals	8.2	8.1	8.2	5.4	8.6	6.3
Life science and health professionals	3.6	3.4	3.5	1.6	3.4	2.1
Teaching professionals	1.6	3.2	2.0	1.1	2.3	1.4
Technicians and associate professionals	7.7	12.1	9.0	6.8	9.4	7.5
Clerks	7.8	18.7	11.0	5.9	22.1	10.6
Service, shop and market sales workers	18.6	35.3	23.5	16.5	32.3	21.0
Skilled agricultural and fishery workers	0.4	0.2	0.4	0.8	0.7	0.8
Craft and related trades workers	11.9	2.2	9.1	16.5	7.8	14.0
Plant and machine operators and assemblers	17.5	6.4	14.3	19.2	2.7	14.4
Elementary occupations	18.4	11.2	16.3	16.1	13.0	15.2

Distribution of employment by occupation (%), population 15+

Persons born in Afghanistan and their native-born children, population 15+

Living in:	Europe	United States	Australia
2008	Thousands	Thousands	Thousands
Native-born children	14.6	53.2	..
Foreign-born	197.8	62.9	11.4
Total	212.4	116.1	..

International students from Afghanistan in OECD countries

Five main destinations	2004	2005	2006	2007	2008	2009
Turkey	186	230	337	388	509	623
United States	109	162	181	274	338	400
United Kingdom	89	99	105	142	136	144
France	101	106	113	122	131	124
Germany	..	..	..	..	70	120
Total	645	743	888	1 162	1 491	1 843

Legal migrant flows to the OECD
Thousands

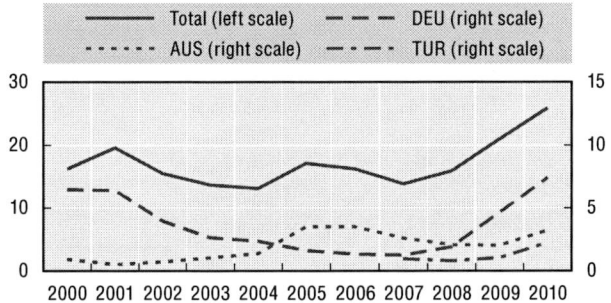

Ten main countries of destination for legal migrants in 2010 (numbers, % of total flows to the country): DEU (7377, 1.1%), AUS (3171, 1.5%), TUR (2188, 7.4%), USA (2017, 0.2%), SWE (1920, 2.5%), CAN (1545, 0.6%), NOR (1417, 1.3%), AUT (1304, 1.3%), GBR (1131, 0.2%), ITA (694, 0.2%).

Desire to emigrate, 2008-10

	Women	15-24	Highly educated	Total	Regional total
Persons who would move permanently, if they had the opportunity to do so (%)	28	31	29	28	9
Of which: Persons who are planning to move permanently in the next 12 months (%)				27	7
Of which: Persons who have already done some preparations for this move (*e.g.* visa application) (%)					40

Three main countries of desired destination: Iran (26%), United States (12%), Pakistan (10%).

StatLink ⟨⟩ http://dx.doi.org/10.1787/888932672251

			World	Region
Total population 2010 (millions)	148.7	**Bangladesh compared to:**		
Population growth 2010 (%)	1.1	Human Development Index (HDI)	146/187	26/31
GDP per capita 2010 (current USD)	675	GDP per capita	161/194	30/33
GDP growth 2010 (%)	6.1	Emigration rate	176/203	30/38
Poverty rate 2005 (USD PPP 2 a day, in %)	81.3	Emigration rate of the highly educated	132/157	20/25

Age structure of the population 0+ (2010): "0-14": 20%; "15-24": 31%; "25-64": 44%; "65+": 5%.
Level of education of the population 15+ (2010): "Low": 56%; "Medium": 40%; "High": 4%.

Emigrant population living in OECD countries

Immigrant population

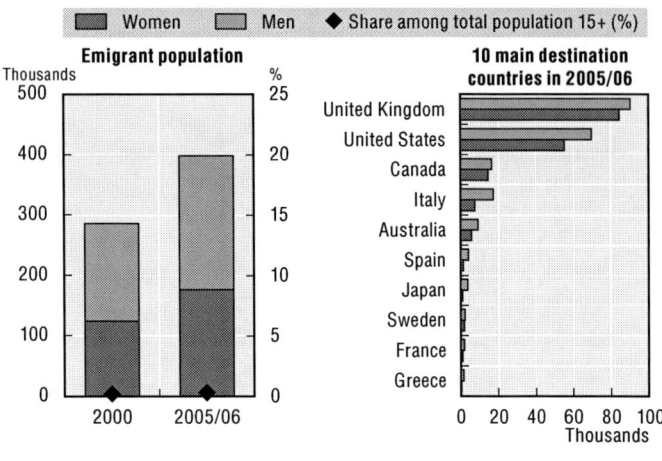

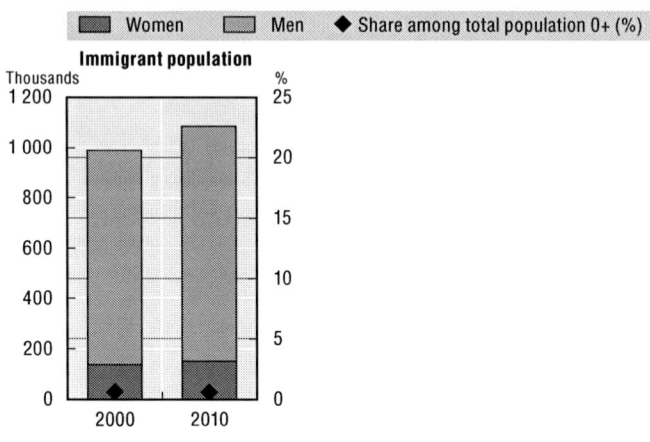

Emigrant population: persons born in Bangladesh living abroad

	2000						2005/06		
	All destinations			OECD destinations			OECD destinations		
Population 15+	Men	Women	Total	Men	Women	Total	Men	Women	Total
Emigrant population (thousands)	2 064.6	1 790.3	3 854.9	161.9	123.6	285.5	222.3	176.1	398.5
Recent emigrants (thousands)	..	..	..	33.0	24.4	57.4	46.1	40.7	86.8
15-24 (%)	10.0	8.5	9.3	17.2	23.1	19.7	13.0	15.7	14.2
25-64 (%)	89.6	91.2	90.3	78.2	73.3	76.1	80.3	79.8	80.1
65+ (%)	0.4	0.3	0.3	4.7	3.6	4.2	6.7	4.5	5.7
Low-educated (%)	65.7	84.7	74.6	43.3	54.7	48.3	33.2	43.3	37.7
Highly educated (%)	5.6	2.0	3.9	33.6	21.8	28.4	43.7	30.4	37.8
Total emigration rates (%)	4.4	4.0	4.2	0.4	0.3	0.3	0.4	0.4	0.4
Emigration rates of the highly educated (%)	5.7	2.7	4.5	2.7	2.0	2.4	4.1	3.2	3.7

Main destinations in 2005/06

	Total		Recent emigrants	Women	Highly educated	15-24	Total in 2000
Population 15+	Thousands	%	%	%	%	%	Thousands
United Kingdom	175.0	43.9	11.6	48.3	27.6	11.5	141.9
United States	125.0	31.4	22.2	44.3	48.8	15.3	82.8
Canada	30.9	7.8	37.1	47.0	61.7	16.2	19.5
Italy	24.6	6.2	39.7	29.9	9.2	16.4	11.5
Australia	14.9	3.7	51.9	38.7	69.5	21.8	7.8
Spain	5.4	1.4	88.6	25.7	–	32.2	1.4
Japan	4.9	1.2	..	22.1	53.2	11.5	5.0
Sweden	4.0	1.0	34.6	43.1	36.8	11.9	3.2
France	2.8	0.7	35.9	36.4	22.9	14.1	1.6
Greece	1.9	0.5	–	–	–	–	4.7

Labour market indicators of persons born in Bangladesh living in OECD countries

Population 15-64	2000			2005/06		
	Men	Women	Total	Men	Women	Total
Employment-population ratio (%)	68.5	25.6	49.5	76.8	30.9	56.4
Unemployment rate (%)	11.4	16.6	12.6	8.4	15.1	10.1
Participation rate (%)	77.3	30.7	56.7	83.8	36.4	62.7
Total employed (thousands)	**97.8**	**29.2**	**127.0**	**152.1**	**49.2**	**201.3**
Employment rates of the highly educated (%)	80.0	48.7	69.3	90.9	58.6	79.2
Unemployment rates of the highly educated (%)	6.3	11.4	7.6	4.6	11.3	6.4
Highly educated in low- and medium-skilled jobs (%)	47.2	49.4	47.7	50.1	52.1	50.6
Highly educated employed (thousands)	**38.7**	**12.2**	**51.0**	**74.9**	**25.4**	**100.2**
Legislators, senior officials and managers	12.7	5.8	11.1	10.1	6.2	9.2
Professionals	10.1	11.8	10.5	10.6	10.4	10.5
Life science and health professionals	1.6	2.1	1.7	1.8	3.1	2.1
Teaching professionals	2.0	5.4	2.7	2.1	2.8	2.2
Technicians and associate professionals	5.6	10.1	6.6	7.3	11.8	8.3
Clerks	5.5	19.9	8.8	5.5	17.7	8.3
Service, shop and market sales workers	37.2	33.4	36.3	11.7	12.6	11.9
Skilled agricultural and fishery workers	0.2	0.2	0.2	0.6	8.4	2.4
Craft and related trades workers	5.6	1.6	4.7	10.6	16.6	12.0
Plant and machine operators and assemblers	10.2	6.6	9.4	16.3	4.2	13.5
Elementary occupations	13.0	10.6	12.4	20.5	11.0	18.3

(Left margin label: Distribution of employment by occupation (%), population 15+)

Persons born in Bangladesh and their native-born children, population 15+

Living in:	Europe	United States	Australia
2008	Thousands	Thousands	Thousands
Native-born children	84.7	31.6	0.7
Foreign-born	253.5	131.7	14.4
Total	338.3	163.3	15.1

International students from Bangladesh in OECD countries

Five main destinations	2004	2005	2006	2007	2008	2009
United Kingdom	1 721	1 947	2 222	2 675	2 817	3 488
United States	3 198	2 881	2 673	2 463	2 307	2 662
Australia	2 950	3 393	3 131	2 902	2 355	2 380
Japan	958	1 110	1 303	1 431	1 515	1 683
Canada	614	..	1 266	894	1 246	1 142
Total	9 628	9 653	10 994	10 898	11 636	13 426

Legal migrant flows to the OECD
Thousands

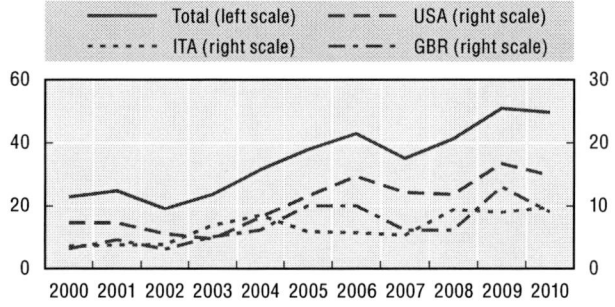

Remittance flows

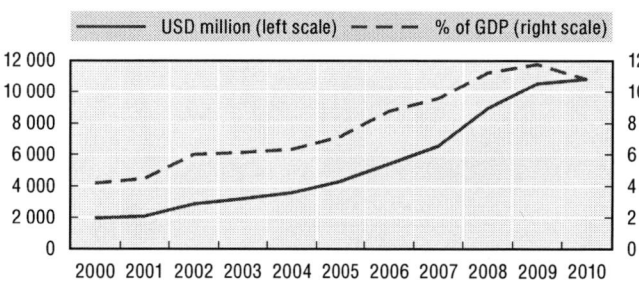

Ten main countries of destination for legal migrants in 2010 (numbers, % of total flows to the country): USA (14819, 1.4%), ITA (9688, 2.3%), GBR (9000, 1.9%), CAN (4365, 1.6%), KOR (2902, 1%), AUS (2114, 1%), ESP (2003, 0.4%), JPN (1083, 0.4%), SWE (957, 1.2%), DEU (743, 0.1%).

Desire to emigrate, 2008-10

	Women	15-24	Highly educated	Total	Regional total
Persons who would move permanently, if they had the opportunity to do so (%)	21	37	..	28	9
Of which: Persons who are planning to move permanently in the next 12 months (%)				7	7
Of which: Persons who have already done some preparations for this move (*e.g.* visa application) (%)					40

Three main countries of desired destination: United States (25%), Saudi Arabia (25%), United Kingdom (11%).

StatLink ᘃᗛᔛ http://dx.doi.org/10.1787/888932672270

Total population 2010 (millions)	14.1	**Cambodia compared to:**	**World**	**Region**
Population growth 2010 (%)	1.1	Human Development Index (HDI)	139/187	22/31
GDP per capita 2010 (current USD)	795	GDP per capita	156/194	29/33
GDP growth 2010 (%)	6.0	Emigration rate	110/203	17/38
Poverty rate 2007 (USD PPP 2 a day, in %)	56.5	Emigration rate of the highly educated	11/157	2/25

Age structure of the population 0+ (2010): "0-14": 22%; "15-24": 32%; "25-64": 42%; "65+": 4%.
Level of education of the population 15+ (2010): "Low": 82%; "Medium": 17%; "High": 1%.

Emigrant population living in OECD countries

Immigrant population

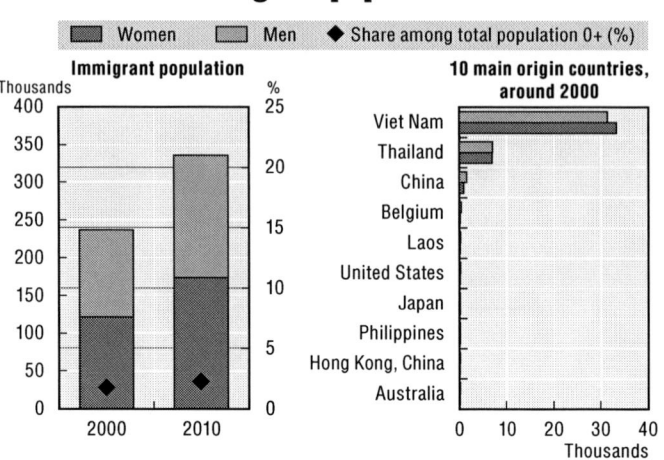

Emigrant population: persons born in Cambodia living abroad

	2000						2005/06		
	All destinations			OECD destinations			OECD destinations		
Population 15+	Men	Women	Total	Men	Women	Total	Men	Women	Total
Emigrant population (thousands)	115.0	124.8	239.8	114.5	124.5	239.1	119.5	135.0	254.5
Recent emigrants (thousands)	..	..	..	6.0	9.1	15.2	7.3	12.8	20.1
15-24 (%)	11.9	11.8	11.8	11.8	11.8	11.8	6.3	6.1	6.2
25-64 (%)	82.2	80.0	81.0	82.3	80.0	81.1	85.3	82.6	83.9
65+ (%)	5.9	8.2	7.1	5.9	8.2	7.1	8.5	11.3	10.0
Low-educated (%)	46.8	59.2	53.2	46.8	59.1	53.2	38.4	51.6	45.4
Highly educated (%)	19.1	12.2	15.5	19.1	12.2	15.5	23.5	16.2	19.7
Total emigration rates (%)	3.2	3.1	3.1	3.2	3.1	3.1	2.8	2.9	2.8
Emigration rates of the highly educated (%)	37.9	55.6	43.7	37.8	55.5	43.6	40.8	47.8	43.6

Main destinations in 2005/06

	Total		Recent emigrants	Women	Highly educated	15-24	Total in 2000
Population 15+	Thousands	%	%	%	%	%	Thousands
United States	139.3	54.8	8.4	53.8	19.8	5.5	132.4
France	57.0	22.4	4.4	51.3	20.0	3.5	55.1
Australia	23.9	9.4	11.1	53.7	18.9	11.3	22.0
Canada	20.3	8.0	6.8	53.4	21.9	7.4	18.7
New Zealand	5.4	2.1	30.1	53.2	8.4	19.4	4.4
Switzerland	1.7	0.7	–	–	–	–	1.8
Japan	1.6	0.6	..	44.7	11.7	0.0	1.2
Belgium	–	–	–	–	–	–	1.0
Netherlands	–	–	–	–	–	–	–
Austria	–	–	–	–	–	–	0.6

Labour market indicators of persons born in Cambodia living in OECD countries

Population 15-64	2000			2005/06		
	Men	Women	Total	Men	Women	Total
Employment-population ratio (%)	68.8	51.0	59.6	76.2	58.7	67.0
Unemployment rate (%)	9.6	13.0	11.2	7.7	10.8	9.1
Participation rate (%)	76.1	58.6	67.1	82.5	65.8	73.8
Total employed (thousands)	**72.6**	**57.1**	**129.7**	**80.3**	**67.3**	**147.6**
Employment rates of the highly educated (%)	79.9	71.9	76.6	90.1	82.0	86.5
Unemployment rates of the highly educated (%)	6.0	6.9	6.4	4.6	8.5	6.2
Highly educated in low- and medium-skilled jobs (%)	35.6	42.0	38.1	41.9	41.0	41.5
Highly educated employed (thousands)	**16.6**	**10.5**	**27.1**	**22.2**	**15.0**	**37.1**
Legislators, senior officials and managers	9.3	7.7	8.7	10.6	9.2	10.0
Professionals	10.2	6.0	8.5	10.1	6.5	8.5
Life science and health professionals	2.1	1.8	2.0	1.7	1.2	1.5
Teaching professionals	0.8	1.0	0.9	0.9	1.4	1.1
Technicians and associate professionals	10.5	11.0	10.7	10.1	11.2	10.6
Clerks	5.2	15.7	9.5	5.8	15.9	10.2
Service, shop and market sales workers	13.5	20.9	16.4	14.6	21.3	17.5
Skilled agricultural and fishery workers	0.7	0.8	0.7	1.7	2.1	1.9
Craft and related trades workers	16.3	7.9	12.9	17.2	6.9	12.7
Plant and machine operators and assemblers	22.4	16.7	20.1	20.8	13.7	17.7
Elementary occupations	11.9	13.3	12.5	9.0	13.3	10.9

Distribution of employment by occupation (%), population 15+

Persons born in Cambodia and their native-born children, population 15+

Living in:	Europe	United States	Australia
2008	Thousands	Thousands	Thousands
Native-born children	24.1	96.3	..
Foreign-born	46.4	163.0	36.4
Total	70.5	259.3	..

International students from Cambodia in OECD countries

Five main destinations	2004	2005	2006	2007	2008	2009
France	715	612	641	644	512	546
Australia	177	173	209	250	311	366
United States	330	348	377	336	369	347
Japan	260	278	282	282	277	289
Korea	37	38	48	67	86	115
Total	1 632	1 535	1 679	1 709	1 771	1 885

Legal migrant flows to the OECD
Thousands

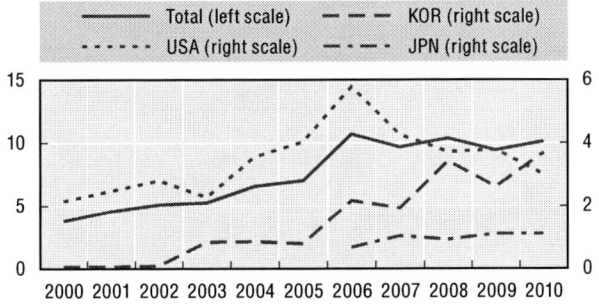

Ten main countries of destination for legal migrants in 2010 (numbers, % of total flows to the country): KOR (3679, 1.3%), USA (2986, 0.3%), JPN (1097, 0.4%), AUS (875, 0.4%), FRA (559, 0.4%), NZL (379, 0.9%), CAN (190, 0%), ITA (81, 0%), DEU (74, 0%), BEL (46, 0%).

Remittance flows

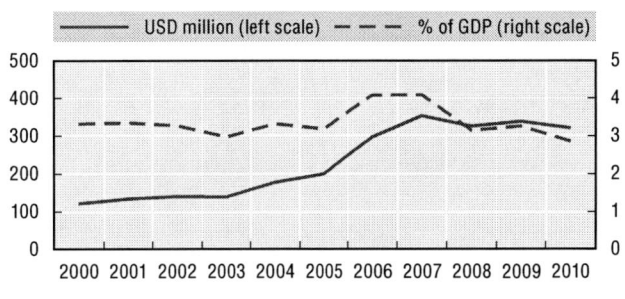

Desire to emigrate, 2008-10

	Women	15-24	Highly educated	Total	Regional total
Persons who would move permanently, if they had the opportunity to do so (%)	35	42	41	35	9
Of which: Persons who are planning to move permanently in the next 12 months (%)				5	7
Of which: Persons who have already done some preparations for this move (*e.g.* visa application) (%)					40

Three main countries of desired destination: United States (67%), Korea (9%), France (5%).

StatLink ⬛⬛⬛ http://dx.doi.org/10.1787/888932672289

			China compared to:	World	Region
Total population 2010 (millions)	1 338.3		Human Development Index (HDI)	101/187	10/31
Population growth 2010 (%)	0.0		GDP per capita	97/194	9/33
GDP per capita 2010 (current USD)	4 428		Emigration rate	191/203	34/38
GDP growth 2010 (%)	10.4		Emigration rate of the highly educated	147/157	24/25
Poverty rate 2005 (USD PPP 2 a day, in %)	36.3				

Age structure of the population 0+ (2010): "0-14": 17%; "15-24": 19%; "25-64": 56%; "65+": 8%.
Level of education of the population 15+ (2010): "Low": 31%; "Medium": 60%; "High": 9%.

Emigrant population living in OECD countries

Immigrant population

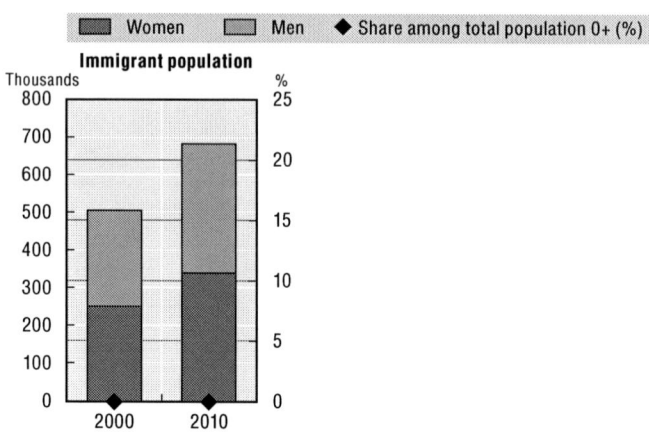

Emigrant population: persons born in China living abroad

	2000						2005/06		
	All destinations			OECD destinations			OECD destinations		
Population 15+	Men	Women	Total	Men	Women	Total	Men	Women	Total
Emigrant population (thousands)	2 297.0	2 467.2	4 764.2	976.3	1 089.8	2 066.1	1 254.1	1 470.4	2 724.5
Recent emigrants (thousands)	..	..	..	217.0	250.7	467.7	298.9	355.7	654.6
15-24 (%)	9.8	9.2	9.5	12.3	11.4	11.8	16.6	15.1	15.8
25-64 (%)	69.0	68.1	68.5	73.1	73.4	73.3	69.1	70.4	69.8
65+ (%)	21.2	22.7	22.0	14.6	15.2	14.9	14.3	14.5	14.4
Low-educated (%)	39.3	46.9	43.3	30.1	34.4	32.4	24.4	27.4	26.0
Highly educated (%)	24.3	20.7	22.4	44.6	38.4	41.3	46.8	42.9	44.7
Total emigration rates (%)	0.5	0.5	0.5	0.2	0.2	0.2	0.2	0.3	0.3
Emigration rates of the highly educated (%)	2.0	2.9	2.3	1.5	2.3	1.8	1.4	2.2	1.7

Main destinations in 2005/06

	Total		Recent emigrants	Women	Highly educated	15-24	Total in 2000
Population 15+	Thousands	%	%	%	%	%	Thousands
United States	1 255.5	46.1	20.6	52.7	46.8	9.7	1 129.6
Canada	454.2	16.7	30.1	53.2	50.7	12.0	318.1
Japan	329.4	12.1	..	61.0	37.2	26.1	227.4
Australia	221.9	8.1	34.6	55.1	48.8	24.2	134.7
United Kingdom	88.7	3.3	54.7	55.6	58.3	32.4	47.8
New Zealand	73.8	2.7	62.0	52.5	36.7	34.2	36.0
France	67.5	2.5	38.0	55.6	37.4	26.6	31.3
Germany	64.9	2.4	42.7	50.9	36.5	13.4	25.6
Italy	53.0	1.9	30.9	46.1	4.2	15.6	35.6
Spain	32.4	1.2	42.7	48.6	6.6	19.3	23.5

Labour market indicators of persons born in China living in OECD countries

Population 15-64	2000			2005/06		
	Men	Women	Total	Men	Women	Total
Employment-population ratio (%)	74.1	58.2	65.9	72.5	59.0	65.4
Unemployment rate (%)	5.7	6.8	6.2	6.2	7.8	6.9
Participation rate (%)	78.6	62.5	70.2	77.2	63.9	70.2
Total employed (thousands)	**531.5**	**447.0**	**978.5**	**673.0**	**608.8**	**1 281.8**
Employment rates of the highly educated (%)	82.1	66.4	74.4	83.8	71.7	77.5
Unemployment rates of the highly educated (%)	4.3	5.7	4.9	5.1	6.8	5.9
Highly educated in low- and medium-skilled jobs (%)	21.7	29.0	24.9	25.4	32.3	28.7
Highly educated employed (thousands)	**281.4**	**221.1**	**502.5**	**363.2**	**333.4**	**696.6**
Legislators, senior officials and managers	14.4	9.0	11.9	17.3	11.1	14.4
Professionals	20.6	16.0	18.5	19.9	17.1	18.6
Life science and health professionals	1.6	2.6	2.1	1.0	2.1	1.5
Teaching professionals	3.5	3.5	3.5	2.7	3.4	3.0
Technicians and associate professionals	9.4	11.4	10.4	8.2	11.8	10.0
Clerks	3.6	12.7	7.7	5.7	15.4	10.4
Service, shop and market sales workers	22.8	22.2	22.5	23.0	23.3	23.1
Skilled agricultural and fishery workers	0.6	0.5	0.6	0.7	1.4	1.0
Craft and related trades workers	10.7	5.5	8.4	8.9	4.3	6.7
Plant and machine operators and assemblers	8.5	11.5	9.8	6.9	6.7	6.8
Elementary occupations	9.4	11.2	10.2	8.1	8.5	8.3

Distribution of employment by occupation (%), population 15+

Persons born in China and their native-born children, population 15+

Living in:	Europe	United States	Australia
2008	Thousands	Thousands	Thousands
Native-born children	85.6	570.4	6.0
Foreign-born	526.6	1 909.3	171.7
Total	612.2	2 479.7	177.7

International students from China in OECD countries

Five main destinations	2004	2005	2006	2007	2008	2009
United States	87 943	92 370	93 672	98 958	110 246	124 225
Japan	76 130	83 264	86 378	80 231	77 916	79 394
Australia	28 309	37 344	42 008	50 418	57 596	70 357
United Kingdom	47 738	52 677	50 753	49 594	45 356	47 033
Korea	6 462	10 093	15 288	23 097	30 552	39 309
Total	291 469	317 933	347 072	352 459	405 024	447 554

Legal migrant flows to the OECD
Thousands

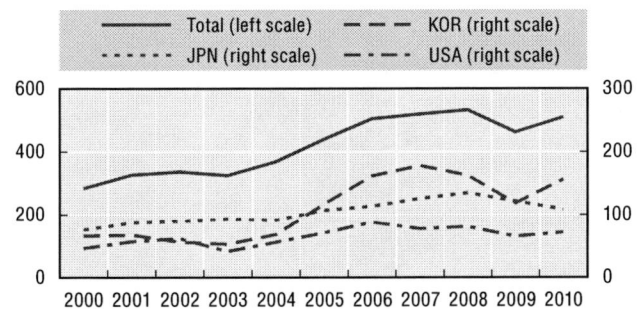

Remittance flows

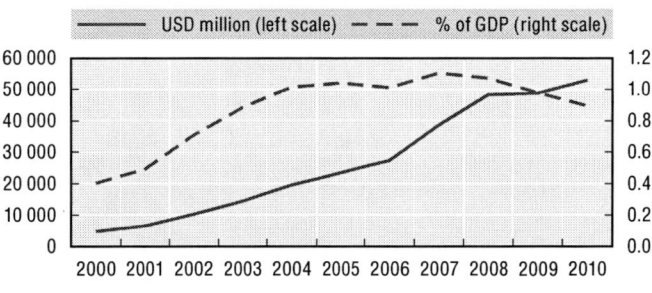

Ten main countries of destination for legal migrants in 2010 (numbers, % of total flows to the country): KOR (155252, 53%), JPN (107930, 37.6%), USA (70863, 6.8%), CAN (30195, 10.8%), GBR (28000, 6%), AUS (25025, 12.1%), ITA (22866, 4%), ESP (17372, 4%), DEU (16248, 2.4%), NZL (5622, 12.7%).

Desire to emigrate, 2008-10

	Women	15-24	Highly educated	Total	Regional total
Persons who would move permanently, if they had the opportunity to do so (%)	6	12	17	7	9
Of which: Persons who are planning to move permanently in the next 12 months (%)				5	7
Of which: Persons who have already done some preparations for this move (*e.g.* visa application) (%)					40

Three main countries of desired destination: United States (32%), Korea (8%), Canada (7%).

StatLink http://dx.doi.org/10.1787/888932672308

Total population 2010 (millions)	0.9	Fiji compared to:	World	Region
Population growth 2010 (%)	1.0	Human Development Index (HDI)	100/187	8/31
GDP per capita 2010 (current USD)	3 706	GDP per capita	104/194	10/33
GDP growth 2010 (%)	0.3	Emigration rate	26/203	7/38
Poverty rate 2010 (USD PPP 2 a day, in %)	..	Emigration rate of the highly educated	12/157	3/25

Age structure of the population 0+ (2010): "0-14": 18%; "15-24": 29%; "25-64": 48%; "65+": 5%.
Level of education of the population 15+ (2010): "Low": 10%; "Medium": 79%; "High": 11%.

Emigrant population living in OECD countries

Immigrant population

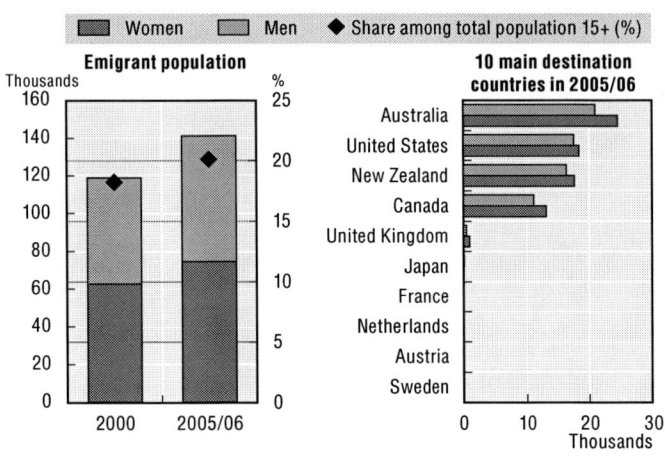

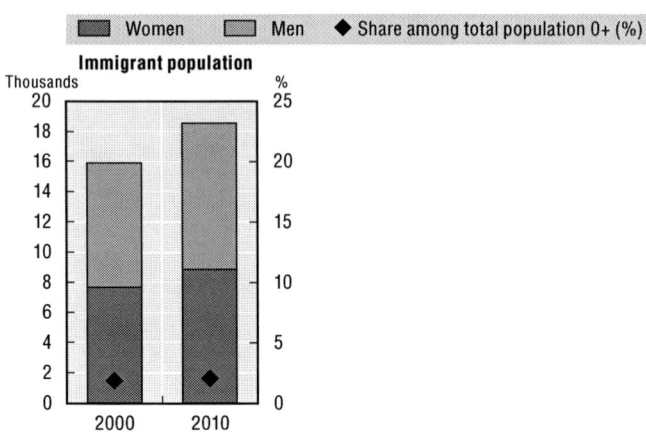

Emigrant population: persons born in Fiji living abroad

Population 15+	2000						2005/06		
	All destinations			OECD destinations			OECD destinations		
	Men	Women	Total	Men	Women	Total	Men	Women	Total
Emigrant population (thousands)	56.3	63.1	119.5	56.1	62.8	119.0	66.5	74.7	141.2
Recent emigrants (thousands)	..	..	..	11.4	13.4	24.8	13.2	15.0	28.2
15-24 (%)	18.0	17.6	17.8	18.1	17.5	17.8	13.7	13.3	13.5
25-64 (%)	76.4	76.2	76.3	76.4	76.2	76.3	78.5	78.8	78.6
65+ (%)	5.5	6.3	5.9	5.6	6.3	5.9	7.8	8.0	7.9
Low-educated (%)	29.1	36.5	33.0	29.0	36.5	32.9	18.6	22.3	20.5
Highly educated (%)	24.3	21.3	22.7	24.4	21.3	22.8	28.3	28.6	28.5
Total emigration rates (%)	17.5	19.4	18.4	17.4	19.3	18.4	19.2	21.3	20.3
Emigration rates of the highly educated (%)	31.3	34.8	32.9	31.3	34.7	32.9	36.5	41.1	38.8

Main destinations in 2005/06

Population 15+	Total		Recent emigrants	Women	Highly educated	15-24	Total in 2000
	Thousands	%	%	%	%	%	Thousands
Australia	45.5	32.2	16.7	54.0	35.0	13.5	40.9
United States	35.8	25.4	13.8	51.2	22.2	12.9	28.7
New Zealand	34.0	24.1	39.7	51.9	26.3	19.0	23.4
Canada	24.3	17.2	9.2	54.2	29.4	7.0	22.3
United Kingdom	–	–	–	–	–	–	3.3
Japan	–	–	–	–	–	–	–
France	–	–	–	–	–	–	0.1

Labour market indicators of persons born in Fiji living in OECD countries

Population 15-64	2000			2005/06		
	Men	Women	Total	Men	Women	Total
Employment-population ratio (%)	76.8	62.6	69.4	81.9	69.2	75.2
Unemployment rate (%)	6.6	8.2	7.4	5.6	5.9	5.8
Participation rate (%)	82.2	68.2	74.9	86.7	73.5	79.8
Total employed (thousands)	**38.4**	**34.3**	**72.7**	**47.6**	**44.5**	**92.1**
Employment rates of the highly educated (%)	89.0	79.0	84.0	94.4	86.4	90.1
Unemployment rates of the highly educated (%)	4.6	6.0	5.3	3.9	3.8	3.9
Highly educated in low- and medium-skilled jobs (%)	35.7	39.7	37.6	37.9	43.6	40.8
Highly educated employed (thousands)	**11.1**	**9.7**	**20.7**	**15.4**	**16.1**	**31.5**

Distribution of employment by occupation (%), population 15+

	Men	Women	Total	Men	Women	Total
Legislators, senior officials and managers	10.6	5.6	8.2	13.9	8.2	11.2
Professionals	14.5	15.6	15.0	12.7	15.3	13.9
Life science and health professionals	2.5	8.1	5.1	1.6	6.1	3.7
Teaching professionals	2.9	4.4	3.6	2.5	4.6	3.5
Technicians and associate professionals	9.5	10.7	10.1	9.8	12.0	10.8
Clerks	8.0	25.1	16.1	9.7	23.7	16.4
Service, shop and market sales workers	9.6	23.1	16.0	9.5	22.4	15.7
Skilled agricultural and fishery workers	0.8	0.4	0.6	1.3	2.1	1.7
Craft and related trades workers	18.7	2.1	10.8	19.7	2.7	11.6
Plant and machine operators and assemblers	14.2	4.6	9.7	12.7	4.4	8.7
Elementary occupations	14.2	12.7	13.5	10.7	9.2	10.0

Persons born in Fiji and their native-born children, population 15+

Living in:	Europe	United States	Australia
2008	Thousands	Thousands	Thousands
Native-born children	1.8	6.9	6.5
Foreign-born	1.6	36.9	52.9
Total	3.4	43.7	59.4

International students from Fiji in OECD countries

Five main destinations	2004	2005	2006	2007	2008	2009
New Zealand	540	450	526	560	566	737
Australia	758	891	848	833	782	689
United States	177	192	183	114	177	189
Japan	27	30	29	35	36	30
United Kingdom	29	33	34	30	23	17
Total	1 547	1 610	1 634	1 586	1 601	1 693

Legal migrant flows to the OECD
Thousands

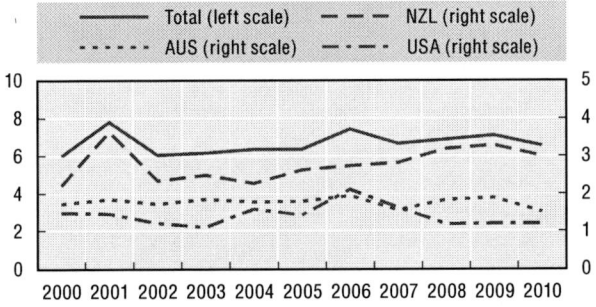

Remittance flows

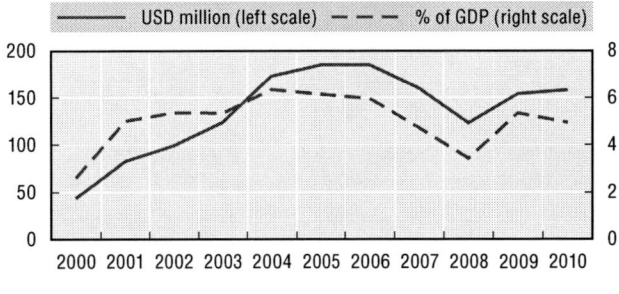

Ten main countries of destination for legal migrants in 2010 (numbers, % of total flows to the country): NZL (2992, 6.8%), AUS (1530, 0.7%), USA (1201, 0.1%), CAN (385, 0.1%), GBR (205, 0%), JPN (111, 0%), KOR (32, 0%), FRA (28, 0%), DEU (28, 0%), AUT (6, 0%).

Desire to emigrate, 2008-10

	Women	15-24	Highly educated	Total	Regional total
Persons who would move permanently, if they had the opportunity to do so (%)	..	..	..	..	9
Of which: Persons who are planning to move permanently in the next 12 months (%)				..	7
Of which: Persons who have already done some preparations for this move (*e.g.* visa application) (%)					40

StatLink ⟲ http://dx.doi.org/10.1787/888932672327

Total population 2010 (millions)	1 170.9		India compared to:	World	Region
Population growth 2010 (%)	1.3		Human Development Index (HDI)	134/187	20/31
GDP per capita 2010 (current USD)	1 475		GDP per capita	135/194	23/33
GDP growth 2010 (%)	8.8		Emigration rate	181/203	32/38
Poverty rate 2005 (USD PPP 2 a day, in %)	75.6		Emigration rate of the highly educated	129/157	19/25

Age structure of the population 0+ (2010): "0-14": 19%; "15-24": 31%; "25-64": 45%; "65+": 5%.
Level of education of the population 15+ (2010): "Low": 54%; "Medium": 41%; "High": 6%.

Emigrant population living in OECD countries

Immigrant population

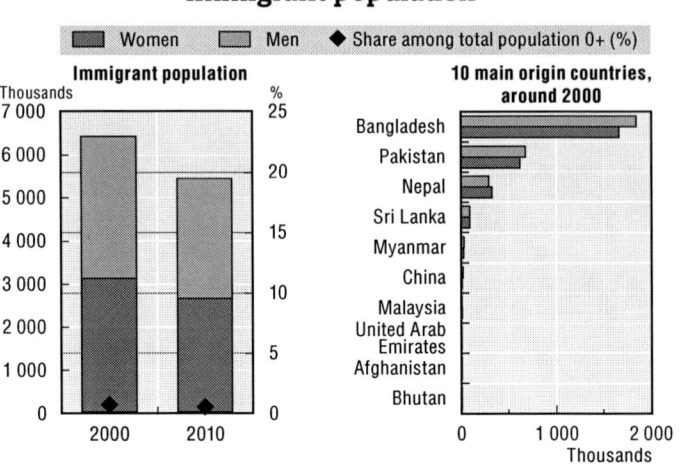

Emigrant population: persons born in India living abroad

	2000						2005/06		
	All destinations			OECD destinations			OECD destinations		
Population 15+	Men	Women	Total	Men	Women	Total	Men	Women	Total
Emigrant population (thousands)	1 271.7	1 366.9	2 638.5	1 027.6	943.0	1 970.6	1 469.5	1 305.7	2 775.2
Recent emigrants (thousands)	..	..	..	264.2	226.6	490.8	417.2	362.9	780.1
15-24 (%)	12.3	14.0	13.2	10.2	11.0	10.6	9.8	9.8	9.8
25-64 (%)	78.0	75.7	76.8	80.0	77.7	78.9	79.7	78.4	79.1
65+ (%)	9.7	10.3	10.0	9.8	11.4	10.6	10.5	11.7	11.1
Low-educated (%)	29.8	47.1	38.8	22.5	31.2	26.7	14.0	19.6	16.6
Highly educated (%)	49.3	34.3	41.5	57.7	47.5	52.8	66.7	59.3	63.3
Total emigration rates (%)	0.4	0.4	0.4	0.3	0.3	0.3	0.4	0.4	0.4
Emigration rates of the highly educated (%)	3.0	4.0	3.4	2.9	3.8	3.2	4.0	4.5	4.2

Main destinations in 2005/06

	Total		Recent emigrants	Women	Highly educated	15-24	Total in 2000
Population 15+	Thousands	%	%	%	%	%	Thousands
United States	1 469.2	52.9	27.4	45.9	74.2	9.2	958.1
United Kingdom	500.7	18.0	28.8	48.9	54.9	7.2	454.5
Canada	430.1	15.5	26.3	50.0	50.2	9.3	306.9
Australia	136.4	4.9	39.9	44.5	66.5	15.9	88.2
Italy	41.9	1.5	42.5	43.9	4.7	22.5	24.0
France	38.6	1.4	19.3	48.9	23.2	15.4	26.4
New Zealand	37.9	1.4	60.8	47.8	54.1	15.5	18.4
Israel	16.4	0.6	13.6	51.7	20.6	4.2	18.7
Switzerland	15.2	0.5	46.9	43.5	53.3	11.4	7.2
Spain	14.5	0.5	26.6	42.2	29.4	–	7.8

Labour market indicators of persons born in India living in OECD countries

Population 15-64	2000 Men	2000 Women	2000 Total	2005/06 Men	2005/06 Women	2005/06 Total
Employment-population ratio (%)	81.9	54.4	68.9	85.7	57.4	72.5
Unemployment rate (%)	4.7	7.9	5.9	4.6	9.0	6.3
Participation rate (%)	86.0	59.0	73.2	89.9	63.0	77.4
Total employed (thousands)	**737.7**	**442.8**	**1 180.5**	**1 102.7**	**640.9**	**1 743.6**
Employment rates of the highly educated (%)	88.6	61.5	76.8	95.0	68.8	83.3
Unemployment rates of the highly educated (%)	3.0	6.5	4.3	3.3	8.0	5.0
Highly educated in low- and medium-skilled jobs (%)	21.7	33.7	25.9	23.6	31.9	26.5
Highly educated employed (thousands)	**474.8**	**254.2**	**729.0**	**803.3**	**442.3**	**1 245.6**
Legislators, senior officials and managers	15.0	8.6	12.4	12.9	6.8	10.5
Professionals	19.8	14.5	17.7	20.9	16.8	19.3
Life science and health professionals	6.7	4.9	6.0	6.4	6.4	6.4
Teaching professionals	2.4	5.0	3.4	1.4	4.8	2.7
Technicians and associate professionals	8.8	10.9	9.7	9.5	15.9	12.0
Clerks	6.4	19.4	11.7	6.5	18.6	11.2
Service, shop and market sales workers	8.3	17.2	11.9	10.0	11.6	10.6
Skilled agricultural and fishery workers	1.3	1.3	1.3	2.5	4.4	3.2
Craft and related trades workers	10.5	2.1	7.1	8.0	3.9	6.4
Plant and machine operators and assemblers	17.3	11.4	14.9	16.5	8.4	13.3
Elementary occupations	12.7	14.5	13.4	12.2	13.2	12.6

Distribution of employment by occupation (%), population 15+

Persons born in India and their native-born children, population 15+

Living in:	Europe	United States	Australia
2008	Thousands	Thousands	Thousands
Native-born children	403.0	602.8	17.8
Foreign-born	935.1	1 720.6	97.0
Total	1 338.1	2 323.4	114.8

International students from India in OECD countries

Five main destinations	2004	2005	2006	2007	2008	2009
United States	79 736	84 044	79 219	85 687	94 664	101 563
United Kingdom	14 625	16 685	19 204	23 833	25 901	34 065
Australia	15 742	20 515	22 357	24 523	26 520	26 573
New Zealand	1 698	1 563	1 777	2 452	4 094	5 710
Canada	1 271	..	2 826	1 812	3 219	3 501
Total	114 398	124 536	127 625	141 086	161 902	180 138

Legal migrant flows to the OECD
Thousands

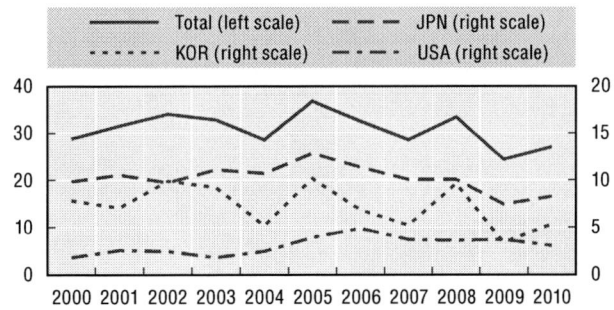

Remittance flows

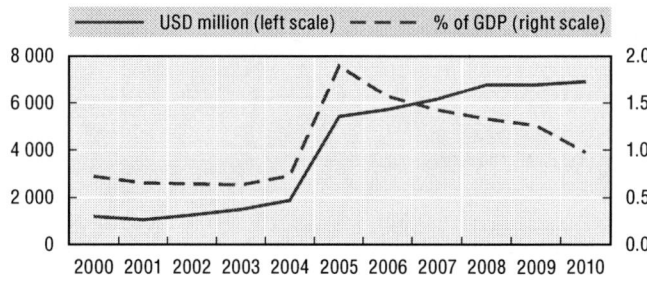

Ten main countries of destination for legal migrants in 2010 (numbers, % of total flows to the country): USA (69162, 6.6%), GBR (68000, 14.7%), CAN (30250, 10.9%), AUS (23512, 11.4%), ITA (15246, 3.6%), DEU (13187, 2%), JPN (4854, 1.1%), ESP (4758, 1.1%), NZL (3976, 9%), NLD (3172, 3.2%).

Desire to emigrate, 2008-10

	Women	15-24	Highly educated	Total	Regional total
Persons who would move permanently, if they had the opportunity to do so (%)	3	9	13	5	9
Of which: Persons who are planning to move permanently in the next 12 months (%)				11	7
Of which: Persons who have already done some preparations for this move (*e.g.* visa application) (%)					40

Three main countries of desired destination: United States (31%), United Kingdom (7%), United Arab Emirates (4%).

StatLink http://dx.doi.org/10.1787/888932672346

			Indonesia compared to:	World	Region
Total population 2010 (millions)		239.9			
Population growth 2010 (%)		1.0	Human Development Index (HDI)	125/187	17/31
GDP per capita 2010 (current USD)		2 946	GDP per capita	116/194	15/33
GDP growth 2010 (%)		6.1	Emigration rate	194/203	36/38
Poverty rate 2009 (USD PPP 2 a day, in %)		50.6	Emigration rate of the highly educated	133/157	21/25

Age structure of the population 0+ (2010): "0-14": 18%; "15-24": 27%; "25-64": 49%; "65+": 6%.
Level of education of the population 15+ (2010): "Low": 70%; "Medium": 28%; "High": 2%.

Emigrant population living in OECD countries

Immigrant population

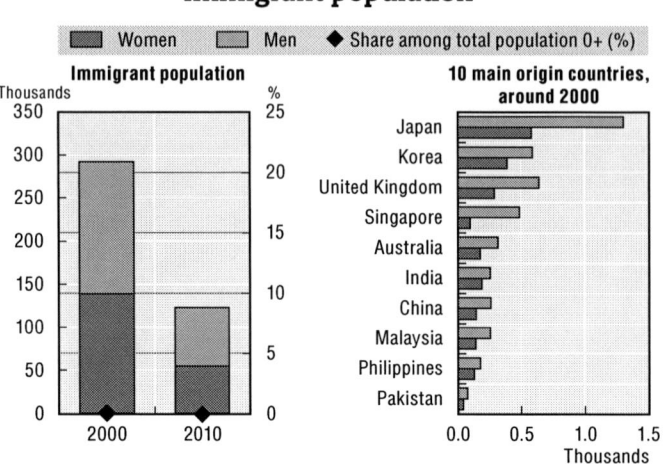

Emigrant population: persons born in Indonesia living abroad

	2000						2005/06		
	All destinations			OECD destinations			OECD destinations		
Population 15+	Men	Women	Total	Men	Women	Total	Men	Women	Total
Emigrant population (thousands)	538.2	551.5	1 089.8	162.3	177.3	339.6	152.8	183.2	336.0
Recent emigrants (thousands)	..	..	..	22.0	26.4	48.4	17.6	26.5	44.0
15-24 (%)	20.7	23.6	22.2	13.7	11.3	12.4	12.8	9.2	10.9
25-64 (%)	71.1	65.8	68.4	65.4	61.8	63.5	64.0	64.9	64.5
65+ (%)	8.2	10.6	9.4	20.9	26.9	24.0	23.1	25.9	24.6
Low-educated (%)	69.1	63.9	66.4	21.0	29.5	25.5	14.0	21.1	17.9
Highly educated (%)	14.8	12.5	13.6	40.4	30.7	35.3	45.2	39.0	41.9
Total emigration rates (%)	0.7	0.7	0.7	0.2	0.2	0.2	0.2	0.2	0.2
Emigration rates of the highly educated (%)	3.8	5.2	4.3	3.2	4.2	3.6	3.4	4.1	3.7

Main destinations in 2005/06

	Total		Recent emigrants	Women	Highly educated	15-24	Total in 2000
Population 15+	Thousands	%	%	%	%	%	Thousands
Netherlands	144.3	43.0	1.9	54.8	30.6	1.7	177.9
United States	82.8	24.6	18.0	55.5	54.1	12.0	70.3
Australia	47.4	14.1	32.4	55.7	52.8	26.2	43.4
Japan	17.4	5.2	..	32.0	21.6	33.2	13.8
Canada	12.7	3.8	20.4	53.1	63.1	13.9	10.0
United Kingdom	7.6	2.3	–	–	–	–	6.1
New Zealand	4.1	1.2	37.6	55.1	42.6	16.1	3.4
France	4.0	1.2	27.3	67.9	44.7	15.8	3.4
Belgium	–	–	–	–	–	–	2.6
Switzerland	2.9	0.9	55.3	56.4	–	–	2.2

Labour market indicators of persons born in Indonesia living in OECD countries

Population 15-64	2000			2005/06		
	Men	Women	Total	Men	Women	Total
Employment-population ratio (%)	69.1	53.0	60.9	75.3	57.6	65.5
Unemployment rate (%)	3.8	5.2	4.4	6.7	7.2	6.9
Participation rate (%)	71.9	55.9	63.7	80.7	62.0	70.4
Total employed (thousands)	**80.6**	**65.3**	**145.9**	**77.1**	**72.4**	**149.5**
Employment rates of the highly educated (%)	75.7	61.2	69.0	88.7	69.9	78.8
Unemployment rates of the highly educated (%)	3.9	5.4	4.5	5.0	6.3	5.6
Highly educated in low- and medium-skilled jobs (%)	21.8	37.5	27.9	29.1	39.7	34.0
Highly educated employed (thousands)	**37.1**	**25.6**	**62.6**	**42.1**	**36.6**	**78.6**
Legislators, senior officials and managers	6.0	3.7	4.9	10.6	6.3	8.5
Professionals	40.4	16.6	29.1	25.5	18.0	21.8
Life science and health professionals	6.7	1.4	4.2	4.5	3.0	3.7
Teaching professionals	8.4	10.4	9.3	3.1	4.1	3.6
Technicians and associate professionals	19.4	22.1	20.7	17.1	16.1	16.6
Clerks	3.8	27.7	15.2	11.0	23.6	17.1
Service, shop and market sales workers	6.9	19.4	12.9	10.9	20.3	15.4
Skilled agricultural and fishery workers	0.5	0.2	0.4	0.5	1.2	0.8
Craft and related trades workers	10.3	1.0	5.9	8.9	1.6	5.4
Plant and machine operators and assemblers	4.8	1.7	3.3	8.0	2.6	5.4
Elementary occupations	7.9	7.5	7.7	7.5	10.5	8.9

Distribution of employment by occupation (%), population 15+

Persons born in Indonesia and their native-born children, population 15+

Living in:	Europe	United States	Australia
2008	Thousands	Thousands	Thousands
Native-born children	269.3	45.6	9.8
Foreign-born	143.1	121.9	46.7
Total	412.4	167.4	56.4

International students from Indonesia in OECD countries

Five main destinations	2004	2005	2006	2007	2008	2009
Australia	10 184	9 293	9 054	10 536	10 242	10 205
United States	8 880	8 105	7 844	7 500	7 700	7 386
Japan	1 474	1 414	1 467	1 541	1 578	1 788
Germany	..	..	..	..	1 579	1 520
United Kingdom	1 107	1 150	1 154	1 092	924	1 029
Total	22 734	21 314	21 503	22 330	24 245	24 271

Legal migrant flows to the OECD
Thousands

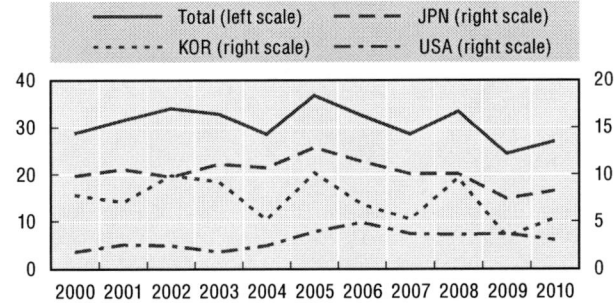

Remittance flows

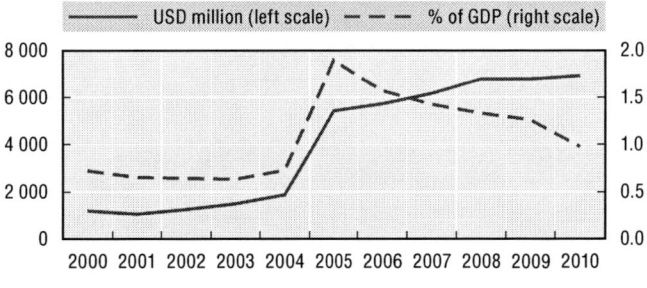

Ten main countries of destination for legal migrants in 2010 (numbers, % of total flows to the country): JPN (8297, 2.9%), KOR (5308, 1.8%), USA (3032, 0.3%), AUS (2449, 1.2%), GBR (2205, 0.5%), DEU (1759, 0.3%), NLD (1227, 0.3%), CAN (735, 0.3%), TUR (320, 1.1%), FRA (225, 0.2%).

Desire to emigrate, 2008-10

	Women	15-24	Highly educated	Total	Regional total
Persons who would move permanently, if they had the opportunity to do so (%)	2	..	..	3	9
Of which: Persons who are planning to move permanently in the next 12 months (%)				..	7
Of which: Persons who have already done some preparations for this move (*e.g.* visa application) (%)					40

StatLink ⬛⬛ *http://dx.doi.org/10.1787/888932672365*

LAOS – Country Notes

Total population 2010 (millions)	6.2	**Laos compared to:**	**World**	**Region**
Population growth 2010 (%)	1.4	Human Development Index (HDI)	138/187	21/31
GDP per capita 2010 (current USD)	1 177	GDP per capita	145/194	27/33
GDP growth 2010 (%)	9.4	Emigration rate	67/203	10/38
Poverty rate 2008 (USD PPP 2 a day, in %)	66.0	Emigration rate of the highly educated	25/157	6/25

Age structure of the population 0+ (2010): "0-14": 23%; "15-24": 35%; "25-64": 39%; "65+": 4%.
Level of education of the population 15+ (2010): "Low": 63%; "Medium": 31%; "High": 6%.

Emigrant population living in OECD countries

Immigrant population

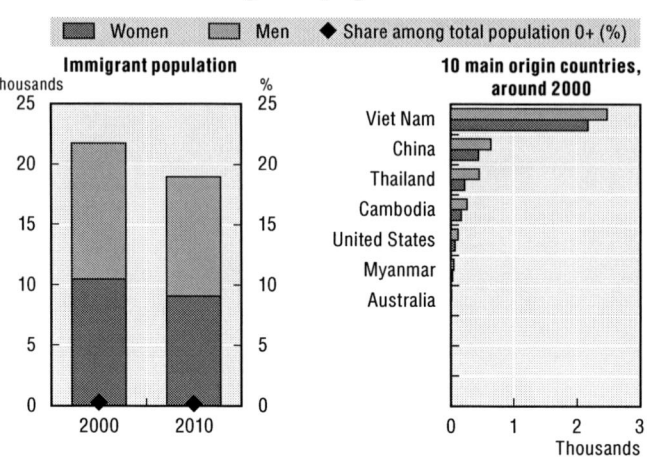

Emigrant population: persons born in Laos living abroad

	2000						2005/06		
	All destinations			OECD destinations			OECD destinations		
Population 15+	Men	Women	Total	Men	Women	Total	Men	Women	Total
Emigrant population (thousands)	137.6	138.4	275.9	132.8	131.4	264.1	126.4	129.7	256.1
Recent emigrants (thousands)	..	..	..	4.4	5.8	10.2	4.2	6.5	10.7
15-24 (%)	13.8	14.0	13.9	13.8	13.7	13.8	3.3	3.8	3.5
25-64 (%)	80.6	78.6	79.6	81.2	79.0	80.1	88.5	86.3	87.4
65+ (%)	5.7	7.4	6.5	5.0	7.3	6.1	8.2	9.9	9.1
Low-educated (%)	45.7	57.6	51.7	43.9	55.8	49.8	34.9	47.1	41.1
Highly educated (%)	15.7	11.7	13.7	16.2	12.3	14.3	22.3	17.2	19.7
Total emigration rates (%)	8.6	8.5	8.5	8.3	8.1	8.2	7.0	7.0	7.0
Emigration rates of the highly educated (%)	23.9	29.2	25.9	23.8	29.2	25.9	24.4	25.2	24.8

Main destinations in 2005/06

	Total		Recent emigrants	Women	Highly educated	15-24	Total in 2000
Population 15+	Thousands	%	%	%	%	%	Thousands
United States	186.0	72.6	5.0	50.6	19.3	3.8	194.8
France	40.3	15.7	1.5	50.5	18.7	1.7	40.6
Canada	14.5	5.7	2.0	50.0	25.0	4.0	14.2
Australia	9.3	3.6	4.7	51.9	23.9	4.4	9.3
Japan	1.6	0.6	..	48.1	11.0	0.0	1.1
Belgium	–	–	–	–	–	–	1.1
Spain	1.2	0.5	–	–	–	–	–
New Zealand	0.9	0.3	1.6	46.0	8.8	10.0	1.0
Sweden	0.4	0.1	19.0	57.9	5.7	13.2	0.4
United Kingdom	–	–	–	–	–	–	0.5

Labour market indicators of persons born in Laos living in OECD countries

Population 15-64	2000			2005/06		
	Men	Women	Total	Men	Women	Total
Employment-population ratio (%)	67.6	53.6	60.7	75.0	62.3	68.7
Unemployment rate (%)	8.4	11.0	9.6	8.5	9.5	9.0
Participation rate (%)	73.8	60.2	67.1	82.0	68.8	75.4
Total employed (thousands)	**84.4**	**64.6**	**149.0**	**85.6**	**71.3**	**156.9**
Employment rates of the highly educated (%)	78.1	70.7	74.9	90.4	82.9	87.0
Unemployment rates of the highly educated (%)	5.0	7.3	6.0	4.8	6.3	5.4
Highly educated in low- and medium-skilled jobs (%)	47.2	46.0	46.7	48.1	41.3	45.3
Highly educated employed (thousands)	**16.4**	**11.2**	**27.5**	**22.9**	**16.6**	**39.6**
Legislators, senior officials and managers	6.1	6.0	6.1	7.6	7.5	7.6
Professionals	6.9	5.8	6.4	9.2	7.8	8.6
Life science and health professionals	1.2	0.9	1.1	1.1	1.1	1.1
Teaching professionals	0.8	1.0	0.9	0.7	1.4	1.0
Technicians and associate professionals	13.0	11.4	12.4	12.5	13.8	13.1
Clerks	5.8	17.7	10.8	6.8	14.9	10.4
Service, shop and market sales workers	7.9	16.7	11.6	8.6	18.3	13.0
Skilled agricultural and fishery workers	1.5	1.6	1.5	2.3	1.7	2.0
Craft and related trades workers	20.6	7.1	15.0	19.1	6.5	13.4
Plant and machine operators and assemblers	25.6	21.2	23.8	24.5	16.8	21.0
Elementary occupations	12.4	12.6	12.5	9.5	12.7	10.9

Distribution of employment by occupation (%), population 15+

Persons born in Laos and their native-born children, population 15+

Living in:	Europe	United States	Australia
2008	Thousands	Thousands	Thousands
Native-born children	28.4	175.1	..
Foreign-born	29.7	216.3	7.3
Total	58.1	391.4	..

International students from Laos in OECD countries

Five main destinations	2004	2005	2006	2007	2008	2009
Japan	231	255	256	257	251	264
Australia	117	111	125	162	162	167
France	168	151	137	132	104	117
United States	65	66	67	46	69	79
Korea	15	15	24	37	35	33
Total	626	613	633	668	689	747

Legal migrant flows to the OECD
Thousands

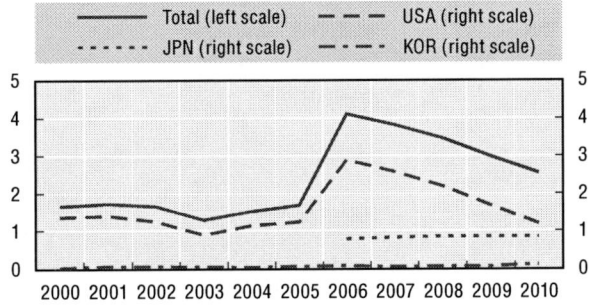

Remittance flows

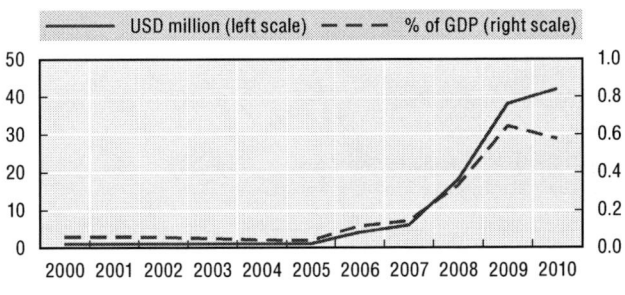

Ten main countries of destination for legal migrants in 2010 (numbers, % of total flows to the country): USA (1200, 0.1%), JPN (855, 0.3%), KOR (117, 0%), FRA (110, 0.1%), AUS (69, 0%), CAN (60, 0%), DEU (51, 0%), SWE (17, 0%), CHE (15, 0%), BEL (14, 0%).

Desire to emigrate, 2008-10

	Women	15-24	Highly educated	Total	Regional total
Persons who would move permanently, if they had the opportunity to do so (%)	12	16	..	12	9
Of which: Persons who are planning to move permanently in the next 12 months (%)				..	7
Of which: Persons who have already done some preparations for this move (*e.g.* visa application) (%)					40

StatLink http://dx.doi.org/10.1787/888932672384

Total population 2010 (millions)	28.4	**Malaysia compared to:**		**World**	**Region**
Population growth 2010 (%)	1.6	Human Development Index (HDI)		61/187	5/31
GDP per capita 2010 (current USD)	8 373	GDP per capita		69/194	5/33
GDP growth 2010 (%)	7.2	Emigration rate		140/203	23/38
Poverty rate 2009 (USD PPP 2 a day, in %)	2.3	Emigration rate of the highly educated		111/157	17/25

Age structure of the population 0+ (2010): "0-14": 18%; "15-24": 30%; "25-64": 47%; "65+": 5%.
Level of education of the population 15+ (2010): "Low": 24%; "Medium": 61%; "High": 15%.

Emigrant population living in OECD countries

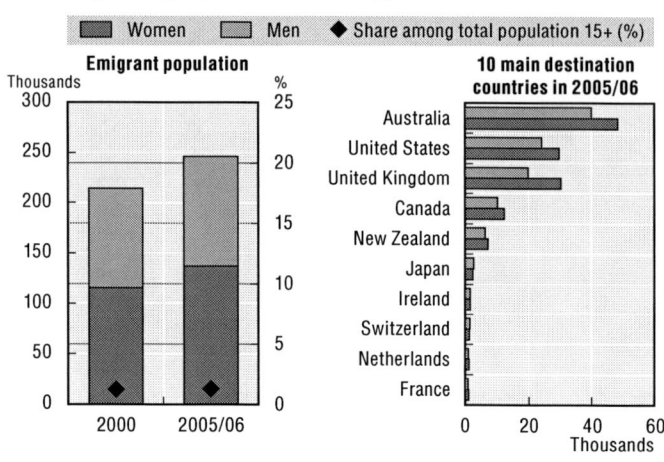

Immigrant population

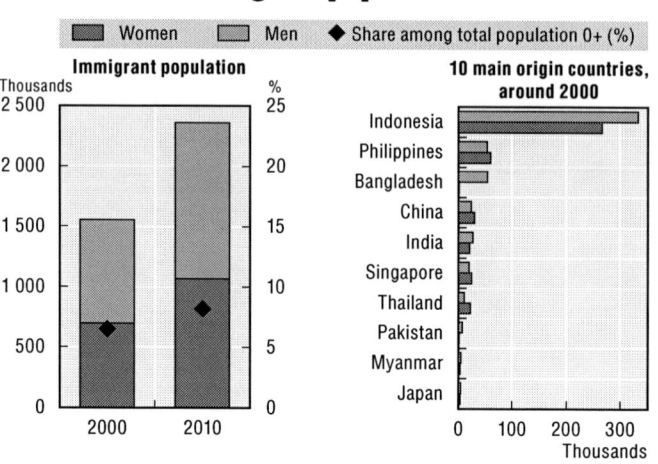

Emigrant population: persons born in Malaysia living abroad

	2000						2005/06		
	All destinations			OECD destinations			OECD destinations		
Population 15+	Men	Women	Total	Men	Women	Total	Men	Women	Total
Emigrant population (thousands)	234.3	298.3	532.6	98.6	115.7	214.3	108.9	137.1	245.9
Recent emigrants (thousands)	..	..	..	16.9	18.8	35.7	22.7	28.3	51.0
15-24 (%)	22.0	17.8	19.7	23.9	19.0	21.2	19.3	16.1	17.5
25-64 (%)	72.0	76.5	74.5	71.2	75.3	73.5	73.0	76.5	74.9
65+ (%)	6.0	5.7	5.9	4.9	5.7	5.3	7.7	7.4	7.6
Low-educated (%)	28.4	42.1	36.1	16.4	22.0	19.4	9.7	13.1	11.6
Highly educated (%)	37.1	25.5	30.6	53.0	47.8	50.2	61.4	56.0	58.4
Total emigration rates (%)	2.9	3.8	3.3	1.2	1.5	1.4	1.2	1.6	1.4
Emigration rates of the highly educated (%)	9.4	9.3	9.4	5.7	6.7	6.2	5.1	6.3	5.6

Main destinations in 2005/06

	Total		Recent emigrants	Women	Highly educated	15-24	Total in 2000
Population 15+	Thousands	%	%	%	%	%	Thousands
Australia	88.3	35.9	24.2	54.8	58.6	21.7	75.1
United States	54.0	21.9	17.7	55.2	58.7	11.0	47.8
United Kingdom	50.1	20.4	21.5	60.5	67.5	17.2	47.5
Canada	22.3	9.1	8.1	54.6	59.3	10.0	20.6
New Zealand	13.5	5.5	33.0	53.3	48.1	23.8	10.7
Japan	5.0	2.0	..	46.8	32.5	32.8	5.5
Ireland	3.2	1.3	59.0	49.5	48.1	32.8	2.0
Switzerland	2.7	1.1	68.4	45.3	49.6	–	1.2
Netherlands	2.0	0.8	–	–	–	–	–
France	2.0	0.8	30.5	55.5	40.8	17.6	1.4

Labour market indicators of persons born in Malaysia living in OECD countries

	2000			2005/06		
Population 15-64	Men	Women	Total	Men	Women	Total
Employment-population ratio (%)	71.5	60.3	65.4	78.5	65.3	71.2
Unemployment rate (%)	6.2	6.1	6.2	4.9	5.1	5.0
Participation rate (%)	76.3	64.2	69.7	82.6	68.9	74.9
Total employed (thousands)	**62.5**	**61.6**	**124.1**	**73.8**	**77.8**	**151.6**
Employment rates of the highly educated (%)	81.7	72.4	76.8	92.2	79.3	85.3
Unemployment rates of the highly educated (%)	4.3	4.2	4.3	3.9	4.0	3.9
Highly educated in low- and medium-skilled jobs (%)	18.5	22.8	20.6	19.3	26.4	22.9
Highly educated employed (thousands)	**38.5**	**36.5**	**75.0**	**52.2**	**52.4**	**104.6**
Distribution of employment by occupation (%), population 15+						
Legislators, senior officials and managers	15.6	9.0	12.3	20.3	10.8	15.3
Professionals	33.7	29.9	31.8	33.9	29.0	31.4
Life science and health professionals	9.6	12.2	10.9	8.2	11.4	9.8
Teaching professionals	3.7	5.4	4.5	5.0	3.7	4.3
Technicians and associate professionals	12.6	18.8	15.8	10.8	19.2	15.2
Clerks	6.9	19.0	13.1	7.1	16.0	11.8
Service, shop and market sales workers	11.9	14.7	13.3	10.2	11.0	10.6
Skilled agricultural and fishery workers	0.5	0.2	0.3	2.4	3.3	2.9
Craft and related trades workers	7.4	1.2	4.2	6.2	3.2	4.6
Plant and machine operators and assemblers	4.6	1.9	3.2	3.5	1.6	2.5
Elementary occupations	6.8	5.3	6.0	4.5	4.9	4.7

Persons born in Malaysia and their native-born children, population 15+

Living in:	Europe	United States	Australia
2008	Thousands	Thousands	Thousands
Native-born children	28.1	23.1	5.7
Foreign-born	62.0	63.0	39.9
Total	90.0	86.1	45.6

International students from Malaysia in OECD countries

Five main destinations	2004	2005	2006	2007	2008	2009
Australia	16 094	15 552	15 358	17 691	18 576	19 970
United Kingdom	11 806	11 474	11 448	11 811	11 727	12 697
United States	6 483	6 415	5 711	5 398	5 434	5 844
Japan	1 841	1 915	2 009	2 052	2 012	2 147
New Zealand	1 062	1 190	1 390	1 727	1 942	2 038
Total	38 267	37 138	37 219	39 883	43 146	46 326

Legal migrant flows to the OECD

Thousands

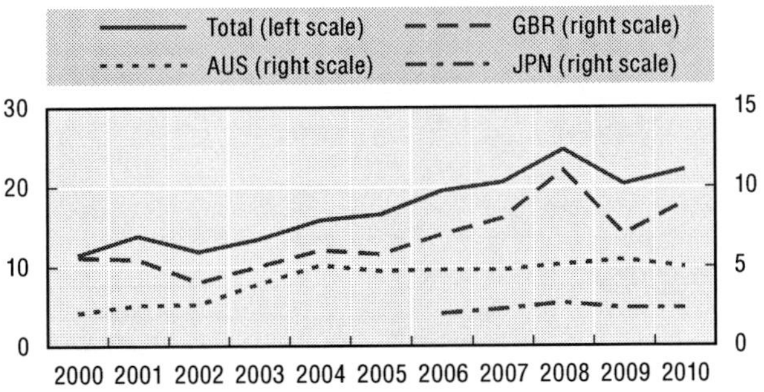

Remittance flows

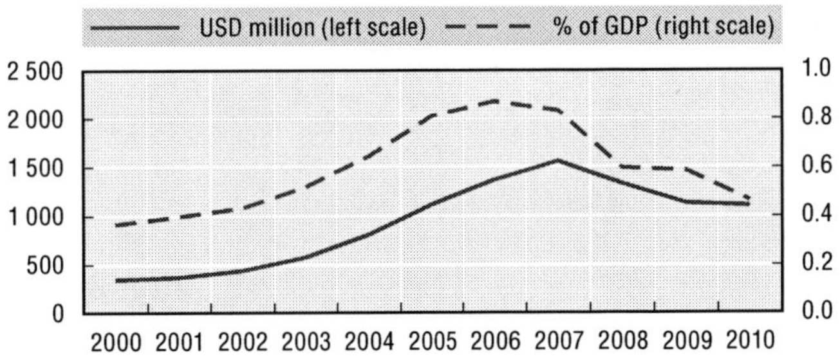

Ten main countries of destination for legal migrants in 2010 (numbers, % of total flows to the country): GBR (9000, 1.9%), AUS (4934, 2.4%), JPN (2318, 0.8%), USA (1714, 0.2%), CAN (900, 0.3%), NZL (710, 1.6%), DEU (618, 0.2%), KOR (581, 0.2%), CHE (259, 0.2%), NLD (255, 0.3%).

Desire to emigrate, 2008-10

	Women	15-24	Highly educated	Total	Regional total
Persons who would move permanently, if they had the opportunity to do so (%)	5	8	14	5	9
Of which: Persons who are planning to move permanently in the next 12 months (%)				. .	7
Of which: Persons who have already done some preparations for this move (*e.g.* visa application) (%)					40

StatLink http://dx.doi.org/10.1787/888932672403

			Myanmar compared to:	World	Region
Total population 2010 (millions)		48.0	Human Development Index (HDI)	149/187	28/31
Population growth 2010 (%)		0.8	GDP per capita	..	..
GDP per capita 2010 (current USD)		..	Emigration rate	193/203	35/38
GDP growth 2010 (%)		10.4	Emigration rate of the highly educated	151/157	25/25
Poverty rate 2010 (USD PPP 2 a day, in %)		..			

Age structure of the population 0+ (2010): "0-14": 19%; "15-24": 26%; "25-64": 51%; "65+": 5%.
Level of education of the population 15+ (2010): "Low": 77%; "Medium": 14%; "High": 9%.

Emigrant population living in OECD countries

Immigrant population

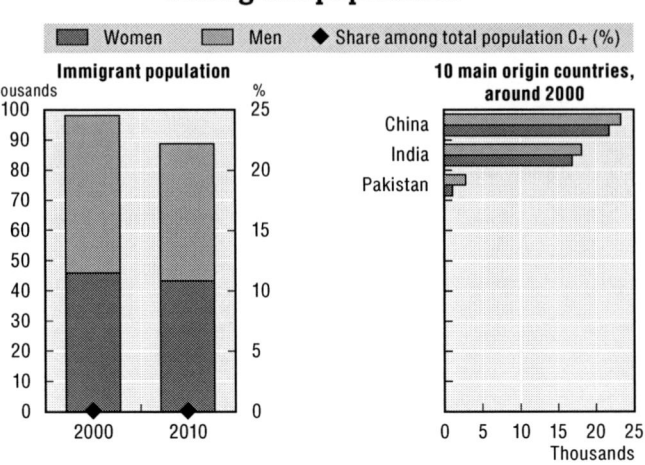

Emigrant population: persons born in Myanmar living abroad

	2000						2005/06		
	All destinations			OECD destinations			OECD destinations		
Population 15+	Men	Women	Total	Men	Women	Total	Men	Women	Total
Emigrant population (thousands)	115.7	104.1	219.8	30.3	31.2	61.4	37.8	40.6	78.4
Recent emigrants (thousands)	..	..	..	5.0	4.8	9.9	10.0	10.9	20.9
15-24 (%)	16.9	20.3	18.5	7.8	7.1	7.5	10.1	9.6	9.8
25-64 (%)	77.7	72.1	75.1	77.5	73.2	75.3	76.1	68.5	72.1
65+ (%)	5.4	7.6	6.4	14.7	19.7	17.2	13.9	21.9	18.0
Low-educated (%)	64.4	70.9	67.5	22.8	31.2	27.0	22.9	27.7	25.3
Highly educated (%)	14.3	16.3	15.2	47.7	41.3	44.5	44.9	43.7	44.3
Total emigration rates (%)	0.7	0.6	0.7	0.2	0.2	0.2	0.2	0.2	0.2
Emigration rates of the highly educated (%)	1.7	2.1	1.9	1.5	1.5	1.5	1.1	1.5	1.3

Main destinations in 2005/06

	Total		Recent emigrants	Women	Highly educated	15-24	Total in 2000
Population 15+	Thousands	%	%	%	%	%	Thousands
United States	49.1	62.6	32.3	49.4	44.6	10.7	31.6
Australia	12.0	15.3	16.3	51.9	38.7	8.9	10.5
United Kingdom	6.5	8.3	–	–	–	–	9.8
Canada	4.9	6.2	20.8	49.6	57.5	8.2	3.6
Japan	2.7	3.5	..	45.2	56.6	11.3	3.5
New Zealand	0.7	1.0	50.8	50.6	39.9	16.9	0.6
Denmark	0.6	0.8	90.2	35.6	17.2	19.0	0.1
Sweden	0.5	0.7	86.2	48.6	20.8	24.3	0.1
Netherlands	–	–	–	–	–	–	–
France	0.3	0.4	30.4	62.1	41.2	4.6	0.6

Labour market indicators of persons born in Myanmar living in OECD countries

Population 15-64	2000			2005/06		
	Men	Women	Total	Men	Women	Total
Employment-population ratio (%)	77.1	60.2	68.6	80.2	64.5	72.4
Unemployment rate (%)	5.7	5.8	5.7	7.8	5.9	7.0
Participation rate (%)	81.8	63.9	72.8	87.0	68.6	77.8
Total employed (thousands)	**17.7**	**14.0**	**31.6**	**23.9**	**18.9**	**42.8**
Employment rates of the highly educated (%)	84.8	70.1	77.7	93.7	75.9	84.7
Unemployment rates of the highly educated (%)	4.4	4.6	4.5	4.6	5.6	5.1
Highly educated in low- and medium-skilled jobs (%)	34.7	38.5	36.4	38.4	42.2	40.1
Highly educated employed (thousands)	**9.4**	**7.3**	**16.7**	**11.8**	**9.8**	**21.7**
Legislators, senior officials and managers	12.4	8.4	10.7	10.0	5.0	7.6
Professionals	20.7	20.1	20.5	15.2	18.0	16.5
Life science and health professionals	8.3	8.7	8.5	3.1	4.2	3.7
Teaching professionals	2.7	5.2	3.8	1.2	2.2	1.7
Technicians and associate professionals	12.0	12.3	12.2	11.1	10.4	10.8
Clerks	6.8	21.7	13.2	6.8	23.8	14.8
Service, shop and market sales workers	8.9	17.1	12.5	14.0	16.6	15.2
Skilled agricultural and fishery workers	0.4	0.2	0.3	0.4	0.1	0.3
Craft and related trades workers	10.6	1.7	6.8	10.9	7.0	9.1
Plant and machine operators and assemblers	12.2	4.2	8.8	20.8	6.4	14.0
Elementary occupations	15.8	14.3	15.2	10.8	12.7	11.7

Distribution of employment by occupation (%), population 15+

Persons born in Myanmar and their native-born children, population 15+

Living in:	Europe	United States	Australia
2008	Thousands	Thousands	Thousands
Native-born children	14.0	21.1	6.5
Foreign-born	7.6	71.1	16.3
Total	21.5	92.2	22.8

International students from Myanmar in OECD countries

Five main destinations	2004	2005	2006	2007	2008	2009
Japan	492	579	627	720	829	922
United States	691	680	673	639	605	656
Australia	211	194	199	289	356	495
United Kingdom	183	202	236	254	234	231
Korea	58	55	71	94	82	104
Total	1 711	1 772	1 886	2 086	2 260	2 593

Legal migrant flows to the OECD
Thousands

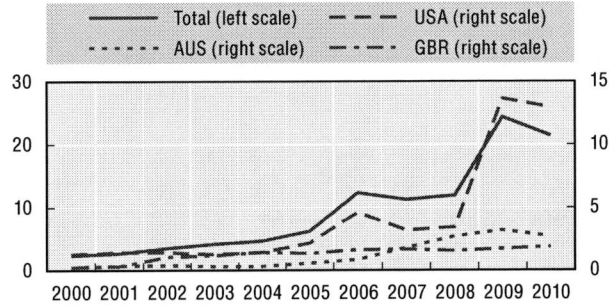

Remittance flows

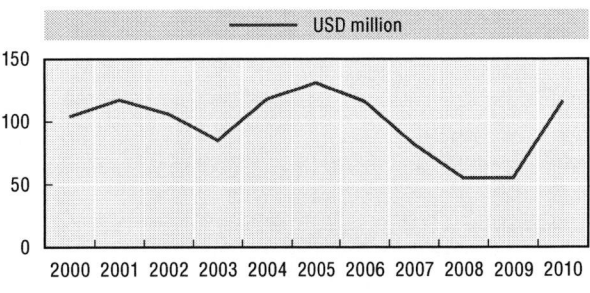

Ten main countries of destination for legal migrants in 2010 (numbers, % of total flows to the country): USA (12925, 1.2%), AUS (2656, 1.3%), GBR (1840, 0.4%), JPN (1139, 0.4%), KOR (618, 0.2%), CAN (450, 0.2%), DEU (446, 0.8%), NZL (349, 0.8%), NOR (279, 0.4%), DNK (227, 0.7%).

Desire to emigrate, 2008-10

	Women	15-24	Highly educated	Total	Regional total
Persons who would move permanently, if they had the opportunity to do so (%)	..	..	..	..	9
Of which: Persons who are planning to move permanently in the next 12 months (%)				..	7
Of which: Persons who have already done some preparations for this move (*e.g.* visa application) (%)					40

StatLink 🔗 http://dx.doi.org/10.1787/888932672422

Total population 2010 (millions)	30.0		Nepal compared to:	World	Region
Population growth 2010 (%)	1.8		Human Development Index (HDI)	157/187	30/31
GDP per capita 2009 (current USD)	438		GDP per capita	176/194	33/33
GDP growth 2010 (%)	4.6		Emigration rate	180/203	31/38
Poverty rate 2004 (USD PPP 2 a day, in %)	77.6		Emigration rate of the highly educated	104/157	14/25

Age structure of the population 0+ (2010): "0-14": 21%; "15-24": 36%; "25-64": 39%; "65+": 4%.
Level of education of the population 15+ (2010): "Low": 67%; "Medium": 31%; "High": 2%.

Emigrant population living in OECD countries

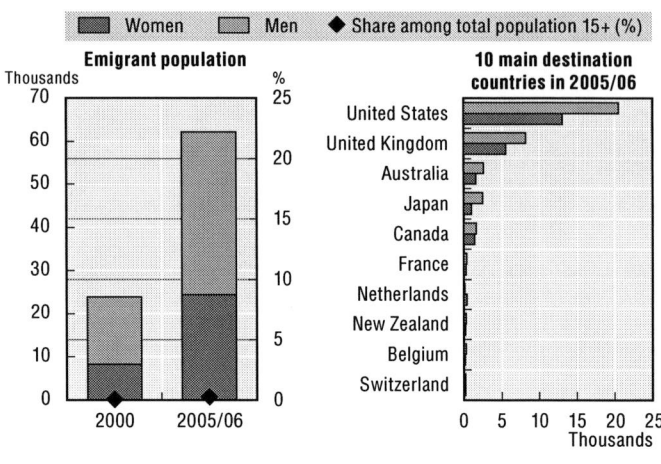

Immigrant population

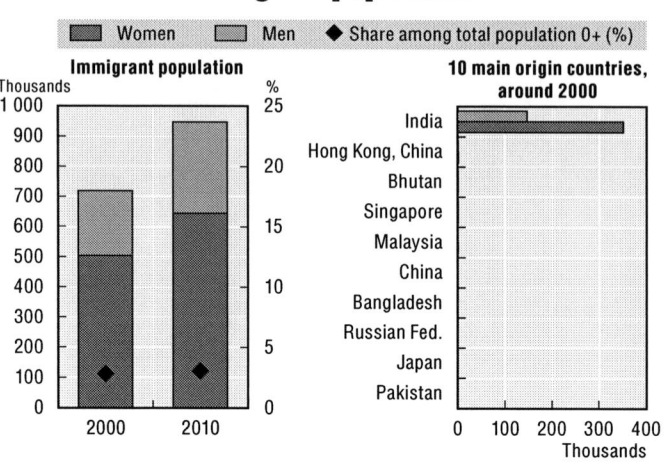

Emigrant population: persons born in Nepal living abroad

	2000						2005/06		
	All destinations			OECD destinations			OECD destinations		
Population 15+	Men	Women	Total	Men	Women	Total	Men	Women	Total
Emigrant population (thousands)	314.8	339.7	654.4	15.7	8.2	23.9	37.7	24.4	62.1
Recent emigrants (thousands)	..	..	..	5.6	3.1	8.7	17.4	14.4	31.7
15-24 (%)	35.3	33.8	34.6	24.2	23.6	24.0	17.6	26.1	21.0
25-64 (%)	64.6	66.1	65.4	75.0	75.2	75.0	81.5	73.0	78.1
65+ (%)	0.1	0.1	0.1	0.9	1.2	1.0	0.9	0.9	0.9
Low-educated (%)	59.1	80.8	70.3	20.9	26.3	22.8	13.4	23.9	17.5
Highly educated (%)	2.3	1.0	1.6	44.3	37.4	41.9	53.9	36.2	46.9
Total emigration rates (%)	4.3	4.4	4.3	0.2	0.1	0.2	0.5	0.3	0.4
Emigration rates of the highly educated (%)	2.1	4.2	2.5	1.9	3.7	2.2	5.7	7.6	6.2

Main destinations in 2005/06

	Total		Recent emigrants	Women	Highly educated	15-24	Total in 2000
Population 15+	Thousands	%	%	%	%	%	Thousands
United States	33.6	54.2	56.4	39.0	54.4	21.6	11.0
United Kingdom	13.7	22.1	57.3	–	–	–	5.2
Australia	4.2	6.8	50.0	38.3	65.1	24.9	2.2
Japan	3.5	5.7	..	29.5	42.0	14.6	2.4
Canada	3.1	5.0	61.3	46.3	57.0	23.0	1.0
France	0.7	1.1	27.7	43.7	29.2	28.4	0.4
Netherlands	–	–	–	–	–	–	–
New Zealand	0.5	0.8	61.4	41.0	54.5	24.1	0.3
Belgium	–	–	–	–	–	–	0.2
Switzerland	–	–	–	–	–	–	0.3

Labour market indicators of persons born in Nepal living in OECD countries

Population 15-64	2000			2005/06		
	Men	Women	Total	Men	Women	Total
Employment-population ratio (%)	74.4	55.1	67.6	81.6	55.5	71.3
Unemployment rate (%)	5.8	8.9	6.7	4.5	13.0	7.3
Participation rate (%)	79.0	60.5	72.4	85.5	63.8	76.9
Total employed (thousands)	**9.7**	**4.0**	**13.7**	**27.9**	**12.5**	**40.4**
Employment rates of the highly educated (%)	77.7	60.8	72.3	90.0	73.8	85.0
Unemployment rates of the highly educated (%)	4.8	8.9	5.9	4.9	12.1	6.8
Highly educated in low- and medium-skilled jobs (%)	39.9	49.6	42.6	42.2	43.0	42.4
Highly educated employed (thousands)	**4.5**	**1.7**	**6.2**	**15.9**	**5.4**	**21.3**
Legislators, senior officials and managers	9.3	3.9	7.6	20.9	1.2	14.6
Professionals	16.1	10.2	14.2	8.8	6.6	8.1
Life science and health professionals	4.1	4.6	4.2	0.5	2.1	1.0
Teaching professionals	2.2	2.5	2.3	0.4	0.2	0.3
Technicians and associate professionals	9.1	8.2	8.8	11.4	12.2	11.6
Clerks	7.6	13.9	9.7	2.9	9.3	4.9
Service, shop and market sales workers	27.1	36.0	30.0	13.0	16.1	14.0
Skilled agricultural and fishery workers	0.7	0.2	0.5	0.3	13.1	4.4
Craft and related trades workers	4.8	0.4	3.3	4.9	15.6	8.4
Plant and machine operators and assemblers	6.3	5.9	6.2	1.8	1.4	1.7
Elementary occupations	18.9	21.4	19.7	27.0	24.5	26.2

Distribution of employment by occupation (%), population 15+

Persons born in Nepal and their native-born children, population 15+

Living in:	Europe	United States	Australia
2008	Thousands	Thousands	Thousands
Native-born children	0.3	5.4	..
Foreign-born	26.7	30.4	8.4
Total	27.0	35.8	..

International students from Nepal in OECD countries

Five main destinations	2004	2005	2006	2007	2008	2009
United States	4 384	5 077	6 276	7 925	8 946	11 391
Australia	616	618	891	2 358	3 314	3 900
Japan	343	457	598	994	1 311	1 457
United Kingdom	394	458	518	635	646	693
Denmark	8	20	19	77	130	428
Total	5 982	6 922	8 685	12 402	15 239	18 926

Legal migrant flows to the OECD
Thousands

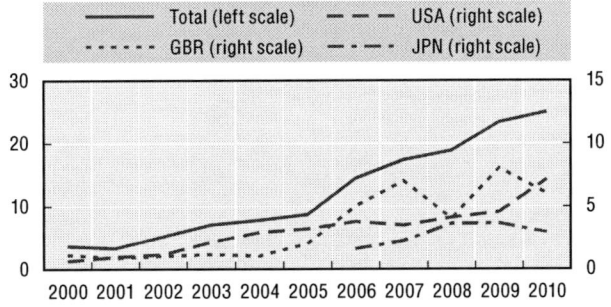

Remittance flows

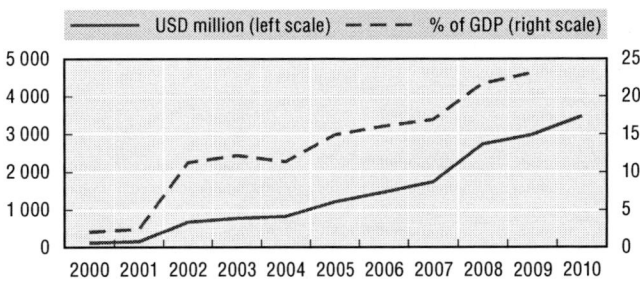

Ten main countries of destination for legal migrants in 2010 (numbers, % of total flows to the country): USA (7115, 0.7%), GBR (6000, 1.3%), JPN (2889, 1%), KOR (2692, 0.9%), CAN (1505, 0.5%), AUS (1285, 0.6%), DEU (559, 0.1%), ESP (512, 0.1%), POL (447, 1.1%), FIN (258, 1.4%).

Desire to emigrate, 2008-10

	Women	15-24	Highly educated	Total	Regional total
Persons who would move permanently, if they had the opportunity to do so (%)	15	25	34	19	9
Of which: Persons who are planning to move permanently in the next 12 months (%)				6	7
Of which: Persons who have already done some preparations for this move (*e.g.* visa application) (%)					40

Three main countries of desired destination: United States (34%), Japan (8%), United Kingdom (8%).

StatLink http://dx.doi.org/10.1787/888932672441

			Pakistan compared to:	World	Region
Total population 2010 (millions)	173.6		Human Development Index (HDI)	145/187	25/31
Population growth 2010 (%)	1.8		GDP per capita	152/194	28/33
GDP per capita 2010 (current USD)	1 019		Emigration rate	152/203	24/38
GDP growth 2010 (%)	4.1		Emigration rate of the highly educated	110/157	16/25
Poverty rate 2006 (USD PPP 2 a day, in %)	61.0				

Age structure of the population 0+ (2010): "0-14": 21%; "15-24": 35%; "25-64": 39%; "65+": 4%.
Level of education of the population 15+ (2010): "Low": 60%; "Medium": 35%; "High": 6%.

Emigrant population living in OECD countries

Immigrant population

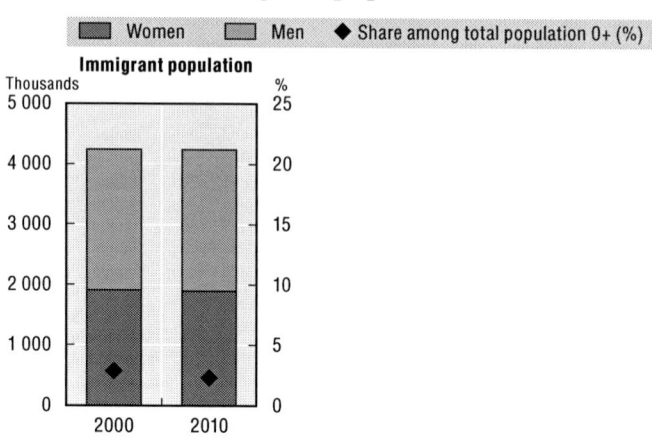

Emigrant population: persons born in Pakistan living abroad

	2000						2005/06		
	All destinations			OECD destinations			OECD destinations		
Population 15+	Men	Women	Total	Men	Women	Total	Men	Women	Total
Emigrant population (thousands)	1 076.4	923.6	2 000.0	375.0	293.7	668.7	471.9	371.2	843.1
Recent emigrants (thousands)	..	..	..	79.8	60.4	140.2	109.7	80.3	190.0
15-24 (%)	5.7	6.3	6.0	13.9	15.4	14.5	13.0	14.4	13.7
25-64 (%)	92.2	91.6	91.9	80.3	78.2	79.3	80.9	78.2	79.7
65+ (%)	2.1	2.1	2.1	5.9	6.4	6.1	6.0	7.4	6.6
Low-educated (%)	52.7	76.1	63.5	41.1	51.6	45.7	29.8	40.7	34.5
Highly educated (%)	17.8	9.0	13.7	35.8	26.7	31.8	43.9	33.2	39.3
Total emigration rates (%)	2.4	2.2	2.3	0.9	0.7	0.8	0.9	0.8	0.8
Emigration rates of the highly educated (%)	4.5	3.9	4.3	3.1	3.6	3.3	5.4	6.4	5.7

Main destinations in 2005/06

	Total		Recent emigrants	Women	Highly educated	15-24	Total in 2000
Population 15+	Thousands	%	%	%	%	%	Thousands
United Kingdom	332.8	39.5	19.4	47.4	28.9	10.1	301.9
United States	246.3	29.2	16.7	44.0	53.9	14.3	197.2
Canada	114.6	13.6	38.3	47.8	59.0	19.2	68.0
Spain	22.2	2.6	47.9	31.1	6.3	24.1	9.7
Italy	18.7	2.2	40.9	27.3	–	13.9	11.8
France	15.3	1.8	19.9	38.2	12.8	13.7	10.8
Australia	14.6	1.7	36.7	41.8	58.3	18.6	9.9
Norway	14.4	1.7	17.3	47.7	12.7	15.3	14.1
Netherlands	11.6	1.4	–	42.7	15.8	19.2	3.5
Greece	10.7	1.3	31.1	–	–	–	10.8

Labour market indicators of persons born in Pakistan living in OECD countries

Population 15-64	2000			2005/06		
	Men	Women	Total	Men	Women	Total
Employment-population ratio (%)	71.6	26.8	51.8	77.7	28.5	56.4
Unemployment rate (%)	9.8	14.3	10.8	7.8	15.4	9.6
Participation rate (%)	79.4	31.3	58.1	84.3	33.7	62.3
Total employed (thousands)	**239.2**	**70.8**	**310.0**	**331.9**	**93.4**	**425.3**
Employment rates of the highly educated (%)	81.7	45.5	68.1	91.1	52.2	76.7
Unemployment rates of the highly educated (%)	6.3	10.3	7.3	6.3	12.6	7.9
Highly educated in low- and medium-skilled jobs (%)	38.9	42.1	39.7	47.6	40.9	46.0
Highly educated employed (thousands)	**98.8**	**33.1**	**131.9**	**161.5**	**50.4**	**211.9**
Legislators, senior officials and managers	13.4	10.0	12.7	14.0	9.3	13.0
Professionals	11.5	14.4	12.1	11.5	12.4	11.7
Life science and health professionals	2.9	3.2	2.9	2.8	4.3	3.0
Teaching professionals	1.4	6.6	2.4	1.4	2.4	1.6
Technicians and associate professionals	6.9	10.8	7.8	4.3	13.7	6.2
Clerks	5.9	19.4	8.9	7.8	19.6	10.1
Service, shop and market sales workers	13.2	25.0	15.8	8.5	13.0	9.4
Skilled agricultural and fishery workers	0.4	0.1	0.3	0.8	6.6	1.9
Craft and related trades workers	9.7	1.6	7.9	11.8	6.4	10.7
Plant and machine operators and assemblers	23.8	7.6	20.2	23.9	6.4	20.4
Elementary occupations	15.1	11.2	14.3	16.1	12.1	15.3

Distribution of employment by occupation (%), population 15+

Persons born in Pakistan and their native-born children, population 15+

Living in:	Europe	United States	Australia
2008	Thousands	Thousands	Thousands
Native-born children	253.1	157.4	..
Foreign-born	451.7	269.8	9.0
Total	704.8	427.1	..

International students from Pakistan in OECD countries

Five main destinations	2004	2005	2006	2007	2008	2009
United Kingdom	4 378	6 547	7 940	9 307	9 303	9 609
United States	7 325	6 576	5 963	5 520	5 351	5 211
Australia	1 100	1 295	1 539	2 090	2 482	2 844
Sweden	4	3	20	62	1 303	2 420
Canada	889	..	1 161	996	1 342	1 439
Total	14 294	15 126	17 484	19 115	22 517	24 800

Legal migrant flows to the OECD
Thousands

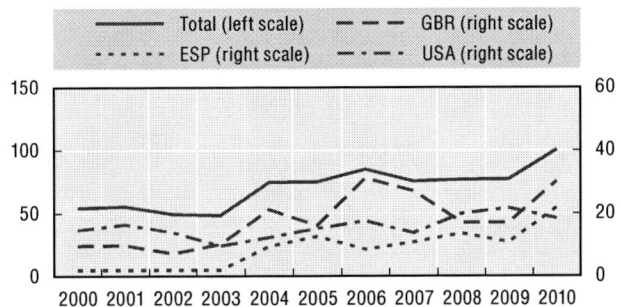

Ten main countries of destination for legal migrants in 2010 (numbers, % of total flows to the country): GBR (30000, 6.5%), ESP (21725, 5%), USA (18258, 1.8%), ITA (10816, 2.5%), CAN (4990, 1.8%), DEU (3310, 0.5%), AUS (2019, 0.6%), KOR (1666, 0.6%), SWE (1575, 2.1%), JPN (1037, 0.4%).

Remittance flows

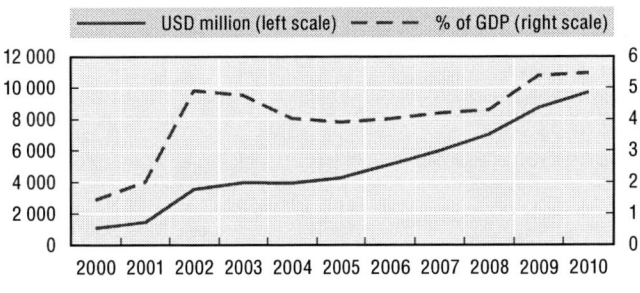

Desire to emigrate, 2008-10

	Women	15-24	Highly educated	Total	Regional total
Persons who would move permanently, if they had the opportunity to do so (%)	8	13	22	11	9
Of which: Persons who are planning to move permanently in the next 12 months (%)				12	7
Of which: Persons who have already done some preparations for this move (*e.g.* visa application) (%)					40

Three main countries of desired destination: Saudi Arabia (37%), United Arab Emirates (13%), United Kingdom (8%).

StatLink ▨▨▨ http://dx.doi.org/10.1787/888932672460

			Papua New Guinea compared to:	World	Region
Total population 2010 (millions)		6.9	Human Development Index (HDI)	153/187	29/31
Population growth 2010 (%)		2.3	GDP per capita	138/194	24/33
GDP per capita 2010 (current USD)		1 382	Emigration rate	154/203	25/38
GDP growth 2010 (%)		8.0	Emigration rate of the highly educated	31/157	8/25
Poverty rate 2010 (USD PPP 2 a day, in %)		..			

Age structure of the population 0+ (2010): "0-14": 19%; "15-24": 39%; "25-64": 39%; "65+": 3%.
Level of education of the population 15+ (2010): "Low": 79%; "Medium": 20%; "High": 1%.

Emigrant population living in OECD countries

Immigrant population

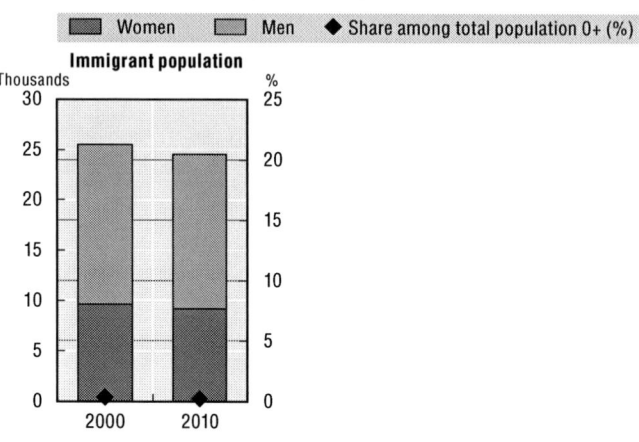

Emigrant population: persons born in Papua New Guinea living abroad

	2000						2005/06		
	All destinations			OECD destinations			OECD destinations		
Population 15+	Men	Women	Total	Men	Women	Total	Men	Women	Total
Emigrant population (thousands)	12.8	15.4	28.1	11.7	14.2	25.9	12.5	15.0	27.5
Recent emigrants (thousands)	..	..	..	1.0	1.4	2.3	1.6	1.8	3.4
15-24 (%)	21.7	18.5	20.0	20.4	17.5	18.8	16.2	10.8	13.2
25-64 (%)	74.4	76.9	75.8	75.6	78.1	77.0	78.9	83.5	81.4
65+ (%)	3.9	4.5	4.2	3.9	4.3	4.1	4.9	5.7	5.4
Low-educated (%)	25.0	35.4	30.6	23.8	35.4	30.1	14.0	21.8	18.2
Highly educated (%)	32.0	32.8	32.4	33.0	34.0	33.5	36.6	41.9	39.5
Total emigration rates (%)	0.8	1.0	0.9	0.7	0.9	0.8	0.7	0.8	0.8
Emigration rates of the highly educated (%)	12.6	33.8	19.1	12.0	32.9	18.3	13.5	40.4	22.0

Main destinations in 2005/06

	Total		Recent emigrants	Women	Highly educated	15-24	Total in 2000
Population 15+	Thousands	%	%	%	%	%	Thousands
Australia	22.5	81.8	8.3	55.7	38.0	10.1	21.8
United Kingdom	–	–	–	–	–	–	0.9
New Zealand	1.1	4.1	18.9	55.3	38.4	23.4	1.0
Netherlands	–	–	–	–	–	–	–
Canada	0.4	1.3	7.3	46.6	53.4	28.8	0.3
Belgium	–	–	–	–	–	–	–
Japan	–	–	–	–	–	–	–
France	–	–	–	–	–	–	0.1
Ireland	–	–	–	–	–	–	–
Switzerland	–	–	–	–	–	–	0.1

Labour market indicators of persons born in Papua New Guinea living in OECD countries

Population 15-64	2000 Men	2000 Women	2000 Total	2005/06 Men	2005/06 Women	2005/06 Total
Employment-population ratio (%)	74.9	61.6	67.7	79.4	68.3	73.4
Unemployment rate (%)	9.2	7.8	8.5	4.4	6.2	5.3
Participation rate (%)	82.6	66.8	74.0	83.0	72.8	77.5
Total employed (thousands)	**8.0**	**7.7**	**15.7**	**8.8**	**8.9**	**17.7**
Employment rates of the highly educated (%)	86.1	76.2	80.7	94.5	83.0	87.8
Unemployment rates of the highly educated (%)	4.9	4.9	4.9	2.6	4.3	3.5
Highly educated in low- and medium-skilled jobs (%)	19.9	24.0	22.0	19.3	19.5	19.4
Highly educated employed (thousands)	**3.1**	**3.3**	**6.4**	**3.8**	**4.5**	**8.2**
Legislators, senior officials and managers	12.4	7.7	10.1	14.2	8.8	11.4
Professionals	22.1	25.6	23.8	24.9	22.1	23.5
Life science and health professionals	3.0	7.3	5.1	4.6	7.1	5.9
Teaching professionals	3.8	7.5	5.7	3.2	6.2	4.8
Technicians and associate professionals	13.1	14.9	14.0	13.9	22.2	18.1
Clerks	5.6	22.5	14.0	7.6	20.4	14.1
Service, shop and market sales workers	11.1	17.6	14.3	9.0	16.7	13.0
Skilled agricultural and fishery workers	2.0	0.5	1.3	2.2	1.2	1.7
Craft and related trades workers	15.6	1.3	8.5	14.1	0.8	7.3
Plant and machine operators and assemblers	6.1	0.7	3.4	6.5	1.3	3.8
Elementary occupations	12.0	9.2	10.6	7.7	6.5	7.1

Distribution of employment by occupation (%), population 15+

Persons born in Papua New Guinea and their native-born children, population 15+

Living in:	Europe	United States	Australia
2008	Thousands	Thousands	Thousands
Native-born children	1.8	..	3.1
Foreign-born	1.0	..	6.7
Total	2.8	..	9.8

International students from Papua New Guinea in OECD countries

Five main destinations	2004	2005	2006	2007	2008	2009
Australia	648	608	524	566	644	672
New Zealand	139	95	85	77	83	81
United States	32	37	66	28	35	55
United Kingdom	56	52	42	30	17	28
Japan	31	33	27	29	25	21
Total	907	828	755	734	814	867

Legal migrant flows to the OECD
Thousands

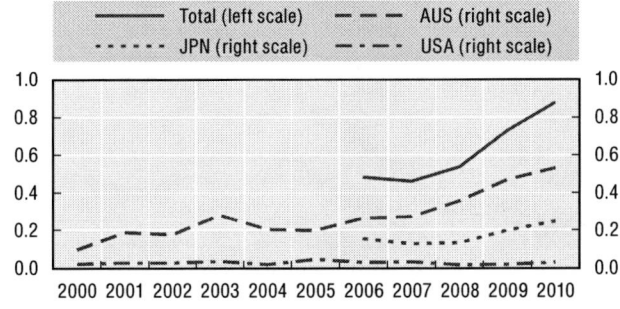

Remittance flows

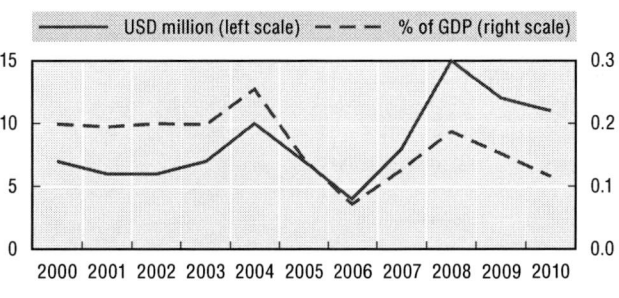

Ten main countries of destination for legal migrants in 2010 (numbers, % of total flows to the country): AUS (532, 0.3%), JPN (247, 0.1%), USA (30, 0%), NZL (22, 0%), CAN (15, 0%), DEU (11, 0%), ITA (11, 0%), KOR (3, 0%), CHE (2, 0%), AUT (1, 0%).

Desire to emigrate, 2008-10

	Women	15-24	Highly educated	Total	Regional total
Persons who would move permanently, if they had the opportunity to do so (%)	..	..	..	..	9
Of which: Persons who are planning to move permanently in the next 12 months (%)				..	7
Of which: Persons who have already done some preparations for this move (*e.g.* visa application) (%)					40

StatLink http://dx.doi.org/10.1787/888932672479

Total population 2010 (millions)	93.3	Philippines compared to:	World	Region
Population growth 2010 (%)	1.7	Human Development Index (HDI)	113/187	14/31
GDP per capita 2010 (current USD)	2 140	GDP per capita	129/194	20/33
GDP growth 2010 (%)	7.6	Emigration rate	87/203	12/38
Poverty rate 2006 (USD PPP 2 a day, in %)	45.0	Emigration rate of the highly educated	87/157	13/25

Age structure of the population 0+ (2010): "0-14": 20%; "15-24": 35%; "25-64": 41%; "65+": 4%.
Level of education of the population 15+ (2010): "Low": 29%; "Medium": 42%; "High": 29%.

Emigrant population living in OECD countries

Immigrant population

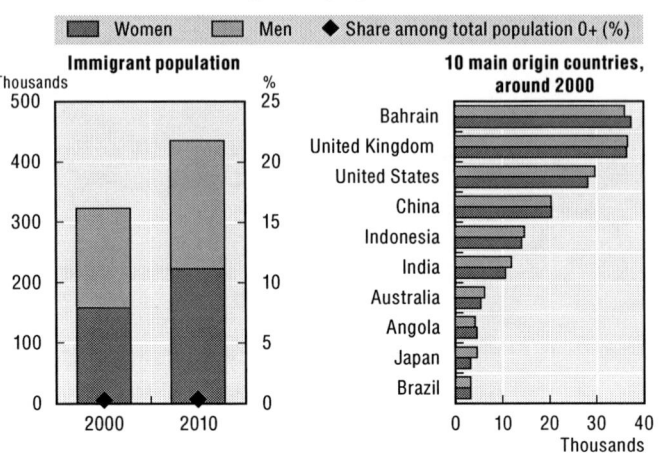

Emigrant population: persons born in Philippines living abroad

	2000						2005/06		
	All destinations			OECD destinations			OECD destinations		
Population 15+	Men	Women	Total	Men	Women	Total	Men	Women	Total
Emigrant population (thousands)	809.2	1 392.8	2 202.1	745.8	1 192.1	1 938.0	966.5	1 535.8	2 502.3
Recent emigrants (thousands)	..	..	..	107.5	168.8	276.4	164.1	256.4	420.5
15-24 (%)	14.2	10.0	11.5	13.9	9.6	11.3	11.8	8.0	9.5
25-64 (%)	76.0	81.4	79.4	75.7	80.5	78.6	76.4	79.6	78.4
65+ (%)	9.8	8.6	9.0	10.5	9.9	10.1	11.8	12.4	12.2
Low-educated (%)	21.2	20.2	20.6	16.2	18.6	17.7	12.8	14.3	13.7
Highly educated (%)	41.5	44.4	43.3	44.2	48.2	46.6	49.4	53.5	51.9
Total emigration rates (%)	3.3	5.5	4.4	3.1	4.8	3.9	3.5	5.4	4.4
Emigration rates of the highly educated (%)	5.4	8.7	7.1	5.3	8.1	6.8	6.2	9.6	8.0

Main destinations in 2005/06

	Total		Recent emigrants	Women	Highly educated	15-24	Total in 2000
Population 15+	Thousands	%	%	%	%	%	Thousands
United States	1 677.2	67.0	14.4	58.7	54.5	8.5	1 356.7
Canada	298.8	11.9	22.1	61.1	64.6	11.4	224.1
Japan	117.3	4.7	..	83.5	31.0	13.9	87.6
Australia	111.9	4.5	16.6	65.9	48.5	14.5	94.6
United Kingdom	75.3	3.0	47.0	66.6	63.4	–	38.1
Italy	75.0	3.0	18.7	58.8	8.9	10.5	46.4
Spain	27.4	1.1	56.2	52.8	19.6	11.5	15.8
New Zealand	13.2	0.5	42.5	65.6	50.0	16.4	8.6
Austria	12.8	0.5	28.2	66.1	18.5	14.2	8.4
Greece	12.5	0.5	13.2	76.0	–	–	6.0

Labour market indicators of persons born in Philippines living in OECD countries

	2000			2005/06		
Population 15-64	Men	Women	Total	Men	Women	Total
Employment-population ratio (%)	77.7	71.7	74.1	82.7	77.7	79.7
Unemployment rate (%)	5.3	4.5	4.9	5.7	4.6	5.0
Participation rate (%)	82.1	75.2	77.9	87.7	81.4	84.0
Total employed (thousands)	**504.4**	**702.3**	**1 206.7**	**679.5**	**949.7**	**1 629.2**
Employment rates of the highly educated (%)	84.7	78.3	80.6	92.7	85.6	88.2
Unemployment rates of the highly educated (%)	3.8	3.3	3.5	4.1	3.7	3.8
Highly educated in low- and medium-skilled jobs (%)	47.6	43.7	45.2	49.0	43.6	45.7
Highly educated employed (thousands)	**249.2**	**398.3**	**647.5**	**365.5**	**577.4**	**942.9**
Legislators, senior officials and managers	5.3	3.7	4.3	4.1	3.5	3.7
Professionals	10.2	10.8	10.6	9.0	9.8	9.5
Life science and health professionals	1.8	4.4	3.5	1.4	3.9	3.0
Teaching professionals	0.7	1.1	0.9	0.3	0.5	0.4
Technicians and associate professionals	11.4	14.2	13.1	10.2	14.7	12.9
Clerks	9.2	16.8	14.0	9.8	14.6	12.7
Service, shop and market sales workers	13.9	26.1	21.6	13.6	22.7	19.2
Skilled agricultural and fishery workers	0.5	0.2	0.3	3.6	3.7	3.7
Craft and related trades workers	13.3	2.1	6.3	12.6	2.6	6.5
Plant and machine operators and assemblers	14.5	5.1	8.6	13.1	4.1	7.6
Elementary occupations	21.8	21.0	21.3	23.3	24.3	23.9

Distribution of employment by occupation (%), population 15+

Persons born in Philippines and their native-born children, population 15+

Living in:	Europe	United States	Australia
2008	Thousands	Thousands	Thousands
Native-born children	36.1	898.5	11.5
Foreign-born	320.1	1 825.7	120.6
Total	356.3	2 724.2	132.0

International students from Philippines in OECD countries

Five main destinations	2004	2005	2006	2007	2008	2009
United States	3 467	3 688	3 891	3 812	4 174	4 157
Australia	674	732	806	882	1 019	1 291
United Kingdom	777	955	935	824	663	1 093
Japan	526	552	574	575	594	583
Canada	111	..	159	132	239	262
Total	6 101	6 327	6 886	6 922	7 687	8 618

Legal migrant flows to the OECD
Thousands

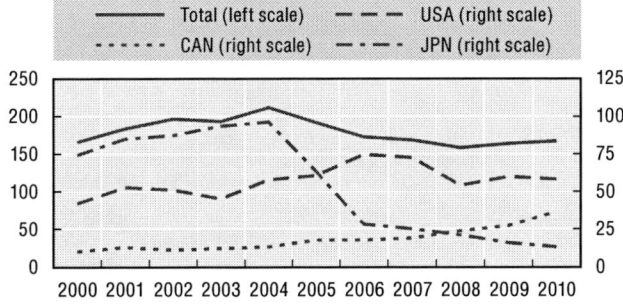

Remittance flows

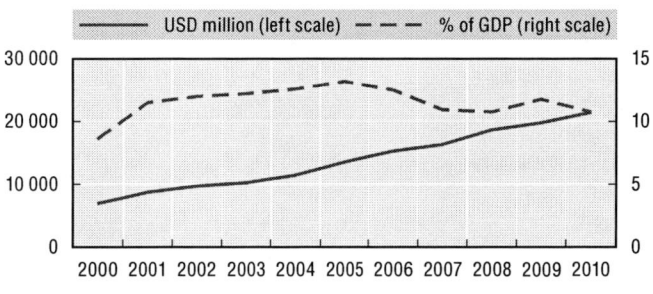

Ten main countries of destination for legal migrants in 2010 (numbers, % of total flows to the country): USA (58173, 5.6%), CAN (36575, 13.1%), JPN (13264, 4.6%), ITA (10745, 2.5%), AUS (10251, 5%), KOR (9079, 3.1%), GBR (9000, 0.8%), DEU (5316, 0.8%), NZL (3896, 8.8%), ESP (2661, 0.6%).

Desire to emigrate, 2008-10

	Women	15-24	Highly educated	Total	Regional total
Persons who would move permanently, if they had the opportunity to do so (%)	20	27	38	21	9
Of which: Persons who are planning to move permanently in the next 12 months (%)				17	7
Of which: Persons who have already done some preparations for this move (*e.g.* visa application) (%)					40

Three main countries of desired destination: United States (42%), Canada (16%), Japan (7%).

StatLink ᵐˢ🔗 http://dx.doi.org/10.1787/888932672498

			World	Region
Total population 2010 (millions)	5.1	**Singapore compared to:**		
Population growth 2010 (%)	1.8	Human Development Index (HDI)	26/187	2/31
GDP per capita 2010 (current USD)	41 122	GDP per capita	21/194	2/33
GDP growth 2010 (%)	14.5	Emigration rate	102/203	14/38
Poverty rate 2010 (USD PPP 2 a day, in %)	..	Emigration rate of the highly educated	82/157	12/25

Age structure of the population 0+ (2010): "0-14": 14%; "15-24": 17%; "25-64": 60%; "65+": 9%.
Level of education of the population 15+ (2010): "Low": 35%; "Medium": 46%; "High": 18%.

Emigrant population living in OECD countries

Immigrant population

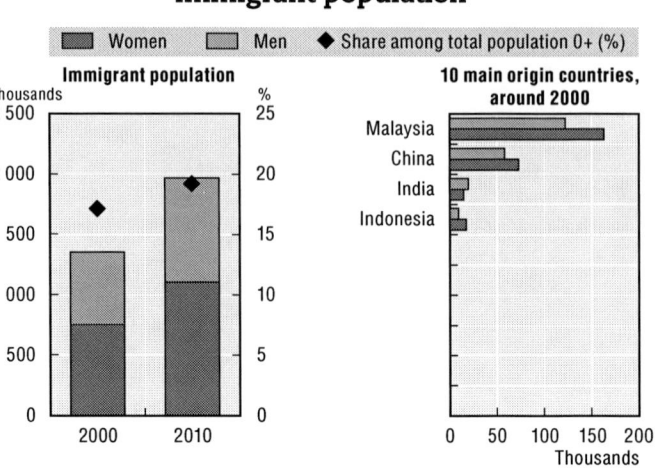

Emigrant population: persons born in Singapore living abroad

	2000						2005/06		
	All destinations			OECD destinations			OECD destinations		
Population 15+	Men	Women	Total	Men	Women	Total	Men	Women	Total
Emigrant population (thousands)	74.8	90.4	165.2	48.5	58.1	106.6	54.5	64.8	119.3
Recent emigrants (thousands)	..	..	..	9.1	10.8	19.9	11.4	13.8	25.2
15-24 (%)	14.7	12.8	13.7	19.3	17.0	18.0	19.7	14.8	17.1
25-64 (%)	78.1	78.9	78.5	76.2	78.0	77.2	74.4	78.2	76.5
65+ (%)	7.2	8.2	7.7	4.6	4.9	4.8	5.8	7.0	6.5
Low-educated (%)	32.4	39.5	36.2	18.3	22.7	20.7	13.1	19.0	16.3
Highly educated (%)	40.6	34.2	37.1	47.6	43.8	45.5	53.8	51.7	52.7
Total emigration rates (%)	4.5	5.4	5.0	3.0	3.6	3.3	3.0	3.6	3.3
Emigration rates of the highly educated (%)	11.2	13.6	12.3	8.6	11.3	9.9	7.7	11.0	9.1

Main destinations in 2005/06

	Total		Recent emigrants	Women	Highly educated	15-24	Total in 2000
Population 15+	Thousands	%	%	%	%	%	Thousands
Australia	35.4	29.7	31.5	55.2	54.1	21.8	30.4
United Kingdom	35.2	29.5	–	51.0	44.1	–	38.5
United States	26.6	22.3	29.4	55.7	63.3	17.2	20.4
Canada	9.6	8.0	12.5	55.2	63.8	16.3	8.9
New Zealand	4.2	3.5	25.3	58.7	46.1	21.1	3.3
Netherlands	2.0	1.7	–	–	–	–	–
France	1.6	1.3	36.8	55.5	51.0	22.9	1.1
Switzerland	1.4	1.2	–	–	–	–	0.6
Japan	1.1	0.9	..	65.6	51.7	0.0	1.1
Denmark	0.4	0.3	38.6	60.6	34.6	22.3	0.3

Labour market indicators of persons born in Singapore living in OECD countries

Population 15-64	2000			2005/06		
	Men	Women	Total	Men	Women	Total
Employment-population ratio (%)	69.7	57.8	63.3	74.5	63.0	68.4
Unemployment rate (%)	5.6	6.1	5.8	4.2	5.4	4.8
Participation rate (%)	73.9	61.6	67.2	77.8	66.7	71.8
Total employed (thousands)	**30.7**	**30.3**	**61.1**	**37.1**	**36.3**	**73.4**
Employment rates of the highly educated (%)	76.7	65.1	70.6	86.2	73.4	79.4
Unemployment rates of the highly educated (%)	4.2	4.7	4.4	3.8	4.3	4.0
Highly educated in low- and medium-skilled jobs (%)	18.2	23.7	20.9	19.4	23.0	21.2
Highly educated employed (thousands)	**16.1**	**15.3**	**31.4**	**22.4**	**21.5**	**43.9**
Legislators, senior officials and managers	19.4	12.1	15.7	21.1	16.2	18.7
Professionals	25.0	22.2	23.6	24.3	21.2	22.7
Life science and health professionals	4.4	5.1	4.8	6.6	4.1	5.4
Teaching professionals	3.9	6.3	5.1	5.5	5.0	5.3
Technicians and associate professionals	14.5	16.7	15.6	12.7	18.1	15.4
Clerks	6.9	24.0	15.4	4.6	16.4	10.5
Service, shop and market sales workers	9.1	16.8	12.9	14.6	9.6	12.1
Skilled agricultural and fishery workers	0.7	0.2	0.5	0.9	5.5	3.2
Craft and related trades workers	10.0	0.7	5.3	4.3	4.4	4.4
Plant and machine operators and assemblers	6.8	1.6	4.2	6.4	2.8	4.6
Elementary occupations	7.6	5.6	6.6	11.1	5.9	8.5

Distribution of employment by occupation (%), population 15+

Persons born in Singapore and their native-born children, population 15+

Living in:	Europe	United States	Australia
2008	Thousands	Thousands	Thousands
Native-born children	26.5	18.8	1.7
Foreign-born	23.2	27.7	11.4
Total	49.7	46.5	13.1

International students from Singapore in OECD countries

Five main destinations	2004	2005	2006	2007	2008	2009
Australia	11 200	10 105	9 555	9 429	9 654	10 394
United States	3 955	3 937	4 048	3 787	3 980	3 923
United Kingdom	3 905	3 628	3 273	3 201	2 898	3 188
Canada	364	..	420	330	355	347
New Zealand	209	209	189	210	188	190
Total	19 956	18 201	17 807	17 351	17 633	18 783

Legal migrant flows to the OECD
Thousands

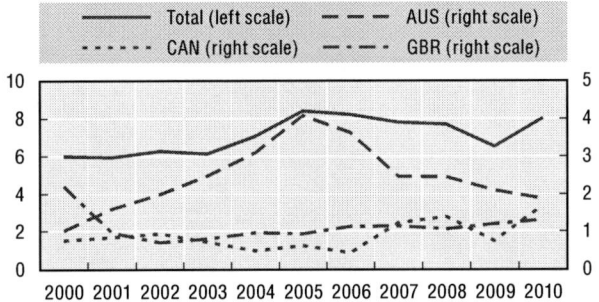

Ten main countries of destination for legal migrants in 2010 (numbers, % of total flows to the country): AUS (1873, 0.9%), CAN (1690, 0.6%), GBR (1309, 0.3%), USA (774, 0.1%), JPN (486, 0.2%), DEU (470, 0.1%), KOR (377, 0.2%), CHE (219, 0.2%), NLD (197, 0.2%), NZL (172, 0.4%).

Desire to emigrate, 2008-10

	Women	15-24	Highly educated	Total	Regional total
Persons who would move permanently, if they had the opportunity to do so (%)	9	16	10	10	9
Of which: Persons who are planning to move permanently in the next 12 months (%)				3	7
Of which: Persons who have already done some preparations for this move (*e.g.* visa application) (%)					40

Three main countries of desired destination: Australia (26%), United States (10%), Canada (7%).

StatLink ⬛⬛ http://dx.doi.org/10.1787/888932672517

Total population 2010 (millions)	20.9	Sri Lanka compared to:	World	Region
Population growth 2010 (%)	0.9	Human Development Index (HDI)	97/187	7/31
GDP per capita 2010 (current USD)	2 375	GDP per capita	127/194	18/33
GDP growth 2010 (%)	8.0	Emigration rate	108/203	15/38
Poverty rate 2007 (USD PPP 2 a day, in %)	29.1	Emigration rate of the highly educated	15/157	4/25

Age structure of the population 0+ (2010): "0-14": 16%; "15-24": 25%; "25-64": 51%; "65+": 8%.
Level of education of the population 15+ (2010): "Low": 39%; "Medium": 58%; "High": 2%.

Emigrant population living in OECD countries

Immigrant population

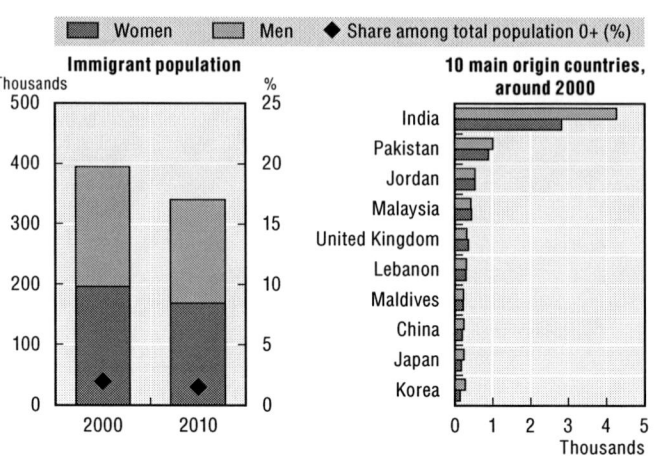

Emigrant population: persons born in Sri Lanka living abroad

	2000						2005/06		
	All destinations			OECD destinations			OECD destinations		
Population 15+	Men	Women	Total	Men	Women	Total	Men	Women	Total
Emigrant population (thousands)	263.8	241.1	504.9	169.2	147.7	317.0	227.2	206.0	433.2
Recent emigrants (thousands)	..	..	..	26.7	30.5	57.2	38.7	42.2	81.0
15-24 (%)	13.3	14.1	13.7	14.6	15.2	14.9	14.0	15.1	14.5
25-64 (%)	83.0	80.8	82.0	79.8	76.8	78.4	79.6	76.8	78.3
65+ (%)	3.7	5.1	4.4	5.6	8.1	6.7	6.4	8.1	7.2
Low-educated (%)	38.1	55.2	46.3	33.4	36.8	35.0	27.2	31.4	29.2
Highly educated (%)	22.5	15.3	19.1	30.6	25.5	28.2	36.7	31.4	34.2
Total emigration rates (%)	3.7	3.4	3.6	2.4	2.1	2.3	3.1	2.7	2.9
Emigration rates of the highly educated (%)	30.5	28.9	29.7	27.2	28.7	27.7	33.6	35.2	34.2

Main destinations in 2005/06

	Total		Recent emigrants	Women	Highly educated	15-24	Total in 2000
Population 15+	Thousands	%	%	%	%	%	Thousands
Canada	103.5	23.9	19.3	49.5	34.8	14.4	83.4
United Kingdom	96.2	22.2	21.1	47.0	49.5	13.0	63.8
Australia	58.8	13.6	19.4	49.7	50.4	12.5	49.7
Italy	37.2	8.6	26.6	45.3	2.4	13.4	21.9
United States	36.2	8.4	22.4	47.5	56.8	8.7	24.2
France	32.5	7.5	14.2	47.7	11.5	14.8	22.3
Switzerland	22.5	5.2	10.9	38.0	–	19.4	20.2
Netherlands	9.4	2.2	–	46.8	–	40.4	–
Norway	7.9	1.8	19.5	48.0	17.0	15.2	7.7
Denmark	7.5	1.7	6.1	50.3	15.9	18.0	7.1

Labour market indicators of persons born in Sri Lanka living in OECD countries

Population 15-64	2000			2005/06		
	Men	Women	Total	Men	Women	Total
Employment-population ratio (%)	77.0	50.6	64.9	82.9	54.7	69.7
Unemployment rate (%)	8.1	14.4	10.5	6.2	14.0	9.2
Participation rate (%)	83.8	59.1	72.5	88.3	63.6	76.8
Total employed (thousands)	**112.7**	**62.8**	**175.6**	**167.9**	**97.2**	**265.1**
Employment rates of the highly educated (%)	86.4	68.2	78.8	96.1	77.7	88.1
Unemployment rates of the highly educated (%)	5.9	8.9	7.0	4.4	8.6	6.0
Highly educated in low- and medium-skilled jobs (%)	29.3	37.3	32.3	34.0	42.3	37.1
Highly educated employed (thousands)	**38.7**	**22.3**	**61.1**	**68.4**	**40.9**	**109.2**
Legislators, senior officials and managers	10.2	5.0	8.3	9.8	6.0	8.4
Professionals	15.2	14.5	15.0	14.2	12.1	13.4
Life science and health professionals	3.6	5.3	4.2	1.7	3.4	2.3
Teaching professionals	1.6	3.4	2.3	1.0	3.1	1.7
Technicians and associate professionals	7.8	10.8	8.9	7.9	11.2	9.1
Clerks	8.8	24.1	14.2	8.6	21.2	13.3
Service, shop and market sales workers	19.2	18.4	19.0	14.7	16.2	15.3
Skilled agricultural and fishery workers	0.4	0.1	0.3	0.3	2.3	1.0
Craft and related trades workers	9.3	2.2	6.8	12.7	6.0	10.3
Plant and machine operators and assemblers	12.4	6.3	10.2	12.2	5.1	9.6
Elementary occupations	16.6	18.5	17.3	18.9	19.7	19.2

Distribution of employment by occupation (%), population 15+

Persons born in Sri Lanka and their native-born children, population 15+

Living in:	Europe	United States	Australia
2008	Thousands	Thousands	Thousands
Native-born children	26.8	6.3	7.4
Foreign-born	270.2	25.9	56.3
Total	297.0	32.2	63.7

International students from Sri Lanka in OECD countries

Five main destinations	2004	2005	2006	2007	2008	2009
Australia	2 117	2 082	2 499	3 550	4 073	4 296
United Kingdom	2 267	2 419	2 765	3 005	3 141	3 553
United States	1 964	2 081	2 234	2 425	2 594	2 927
Japan	615	765	867	1 155	1 197	1 098
Canada	161	..	252	186	271	309
Total	7 603	7 855	9 125	10 915	12 049	13 065

Legal migrant flows to the OECD
Thousands

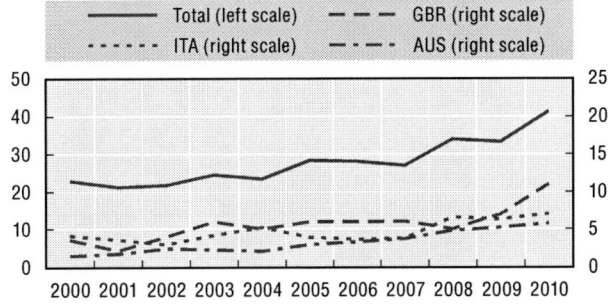

Remittance flows

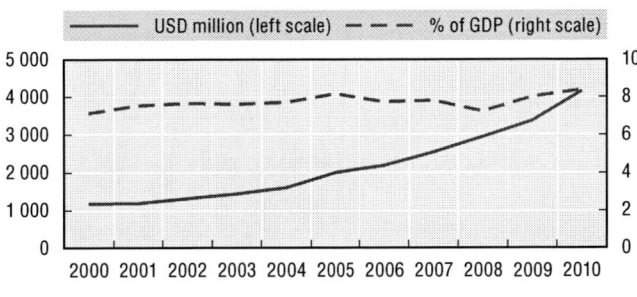

Ten main countries of destination for legal migrants in 2010 (numbers, % of total flows to the country): GBR (11000, 2.4%), ITA (7105, 1.7%), AUS (5760, 2.8%), KOR (4202, 1.4%), CAN (4180, 1.5%), FRA (2366, 1.7%), USA (2036, 0.4%), JPN (1200, 0.4%), DEU (1181, 0.2%), NZL (826, 1.9%).

Desire to emigrate, 2008-10

	Women	15-24	Highly educated	Total	Regional total
Persons who would move permanently, if they had the opportunity to do so (%)	16	29	..	17	9
Of which: Persons who are planning to move permanently in the next 12 months (%)				10	7
Of which: Persons who have already done some preparations for this move (*e.g.* visa application) (%)					40

Three main countries of desired destination: Australia (17%), United Kingdom (13%), Japan (10%).

StatLink 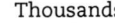 *http://dx.doi.org/10.1787/888932672536*

Total population 2010 (millions)	69.1	Thailand compared to:	World	Region
Population growth 2010 (%)	0.6	Human Development Index (HDI)	103/187	11/31
GDP per capita 2010 (current USD)	4 608	GDP per capita	92/194	8/33
GDP growth 2010 (%)	7.8	Emigration rate	159/203	27/38
Poverty rate 2004 (USD PPP 2 a day, in %)	11.5	Emigration rate of the highly educated	141/157	22/25

Age structure of the population 0+ (2010): "0-14": 15%; "15-24": 21%; "25-64": 55%; "65+": 9%.
Level of education of the population 15+ (2010): "Low": 60%; "Medium": 28%; "High": 12%.

Emigrant population living in OECD countries

Immigrant population

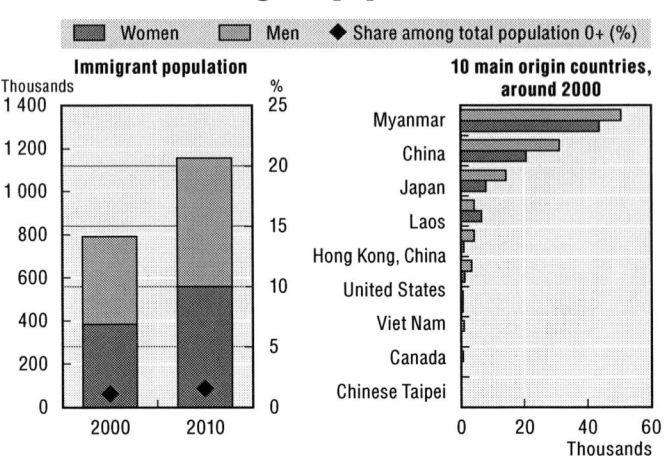

Emigrant population: persons born in Thailand living abroad

	2000						2005/06		
	All destinations			OECD destinations			OECD destinations		
Population 15+	Men	Women	Total	Men	Women	Total	Men	Women	Total
Emigrant population (thousands)	112.1	229.3	341.3	90.8	180.0	270.8	113.0	233.9	346.9
Recent emigrants (thousands)	..	..	..	15.8	33.9	49.7	19.4	59.2	78.6
15-24 (%)	38.8	22.0	27.5	38.7	21.8	27.5	30.8	16.0	20.8
25-64 (%)	59.0	76.0	70.4	59.6	76.3	70.7	66.1	80.6	75.9
65+ (%)	2.2	2.1	2.1	1.7	1.9	1.8	3.1	3.4	3.3
Low-educated (%)	39.0	50.1	46.4	28.1	41.7	37.1	22.4	34.6	30.6
Highly educated (%)	29.1	21.5	24.0	34.6	26.3	29.1	36.2	32.0	33.4
Total emigration rates (%)	0.5	1.0	0.7	0.4	0.7	0.6	0.5	0.9	0.7
Emigration rates of the highly educated (%)	2.5	3.3	2.9	2.4	3.1	2.8	1.9	2.9	2.5

Main destinations in 2005/06

	Total		Recent emigrants	Women	Highly educated	15-24	Total in 2000
Population 15+	Thousands	%	%	%	%	%	Thousands
United States	191.9	55.3	17.4	60.0	39.4	21.3	147.2
Australia	27.4	7.9	35.5	67.5	42.2	26.4	20.6
Japan	25.5	7.4	..	77.3	16.5	10.3	22.5
Sweden	17.2	5.0	46.9	82.6	17.9	16.3	12.1
France	12.7	3.7	23.8	69.5	26.0	25.8	8.0
United Kingdom	10.9	3.2	–	87.3	–	–	14.3
Canada	9.8	2.8	16.9	60.2	39.3	41.4	7.3
Denmark	7.4	2.1	26.3	83.3	12.7	17.1	5.5
Netherlands	6.6	1.9	34.3	84.2	–	–	2.1
Switzerland	6.3	1.8	60.3	82.4	20.2	26.7	8.7

Labour market indicators of persons born in Thailand living in OECD countries

Population 15-64	2000			2005/06		
	Men	Women	Total	Men	Women	Total
Employment-population ratio (%)	60.8	53.5	56.2	69.8	58.5	62.4
Unemployment rate (%)	8.8	9.3	9.1	9.3	8.2	8.6
Participation rate (%)	66.7	59.0	61.8	76.9	63.7	68.3
Total employed (thousands)	**48.2**	**75.2**	**123.4**	**67.9**	**107.6**	**175.4**
Employment rates of the highly educated (%)	71.0	61.5	65.4	83.5	71.7	76.0
Unemployment rates of the highly educated (%)	4.7	5.8	5.3	7.9	6.2	6.9
Highly educated in low- and medium-skilled jobs (%)	42.3	47.6	45.2	44.7	52.7	49.6
Highly educated employed (thousands)	**20.0**	**24.9**	**44.9**	**27.9**	**43.3**	**71.2**
Legislators, senior officials and managers	9.4	6.2	7.2	10.2	4.5	6.0
Professionals	9.5	5.5	6.6	7.2	5.7	6.1
Life science and health professionals	1.1	0.8	0.9	0.7	0.7	0.7
Teaching professionals	1.6	1.2	1.3	0.8	0.8	0.8
Technicians and associate professionals	7.2	6.7	6.9	7.2	7.1	7.1
Clerks	6.1	9.6	8.6	7.3	8.7	8.3
Service, shop and market sales workers	28.5	32.2	31.2	31.1	29.6	30.0
Skilled agricultural and fishery workers	1.4	1.0	1.1	1.6	3.4	2.9
Craft and related trades workers	10.5	3.3	5.4	11.4	4.5	6.3
Plant and machine operators and assemblers	10.2	7.1	8.0	8.8	6.6	7.2
Elementary occupations	17.2	28.4	25.1	13.9	29.0	25.0

Distribution of employment by occupation (%), population 15+

Persons born in Thailand and their native-born children, population 15+

Living in:	Europe	United States	Australia
2008	Thousands	Thousands	Thousands
Native-born children	11.7	94.7	..
Foreign-born	85.3	144.6	22.0
Total	97.0	239.3	..

International students from Thailand in OECD countries

Five main destinations	2004	2005	2006	2007	2008	2009
United States	8 937	9 021	9 076	9 082	9 014	8 592
United Kingdom	3 754	3 940	4 206	4 543	4 181	4 674
Australia	5 449	4 923	4 659	4 884	4 573	4 377
Japan	1 604	1 631	1 623	1 722	1 975	2 193
France	618	602	744	797	783	768
Total	21 390	20 734	21 416	21 991	22 480	22 883

Legal migrant flows to the OECD
Thousands

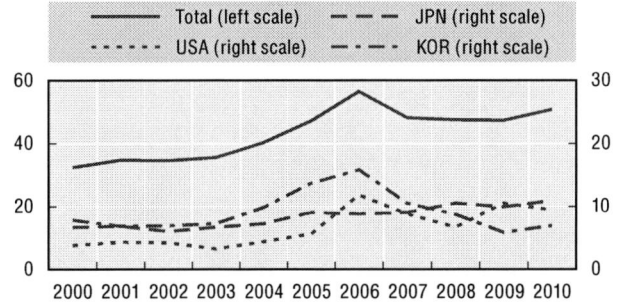

Remittance flows

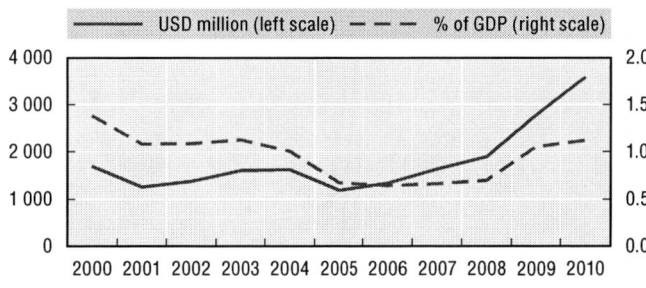

Ten main countries of destination for legal migrants in 2010 (numbers, % of total flows to the country): JPN (10868, 3.8%), USA (9384, 0.9%), KOR (6884, 2.3%), GBR (6000, 1.3%), DEU (3342, 0.5%), SWE (2775, 3.6%), AUS (2558, 1.8%), NOR (1171, 1.8%), CHE (877, 0.7%), FRA (849, 0.6%).

Desire to emigrate, 2008-10

	Women	15-24	Highly educated	Total	Regional total
Persons who would move permanently, if they had the opportunity to do so (%)	3	..	7	4	9
Of which: Persons who are planning to move permanently in the next 12 months (%)				..	7
Of which: Persons who have already done some preparations for this move (*e.g.* visa application) (%)					40

StatLink ⬛⬛ http://dx.doi.org/10.1787/888932672555

Total population 2010 (millions)	0.1	**Tonga compared to:**	**World**	**Region**
Population growth 2010 (%)	0.5	Human Development Index (HDI)	90/187	6/31
GDP per capita 2010 (current USD)	3 347	GDP per capita	107/194	11/33
GDP growth 2010 (%)	−0.5	Emigration rate	6/203	4/38
Poverty rate 2010 (USD PPP 2 a day, in %)	..	Emigration rate of the highly educated	6/157	1/25

Age structure of the population 0+ (2010): "0-14": 18%; "15-24": 38%; "25-64": 38%; "65+": 6%.
Level of education of the population 15+ (2010): "Low": 13%; "Medium": 80%; "High": 7%.

Emigrant population living in OECD countries

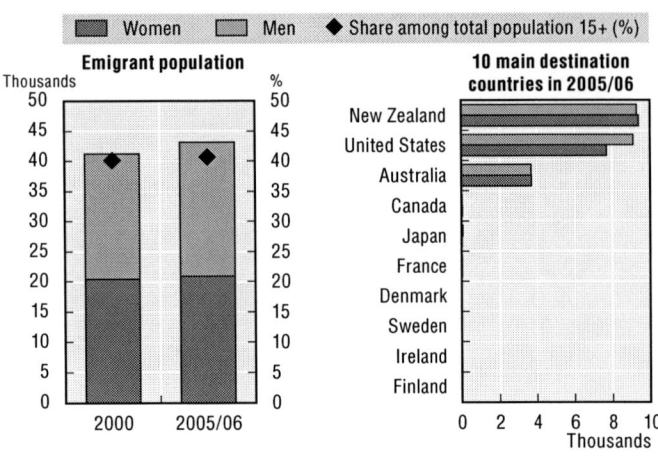

Immigrant population

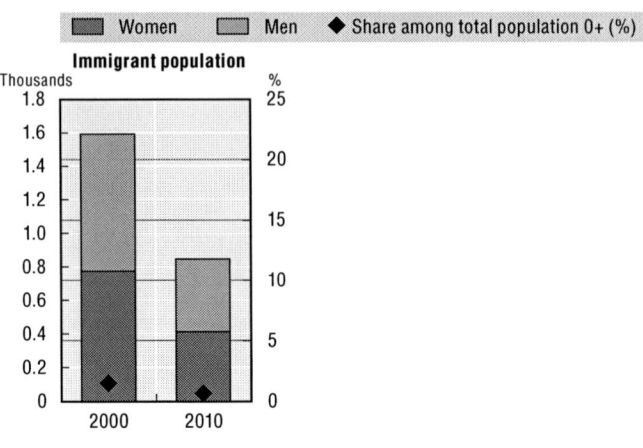

Emigrant population: persons born in Tonga living abroad

	2000						2005/06		
	All destinations			OECD destinations			OECD destinations		
Population 15+	Men	Women	Total	Men	Women	Total	Men	Women	Total
Emigrant population (thousands)	20.8	20.5	41.3	20.8	20.4	41.2	22.2	20.9	43.1
Recent emigrants (thousands)	..	..	..	3.2	3.2	6.4	3.1	2.9	6.1
15-24 (%)	12.8	13.5	13.1	12.8	13.5	13.1	10.4	10.1	10.3
25-64 (%)	79.8	78.2	79.0	79.8	78.2	79.0	79.6	79.1	79.3
65+ (%)	7.5	8.4	7.9	7.4	8.3	7.9	10.0	10.8	10.4
Low-educated (%)	40.0	38.5	39.2	40.0	38.5	39.3	33.1	28.3	30.8
Highly educated (%)	10.5	10.8	10.7	10.5	10.8	10.7	11.3	14.9	13.0
Total emigration rates (%)	40.8	40.3	40.5	40.6	40.3	40.3	41.6	40.3	41.0
Emigration rates of the highly educated (%)	49.0	55.2	51.9	48.9	55.0	51.7	50.3	62.3	56.3

Main destinations in 2005/06

	Total		Recent emigrants	Women	Highly educated	15-24	Total in 2000
Population 15+	Thousands	%	%	%	%	%	Thousands
New Zealand	18.7	43.4	19.4	50.3	9.3	13.3	16.5
United States	16.8	39.0	12.7	45.8	16.3	7.9	16.7
Australia	7.4	17.1	9.4	50.0	13.9	7.7	7.3
Canada	–	–	–	–	–	–	0.1
Japan	–	–	–	–	–	–	–
France	–	–	–	–	–	–	0.2

Labour market indicators of persons born in Tonga living in OECD countries

Population 15-64	2000			2005/06		
	Men	Women	Total	Men	Women	Total
Employment-population ratio (%)	69.9	50.7	60.5	71.3	55.5	63.7
Unemployment rate (%)	10.0	12.0	10.9	9.4	10.8	10.0
Participation rate (%)	77.7	57.6	67.8	78.7	62.2	70.8
Total employed (thousands)	**12.0**	**8.5**	**20.5**	**12.9**	**9.4**	**22.3**
Employment rates of the highly educated (%)	74.8	68.3	71.5	85.1	73.9	79.1
Unemployment rates of the highly educated (%)	7.7	5.3	6.6	8.6	8.7	8.6
Highly educated in low- and medium-skilled jobs (%)	57.2	50.6	54.1	51.3	55.1	53.2
Highly educated employed (thousands)	**1.4**	**1.3**	**2.7**	**1.7**	**1.7**	**3.5**
Legislators, senior officials and managers	3.5	3.0	3.3	6.0	4.5	5.4
Professionals	4.0	12.6	7.6	3.5	10.3	6.2
Life science and health professionals	0.7	7.6	3.5	0.2	5.1	2.2
Teaching professionals	0.8	2.9	1.7	0.6	2.7	1.4
Technicians and associate professionals	4.1	6.1	4.9	4.9	6.2	5.4
Clerks	6.0	14.3	9.5	7.4	13.6	9.9
Service, shop and market sales workers	6.0	24.4	13.6	5.0	21.7	11.7
Skilled agricultural and fishery workers	4.2	1.6	3.1	5.6	2.6	4.4
Craft and related trades workers	16.5	2.1	10.5	22.5	8.2	16.7
Plant and machine operators and assemblers	29.8	11.6	22.3	21.8	12.0	17.8
Elementary occupations	25.8	24.3	25.2	23.3	21.0	22.3

Left margin label: Distribution of employment by occupation (%), population 15+

Persons born in Tonga and their native-born children, population 15+

Living in:	Europe	United States	Australia
2008	Thousands	Thousands	Thousands
Native-born children	..	10.0	2.2
Foreign-born	..	12.4	9.6
Total	..	22.4	11.7

International students from Tonga in OECD countries

Five main destinations	2004	2005	2006	2007	2008	2009
New Zealand	281	257	227	323	160	245
United States	111	152	174	48	201	113
Australia	58	54	53	65	58	53
Japan	27	34	36	29	27	31
United Kingdom	10	11	4	2	4	5
Total	493	512	499	470	456	453

Legal migrant flows to the OECD
Thousands

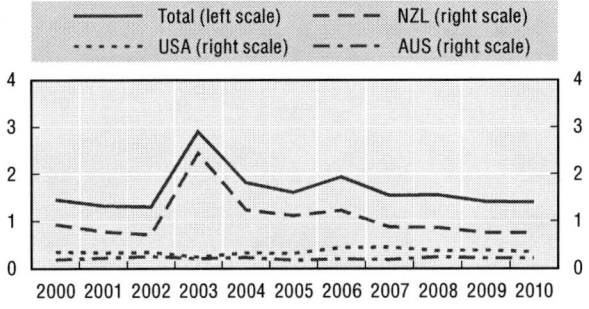

Remittance flows

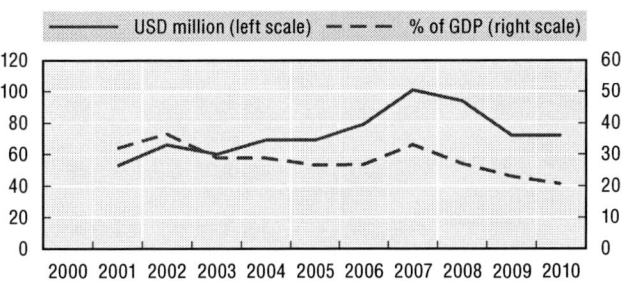

Ten main countries of destination for legal migrants in 2010 (numbers, % of total flows to the country): NZL (751, 1.7%), USA (343, 0%), AUS (211, 0.1%), JPN (72, 0%), FRA (12, 0%), CAN (5, 0%), DEU (4, 0%), KOR (2, 0%), IRL (1, 0%), ITA (1, 0%).

Desire to emigrate, 2008-10

	Women	15-24	Highly educated	Total	Regional total
Persons who would move permanently, if they had the opportunity to do so (%)	..	..	..	..	9
Of which: Persons who are planning to move permanently in the next 12 months (%)				..	7
Of which: Persons who have already done some preparations for this move (*e.g.* visa application) (%)					40

StatLink http://dx.doi.org/10.1787/888932672574

				World	Region
Total population 2010 (millions)	86.9	**Viet Nam compared to:**		**World**	**Region**
Population growth 2010 (%)	1.1	Human Development Index (HDI)		128/187	19/31
GDP per capita 2010 (current USD)	1 224	GDP per capita		142/194	26/33
GDP growth 2010 (%)	6.8	Emigration rate		109/203	16/38
Poverty rate 2008 (USD PPP 2 a day, in %)	38.5	Emigration rate of the highly educated		46/157	10/25

Age structure of the population 0+ (2010): "0-14": 20%; "15-24": 24%; "25-64": 50%; "65+": 6%.
Level of education of the population 15+ (2010): "Low": 62%; "Medium": 32%; "High": 6%.

Emigrant population living in OECD countries

Immigrant population

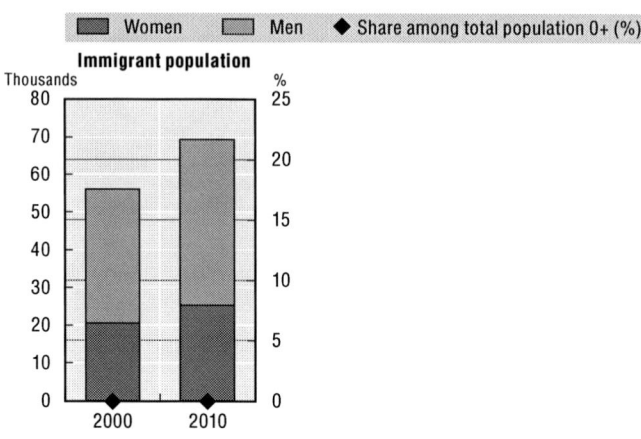

Emigrant population: persons born in Viet Nam living abroad

	2000						2005/06		
	All destinations			OECD destinations			OECD destinations		
Population 15+	Men	Women	Total	Men	Women	Total	Men	Women	Total
Emigrant population (thousands)	808.0	820.7	1 628.8	747.4	768.6	1 515.9	854.6	903.1	1 757.7
Recent emigrants (thousands)	..	..	..	63.0	86.1	149.1	59.0	97.6	156.6
15-24 (%)	13.3	13.1	13.2	12.5	12.1	12.3	8.6	8.2	8.4
25-64 (%)	80.4	79.1	79.8	81.1	79.9	80.5	82.3	81.1	81.7
65+ (%)	6.3	7.8	7.0	6.5	8.0	7.2	9.0	10.7	9.9
Low-educated (%)	38.4	47.9	43.2	36.5	46.1	41.3	29.1	37.7	33.5
Highly educated (%)	24.5	19.5	22.0	26.1	20.6	23.3	30.4	25.1	27.7
Total emigration rates (%)	3.0	3.0	3.0	2.8	2.8	2.8	2.8	2.9	2.9
Emigration rates of the highly educated (%)	17.4	19.9	18.4	17.1	19.8	18.2	14.5	16.6	15.4

Main destinations in 2005/06

	Total		Recent emigrants	Women	Highly educated	15-24	Total in 2000
Population 15+	Thousands	%	%	%	%	%	Thousands
United States	1 086.4	61.8	9.8	51.4	30.1	7.9	938.2
Canada	160.2	9.1	5.8	52.2	30.1	6.6	147.3
Australia	156.8	8.9	7.8	53.0	25.5	8.2	150.7
France	109.7	6.2	6.3	53.6	32.7	5.4	106.4
Germany	98.9	5.6	8.5	51.5	9.4	10.6	66.9
Czech Republic	34.9	2.0	..	35.4	8.1	9.4	13.7
United Kingdom	20.9	1.2	–	51.1	–	–	22.7
Japan	17.8	1.0	..	49.4	14.5	34.5	10.5
Norway	11.8	0.7	10.9	51.1	16.3	13.3	11.5
Sweden	11.0	0.6	16.1	53.7	11.2	13.9	9.8

Labour market indicators of persons born in Viet Nam living in OECD countries

Population 15-64	2000			2005/06		
	Men	Women	Total	Men	Women	Total
Employment-population ratio (%)	71.5	57.3	64.3	76.5	62.7	69.4
Unemployment rate (%)	7.4	8.1	7.7	7.6	8.3	7.9
Participation rate (%)	77.2	62.4	69.7	82.8	68.4	75.4
Total employed (thousands)	**471.2**	**388.3**	**859.5**	**554.9**	**477.3**	**1 032.1**
Employment rates of the highly educated (%)	81.6	74.0	78.1	90.0	81.0	85.8
Unemployment rates of the highly educated (%)	4.5	5.0	4.7	4.8	5.2	5.0
Highly educated in low- and medium-skilled jobs (%)	33.1	38.3	35.3	35.7	38.0	36.7
Highly educated employed (thousands)	**144.1**	**111.6**	**255.6**	**198.8**	**159.0**	**357.8**
Legislators, senior officials and managers	7.9	5.6	7.0	11.6	9.1	10.4
Professionals	15.2	12.6	14.2	14.4	11.7	13.1
Life science and health professionals	3.3	3.7	3.4	2.5	2.9	2.7
Teaching professionals	1.5	1.5	1.5	1.1	2.0	1.5
Technicians and associate professionals	9.9	10.0	9.9	8.8	10.8	9.7
Clerks	5.4	14.4	8.8	5.5	13.5	9.2
Service, shop and market sales workers	11.4	18.3	14.0	15.3	25.9	20.1
Skilled agricultural and fishery workers	0.7	0.5	0.6	1.3	1.1	1.2
Craft and related trades workers	17.8	6.4	13.4	17.3	5.2	11.7
Plant and machine operators and assemblers	18.8	18.5	18.7	16.7	11.9	14.5
Elementary occupations	13.1	13.7	13.3	8.8	10.8	9.7

Left margin label: Distribution of employment by occupation (%), population 15+

Persons born in Viet Nam and their native-born children, population 15+

Living in:	Europe	United States	Australia
2008	Thousands	Thousands	Thousands
Native-born children	119.7	499.4	4.7
Foreign-born	260.4	1 064.6	111.6
Total	380.1	1 564.0	116.2

International students from Viet Nam in OECD countries

Five main destinations	2004	2005	2006	2007	2008	2009
United States	3 165	3 833	4 760	6 169	8 778	12 612
Australia	2 619	2 755	3 081	4 042	5 446	7 648
France	2 950	3 735	4 658	5 164	5 133	5 803
Japan	1 340	1 563	1 734	2 087	2 541	2 895
United Kingdom	703	1 111	1 448	1 686	1 791	2 064
Total	11 917	14 563	18 155	22 070	28 516	36 163

Legal migrant flows to the OECD
Thousands

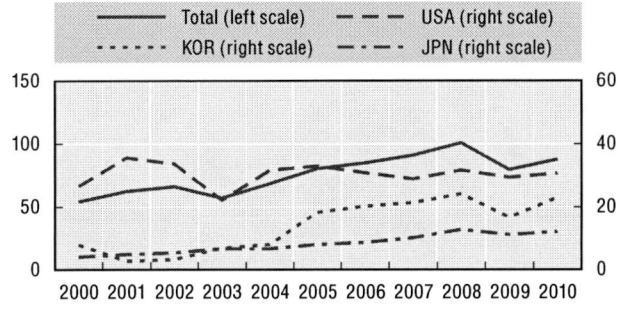

Remittance flows

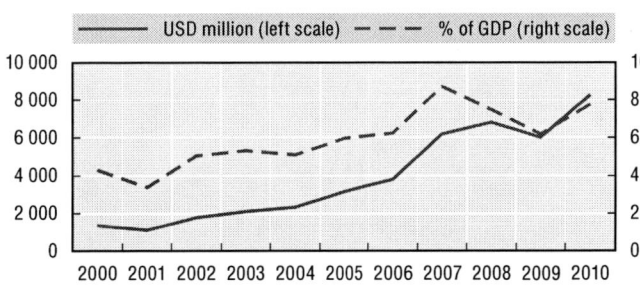

Ten main countries of destination for legal migrants in 2010 (numbers, % of total flows to the country): USA (30632, 2.9%), KOR (22934, 7.8%), JPN (11932, 4.2%), DEU (4310, 0.6%), AUS (3850, 1.9%), GBR (3000, 0.6%), POL (2402, 0.7%), CAN (1895, 0.7%), CZE (1422, 5.6%), FRA (1086, 0.8%).

Desire to emigrate, 2008-10

	Women	15-24	Highly educated	Total	Regional total
Persons who would move permanently, if they had the opportunity to do so (%)	18	28	21	17	9
Of which: Persons who are planning to move permanently in the next 12 months (%)				5	7
Of which: Persons who have already done some preparations for this move (*e.g.* visa application) (%)					40

Three main countries of desired destination: United States (40%), Korea (8%), Australia (8%).

StatLink ᴹᴵˢᴸ http://dx.doi.org/10.1787/888932672593

Connecting with Emigrants
A Global Profile of Diasporas
© OECD 2012

Chapter 3

Latin America and the Caribbean

This chapter looks at recent migration flows and diasporas from Latin America and the Caribbean countries to the OECD area. It shows that in 2010 almost 900 000 new migrants from the region settled in OECD countries, accounting for about 17% of total immigration flows. In 2005/06 there were 14 million emigrants (almost 25 million when including Mexico and Chile), 15 years old or older, from the region in OECD countries, of which 53% were women and 24% held a tertiary diploma. Total emigration rate for those over 15 years of age reached 4.4% for the region as a whole. The emigration rate for the highly educated was close to 11%. Future challenges refer notably to integration of immigrants and their children in destination countries as well as to the mobilisation of the diaspora to support economic development in origin countries.

This chapter also contains 22 country notes for Argentina, Barbados, Belize, Bolivia, Brazil, Colombia, Costa Rica, Cuba, Dominican Republic, Ecuador, El Salvador, Guatemala, Haiti, Honduras, Jamaica, Nicaragua, Panama, Paraguay, Peru, Trinidad and Tobago, Uruguay and Venezuela.

1. Historical migration patterns

Latin America and the Caribbean is a region[1] characterised by profound changes in mobility and migration. After a period of welcoming migrants, like the whole of the American continent, it has become essentially a region of emigration over the last half-century. Political problems, dictatorships, armed conflicts and deep instability in many countries throughout that period have all contributed to massive migration flows. This trend has been reinforced by strong population growth in almost all countries in the area, combined with endemic poverty and chronic underemployment. Recent years apart, its unfavourable socioeconomic situation and proximity to the epicentre of the globalisation process have made this the region with the most pronounced South-North migration flows (Escobar Latapi, 2010).

Looking more closely at the recent period, the years following the "lost decade" of the 1980s have seen crucial changes in the circumstances that shape migration trends. From 1990 to 1999, weak economic growth was unable to reduce the high unemployment rate (10% overall), and almost half of the population lived in poverty. The immediate pre- and post-millennium years saw a general deterioration in the situation and, in some cases, the onset of an acute crisis: unemployment climbed to over 15% in several countries, where recession took hold and wages collapsed. Finally, the recovery began to gather pace from 2003, but at a different rate and with different results from country to country. Economic growth varied from 5% to 10%, first in Argentina, Cuba, Panama and Uruguay, then in Brazil, Chile and Colombia, and lastly (to a lesser extent) in Mexico (Koolhaas *et al.*, 2010). Unemployment fell significantly and some countries neared full employment, while shortages of qualified workers were felt here and there. The crisis of 2008 had little fundamental effect on this situation, and the region enjoyed a quick recovery. But debt levels in the major OECD countries and the European slowdown from the beginning of the decade, combined with uncertainties over the course of the financial situation in North America, began to affect the emerging economies, notably Brazil.

Intra-regional migration, traditionally quite modest compared with other regions of the world (South Asia and Africa), has risen significantly over the past two decades. Local migration flows more usually concern emigration countries such as Nicaragua and El Salvador to Costa Rica (and Mexico); Colombia to Venezuela and Ecuador; Ecuador and Peru to Chile; Paraguay and Bolivia to Argentina and Brazil. However, these bilateral cross-border migration trends are becoming more complex. Recent low-skilled migrants are now sometimes travelling much farther, while professionals and students are no longer heading to Europe or the United States as they increasingly choose to move to emerging countries in the region (Meyer, 2010).

These recent developments have a very clear impact on migration dynamics. Aspects of the new forms of migration include returns to the home country, more highly diversified destinations, social transformations in migrant populations, the growth of associations and the proliferation of cross-border networks.

Initial findings based on survey data and limited statistical observations do help to illustrate these trends (Luchilo, 2011; Hernandez *et al.*, 2011). They show, *inter alia*, an increase in the skill levels of migrant populations and the feminisation and multi-polarisation of Latin American migrants. Some of these findings are confirmed by the data included in the present publication. Their presentation and analysis can help shape new public and institutional policies to better address these emerging challenges.

2. Current profiles of emigrant populations

Flows and stocks

In 2005/06, the Latin American and Caribbean migrant population aged 15 and over in the OECD area countries totalled 14 million (almost 25 million when including Mexico and Chile) (Figure 3.2). This represents one-eighth of the world's migrants to the OECD area, a proportion equivalent to the region's demographic weight in the world population. If the figures for intra-regional and non-OECD migration – non-negligible (15% in 2000) and recently on the rise – were included, the stock of migrants would be significantly larger.

Latin America clearly continues to be a region of intense mobility despite a slight slowdown in flows that predated the onset of the financial crisis. After peaking at almost 800 000 Latin American migrants to the OECD area in 2006, the number fell to 588 000 in 2010, a level equivalent to that of 2004 (Figure 3.1). And these figures include only declared migrants, which excludes those who migrate illegally or who stay as illegal immigrants in the host countries (estimated at 30% for Mexican and Central American migrants in the United States) (Escobar Latapi, 2010).

Remittances grew significantly throughout the decade, tripling to a peak in 2008 at USD 40 billion and remaining very high during the crisis, despite a decline in 2010 to USD 36 billion. A recovery in remittances was noted in most countries from mid-2010. The main recipient countries are Brazil, Colombia and Guatemala, which each recorded over USD 4 billion in 2010.

Figure 3.1. **Migrant flows from Latin America and the Caribbean to OECD countries and remittance flows, 2000-10**

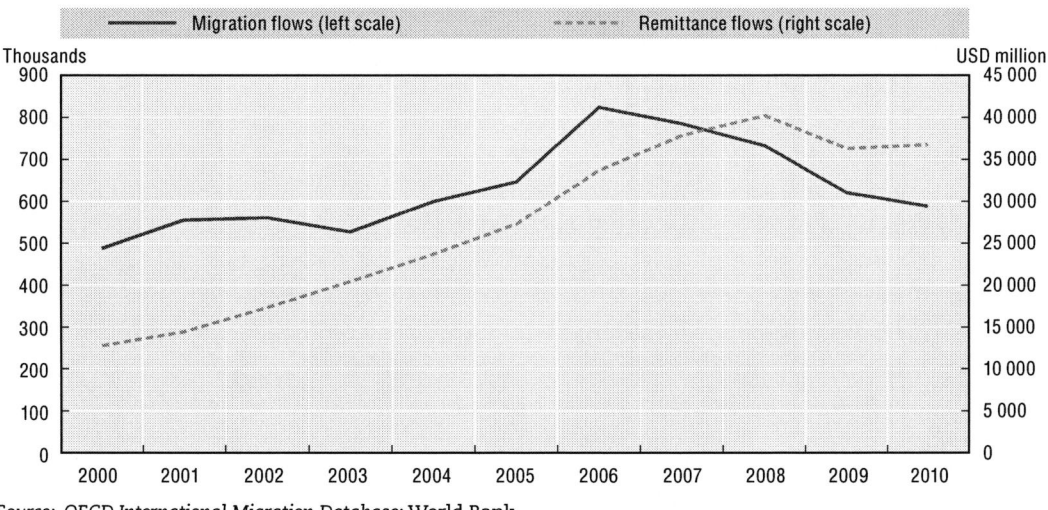

Source: OECD International Migration Database; World Bank.

StatLink ᴍᴤ🖼 http://dx.doi.org/10.1787/888932671966

Migrant numbers differ considerably, depending on the country. Mexico leads the way with some 11 million migrants in 2005/06.[2] This is at least ten times the levels recorded by the other main emigration countries, such as Puerto Rico, El Salvador, Cuba, Ecuador and Colombia (Figure 3.2). Regional demographic giant Brazil ranks only seventh on the list, among incomparably smaller countries such as Jamaica, the Dominican Republic and Guatemala. Countries whose expatriate populations grew the most are the Andean nations of Ecuador and Bolivia and, in the Southern Cone, Argentina, Paraguay and Uruguay, which almost doubled the size of their diasporas between 2000 and 2005. This sudden surge can be explained by domestic economic problems at the beginning of the decade, and the moderate level of migration to the OECD area in the years immediately before.

Figure 3.2. **Total and highly educated emigrant population aged 15 and over from Latin America and the Caribbean in the OECD area, 2005/06**

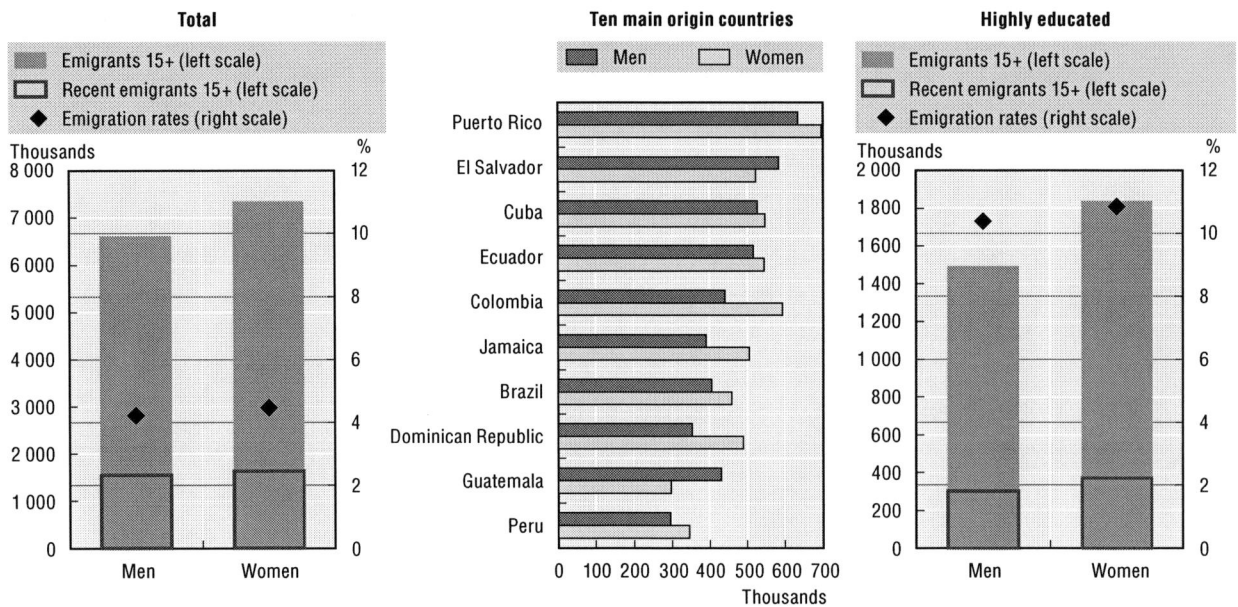

Source: Database on Immigrants in OECD Countries (DIOC 2005/06).

StatLink ᴹᴸᴴ http://dx.doi.org/10.1787/888932671985

Over the period in question, new destinations – Spain in particular – emerged as magnets in a context of strong migration growth (Figure 3.3). In 2000 the United States attracted 75% of all migrants from Latin America and the Caribbean, the other OECD countries and those outside the area accounting for only 13% each (OECD, 2010). Spain, which took in only 4.5% of all Latin American migrants to the OECD countries in 2000, admitted nearly 20% five years later. Figures for Canada over the same period progressed from 3.5% to 6.4%. While the United States remains the top host country for most migrants from the region, nationals from Argentina, Bolivia, Ecuador, Paraguay and Uruguay opted for Spain as their destination of choice. In any event, the appeal of the United States is less overriding than in the past. Competitors are emerging on the American continent and elsewhere, and flows are becoming more diversified. While Spain's current economic difficulties and the resultant slowdown of immigration are changing the situation, recent flows are not all turning back to the United States.

Figure 3.3. **Emigrant populations and migrant flows from Latin America and the Caribbean to the five main destinations within the OECD area, population aged 15 and over**

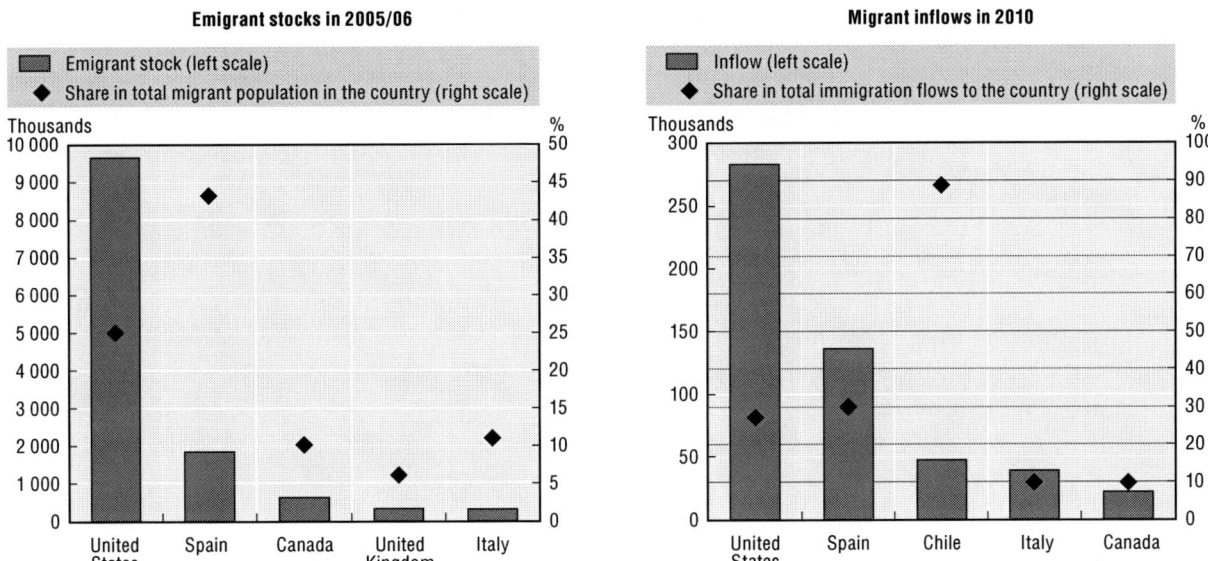

Source: Database on Immigrants in OECD Countries (DIOC 2005/06); OECD International Migration Database.

StatLink ᵐˢᵖ http://dx.doi.org/10.1787/888932672004

Characteristics of emigrant populations

The 25-64 age group accounts for three-quarters of all migrants (Table 3.1). On average, one-third of migrants from Latin America and the Caribbean are highly skilled. Educational attainment is usually low for Bolivia, Peru and Colombia but high for other countries, particularly Argentina and Uruguay.

Table 3.1. **Characteristics of migrants from Latin America and the Caribbean in the OECD area, by gender, 2005/06**

Percentage

	Regional averages (unweighted)			Regional total (weighted)		
	Men	Women	Total	Men	Women	Total
15-24	13.6	12.5	13.0	14.4	12.3	13.3
25-64	74.4	74.5	74.4	76.5	75.5	76.0
65+	12.3	13.3	12.8	9.1	12.3	10.8
Low-educated	27.9	26.7	27.2	35.5	33.2	34.3
Highly educated	28.7	29.8	29.8	22.8	25.3	24.1
Total emigration rates	16.7	18.0	17.4	4.2	4.5	4.4
Emigration rates of the highly educated	26.9	27.1	26.9	10.4	10.9	10.6

Source: Database on Immigrants in OECD Countries (DIOC 2005/06).

StatLink ᵐˢᵖ http://dx.doi.org/10.1787/888932675025

There are some surprises in student migration from Latin America. The English-speaking countries are noticeably losing their influence. Between 2004 and 2009, the number of Latin American students choosing to pursue higher education in the United States dropped by 10%, while the percentage of those travelling to the United Kingdom remained stable. At the same time, the attractiveness of Canada rose by 32%, France by 51% and Spain by 440%. The case of Spain merits close scrutiny. Between 2004 and 2008, immigration increased at a faster rate than in the other two countries, but in a similar proportion. Between 2008 and 2009 there was an abrupt change, with a massive influx of Latin American students to Spain. This remarkable growth can be explained by demand for higher education in the countries of origin far outstripping domestic supply, as well as by the introduction of targeted measures, particularly in Europe, to tap this pool of student talent. Australia, Germany and Chile also emerge as host countries. Mexico remains surprisingly absent, while the other major countries of education in the region (Argentina and especially Brazil) are also attracting increasing numbers of students.

Overall, just under one-tenth of Latin American migrants in OECD countries were unemployed in 2005/06, with a slightly higher jobless rate for women than for men (Table 3.2). Among the highly skilled population (more active and with a higher employment rate than the group as a whole), participation in the labour market is markedly higher for men than for women (a difference of almost 10 percentage points) and unemployment lower by two points. While senior managers and highly skilled workers are mostly men, women are overrepresented in the education sector, office and retail jobs, and occupations classified as elementary (i.e. unskilled).

From the beginning to the middle of the decade, the imbalance between migrants' skills and job opportunities in the host countries increased. The percentage of higher education graduates working in medium or low-skilled jobs rose for most Latin American migrant groups. That proportion exceeded 60% for migrants from Bolivia, Ecuador, Guatemala and Honduras. Less than 40% of skilled migrants from Argentina, Jamaica, Venezuela and Panama fell into this category. Nevertheless, the general skills wastage increased. This skills-to-jobs imbalance shows that while migrants with qualifications find employment more easily, their qualifications are often devalued in the process.

Table 3.2. **Labour market characteristics of migrants from Latin America and the Caribbean in the OECD area, by gender, 2005/06**

	Regional averages (unweighted)			Regional total (weighted)		
	Men	Women	Total	Men	Women	Total
Employment rate (%)	78.8	67.7	73.1	73.5	57.2	64.9
Unemployment rate (%)	9.2	10.1	9.5	7.6	10.1	8.8
Participation rate (%)	86.6	74.8	80.3	79.6	63.7	71.2
Total employed (thousands)	**4 672**	**4 059**	**8 730**			
Employment rate of the highly educated (%)	88.4	77.9	82.6	81.9	69.9	75.3
Unemployment rate of the highly educated (%)	5.0	6.2	5.6	5.4	7.5	6.5
Participation rate of the highly educated (%)	93.0	83.0	87.5	86.6	75.5	80.5
Highly educated employed (thousands)	**1 196**	**1 261**	**2 457**			
Persons with tertiary degrees in low- or medium-skilled jobs (%)	46.1	44.0	45.0	49.0	46.7	47.8

Source: Database on Immigrants in OECD Countries (DIOC 2005/06).

StatLink ⫘⫘⫘ http://dx.doi.org/10.1787/888932675044

Emigration rates and the "brain drain"

Between 2000 and 2005/06, the overall migration rate and the proportion of higher education graduates both progressed, but the latter to a significantly greater extent. In other words, the proportion of skilled migrants rose considerably during the first half of the 2000s. This occurred at the same time as an impressive increase in the number of graduates in the source countries as a result of the expansion of higher education over the past two decades.

This increase surpassed even recent forecasts, which aimed to compensate for the lack of updated quantitative data. Trends from 1990 to 2000 had been projected into the mid-2000s to estimate the scale of the brain drain (Lozano and Gandini, 2009). According to these forecasts, the average rate per country was to increase by only 0.07 points, with rates even falling in almost half of the source countries thanks to their growing number of graduates. But in fact the rate rose by an average of 2.5 points, with increases in almost all countries. It stands today at 10.6% for the region as a whole, but with considerable disparities.

A small group of five Caribbean islands register expatriation rates in excess of 50%. The rates for five other small countries in Central America and the Caribbean range between 20% and 50%. The countries of the Andean region and Central America have rates of 10% to 20%. Lastly, Brazil is noted as having a much lower rate (below or equal to 3%), although this is rising significantly. Clear trends can be identified in those countries with a propensity towards migration: geographical isolation, low critical mass and limited economic development (Dumont et al., 2010). The variations between 2000 and 2005 show that migration grew fastest in small countries: Guatemala, El Salvador, Uruguay and Paraguay. Their exposure to migratory dynamics is probably magnified by their relative dependence on the outside world.

3. Future trends and challenges

Migration conditions are being profoundly affected by economic difficulties in the OECD countries and the dynamism of the Latin American countries. However, most countries had already witnessed a downturn in their migration flows before the crisis took hold in 2008. Indeed, most of them recorded peaks in emigration rates in 2006. Rates in Honduras, Haiti, Peru and Paraguay reached their highest levels in 2007, followed by Ecuador and Mexico a year later, before declining in subsequent years. As a result, it seems that migration from the region entered a new phase in the second half of the 2000s as a result of several factors: economic reversals in the host and source countries, increasingly restrictive policies in the former, and shifting migration patterns in the latter. The drastic fall in migration to Spain is a result of the country's worsening labour market. Initial data and anecdotal evidence point towards this reversal in the trend: after the huge wave of migration to Spain in the first half of the decade, more and more expatriates are now returning home, and some of the Iberian peninsula's native-born population are even starting to leave to find new Eldorados in the emerging countries of the region. Nevertheless, a complete and rapid turnaround in migration flows seems unlikely, even if the economic situation, particularly in Europe, indicates that the need for foreign labour will remain limited in the near and medium term.

For the coming period of instability, the view of migration being restricted to the North-South axis no longer holds true. Increased regional movement does, however, look far more likely. Also, it is inconceivable that Europe will be deserted following the many cross-border networks that have been built up on the continent over the past 20 years. Moreover, the resilience of remittances in spite of the crisis is a sign of the permanence of ties, the interdependence of the source and host regions, and the lasting settlement of people in connected locations. This tangible link between migration – or mobility – and development raises new policy challenges. In a multi-polar world, it is no longer a matter of one-way co-operation along fixed and unchanging asymmetric lines (Khadria and Meyer, 2011).

Since the 1990s, Latin America has shown the way for promising and creative diaspora networks. The region is now striving to better understand and monitor on a daily basis the complex migration patterns it is undergoing and that are affecting it. The MICAL Observatory of the International Migration of Latin American diasporas and professionals aims to inform the decisions that need to be taken in this field by all concerned stakeholders, from migrants to governments by way of associations. This knowledge is vital to action. It supplies inputs for the co-operation networks that diaspora incubators provide with instruments and mechanisms to further their construction and their work.[3] Such initiatives are important for strengthening cultural and business links. This is at least one of the lessons to be learned from the experience of Latin American migration to the OECD countries.

Notes

1. The Latin America and the Caribbean region does not include OECD countries, *i.e.* Mexico and Chile.

2. Mexico is not covered in this chapter as it is included in Chapter 4 on OECD countries.

3. CIDESAL (Création d'Incubateurs des Diasporas du Savoir pour l'Amérique Latine) and MICAL (Migration of Knowledge Workers of Latin America), supported by the EuropeAid programme (European Commission), *www.observatoriodiasporas.com*.

Country Notes

Latin America and the Caribbean

Total population 2010 (millions)	40.4	**Argentina compared to:** **World** **Region**	
Population growth 2010 (%)	0.9	Human Development Index (HDI)	45/187	1/31
GDP per capita 2010 (current USD)	9 124	GDP per capita	66/194	10/36
GDP growth 2010 (%)	9.2	Emigration rate	127/203	34/38
Poverty rate 2009 (USD PPP 2 a day, in %)	2.4	Emigration rate of the highly educated	100/157	19/24

Age structure of the population 0+ (2010): "0-14": 17%; "15-24": 25%; "25-64": 48%; "65+": 11%.
Level of education of the population 15+ (2010): "Low": 43%; "Medium": 45%; "High": 12%.

Emigrant population living in OECD countries

Immigrant population

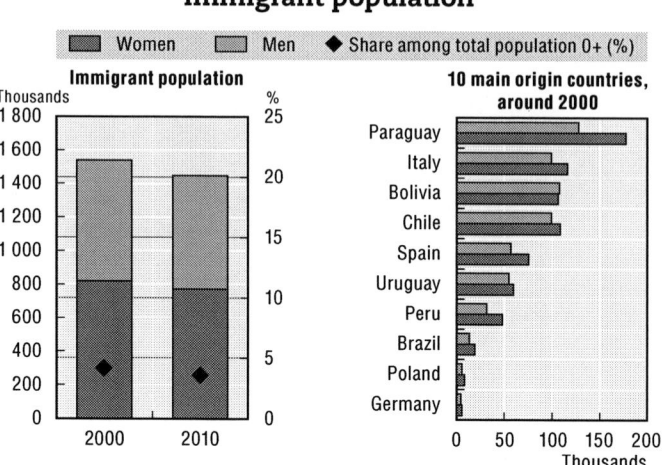

Emigrant population: persons born in Argentina living abroad

	2000						2005/06		
	All destinations			OECD destinations			OECD destinations		
Population 15+	Men	Women	Total	Men	Women	Total	Men	Women	Total
Emigrant population (thousands)	253.0	265.4	518.4	187.0	202.1	389.1	310.4	328.6	638.9
Recent emigrants (thousands)	..	..	..	31.8	32.2	64.0	123.1	117.0	240.2
15-24 (%)	16.3	15.7	16.0	14.3	13.3	13.8	12.6	12.7	12.6
25-64 (%)	73.1	68.1	70.5	75.0	70.2	72.5	78.7	73.8	76.2
65+ (%)	10.7	16.2	13.5	10.7	16.4	13.7	8.7	13.5	11.2
Low-educated (%)	31.7	34.4	33.1	29.9	31.9	30.9	25.9	24.8	25.3
Highly educated (%)	31.2	29.7	30.4	33.4	31.9	32.7	35.9	39.0	37.5
Total emigration rates (%)	1.9	1.9	1.9	1.3	1.4	1.3	2.2	2.2	2.2
Emigration rates of the highly educated (%)	7.9	5.2	6.3	6.1	4.3	5.0	8.9	7.0	7.7

Main destinations in 2005/06

	Total		Recent emigrants	Women	Highly educated	15-24	Total in 2000
Population 15+	Thousands	%	%	%	%	%	Thousands
Spain	269.7	42.2	83.8	49.3	34.4	14.4	92.7
United States	163.7	25.6	18.2	48.2	40.4	8.3	120.8
Italy	55.3	8.7	30.5	58.3	18.0	10.0	48.8
Chile	35.1	5.5	15.1	64.2	30.2	36.3	35.1
Israel	34.8	5.5	28.3	57.9	56.0	10.4	31.9
Canada	18.1	2.8	28.9	50.6	51.1	10.4	12.7
Australia	11.0	1.7	10.3	51.9	34.7	6.6	10.2
France	10.9	1.7	23.9	55.5	57.4	7.7	9.1
United Kingdom	10.7	1.7	–	61.6	61.6	–	6.5
Mexico	10.2	1.6	..	38.0	62.9	3.0	5.9

Labour market indicators of persons born in Argentina living in OECD countries

Population 15-64	2000			2005/06		
	Men	Women	Total	Men	Women	Total
Employment-population ratio (%)	75.7	54.2	64.9	85.2	62.1	73.7
Unemployment rate (%)	8.7	12.1	10.2	6.7	13.5	9.7
Participation rate (%)	82.9	61.6	72.2	91.4	71.8	81.6
Total employed (thousands)	**123.7**	**89.6**	**213.3**	**237.6**	**173.5**	**411.2**
Employment rates of the highly educated (%)	84.9	66.5	75.5	97.3	79.6	87.8
Unemployment rates of the highly educated (%)	6.0	9.3	7.5	5.3	12.8	9.0
Highly educated in low- and medium-skilled jobs (%)	22.3	26.4	24.1	33.8	35.2	34.5
Highly educated employed (thousands)	**47.1**	**38.4**	**85.5**	**93.4**	**81.1**	**174.4**
Legislators, senior officials and managers	13.2	8.0	11.1	7.4	5.6	6.6
Professionals	17.0	20.4	18.4	13.4	16.1	14.5
Life science and health professionals	2.2	3.1	2.6	2.6	4.3	3.3
Teaching professionals	2.4	5.4	3.6	1.8	4.2	2.8
Technicians and associate professionals	14.1	17.2	15.4	13.9	14.4	14.1
Clerks	5.3	13.1	8.4	4.6	10.8	7.2
Service, shop and market sales workers	11.3	20.6	15.0	13.8	27.8	19.7
Skilled agricultural and fishery workers	1.3	0.7	1.0	1.1	0.3	0.8
Craft and related trades workers	18.3	3.7	12.4	25.8	3.9	16.5
Plant and machine operators and assemblers	8.8	2.7	6.3	8.1	2.4	5.7
Elementary occupations	10.7	13.7	11.9	11.5	18.8	14.6

Left vertical label: Distribution of employment by occupation (%), population 15+

Persons born in Argentina and their native-born children, population 15+

Living in:	Europe	United States	Australia
2008	Thousands	Thousands	Thousands
Native-born children	87.4	81.1	0.9
Foreign-born	348.0	144.3	10.4
Total	435.4	225.5	11.3

International students from Argentina in OECD countries

Five main destinations	2004	2005	2006	2007	2008	2009
United States	3 644	3 513	3 140	2 875	2 538	2 341
Spain	802	932	975	967	1 016	2 297
France	838	779	746	662	768	753
Italy	407	416	420	560	469	419
Germany	..	..	..	..	431	388
Total	6 631	6 297	6 046	5 983	6 521	7 195

Legal migrant flows to the OECD
Thousands

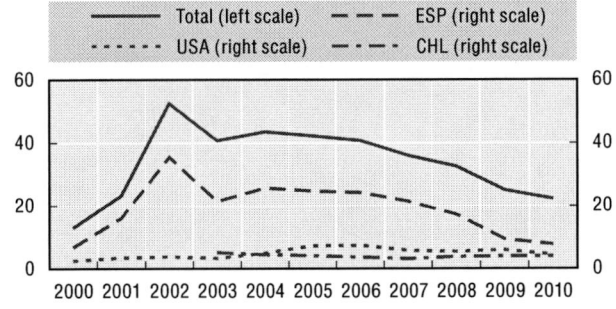

Remittance flows

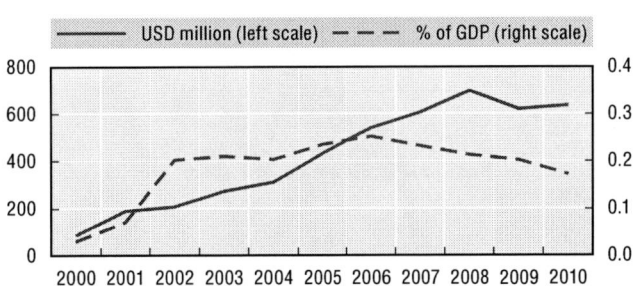

Ten main countries of destination for legal migrants in 2010 (numbers, % of total flows to the country): ESP (7567, 1.8%), USA (4399, 0.4%), CHL (3806, 6%), MEX (1443, 5.5%), ITA (1195, 0.3%), DEU (921, 0.1%), CAN (445, 0.1%), JPN (370, 0.1%), ISR (337, 2%), FRA (271, 0.2%).

Desire to emigrate, 2008-10

	Women	15-24	Highly educated	Total	Regional total
Persons who would move permanently, if they had the opportunity to do so (%)	15	31	..	16	22
Of which: Persons who are planning to move permanently in the next 12 months (%)				7	11
Of which: Persons who have already done some preparations for this move (*e.g.* visa application) (%)					29

Three main countries of desired destination: Spain (28%), United States (16%), Brazil (10%).

StatLink ⟶ http://dx.doi.org/10.1787/888932672612

		Barbados compared to:	World	Region
Total population 2010 (millions)	0.3	Human Development Index (HDI)	47/187	2/31
Population growth 2010 (%)	0.2	GDP per capita	47/194	4/36
GDP per capita 2010 (current USD)	15 035	Emigration rate	20/203	11/38
GDP growth 2009 (%)	−5.3	Emigration rate of the highly educated	1/157	1/24
Poverty rate 2010 (USD PPP 2 a day, in %)	..			

Age structure of the population 0+ (2010): "0-14": 15%; "15-24": 18%; "25-64": 57%; "65+": 11%.
Level of education of the population 15+ (2010): "Low": 10%; "Medium": 85%; "High": 5%.

Emigrant population living in OECD countries

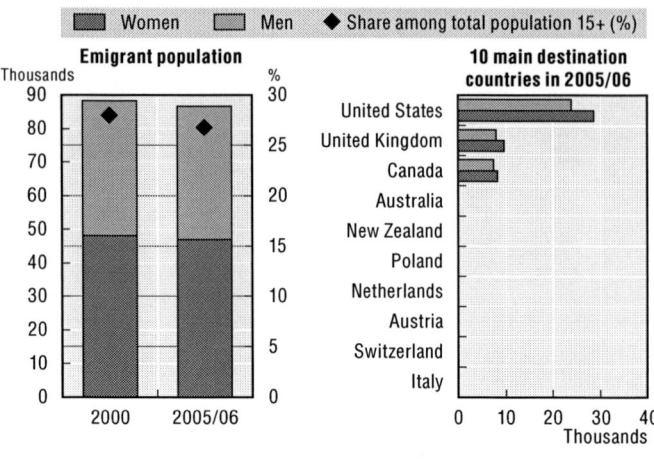

Immigrant population

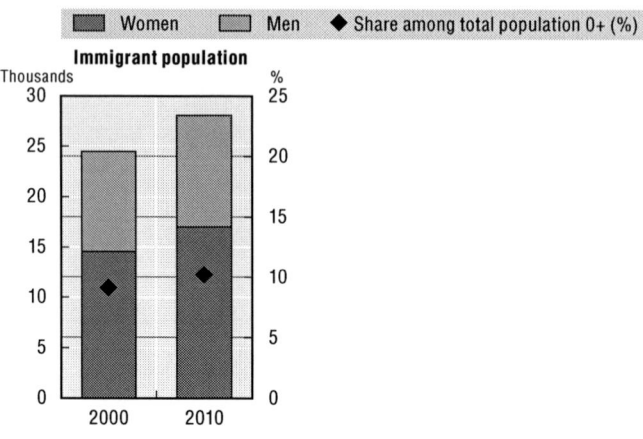

Emigrant population: persons born in Barbados living abroad

	2000						2005/06		
	All destinations			OECD destinations			OECD destinations		
Population 15+	Men	Women	Total	Men	Women	Total	Men	Women	Total
Emigrant population (thousands)	41.2	49.0	90.1	40.3	48.1	88.4	39.8	46.9	86.7
Recent emigrants (thousands)	..	..	..	2.4	2.7	5.1	2.2	1.9	4.1
15-24 (%)	6.4	6.0	6.2	6.4	6.0	6.2	4.9	4.5	4.7
25-64 (%)	75.1	75.7	75.5	75.9	76.4	76.2	71.3	72.9	72.2
65+ (%)	18.5	18.3	18.4	17.7	17.6	17.7	23.8	22.5	23.1
Low-educated (%)	33.8	29.7	31.5	33.4	29.2	31.1	18.8	16.0	17.3
Highly educated (%)	24.1	29.4	27.0	24.3	29.7	27.3	32.3	40.6	36.8
Total emigration rates (%)	27.6	29.2	28.5	27.2	28.8	28.0	26.0	27.5	26.8
Emigration rates of the highly educated (%)	89.7	90.9	90.4	89.6	90.9	90.4	90.7	78.2	82.8

Main destinations in 2005/06

	Total		Recent emigrants	Women	Highly educated	15-24	Total in 2000
Population 15+	Thousands	%	%	%	%	%	Thousands
United States	52.5	60.5	5.4	54.6	31.1	5.5	51.7
United Kingdom	17.5	20.2	–	54.8	54.5	–	21.2
Canada	15.7	18.1	3.8	52.7	45.1	4.0	14.8
Australia	0.3	0.4	10.5	48.2	35.0	1.2	0.2
New Zealand	–	–	–	–	–	–	0.1

Labour market indicators of persons born in Barbados living in OECD countries

Population 15-64	2000			2005/06		
	Men	Women	Total	Men	Women	Total
Employment-population ratio (%)	77.8	71.3	74.2	78.3	78.0	78.2
Unemployment rate (%)	6.3	6.3	6.3	8.0	6.8	7.3
Participation rate (%)	83.0	76.1	79.2	85.1	83.7	84.4
Total employed (thousands)	**25.0**	**27.8**	**52.8**	**23.6**	**26.9**	**50.5**
Employment rates of the highly educated (%)	86.4	80.8	83.0	87.7	88.6	88.2
Unemployment rates of the highly educated (%)	4.5	3.5	4.0	4.6	3.7	4.1
Highly educated in low- and medium-skilled jobs (%)	35.6	33.7	34.5	38.8	41.7	40.6
Highly educated employed (thousands)	**7.2**	**10.3**	**17.5**	**8.6**	**13.1**	**21.7**
Legislators, senior officials and managers	10.5	6.4	8.4	20.2	9.1	14.2
Professionals	11.3	13.9	12.6	15.7	10.0	12.6
Life science and health professionals	0.7	0.4	0.5	0.2	0.1	0.1
Teaching professionals	2.8	4.2	3.5	0.1	0.2	0.2
Technicians and associate professionals	11.6	22.0	16.8	11.6	16.7	14.3
Clerks	8.5	24.7	16.5	6.3	30.4	19.2
Service, shop and market sales workers	9.7	20.7	15.2	10.4	11.0	10.7
Skilled agricultural and fishery workers	0.6	0.0	0.3	1.3	14.0	8.2
Craft and related trades workers	17.2	0.7	9.0	10.6	1.9	6.0
Plant and machine operators and assemblers	15.0	3.2	9.1	12.9	1.7	6.9
Elementary occupations	15.5	8.4	12.0	7.4	5.2	6.2

Distribution of employment by occupation (%), population 15+

Persons born in Barbados and their native-born children, population 15+

Living in:	Europe	United States	Australia
2008	Thousands	Thousands	Thousands
Native-born children	32.9	58.4	..
Foreign-born	11.8	87.9	1.6
Total	44.6	146.3	..

International students from Barbados in OECD countries

Five main destinations	2004	2005	2006	2007	2008	2009
United States	569	516	484	450	403	445
United Kingdom	468	479	491	414	342	322
Canada	165	..	201	186	210	170
Australia	12	15	13	5	5	9
France	2	5	7	7	5	5
Total	1 221	1 020	1 200	1 065	972	960

Legal migrant flows to the OECD
Thousands

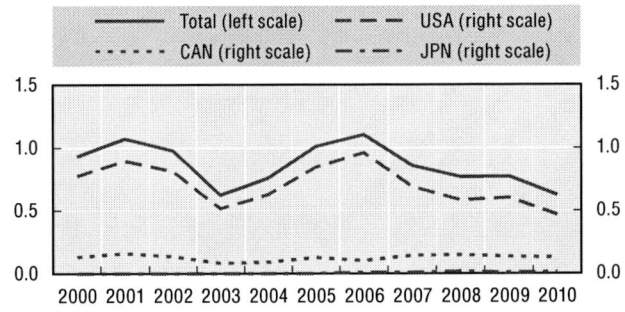

Remittance flows

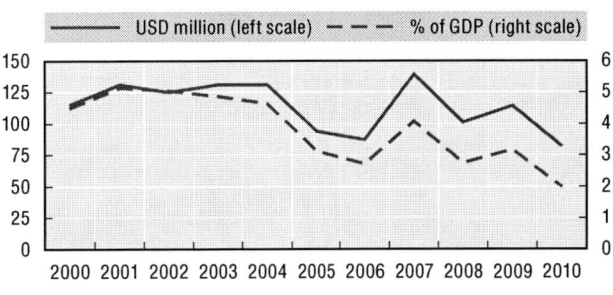

Ten main countries of destination for legal migrants in 2010 (numbers, % of total flows to the country): USA (465, 0%), CAN (125, 0%), JPN (9, 0%), DEU (5, 0%), NZL (4, 0%), AUT (3, 0%), ESP (3, 0%), CHE (3, 0%), AUS (1, 0%), ISL (1, 0%).

Desire to emigrate, 2008-10

	Women	15-24	Highly educated	Total	Regional total
Persons who would move permanently, if they had the opportunity to do so (%)	..	..	..	..	22
Of which: Persons who are planning to move permanently in the next 12 months (%)				..	11
Of which: Persons who have already done some preparations for this move (*e.g.* visa application) (%)					29

StatLink http://dx.doi.org/10.1787/888932672631

BELIZE – Country Notes

		Belize compared to:	World	Region
Total population 2010 (millions)	0.3	Human Development Index (HDI)	93/187	21/31
Population growth 2010 (%)	3.4	GDP per capita	101/194	22/36
GDP per capita 2010 (current USD)	4 064	Emigration rate	24/203	14/38
GDP growth 2010 (%)	2.9	Emigration rate of the highly educated	9/157	6/24
Poverty rate 2010 (USD PPP 2 a day, in %)	..			

Age structure of the population 0+ (2010): "0-14": 21%; "15-24": 35%; "25-64": 40%; "65+": 4%.
Level of education of the population 15+ (2010): "Low": 52%; "Medium": 39%; "High": 9%.

Emigrant population living in OECD countries

Immigrant population

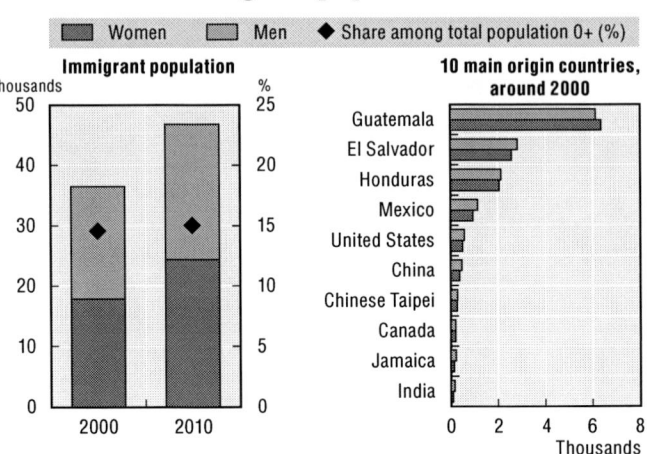

Emigrant population: persons born in Belize living abroad

	2000						2005/06		
	All destinations			OECD destinations			OECD destinations		
Population 15+	Men	Women	Total	Men	Women	Total	Men	Women	Total
Emigrant population (thousands)	18.8	25.6	44.4	17.9	24.7	42.6	21.6	28.1	49.7
Recent emigrants (thousands)	..	..	..	2.1	2.8	4.9	1.9	2.4	4.3
15-24 (%)	16.4	12.6	14.2	16.0	11.9	13.6	10.8	10.7	10.7
25-64 (%)	75.2	75.8	75.6	75.7	76.4	76.1	76.8	75.1	75.8
65+ (%)	8.4	11.5	10.2	8.3	11.6	10.3	12.4	14.3	13.4
Low-educated (%)	33.2	31.6	32.3	31.4	30.1	30.6	22.8	24.3	23.7
Highly educated (%)	19.3	20.6	20.0	19.6	21.0	20.4	27.2	26.8	27.0
Total emigration rates (%)	20.2	26.1	23.2	19.4	25.3	22.5	20.0	24.8	22.4
Emigration rates of the highly educated (%)	39.8	51.4	45.9	39.0	51.1	45.4	46.3	52.5	49.6

Main destinations in 2005/06

	Total		Recent emigrants	Women	Highly educated	15-24	Total in 2000
Population 15+	Thousands	%	%	%	%	%	Thousands
United States	44.7	89.9	9.1	56.8	27.3	10.9	39.0
Mexico	1.9	3.8	..	40.5	20.9	5.4	1.0
Canada	1.9	3.8	11.5	46.4	21.6	19.3	1.4
United Kingdom	–	–	–	–	–	–	1.1

Labour market indicators of persons born in Belize living in OECD countries

Population 15-64	2000			2005/06		
	Men	Women	Total	Men	Women	Total
Employment-population ratio (%)	73.7	62.5	67.3	75.9	63.0	68.7
Unemployment rate (%)	8.0	8.7	8.4	8.3	10.1	9.2
Participation rate (%)	80.1	68.4	73.4	82.7	70.1	75.7
Total employed (thousands)	**12.1**	**13.6**	**25.7**	**14.3**	**14.9**	**29.2**
Employment rates of the highly educated (%)	84.9	78.7	81.2	89.5	82.5	85.5
Unemployment rates of the highly educated (%)	5.0	6.2	5.7	4.1	3.1	3.6
Highly educated in low- and medium-skilled jobs (%)	46.0	41.6	43.5	46.5	36.6	40.9
Highly educated employed (thousands)	**2.8**	**3.9**	**6.7**	**4.5**	**5.5**	**10.0**
Legislators, senior officials and managers	5.5	7.4	6.5	7.1	1.9	4.3
Professionals	10.5	16.1	13.4	6.6	6.1	6.3
Life science and health professionals	4.0	0.7	1.7	8.3	0.6	1.1
Teaching professionals	4.5	5.9	5.4	–	–	–
Technicians and associate professionals	7.0	14.2	10.7	6.6	29.7	18.8
Clerks	8.6	19.7	14.3	5.2	40.3	23.8
Service, shop and market sales workers	8.6	25.7	17.4	6.3	9.9	8.2
Skilled agricultural and fishery workers	5.8	1.2	3.5	15.7	2.9	8.9
Craft and related trades workers	22.7	1.2	11.7	22.3	–	10.5
Plant and machine operators and assemblers	14.6	6.9	10.7	19.0	3.4	10.7
Elementary occupations	16.5	7.5	11.9	11.2	5.8	8.3

Distribution of employment by occupation (%), population 15+

Persons born in Belize and their native-born children, population 15+

Living in:	Europe	United States	Australia
2008	Thousands	Thousands	Thousands
Native-born children	1.4	18.9	..
Foreign-born	1.0	34.7	..
Total	2.4	53.6	..

International students from Belize in OECD countries

Five main destinations	2004	2005	2006	2007	2008	2009
United States	501	469	478	464	491	460
Canada	11	..	18	27	32	44
United Kingdom	44	46	40	30	25	34
Germany	..	..	..	..	10	8
Spain	1	1	1	3	2	3
Total	559	523	543	529	568	562

Legal migrant flows to the OECD
Thousands

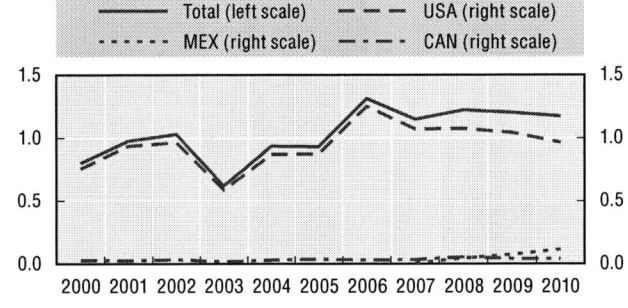

Remittance flows

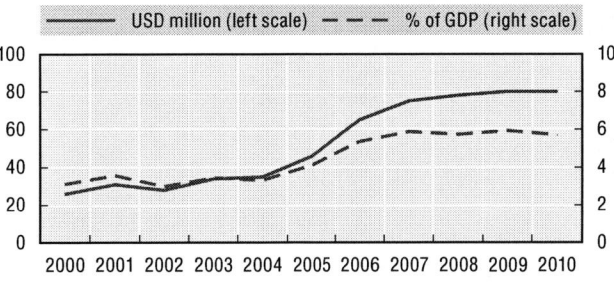

Ten main countries of destination for legal migrants in 2010 (numbers, % of total flows to the country): USA (965, 0.1%), MEX (113, 0.4%), CAN (40, 0%), JPN (27, 0%), DEU (11, 0%), KOR (3, 0%), ESP (3, 0%), ITA (2, 0%), NOR (2, 0%), CHE (2, 0%).

Desire to emigrate, 2008-10

	Women	15-24	Highly educated	Total	Regional total
Persons who would move permanently, if they had the opportunity to do so (%)	..	..	..	..	22
Of which: Persons who are planning to move permanently in the next 12 months (%)				..	11
Of which: Persons who have already done some preparations for this move (*e.g.* visa application) (%)					29

StatLink ᵃᵈˢᵖ *http://dx.doi.org/10.1787/888932672650*

		Bolivia compared to:	World	Region
Total population 2010 (millions)	9.9	Human Development Index (HDI)	108/187	26/31
Population growth 2010 (%)	1.6	GDP per capita	132/194	29/36
GDP per capita 2010 (current USD)	1 979	Emigration rate	105/203	32/38
GDP growth 2010 (%)	4.1	Emigration rate of the highly educated	122/157	22/24
Poverty rate 2007 (USD PPP 2 a day, in %)	25.1			

Age structure of the population 0+ (2010): "0-14": 20%; "15-24": 36%; "25-64": 39%; "65+": 5%.
Level of education of the population 15+ (2010): "Low": 30%; "Medium": 53%; "High": 17%.

Emigrant population living in OECD countries

Immigrant population

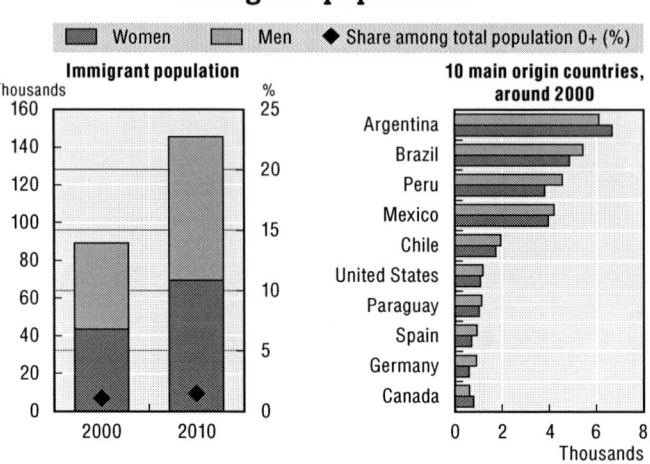

Emigrant population: persons born in Bolivia living abroad

	2000						2005/06		
	All destinations			OECD destinations			OECD destinations		
Population 15+	Men	Women	Total	Men	Women	Total	Men	Women	Total
Emigrant population (thousands)	165.9	166.5	332.4	42.0	45.7	87.7	84.9	108.3	193.2
Recent emigrants (thousands)	..	..	..	9.8	10.5	20.3	43.1	60.1	103.2
15-24 (%)	17.6	18.4	18.0	19.8	17.6	18.7	21.3	17.7	19.3
25-64 (%)	73.5	72.7	73.1	74.7	75.9	75.3	74.6	77.9	76.5
65+ (%)	8.8	8.9	8.9	5.5	6.5	6.0	4.1	4.4	4.3
Low-educated (%)	60.2	63.7	62.0	26.9	30.0	28.5	29.9	31.5	30.8
Highly educated (%)	12.6	10.5	11.6	30.3	25.8	28.0	26.9	22.2	24.3
Total emigration rates (%)	6.3	6.1	6.2	1.5	1.8	1.5	3.0	3.6	3.3
Emigration rates of the highly educated (%)	5.6	5.6	5.6	3.2	3.8	3.4	4.7	5.7	5.1

Main destinations in 2005/06

	Total		Recent emigrants	Women	Highly educated	15-24	Total in 2000
Population 15+	Thousands	%	%	%	%	%	Thousands
Spain	94.0	48.6	92.7	58.7	12.6	23.7	12.4
United States	67.7	35.0	17.3	52.4	37.2	12.3	50.1
Chile	8.4	4.4	28.2	60.9	15.2	21.9	10.5
Italy	3.6	1.9	52.3	55.3	–	32.6	1.7
Mexico	3.4	1.8	..	47.5	91.8	6.7	1.3
Canada	3.2	1.6	18.5	55.7	37.4	28.7	2.3
Japan	3.2	1.6	..	46.2	24.6	18.7	2.2
Sweden	2.6	1.3	20.9	47.7	31.8	14.7	2.2
France	1.9	1.0	38.5	57.7	44.6	26.8	0.9
Switzerland	1.7	0.9	–	69.5	–	–	1.1

Labour market indicators of persons born in Bolivia living in OECD countries

Population 15-64	2000			2005/06		
	Men	Women	Total	Men	Women	Total
Employment-population ratio (%)	72.5	54.6	63.1	80.4	73.3	76.4
Unemployment rate (%)	7.7	10.2	8.8	11.2	9.8	10.4
Participation rate (%)	78.5	60.7	69.2	90.5	81.2	85.3
Total employed (thousands)	**26.9**	**22.1**	**49.0**	**62.6**	**73.4**	**136.0**
Employment rates of the highly educated (%)	81.3	63.8	72.7	92.5	82.3	87.2
Unemployment rates of the highly educated (%)	5.5	7.6	6.4	10.0	8.6	9.3
Highly educated in low- and medium-skilled jobs (%)	40.3	44.2	42.0	58.7	64.2	61.4
Highly educated employed (thousands)	**9.1**	**6.8**	**15.9**	**17.0**	**16.7**	**33.7**
Legislators, senior officials and managers	6.9	6.4	6.7	0.9	3.1	2.2
Professionals	13.5	10.8	12.3	4.3	1.3	2.5
Life science and health professionals	2.9	1.5	2.3	1.1	0.4	0.7
Teaching professionals	0.8	2.3	1.4	0.5	0.4	0.4
Technicians and associate professionals	8.8	10.0	9.3	3.2	1.9	2.4
Clerks	4.4	8.5	6.2	1.1	3.3	2.4
Service, shop and market sales workers	11.8	20.5	15.7	12.4	25.4	19.9
Skilled agricultural and fishery workers	7.1	1.9	4.7	3.7	0.5	1.8
Craft and related trades workers	19.6	3.4	12.3	35.2	2.2	16.0
Plant and machine operators and assemblers	12.1	4.1	8.5	6.5	0.6	3.1
Elementary occupations	15.8	34.5	24.2	32.6	61.9	49.6

Distribution of employment by occupation (%), population 15+

Persons born in Bolivia and their native-born children, population 15+

Living in:	Europe	United States	Australia
2008	Thousands	Thousands	Thousands
Native-born children	11.1	31.3	..
Foreign-born	265.5	63.9	..
Total	276.7	95.1	..

International students from Bolivia in OECD countries

Five main destinations	2004	2005	2006	2007	2008	2009
United States	1 004	1 053	1 030	1 015	965	1 049
Spain	86	152	171	244	241	749
France	185	203	238	242	310	288
Germany	..	..	..	..	169	170
Italy	80	92	105	131	138	161
Total	1 535	1 668	1 766	1 825	2 482	2 846

Legal migrant flows to the OECD
Thousands

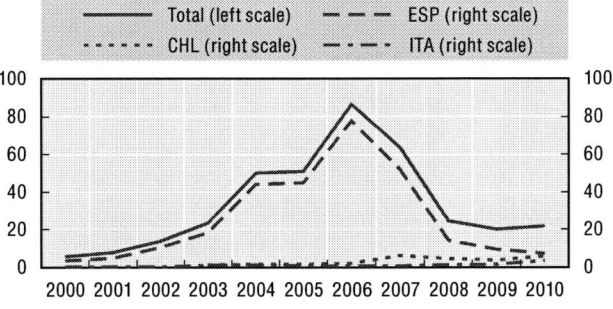

Remittance flows

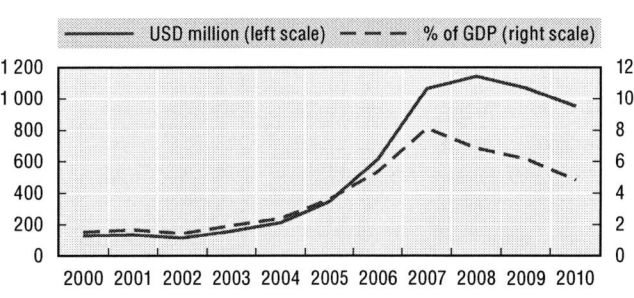

Ten main countries of destination for legal migrants in 2010 (numbers, % of total flows to the country): ESP (7390, 1.7%), CHL (5836, 9.2%), ITA (3362, 0.8%), USA (2253, 0.2%), GBR (1014, 0.2%), SWE (320, 0.4%), DEU (288, 0.2%), CHE (247, 0.2%), JPN (181, 0.1%), MEX (176, 0.7%).

Desire to emigrate, 2008-10

	Women	15-24	Highly educated	Total	Regional total
Persons who would move permanently, if they had the opportunity to do so (%)	21	33	30	24	22
Of which: Persons who are planning to move permanently in the next 12 months (%)				18	11
Of which: Persons who have already done some preparations for this move (*e.g.* visa application) (%)					29

Three main countries of desired destination: Spain (24%), Argentina (20%), United States (14%).

StatLink *StatLink* http://dx.doi.org/10.1787/888932672669

Total population 2010 (millions)	194.9	Brazil compared to:	World	Region
Population growth 2010 (%)	0.9	Human Development Index (HDI)	84/187	18/31
GDP per capita 2010 (current USD)	10 710	GDP per capita	59/194	9/36
GDP growth 2010 (%)	7.5	Emigration rate	162/203	37/38
Poverty rate 2009 (USD PPP 2 a day, in %)	9.9	Emigration rate of the highly educated	140/157	24/24

Age structure of the population 0+ (2010): "0-14": 17%; "15-24": 25%; "25-64": 50%; "65+": 7%.
Level of education of the population 15+ (2010): "Low": 48%; "Medium": 44%; "High": 7%.

Emigrant population living in OECD countries

Immigrant population

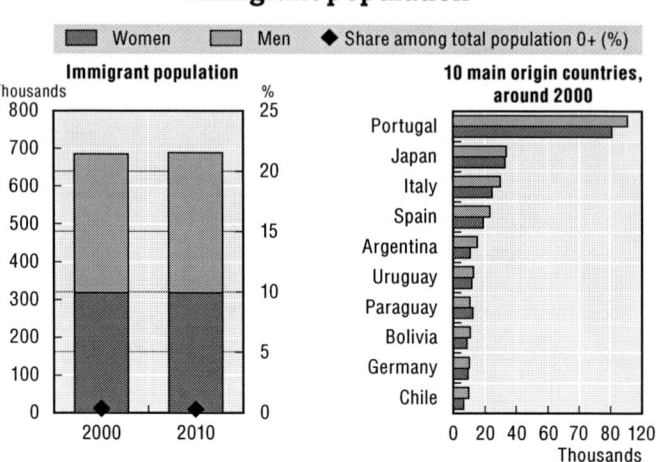

Emigrant population: persons born in Brazil living abroad

	2000						2005/06		
	All destinations			OECD destinations			OECD destinations		
Population 15+	Men	Women	Total	Men	Women	Total	Men	Women	Total
Emigrant population (thousands)	326.5	376.0	702.5	255.2	299.6	554.8	407.1	460.1	867.2
Recent emigrants (thousands)	..	..	..	56.7	73.0	129.7	133.2	148.1	281.3
15-24 (%)	22.2	19.3	20.6	23.4	19.7	21.4	20.1	16.9	18.4
25-64 (%)	73.5	74.3	73.9	73.5	75.1	74.4	77.6	78.7	78.2
65+ (%)	4.3	6.4	5.4	3.0	5.2	4.2	2.3	4.3	3.4
Low-educated (%)	41.6	40.1	40.8	32.0	31.9	31.9	30.6	28.9	29.7
Highly educated (%)	22.1	24.3	23.3	26.2	28.1	27.2	26.4	29.8	28.2
Total emigration rates (%)	0.5	0.6	0.6	0.4	0.5	0.4	0.6	0.7	0.6
Emigration rates of the highly educated (%)	2.0	2.0	2.0	1.8	1.8	1.8	2.7	2.7	2.7

Main destinations in 2005/06

	Total		Recent emigrants	Women	Highly educated	15-24	Total in 2000
Population 15+	Thousands	%	%	%	%	%	Thousands
United States	340.1	39.2	35.2	51.2	33.0	16.7	199.6
Japan	179.8	20.7	..	44.4	19.1	21.0	157.9
Portugal	90.9	10.5	64.9	54.2	14.1	18.3	45.2
Spain	66.6	7.7	73.9	62.5	20.3	16.2	29.3
Italy	43.3	5.0	26.6	65.9	14.1	17.5	34.8
United Kingdom	34.6	4.0	66.7	46.9	53.6	21.3	14.0
France	24.4	2.8	30.9	61.9	40.6	29.3	13.1
Switzerland	17.8	2.1	56.3	77.6	29.5	14.3	13.0
Canada	16.8	1.9	30.7	54.8	57.0	14.2	12.5
Netherlands	9.8	1.1	20.8	69.3	30.3	22.9	2.1

Labour market indicators of persons born in Brazil living in OECD countries

Population 15-64	2000			2005/06		
	Men	Women	Total	Men	Women	Total
Employment-population ratio (%)	74.0	53.4	62.3	81.7	62.0	70.9
Unemployment rate (%)	6.0	11.4	8.7	7.0	11.2	9.1
Participation rate (%)	78.8	60.3	68.2	87.9	69.8	78.0
Total employed (thousands)	**116.7**	**111.4**	**228.1**	**239.3**	**220.3**	**459.7**
Employment rates of the highly educated (%)	81.2	60.8	69.2	90.4	72.9	80.3
Unemployment rates of the highly educated (%)	4.3	8.9	6.7	7.0	9.1	8.1
Highly educated in low- and medium-skilled jobs (%)	31.7	40.5	36.2	42.7	48.0	45.5
Highly educated employed (thousands)	**38.6**	**40.8**	**79.4**	**70.4**	**76.6**	**147.0**
Legislators, senior officials and managers	11.2	6.9	9.0	7.4	6.0	6.7
Professionals	16.3	15.9	16.1	11.1	9.0	10.0
Life science and health professionals	2.1	2.7	2.4	1.5	1.6	1.5
Teaching professionals	2.4	4.3	3.4	1.9	3.4	2.7
Technicians and associate professionals	13.0	14.4	13.7	10.1	10.1	10.1
Clerks	5.1	12.9	9.1	3.5	8.9	6.3
Service, shop and market sales workers	11.9	24.5	18.3	14.4	31.0	23.0
Skilled agricultural and fishery workers	1.1	1.0	1.1	2.0	1.4	1.7
Craft and related trades workers	21.6	3.1	12.1	21.8	3.5	12.3
Plant and machine operators and assemblers	7.8	2.7	5.2	9.4	1.5	5.3
Elementary occupations	11.8	18.5	15.3	19.4	28.4	24.1

Distribution of employment by occupation (%), population 15+

Persons born in Brazil and their native-born children, population 15+

Living in:	Europe	United States	Australia
2008	Thousands	Thousands	Thousands
Native-born children	73.5	113.0	0.9
Foreign-born	363.9	387.7	3.9
Total	437.4	500.7	4.8

International students from Brazil in OECD countries

Five main destinations	2004	2005	2006	2007	2008	2009
United States	7 799	7 566	7 258	7 284	7 586	8 623
France	1 759	1 846	2 112	2 580	2 941	3 379
Portugal	..	..	..	..	1 713	2 252
Germany	..	..	..	..	1 803	1 919
Spain	574	685	663	737	964	1 859
Total	13 239	12 941	13 589	14 614	19 808	23 324

Legal migrant flows to the OECD
Thousands

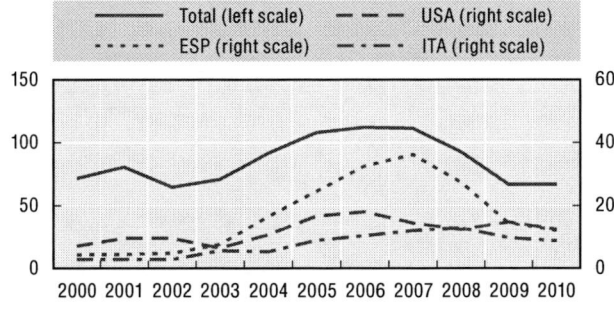

Remittance flows

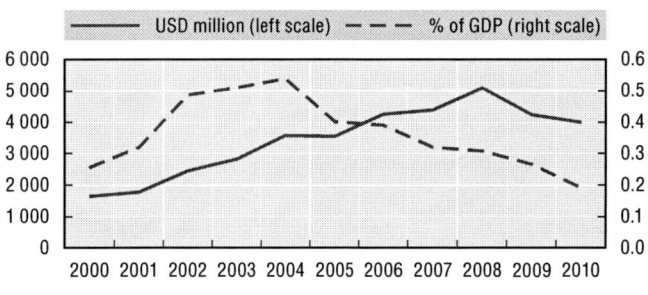

Ten main countries of destination for legal migrants in 2010 (numbers, % of total flows to the country): USA (12258, 1.2%), ESP (11883, 2.8%), ITA (8566, 2%), DEU (6127, 0.9%), JPN (4719, 1.6%), PRT (3442, 12.6%), CAN (2600, 1.9%), CHE (2473, 1.9%), FRA (2364, 1.7%), GBR (2321, 0.5%).

Desire to emigrate, 2008-10

	Women	15-24	Highly educated	Total	Regional total
Persons who would move permanently, if they had the opportunity to do so (%)	13	29	..	15	22
Of which: Persons who are planning to move permanently in the next 12 months (%)				9	11
Of which: Persons who have already done some preparations for this move (*e.g.* visa application) (%)					29

Three main countries of desired destination: United States (35%), Italy (7%), Spain (6%).

StatLink http://dx.doi.org/10.1787/888932672688

			Colombia compared to:	World	Region
Total population 2010 (millions)		46.3	Human Development Index (HDI)	87/187	20/31
Population growth 2010 (%)		1.4	GDP per capita	83/194	18/36
GDP per capita 2010 (current USD)		6 225	Emigration rate	104/203	31/38
GDP growth 2010 (%)		4.3	Emigration rate of the highly educated	67/157	14/24
Poverty rate 2006 (USD PPP 2 a day, in %)		27.9			

Age structure of the population 0+ (2010): "0-14": 18%; "15-24": 29%; "25-64": 47%; "65+": 6%.
Level of education of the population 15+ (2010): "Low": 47%; "Medium": 44%; "High": 8%.

Emigrant population living in OECD countries

Immigrant population

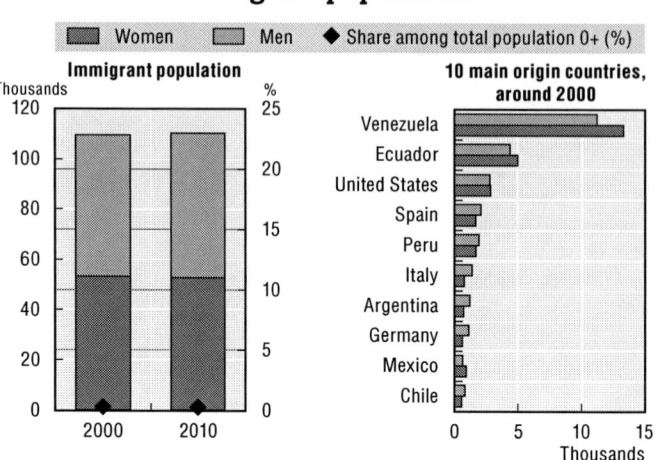

Emigrant population: persons born in Colombia living abroad

	2000						2005/06		
	All destinations			OECD destinations			OECD destinations		
Population 15+	Men	Women	Total	Men	Women	Total	Men	Women	Total
Emigrant population (thousands)	621.4	745.8	1 367.2	300.9	395.6	696.5	442.0	594.2	1 036.3
Recent emigrants (thousands)	..	..	..	101.3	138.8	240.1	162.9	214.0	376.8
15-24 (%)	14.0	12.2	13.0	18.4	14.8	16.3	17.1	12.7	14.6
25-64 (%)	79.7	79.8	79.7	76.9	78.5	77.8	77.3	79.2	78.4
65+ (%)	6.3	8.0	7.2	4.8	6.7	5.9	5.7	8.0	7.0
Low-educated (%)	54.2	53.6	53.9	32.3	35.3	34.0	25.4	26.5	26.0
Highly educated (%)	16.5	15.8	16.1	26.2	24.3	25.1	31.1	29.8	30.4
Total emigration rates (%)	4.4	4.9	4.6	2.1	2.7	2.4	2.8	3.6	3.2
Emigration rates of the highly educated (%)	7.0	8.0	7.5	5.5	6.6	6.0	10.2	12.8	11.5

Main destinations in 2005/06

	Total		Recent emigrants	Women	Highly educated	15-24	Total in 2000
Population 15+	Thousands	%	%	%	%	%	Thousands
United States	574.4	55.4	16.8	55.9	34.6	11.0	472.0
Spain	322.0	31.1	79.5	59.8	18.5	16.9	143.5
Canada	35.7	3.4	60.5	54.0	53.7	18.1	15.8
United Kingdom	20.6	2.0	–	64.1	48.1	–	10.9
France	17.3	1.7	26.7	57.7	36.9	28.2	9.2
Italy	16.5	1.6	26.7	61.2	10.4	30.7	12.9
Switzerland	7.4	0.7	39.1	58.9	37.0	23.4	4.6
Sweden	7.3	0.7	20.8	48.9	24.8	40.6	5.8
Netherlands	7.2	0.7	–	62.2	–	34.9	–
Mexico	5.5	0.5	..	62.9	60.8	12.9	5.5

Labour market indicators of persons born in Colombia living in OECD countries

Population 15-64	2000			2005/06		
	Men	Women	Total	Men	Women	Total
Employment-population ratio (%)	68.7	53.9	60.4	80.8	66.1	72.4
Unemployment rate (%)	10.0	13.0	11.5	7.6	11.3	9.6
Participation rate (%)	76.4	61.9	68.3	87.4	74.5	80.1
Total employed (thousands)	**193.6**	**195.5**	**389.1**	**329.4**	**354.2**	**683.6**
Employment rates of the highly educated (%)	77.6	60.2	68.0	91.9	78.5	84.3
Unemployment rates of the highly educated (%)	7.0	9.7	8.4	5.5	8.9	7.3
Highly educated in low- and medium-skilled jobs (%)	44.0	47.4	45.7	47.3	53.7	50.6
Highly educated employed (thousands)	**57.5**	**55.2**	**112.7**	**112.0**	**120.1**	**232.1**
Legislators, senior officials and managers	5.3	3.3	4.2	3.1	2.9	3.0
Professionals	9.4	7.8	8.5	10.1	5.2	7.4
Life science and health professionals	1.7	0.9	1.3	1.7	1.1	1.4
Teaching professionals	1.2	2.1	1.7	1.1	1.5	1.4
Technicians and associate professionals	8.0	8.4	8.2	5.1	6.2	5.7
Clerks	4.5	8.7	6.8	3.2	8.5	6.1
Service, shop and market sales workers	14.2	25.0	20.1	14.4	31.8	23.9
Skilled agricultural and fishery workers	2.7	0.7	1.6	2.2	0.6	1.4
Craft and related trades workers	23.7	4.0	13.0	29.7	2.4	14.7
Plant and machine operators and assemblers	9.1	2.8	5.7	7.9	1.7	4.5
Elementary occupations	23.1	39.2	31.8	24.0	40.7	33.1

Distribution of employment by occupation (%), population 15+

Persons born in Colombia and their native-born children, population 15+

Living in:	Europe	United States	Australia
2008	Thousands	Thousands	Thousands
Native-born children	16.3	308.6	..
Foreign-born	413.0	602.9	7.3
Total	429.3	911.5	..

International students from Colombia in OECD countries

Five main destinations	2004	2005	2006	2007	2008	2009
United States	7 533	7 660	7 078	6 899	6 669	6 898
Spain	797	1 045	929	1 343	1 361	4 501
France	1 754	1 783	2 028	2 288	2 281	2 494
Germany	..	..	..	..	1 074	1 191
Australia	608	536	518	623	740	901
Total	12 187	12 061	12 085	13 004	15 017	18 868

Legal migrant flows to the OECD
Thousands

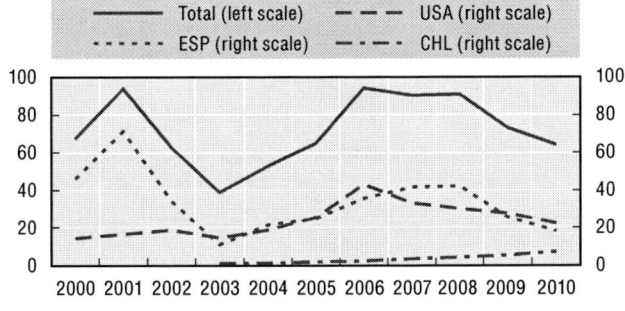

Remittance flows

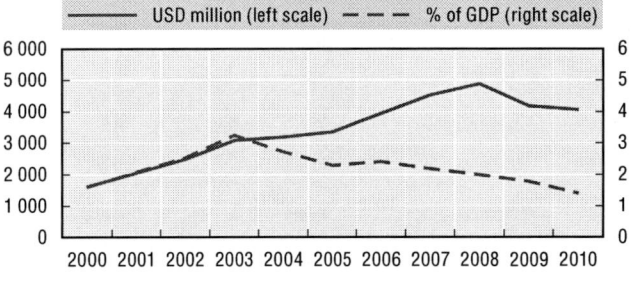

Ten main countries of destination for legal migrants in 2010 (numbers, % of total flows to the country): USA (22406, 2.2%), ESP (18089, 4.2%), CHL (7191, 11.3%), CAN (4800, 1.7%), MEX (2312, 8.8%), ITA (2132, 0.5%), DEU (1954, 0.2%), GBR (1151, 0.2%), FRA (823, 0.6%), AUS (785, 0.4%).

Desire to emigrate, 2008-10

	Women	15-24	Highly educated	Total	Regional total
Persons who would move permanently, if they had the opportunity to do so (%)	28	46	33	32	22
Of which: Persons who are planning to move permanently in the next 12 months (%)				11	11
Of which: Persons who have already done some preparations for this move (*e.g.* visa application) (%)					29

Three main countries of desired destination: United States (27%), Spain (26%), Canada (8%).

StatLink ᴹᴸᴾ *http://dx.doi.org/10.1787/888932672707*

		Costa Rica compared to:	World	Region
Total population 2010 (millions)	4.7	Human Development Index (HDI)	69/187	10/31
Population growth 2010 (%)	1.5	GDP per capita	71/194	11/36
GDP per capita 2010 (current USD)	7 691	Emigration rate	106/203	33/38
GDP growth 2010 (%)	4.2	Emigration rate of the highly educated	113/157	20/24
Poverty rate 2009 (USD PPP 2 a day, in %)	5.4			

Age structure of the population 0+ (2010): "0-14": 19%; "15-24": 25%; "25-64": 50%; "65+": 7%.
Level of education of the population 15+ (2010): "Low": 40%; "Medium": 44%; "High": 16%.

Emigrant population living in OECD countries

Immigrant population

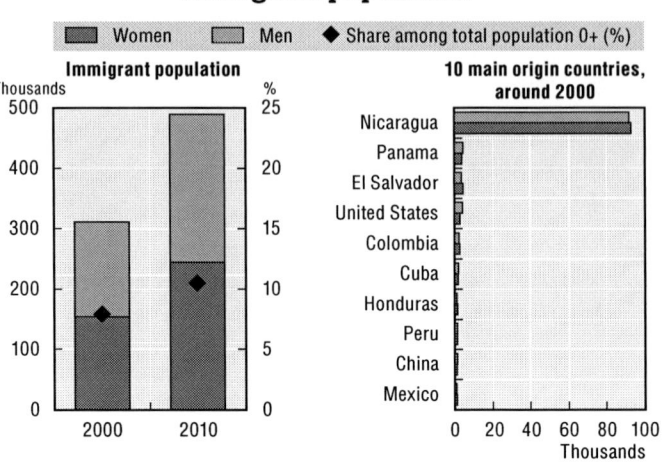

Emigrant population: persons born in Costa Rica living abroad

	2000						2005/06		
	All destinations			OECD destinations			OECD destinations		
Population 15+	Men	Women	Total	Men	Women	Total	Men	Women	Total
Emigrant population (thousands)	41.0	47.6	88.6	35.4	40.9	76.4	47.9	48.7	96.6
Recent emigrants (thousands)	..	..	..	10.3	8.9	19.2	9.7	7.7	17.4
15-24 (%)	19.8	17.1	18.4	18.7	16.0	17.3	16.3	11.1	13.7
25-64 (%)	73.8	72.6	73.2	75.8	74.5	75.1	76.5	76.2	76.3
65+ (%)	6.4	10.2	8.4	5.5	9.5	7.6	7.2	12.8	10.0
Low-educated (%)	34.0	32.5	33.2	32.7	30.4	31.5	28.8	24.3	26.5
Highly educated (%)	25.6	23.9	24.7	24.9	24.6	24.7	24.9	30.7	27.8
Total emigration rates (%)	2.9	3.5	3.2	2.5	3.0	2.8	3.0	3.1	3.0
Emigration rates of the highly educated (%)	4.8	5.4	5.1	4.1	4.8	4.4	5.0	6.2	5.6

Main destinations in 2005/06

	Total		Recent emigrants	Women	Highly educated	15-24	Total in 2000
Population 15+	Thousands	%	%	%	%	%	Thousands
United States	86.5	89.6	17.3	49.8	26.5	13.1	68.1
Canada	3.3	3.4	23.6	52.6	35.0	28.4	2.2
Spain	1.5	1.5	–	–	–	–	1.2
Italy	–	–	–	–	–	–	0.6
Mexico	0.8	0.8	..	40.5	18.2	37.0	1.8
Switzerland	–	–	–	–	–	–	0.4
France	0.6	0.6	33.8	61.2	48.1	27.7	0.4
Portugal	–	–	–	–	–	–	–
Netherlands	–	–	–	–	–	–	–
Australia	–	–	–	–	–	–	0.1

Labour market indicators of persons born in Costa Rica living in OECD countries

Population 15-64	2000			2005/06		
	Men	Women	Total	Men	Women	Total
Employment-population ratio (%)	77.1	55.1	65.6	81.1	60.5	71.0
Unemployment rate (%)	4.7	8.9	6.6	7.3	8.4	7.7
Participation rate (%)	80.8	60.5	70.2	87.4	66.0	77.0
Total employed (thousands)	**25.7**	**20.3**	**46.1**	**35.5**	**25.3**	**60.8**
Employment rates of the highly educated (%)	85.8	67.1	75.8	95.8	76.4	84.9
Unemployment rates of the highly educated (%)	2.7	4.9	3.8	4.3	5.2	4.8
Highly educated in low- and medium-skilled jobs (%)	40.3	39.7	40.0	42.3	42.9	42.6
Highly educated employed (thousands)	**7.1**	**6.4**	**13.5**	**9.8**	**9.9**	**19.7**
Legislators, senior officials and managers	9.2	5.3	7.3	8.4	18.1	14.0
Professionals	19.5	20.5	20.0	15.0	12.2	13.4
Life science and health professionals	5.1	1.0	3.1	8.7	4.2	5.7
Teaching professionals	3.9	5.6	4.7	2.2	2.8	2.6
Technicians and associate professionals	14.7	16.4	15.5	5.5	7.3	6.6
Clerks	5.3	15.8	10.3	5.1	11.2	8.6
Service, shop and market sales workers	15.0	21.3	18.0	17.6	33.9	26.9
Skilled agricultural and fishery workers	1.5	1.5	1.5	2.2	1.2	1.6
Craft and related trades workers	9.3	2.0	5.8	28.3	4.6	14.7
Plant and machine operators and assemblers	8.5	5.8	7.2	5.4	1.6	3.2
Elementary occupations	17.0	11.4	14.3	12.7	9.8	11.0

Distribution of employment by occupation (%), population 15+

Persons born in Costa Rica and their native-born children, population 15+

Living in:	Europe	United States	Australia
2008	Thousands	Thousands	Thousands
Native-born children	0.4	46.7	..
Foreign-born	3.6	96.0	..
Total	4.1	142.7	..

International students from Costa Rica in OECD countries

Five main destinations	2004	2005	2006	2007	2008	2009
United States	907	935	928	960	928	1 010
Spain	28	33	131	87	110	207
Germany	..	..	..	..	112	124
France	70	64	87	85	96	85
Canada	47	..	51	54	70	71
Total	1 160	1 134	1 298	1 306	1 500	1 673

Legal migrant flows to the OECD
Thousands

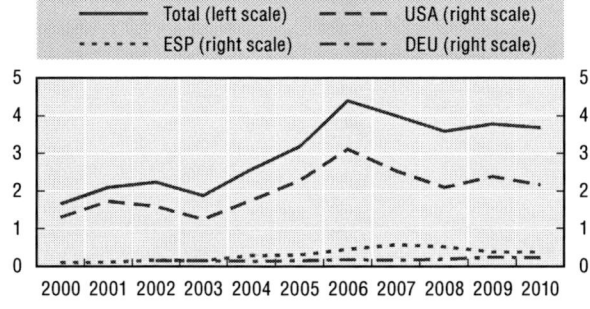

Remittance flows

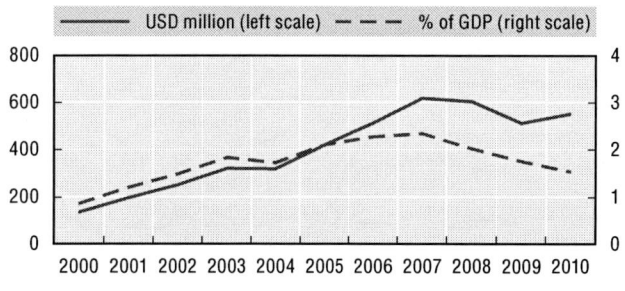

Ten main countries of destination for legal migrants in 2010 (numbers, % of total flows to the country): USA (2164, 0.2%), ESP (378, 0.1%), DEU (222, 0%), CAN (205, 0.1%), MEX (162, 0.6%), JPN (98, 0%), CHL (97, 0%), ITA (68, 0%), CHE (66, 0.1%), NLD (52, 0.1%).

Desire to emigrate, 2008-10

	Women	15-24	Highly educated	Total	Regional total
Persons who would move permanently, if they had the opportunity to do so (%)	16	32	18	20	22
Of which: Persons who are planning to move permanently in the next 12 months (%)				12	11
Of which: Persons who have already done some preparations for this move (*e.g.* visa application) (%)					29

Three main countries of desired destination: United States (31%), Spain (11%), Canada (8%).

StatLink http://dx.doi.org/10.1787/888932672726

Total population 2010 (millions)	11.3		Cuba compared to:	World	Region
Population growth 2010 (%)	0.0		Human Development Index (HDI)	51/187	4/31
GDP per capita 2008 (current USD)	5 565		GDP per capita	191/194	34/36
GDP growth 2008 (%)	4.3		Emigration rate	46/203	20/38
Poverty rate 2010 (USD PPP 2 a day, in %)	..		Emigration rate of the highly educated	22/157	8/24

Age structure of the population 0+ (2010): "0-14": 14%; "15-24": 17%; "25-64": 56%; "65+": 12%.
Level of education of the population 15+ (2010): "Low": 19%; "Medium": 66%; "High": 15%.

Emigrant population living in OECD countries

Immigrant population

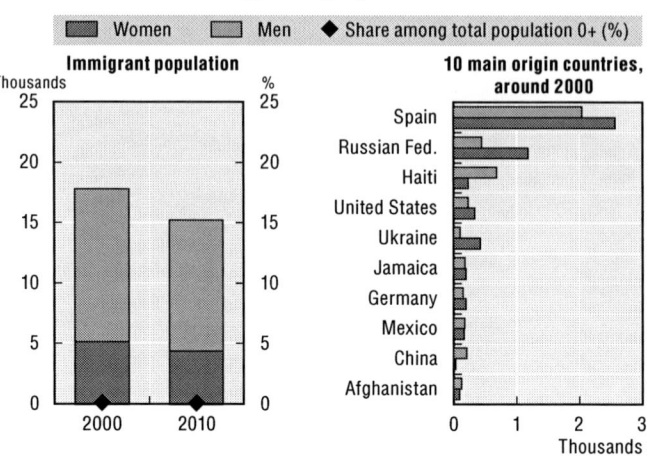

Emigrant population: persons born in Cuba living abroad

	2000						2005/06		
	All destinations			OECD destinations			OECD destinations		
Population 15+	Men	Women	Total	Men	Women	Total	Men	Women	Total
Emigrant population (thousands)	475.7	500.8	976.6	450.0	477.5	927.5	527.6	548.4	1 076.0
Recent emigrants (thousands)	..	..	..	75.3	73.4	148.7	81.9	83.3	165.2
15-24 (%)	5.1	5.2	5.2	5.1	5.0	5.0	5.8	6.3	6.0
25-64 (%)	72.0	65.1	68.4	72.0	65.1	68.5	69.4	61.8	65.6
65+ (%)	22.9	29.8	26.4	22.9	29.8	26.5	24.8	31.9	28.4
Low-educated (%)	39.4	40.1	39.7	40.6	40.9	40.8	28.4	30.1	29.3
Highly educated (%)	25.7	24.2	25.0	24.5	23.5	24.0	29.6	28.2	28.9
Total emigration rates (%)	9.8	10.1	9.9	9.3	9.7	9.5	10.4	10.7	10.6
Emigration rates of the highly educated (%)	32.8	26.7	29.4	30.6	25.2	27.5	28.2	24.3	26.1

Main destinations in 2005/06

	Total		Recent emigrants	Women	Highly educated	15-24	Total in 2000
Population 15+	Thousands	%	%	%	%	%	Thousands
United States	946.5	88.0	12.4	50.2	27.4	5.4	851.7
Spain	82.0	7.6	66.1	53.4	39.5	9.5	45.2
Italy	15.3	1.4	50.6	82.7	12.1	19.0	8.2
Mexico	9.8	0.9	..	50.3	59.7	6.7	6.3
Canada	8.7	0.8	45.3	51.7	55.5	13.5	4.9
France	3.2	0.3	44.2	58.0	40.8	11.2	1.6
Chile	1.8	0.2	28.4	58.0	87.2	8.0	3.0
Sweden	1.8	0.2	32.6	45.2	53.0	13.3	1.5
Switzerland	1.3	0.1	–	–	–	–	1.1

Labour market indicators of persons born in Cuba living in OECD countries

Population 15-64	2000			2005/06		
	Men	Women	Total	Men	Women	Total
Employment-population ratio (%)	73.8	57.6	65.8	83.5	65.1	74.5
Unemployment rate (%)	6.7	9.6	8.0	7.1	9.4	8.1
Participation rate (%)	79.1	63.8	71.5	89.9	71.8	81.1
Total employed (thousands)	**254.6**	**192.4**	**447.1**	**328.0**	**240.9**	**568.9**
Employment rates of the highly educated (%)	86.9	72.7	79.8	97.5	82.8	90.3
Unemployment rates of the highly educated (%)	4.2	6.4	5.2	4.9	7.0	5.8
Highly educated in low- and medium-skilled jobs (%)	40.4	39.8	40.1	49.7	48.3	49.1
Highly educated employed (thousands)	**80.1**	**66.3**	**146.4**	**119.4**	**94.8**	**214.2**
Legislators, senior officials and managers	10.8	5.9	8.5	5.9	4.1	5.0
Professionals	22.2	15.2	19.0	16.9	11.2	14.2
Life science and health professionals	4.0	2.0	3.0	2.4	3.0	2.7
Teaching professionals	4.2	5.5	4.8	2.9	4.2	3.5
Technicians and associate professionals	10.5	12.8	11.6	9.0	9.8	9.4
Clerks	5.2	13.7	9.1	4.8	14.8	9.6
Service, shop and market sales workers	14.6	26.4	20.1	21.2	34.8	27.7
Skilled agricultural and fishery workers	1.2	0.7	0.9	1.8	1.6	1.7
Craft and related trades workers	15.2	4.4	10.2	15.9	3.0	9.7
Plant and machine operators and assemblers	9.6	3.7	6.9	7.3	1.2	4.4
Elementary occupations	10.7	17.2	13.7	17.2	19.5	18.3

Distribution of employment by occupation (%), population 15+

Persons born in Cuba and their native-born children, population 15+

Living in:	Europe	United States	Australia
2008	Thousands	Thousands	Thousands
Native-born children	29.1	424.8	..
Foreign-born	128.4	1 000.8	1.6
Total	157.5	1 425.6	..

International students from Cuba in OECD countries

Five main destinations	2004	2005	2006	2007	2008	2009
Spain	225	255	366	421	390	779
Italy	95	103	113	126	115	137
Germany	..	..	..	..	110	104
France	78	84	78	77	96	87
United States	132	198	123	101	82	83
Total	636	703	773	846	1 028	1 391

Legal migrant flows to the OECD
Thousands

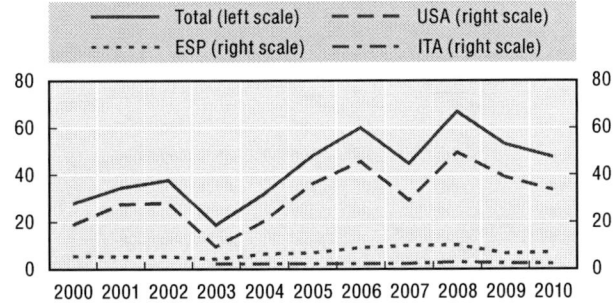

Ten main countries of destination for legal migrants in 2010 (numbers, % of total flows to the country): USA (33573, 3.2%), ESP (6811, 1.6%), ITA (2088, 0.5%), MEX (1847, 7.1%), CAN (945, 0.3%), DEU (641, 0.1%), CHL (438, 0.2%), FRA (236, 0.2%), CHE (193, 0.1%), JPN (172, 0.1%).

Desire to emigrate, 2008-10

	Women	15-24	Highly educated	Total	Regional total
Persons who would move permanently, if they had the opportunity to do so (%)	..	..	..	..	22
Of which: Persons who are planning to move permanently in the next 12 months (%)				..	11
Of which: Persons who have already done some preparations for this move (*e.g.* visa application) (%)					29

StatLink http://dx.doi.org/10.1787/888932672745

		Dominican Republic compared to:	World	Region
Total population 2010 (millions)	9.9	Human Development Index (HDI)	98/187	22/31
Population growth 2010 (%)	1.3	GDP per capita	91/194	21/36
GDP per capita 2010 (current USD)	5 215	Emigration rate	41/203	18/38
GDP growth 2010 (%)	7.8	Emigration rate of the highly educated	56/157	13/24
Poverty rate 2007 (USD PPP 2 a day, in %)	13.6			

Age structure of the population 0+ (2010): "0-14": 19%; "15-24": 31%; "25-64": 44%; "65+": 6%.
Level of education of the population 15+ (2010): "Low": 47%; "Medium": 35%; "High": 18%.

Emigrant population living in OECD countries

Immigrant population

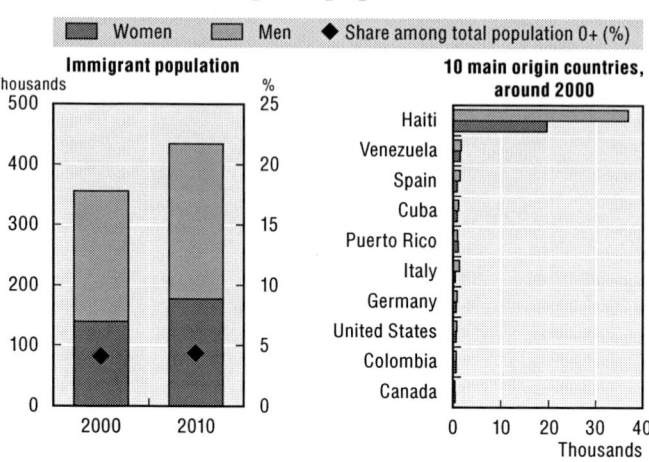

Emigrant population: persons born in the Dominican Republic living abroad

	2000						2005/06		
	All destinations			OECD destinations			OECD destinations		
Population 15+	Men	Women	Total	Men	Women	Total	Men	Women	Total
Emigrant population (thousands)	334.2	442.3	776.5	300.1	395.5	695.5	352.9	488.1	841.0
Recent emigrants (thousands)	..	..	..	51.5	67.0	118.6	63.6	78.9	142.5
15-24 (%)	18.4	15.2	16.6	18.3	15.2	16.6	18.1	13.5	15.4
25-64 (%)	76.1	76.9	76.6	76.2	76.8	76.5	73.9	76.0	75.1
65+ (%)	5.5	7.9	6.8	5.5	8.0	6.9	8.1	10.6	9.5
Low-educated (%)	53.6	53.2	53.4	53.8	53.0	53.3	43.1	44.1	43.6
Highly educated (%)	11.8	12.4	12.1	11.8	12.8	12.4	15.6	17.0	16.4
Total emigration rates (%)	10.5	13.4	12.0	9.5	12.2	10.8	10.1	13.4	11.8
Emigration rates of the highly educated (%)	9.1	13.5	11.2	8.2	12.5	10.3	10.0	15.1	12.6

Main destinations in 2005/06

	Total		Recent emigrants	Women	Highly educated	15-24	Total in 2000
Population 15+	Thousands	%	%	%	%	%	Thousands
United States	732.9	87.1	13.8	56.6	17.6	14.2	633.3
Spain	70.9	8.4	62.2	66.2	6.3	23.3	36.8
Italy	16.6	2.0	25.9	74.2	–	24.4	12.9
Canada	6.4	0.8	17.9	55.1	24.1	22.3	4.5
Netherlands	4.3	0.5	–	73.2	–	–	–
Switzerland	3.7	0.4	47.8	69.3	–	–	4.5
Austria	–	–	–	–	–	–	–
France	1.3	0.2	41.9	65.4	30.3	21.0	0.3
United Kingdom	–	–	–	–	–	–	0.4
Belgium	–	–	–	–	–	–	0.9

Labour market indicators of persons born in the Dominican Republic living in OECD countries

Population 15-64	2000			2005/06		
	Men	Women	Total	Men	Women	Total
Employment-population ratio (%)	59.7	47.5	52.9	73.9	62.3	67.2
Unemployment rate (%)	11.3	15.1	13.3	9.8	11.3	10.6
Participation rate (%)	67.3	56.0	61.0	81.9	70.2	75.2
Total employed (thousands)	**169.0**	**172.2**	**341.3**	**236.2**	**268.9**	**505.1**
Employment rates of the highly educated (%)	77.9	64.9	70.3	90.6	82.6	85.8
Unemployment rates of the highly educated (%)	5.4	8.6	7.1	5.6	6.3	6.0
Highly educated in low- and medium-skilled jobs (%)	55.2	52.8	53.9	60.1	57.2	58.4
Highly educated employed (thousands)	**26.8**	**31.7**	**58.6**	**45.2**	**61.5**	**106.7**
Legislators, senior officials and managers	5.0	2.3	3.1	1.8	3.7	3.0
Professionals	6.0	3.8	4.5	1.9	1.4	1.6
Life science and health professionals	2.0	0.7	1.0	0.1	0.1	0.1
Teaching professionals	1.2	1.1	1.1	0.0	0.1	0.1
Technicians and associate professionals	7.0	6.1	6.4	5.7	1.8	3.2
Clerks	4.5	5.9	5.5	2.5	4.4	3.7
Service, shop and market sales workers	17.9	24.0	22.2	12.0	34.0	26.3
Skilled agricultural and fishery workers	1.1	0.6	0.7	3.3	0.3	1.3
Craft and related trades workers	25.0	5.1	10.9	33.4	3.5	14.1
Plant and machine operators and assemblers	12.9	4.3	6.8	6.9	1.5	3.4
Elementary occupations	20.5	47.9	40.0	32.6	49.4	43.5

Distribution of employment by occupation (%), population 15+

Persons born in the Dominican Republic and their native-born children, population 15+

Living in:	Europe	United States	Australia
2008	Thousands	Thousands	Thousands
Native-born children	4.1	596.4	..
Foreign-born	153.6	904.4	..
Total	157.6	1 500.8	..

International students from the Dominican Republic in OECD countries

Five main destinations	2004	2005	2006	2007	2008	2009
United States	998	907	906	982	1 160	1 364
Spain	61	173	210	222	223	731
Canada	169	..	81	99	155	123
France	95	55	97	116	71	104
Italy	32	39	61	63	73	87
Total	1 409	1 223	1 394	1 531	1 790	2 505

Legal migrant flows to the OECD
Thousands

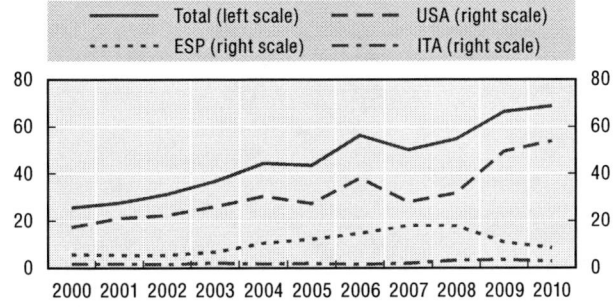

Remittance flows

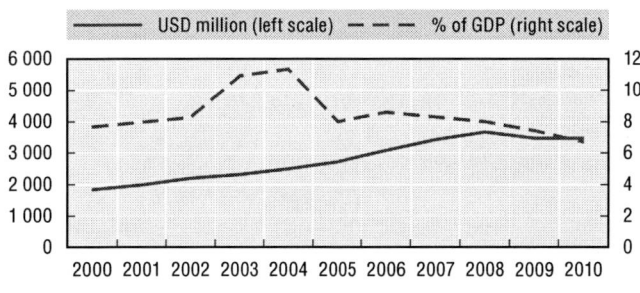

Ten main countries of destination for legal migrants in 2010 (numbers, % of total flows to the country): USA (53870, 5.2%), ESP (8337, 1.9%), ITA (2742, 0.6%), CHL (1038, 1.6%), DEU (568, 0.1%), CAN (490, 0.2%), CHE (419, 0.3%), FRA (394, 0.3%), MEX (195, 0.7%), NLD (148, 0.1%).

Desire to emigrate, 2008-10

	Women	15-24	Highly educated	Total	Regional total
Persons who would move permanently, if they had the opportunity to do so (%)	51	61	43	52	22
Of which: Persons who are planning to move permanently in the next 12 months (%)				10	11
Of which: Persons who have already done some preparations for this move (*e.g.* visa application) (%)					29

Three main countries of desired destination: United States (48%), Spain (29%), Puerto Rico (4%).

StatLink ⟐⟐ *http://dx.doi.org/10.1787/888932672764*

		Ecuador compared to:	World	Region
Total population 2010 (millions)	14.5	Human Development Index (HDI)	83/187	17/31
Population growth 2010 (%)	1.4	GDP per capita	102/194	23/36
GDP per capita 2010 (current USD)	4 008	Emigration rate	45/203	19/38
GDP growth 2010 (%)	3.6	Emigration rate of the highly educated	73/157	17/24
Poverty rate 2009 (USD PPP 2 a day, in %)	13.6			

Age structure of the population 0+ (2010): "0-14": 19%; "15-24": 30%; "25-64": 45%; "65+": 6%.
Level of education of the population 15+ (2010): "Low": 49%; "Medium": 35%; "High": 16%.

Emigrant population living in OECD countries

Immigrant population

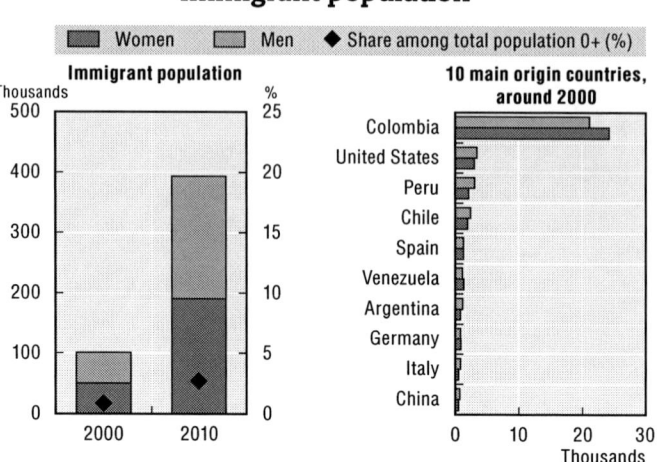

Emigrant population: persons born in Ecuador living abroad

	2000						2005/06		
	All destinations			OECD destinations			OECD destinations		
Population 15+	Men	Women	Total	Men	Women	Total	Men	Women	Total
Emigrant population (thousands)	278.3	281.1	559.4	255.5	256.5	512.1	518.5	548.3	1 066.8
Recent emigrants (thousands)	..	..	..	109.8	108.8	218.7	271.1	294.7	565.8
15-24 (%)	21.3	18.9	20.1	22.1	19.3	20.7	19.0	18.4	18.7
25-64 (%)	74.9	75.1	75.0	74.6	75.1	74.9	77.9	76.7	77.3
65+ (%)	3.8	6.0	4.9	3.3	5.6	4.5	3.0	4.9	4.0
Low-educated (%)	51.1	47.3	49.2	50.7	46.4	48.6	46.9	43.8	45.3
Highly educated (%)	14.5	16.1	15.3	14.3	16.3	15.3	14.6	15.4	15.0
Total emigration rates (%)	6.5	6.5	6.5	5.9	6.0	5.9	10.6	11.0	10.8
Emigration rates of the highly educated (%)	6.7	7.4	7.0	5.9	6.9	6.3	9.9	11.5	10.7

Main destinations in 2005/06

	Total		Recent emigrants	Women	Highly educated	15-24	Total in 2000
Population 15+	Thousands	%	%	%	%	%	Thousands
Spain	608.6	57.0	78.9	52.6	10.9	21.7	190.0
United States	372.9	35.0	18.3	47.8	20.5	13.2	280.5
Italy	47.2	4.4	46.8	61.8	7.8	23.5	12.2
Canada	13.2	1.2	14.4	53.7	37.0	11.1	10.7
Chile	6.0	0.6	38.8	51.6	46.1	31.3	7.9
United Kingdom	–	–	–	–	–	–	2.4
France	2.9	0.3	36.2	64.3	37.6	24.1	1.1
Belgium	–	–	–	–	–	–	1.0
Switzerland	2.0	0.2	61.9	61.3	–	–	1.4
Netherlands	2.0	0.2	–	–	–	–	–

Labour market indicators of persons born in Ecuador living in OECD countries

Population 15-64	2000			2005/06		
	Men	Women	Total	Men	Women	Total
Employment-population ratio (%)	72.6	57.6	65.2	85.4	67.9	76.5
Unemployment rate (%)	9.5	12.5	10.9	6.4	11.4	8.7
Participation rate (%)	80.3	65.9	73.2	91.3	76.6	83.8
Total employed (thousands)	**178.6**	**138.6**	**317.3**	**423.7**	**350.4**	**774.1**
Employment rates of the highly educated (%)	79.0	64.8	71.4	95.6	81.0	87.9
Unemployment rates of the highly educated (%)	7.5	8.6	8.0	4.6	8.5	6.5
Highly educated in low- and medium-skilled jobs (%)	55.2	56.3	55.7	70.9	73.6	72.2
Highly educated employed (thousands)	**27.7**	**26.1**	**53.7**	**65.7**	**60.2**	**125.9**
Legislators, senior officials and managers	2.2	2.3	2.2	0.9	0.3	0.6
Professionals	4.0	4.1	4.1	1.7	0.6	1.1
Life science and health professionals	0.4	0.4	0.4	0.4	0.2	0.3
Teaching professionals	0.4	0.9	0.6	0.3	0.1	0.2
Technicians and associate professionals	4.2	4.9	4.5	0.9	1.9	1.4
Clerks	3.0	6.2	4.5	1.8	4.0	2.8
Service, shop and market sales workers	12.1	18.7	15.2	9.7	26.6	17.9
Skilled agricultural and fishery workers	3.7	0.6	2.2	2.2	0.5	1.3
Craft and related trades workers	25.6	4.2	15.4	35.5	2.8	19.6
Plant and machine operators and assemblers	10.5	4.6	7.7	11.0	2.7	6.9
Elementary occupations	34.9	54.3	44.2	36.3	60.7	48.1

(Left margin label: Distribution of employment by occupation (%), population 15+)

Persons born in Ecuador and their native-born children, population 15+

Living in:	Europe	United States	Australia
2008	Thousands	Thousands	Thousands
Native-born children	9.3	206.4	0.8
Foreign-born	780.1	417.6	..
Total	789.4	624.0	..

International students from Ecuador in OECD countries

Five main destinations	2004	2005	2006	2007	2008	2009
Spain	135	358	392	435	478	2 461
United States	2 345	2 274	2 250	2 260	2 154	2 231
Italy	207	276	329	421	468	582
France	291	294	299	299	275	443
Germany	..	..	..	..	318	330
Total	3 267	3 427	3 602	3 805	4 655	6 744

Legal migrant flows to the OECD
Thousands

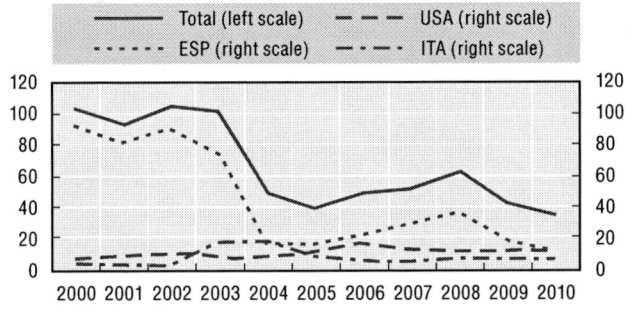

Remittance flows

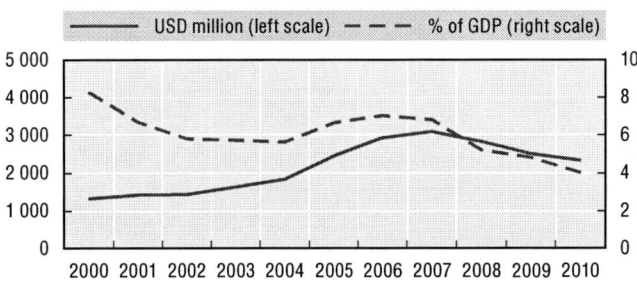

Ten main countries of destination for legal migrants in 2010 (numbers, % of total flows to the country): USA (11492, 1.1%), ESP (10967, 2.5%), ITA (6168, 1.5%), CHL (2476, 3.9%), GBR (735, 0.2%), DEU (666, 0.1%), BEL (490, 0.1%), CAN (385, 0.1%), CHE (345, 0.3%), MEX (232, 0.9%).

Desire to emigrate, 2008-10

	Women	15-24	Highly educated	Total	Regional total
Persons who would move permanently, if they had the opportunity to do so (%)	21	30	21	21	22
Of which: Persons who are planning to move permanently in the next 12 months (%)				13	11
Of which: Persons who have already done some preparations for this move (e.g. visa application) (%)					29

Three main countries of desired destination: United States (33%), Spain (26%), Italy (8%).

StatLink ▬▬ http://dx.doi.org/10.1787/888932672783

			El Salvador compared to:	World	Region
Total population 2010 (millions)		6.2	Human Development Index (HDI)	105/187	24/31
Population growth 2010 (%)		0.5	GDP per capita	106/194	24/36
GDP per capita 2010 (current USD)		3 426	Emigration rate	27/203	15/38
GDP growth 2010 (%)		1.4	Emigration rate of the highly educated	28/157	10/24
Poverty rate 2008 (USD PPP 2 a day, in %)		15.2			

Age structure of the population 0+ (2010): "0-14": 22%; "15-24": 32%; "25-64": 39%; "65+": 7%.
Level of education of the population 15+ (2010): "Low": 52%; "Medium": 38%; "High": 10%.

Emigrant population living in OECD countries

Immigrant population

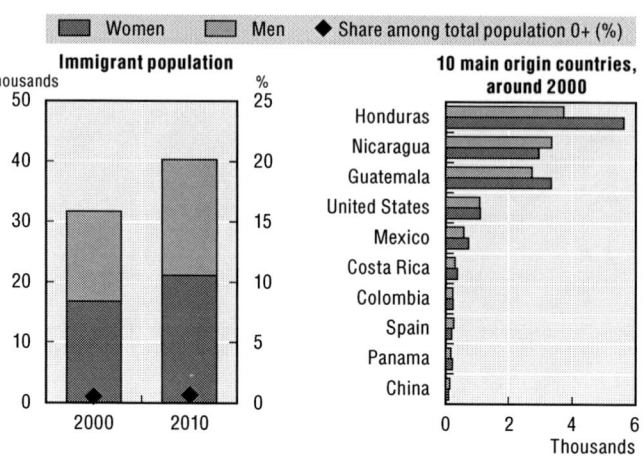

Emigrant population: persons born in El Salvador living abroad

	2000						2005/06		
	All destinations			OECD destinations			OECD destinations		
Population 15+	Men	Women	Total	Men	Women	Total	Men	Women	Total
Emigrant population (thousands)	444.3	428.2	872.6	428.5	407.3	835.8	584.3	523.1	1 107.4
Recent emigrants (thousands)	..	..	..	77.5	60.3	137.8	96.4	74.4	170.9
15-24 (%)	21.8	17.9	19.9	21.9	17.9	20.0	13.3	11.2	12.3
25-64 (%)	75.6	76.6	76.1	75.9	76.8	76.3	83.6	81.3	82.5
65+ (%)	2.6	5.6	4.1	2.2	5.3	3.7	3.1	7.5	5.2
Low-educated (%)	63.6	62.8	63.2	63.6	62.5	63.0	54.0	53.4	53.7
Highly educated (%)	7.8	8.0	7.9	7.6	7.9	7.7	9.9	11.4	10.6
Total emigration rates (%)	18.8	17.1	18.0	18.3	16.4	17.3	21.7	18.6	20.1
Emigration rates of the highly educated (%)	16.4	16.4	16.4	15.4	15.6	15.5	22.1	23.2	22.7

Main destinations in 2005/06

	Total		Recent emigrants	Women	Highly educated	15-24	Total in 2000
Population 15+	Thousands	%	%	%	%	%	Thousands
United States	1 032.7	93.3	15.9	47.0	9.5	12.0	775.0
Canada	42.6	3.8	5.5	49.5	29.5	15.3	37.0
Australia	9.2	0.8	1.4	51.9	30.7	19.0	8.8
Italy	6.8	0.6	–	54.1	–	25.0	3.6
Mexico	5.0	0.4	..	54.9	12.3	4.3	5.3
Spain	4.2	0.4	94.0	55.0	29.7	–	1.8
Sweden	2.4	0.2	10.6	49.1	21.9	19.0	2.2
United Kingdom	–	–	–	–	–	–	0.4
France	1.3	0.1	33.0	47.3	35.3	35.3	0.7
Chile	0.5	0.0	0.0	22.2	100.0	0.0	0.2

Labour market indicators of persons born in El Salvador living in OECD countries

Population 15-64	2000			2005/06		
	Men	Women	Total	Men	Women	Total
Employment-population ratio (%)	70.1	52.4	61.6	85.7	65.7	76.5
Unemployment rate (%)	6.8	10.6	8.4	6.0	8.7	7.1
Participation rate (%)	75.2	58.5	67.2	91.1	72.0	82.3
Total employed (thousands)	**292.7**	**201.1**	**493.8**	**481.1**	**315.2**	**796.3**
Employment rates of the highly educated (%)	80.8	69.6	75.2	95.2	81.6	88.4
Unemployment rates of the highly educated (%)	5.6	5.9	5.7	4.7	5.9	5.3
Highly educated in low- and medium-skilled jobs (%)	56.9	53.3	55.2	62.6	55.7	59.4
Highly educated employed (thousands)	**25.2**	**21.4**	**46.6**	**50.2**	**43.3**	**93.4**
Legislators, senior officials and managers	4.2	3.3	3.8	4.0	3.7	3.9
Professionals	6.9	6.3	6.6	7.8	8.6	8.2
Life science and health professionals	1.0	2.3	1.7	0.6	4.4	2.5
Teaching professionals	1.2	2.0	1.6	1.1	3.4	2.3
Technicians and associate professionals	7.9	10.2	8.9	8.1	10.9	9.4
Clerks	6.8	16.2	11.1	6.7	14.1	10.1
Service, shop and market sales workers	10.8	24.2	16.9	10.9	23.2	16.6
Skilled agricultural and fishery workers	1.3	0.7	1.0	1.3	2.4	1.8
Craft and related trades workers	19.6	4.0	12.5	21.3	5.2	13.9
Plant and machine operators and assemblers	18.2	9.4	14.2	17.4	6.4	12.3
Elementary occupations	24.3	25.7	25.0	22.4	25.3	23.8

Distribution of employment by occupation (%), population 15+

Persons born in El Salvador and their native-born children, population 15+

Living in:	Europe	United States	Australia
2008	Thousands	Thousands	Thousands
Native-born children	3.0	682.1	..
Foreign-born	17.9	978.6	1.0
Total	20.9	1 660.7	..

International students from El Salvador in OECD countries

Five main destinations	2004	2005	2006	2007	2008	2009
United States	976	1 005	972	1 054	941	1 165
Spain	29	80	126	151	101	232
France	106	106	126	148	151	170
Germany	..	..	..	..	72	76
Chile	..	..	..	..	85	57
Total	1 229	1 283	1 350	1 507	1 536	1 897

Legal migrant flows to the OECD
Thousands

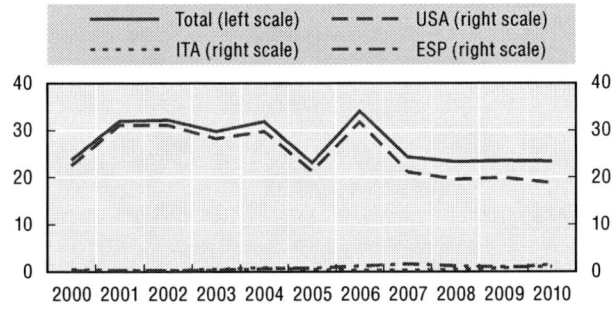

Remittance flows

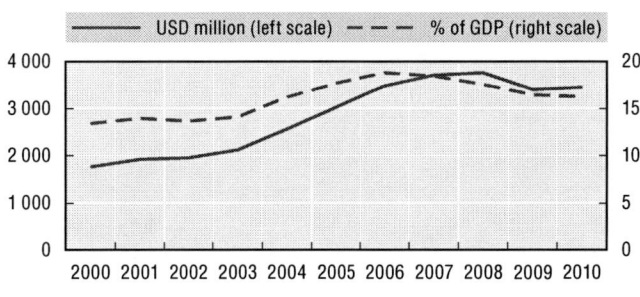

Ten main countries of destination for legal migrants in 2010 (numbers, % of total flows to the country): USA (18806, 1.8%), ITA (1535, 0.4%), ESP (993, 0.2%), CAN (765, 0.3%), MEX (708, 2.7%), CHL (122, 0.2%), JPN (115, 0%), DEU (96, 0%), SWE (63, 0.1%), AUS (61, 0%).

Desire to emigrate, 2008-10

	Women	15-24	Highly educated	Total	Regional total
Persons who would move permanently, if they had the opportunity to do so (%)	42	51	54	43	22
Of which: Persons who are planning to move permanently in the next 12 months (%)				10	11
Of which: Persons who have already done some preparations for this move (*e.g.* visa application) (%)					29

Three main countries of desired destination: United States (56%), Canada (13%), Spain (10%).

StatLink ⬛🔗 http://dx.doi.org/10.1787/888932672802

GUATEMALA – Country Notes

			World	Region
Total population 2010 (millions)	14.4	**Guatemala compared to:**		
Population growth 2010 (%)	2.5	Human Development Index (HDI)	131/187	30/31
GDP per capita 2010 (current USD)	2 862	GDP per capita	120/194	26/36
GDP growth 2010 (%)	2.8	Emigration rate	53/203	23/38
Poverty rate 2006 (USD PPP 2 a day, in %)	24.3	Emigration rate of the highly educated	20/157	7/24

Age structure of the population 0+ (2010): "0-14": 20%; "15-24": 41%; "25-64": 34%; "65+": 4%.
Level of education of the population 15+ (2010): "Low": 76%; "Medium": 22%; "High": 2%.

Emigrant population living in OECD countries

Immigrant population

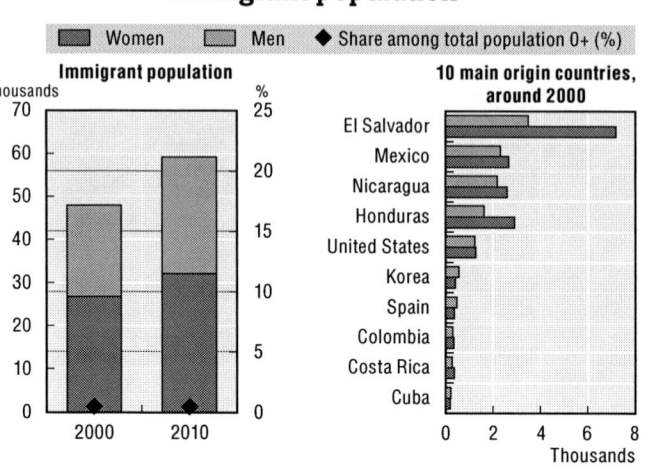

Emigrant population: persons born in Guatemala living abroad

	2000						2005/06		
	All destinations			OECD destinations			OECD destinations		
Population 15+	Men	Women	Total	Men	Women	Total	Men	Women	Total
Emigrant population (thousands)	281.4	232.2	513.6	267.8	217.9	485.6	429.9	297.3	727.2
Recent emigrants (thousands)	..	..	..	70.7	38.2	108.9	128.9	56.4	185.3
15-24 (%)	26.1	20.4	23.5	26.1	20.0	23.3	20.3	16.2	18.6
25-64 (%)	71.5	74.3	72.8	71.7	74.9	73.1	77.1	77.4	77.2
65+ (%)	2.4	5.3	3.7	2.2	5.2	3.5	2.7	6.4	4.2
Low-educated (%)	65.1	63.0	64.2	64.9	62.2	63.7	59.6	55.3	57.9
Highly educated (%)	8.2	8.9	8.5	8.0	8.9	8.4	9.1	11.8	10.2
Total emigration rates (%)	8.5	6.6	7.6	8.2	6.2	7.2	11.1	7.3	9.1
Emigration rates of the highly educated (%)	18.5	24.3	20.9	17.3	23.2	19.7	25.5	34.5	29.1

Main destinations in 2005/06

	Total		Recent emigrants	Women	Highly educated	15-24	Total in 2000
Population 15+	Thousands	%	%	%	%	%	Thousands
United States	681.3	93.7	26.8	39.7	9.6	18.8	446.1
Mexico	22.4	3.1	..	60.6	3.0	12.3	21.6
Canada	14.9	2.1	6.4	49.3	32.8	16.9	12.5
Spain	3.6	0.5	58.3	85.9	36.7	–	1.4
Italy	1.4	0.2	–	71.7	–	–	1.0
France	1.0	0.1	21.2	56.1	36.1	40.7	0.7
Belgium	–	–	–	–	–	–	0.4
Sweden	0.6	0.1	8.2	46.4	22.9	36.6	0.5
Netherlands	–	–	–	–	–	–	–
Switzerland	–	–	–	–	–	–	0.4

Labour market indicators of persons born in Guatemala living in OECD countries

Population 15-64	2000			2005/06		
	Men	Women	Total	Men	Women	Total
Employment-population ratio (%)	70.5	47.6	60.4	86.3	56.8	74.5
Unemployment rate (%)	6.7	10.9	8.2	5.6	10.3	7.1
Participation rate (%)	75.6	53.4	65.8	91.4	63.3	80.2
Total employed (thousands)	**184.4**	**98.1**	**282.5**	**359.2**	**157.0**	**516.3**
Employment rates of the highly educated (%)	80.5	65.2	73.2	94.5	76.4	86.0
Unemployment rates of the highly educated (%)	4.2	7.1	5.4	4.7	6.0	5.3
Highly educated in low- and medium-skilled jobs (%)	55.6	53.9	54.9	66.2	54.2	61.2
Highly educated employed (thousands)	**16.5**	**12.0**	**28.5**	**33.6**	**23.8**	**57.3**
Legislators, senior officials and managers	5.9	3.6	4.9	4.8	3.2	4.0
Professionals	8.6	9.0	8.8	13.2	17.5	15.4
Life science and health professionals	2.7	5.2	4.0	6.7	2.0	3.4
Teaching professionals	5.8	3.6	4.7	1.7	4.6	3.7
Technicians and associate professionals	6.6	11.0	8.5	7.5	10.2	8.9
Clerks	6.7	18.8	12.0	7.4	19.3	13.5
Service, shop and market sales workers	12.0	24.2	17.3	14.4	29.4	22.0
Skilled agricultural and fishery workers	1.3	0.5	1.0	2.1	0.5	1.3
Craft and related trades workers	17.0	3.3	11.0	19.2	2.5	10.6
Plant and machine operators and assemblers	19.3	9.0	14.8	12.0	3.9	7.9
Elementary occupations	22.6	20.6	21.8	19.5	13.4	16.4

(left axis label: Distribution of employment by occupation (%), population 15+)

Persons born in Guatemala and their native-born children, population 15+

Living in:	Europe	United States	Australia
2008	Thousands	Thousands	Thousands
Native-born children	1.3	428.3	..
Foreign-born	8.7	730.3	..
Total	10.0	1 158.6	..

International students from Guatemala in OECD countries

Five main destinations	2004	2005	2006	2007	2008	2009
United States	1 030	1 083	1 042	1 036	1 020	1 076
Spain	11	35	57	79	93	176
France	85	73	91	84	94	92
Germany	..	..	..	..	86	85
Chile	..	..	..	..	134	79
Total	1 257	1 286	1 320	1 342	1 602	1 731

Legal migrant flows to the OECD
Thousands

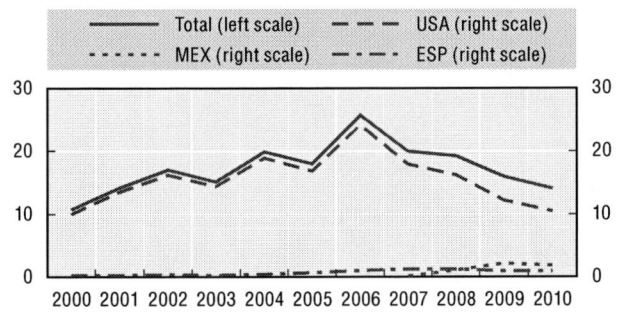

Remittance flows

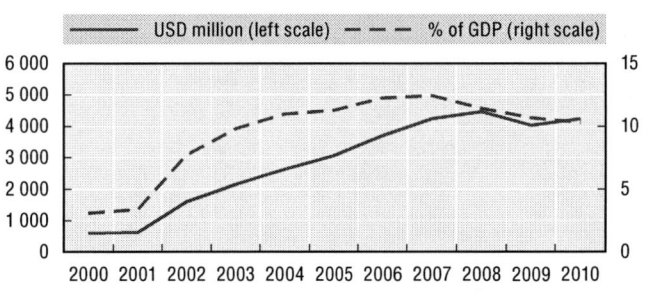

Ten main countries of destination for legal migrants in 2010 (numbers, % of total flows to the country): USA (10467, 1%), MEX (1799, 6.9%), ESP (867, 0.2%), CAN (270, 0.1%), DEU (110, 0%), ITA (104, 0%), JPN (104, 0.2%), CHL (97, 0.2%), KOR (37, 0%), BEL (32, 0%).

Desire to emigrate, 2008-10

	Women	15-24	Highly educated	Total	Regional total
Persons who would move permanently, if they had the opportunity to do so (%)	23	32	28	24	22
Of which: Persons who are planning to move permanently in the next 12 months (%)				11	11
Of which: Persons who have already done some preparations for this move (e.g. visa application) (%)					29

Three main countries of desired destination: United States (46%), Spain (17%), Canada (9%).

StatLink http://dx.doi.org/10.1787/888932672821

			Haiti compared to:	World	Region
Total population 2010 (millions)		10.0	Human Development Index (HDI)	158/187	31/31
Population growth 2010 (%)		1.3	GDP per capita	162/194	31/36
GDP per capita 2010 (current USD)		671	Emigration rate	51/203	22/38
GDP growth 2010 (%)		-5.1	Emigration rate of the highly educated	3/157	3/24
Poverty rate 2001 (USD PPP 2 a day, in %)		72.2			

Age structure of the population 0+ (2010): "0-14": 21%; "15-24": 36%; "25-64": 39%; "65+": 4%.
Level of education of the population 15+ (2010): "Low": 69%; "Medium": 30%; "High": 1%.

Emigrant population living in OECD countries

Immigrant population

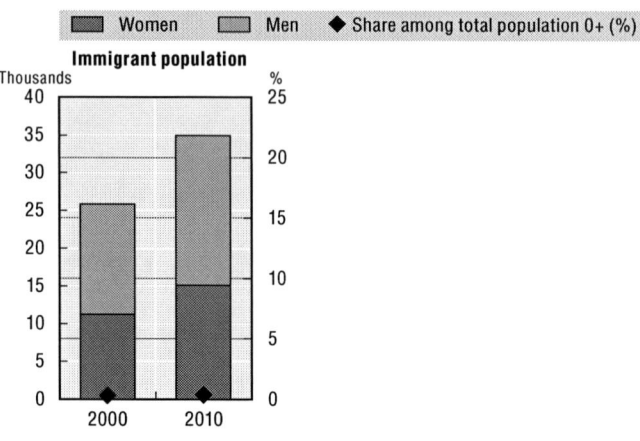

Emigrant population: persons born in Haiti living abroad

	2000						2005/06		
	All destinations			OECD destinations			OECD destinations		
Population 15+	Men	Women	Total	Men	Women	Total	Men	Women	Total
Emigrant population (thousands)	255.7	267.3	523.0	216.6	246.3	462.9	275.6	318.3	593.9
Recent emigrants (thousands)	..	..	..	33.4	38.7	72.1	36.6	46.8	83.5
15-24 (%)	16.9	15.3	16.1	14.9	14.1	14.5	12.1	11.3	11.7
25-64 (%)	76.4	75.3	75.8	78.4	76.1	77.2	78.2	76.4	77.2
65+ (%)	6.8	9.5	8.1	6.6	9.9	8.4	9.8	12.3	11.1
Low-educated (%)	45.3	45.1	45.2	37.2	41.2	39.3	26.9	31.1	29.2
Highly educated (%)	18.2	17.8	18.0	21.0	19.1	20.0	26.0	23.7	24.8
Total emigration rates (%)	9.3	9.2	9.3	8.0	8.6	8.3	8.9	9.7	9.3
Emigration rates of the highly educated (%)	75.3	66.3	70.4	75.0	66.1	70.2	82.5	69.7	75.4

Main destinations in 2005/06

	Total		Recent emigrants	Women	Highly educated	15-24	Total in 2000
Population 15+	Thousands	%	%	%	%	%	Thousands
United States	497.7	83.8	14.2	53.1	23.9	11.3	391.3
Canada	60.5	10.2	13.6	56.1	36.8	11.3	49.7
France	31.4	5.3	16.6	55.5	13.9	18.6	18.7
Belgium	–	–	–	–	–	–	0.9
Spain	–	–	–	–	–	–	0.3
Switzerland	–	–	–	–	–	–	1.0
Italy	–	–	–	–	–	–	0.3
United Kingdom	–	–	–	–	–	–	0.2

Labour market indicators of persons born in Haiti living in OECD countries

Population 15-64	2000			2005/06		
	Men	Women	Total	Men	Women	Total
Employment-population ratio (%)	67.6	60.8	64.0	78.0	70.5	74.0
Unemployment rate (%)	10.4	12.2	11.3	10.6	10.4	10.5
Participation rate (%)	75.4	69.3	72.2	87.3	78.7	82.7
Total employed (thousands)	**136.5**	**134.8**	**271.3**	**191.9**	**195.3**	**387.2**
Employment rates of the highly educated (%)	78.4	75.7	77.0	93.7	87.6	90.5
Unemployment rates of the highly educated (%)	6.8	6.4	6.6	8.7	7.0	7.9
Highly educated in low- and medium-skilled jobs (%)	48.1	38.9	43.5	53.1	39.8	46.4
Highly educated employed (thousands)	**33.6**	**34.0**	**67.7**	**56.1**	**57.6**	**113.7**
Legislators, senior officials and managers	4.6	1.8	3.1	4.1	4.5	4.3
Professionals	11.3	14.2	12.9	10.9	13.0	12.0
Life science and health professionals	1.7	0.6	1.1	1.3	0.6	0.9
Teaching professionals	1.0	1.3	1.1	1.0	1.7	1.4
Technicians and associate professionals	8.1	12.2	10.3	9.0	13.0	11.1
Clerks	8.1	13.5	11.0	8.4	13.7	11.2
Service, shop and market sales workers	11.5	23.8	18.1	15.7	27.2	21.8
Skilled agricultural and fishery workers	0.5	0.1	0.3	1.1	0.1	0.6
Craft and related trades workers	16.0	2.4	8.7	15.9	2.6	8.8
Plant and machine operators and assemblers	23.1	11.7	17.0	20.1	4.9	12.0
Elementary occupations	16.7	20.5	18.7	14.7	21.1	18.1

Distribution of employment by occupation (%), population 15+

Persons born in Haiti and their native-born children, population 15+

Living in:	Europe	United States	Australia
2008	Thousands	Thousands	Thousands
Native-born children	23.1	289.0	..
Foreign-born	48.8	402.9	..
Total	71.9	691.9	..

International students from Haiti in OECD countries

Five main destinations	2004	2005	2006	2007	2008	2009
France	912	1 026	1 256	1 428	1 289	1 320
Canada	692	..	243	867	868	878
United States	1 074	1 047	1 066	1 189	873	843
Switzerland	..	..	..	..	20	24
Chile	..	..	..	..	26	23
Total	2 702	2 094	2 585	3 518	3 125	3 152

Legal migrant flows to the OECD
Thousands

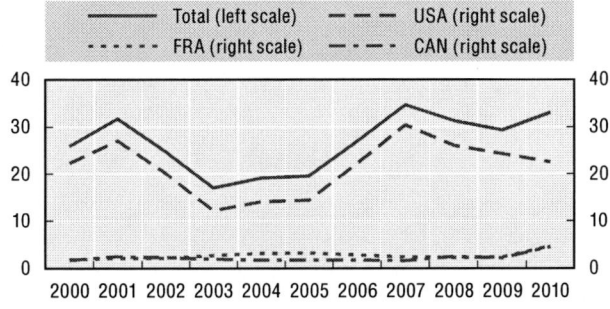

Remittance flows

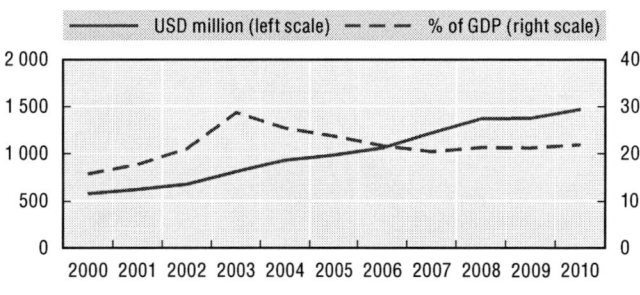

Ten main countries of destination for legal migrants in 2010 (numbers, % of total flows to the country): USA (22582, 2.2%), FRA (4678, 3.4%), CAN (4550, 1.6%), CHL (674, 1.1%), DEU (128, 0%), CHE (75, 0.1%), MEX (73, 0%), ESP (71, 0%), ITA (59, 0%), BEL (58, 0.1%).

Desire to emigrate, 2008-10

	Women	15-24	Highly educated	Total	Regional total
Persons who would move permanently, if they had the opportunity to do so (%)	52	60	53	54	22
Of which: Persons who are planning to move permanently in the next 12 months (%)				21	11
Of which: Persons who have already done some preparations for this move (*e.g.* visa application) (%)					29

Three main countries of desired destination: United States (43%), France (13%), Canada (12%).

StatLink ⚙ http://dx.doi.org/10.1787/888932672840

			Honduras compared to:	World	Region
Total population 2010 (millions)		7.6	Human Development Index (HDI)	120/187	28/31
Population growth 2010 (%)		2.0	GDP per capita	131/194	28/36
GDP per capita 2010 (current USD)		2 026	Emigration rate	48/203	21/38
GDP growth 2010 (%)		2.8	Emigration rate of the highly educated	37/157	11/24
Poverty rate 2007 (USD PPP 2 a day, in %)		35.4			

Age structure of the population 0+ (2010): "0-14": 21%; "15-24": 37%; "25-64": 38%; "65+": 4%.
Level of education of the population 15+ (2010): "Low": 51%; "Medium": 42%; "High": 7%.

Emigrant population living in OECD countries

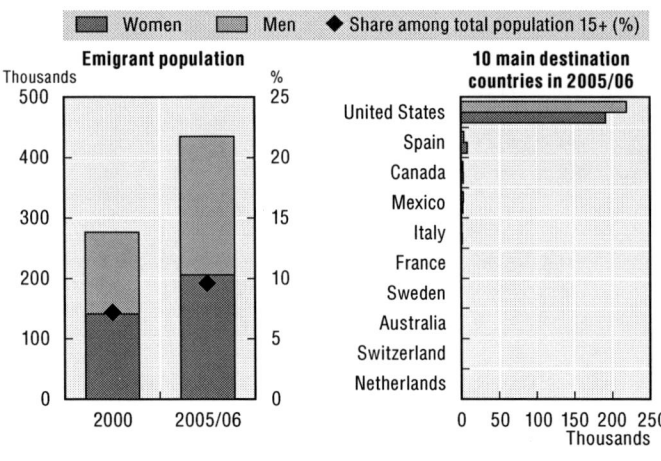

Immigrant population

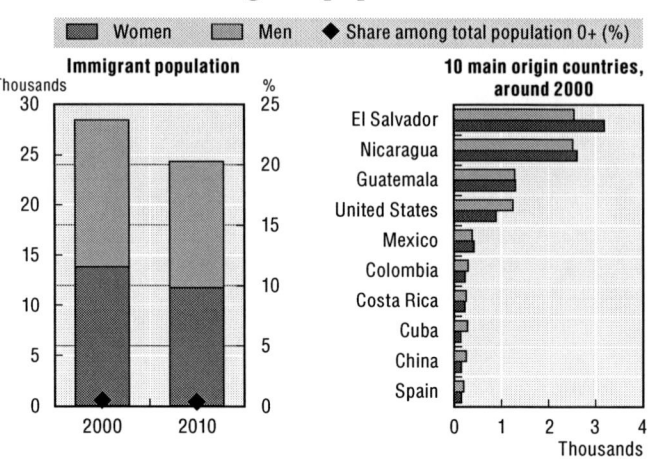

Emigrant population: persons born in Honduras living abroad

	2000						2005/06		
	All destinations			OECD destinations			OECD destinations		
Population 15+	Men	Women	Total	Men	Women	Total	Men	Women	Total
Emigrant population (thousands)	149.3	159.3	308.6	135.1	140.7	275.9	229.1	206.1	435.2
Recent emigrants (thousands)	..	..	..	47.0	35.8	82.8	70.2	50.0	120.2
15-24 (%)	26.4	20.9	23.5	25.3	19.2	22.2	20.7	16.4	18.7
25-64 (%)	70.0	72.9	71.5	71.6	75.2	73.5	76.8	77.5	77.1
65+ (%)	3.6	6.2	4.9	3.1	5.6	4.4	2.5	6.1	4.2
Low-educated (%)	62.6	56.3	59.4	60.9	53.5	57.1	57.6	46.6	52.4
Highly educated (%)	9.5	11.0	10.2	9.7	11.5	10.6	9.7	15.5	12.4
Total emigration rates (%)	7.9	8.1	8.0	7.2	7.2	7.2	10.3	9.0	9.6
Emigration rates of the highly educated (%)	13.1	17.8	15.3	12.2	16.7	14.3	15.2	20.7	18.0

Main destinations in 2005/06

	Total		Recent emigrants	Women	Highly educated	15-24	Total in 2000
Population 15+	Thousands	%	%	%	%	%	Thousands
United States	410.4	94.3	27.0	46.6	11.6	18.1	263.6
Spain	11.5	2.6	82.3	69.8	32.1	33.8	2.6
Canada	5.1	1.2	11.6	53.2	30.6	25.6	4.0
Mexico	4.7	1.1	..	41.8	15.4	22.2	3.4
Italy	2.0	0.5	–	56.2	–	–	0.6
France	0.4	0.1	23.9	73.5	37.9	34.6	0.4
Sweden	–	–	–	–	–	–	0.2
Australia	–	–	–	–	–	–	–
Switzerland	–	–	–	–	–	–	0.2

Labour market indicators of persons born in Honduras living in OECD countries

Population 15-64	2000			2005/06		
	Men	Women	Total	Men	Women	Total
Employment-population ratio (%)	69.6	50.4	59.9	81.2	59.7	71.2
Unemployment rate (%)	8.1	12.4	10.0	8.6	12.0	9.9
Participation rate (%)	75.8	57.5	66.6	88.9	67.8	79.1
Total employed (thousands)	**91.1**	**66.8**	**157.9**	**179.9**	**114.1**	**294.0**
Employment rates of the highly educated (%)	82.0	66.4	73.3	95.1	76.8	84.4
Unemployment rates of the highly educated (%)	4.5	6.4	5.5	6.3	8.3	7.4
Highly educated in low- and medium-skilled jobs (%)	58.3	54.6	56.5	68.6	59.5	63.8
Highly educated employed (thousands)	**10.2**	**10.3**	**20.6**	**18.9**	**21.4**	**40.3**
Legislators, senior officials and managers	8.1	5.5	6.7	3.0	1.1	1.8
Professionals	13.6	6.9	10.0	7.5	7.0	7.2
Life science and health professionals	13.5	1.5	6.5	7.2	4.9	5.6
Teaching professionals	1.7	1.1	1.4	0.2	0.3	0.3
Technicians and associate professionals	8.7	11.0	10.0	1.7	4.3	3.3
Clerks	5.3	15.8	11.0	2.7	6.1	4.8
Service, shop and market sales workers	11.3	19.8	16.0	27.6	31.8	30.2
Skilled agricultural and fishery workers	4.5	1.9	3.1	0.9	0.3	0.5
Craft and related trades workers	19.4	3.4	10.7	27.0	1.2	11.0
Plant and machine operators and assemblers	14.4	8.0	10.9	7.2	1.2	3.5
Elementary occupations	14.6	27.5	21.7	22.4	47.0	37.7

Distribution of employment by occupation (%), population 15+

Persons born in Honduras and their native-born children, population 15+

Living in:	Europe	United States	Australia
2008	Thousands	Thousands	Thousands
Native-born children	0.4	235.3	..
Foreign-born	21.4	564.2	..
Total	21.7	799.4	..

International students from Honduras in OECD countries

Five main destinations	2004	2005	2006	2007	2008	2009
United States	1 089	1 191	1 079	1 121	1 069	1 206
Spain	28	76	54	92	83	174
France	21	26	31	39	42	42
Canada	32	..	33	36	41	41
Germany	..	..	..	..	46	40
Total	1 208	1 345	1 264	1 357	1 399	1 629

Legal migrant flows to the OECD
Thousands

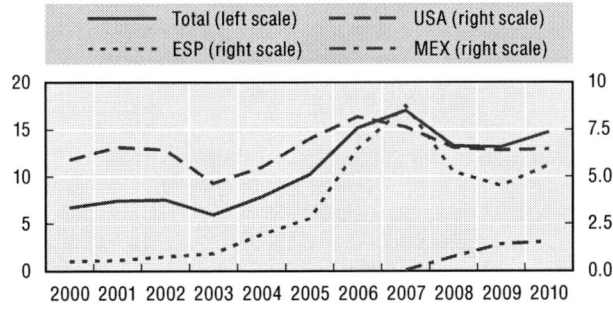

Remittance flows

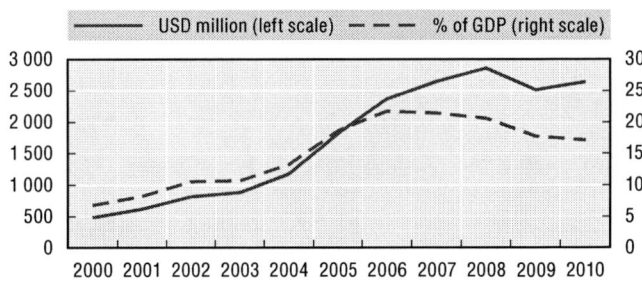

Ten main countries of destination for legal migrants in 2010 (numbers, % of total flows to the country): USA (6448, 0.6%), ESP (5603, 1.3%), MEX (1544, 5.9%), CAN (375, 0.1%), ITA (274, 0.1%), CHL (128, 0.2%), DEU (116, 0%), GBR (53, 0%), CHE (30, 0%), JPN (27, 0%).

Desire to emigrate, 2008-10

	Women	15-24	Highly educated	Total	Regional total
Persons who would move permanently, if they had the opportunity to do so (%)	36	44	43	36	22
Of which: Persons who are planning to move permanently in the next 12 months (%)				18	11
Of which: Persons who have already done some preparations for this move (*e.g.* visa application) (%)					29

Three main countries of desired destination: United States (49%), Spain (29%), Canada (4%).

StatLink ⬛🖻 *http://dx.doi.org/10.1787/888932672859*

Total population 2010 (millions)	2.7	**Jamaica compared to:**	**World**	**Region**	
Population growth 2010 (%)	0.2	Human Development Index (HDI)	79/187	13/31	
GDP per capita 2010 (current USD)	5 274	GDP per capita	89/194	20/36	
GDP growth 2010 (%)	−0.6	Emigration rate	14/203	6/38	
Poverty rate 2004 (USD PPP 2 a day, in %)	5.9	Emigration rate of the highly educated	7/157	5/24	

Age structure of the population 0+ (2010): "0-14": 18%; "15-24": 29%; "25-64": 45%; "65+": 8%.
Level of education of the population 15+ (2010): "Low": 22%; "Medium": 62%; "High": 16%.

Emigrant population living in OECD countries

Immigrant population

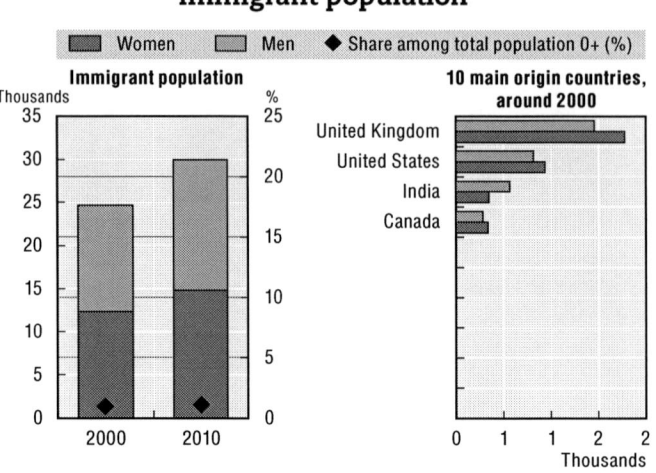

Emigrant population: persons born in Jamaica living abroad

	2000						2005/06		
	All destinations			OECD destinations			OECD destinations		
Population 15+	Men	Women	Total	Men	Women	Total	Men	Women	Total
Emigrant population (thousands)	346.3	445.5	791.8	345.3	444.4	789.7	390.1	504.7	894.8
Recent emigrants (thousands)	..	..	..	33.8	41.9	75.7	38.9	49.2	88.1
15-24 (%)	12.7	10.7	11.6	12.7	10.7	11.6	10.9	8.9	9.7
25-64 (%)	74.1	75.2	74.7	74.1	75.2	74.7	72.3	73.5	73.0
65+ (%)	13.2	14.1	13.7	13.2	14.0	13.7	16.8	17.6	17.3
Low-educated (%)	38.4	30.9	34.2	38.4	30.9	34.1	25.1	22.0	23.4
Highly educated (%)	20.5	28.4	24.9	20.5	28.4	24.9	25.3	34.6	30.6
Total emigration rates (%)	29.1	33.3	31.3	29.1	33.2	31.3	30.5	34.8	32.8
Emigration rates of the highly educated (%)	46.1	47.7	47.1	46.0	47.6	47.0	49.3	51.3	50.6

Main destinations in 2005/06

	Total		Recent emigrants	Women	Highly educated	15-24	Total in 2000
Population 15+	Thousands	%	%	%	%	%	Thousands
United States	615.2	68.8	11.4	56.1	28.6	10.5	528.9
United Kingdom	151.5	16.9	6.2	57.0	28.4	7.3	141.9
Canada	122.9	13.7	6.4	57.5	42.4	9.0	116.4
Italy	1.0	0.1	–	–	–	–	0.2
Belgium	–	–	–	–	–	–	0.2
Australia	0.8	0.1	15.3	49.0	50.0	6.3	0.5
Switzerland	–	–	–	–	–	–	0.4
Netherlands	–	–	–	–	–	–	–
France	0.4	0.0	33.2	68.2	55.2	8.5	0.4
Ireland	–	–	–	–	–	–	0.1

Labour market indicators of persons born in Jamaica living in OECD countries

Population 15-64	2000			2005/06		
	Men	Women	Total	Men	Women	Total
Employment-population ratio (%)	74.3	71.3	72.6	78.6	77.1	77.8
Unemployment rate (%)	8.5	7.3	7.9	9.6	7.6	8.5
Participation rate (%)	81.2	77.0	78.8	87.0	83.5	85.0
Total employed (thousands)	**217.6**	**268.4**	**486.0**	**253.6**	**315.0**	**568.6**
Employment rates of the highly educated (%)	87.0	82.5	84.1	94.4	89.2	91.1
Unemployment rates of the highly educated (%)	4.4	4.3	4.3	6.0	4.8	5.2
Highly educated in low- and medium-skilled jobs (%)	42.0	34.3	37.1	46.1	35.1	39.2
Highly educated employed (thousands)	**55.1**	**95.4**	**150.6**	**76.4**	**129.2**	**205.6**
Legislators, senior officials and managers	8.9	6.0	7.3	7.2	4.6	5.7
Professionals	9.0	13.4	11.4	9.1	15.4	12.6
Life science and health professionals	0.6	0.4	0.5	0.0	2.1	1.2
Teaching professionals	1.9	4.0	3.1	1.2	4.2	2.9
Technicians and associate professionals	8.8	17.2	13.4	8.5	15.1	12.1
Clerks	7.0	22.5	15.5	6.4	17.1	12.3
Service, shop and market sales workers	9.2	25.3	18.0	12.9	14.0	13.5
Skilled agricultural and fishery workers	0.9	0.1	0.4	3.1	16.1	10.2
Craft and related trades workers	21.2	1.1	10.2	13.2	2.8	7.5
Plant and machine operators and assemblers	19.2	4.4	11.1	16.8	2.9	9.1
Elementary occupations	15.9	10.1	12.7	19.8	10.9	14.9

Distribution of employment by occupation (%), population 15+

Persons born in Jamaica and their native-born children, population 15+

Living in:	Europe	United States	Australia
2008	Thousands	Thousands	Thousands
Native-born children	162.9	281.7	..
Foreign-born	100.9	672.6	..
Total	263.8	954.3	..

International students from Jamaica in OECD countries

Five main destinations	2004	2005	2006	2007	2008	2009
United States	4 994	4 562	4 314	4 201	3 875	3 838
United Kingdom	979	938	847	807	631	550
Canada	205	..	297	237	302	281
France	17	16	17	15	22	26
Australia	20	17	16	12	17	16
Total	6 228	5 576	5 511	5 295	4 898	4 766

Legal migrant flows to the OECD
Thousands

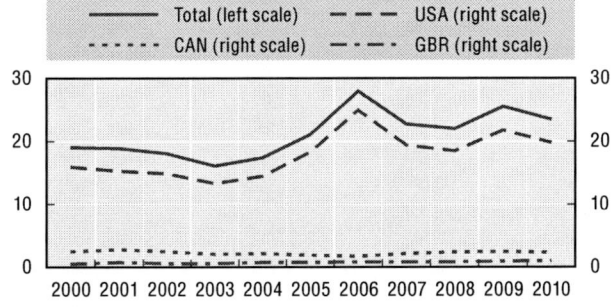

Remittance flows

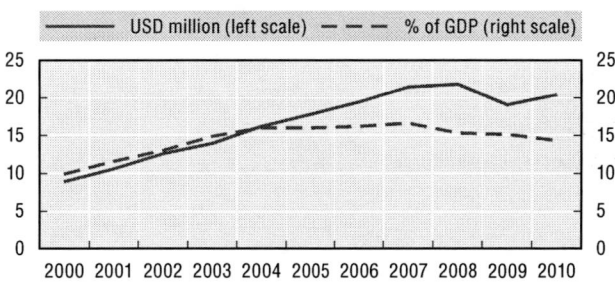

Ten main countries of destination for legal migrants in 2010 (numbers, % of total flows to the country): USA (19825, 1.9%), CAN (2255, 0.8%), GBR (930, 0.2%), JPN (145, 0.1%), DEU (102, 0%), CHE (35, 0%), BEL (23, 0%), FRA (22, 0%), NLD (22, 0%), ITA (18, 0%).

Desire to emigrate, 2008-10

	Women	15-24	Highly educated	Total	Regional total
Persons who would move permanently, if they had the opportunity to do so (%)	..	..	..	..	22
Of which: Persons who are planning to move permanently in the next 12 months (%)				..	11
Of which: Persons who have already done some preparations for this move (*e.g.* visa application) (%)					29

StatLink http://dx.doi.org/10.1787/888932672878

		Nicaragua compared to:	World	Region
Total population 2010 (millions)	5.8			
Population growth 2010 (%)	1.4	Human Development Index (HDI)	129/187	29/31
GDP per capita 2010 (current USD)	1 132	GDP per capita	148/194	30/36
GDP growth 2010 (%)	7.6	Emigration rate	68/203	27/38
Poverty rate 2005 (USD PPP 2 a day, in %)	31.9	Emigration rate of the highly educated	69/157	16/24

Age structure of the population 0+ (2010): "0-14": 21%; "15-24": 34%; "25-64": 40%; "65+": 5%.
Level of education of the population 15+ (2010): "Low": 51%; "Medium": 33%; "High": 16%.

Emigrant population living in OECD countries

Immigrant population

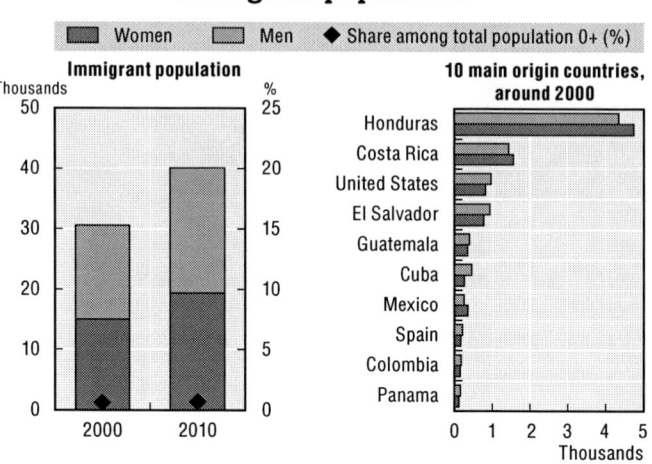

Emigrant population: persons born in Nicaragua living abroad

	2000						2005/06		
	All destinations			OECD destinations			OECD destinations		
Population 15+	Men	Women	Total	Men	Women	Total	Men	Women	Total
Emigrant population (thousands)	205.4	226.0	431.3	101.2	120.0	221.2	119.5	135.1	254.7
Recent emigrants (thousands)	..	..	..	10.5	13.4	23.9	13.1	10.9	23.9
15-24 (%)	26.5	23.9	25.1	21.8	17.7	19.6	12.3	10.0	11.1
25-64 (%)	68.1	68.4	68.3	73.4	73.0	73.2	80.5	77.1	78.7
65+ (%)	5.4	7.6	6.6	4.8	9.3	7.3	7.2	12.9	10.2
Low-educated (%)	62.6	60.5	61.5	40.1	41.2	40.7	27.7	29.4	28.6
Highly educated (%)	12.1	10.9	11.5	19.7	16.7	18.1	24.1	24.7	24.4
Total emigration rates (%)	12.1	12.9	12.5	6.4	7.3	6.8	6.7	7.3	7.0
Emigration rates of the highly educated (%)	8.8	15.2	11.1	7.1	12.7	9.1	8.4	15.2	11.0

Main destinations in 2005/06

	Total		Recent emigrants	Women	Highly educated	15-24	Total in 2000
Population 15+	Thousands	%	%	%	%	%	Thousands
United States	238.9	93.8	9.3	52.7	23.4	10.6	205.9
Canada	9.2	3.6	4.3	51.0	43.3	17.2	9.1
Spain	1.6	0.6	96.0	72.2	–	–	1.0
Mexico	1.1	0.4	..	61.9	39.0	11.8	2.4
Italy	–	–	–	–	–	–	0.5
Netherlands	–	–	–	–	–	–	–
Australia	0.7	0.3	2.7	53.3	34.0	13.4	0.5
France	0.5	0.2	20.0	63.5	46.1	21.6	0.4
Sweden	0.4	0.2	27.7	56.8	31.9	28.4	0.4
Belgium	–	–	–	–	–	–	0.1

Labour market indicators of persons born in Nicaragua living in OECD countries

Population 15-64	2000			2005/06		
	Men	Women	Total	Men	Women	Total
Employment-population ratio (%)	68.4	53.7	60.6	84.0	67.2	75.3
Unemployment rate (%)	7.1	10.4	8.7	6.2	8.4	7.2
Participation rate (%)	73.6	60.0	66.4	89.5	73.4	81.2
Total employed (thousands)	**65.7**	**58.3**	**124.0**	**92.6**	**78.6**	**171.2**
Employment rates of the highly educated (%)	81.3	68.1	74.6	96.3	80.4	87.7
Unemployment rates of the highly educated (%)	4.5	6.0	5.2	5.4	5.8	5.6
Highly educated in low- and medium-skilled jobs (%)	52.5	55.4	53.9	61.1	55.8	58.5
Highly educated employed (thousands)	**15.3**	**13.0**	**28.2**	**24.1**	**23.6**	**47.8**
Legislators, senior officials and managers	5.5	3.9	4.8	6.5	2.3	4.2
Professionals	11.1	10.5	10.8	14.1	12.9	13.4
Life science and health professionals	12.9	7.1	10.1	18.9	11.5	13.6
Teaching professionals	0.7	7.7	4.0	1.4	2.0	1.9
Technicians and associate professionals	9.5	11.6	10.5	8.0	10.9	9.6
Clerks	5.8	19.6	12.3	10.3	14.8	12.8
Service, shop and market sales workers	15.1	25.0	19.8	9.4	30.6	21.0
Skilled agricultural and fishery workers	1.4	0.0	0.8	0.6	0.4	0.5
Craft and related trades workers	15.9	2.8	9.7	14.5	1.4	7.3
Plant and machine operators and assemblers	12.1	6.4	9.4	14.9	3.6	8.7
Elementary occupations	23.6	20.2	22.0	21.7	23.2	22.5

(Left margin label: Distribution of employment by occupation (%), population 15+)

Persons born in Nicaragua and their native-born children, population 15+

Living in:	Europe	United States	Australia
2008	Thousands	Thousands	Thousands
Native-born children	3.8	165.2	..
Foreign-born	9.6	211.0	..
Total	13.4	376.2	..

International students from Nicaragua in OECD countries

Five main destinations	2004	2005	2006	2007	2008	2009
United States	473	703	425	418	389	441
Spain	26	29	20	31	25	102
Sweden	6	6	6	3	11	37
France	26	25	23	32	35	36
Chile	..	..	..	..	49	35
Total	618	814	543	557	615	756

Legal migrant flows to the OECD
Thousands

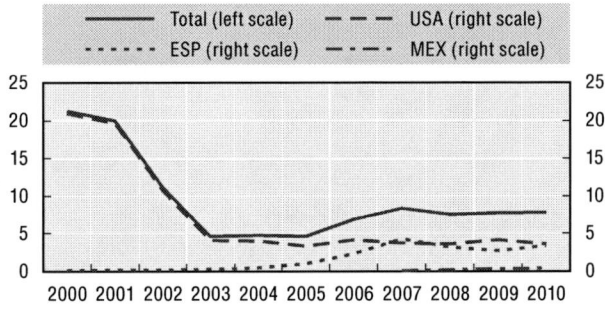

Remittance flows

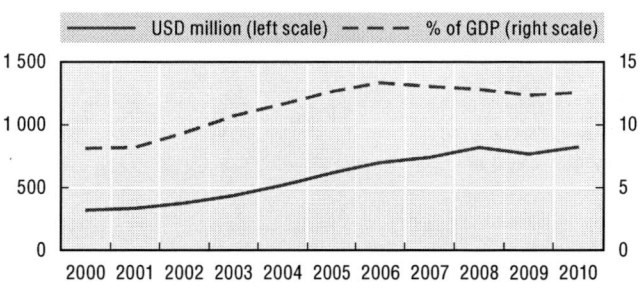

Ten main countries of destination for legal migrants in 2010 (numbers, % of total flows to the country): USA (3565, 0.3%), ESP (3377, 0.8%), MEX (350, 1.3%), CAN (85, 0%), DEU (77, 0%), JPN (77, 0%), ITA (75, 0.1%), CHL (64, 0.1%), CHE (39, 0%), SWE (38, 0%).

Desire to emigrate, 2008-10

	Women	15-24	Highly educated	Total	Regional total
Persons who would move permanently, if they had the opportunity to do so (%)	39	50	49	40	22
Of which: Persons who are planning to move permanently in the next 12 months (%)				14	11
Of which: Persons who have already done some preparations for this move (e.g. visa application) (%)					29

Three main countries of desired destination: United States (47%), Spain (15%), Costa Rica (14%).

StatLink ⬛⬛⬛ http://dx.doi.org/10.1787/888932672897

Total population 2010 (millions)	3.5	Panama compared to:	World	Region
Population growth 2010 (%)	1.6	Human Development Index (HDI)	58/187	6/31
GDP per capita 2010 (current USD)	7 589	GDP per capita	73/194	12/36
GDP growth 2010 (%)	4.8	Emigration rate	72/203	28/38
Poverty rate 2009 (USD PPP 2 a day, in %)	9.5	Emigration rate of the highly educated	68/157	15/24

Age structure of the population 0+ (2010): "0-14": 17%; "15-24": 29%; "25-64": 47%; "65+": 7%.
Level of education of the population 15+ (2010): "Low": 35%; "Medium": 44%; "High": 21%.

Emigrant population living in OECD countries

Immigrant population

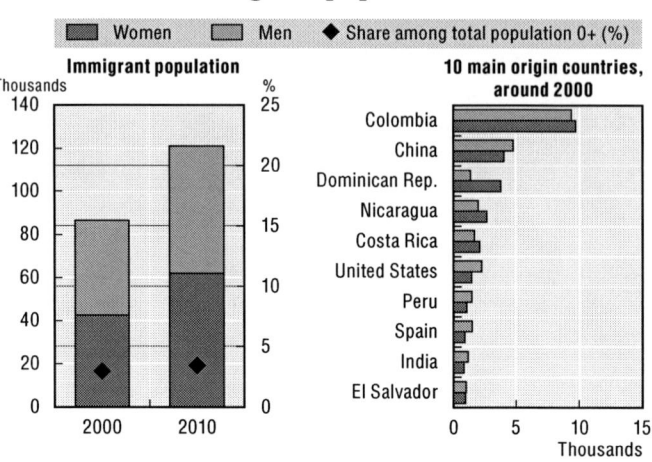

Emigrant population: persons born in Panama living abroad

	2000						2005/06		
	All destinations			OECD destinations			OECD destinations		
Population 15+	Men	Women	Total	Men	Women	Total	Men	Women	Total
Emigrant population (thousands)	63.9	92.0	155.9	56.0	84.3	140.4	60.2	90.5	150.8
Recent emigrants (thousands)	..	..	..	5.5	9.8	15.3	4.4	8.0	12.4
15-24 (%)	15.2	11.8	13.2	14.7	11.0	12.5	13.3	9.6	11.0
25-64 (%)	75.8	75.2	75.4	76.3	75.9	76.1	72.9	73.0	73.0
65+ (%)	9.1	13.0	11.4	9.1	13.1	11.5	13.8	17.4	16.0
Low-educated (%)	19.7	20.2	20.0	15.5	18.0	17.0	11.8	12.9	12.5
Highly educated (%)	34.3	30.3	31.9	35.7	31.0	32.9	39.4	36.6	37.7
Total emigration rates (%)	5.9	8.4	7.2	5.2	7.8	6.5	5.1	7.5	6.3
Emigration rates of the highly educated (%)	11.4	12.0	11.7	10.5	11.3	10.9	10.4	11.8	11.2

Main destinations in 2005/06

	Total		Recent emigrants	Women	Highly educated	15-24	Total in 2000
Population 15+	Thousands	%	%	%	%	%	Thousands
United States	139.7	92.7	7.1	60.4	36.6	10.8	131.5
Spain	3.1	2.1	86.5	64.0	53.1	–	2.1
Canada	2.9	1.9	10.7	52.3	48.5	16.9	2.3
United Kingdom	–	–	–	–	–	–	0.4
Italy	1.0	0.7	–	–	–	–	0.7
Netherlands	–	–	–	–	–	–	–
Mexico	0.6	0.4	..	44.9	70.9	3.7	1.5
Switzerland	–	–	–	–	–	–	0.3
France	0.3	0.2	29.6	63.4	65.9	21.1	0.3
Chile	–	–	–	–	–	–	0.5

Labour market indicators of persons born in Panama living in OECD countries

Population 15-64	2000			2005/06		
	Men	Women	Total	Men	Women	Total
Employment-population ratio (%)	76.0	64.8	69.4	80.8	70.6	74.8
Unemployment rate (%)	5.8	6.4	6.2	5.6	6.8	6.3
Participation rate (%)	80.7	69.2	73.9	85.7	75.8	79.8
Total employed (thousands)	**38.6**	**47.3**	**85.9**	**41.5**	**52.4**	**93.9**
Employment rates of the highly educated (%)	86.7	76.3	80.8	92.1	81.6	85.9
Unemployment rates of the highly educated (%)	3.8	3.0	3.4	3.2	5.5	4.5
Highly educated in low- and medium-skilled jobs (%)	37.6	35.7	36.6	40.2	37.9	38.9
Highly educated employed (thousands)	**15.9**	**18.5**	**34.4**	**18.5**	**23.2**	**41.7**
Legislators, senior officials and managers	13.0	10.0	11.5	8.0	11.1	9.6
Professionals	17.2	17.8	17.5	35.9	10.3	22.2
Life science and health professionals	5.2	3.9	4.5	2.8	7.2	5.2
Teaching professionals	0.9	2.8	1.9	0.3	0.6	0.5
Technicians and associate professionals	17.1	20.9	19.0	7.5	8.1	7.8
Clerks	11.7	17.4	14.4	7.2	26.2	17.3
Service, shop and market sales workers	10.4	16.2	13.2	9.1	36.4	23.6
Skilled agricultural and fishery workers	0.7	0.5	0.6	0.3	–	0.1
Craft and related trades workers	10.4	1.7	6.2	9.6	1.1	5.1
Plant and machine operators and assemblers	10.7	6.7	8.7	6.6	1.6	3.9
Elementary occupations	8.7	8.7	8.7	15.9	5.3	10.2

Distribution of employment by occupation (%), population 15+

Persons born in Panama and their native-born children, population 15+

Living in:	Europe	United States	Australia
2008	Thousands	Thousands	Thousands
Native-born children	1.6	91.4	..
Foreign-born	3.0	93.3	..
Total	4.7	184.7	..

International students from Panama in OECD countries

Five main destinations	2004	2005	2006	2007	2008	2009
United States	958	1 053	1 059	995	1 131	1 114
Spain	26	44	44	69	76	179
Chile	..	..	..	..	150	104
Canada	38	..	30	30	42	54
United Kingdom	39	48	42	30	39	46
Total	1 126	1 205	1 248	1 208	1 568	1 640

Legal migrant flows to the OECD
Thousands

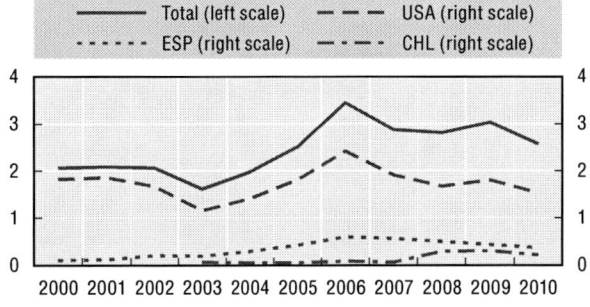

Remittance flows

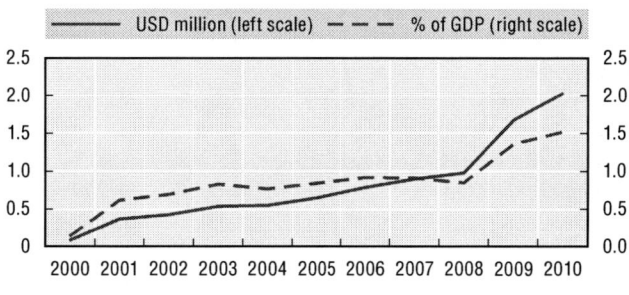

Ten main countries of destination for legal migrants in 2010 (numbers, % of total flows to the country): USA (1536, 0.1%), ESP (371, 0.1%), CHL (213, 0.3%), MEX (92, 0.4%), CAN (85, 0%), DEU (66, 0%), JPN (56, 0%), ITA (36, 0%), CHE (30, 0%), BEL (15, 0%).

Desire to emigrate, 2008-10

	Women	15-24	Highly educated	Total	Regional total
Persons who would move permanently, if they had the opportunity to do so (%)	13	23	15	14	22
Of which: Persons who are planning to move permanently in the next 12 months (%)				10	11
Of which: Persons who have already done some preparations for this move (*e.g.* visa application) (%)					29

Three main countries of desired destination: United States (51%), Spain (11%), Canada (7%).

StatLink 🔗 http://dx.doi.org/10.1787/888932672916

		Paraguay compared to:	World	Region
Total population 2010 (millions)	6.5	Human Development Index (HDI)	107/187	25/31
Population growth 2010 (%)	1.8	GDP per capita	121/194	27/36
GDP per capita 2010 (current USD)	2 840	Emigration rate	143/203	36/38
GDP growth 2010 (%)	15.0	Emigration rate of the highly educated	89/157	18/24
Poverty rate 2008 (USD PPP 2 a day, in %)	13.2			

Age structure of the population 0+ (2010): "0-14": 20%; "15-24": 34%; "25-64": 41%; "65+": 5%.
Level of education of the population 15+ (2010): "Low": 42%; "Medium": 52%; "High": 6%.

Emigrant population living in OECD countries

Immigrant population

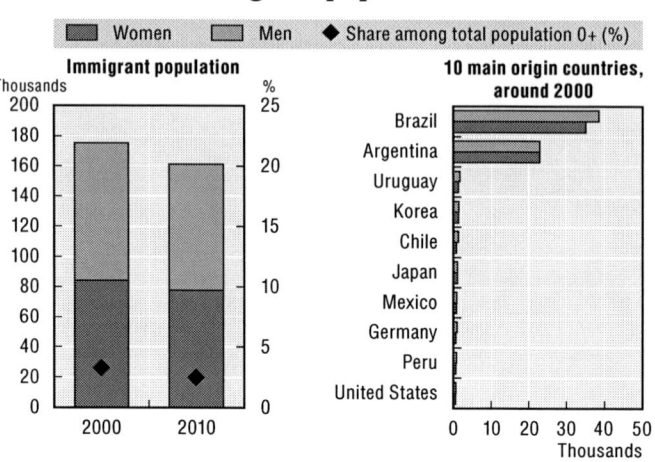

Emigrant population: persons born in Paraguay living abroad

	2000						2005/06		
	All destinations			OECD destinations			OECD destinations		
Population 15+	Men	Women	Total	Men	Women	Total	Men	Women	Total
Emigrant population (thousands)	150.4	204.2	354.6	9.5	11.6	21.1	21.0	23.8	44.7
Recent emigrants (thousands)	..	..	..	1.5	1.8	3.3	8.3	10.8	19.1
15-24 (%)	13.3	14.4	14.0	15.8	14.4	15.0	16.4	25.0	21.0
25-64 (%)	72.7	72.1	72.4	80.7	79.3	80.0	80.1	69.8	74.6
65+ (%)	14.0	13.4	13.7	3.5	6.3	5.0	3.6	5.2	4.4
Low-educated (%)	82.4	82.1	82.2	37.3	37.7	37.5	34.7	34.3	34.5
Highly educated (%)	4.2	3.9	4.1	23.7	23.6	23.7	24.2	22.6	23.4
Total emigration rates (%)	8.3	11.1	9.7	0.5	0.7	0.6	1.1	1.2	1.2
Emigration rates of the highly educated (%)	5.5	6.8	6.2	2.0	2.4	2.2	10.2	7.1	8.3

Main destinations in 2005/06

	Total		Recent emigrants	Women	Highly educated	15-24	Total in 2000
Population 15+	Thousands	%	%	%	%	%	Thousands
Spain	16.2	36.2	94.0	58.9	18.8	21.9	2.1
United States	14.5	32.3	19.5	50.5	26.4	24.5	9.2
Canada	7.4	16.6	10.2	48.5	21.4	14.4	5.0
Japan	1.4	3.2	..	49.6	13.3	0.0	1.0
Chile	1.4	3.1	36.6	34.0	44.8	25.1	1.0
Switzerland	–	–	–	–	–	–	0.3
France	0.7	1.5	33.9	61.3	39.7	25.2	0.7
United Kingdom	–	–	–	–	–	–	0.3
Belgium	–	–	–	–	–	–	0.2
Australia	0.3	0.7	14.1	55.1	29.4	11.8	0.1

Labour market indicators of persons born in Paraguay living in OECD countries

Population 15-64	2000			2005/06		
	Men	Women	Total	Men	Women	Total
Employment-population ratio (%)	77.0	57.6	66.4	82.5	71.2	76.5
Unemployment rate (%)	7.0	7.7	7.3	6.1	7.9	7.0
Participation rate (%)	82.9	62.4	71.7	87.9	77.3	82.3
Total employed (thousands)	**6.6**	**5.9**	**12.5**	**15.9**	**15.4**	**31.2**
Employment rates of the highly educated (%)	83.1	70.7	76.3	85.7	78.7	82.1
Unemployment rates of the highly educated (%)	6.7	6.0	6.4	2.1	6.4	4.2
Highly educated in low- and medium-skilled jobs (%)	33.1	43.0	38.1	54.2	63.7	58.6
Highly educated employed (thousands)	**1.7**	**1.8**	**3.5**	**4.1**	**3.7**	**7.7**
Legislators, senior officials and managers	13.3	4.6	9.3	3.3	1.4	2.4
Professionals	8.2	9.7	8.9	6.1	3.7	4.9
Life science and health professionals	0.5	1.9	1.2	0.4	1.0	0.7
Teaching professionals	1.0	0.9	0.9	2.4	1.1	1.7
Technicians and associate professionals	8.1	13.6	10.6	3.2	2.8	3.0
Clerks	3.9	13.4	8.3	3.6	6.0	4.8
Service, shop and market sales workers	6.1	24.6	14.7	4.5	28.3	16.7
Skilled agricultural and fishery workers	4.1	2.4	3.3	3.3	3.5	3.4
Craft and related trades workers	28.3	7.5	18.6	38.1	4.1	20.6
Plant and machine operators and assemblers	16.4	6.0	11.6	11.2	2.4	6.7
Elementary occupations	11.5	18.2	14.6	26.7	47.7	37.5

Distribution of employment by occupation (%), population 15+

Persons born in Paraguay and their native-born children, population 15+

Living in:	Europe	United States	Australia
2008	Thousands	Thousands	Thousands
Native-born children	2.4	19.2	..
Foreign-born	73.4	12.8	..
Total	75.8	32.0	..

International students from Paraguay in OECD countries

Five main destinations	2004	2005	2006	2007	2008	2009
United States	343	319	332	348	377	374
Spain	15	40	57	87	98	258
France	64	58	76	73	90	78
Italy	20	26	28	30	32	48
Korea	36	37	31	35	36	42
Total	563	556	600	651	841	965

Legal migrant flows to the OECD
Thousands

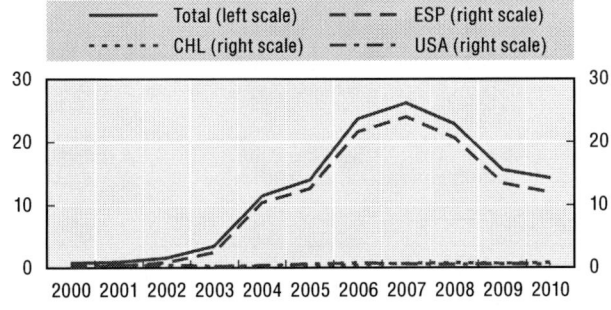

Ten main countries of destination for legal migrants in 2010 (numbers, % of total flows to the country): ESP (11907, 2.8%), CHL (710, 1.1%), USA (467, 0%), ITA (320, 0.1%), JPN (242, 0.1%), DEU (195, 0%), CAN (120, 0.2%), MEX (55, 0.2%), BEL (38, 0%), CHE (37, 0%).

Remittance flows

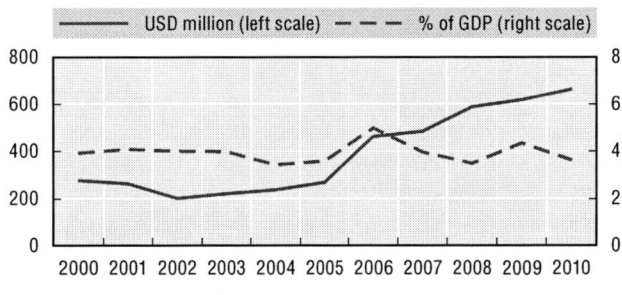

Desire to emigrate, 2008-10

	Women	15-24	Highly educated	Total	Regional total
Persons who would move permanently, if they had the opportunity to do so (%)	18	31	24	19	22
Of which: Persons who are planning to move permanently in the next 12 months (%)				13	11
Of which: Persons who have already done some preparations for this move (*e.g.* visa application) (%)					29

Three main countries of desired destination: Argentina (36%), Brazil (16%), Spain (13%).

StatLink http://dx.doi.org/10.1787/888932672935

			Peru compared to:	World	Region
Total population 2010 (millions)		29.1	Human Development Index (HDI)	80/187	14/31
Population growth 2010 (%)		1.1	GDP per capita	87/194	19/36
GDP per capita 2010 (current USD)		5 401	Emigration rate	101/203	30/38
GDP growth 2010 (%)		8.8	Emigration rate of the highly educated	120/157	21/24
Poverty rate 2009 (USD PPP 2 a day, in %)		14.7			

Age structure of the population 0+ (2010): "0-14": 19%; "15-24": 30%; "25-64": 45%; "65+": 6%.
Level of education of the population 15+ (2010): "Low": 25%; "Medium": 55%; "High": 20%.

Emigrant population living in OECD countries

Immigrant population

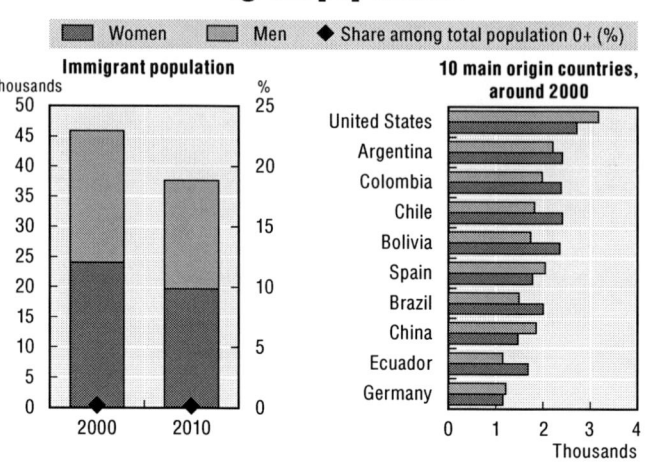

Emigrant population: persons born in Peru living abroad

	2000						2005/06		
	All destinations			OECD destinations			OECD destinations		
Population 15+	Men	Women	Total	Men	Women	Total	Men	Women	Total
Emigrant population (thousands)	277.3	326.6	603.9	205.1	246.8	451.9	310.3	369.0	679.3
Recent emigrants (thousands)	..	..	..	40.7	51.8	92.5	80.7	101.1	181.8
15-24 (%)	15.7	15.1	15.4	15.8	14.2	15.0	14.7	13.7	14.1
25-64 (%)	78.8	78.7	78.7	78.4	78.7	78.6	78.3	78.1	78.2
65+ (%)	5.5	6.2	5.9	5.8	7.1	6.5	7.0	8.2	7.7
Low-educated (%)	23.7	27.0	25.5	23.7	26.8	25.4	19.9	21.0	20.5
Highly educated (%)	28.3	25.2	26.6	29.4	26.7	27.9	33.6	31.7	32.5
Total emigration rates (%)	3.2	3.7	3.5	2.2	2.8	2.4	3.2	3.8	3.5
Emigration rates of the highly educated (%)	4.3	4.5	4.4	3.2	3.6	3.4	5.7	5.4	5.5

Main destinations in 2005/06

	Total		Recent emigrants	Women	Highly educated	15-24	Total in 2000
Population 15+	Thousands	%	%	%	%	%	Thousands
United States	378.6	55.7	19.8	52.0	33.5	12.0	261.9
Spain	116.0	17.1	73.5	57.2	30.6	16.3	47.9
Italy	51.7	7.6	28.0	61.0	14.2	14.3	28.8
Chile	38.0	5.6	54.0	61.3	33.3	24.0	35.6
Japan	32.3	4.8	..	46.5	29.5	16.5	27.2
Canada	21.8	3.2	21.4	54.9	51.7	14.1	16.6
France	8.9	1.3	22.9	59.1	46.3	16.7	5.8
Australia	6.1	0.9	17.1	57.0	46.7	12.0	5.1
Sweden	5.4	0.8	23.2	54.0	41.0	17.3	4.6
Switzerland	5.3	0.8	27.7	74.6	35.4	–	5.1

Labour market indicators of persons born in Peru living in OECD countries

Population 15-64	2000			2005/06		
	Men	Women	Total	Men	Women	Total
Employment-population ratio (%)	74.0	60.4	66.5	84.5	67.8	75.4
Unemployment rate (%)	7.5	9.7	8.6	6.1	9.8	7.9
Participation rate (%)	80.0	66.8	72.8	89.9	75.2	81.9
Total employed (thousands)	**129.9**	**128.9**	**258.8**	**225.0**	**215.4**	**440.5**
Employment rates of the highly educated (%)	82.6	66.1	73.8	95.6	79.6	87.0
Unemployment rates of the highly educated (%)	5.3	8.8	7.0	4.1	9.0	6.5
Highly educated in low- and medium-skilled jobs (%)	47.0	50.7	48.7	56.5	59.9	58.1
Highly educated employed (thousands)	**42.8**	**39.0**	**81.8**	**83.6**	**76.7**	**160.3**
Legislators, senior officials and managers	7.3	3.4	5.1	3.8	2.3	3.0
Professionals	11.9	7.8	9.6	6.9	4.7	5.7
Life science and health professionals	2.4	1.3	1.8	1.1	0.5	0.8
Teaching professionals	1.1	1.5	1.3	0.6	0.9	0.8
Technicians and associate professionals	10.0	8.5	9.2	9.5	7.0	8.2
Clerks	6.0	9.2	7.8	6.8	9.6	8.3
Service, shop and market sales workers	14.5	17.8	16.3	13.1	23.7	18.8
Skilled agricultural and fishery workers	1.7	0.3	0.9	1.1	0.3	0.6
Craft and related trades workers	18.5	2.2	9.4	31.3	2.7	15.9
Plant and machine operators and assemblers	9.5	2.2	5.4	8.1	2.6	5.2
Elementary occupations	20.6	48.6	36.3	19.4	47.2	34.3

Distribution of employment by occupation (%), population 15+

Persons born in Peru and their native-born children, population 15+

Living in:	Europe	United States	Australia
2008	Thousands	Thousands	Thousands
Native-born children	12.8	149.6	..
Foreign-born	291.0	331.9	5.8
Total	303.8	481.5	..

International students from Peru in OECD countries

Five main destinations	2004	2005	2006	2007	2008	2009
United States	3 771	3 792	3 644	3 783	3 676	3 539
Spain	378	654	1 035	1 319	1 368	3 489
Italy	687	782	993	1 243	1 430	1 591
France	498	506	620	688	790	937
Germany	..	..	..	..	641	671
Total	6 066	6 354	7 201	8 179	10 740	12 311

Legal migrant flows to the OECD
Thousands

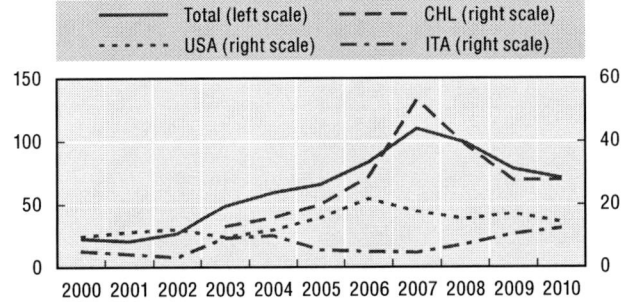

Remittance flows

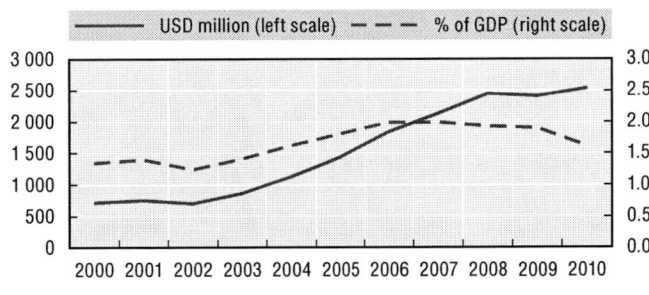

Ten main countries of destination for legal migrants in 2010 (numbers, % of total flows to the country): CHL (27714, 43.5%), USA (14247, 1.4%), ITA (12166, 2.9%), ESP (10045, 2.3%), CAN (1270, 0.5%), JPN (1193, 0.4%), DEU (862, 3.2%), MEX (825, 3.2%), FRA (434, 0.3%), AUS (358, 0.2%).

Desire to emigrate, 2008-10

	Women	15-24	Highly educated	Total	Regional total
Persons who would move permanently, if they had the opportunity to do so (%)	35	50	31	38	22
Of which: Persons who are planning to move permanently in the next 12 months (%)				10	11
Of which: Persons who have already done some preparations for this move (*e.g.* visa application) (%)					29

Three main countries of desired destination: Spain (25%), United States (21%), Italy (8%).

StatLink http://dx.doi.org/10.1787/888932672954

Total population 2010 (millions)	1.3	Trinidad and Tobago compared to:	World	Region
Population growth 2010 (%)	0.4	Human Development Index (HDI)	62/187	8/31
GDP per capita 2010 (current USD)	15 359	GDP per capita	46/194	3/36
GDP growth 2010 (%)	0.1	Emigration rate	23/203	13/38
Poverty rate 2010 (USD PPP 2 a day, in %)	..	Emigration rate of the highly educated	4/157	4/24

Age structure of the population 0+ (2010): "0-14": 18%; "15-24": 21%; "25-64": 55%; "65+": 7%.
Level of education of the population 15+ (2010): "Low": 26%; "Medium": 69%; "High": 5%.

Emigrant population living in OECD countries

Immigrant population

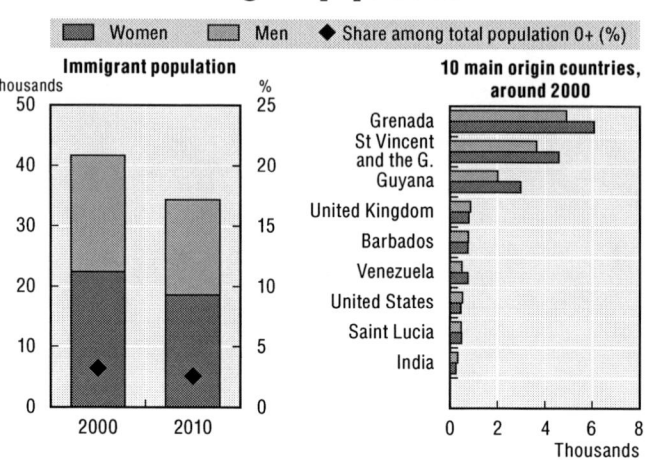

Emigrant population: persons born in Trinidad and Tobago living abroad

	2000						2005/06		
	All destinations			OECD destinations			OECD destinations		
Population 15+	Men	Women	Total	Men	Women	Total	Men	Women	Total
Emigrant population (thousands)	120.3	157.3	277.6	118.8	155.5	274.3	136.0	176.0	312.0
Recent emigrants (thousands)	..	..	..	14.0	17.9	31.8	12.1	15.1	27.2
15-24 (%)	13.8	11.4	12.4	13.9	11.5	12.5	11.7	11.4	11.6
25-64 (%)	77.8	79.2	78.6	77.9	79.3	78.7	76.7	77.4	77.1
65+ (%)	8.4	9.4	9.0	8.2	9.2	8.8	11.6	11.2	11.3
Low-educated (%)	24.7	22.9	23.7	24.5	22.7	23.5	14.8	14.7	14.8
Highly educated (%)	28.8	30.4	29.7	29.0	30.6	29.9	34.2	36.6	35.6
Total emigration rates (%)	20.5	24.3	22.5	20.3	24.1	22.3	21.3	25.0	23.3
Emigration rates of the highly educated (%)	69.2	76.8	73.4	69.0	76.7	73.3	71.9	75.6	74.0

Main destinations in 2005/06

	Total		Recent emigrants	Women	Highly educated	15-24	Total in 2000
Population 15+	Thousands	%	%	%	%	%	Thousands
United States	224.1	71.8	9.1	56.2	29.4	12.2	188.0
Canada	66.1	21.2	5.6	54.7	48.8	9.2	63.1
United Kingdom	18.7	6.0	–	63.9	67.2	–	20.6
Australia	1.2	0.4	9.6	51.3	43.5	5.4	1.0
Netherlands	–	–	–	–	–	–	–
France	–	–	–	–	–	–	0.3
Ireland	–	–	–	–	–	–	0.2
Italy	–	–	–	–	–	–	0.1
Sweden	–	–	–	–	–	–	0.2
New Zealand	–	–	–	–	–	–	0.2

Labour market indicators of persons born in Trinidad and Tobago living in OECD countries

Population 15-64	2000			2005/06		
	Men	Women	Total	Men	Women	Total
Employment-population ratio (%)	76.1	67.6	71.3	79.6	71.3	74.9
Unemployment rate (%)	7.1	7.1	7.1	7.8	7.4	7.6
Participation rate (%)	82.0	72.7	76.8	86.4	77.0	81.1
Total employed (thousands)	**82.6**	**95.1**	**177.6**	**95.2**	**110.5**	**205.7**
Employment rates of the highly educated (%)	86.3	78.9	82.0	92.9	84.5	87.9
Unemployment rates of the highly educated (%)	3.8	4.4	4.1	5.4	4.1	4.6
Highly educated in low- and medium-skilled jobs (%)	37.2	33.9	35.4	40.4	34.7	37.1
Highly educated employed (thousands)	**27.6**	**35.6**	**63.2**	**36.6**	**48.9**	**85.5**
Legislators, senior officials and managers	12.5	7.9	10.0	9.6	6.2	7.7
Professionals	15.6	14.6	15.1	17.3	18.5	18.0
Life science and health professionals	5.2	2.4	3.5	16.8	6.4	10.1
Teaching professionals	5.1	6.0	5.6	0.5	12.7	8.4
Technicians and associate professionals	13.0	24.5	19.1	16.5	27.1	22.3
Clerks	10.1	26.4	18.7	10.5	22.6	17.1
Service, shop and market sales workers	9.1	16.6	13.1	9.4	14.3	12.1
Skilled agricultural and fishery workers	0.6	0.1	0.4	0.9	2.1	1.6
Craft and related trades workers	16.7	1.2	8.5	15.8	1.4	7.9
Plant and machine operators and assemblers	12.6	3.7	7.9	10.5	2.8	6.3
Elementary occupations	9.7	5.0	7.2	9.4	5.1	7.0

(Left side vertical label: Distribution of employment by occupation (%), population 15+)

Persons born in Trinidad and Tobago and their native-born children, population 15+

Living in:	Europe	United States	Australia
2008	Thousands	Thousands	Thousands
Native-born children	19.0	140.7	..
Foreign-born	16.6	241.6	1.6
Total	35.6	382.3	..

International students from Trinidad and Tobago in OECD countries

Five main destinations	2004	2005	2006	2007	2008	2009
United States	3 638	3 060	3 028	2 976	2 643	2 434
Canada	371	..	561	573	736	1 162
United Kingdom	683	767	849	878	834	835
France	35	41	43	47	42	36
Australia	7	13	23	23	23	24
Total	4 745	3 894	4 525	4 516	4 334	4 555

Legal migrant flows to the OECD
Thousands

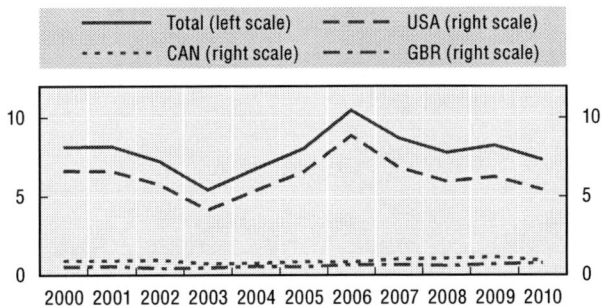

Remittance flows

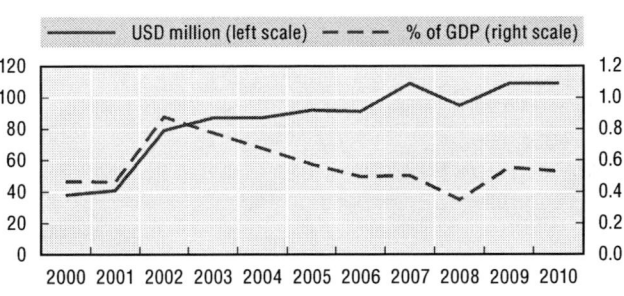

Ten main countries of destination for legal migrants in 2010 (numbers, % of total flows to the country): USA (5435, 0.5%), CAN (910, 0.3%), GBR (733, 0.2%), JPN (61, 0%), DEU (54, 0%), AUS (26, 0%), SWE (19, 0%), FRA (17, 0%), NLD (15, 0%), DNK (12, 0%).

Desire to emigrate, 2008-10

	Women	15-24	Highly educated	Total	Regional total
Persons who would move permanently, if they had the opportunity to do so (%)	20	28	..	20	22
Of which: Persons who are planning to move permanently in the next 12 months (%)				..	11
Of which: Persons who have already done some preparations for this move (*e.g.* visa application) (%)					29

StatLink http://dx.doi.org/10.1787/888932672973

			Uruguay compared to:	World	Region
Total population 2010 (millions)		3.4	Human Development Index (HDI)	48/187	3/31
Population growth 2010 (%)		0.3	GDP per capita	56/194	8/36
GDP per capita 2010 (current USD)		11 996	Emigration rate	79/203	29/38
GDP growth 2010 (%)		8.5	Emigration rate of the highly educated	50/157	12/24
Poverty rate 2009 (USD PPP 2 a day, in %)		0.2			

Age structure of the population 0+ (2010): "0-14": 15%; "15-24": 22%; "25-64": 48%; "65+": 14%.
Level of education of the population 15+ (2010): "Low": 43%; "Medium": 49%; "High": 8%.

Emigrant population living in OECD countries

Immigrant population

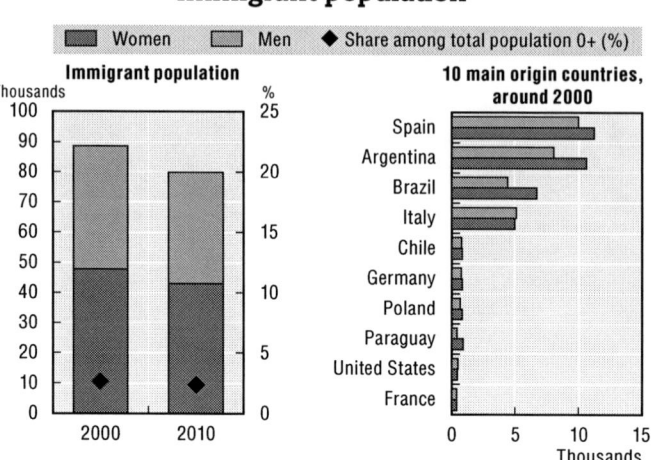

Emigrant population: persons born in Uruguay living abroad

	2000						2005/06		
	All destinations			OECD destinations			OECD destinations		
Population 15+	Men	Women	Total	Men	Women	Total	Men	Women	Total
Emigrant population (thousands)	113.0	117.7	230.7	39.3	41.6	80.9	71.6	81.4	153.1
Recent emigrants (thousands)	..	..	..	5.3	5.5	10.8	25.8	31.4	57.2
15-24 (%)	9.0	8.7	8.9	8.9	7.8	8.3	8.6	12.7	10.8
25-64 (%)	81.4	76.6	78.9	83.9	79.9	81.8	83.7	77.3	80.3
65+ (%)	9.6	14.7	12.2	7.2	12.3	9.8	7.6	10.1	8.9
Low-educated (%)	49.1	47.8	48.4	33.6	33.8	33.7	35.6	30.8	33.0
Highly educated (%)	16.2	17.5	16.9	27.3	29.2	28.3	23.4	26.0	24.8
Total emigration rates (%)	8.7	8.2	8.4	3.1	3.1	3.1	5.6	5.8	5.7
Emigration rates of the highly educated (%)	10.8	17.8	13.6	6.3	11.2	8.2	18.5	14.1	15.7

Main destinations in 2005/06

	Total		Recent emigrants	Women	Highly educated	15-24	Total in 2000
Population 15+	Thousands	%	%	%	%	%	Thousands
Spain	68.4	44.7	91.0	56.2	20.0	15.1	21.8
United States	45.1	29.4	24.7	49.8	24.9	8.8	24.7
Australia	9.2	6.0	2.7	52.5	20.4	3.1	9.2
Canada	6.8	4.5	11.3	50.4	38.9	6.7	6.0
Italy	6.6	4.3	17.5	50.5	14.7	–	4.7
Israel	4.9	3.2	9.1	55.0	54.7	6.4	4.4
Sweden	2.2	1.5	17.3	50.2	32.4	3.8	2.3
France	2.1	1.4	19.4	56.6	56.0	5.4	1.6
Chile	1.9	1.2	23.7	34.4	31.0	24.3	2.1
Switzerland	1.6	1.0	–	–	–	–	1.0

Labour market indicators of persons born in Uruguay living in OECD countries

Population 15-64	2000 Men	2000 Women	2000 Total	2005/06 Men	2005/06 Women	2005/06 Total
Employment-population ratio (%)	78.6	58.9	68.7	87.8	63.4	75.1
Unemployment rate (%)	8.7	10.9	9.6	6.2	12.9	9.3
Participation rate (%)	86.1	66.1	76.1	93.7	72.8	82.8
Total employed (thousands)	**27.4**	**20.6**	**48.0**	**56.9**	**44.9**	**101.8**
Employment rates of the highly educated (%)	85.2	71.3	77.8	96.5	85.4	90.3
Unemployment rates of the highly educated (%)	5.4	8.2	6.7	5.1	9.6	7.5
Highly educated in low- and medium-skilled jobs (%)	30.3	32.2	31.2	49.0	53.5	51.3
Highly educated employed (thousands)	**8.3**	**7.9**	**16.2**	**13.7**	**14.5**	**28.3**
Legislators, senior officials and managers	10.1	6.9	8.7	4.2	3.7	4.0
Professionals	14.7	16.6	15.5	7.3	7.8	7.6
Life science and health professionals	2.1	4.3	3.0	0.6	2.3	1.4
Teaching professionals	2.5	3.5	2.9	0.3	1.9	1.0
Technicians and associate professionals	12.1	16.0	13.8	9.7	9.2	9.5
Clerks	4.3	14.6	8.6	3.5	11.6	7.2
Service, shop and market sales workers	10.6	21.6	15.2	14.4	36.0	24.4
Skilled agricultural and fishery workers	1.3	1.0	1.2	1.1	0.3	0.7
Craft and related trades workers	21.9	2.9	13.9	34.2	1.4	19.1
Plant and machine operators and assemblers	12.4	3.7	8.8	11.0	2.6	7.1
Elementary occupations	12.7	16.6	14.4	14.5	27.3	20.4

Left vertical label: Distribution of employment by occupation (%), population 15+

Persons born in Uruguay and their native-born children, population 15+

Living in:	Europe	United States	Australia
2008	Thousands	Thousands	Thousands
Native-born children	14.8	23.3	0.8
Foreign-born	123.8	29.8	14.3
Total	138.6	53.1	15.1

International students from Uruguay in OECD countries

Five main destinations	2004	2005	2006	2007	2008	2009
United States	532	549	527	487	458	440
Spain	72	140	124	153	140	410
France	71	76	96	99	140	95
Canada	24	..	21	42	36	46
Chile	..	..	..	..	89	42
Total	834	881	871	908	1 021	1 202

Legal migrant flows to the OECD
Thousands

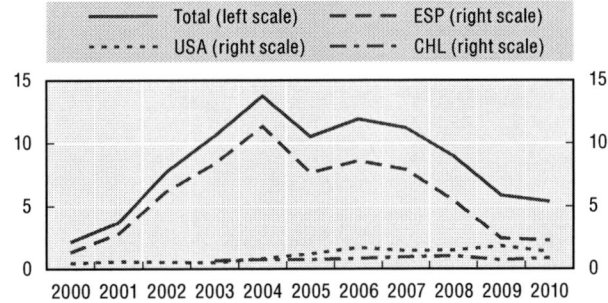

Remittance flows

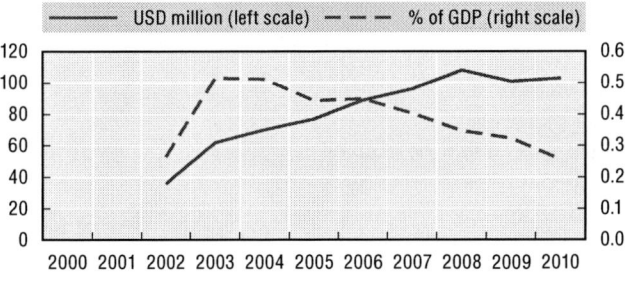

Ten main countries of destination for legal migrants in 2010 (numbers, % of total flows to the country): ESP (2227, 0.5%), USA (1331, 0.1%), CHL (838, 1.3%), MEX (232, 0.9%), ITA (140, 0%), CAN (110, 0%), ISR (90, 0%), DEU (67, 0%), JPN (61, 0%), CHE (52, 0%).

Desire to emigrate, 2008-10

	Women	15-24	Highly educated	Total	Regional total
Persons who would move permanently, if they had the opportunity to do so (%)	14	22	13	14	22
Of which: Persons who are planning to move permanently in the next 12 months (%)				9	11
Of which: Persons who have already done some preparations for this move (*e.g.* visa application) (%)					29

Three main countries of desired destination: Spain (33%), United States (17%), Brazil (13%).

StatLink ᵐˢ⁹ http://dx.doi.org/10.1787/888932672992

Total population 2010 (millions)	28.8	**Venezuela compared to:**	**World**	**Region**
Population growth 2010 (%)	1.6	Human Development Index (HDI)	72/187	12/31
GDP per capita 2010 (current USD)	13 590	GDP per capita	51/194	6/36
GDP growth 2010 (%)	−1.5	Emigration rate	130/203	35/38
Poverty rate 2006 (USD PPP 2 a day, in %)	10.6	Emigration rate of the highly educated	124/157	23/24

Age structure of the population 0+ (2010): "0-14": 19%; "15-24": 29%; "25-64": 46%; "65+": 6%.
Level of education of the population 15+ (2010): "Low": 60%; "Medium": 20%; "High": 20%.

Emigrant population living in OECD countries

Immigrant population

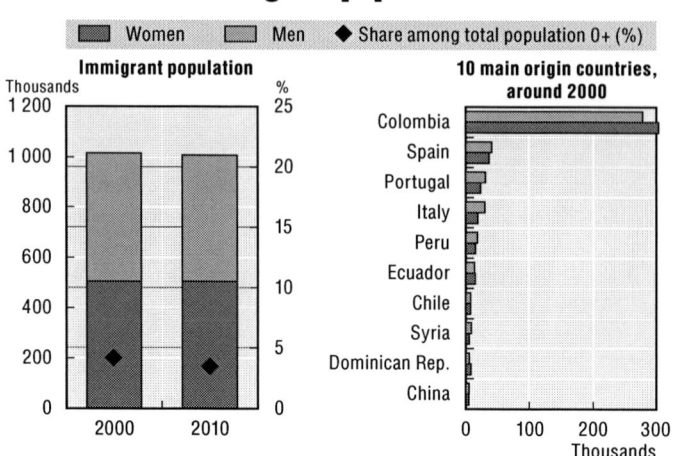

Emigrant population: persons born in Venezuela living abroad

	2000						2005/06		
	All destinations			OECD destinations			OECD destinations		
Population 15+	Men	Women	Total	Men	Women	Total	Men	Women	Total
Emigrant population (thousands)	130.0	150.7	280.7	110.2	127.6	237.8	164.6	186.7	351.3
Recent emigrants (thousands)	..	..	..	24.6	29.6	54.2	37.0	48.2	85.3
15-24 (%)	26.7	23.4	24.9	22.7	19.6	21.0	19.5	15.2	17.2
25-64 (%)	71.6	73.4	72.6	75.7	77.3	76.6	78.1	81.3	79.8
65+ (%)	1.7	3.2	2.5	1.6	3.1	2.4	2.4	3.5	3.0
Low-educated (%)	30.0	28.5	29.2	27.6	26.7	27.1	21.8	20.7	21.3
Highly educated (%)	34.8	34.7	34.7	37.0	36.6	36.8	43.1	45.2	44.2
Total emigration rates (%)	1.6	1.8	1.7	1.3	1.6	1.4	1.8	2.0	1.9
Emigration rates of the highly educated (%)	4.2	3.9	4.0	3.8	3.5	3.6	5.1	4.8	4.9

Main destinations in 2005/06

	Total		Recent emigrants	Women	Highly educated	15-24	Total in 2000
Population 15+	Thousands	%	%	%	%	%	Thousands
United States	155.9	44.4	25.2	53.0	52.5	16.8	99.2
Spain	97.0	27.6	81.2	50.8	41.2	17.8	60.2
Italy	36.6	10.4	8.4	52.8	19.5	6.9	34.2
Portugal	24.5	7.0	–	57.3	–	35.1	18.5
Canada	10.3	2.9	37.2	53.8	65.7	18.1	7.1
Mexico	7.7	2.2	..	55.3	82.0	5.4	2.4
France	4.6	1.3	28.0	55.2	52.6	23.0	2.8
Switzerland	2.7	0.8	54.1	80.0	65.7	–	1.8
United Kingdom	–	–	–	–	–	–	3.6
Netherlands	2.4	0.7	–	–	–	–	–

Labour market indicators of persons born in Venezuela living in OECD countries

Population 15-64	2000			2005/06		
	Men	Women	Total	Men	Women	Total
Employment-population ratio (%)	68.9	48.8	58.2	80.2	55.7	67.2
Unemployment rate (%)	9.0	14.3	11.4	7.8	13.4	10.4
Participation rate (%)	75.7	56.9	65.7	87.0	64.3	75.0
Total employed (thousands)	**74.4**	**59.9**	**134.3**	**127.0**	**99.3**	**226.3**
Employment rates of the highly educated (%)	78.5	58.9	68.0	93.1	72.9	82.0
Unemployment rates of the highly educated (%)	6.1	10.7	8.3	4.5	13.5	8.9
Highly educated in low- and medium-skilled jobs (%)	31.8	32.1	31.9	34.8	41.2	37.8
Highly educated employed (thousands)	**31.3**	**26.9**	**58.2**	**60.9**	**51.9**	**112.8**
Legislators, senior officials and managers	12.6	7.7	10.4	10.6	6.9	9.0
Professionals	14.6	19.0	16.6	12.3	17.3	14.5
Life science and health professionals	1.4	3.6	2.4	1.8	5.2	3.3
Teaching professionals	2.5	5.5	3.8	2.3	5.1	3.5
Technicians and associate professionals	15.5	18.6	16.9	16.1	13.2	14.8
Clerks	6.5	15.6	10.6	5.2	20.2	11.7
Service, shop and market sales workers	13.7	20.7	16.9	12.9	19.7	15.9
Skilled agricultural and fishery workers	1.8	0.8	1.3	1.3	1.3	1.3
Craft and related trades workers	17.9	4.3	11.7	20.6	3.7	13.2
Plant and machine operators and assemblers	8.9	2.2	5.9	9.2	2.7	6.4
Elementary occupations	8.4	11.2	9.7	11.0	15.0	12.7

Distribution of employment by occupation (%), population 15+

Persons born in Venezuela and their native-born children, population 15+

Living in:	Europe	United States	Australia
2008	Thousands	Thousands	Thousands
Native-born children	28.5	57.2	..
Foreign-born	80.6	132.7	..
Total	109.2	189.9	..

International students from Venezuela in OECD countries

Five main destinations	2004	2005	2006	2007	2008	2009
United States	5 575	5 514	4 962	4 623	4 451	4 601
Spain	488	571	595	780	987	1 897
France	405	396	393	438	492	551
Germany	..	..	..	..	293	332
United Kingdom	350	322	324	350	310	329
Total	7 455	7 173	6 878	6 842	7 465	8 740

Legal migrant flows to the OECD
Thousands

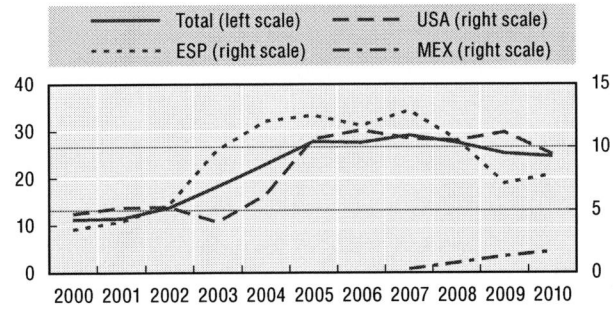

Remittance flows

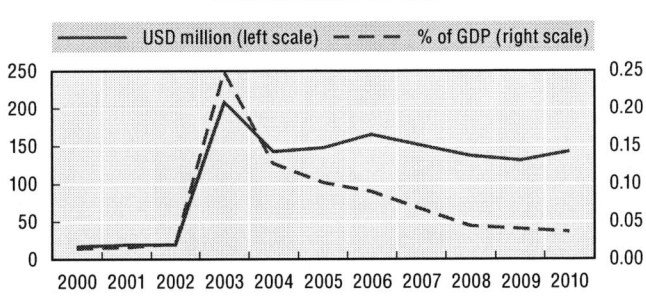

Ten main countries of destination for legal migrants in 2010 (numbers, % of total flows to the country): USA (9409, 0.9%), ESP (7791, 1.8%), MEX (1664, 6.4%), GBR (1098, 0.2%), CAN (1005, 0.4%), ITA (802, 0.2%), CHL (741, 0.1%), DEU (527, 0.1%), AUS (388, 0.2%), FRA (192, 0.1%).

Desire to emigrate, 2008-10

	Women	15-24	Highly educated	Total	Regional total
Persons who would move permanently, if they had the opportunity to do so (%)	12	18	13	12	22
Of which: Persons who are planning to move permanently in the next 12 months (%)				8	11
Of which: Persons who have already done some preparations for this move (*e.g.* visa application) (%)					29

Three main countries of desired destination: United States (32%), Spain (21%), Mexico (8%).

StatLink http://dx.doi.org/10.1787/888932673011

Chapter 4

OECD Countries

This chapter looks at recent migration flows and diasporas from OECD countries to the OECD area. It shows that in 2010 almost 1.6 million new migrants from the region settled in OECD countries, accounting for about 30% of total immigration flows. In 2005/06 there were 39.5 million emigrants, 15 years old or older, from the region in OECD countries, of which 50% were women and 24% hold a tertiary diploma. Total emigration rate for those over 15 years of age reached 3.8% for the region as a whole. The emigration rate for the highly educated was of similar level. Future challenges relate notably to the management of labour migration in the context of demographic ageing and low economic growth.

This chapter also contains 34 country notes for all OECD countries.

1. Historical migration patterns

In 2010, the OECD area, consisting of 34 member countries,[1] registered an average GDP per capita of USD 35 000 (in purchasing power parities). The high living standards characterising the OECD area, comprising mostly high-income countries,[2] are one of the pull factors for migration from less developed regions; however, there are also important movements within the area. In 2000, about two-thirds of the global migrant population lived in the OECD area and half were born in another OECD country.

The size and characteristics of international migrant populations in OECD countries are the result of accumulated migration waves, which have been responding to economic and geopolitical events and which are determined by geographic and linguistic proximity, as well as institutional and historical settings. Reconstruction and economic development after the Second World War induced large-scale temporary labour migration through "guest worker" programmes in many OECD countries, notably the United States and countries in North-western Europe. Decolonisation in the 1950s/1960s led to an increase of migrant flows of foreigners and repatriates from former colonies to the OECD area; further major-scale migration took place following the breakup of the Soviet Union in 1989, especially ethnic migration for resettlement from Central and Eastern European countries to Western Europe. More recently, in the 1990s and 2000s, regional conflicts have induced large migration flows of humanitarian migrants, notably from the former Yugoslavia, Iraq and Afghanistan (OECD, 2011).

The OECD settlement countries, namely Australia, Canada, New Zealand, the United States and Israel,[3] were established by migration, mainly from Europe. In Australia, Canada and New Zealand, permanent migration accounts for a large share of overall migration and plays an important role in population growth. These countries introduced selective migration schemes to attract more highly educated migrants. Inflows of permanent labour migration to these countries have been steadily increasing over the past 50 years, but the origin of labour migrants diversified since the late 1990s, away from predominant European migration to increasing migration from Asian non-OECD countries.

Mexican migration to the United States is a special migration corridor within the OECD area because of its magnitude: 11 million Mexican-born persons lived in the United States in 2005/06, representing the largest diaspora in the OECD area. This large inflow can be traced back to the Bracero programme, implemented by the United States in 1942, to fill labour shortages in low-skilled occupations with Mexican workers, mainly in agriculture. Until the end of this agreement in 1964, 4.6 million temporary workers from Mexico were recruited to the United States, but Mexican migration continued in high numbers and irregular migration progressively increased. Large-scale regularisation of immigrant workers took place in 1986, but due to continuing labour demand and limited legal entry channels, irregular migration continued. The number of irregular migrants in the United States is estimated at 11 million in 2009, of which about 60% are from Mexico.

Israel, another country built on immigration, experienced two significant migration waves: the first at its creation in 1948 and the second in the early 1990s following the breakup of the Soviet Union, when more than 870 000 permanent immigrants settled there. Since its founding, Israel has accepted about 2.8 million immigrants and represents one of the OECD countries with the highest share of immigrants among total population (Chaloff, 2011).

In Europe, foreign labour recruitment after the Second World War largely contributed to shaping the profile of migrant populations. Belgium and Switzerland were the first Western European countries to actively recruit workers abroad by signing guest worker agreements with Italy in 1946 and 1948, respectively. Other Western European countries also concluded labour recruitment agreements to fill labour shortages mainly in low-skilled occupations with Southern European countries (*e.g.* Italy, Portugal, Spain, Greece) and Mediterranean countries (*e.g.* Turkey, Morocco), and attracted migrants from former colonies (*e.g.* Algeria). After the first oil shock in 1973, labour recruitment was stopped and labour migration decreased, but migration for family reunification increased. Thereafter, the total foreign-born population generally either rose (for example in the cases of France, Belgium and the Netherlands) or was fairly stable (as in Germany and Switzerland). Until the late 1990s, migration was predominantly for family and humanitarian reasons. After the breakup of the Soviet Union there were large flows of ethnic minorities to Western Europe. Most of these migrants moved to Germany, which has registered more than 3 million incoming (*Spät*) *Aussiedler* from Poland, the Russian Federation and Romania since 1989. Similar movements were observed in Finland and Hungary, but to a smaller extent. During the 1990s, Italy, Greece, Spain and Portugal, traditionally countries of emigration, became countries of immigration. Ireland and these Southern European countries experienced significant economic growth, which induced large labour migration flows to respond to increasing labour needs, primarily involving low-skilled jobs in construction, hospitality and the household sector. Migration to these new immigration countries was mainly from North Africa, Romania and Bulgaria. The enlargements of the European Union in 2004[4] and in 2008[5] induced new migration flows – notably to the United Kingdom and Ireland, but also to Norway and Germany. In 2010, 37% of permanent migration flows within the European Economic Area is due to free labour mobility (OECD, 2012).

The two Asian OECD countries, Korea and Japan, are significantly less exposed to international migration. The foreign population in Japan was shaped mainly by migration inflows before 1952, mostly from Korea, and immigration of less educated descendants of Japanese emigrants from Brazil and Peru since 1990. More recently, the Japanese government tried to attract more highly skilled foreign labour. In 2009, 2.2 million foreigners lived in Japan, most of which were Chinese (31%), Korean (27%) and Brazilian (12%). The foreign population in Korea reached about 920 000 in 2009 and accounted for 2.4% of total population. Citizens of China represented about 50% of the foreign population in 2009, followed by citizens of the United States and Viet Nam (13% and 10%, respectively) (Chaloff, 2012).

2. Current profile of emigrant populations

Flows and stocks

Migration within the OECD area continues in high numbers, although it represents a smaller share of global movements than in the past. In 2010, about 1.6 million migrants originating from the OECD area moved to another OECD country (Figure 4.1). The magnitude of migration flows from OECD countries decreased slightly since 2007, by 200 000, because of the economic crisis. Still, flows within the OECD area increased by nearly 350 000 since 2000.

The main origin countries of permanent intra-OECD-area migration flows in 2010 were Poland (223 000), Mexico (156 000), the United States, the United Kingdom and Germany (138 000, 117 000 and 117 000 respectively). The figure for Mexican migrant flows is relatively small because only permanent legal migration to the United States is included in the statistics and a large share of Mexican migration to the United States is irregular. The high number of persons migrating from Poland, however, includes temporary migration to Germany.[6] This is also the reason for the ranking of the main OECD destinations of intra-OECD migrant flows in 2010 (Figure 4.3). Most OECD migration is to Germany (291 000), including temporary migration; the country represents one-fifth of total migrant flows within the OECD area, followed by the United States and the United Kingdom (18% and 8%, respectively).

Remittance flows more than doubled to OECD countries from 2000 to 2010, peaking at USD 141 billion in 2008. The largest remittance flows are to the countries with large emigrant populations, Mexico (USD 22 billion), France (USD 15 billion) and Germany (USD 11 billion). The highest increases between 2000 and 2009 in flows are observed for Eastern European OECD countries, notably Poland, the Slovak Republic, the Czech Republic and Estonia.

Figure 4.1. **Migrant flows from the OECD to other OECD countries and remittance flows, 2000-10**

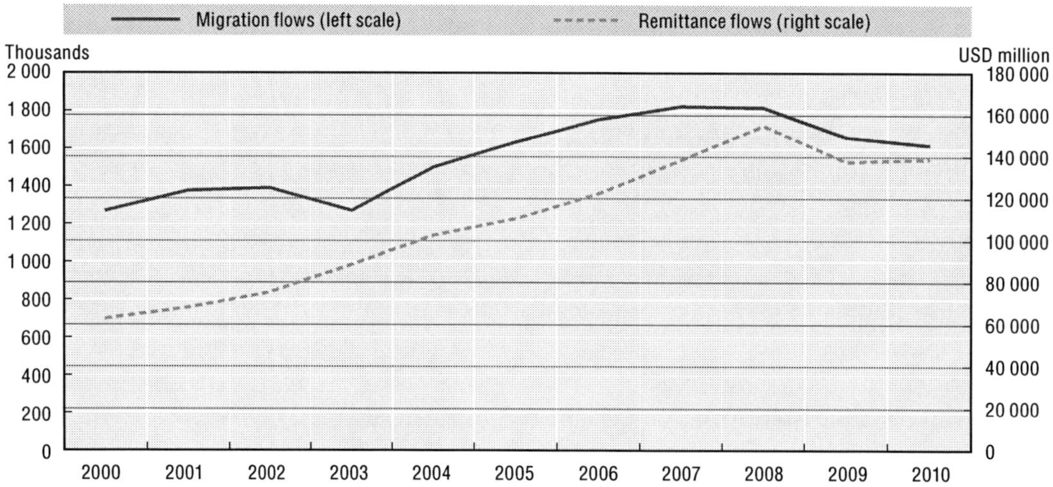

Source: OECD International Migration Database; World Bank.

StatLink ᴍᴤ᠍ᴪ http://dx.doi.org/10.1787/888932672023

The population migrating within the OECD area reached 39.5 million in 2005/06; 5 million of these are recent migrants, i.e. persons having a residency of five years or less in the destination country (Figure 4.2). The main origin countries are Mexico with an emigrant population of nearly 11 million, the United Kingdom (3.4 million), Germany (3 million), Poland (2.8 million) and Turkey (2.6 million). The same countries ranked highest among the top countries of origin for recent migrants with the exception of Poland, which became the second most important country of origin within the OECD area after Mexico. Ireland is the only OECD country that has experienced a net decrease of its emigrant population overseas, probably because of return migration during its economic boom.

At the other end of the spectrum, many OECD countries have very small emigrant populations, especially in Northern Europe. The emigrant populations of Iceland, Norway, Denmark and Sweden, as well as of Luxembourg, Estonia, Slovenia and Israel, range from 28 000 (Iceland) to 224 000 (Sweden).

Figure 4.2. **Total and highly educated emigrant population aged 15
and over from the OECD in the OECD area, 2005/06**

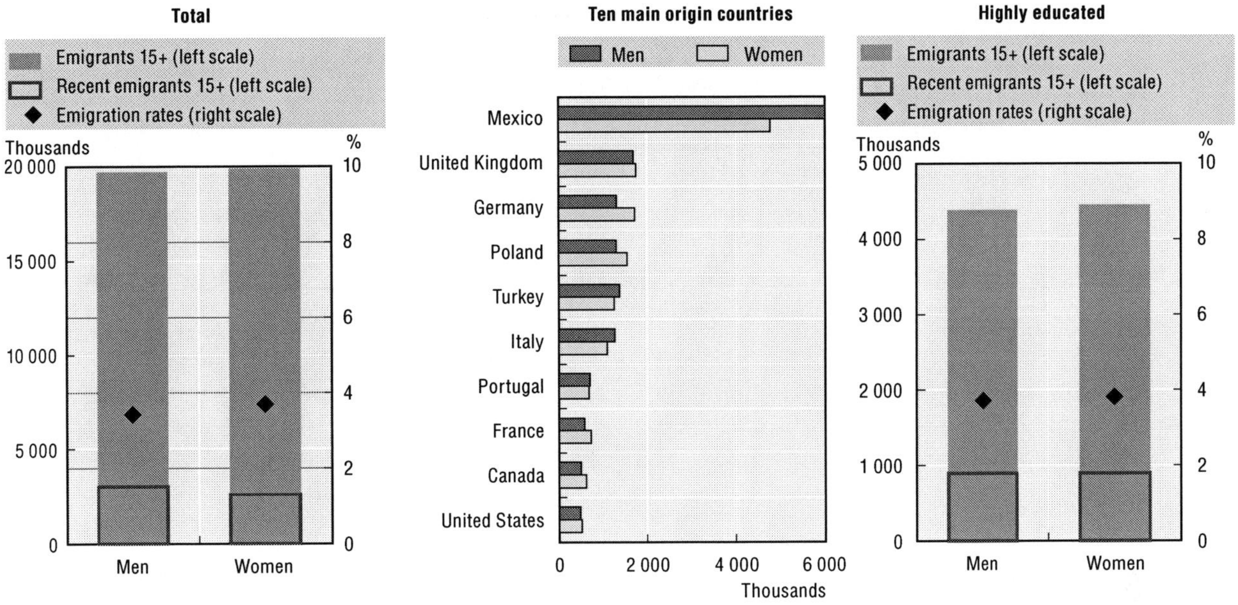

Total

Emigrants 15+ (left scale)
Recent emigrants 15+ (left scale)
◆ Emigration rates (right scale)

Ten main origin countries

■ Men   □ Women

Highly educated

Emigrants 15+ (left scale)
Recent emigrants 15+ (left scale)
◆ Emigration rates (right scale)

The United States is the main destination for migrants born in the OECD area
(16.7 million migrants), followed by Germany (4.6 million), Canada (2.4 million), France
(2.3 million) and Australia (2.3 million) (Figure 4.3). These five destinations account for 75%
of the total OECD emigrant population.

Figure 4.3. **Emigrant populations and migrant flows from the OECD
to the five main destinations within the OECD area, population aged 15 and over**

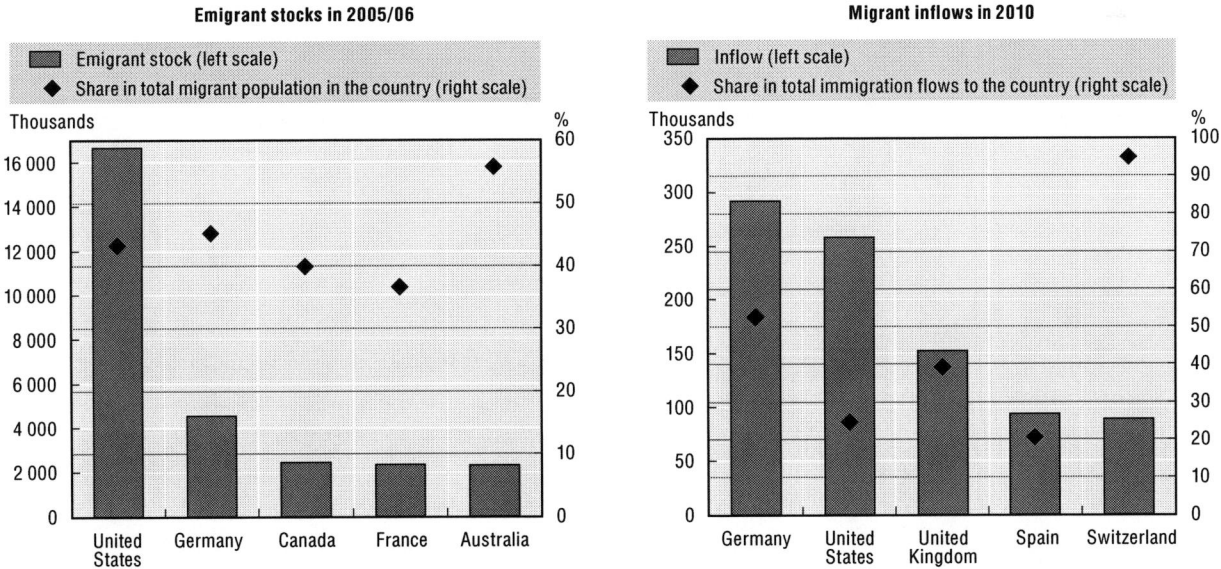

Emigrant stocks in 2005/06

Emigrant stock (left scale)
◆ Share in total migrant population in the country (right scale)

Migrant inflows in 2010

Inflow (left scale)
◆ Share in total immigration flows to the country (right scale)

Characteristics of emigrant populations

Despite increasing migrant populations, the characteristics of most OECD migrant communities changed only slightly. Movements within the OECD area remain highly selective. The number of migrant women born in OECD countries is on a par with the number of migrant men. Among recent emigrants there are slightly more men, mainly because of their importance in the emigration from Mexico.

The age structure of the emigrant population from OECD countries reveals the importance of older migration waves within the OECD area, since one out of six OECD emigrants is aged 65 or older, and only 11% are aged between 15 and 24 (Table 4.1). The share of young emigrants, aged 15 to 24, decreased or remained stable between 2000 and 2005/06 in most migrant groups, except for Estonia and Poland (+4 and +3 percentage points, respectively).

Korea is the main OECD country of origin of international students (119 000 students abroad), followed by Germany and France (67 000 and 50 000, respectively). The number of international students born in Germany nearly doubled between 2004 and 2009 – the highest increase among all OECD countries in absolute numbers (+31 000). The growth of the international student population abroad was particularly high for those migrating from Poland: the number tripled between 2004 and 2009.[7] The number of international students of two origin countries decreased in the period under review, Japan and Greece. The main destinations for international students are the United States (222 000) and the United Kingdom (137 000); the two together accounted for more than 50% of all international students from the OECD studying in other OECD countries in 2009.

Table 4.1. **Characteristics of migrants from the OECD in the OECD area, by gender, 2005/06**

Percentage

	Regional averages (unweighted)			Regional total (weighted)		
	Men	Women	Total	Men	Women	Total
15-24	10.0	9.0	9.4	11.6	10.3	11.0
25-64	71.8	68.8	70.2	74.1	70.7	72.4
65+	18.3	22.1	20.3	14.2	19.0	16.6
Low-educated	25.5	29.3	27.5	39.8	40.2	40.0
Highly educated	34.9	32.2	33.5	23.4	24.0	23.7
Total emigration rates	5.6	5.7	5.6	3.4	3.7	3.8
Emigration rates of the highly educated	7.8	7.9	7.8	3.7	3.8	3.8

Source: Database on Immigrants in OECD Countries (DIOC 2005/06).

StatLink http://dx.doi.org/10.1787/888932675063

On average,[8] in 2005/06 28% of the OECD emigrant population was less educated, while about one-third (34%) held tertiary diplomas (Table 4.1). Migrant men from OECD countries have on average slightly higher educational attainment levels than migrant women. Half of migrant populations from Southern European countries, such as Portugal, Italy, Greece and Spain is low educated. This percentage reaches more than 60% for emigrants from Mexico and Turkey. In contrast, one of every two emigrants from Asian OECD countries, as well as from the United States, Australia and Israel, are highly educated. The educational attainment level of all OECD emigrant populations increased between 2000 and 2005/06, but particularly among migrants from Ireland (+15 percentage points[9]), Sweden (+8 percentage points), Canada and Belgium (+7 percentage points each).

Most of the highly educated emigrant populations from Europe live in English-speaking countries, mainly the United States. Looking closely at bilateral migration stocks of the highly educated, more than 60% of the French-born in the United Kingdom hold tertiary diplomas. The United Kingdom is also the number one destination for young emigrants from France, indicating recent highly skilled migration from France to the United Kingdom. In the other direction, however, the migration of persons born in the United Kingdom and living in France is characterised by an older and less educated population, because of the importance of retirees. Young migrants from the United Kingdom are more attracted to English-speaking destinations within the OECD area, such as the United States and Australia. The share of highly educated persons born in the United Kingdom is particularly high among emigrant populations in Canada and the United States, while migration to Australia is less educated.

The educational attainment levels of OECD emigrants are often reflected in the skill level of the jobs in which they are employed. On average in 2005/06,[10] almost half of OECD emigrants work in highly skilled occupations: legislators, senior officials, managers, professionals and technicians or associate professionals. More than 45% of emigrants born in the United States, Iceland and Israel are employed in highly skilled occupations and face a relatively low incidence of overqualification, *i.e.* persons with tertiary degrees in low-skilled jobs. Overall, about 30% of highly educated persons from the OECD is overqualified (Table 4.2).

Table 4.2. **Labour market characteristics of migrants from the OECD in the OECD area, by gender, 2005/06**

	Regional averages (unweighted)			Regional total (weighted)		
	Men	Women	Total	Men	Women	Total
Employment rate (%)	80.3	61.4	70.5	70.0	47.0	58.5
Unemployment rate (%)	5.5	7.9	6.6	6.7	8.9	7.6
Participation rate (%)	84.9	66.5	75.4	75.0	51.6	63.3
Total employed (thousands)	**13 034**	**8 728**	**21 762**			
Employment rate of the highly educated (%)	89.3	72.5	80.6	78.4	65.1	71.7
Unemployment rate of the highly educated (%)	3.4	6.5	4.9	3.8	5.4	4.6
Participation rate of the highly educated (%)	92.4	77.5	84.7	81.5	68.8	75.1
Highly educated employed (thousands)	**3 528**	**3 000**	**6 528**			
Persons with tertiary degrees in low- or medium-skilled jobs (%)	26.9	29.9	28.2	29.7	31.4	30.5

Source: Database on Immigrants in OECD Countries (DIOC 2005/06).

StatLink ⟳ *http://dx.doi.org/10.1787/888932675082*

Emigration rates and the "brain drain"

The increase in and selectivity of migration within the OECD area particularly affect smaller OECD origin countries; the magnitude, however, remains moderate. In 2005/06, the weighted average of the total emigration rate in the OECD area reached 3.8% (non-weighted average: 5.6%). The highest emigration rate is observed for Ireland, where 16% of total population aged 15 and over lives abroad. The countries that follow are Portugal, Mexico (13% each), New Zealand (12%) and Iceland (11%). Japan and the United States, which have the largest populations in the OECD area, only have 1% or less of their population abroad. Compared to 2000, total emigration rates remained stable or increased only slightly in most OECD countries.

Emigration rates (weighted average) of the highly educated – the so-called "brain drain" – was equal to 3.8% (non-weighted average: 7.8%) in 2005/06, which is not significantly different from the total emigration rate. The highest figures are observed for Ireland and Luxembourg, where 18% of the highly educated population lives in another OECD country. However, two-thirds of the OECD origin countries have less than 10% of their highly educated population abroad.

Between 2000 and 2005/06, emigration rates of the highly educated increased most in Luxembourg (+5.3 percentage points), Portugal and Poland (+3.6 percentage points); they decreased in a small number of countries, namely Finland (-–5 percentage points), Greece and Ireland (–1.8 percentage points).

In 10 out of 34 OECD countries, highly educated women are more prone to leave their origin country than highly educated men. On OECD average, emigration rates of highly educated women exceed those of men, but only by 0.1 percentage points. This hides large variations of gender differences in individual countries. Broken down by detailed origin countries, the greatest differences among men and women occur for persons born in Switzerland, where 16% of highly educated women lived in another OECD country in 2005/06 and only 9% of highly educated men did. The "brain drain" for Germany and Finland is characterised by a gender gap of 3 percentage points in favour of women. In the United Kingdom, Italy and Portugal, men are overrepresented in highly educated emigration, representing a gender gap of 3 percentage points.

3. Future trends and challenges

Future developments in emigration from OECD countries to other OECD countries and to non-OECD countries will be strongly determined by the evolution of the economic situation in both OECD countries and in emerging economies. Large emerging economies are rapidly expanding their activities in research and development and are moving up the value chain. Emerging economies are now competing with OECD countries to attract talents, and it is most likely that this trend will continue and strengthen. In this context, there may occur increasing outflows of highly educated workers from OECD countries to large emerging economies.

Several OECD countries were hard hit by the economic crisis in 2008; those that became countries of immigration in the 2000s, such as Ireland and Southern European countries, were especially affected. In these countries, immigrants and the native-born population – especially the young, both the low-educated and the highly educated, faced high unemployment in 2010, and the economic situation seems unlikely to recover soon. This can be expected to push immigrants to return or to migrate to another country and fuel emigration of the native-born, particularly the highly educated, to other countries offering job opportunities. This development could change the current migration corridors within the OECD area and reactivate migration flows from Southern European countries to other OECD countries, notably to North-western Europe. Southern European OECD countries may lose young and talented workers to other OECD countries in the coming years.

The recruitment of foreign labour from other OECD countries and from non-OECD countries is expected to gain even more importance in view of the fact that many OECD countries face the issues of an ageing population, declining youth cohorts, and large retiring baby-boom generations – all leading to a decreasing workforce. This development challenges social security systems and to some extent potential economic growth. The demographic change in OECD countries might lead to long-term labour shortages in certain occupations and sectors, for example in the care and health sectors. Despite an increase in the labour force participation of women and of older workers, matching labour needs with labour supply might be a challenge for OECD countries. Migration is seen as one means to respond to the labour market needs in the OECD area to support social security systems, to stay internationally competitive, and to fuel economic growth. In this respect, the focus is often on immigration of highly educated workers, but many OECD countries also need workers to fill low-skilled jobs in agriculture, construction and the care sector. Better management of labour migration remains a challenge in OECD countries to indeed match labour supply with current and future labour demand.

Notes

1. Australia, Austria, Belgium, Canada, Chile, the Czech Republic, Denmark, Estonia, Finland, France, Germany, Greece, Hungary, Iceland, Ireland, Israel, Italy, Japan, Korea, Luxembourg, Mexico, the Netherlands, New Zealand, Norway, Poland, Portugal, the Slovak Republic, Slovenia, Spain, Sweden, Switzerland, Turkey, the United Kingdom and the United States.

2. Income groups are classified according to the World Bank Classification of Economies 2011: high-income countries are above USD 12 275 and upper-middle-income countries between USD 3 975 and USD 12 275. The OECD includes three upper-middle-income countries: Chile, Mexico and Turkey.

3. The statistical data for Israel are supplied by and under the responsibility of the relevant Israeli authorities. The use of such data by the OECD is without prejudice to the status of the Golan Heights, East Jerusalem and Israeli settlements in the West Bank under the terms of international law.

4. Eight countries joined the European Union in 2004: Czech Republic, Estonia, Hungary, Latvia, Lithuania, Poland, the Slovak Republic and Slovenia; these are often referred to as EU8.

5. Two additional countries joined the European Union in 2007: Bulgaria and Romania; these are often referred to as EU2.

6. As stated earlier in note 4 of Chapter 1, migration flow data are derived from national administrative data sources that utilise different definitions of "flows", a comparability issue that has to be kept in mind (Lemaître, 2005).

7. Data are only available from 2007 onwards for Germany, where about one-third of all international students from Poland studied in 2009. However, the international student population born in Poland doubled between 2004 and 2009, without taking into account Germany.

8. This average presents the non-weighted figure. The weighted average is for highly educated 24% and 40% for the others.

9. The increase in the share of highly educated among Irish-born emigrants may be due to the change of educational classification in the data of the main destination country, the United Kingdom.

10. This average presents the non-weighted figure.

Country Notes

OECD Countries

			Australia compared to:	World	Region
Total population 2010 (millions)		22.3	Human Development Index (HDI)	2/187	2/34
Population growth 2010 (%)		1.7	GDP per capita	19/194	14/34
GDP per capita 2009 (current USD)		42 131	Emigration rate	128/203	31/34
GDP growth 2009 (%)		1.3	Emigration rate of the highly educated	138/157	30/34
Poverty rate 2010 (USD PPP 2 a day, in %)		..			

Age structure of the population 0+ (2010): "0-14": 14%; "15-24": 19%; "25-64": 53%; "65+": 13%.
Level of education of the population 15+ (2010): "Low": 4%; "Medium": 62%; "High": 35%.

Emigrant population living in OECD countries

Immigrant population

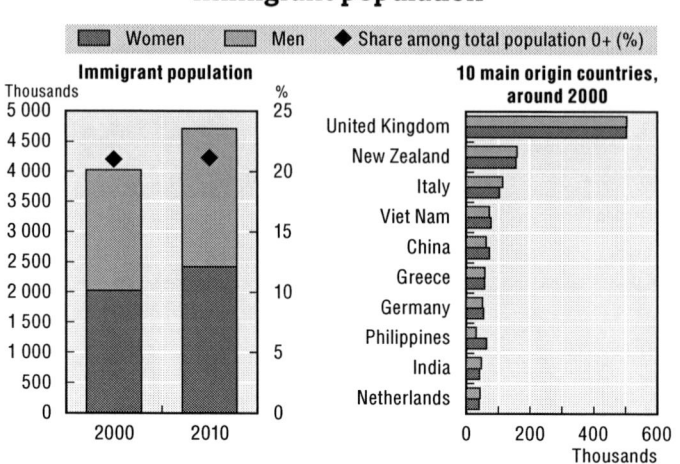

Emigrant population: persons born in Australia living abroad

	2000						2005/06		
	All destinations			OECD destinations			OECD destinations		
Population 15+	Men	Women	Total	Men	Women	Total	Men	Women	Total
Emigrant population (thousands)	147.9	174.1	322.0	132.8	159.9	292.7	159.0	165.5	324.5
Recent emigrants (thousands)	..	..	..	30.7	27.6	58.3	41.9	40.9	82.8
15-24 (%)	15.8	16.3	16.1	15.3	15.5	15.4	13.6	14.7	14.1
25-64 (%)	77.6	73.5	75.3	78.0	74.0	75.8	80.2	74.6	77.4
65+ (%)	6.6	10.2	8.6	6.7	10.5	8.8	6.2	10.7	8.5
Low-educated (%)	18.7	18.2	18.4	17.7	17.0	17.3	14.1	15.1	14.6
Highly educated (%)	46.4	41.6	43.8	47.4	42.5	44.7	51.2	47.5	49.4
Total emigration rates (%)	1.9	2.2	2.1	1.7	2.0	1.9	1.9	2.0	1.9
Emigration rates of the highly educated (%)	3.7	2.3	2.9	3.4	2.2	2.6	4.2	2.2	2.9

Main destinations in 2005/06

	Total		Recent emigrants	Women	Highly educated	15-24	Total in 2000
Population 15+	Thousands	%	%	%	%	%	Thousands
United Kingdom	105.5	32.5	37.6	50.2	60.0	12.5	96.9
United States	78.7	24.2	26.8	50.9	55.1	11.1	64.4
New Zealand	48.9	15.1	19.6	54.4	28.5	24.2	42.0
Canada	20.4	6.3	16.8	51.2	62.1	11.4	17.7
Italy	16.9	5.2	–	50.3	12.5	–	17.2
Greece	8.8	2.7	–	51.3	34.4	–	19.4
Netherlands	7.9	2.4	–	51.1	31.1	–	3.4
Japan	6.4	2.0	..	35.1	84.9	16.2	5.6
Ireland	5.1	1.6	53.2	51.6	53.0	23.8	4.4
France	4.7	1.5	32.7	56.7	57.8	16.4	3.7

Labour market indicators of persons born in Australia living in OECD countries

Population 15-64	2000			2005/06		
	Men	Women	Total	Men	Women	Total
Employment-population ratio (%)	83.1	68.1	75.1	86.5	71.3	78.8
Unemployment rate (%)	5.8	6.3	6.1	4.9	4.7	4.8
Participation rate (%)	88.2	72.8	79.9	90.9	74.8	82.8
Total employed (thousands)	**95.8**	**91.6**	**187.4**	**121.4**	**101.4**	**222.8**
Employment rates of the highly educated (%)	91.5	77.5	84.2	97.0	83.5	90.4
Unemployment rates of the highly educated (%)	3.3	4.2	3.7	3.0	3.6	3.3
Highly educated in low- and medium-skilled jobs (%)	18.4	23.7	21.0	14.5	22.2	18.0
Highly educated employed (thousands)	**49.4**	**46.2**	**95.6**	**67.4**	**55.8**	**123.2**
Legislators, senior officials and managers	18.5	12.7	15.6	22.9	17.9	20.6
Professionals	24.3	22.4	23.3	25.8	20.5	23.4
Life science and health professionals	2.3	2.7	2.5	2.2	3.4	2.7
Teaching professionals	4.9	8.8	6.9	5.6	9.0	7.2
Technicians and associate professionals	15.5	18.8	17.2	15.0	19.1	16.9
Clerks	6.0	21.6	13.9	4.7	20.1	11.8
Service, shop and market sales workers	8.7	16.0	12.4	7.3	9.3	8.2
Skilled agricultural and fishery workers	2.2	1.5	1.8	2.7	3.2	2.9
Craft and related trades workers	12.3	1.4	6.7	9.7	2.3	6.3
Plant and machine operators and assemblers	6.1	1.5	3.7	4.7	1.4	3.2
Elementary occupations	6.5	4.2	5.3	5.2	5.7	5.5

Distribution of employment by occupation (%), population 15+

Persons born in Australia and their native-born children, population 15+

Living in:	Europe	United States
2008	Thousands	Thousands
Native-born children	50.5	45.3
Foreign-born	108.4	54.6
Total	158.9	100.0

International students from Australia in OECD countries

Five main destinations	2004	2005	2006	2007	2008	2009
United States	2 706	2 777	2 906	2 859	3 091	3 150
New Zealand	2 590	2 742	2 781	2 750	2 809	2 943
United Kingdom	1 501	1 611	1 607	1 771	1 610	1 647
Germany	..	..	..	..	318	338
Japan	346	337	333	361	337	326
Total	8 257	8 366	9 004	9 044	9 091	9 456

Legal migrant flows to the OECD
Thousands

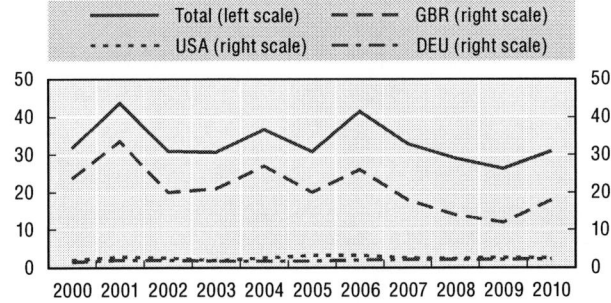

Remittance flows

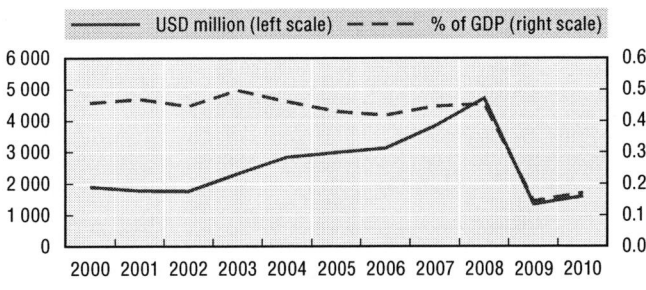

Ten main countries of destination for legal migrants in 2010 (numbers, % of total flows to the country): GBR (18000, 3.9%), USA (2512, 0.2%), DEU (2225, 0.3%), KOR (1555, 0.5%), CAN (1130, 0.4%), JPN (1123, 0.4%), NLD (806, 0.4%), CHE (513, 0.4%), FRA (376, 0.3%), SWE (319, 0.4%).

Desire to emigrate, 2008-10

	Women	15-24	Highly educated	Total	Regional total
Persons who would move permanently, if they had the opportunity to do so (%)	8	..	8	8	16
Of which: Persons who are planning to move permanently in the next 12 months (%)				..	6
Of which: Persons who have already done some preparations for this move (*e.g.* visa application) (%)					39

StatLink 🔗 http://dx.doi.org/10.1787/888932673030

Total population 2010 (millions)	8.4		Austria compared to:	World	Region
Population growth 2010 (%)	0.2		Human Development Index (HDI)	19/187	17/34
GDP per capita 2010 (current USD)	45 209		GDP per capita	15/194	10/34
GDP growth 2010 (%)	2.3		Emigration rate	76/203	13/34
Poverty rate 2010 (USD PPP 2 a day, in %)	..		Emigration rate of the highly educated	58/157	5/34

Age structure of the population 0+ (2010): "0-14": 12%; "15-24": 15%; "25-64": 55%; "65+": 18%.
Level of education of the population 15+ (2010): "Low": 25%; "Medium": 63%; "High": 12%.

Emigrant population living in OECD countries

Immigrant population

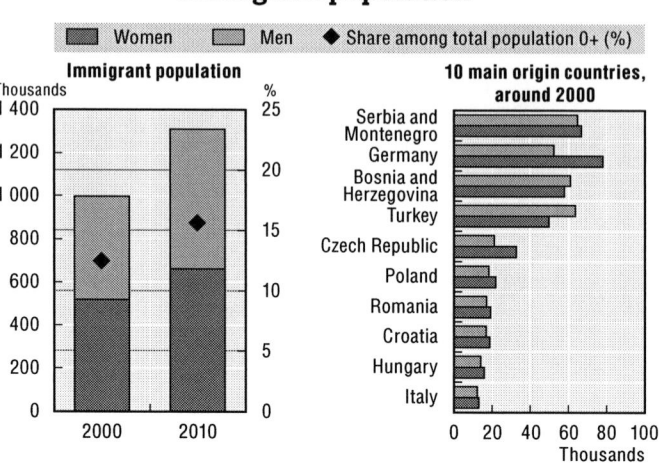

Emigrant population: persons born in Austria living abroad

	2000						2005/06		
	All destinations			OECD destinations			OECD destinations		
Population 15+	Men	Women	Total	Men	Women	Total	Men	Women	Total
Emigrant population (thousands)	186.4	229.7	416.1	166.3	208.1	374.4	202.1	227.6	429.6
Recent emigrants (thousands)	..	..	..	8.2	8.8	17.0	19.1	17.2	36.3
15-24 (%)	4.1	3.9	4.0	2.7	2.6	2.7	4.3	3.1	3.7
25-64 (%)	74.7	64.6	69.1	75.5	65.1	69.7	70.0	64.0	66.8
65+ (%)	21.2	31.4	26.9	21.8	32.3	27.6	25.7	32.9	29.5
Low-educated (%)	15.8	32.3	24.8	14.3	32.1	24.0	12.3	25.9	19.5
Highly educated (%)	36.0	22.2	28.5	36.9	22.1	28.8	39.7	26.4	32.7
Total emigration rates (%)	5.4	6.2	5.8	4.8	5.6	5.2	5.6	6.0	5.8
Emigration rates of the highly educated (%)	12.8	12.3	12.6	11.8	11.2	11.5	12.0	12.6	12.3

Main destinations in 2005/06

	Total		Recent emigrants	Women	Highly educated	15-24	Total in 2000
Population 15+	Thousands	%	%	%	%	%	Thousands
Germany	189.2	44.0	8.2	47.8	29.6	3.1	128.1
United States	59.9	13.9	7.7	56.1	44.9	4.4	68.1
Switzerland	57.0	13.3	15.8	61.7	23.8	2.8	53.5
Canada	21.0	4.9	2.1	51.4	43.9	3.2	22.1
Australia	17.6	4.1	3.6	47.2	24.8	2.7	18.9
United Kingdom	16.1	3.7	–	63.5	71.8	–	18.9
Italy	15.6	3.6	9.5	69.8	18.0	–	15.7
France	11.6	2.7	12.9	61.9	37.8	6.3	11.6
Netherlands	6.5	1.5	–	45.1	–	–	1.6
Sweden	5.6	1.3	9.8	44.3	26.4	2.4	4.9

Labour market indicators of persons born in Austria living in OECD countries

Population 15-64	2000			2005/06		
	Men	Women	Total	Men	Women	Total
Employment-population ratio (%)	84.3	64.2	73.9	82.8	65.0	73.8
Unemployment rate (%)	2.1	3.1	2.6	3.9	2.6	3.3
Participation rate (%)	86.1	66.2	75.9	86.1	66.7	76.4
Total employed (thousands)	**106.3**	**86.0**	**192.2**	**120.7**	**95.5**	**216.2**
Employment rates of the highly educated (%)	85.2	80.8	83.5	92.5	76.8	85.8
Unemployment rates of the highly educated (%)	1.5	2.8	2.0	1.9	3.0	2.3
Highly educated in low- and medium-skilled jobs (%)	14.2	26.3	18.3	12.7	21.6	15.7
Highly educated employed (thousands)	**45.1**	**25.9**	**71.0**	**55.4**	**34.0**	**89.4**
Legislators, senior officials and managers	11.4	11.0	11.2	19.4	6.1	14.0
Professionals	31.0	15.5	25.4	23.0	18.6	21.2
Life science and health professionals	0.9	1.7	1.2	1.4	1.5	1.4
Teaching professionals	1.8	5.6	3.1	1.3	4.1	2.4
Technicians and associate professionals	18.5	19.2	18.7	20.7	18.3	19.7
Clerks	2.7	20.0	8.9	5.6	24.6	13.3
Service, shop and market sales workers	5.3	22.1	11.3	8.0	24.1	14.5
Skilled agricultural and fishery workers	1.0	1.2	1.1	0.9	1.3	1.1
Craft and related trades workers	22.5	2.7	15.4	14.2	2.1	9.3
Plant and machine operators and assemblers	4.7	1.8	3.7	5.6	0.6	3.5
Elementary occupations	3.0	6.6	4.3	2.1	3.8	2.8

(Left margin label: Distribution of employment by occupation (%), population 15+)

Persons born in Austria and their native-born children, population 15+

Living in:	Europe	United States	Australia
2008	Thousands	Thousands	Thousands
Native-born children	305.4	163.4	22.8
Foreign-born	266.9	93.8	20.9
Total	572.3	257.1	43.7

International students from Austria in OECD countries

Five main destinations	2004	2005	2006	2007	2008	2009
Germany	..	..	..	..	4 508	5 442
United Kingdom	1 308	1 326	1 368	1 430	1 416	1 382
United States	899	924	873	862	887	894
Switzerland	..	..	..	..	712	807
France	495	398	419	424	492	433
Total	3 784	3 744	3 807	3 948	9 008	10 297

Legal migrant flows to the OECD
Thousands

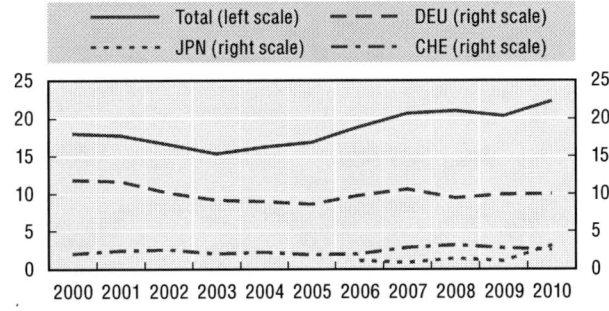

Remittance flows

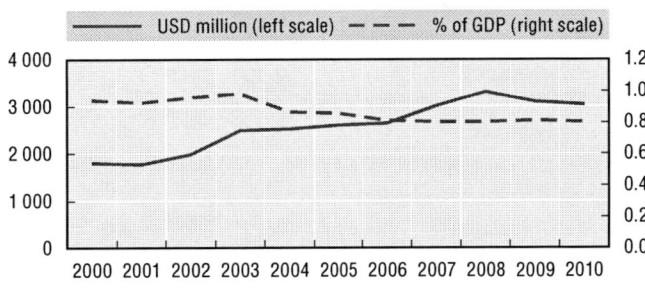

Ten main countries of destination for legal migrants in 2010 (numbers, % of total flows to the country): DEU (10039, 1.5%), JPN (3087, 1.1%), CHE (2579, 2%), GBR (1379, 0.3%), ESP (778, 0.2%), HUN (585, 2.5%), NLD (490, 0%), USA (442, 0%), CZE (385, 1.5%), ITA (343, 0.1%).

Desire to emigrate, 2008-10

	Women	15-24	Highly educated	Total	Regional total
Persons who would move permanently, if they had the opportunity to do so (%)	9	22	9	9	16
Of which: Persons who are planning to move permanently in the next 12 months (%)				..	6
Of which: Persons who have already done some preparations for this move (e.g. visa application) (%)					39

StatLink 🔗 http://dx.doi.org/10.1787/888932673049

		Belgium compared to:	World	Region
Total population 2010 (millions)	10.9	Human Development Index (HDI)	18/187	16/34
Population growth 2010 (%)	0.8	GDP per capita	17/194	12/34
GDP per capita 2010 (current USD)	43 144	Emigration rate	90/203	18/34
GDP growth 2010 (%)	2.3	Emigration rate of the highly educated	102/157	19/34
Poverty rate 2010 (USD PPP 2 a day, in %)	..			

Age structure of the population 0+ (2010): "0-14": 12%; "15-24": 17%; "25-64": 54%; "65+": 17%.
Level of education of the population 15+ (2010): "Low": 21%; "Medium": 55%; "High": 24%.

Emigrant population living in OECD countries

Immigrant population

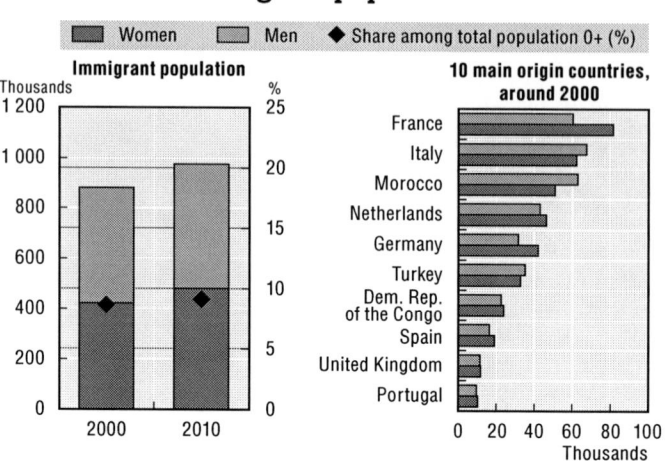

Emigrant population: persons born in Belgium living abroad

	2000						2005/06		
	All destinations			OECD destinations			OECD destinations		
Population 15+	Men	Women	Total	Men	Women	Total	Men	Women	Total
Emigrant population (thousands)	160.1	209.0	369.1	149.3	198.5	347.8	178.4	218.0	396.3
Recent emigrants (thousands)	..	..	..	18.6	17.6	36.2	26.6	23.6	50.1
15-24 (%)	10.6	8.5	9.4	10.3	8.0	8.9	9.2	7.2	8.1
25-64 (%)	71.8	65.3	68.1	71.9	65.4	68.2	74.7	69.5	71.9
65+ (%)	17.6	26.2	22.5	17.8	26.7	22.9	16.0	23.3	20.1
Low-educated (%)	30.5	37.9	34.7	30.9	38.2	35.1	22.3	28.5	25.7
Highly educated (%)	36.4	28.7	32.0	36.1	28.7	31.9	43.1	34.6	38.5
Total emigration rates (%)	3.8	4.6	4.2	3.5	4.4	4.0	4.1	4.7	4.4
Emigration rates of the highly educated (%)	5.9	5.7	5.8	5.5	5.4	5.4	7.0	6.3	6.6

Main destinations in 2005/06

	Total		Recent emigrants	Women	Highly educated	15-24	Total in 2000
Population 15+	Thousands	%	%	%	%	%	Thousands
France	125.5	31.7	17.5	56.6	36.3	8.8	115.3
Italy	42.7	10.8	2.3	59.2	13.8	4.0	41.1
United States	39.3	9.9	12.1	53.8	48.7	12.3	36.9
Netherlands	36.3	9.2	12.8	58.5	28.5	7.1	41.0
Spain	35.1	8.9	33.4	52.6	43.3	10.3	26.1
United Kingdom	22.8	5.7	–	50.6	64.1	–	19.1
Canada	20.5	5.2	5.7	50.8	46.8	4.0	20.3
Germany	18.0	4.5	–	54.3	37.6	–	–
Luxembourg	17.8	4.5	20.5	48.7	47.3	7.2	13.5
Switzerland	12.7	3.2	33.4	53.4	60.2	–	10.1

Labour market indicators of persons born in Belgium living in OECD countries

Population 15-64	2000			2005/06		
	Men	Women	Total	Men	Women	Total
Employment-population ratio (%)	76.4	54.9	64.7	80.8	59.0	69.2
Unemployment rate (%)	7.1	10.0	8.5	5.7	9.5	7.5
Participation rate (%)	82.3	61.0	70.7	85.7	65.2	74.8
Total employed (thousands)	**92.1**	**79.8**	**172.0**	**116.6**	**96.3**	**212.9**
Employment rates of the highly educated (%)	88.0	69.2	78.1	92.1	78.4	85.4
Unemployment rates of the highly educated (%)	3.5	5.7	4.5	3.3	6.1	4.6
Highly educated in low- and medium-skilled jobs (%)	15.7	23.0	19.1	17.0	25.2	20.7
Highly educated employed (thousands)	**40.6**	**35.6**	**76.1**	**58.4**	**46.9**	**105.3**
Legislators, senior officials and managers	16.4	9.3	13.1	16.1	8.9	12.8
Professionals	20.5	17.1	18.9	22.8	19.9	21.5
Life science and health professionals	2.8	2.6	2.7	3.2	4.4	3.7
Teaching professionals	2.4	4.4	3.3	3.3	6.5	4.8
Technicians and associate professionals	16.1	23.8	19.7	17.4	22.4	19.7
Clerks	5.1	17.1	10.7	5.5	16.3	10.4
Service, shop and market sales workers	7.8	17.2	12.2	7.5	16.0	11.4
Skilled agricultural and fishery workers	3.2	2.1	2.6	2.4	2.8	2.6
Craft and related trades workers	15.3	3.0	9.6	13.1	3.3	8.6
Plant and machine operators and assemblers	9.0	2.5	6.0	9.7	2.4	6.4
Elementary occupations	6.6	7.9	7.2	5.5	7.9	6.6

Distribution of employment by occupation (%), population 15+

Persons born in Belgium and their native-born children, population 15+

Living in:	Europe	United States	Australia
2008	Thousands	Thousands	Thousands
Native-born children	485.3	54.2	1.9
Foreign-born	261.5	26.7	6.6
Total	746.7	80.9	8.5

International students from Belgium in OECD countries

Five main destinations	2004	2005	2006	2007	2008	2009
France	2 841	2 623	2 725	2 663	2 763	2 974
United Kingdom	2 418	2 400	2 487	2 560	2 475	2 564
Netherlands	..	1 088	1 065	991	974	974
Germany	..	..	..	..	841	849
United States	823	776	781	719	813	844
Total	7 266	7 868	8 135	8 319	9 098	9 899

Legal migrant flows to the OECD
Thousands

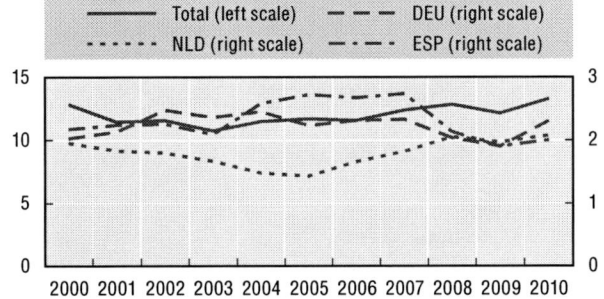

Remittance flows

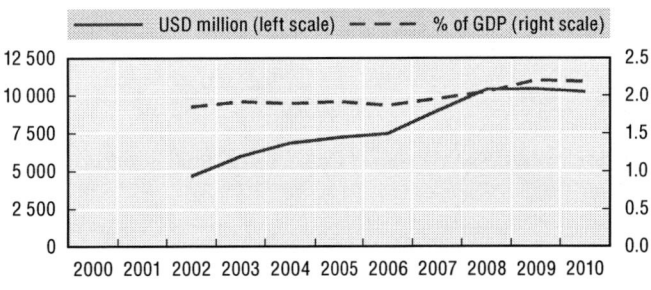

Ten main countries of destination for legal migrants in 2010 (numbers, % of total flows to the country): DEU (2303, 0.3%), NLD (2075, 2.1%), ESP (2005, 0.5%), LUX (1171, 7.5%), CHE (1076, 0.8%), CAN (635, 0.2%), USA (592, 0.1%), GBR (582, 0.1%), JPN (444, 0.2%), ITA (376, 0.1%).

Desire to emigrate, 2008-10

	Women	15-24	Highly educated	Total	Regional total
Persons who would move permanently, if they had the opportunity to do so (%)	16	24	23	19	16
Of which: Persons who are planning to move permanently in the next 12 months (%)				6	6
Of which: Persons who have already done some preparations for this move (*e.g.* visa application) (%)					39

Three main countries of desired destination: France (28%), Spain (19%), Italy (6%).

StatLink http://dx.doi.org/10.1787/888932673068

Total population 2010 (millions)	34.1		Canada compared to:	World	Region
Population growth 2010 (%)	1.1		Human Development Index (HDI)	6/187	7/34
GDP per capita 2010 (current USD)	46 236		GDP per capita	14/194	9/34
GDP growth 2010 (%)	3.2		Emigration rate	94/203	22/34
Poverty rate 2010 (USD PPP 2 a day, in %)	..		Emigration rate of the highly educated	99/157	18/34

Age structure of the population 0+ (2010): "0-14": 13%; "15-24": 16%; "25-64": 56%; "65+": 14%.
Level of education of the population 15+ (2010): "Low": 7%; "Medium": 66%; "High": 27%.

Emigrant population living in OECD countries

Immigrant population

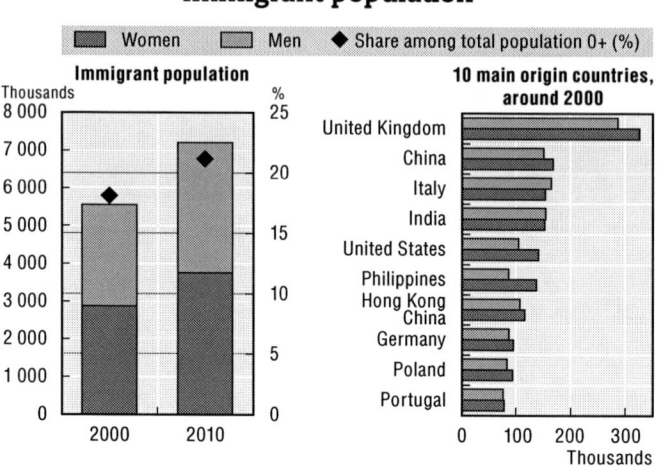

Emigrant population: persons born in Canada living abroad

	2000						2005/06		
	All destinations			OECD destinations			OECD destinations		
Population 15+	Men	Women	Total	Men	Women	Total	Men	Women	Total
Emigrant population (thousands)	488.0	605.7	1 093.6	475.0	593.8	1 068.7	503.6	618.4	1 122.0
Recent emigrants (thousands)	..	..	..	77.1	77.4	154.5	71.1	75.9	147.0
15-24 (%)	10.5	8.9	9.6	10.2	8.6	9.3	10.2	8.6	9.3
25-64 (%)	68.1	62.4	64.9	68.1	62.3	64.9	70.4	65.0	67.4
65+ (%)	21.4	28.7	25.4	21.7	29.0	25.8	19.4	26.4	23.3
Low-educated (%)	18.0	19.1	18.6	17.9	19.0	18.5	13.3	13.5	13.4
Highly educated (%)	44.0	37.2	40.2	43.9	37.1	40.1	50.0	44.6	47.1
Total emigration rates (%)	3.8	4.6	4.2	3.7	4.5	4.1	3.7	4.4	4.1
Emigration rates of the highly educated (%)	6.3	6.4	6.3	6.1	6.3	6.2	6.8	7.0	6.9

Main destinations in 2005/06

	Total		Recent emigrants	Women	Highly educated	15-24	Total in 2000
Population 15+	Thousands	%	%	%	%	%	Thousands
United States	907.9	80.9	12.3	55.4	45.9	8.7	868.8
United Kingdom	58.2	5.2	15.7	56.5	65.9	10.8	66.9
Australia	28.9	2.6	22.9	52.7	56.5	11.8	24.7
Italy	19.9	1.8	–	62.3	21.1	–	22.6
France	19.3	1.7	27.6	55.4	56.1	14.7	16.2
Germany	12.8	1.1	..	42.4	51.1	–	–
Switzerland	8.7	0.8	49.2	59.8	50.7	16.3	6.6
New Zealand	8.2	0.7	27.0	56.1	50.8	13.1	6.9
Netherlands	7.5	0.7	–	56.8	36.1	–	1.5
Japan	7.1	0.6	..	32.4	90.6	14.9	6.6

Labour market indicators of persons born in Canada living in OECD countries

Population 15-64	2000			2005/06		
	Men	Women	Total	Men	Women	Total
Employment-population ratio (%)	84.4	66.5	74.9	84.2	67.4	75.3
Unemployment rate (%)	3.8	4.5	4.1	4.6	4.8	4.7
Participation rate (%)	87.7	69.7	78.1	88.3	70.8	79.1
Total employed (thousands)	**306.8**	**274.8**	**581.6**	**331.3**	**298.4**	**629.7**
Employment rates of the highly educated (%)	91.9	74.3	82.8	94.8	77.2	85.6
Unemployment rates of the highly educated (%)	2.1	3.0	2.5	3.2	3.8	3.5
Highly educated in low- and medium-skilled jobs (%)	22.9	24.0	23.4	22.2	23.8	23.0
Highly educated employed (thousands)	**159.8**	**138.4**	**298.2**	**193.9**	**172.6**	**366.5**
Legislators, senior officials and managers	19.2	11.6	15.4	21.9	13.5	17.8
Professionals	25.8	25.5	25.7	24.5	28.8	26.6
Life science and health professionals	2.1	3.3	2.7	1.3	2.6	1.9
Teaching professionals	5.5	9.6	7.5	5.3	12.7	8.9
Technicians and associate professionals	16.0	20.3	18.1	23.2	25.7	24.4
Clerks	5.1	19.3	12.2	5.0	15.1	9.9
Service, shop and market sales workers	8.7	14.9	11.8	7.1	9.0	8.0
Skilled agricultural and fishery workers	1.4	0.7	1.1	1.8	1.6	1.7
Craft and related trades workers	11.2	1.6	6.4	7.8	1.9	4.9
Plant and machine operators and assemblers	5.8	1.3	3.6	4.0	1.4	2.7
Elementary occupations	6.7	4.8	5.8	4.1	3.1	3.6

Distribution of employment by occupation (%), population 15+

Persons born in Canada and their native-born children, population 15+

Living in:	Europe	United States	Australia
2008	Thousands	Thousands	Thousands
Native-born children	112.8	948.9	10.6
Foreign-born	69.6	666.2	17.3
Total	182.3	1 615.1	27.9

International students from Canada in OECD countries

Five main destinations	2004	2005	2006	2007	2008	2009
United States	27 017	29 391	29 203	28 905	29 082	29 209
United Kingdom	3 890	4 192	4 640	5 010	5 003	5 350
Australia	3 100	3 436	3 785	4 039	4 321	4 390
France	1 267	1 210	1 293	1 302	1 378	1 373
Ireland	..	..	..	..	575	605
Total	36 494	39 651	40 515	40 878	42 616	43 667

Legal migrant flows to the OECD
Thousands

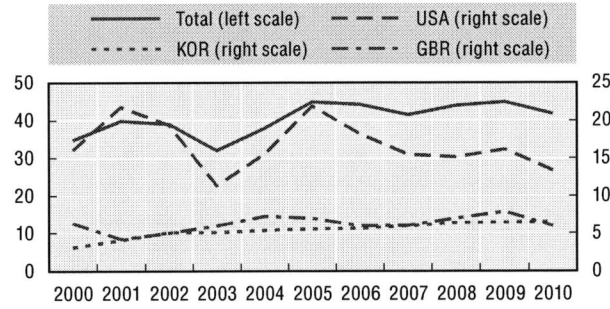

Ten main countries of destination for legal migrants in 2010 (numbers, % of total flows to the country): USA (13328, 1.3%), KOR (6505, 2.2%), GBR (6000, 1.3%), DEU (2891, 0.4%), JPN (2696, 0.9%), AUS (1938, 0.9%), CHE (1080, 0.7%), FRA (1002, 0.7%), NLD (806, 0.8%), MEX (748, 2.9%).

Desire to emigrate, 2008-10

	Women	15-24	Highly educated	Total	Regional total
Persons who would move permanently, if they had the opportunity to do so (%)	9	16	10	10	16
Of which: Persons who are planning to move permanently in the next 12 months (%)				..	6
Of which: Persons who have already done some preparations for this move (*e.g.* visa application) (%)					39

StatLink ⟨⟩ http://dx.doi.org/10.1787/888932673087

Total population 2010 (millions)	17.1
Population growth 2010 (%)	0.9
GDP per capita 2010 (current USD)	12 431
GDP growth 2010 (%)	5.2
Poverty rate 2009 (USD PPP 2 a day, in %)	0.0

Chile compared to:	World	Region
Human Development Index (HDI)	43/187	32/34
GDP per capita	54/194	31/34
Emigration rate	120/203	29/34
Emigration rate of the highly educated	137/157	29/34

Age structure of the population 0+ (2010): "0-14": 17%; "15-24": 22%; "25-64": 51%; "65+": 9%.
Level of education of the population 15+ (2010): "Low": 25%; "Medium": 48%; "High": 27%.

Emigrant population living in OECD countries

Immigrant population

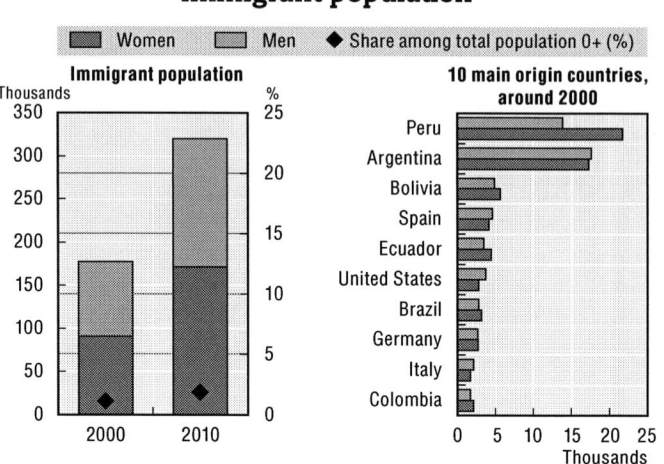

Emigrant population: persons born in Chile living abroad

	2000						2005/06		
	All destinations			OECD destinations			OECD destinations		
Population 15+	Men	Women	Total	Men	Women	Total	Men	Women	Total
Emigrant population (thousands)	229.5	241.5	471.0	101.3	108.4	209.7	128.9	144.9	273.8
Recent emigrants (thousands)	..	..	..	13.5	15.0	28.5	25.7	29.1	54.7
15-24 (%)	10.2	9.2	9.7	14.2	12.2	13.2	13.3	10.5	11.8
25-64 (%)	79.2	78.1	78.6	80.2	77.9	79.0	79.5	76.9	78.2
65+ (%)	10.7	12.7	11.7	5.6	9.9	7.9	7.2	12.5	10.0
Low-educated (%)	47.7	48.6	48.1	24.5	27.2	25.9	20.2	20.7	20.5
Highly educated (%)	20.5	18.9	19.7	31.7	30.3	31.0	36.1	36.2	36.2
Total emigration rates (%)	4.0	4.1	4.1	1.8	1.9	1.8	2.1	2.3	2.2
Emigration rates of the highly educated (%)	3.9	3.9	3.9	2.6	2.8	2.7	3.0	3.5	3.3

Main destinations in 2005/06

	Total		Recent emigrants	Women	Highly educated	15-24	Total in 2000
Population 15+	Thousands	%	%	%	%	%	Thousands
United States	87.0	31.8	14.6	52.2	40.1	10.8	75.8
Spain	55.0	20.1	75.2	53.6	34.8	15.5	15.5
Sweden	27.4	10.0	9.8	49.9	18.6	11.9	26.2
Canada	26.4	9.6	6.9	51.3	45.1	8.2	24.2
Australia	22.7	8.3	4.0	52.4	28.3	8.4	22.5
France	12.0	4.4	13.3	52.0	43.7	14.5	9.9
Italy	8.0	2.9	13.4	65.1	15.7	17.0	7.9
Norway	5.6	2.1	10.2	46.9	22.4	18.5	5.5
Switzerland	5.3	1.9	23.3	58.4	34.7	–	4.9
United Kingdom	–	–	–	–	–	–	4.8

Labour market indicators of persons born in Chile living in OECD countries

Population 15-64	2000			2005/06		
	Men	Women	Total	Men	Women	Total
Employment-population ratio (%)	75.4	57.2	66.2	79.2	61.4	70.0
Unemployment rate (%)	8.1	10.0	8.9	8.1	12.3	10.0
Participation rate (%)	82.0	63.6	72.7	86.2	70.0	77.8
Total employed (thousands)	**60.6**	**47.2**	**107.8**	**82.3**	**68.6**	**151.0**
Employment rates of the highly educated (%)	82.8	68.7	75.7	92.5	78.5	85.1
Unemployment rates of the highly educated (%)	5.7	6.7	6.2	7.4	9.3	8.3
Highly educated in low- and medium-skilled jobs (%)	34.8	36.4	35.5	40.8	35.8	38.4
Highly educated employed (thousands)	**22.9**	**19.1**	**42.0**	**34.0**	**31.6**	**65.6**
Legislators, senior officials and managers	7.0	4.7	6.0	6.6	4.4	5.6
Professionals	13.6	13.8	13.7	11.6	15.7	13.5
Life science and health professionals	1.2	2.9	2.0	0.8	5.2	2.9
Teaching professionals	3.1	4.5	3.7	2.2	4.1	3.1
Technicians and associate professionals	10.8	13.8	12.2	9.3	13.9	11.5
Clerks	6.1	14.6	10.0	4.6	12.0	8.1
Service, shop and market sales workers	10.9	26.4	18.0	11.7	25.5	18.1
Skilled agricultural and fishery workers	0.7	0.2	0.5	1.1	0.2	0.7
Craft and related trades workers	19.5	2.4	11.7	25.6	2.5	14.8
Plant and machine operators and assemblers	13.8	4.5	9.6	14.8	2.4	9.0
Elementary occupations	17.6	19.4	18.4	14.5	23.3	18.6

Distribution of employment by occupation (%), population 15+

Persons born in Chile and their native-born children, population 15+

Living in:	Europe	United States	Australia
2008	Thousands	Thousands	Thousands
Native-born children	31.4	29.6	8.8
Foreign-born	175.4	66.2	27.5
Total	206.8	95.8	36.3

International students from Chile in OECD countries

Five main destinations	2004	2005	2006	2007	2008	2009
United States	1 612	3 436	1 605	1 605	1 687	1 921
Spain	427	502	512	134	748	1 434
France	512	531	613	650	738	761
Germany	..	..	..	..	585	626
United Kingdom	295	312	360	380	369	393
Total	3 419	5 233	3 727	3 529	5 017	6 251

Legal migrant flows to the OECD
Thousands

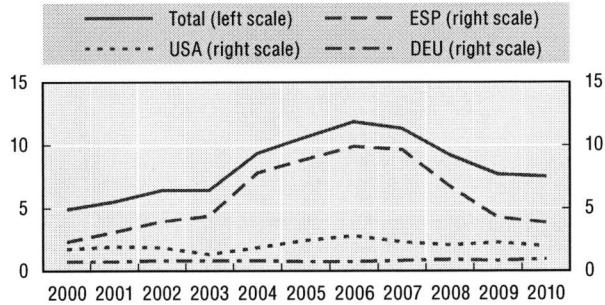

Remittance flows

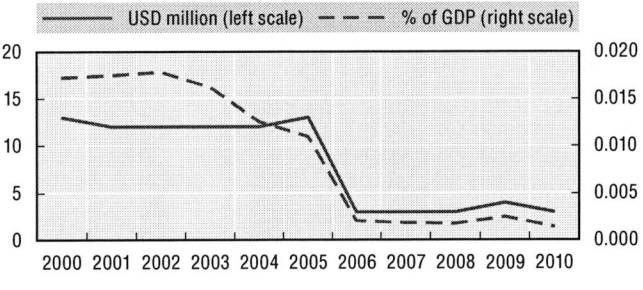

Ten main countries of destination for legal migrants in 2010 (numbers, % of total flows to the country): ESP (3829, 0.9%), USA (1950, 0.2%), DEU (931, 0.1%), MEX (426, 1.6%), SWE (379, 0.5%), CAN (360, 0.1%), ITA (332, 0.2%), FRA (258, 0.2%), AUS (240, 0.1%), CHE (230, 0.2%).

Desire to emigrate, 2008-10

	Women	15-24	Highly educated	Total	Regional total
Persons who would move permanently, if they had the opportunity to do so (%)	22	44	35	26	16
Of which: Persons who are planning to move permanently in the next 12 months (%)				9	6
Of which: Persons who have already done some preparations for this move (*e.g.* visa application) (%)					39

Three main countries of desired destination: Spain (26%), United States (19%), Australia (7%).

StatLink ᴬᴵˢᴾ *http://dx.doi.org/10.1787/888932673106*

Total population 2010 (millions)	10.5		Czech Republic compared to:	World	Region
Population growth 2010 (%)	0.4		Human Development Index (HDI)	27/187	24/34
GDP per capita 2010 (current USD)	18 245		GDP per capita	41/194	27/34
GDP growth 2010 (%)	2.3		Emigration rate	100/203	25/34
Poverty rate 2010 (USD PPP 2 a day, in %)	..		Emigration rate of the highly educated	81/157	11/34

Age structure of the population 0+ (2010): "0-14": 13%; "15-24": 14%; "25-64": 58%; "65+": 15%.
Level of education of the population 15+ (2010): "Low": 14%; "Medium": 75%; "High": 11%.

Emigrant population living in OECD countries

Immigrant population

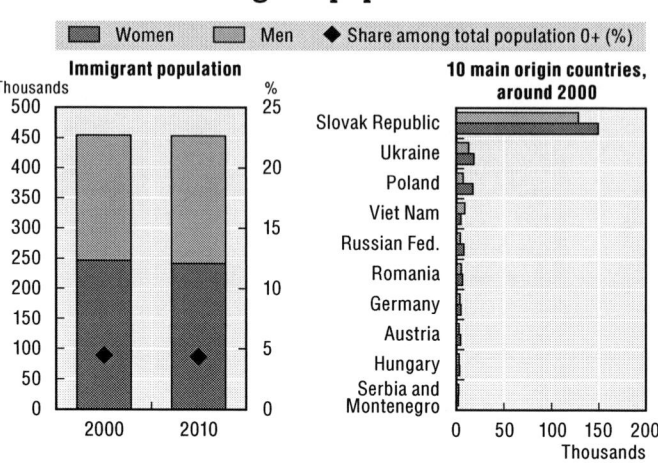

Emigrant population: persons born in the Czech Republic living abroad

	2000						2005/06		
	All destinations			OECD destinations			OECD destinations		
Population 15+	Men	Women	Total	Men	Women	Total	Men	Women	Total
Emigrant population (thousands)	117.3	163.9	281.1	71.5	109.3	180.8	129.9	179.7	309.6
Recent emigrants (thousands)	..	..	..	2.7	9.5	12.2	19.7	23.5	43.1
15-24 (%)	11.0	9.9	10.3	4.9	6.5	5.9	7.4	6.5	6.9
25-64 (%)	66.4	66.6	66.5	66.5	66.3	66.4	61.7	63.6	62.8
65+ (%)	22.6	23.5	23.1	28.7	27.2	27.8	30.9	29.9	30.3
Low-educated (%)	16.6	28.9	23.8	15.4	29.4	23.9	14.0	23.8	19.7
Highly educated (%)	30.9	20.6	24.9	35.6	22.8	27.9	38.9	27.6	32.3
Total emigration rates (%)	2.8	3.6	3.2	1.7	2.4	2.1	3.0	3.8	3.4
Emigration rates of the highly educated (%)	6.3	8.6	7.2	4.5	6.5	5.3	8.6	10.4	9.4

Main destinations in 2005/06

	Total		Recent emigrants	Women	Highly educated	15-24	Total in 2000
Population 15+	Thousands	%	%	%	%	%	Thousands
Germany	98.1	31.7	3.0	59.7	25.2	–	44.1
Austria	49.1	15.8	4.0	61.9	20.0	–	53.9
United States	30.7	9.9	18.3	54.8	48.0	7.2	–
United Kingdom	27.1	8.8	74.2	46.6	39.5	32.2	11.5
Canada	22.0	7.1	4.3	51.1	61.0	3.6	16.0
Switzerland	15.7	5.1	21.3	62.9	40.6	–	10.8
Israel	10.0	3.2	2.8	53.8	30.0	3.0	13.0
France	8.3	2.7	19.0	64.9	35.7	8.6	3.4
Italy	7.6	2.4	14.2	84.5	16.5	–	6.7
Australia	7.1	2.3	11.8	50.7	42.6	3.8	6.7

Labour market indicators of persons born in the Czech Republic living in OECD countries

Population 15-64	2000			2005/06		
	Men	Women	Total	Men	Women	Total
Employment-population ratio (%)	79.3	60.0	67.9	79.2	58.8	67.3
Unemployment rate (%)	5.6	6.1	5.8	4.0	9.0	6.6
Participation rate (%)	84.0	63.9	72.1	82.5	64.6	72.0
Total employed (thousands)	**38.8**	**42.1**	**80.9**	**68.5**	**71.5**	**140.0**
Employment rates of the highly educated (%)	88.6	77.8	83.0	93.2	72.7	82.5
Unemployment rates of the highly educated (%)	3.2	3.7	3.5	2.3	4.1	3.1
Highly educated in low- and medium-skilled jobs (%)	22.8	31.8	27.1	30.8	34.9	32.6
Highly educated employed (thousands)	**16.5**	**15.5**	**31.9**	**32.2**	**26.9**	**59.1**
Legislators, senior officials and managers	13.9	7.3	10.5	8.7	4.3	6.4
Professionals	20.7	15.4	18.0	21.1	12.4	16.5
Life science and health professionals	3.6	3.1	3.3	3.7	2.5	3.1
Teaching professionals	3.2	4.0	3.6	2.2	2.6	2.4
Technicians and associate professionals	15.5	20.7	18.2	11.8	26.1	19.3
Clerks	4.7	17.3	11.3	3.7	18.0	11.2
Service, shop and market sales workers	8.0	24.9	16.8	6.7	19.2	13.3
Skilled agricultural and fishery workers	1.0	0.7	0.9	1.3	3.9	2.7
Craft and related trades workers	20.5	2.8	11.3	18.4	3.2	10.4
Plant and machine operators and assemblers	7.9	1.8	4.7	15.9	2.8	9.0
Elementary occupations	7.8	9.2	8.5	11.5	10.0	10.7

Distribution of employment by occupation (%), population 15+

Persons born in the Czech Republic and their native-born children, population 15+

Living in:	Europe	United States	Australia
2008	Thousands	Thousands	Thousands
Native-born children	214.2	36.4	11.9
Foreign-born	259.8	42.0	24.2
Total	474.1	78.4	36.2

International students from the Czech Republic in OECD countries

Five main destinations	2004	2005	2006	2007	2008	2009
Slovak Republic	428	426	467	474	2 584	3 280
Germany	..	..	..	..	1 646	1 500
United Kingdom	359	606	875	1 152	1 301	1 316
United States	1 052	942	960	934	923	910
France	662	654	694	752	751	751
Total	3 108	3 278	3 702	3 990	7 917	8 675

Legal migrant flows to the OECD
Thousands

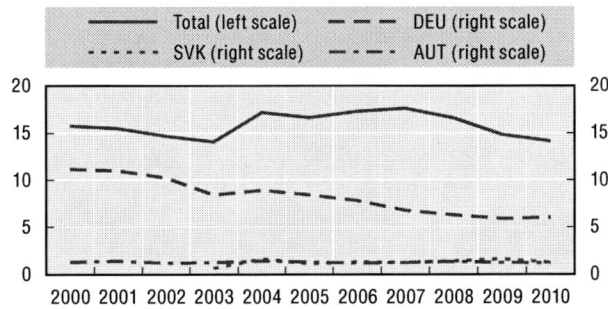

Remittance flows

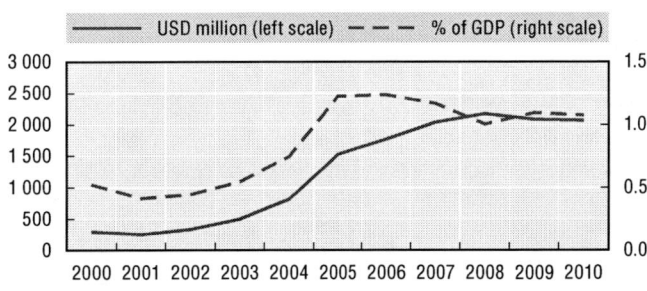

Ten main countries of destination for legal migrants in 2010 (numbers, % of total flows to the country): DEU (6063, 0.9%), SVK (1214, 9.6%), AUT (1170, 1.2%), ESP (803, 0.2%), NLD (701, 0.7%), CHE (529, 0.4%), BEL (525, 0.2%), JPN (512, 0.2%), ITA (496, 0.1%), NOR (238, 0.4%).

Desire to emigrate, 2008-10

	Women	15-24	Highly educated	Total	Regional total
Persons who would move permanently, if they had the opportunity to do so (%)	10	23	13	10	16
Of which: Persons who are planning to move permanently in the next 12 months (%)				..	6
Of which: Persons who have already done some preparations for this move (*e.g.* visa application) (%)					39

StatLink http://dx.doi.org/10.1787/888932673125

		Denmark compared to:	World	Region
Total population 2010 (millions)	5.5			
Population growth 2010 (%)	0.4	Human Development Index (HDI)	16/187	14/34
GDP per capita 2010 (current USD)	55 891	GDP per capita	8/194	4/34
GDP growth 2010 (%)	1.7	Emigration rate	96/203	24/34
Poverty rate 2010 (USD PPP 2 a day, in %)	..	Emigration rate of the highly educated	88/157	13/34

Age structure of the population 0+ (2010): "0-14": 12%; "15-24": 18%; "25-64": 53%; "65+": 16%.
Level of education of the population 15+ (2010): "Low": 41%; "Medium": 38%; "High": 21%.

Emigrant population living in OECD countries

Immigrant population

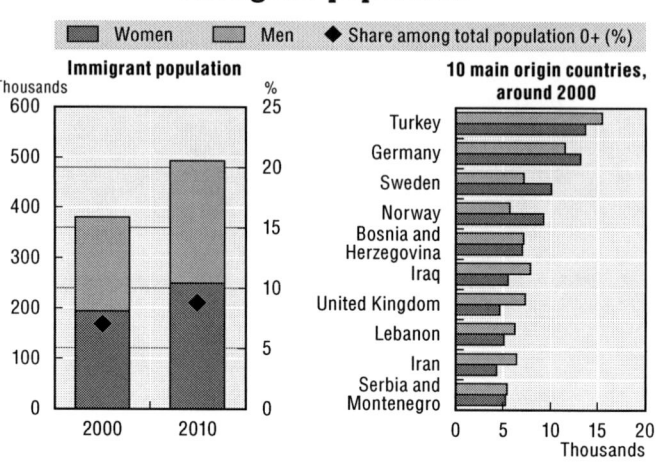

Emigrant population: persons born in Denmark living abroad

	2000						2005/06		
	All destinations			OECD destinations			OECD destinations		
Population 15+	Men	Women	Total	Men	Women	Total	Men	Women	Total
Emigrant population (thousands)	79.3	87.8	167.1	74.7	83.4	158.1	86.3	97.2	183.5
Recent emigrants (thousands)	..	..	..	12.7	10.6	23.2	16.5	13.7	30.1
15-24 (%)	7.5	8.3	8.0	6.9	7.8	7.4	5.4	6.4	5.9
25-64 (%)	70.3	69.6	70.0	70.5	69.8	70.1	69.7	67.5	68.5
65+ (%)	22.2	22.0	22.1	22.6	22.4	22.5	24.9	26.1	25.5
Low-educated (%)	22.6	21.9	22.2	22.4	21.6	22.0	17.9	15.7	16.7
Highly educated (%)	36.9	35.4	36.1	37.2	35.9	36.5	42.6	40.7	41.6
Total emigration rates (%)	3.6	3.8	3.7	3.4	3.6	3.5	3.8	4.2	4.0
Emigration rates of the highly educated (%)	7.0	8.0	7.5	6.7	7.7	7.2	7.4	8.7	8.0

Main destinations in 2005/06

	Total		Recent emigrants	Women	Highly educated	15-24	Total in 2000
Population 15+	Thousands	%	%	%	%	%	Thousands
Sweden	41.9	22.9	28.0	46.4	29.0	5.7	33.1
United States	31.2	17.0	16.2	54.9	54.1	5.5	32.4
Norway	21.6	11.7	15.5	50.5	32.1	6.9	21.6
Canada	17.6	9.6	1.5	47.3	37.0	1.2	18.1
United Kingdom	16.8	9.1	–	57.2	60.3	–	17.0
Germany	14.6	8.0	–	55.9	37.1	–	–
Australia	8.6	4.7	9.0	46.9	34.6	4.3	8.6
France	6.0	3.2	29.1	61.4	55.6	5.7	5.3
Switzerland	5.2	2.8	29.5	63.7	45.8	–	3.9
Netherlands	2.9	1.6	–	69.1	–	–	–

Labour market indicators of persons born in Denmark living in OECD countries

Population 15-64	2000			2005/06		
	Men	Women	Total	Men	Women	Total
Employment-population ratio (%)	84.0	64.9	73.4	89.9	67.3	77.3
Unemployment rate (%)	4.6	4.9	4.8	2.4	4.0	3.2
Participation rate (%)	88.0	68.3	77.1	92.1	70.1	79.8
Total employed (thousands)	**32.4**	**31.2**	**63.6**	**39.4**	**37.3**	**76.7**
Employment rates of the highly educated (%)	89.1	71.1	79.4	96.1	78.8	87.0
Unemployment rates of the highly educated (%)	3.0	4.2	3.5	2.0	4.6	3.2
Highly educated in low- and medium-skilled jobs (%)	19.8	27.8	23.6	17.5	23.4	20.3
Highly educated employed (thousands)	**16.2**	**15.0**	**31.2**	**22.0**	**19.5**	**41.6**
Legislators, senior officials and managers	20.0	9.8	15.0	26.1	12.6	19.5
Professionals	19.6	18.3	19.0	20.5	24.4	22.4
Life science and health professionals	3.5	4.0	3.7	2.7	2.9	2.8
Teaching professionals	3.0	5.2	4.1	4.5	7.1	5.8
Technicians and associate professionals	14.6	20.8	17.6	13.1	20.5	16.7
Clerks	4.5	17.8	11.0	4.2	15.3	9.6
Service, shop and market sales workers	6.6	22.2	14.2	5.9	17.2	11.4
Skilled agricultural and fishery workers	2.5	0.9	1.7	1.7	0.9	1.3
Craft and related trades workers	15.9	1.8	9.0	13.8	2.1	8.1
Plant and machine operators and assemblers	10.9	2.5	6.8	9.5	2.0	5.8
Elementary occupations	5.3	6.0	5.7	5.2	5.2	5.2

Distribution of employment by occupation (%), population 15+

Persons born in Denmark and their native-born children, population 15+

Living in:	Europe	United States	Australia
2008	Thousands	Thousands	Thousands
Native-born children	91.3	27.3	7.6
Foreign-born	95.2	26.5	9.5
Total	186.5	53.8	17.1

International students from Denmark in OECD countries

Five main destinations	2004	2005	2006	2007	2008	2009
United Kingdom	1 662	1 661	1 603	1 567	1 516	1 526
United States	859	926	932	984	899	983
Germany	..	..	..	..	354	333
Sweden	176	170	149	143	161	222
Australia	108	132	125	140	145	188
Total	3 475	3 411	3 459	3 367	3 749	4 026

Legal migrant flows to the OECD
Thousands

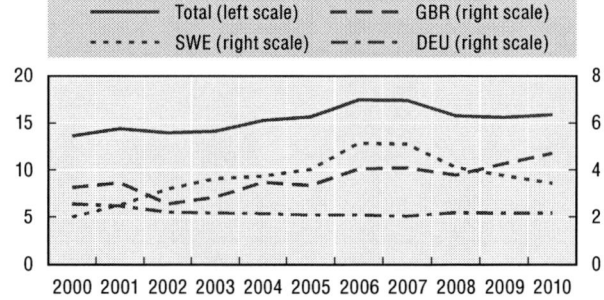

Remittance flows

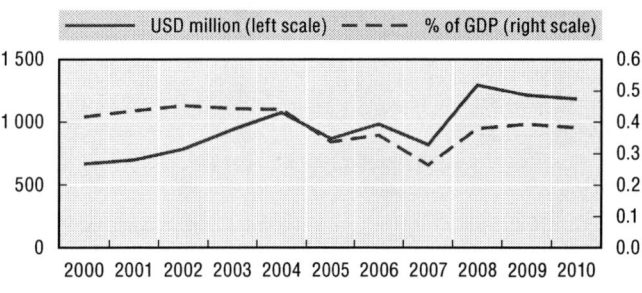

Ten main countries of destination for legal migrants in 2010 (numbers, % of total flows to the country): GBR (4709, 1%), SWE (3437, 4.5%), DEU (2171, 0.3%), NOR (1373, 2.1%), ESP (749, 0.2%), CHE (572, 0.4%), USA (518, 0.4%), NLD (394, 0.4%), JPN (263, 0.1%), BEL (258, 0.3%).

Desire to emigrate, 2008-10

	Women	15-24	Highly educated	Total	Regional total
Persons who would move permanently, if they had the opportunity to do so (%)	13	27	19	15	16
Of which: Persons who are planning to move permanently in the next 12 months (%)				2	6
Of which: Persons who have already done some preparations for this move (*e.g.* visa application) (%)					39

Three main countries of desired destination: United States (13%), Spain (10%), Sweden (9%).

StatLink http://dx.doi.org/10.1787/888932673144

Total population 2010 (millions)	1.3	**Estonia compared to:**	**World**	**Region**
Population growth 2010 (%)	0.0	Human Development Index (HDI)	34/187	27/34
GDP per capita 2010 (current USD)	14 345	GDP per capita	48/194	29/34
GDP growth 2010 (%)	3.1	Emigration rate	91/203	19/34
Poverty rate 2004 (USD PPP 2 a day, in %)	1.5	Emigration rate of the highly educated	119/157	25/34

Age structure of the population 0+ (2010): "0-14": 14%; "15-24": 15%; "25-64": 54%; "65+": 17%.
Level of education of the population 15+ (2010): "Low": 6%; "Medium": 67%; "High": 27%.

Emigrant population living in OECD countries

Immigrant population

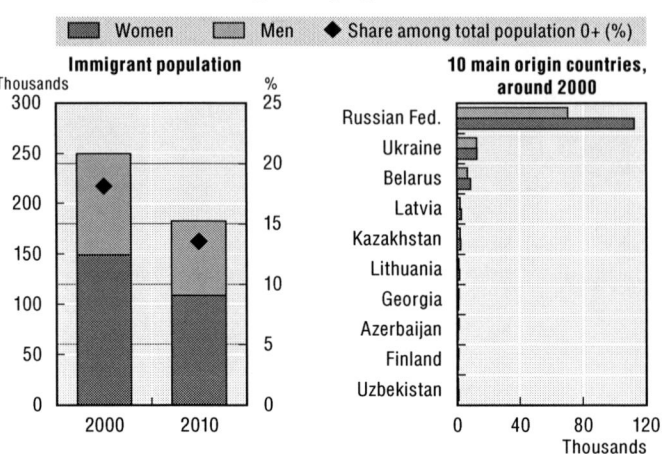

Emigrant population: persons born in Estonia living abroad

	2000						2005/06		
	All destinations			OECD destinations			OECD destinations		
Population 15+	Men	Women	Total	Men	Women	Total	Men	Women	Total
Emigrant population (thousands)	52.3	62.9	115.2	15.1	21.9	37.0	20.8	31.4	52.2
Recent emigrants (thousands)	..	..	..	1.3	3.2	4.5	6.7	8.5	15.2
15-24 (%)	20.5	17.6	18.9	13.3	12.4	12.8	19.9	15.1	17.0
25-64 (%)	65.7	65.2	65.4	46.7	47.8	47.4	48.9	54.9	52.5
65+ (%)	13.8	17.2	15.7	40.0	39.7	39.8	31.1	30.0	30.5
Low-educated (%)	20.8	18.3	19.4	28.7	27.6	28.0	29.8	21.1	24.6
Highly educated (%)	31.2	32.7	32.0	33.5	32.9	33.1	34.5	35.9	35.3
Total emigration rates (%)	9.4	9.3	9.3	2.9	3.4	3.2	3.9	4.8	4.4
Emigration rates of the highly educated (%)	13.4	10.6	11.7	4.4	3.8	4.1	5.9	5.4	5.6

Main destinations in 2005/06

	Total		Recent emigrants	Women	Highly educated	15-24	Total in 2000
Population 15+	Thousands	%	%	%	%	%	Thousands
Finland	12.0	23.0	45.3	54.4	12.8	22.8	6.2
United States	9.5	18.3	13.6	61.3	46.9	16.2	8.7
Sweden	9.4	18.0	30.4	60.1	39.1	7.3	6.2
Canada	5.3	10.2	4.1	58.5	45.8	6.0	6.3
United Kingdom	–	–	–	–	–	–	1.8
Ireland	2.2	4.2	92.8	51.1	25.0	37.8	0.5
Australia	1.9	3.7	5.0	56.2	32.8	2.3	2.2
Germany	–	–	..	–	–	–	1.0
Israel	1.8	3.4	14.7	48.5	55.4	28.3	1.0
Denmark	0.7	1.3	53.0	75.1	36.4	32.8	0.5

Labour market indicators of persons born in Estonia living in OECD countries

Population 15-64	2000			2005/06		
	Men	Women	Total	Men	Women	Total
Employment-population ratio (%)	68.1	55.9	61.1	77.6	69.2	72.9
Unemployment rate (%)	11.2	12.9	12.1	6.6	11.9	9.5
Participation rate (%)	76.7	64.2	69.5	83.1	78.6	80.5
Total employed (thousands)	**5.1**	**5.7**	**10.7**	**9.5**	**11.0**	**20.5**
Employment rates of the highly educated (%)	82.7	64.0	71.4	82.0	86.2	84.6
Unemployment rates of the highly educated (%)	6.8	8.3	7.6	3.6	12.6	9.3
Highly educated in low- and medium-skilled jobs (%)	..	..	..	44.0	42.1	42.8
Highly educated employed (thousands)	**2.1**	**2.4**	**4.5**	**3.1**	**5.0**	**8.1**
Legislators, senior officials and managers	9.3	4.4	6.6	5.7	2.9	4.1
Professionals	19.6	18.3	18.9	10.5	10.9	10.7
Life science and health professionals	2.9	2.6	2.7	1.8	2.9	2.4
Teaching professionals	4.8	6.8	6.0	1.6	3.4	2.6
Technicians and associate professionals	12.6	14.2	13.5	4.9	18.0	12.2
Clerks	4.2	14.0	9.6	2.6	13.4	8.6
Service, shop and market sales workers	6.8	26.1	17.4	12.8	21.2	17.5
Skilled agricultural and fishery workers	2.5	1.4	1.9	0.9	2.6	1.8
Craft and related trades workers	20.5	2.2	10.4	22.6	4.0	12.2
Plant and machine operators and assemblers	14.2	4.5	8.9	24.0	5.9	13.8
Elementary occupations	10.4	14.9	12.9	16.1	19.6	18.1

Distribution of employment by occupation (%), population 15+

Persons born in Estonia and their native-born children, population 15+

Living in:	Europe	United States	Australia
2008	Thousands	Thousands	Thousands
Native-born children	25.2	..	3.3
Foreign-born	16.2	..	3.8
Total	41.4	..	7.1

International students from Estonia in OECD countries

Five main destinations	2004	2005	2006	2007	2008	2009
United Kingdom	103	187	362	533	658	839
Germany	..	..	..	..	579	540
United States	271	296	332	245	245	266
Denmark	24	20	22	32	58	157
Sweden	26	38	25	27	92	114
Total	696	898	1 065	1 129	1 966	2 249

Legal migrant flows to the OECD
Thousands

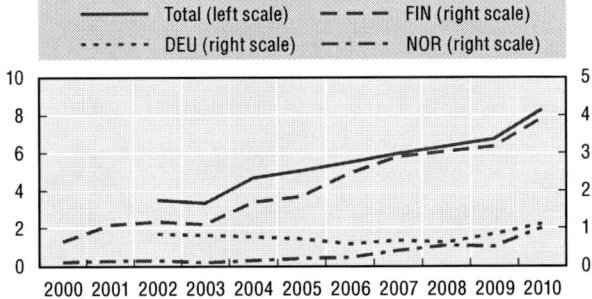

Remittance flows

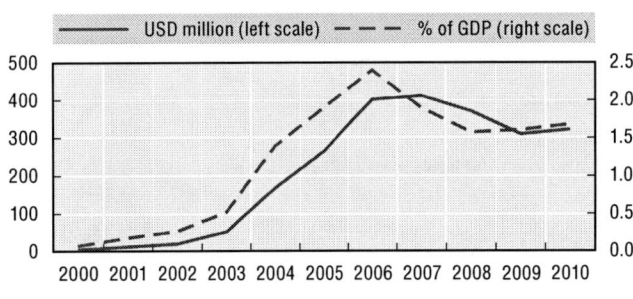

Ten main countries of destination for legal migrants in 2010 (numbers, % of total flows to the country): FIN (3909, 21.9%), DEU (1110, 0.2%), NOR (1008, 1.6%), SWE (491, 0.6%), NLD (312, 0.3%), USA (260, 0%), ESP (241, 0.6%), DNK (190, 0.6%), ITA (124, 0%), BEL (116, 0.1%).

Desire to emigrate, 2008-10

	Women	15-24	Highly educated	Total	Regional total
Persons who would move permanently, if they had the opportunity to do so (%)	22	41	20	21	16
Of which: Persons who are planning to move permanently in the next 12 months (%)				..	6
Of which: Persons who have already done some preparations for this move (*e.g.* visa application) (%)					39

StatLink http://dx.doi.org/10.1787/888932673163

Total population 2010 (millions)	5.4	Finland compared to:	World	Region
Population growth 2010 (%)	0.5	Human Development Index (HDI)	22/187	20/34
GDP per capita 2010 (current USD)	44 512	GDP per capita	16/194	11/34
GDP growth 2010 (%)	3.6	Emigration rate	75/203	12/34
Poverty rate 2010 (USD PPP 2 a day, in %)	..	Emigration rate of the highly educated	107/157	22/34

Age structure of the population 0+ (2010): "0-14": 12%; "15-24": 17%; "25-64": 54%; "65+": 17%.
Level of education of the population 15+ (2010): "Low": 33%; "Medium": 43%; "High": 25%.

Emigrant population living in OECD countries

Immigrant population

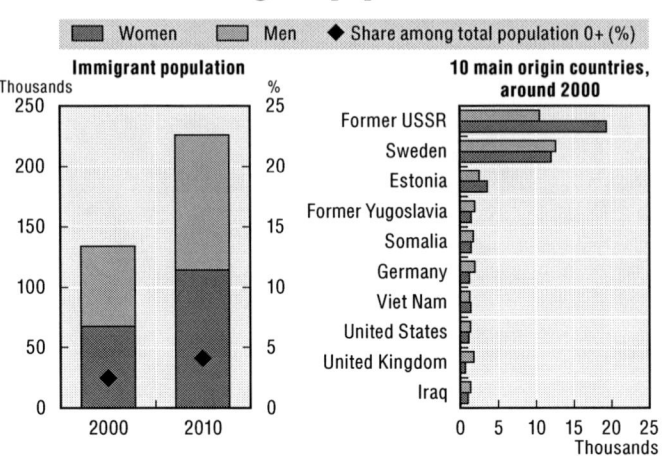

Emigrant population: persons born in Finland living abroad

	2000						2005/06		
	All destinations			OECD destinations			OECD destinations		
Population 15+	Men	Women	Total	Men	Women	Total	Men	Women	Total
Emigrant population (thousands)	106.2	156.5	262.7	103.2	153.0	256.2	104.2	166.5	270.7
Recent emigrants (thousands)	..	..	..	10.1	17.3	27.4	9.4	14.1	23.5
15-24 (%)	3.8	4.7	4.4	3.6	4.6	4.2	2.9	2.9	2.9
25-64 (%)	80.2	76.9	78.2	80.2	77.1	78.3	71.2	68.5	69.5
65+ (%)	16.0	18.3	17.4	16.1	18.4	17.5	25.9	28.6	27.5
Low-educated (%)	35.4	28.6	31.3	35.8	28.7	31.5	31.2	23.7	26.7
Highly educated (%)	19.4	28.3	24.7	18.8	28.1	24.4	22.2	33.2	28.9
Total emigration rates (%)	4.9	6.7	5.8	4.8	6.5	5.7	4.7	6.9	5.9
Emigration rates of the highly educated (%)	6.8	16.3	11.3	6.4	15.9	10.9	4.1	7.3	5.9

Main destinations in 2005/06

	Total		Recent emigrants	Women	Highly educated	15-24	Total in 2000
Population 15+	Thousands	%	%	%	%	%	Thousands
Sweden	179.3	66.2	5.1	59.1	18.2	1.7	171.7
United States	18.7	6.9	16.8	61.6	54.4	8.2	21.1
Germany	12.9	4.7	–	65.1	56.5	–	–
Canada	12.8	4.7	1.8	57.5	39.7	2.0	14.1
Australia	7.8	2.9	6.3	55.9	27.2	2.4	8.0
United Kingdom	7.5	2.8	–	85.9	–	–	10.4
Norway	6.1	2.2	28.4	60.1	37.9	5.9	6.3
Spain	5.8	2.2	57.4	63.4	25.6	–	4.8
Switzerland	3.6	1.3	–	76.4	53.4	–	3.6
Denmark	3.4	1.3	43.9	68.5	39.9	6.1	3.4

Labour market indicators of persons born in Finland living in OECD countries

Population 15-64	2000			2005/06		
	Men	Women	Total	Men	Women	Total
Employment-population ratio (%)	73.7	61.6	65.8	82.3	68.7	73.0
Unemployment rate (%)	6.0	6.5	6.3	2.4	5.7	4.5
Participation rate (%)	78.4	65.9	70.2	84.3	72.8	76.5
Total employed (thousands)	**16.2**	**25.4**	**41.6**	**17.9**	**31.8**	**49.6**
Employment rates of the highly educated (%)	85.1	69.5	74.8	92.7	76.6	81.5
Unemployment rates of the highly educated (%)	3.4	5.1	4.4	1.8	7.1	5.3
Highly educated in low- and medium-skilled jobs (%)	16.5	20.1	18.9	21.2	21.9	21.7
Highly educated employed (thousands)	**8.5**	**13.5**	**22.0**	**10.3**	**18.6**	**28.9**
Legislators, senior officials and managers	8.9	5.0	6.6	9.1	6.0	7.2
Professionals	12.7	17.0	15.3	14.5	18.3	16.8
Life science and health professionals	1.0	3.0	2.2	1.0	3.2	2.3
Teaching professionals	2.5	5.2	4.1	2.6	5.4	4.3
Technicians and associate professionals	14.1	19.5	17.3	14.7	19.9	17.8
Clerks	4.6	13.8	10.0	4.5	13.6	10.0
Service, shop and market sales workers	5.4	27.0	18.2	5.4	26.3	18.0
Skilled agricultural and fishery workers	1.1	0.3	0.6	1.1	0.8	0.9
Craft and related trades workers	24.9	2.1	11.3	22.9	1.5	10.0
Plant and machine operators and assemblers	21.7	5.7	12.2	21.4	5.1	11.6
Elementary occupations	6.6	9.6	8.4	6.5	8.4	7.6

Distribution of employment by occupation (%), population 15+

Persons born in Finland and their native-born children, population 15+

Living in:	Europe	United States	Australia
2008	Thousands	Thousands	Thousands
Native-born children	253.2	34.9	5.4
Foreign-born	128.6	10.1	5.1
Total	381.8	45.1	10.5

International students from Finland in OECD countries

Five main destinations	2004	2005	2006	2007	2008	2009
United Kingdom	1 883	1 754	1 787	1 699	1 666	1 680
Sweden	562	557	630	622	1 124	1 310
United States	619	595	630	579	673	741
Germany	..	..	..	..	596	649
Estonia	..	279	398	441	586	602
Total	3 835	3 932	4 332	4 261	5 693	6 178

Legal migrant flows to the OECD
Thousands

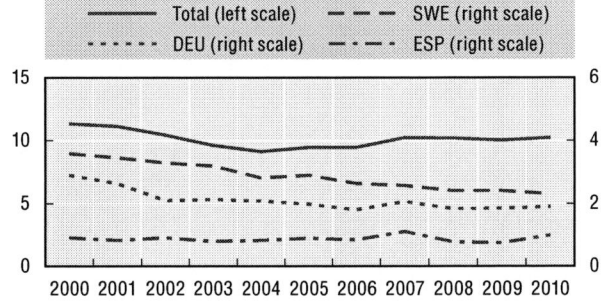

Remittance flows

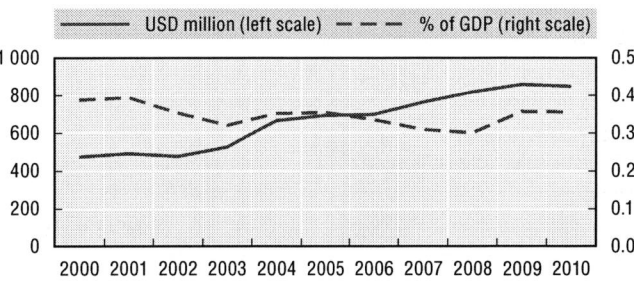

Ten main countries of destination for legal migrants in 2010 (numbers, % of total flows to the country): SWE (2300, 3%), DEU (1901, 0.3%), ESP (978, 0.2%), GBR (705, 0.2%), NOR (558, 0.9%), NLD (541, 0.5%), JPN (529, 0.4%), CHE (469, 0.4%), BEL (404, 0.4%), USA (397, 0%).

Desire to emigrate, 2008-10

	Women	15-24	Highly educated	Total	Regional total
Persons who would move permanently, if they had the opportunity to do so (%)	10	17	..	11	16
Of which: Persons who are planning to move permanently in the next 12 months (%)				..	6
Of which: Persons who have already done some preparations for this move (*e.g.* visa application) (%)					39

StatLink 📊 http://dx.doi.org/10.1787/888932673182

Total population 2010 (millions)	64.9
Population growth 2010 (%)	0.5
GDP per capita 2010 (current USD)	39 460
GDP growth 2010 (%)	1.5
Poverty rate 2010 (USD PPP 2 a day, in %)	..

France compared to:	World	Region
Human Development Index (HDI)	20/187	19/34
GDP per capita	25/194	17/34
Emigration rate	116/203	28/34
Emigration rate of the highly educated	125/157	27/34

Age structure of the population 0+ (2010): "0-14": 13%; "15-24": 19%; "25-64": 52%; "65+": 16%.
Level of education of the population 15+ (2010): "Low": 16%; "Medium": 64%; "High": 20%.

Emigrant population living in OECD countries

Immigrant population

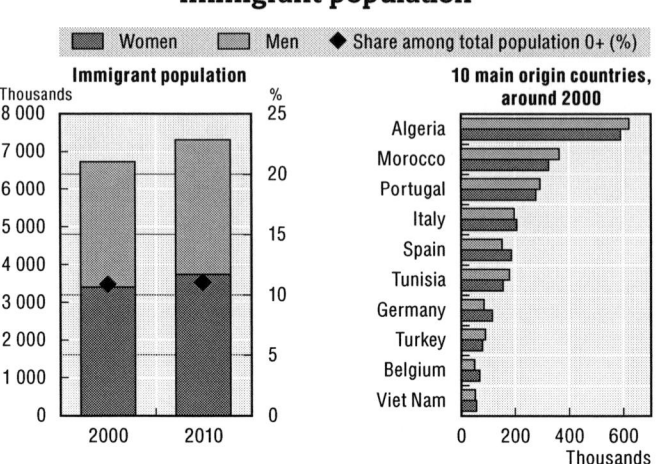

Emigrant population: persons born in France living abroad

	2000						2005/06		
	All destinations			OECD destinations			OECD destinations		
Population 15+	Men	Women	Total	Men	Women	Total	Men	Women	Total
Emigrant population (thousands)	533.4	675.2	1 208.6	500.2	644.8	1 145.0	579.2	718.7	1 297.9
Recent emigrants (thousands)	..	..	..	77.3	77.9	155.3	106.9	107.1	214.0
15-24 (%)	12.3	10.7	11.4	12.0	10.2	11.0	9.4	7.8	8.5
25-64 (%)	73.7	69.0	71.0	74.2	69.5	71.5	77.3	71.3	74.0
65+ (%)	14.0	20.4	17.6	13.8	20.3	17.5	13.3	20.9	17.5
Low-educated (%)	31.3	33.7	32.6	32.2	34.0	33.2	26.8	28.8	27.9
Highly educated (%)	36.0	33.4	34.5	35.5	33.4	34.3	40.6	38.4	39.4
Total emigration rates (%)	2.2	2.6	2.4	2.0	2.4	2.2	2.3	2.6	2.5
Emigration rates of the highly educated (%)	4.2	4.5	4.3	3.9	4.3	4.1	4.9	5.2	5.0

Main destinations in 2005/06

	Total		Recent emigrants	Women	Highly educated	15-24	Total in 2000
Population 15+	Thousands	%	%	%	%	%	Thousands
United States	199.2	15.3	16.1	55.0	54.3	8.2	188.6
Spain	173.3	13.3	43.2	52.8	34.4	6.2	150.3
Belgium	146.8	11.3	15.5	59.3	22.6	7.5	141.9
Italy	128.0	9.9	7.4	59.3	14.3	3.9	125.5
United Kingdom	108.3	8.3	37.3	59.3	69.9	15.6	85.3
Switzerland	107.0	8.2	29.6	56.3	37.1	4.2	93.9
Germany	90.3	7.0	18.6	55.5	43.4	5.2	55.2
Canada	88.0	6.8	18.7	48.2	63.6	8.8	75.6
Portugal	81.2	6.3	6.5	51.8	19.1	21.0	82.0
Poland	40.3	3.1	–	55.2	10.3	–	32.5

Labour market indicators of persons born in France living in OECD countries

Population 15-64	2000			2005/06		
	Men	Women	Total	Men	Women	Total
Employment-population ratio (%)	78.2	59.6	68.1	79.2	63.3	70.8
Unemployment rate (%)	6.2	8.9	7.5	6.4	7.8	7.0
Participation rate (%)	83.4	65.5	73.7	84.6	68.7	76.1
Total employed (thousands)	**315.0**	**287.3**	**602.4**	**391.1**	**355.0**	**746.1**
Employment rates of the highly educated (%)	86.7	73.4	79.4	93.1	80.3	86.2
Unemployment rates of the highly educated (%)	3.7	5.3	4.5	4.5	5.0	4.7
Highly educated in low- and medium-skilled jobs (%)	21.3	25.2	23.3	19.1	25.2	22.1
Highly educated employed (thousands)	**132.0**	**135.3**	**267.4**	**189.7**	**190.9**	**380.7**
Legislators, senior officials and managers	15.0	9.0	12.1	15.1	9.8	12.6
Professionals	18.3	23.3	20.7	21.8	24.7	23.2
Life science and health professionals	1.1	2.3	1.7	1.2	2.4	1.8
Teaching professionals	2.5	8.7	5.5	3.1	11.3	7.1
Technicians and associate professionals	12.5	15.5	13.9	15.0	18.0	16.4
Clerks	6.1	18.4	11.9	5.5	17.2	11.1
Service, shop and market sales workers	12.4	18.2	15.1	8.9	14.0	11.4
Skilled agricultural and fishery workers	1.3	0.7	1.0	1.5	3.3	2.3
Craft and related trades workers	18.9	3.8	11.8	16.4	3.8	10.4
Plant and machine operators and assemblers	8.5	2.7	5.8	9.7	2.0	6.0
Elementary occupations	7.0	8.5	7.7	5.6	7.2	6.4

Distribution of employment by occupation (%), population 15+

Persons born in France and their native-born children, population 15+

Living in:	Europe	United States	Australia
2008	Thousands	Thousands	Thousands
Native-born children	792.0	140.0	1.1
Foreign-born	618.0	196.5	18.2
Total	1 410.0	336.6	19.4

International students from France in OECD countries

Five main destinations	2004	2005	2006	2007	2008	2009
United Kingdom	11 295	11 685	12 456	13 068	12 685	13 089
United States	6 818	6 847	6 876	6 852	7 058	7 299
Canada	6 195	..	6 252	4 698	4 880	5 992
Belgium	6 238	7 583	9 171	8 949	2 091	5 651
Switzerland	..	..	..	..	4 895	5 413
Total	34 855	30 887	40 155	39 561	41 778	50 138

Legal migrant flows to the OECD
Thousands

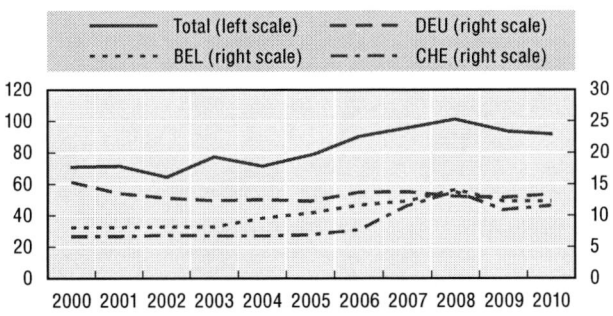

Remittance flows

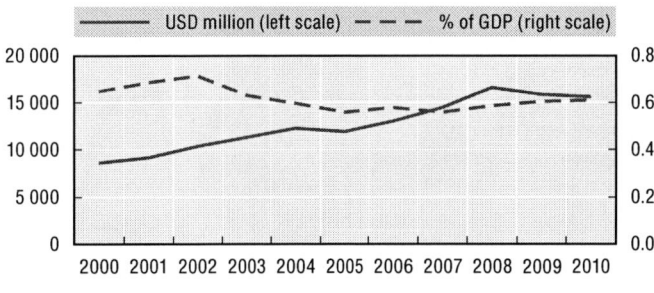

Ten main countries of destination for legal migrants in 2010 (numbers, % of total flows to the country): DEU (13349, 2%), BEL (12272, 12%), CHE (11548, 8.8%), GBR (11000, 2.4%), ESP (8628, 2%), CAN (6935, 2.5%), JPN (3984, 0.4%), USA (3861, 0.4%), NLD (2928, 2.9%), LUX (2909, 18.6%).

Desire to emigrate, 2008-10

	Women	15-24	Highly educated	Total	Regional total
Persons who would move permanently, if they had the opportunity to do so (%)	17	37	26	20	16
Of which: Persons who are planning to move permanently in the next 12 months (%)				7	6
Of which: Persons who have already done some preparations for this move (*e.g.* visa application) (%)					39

Three main countries of desired destination: Canada (21%), United States (11%), Spain (10%).

StatLink ⟿ *http://dx.doi.org/10.1787/888932673201*

			Germany compared to:	World	Region
Total population 2010 (millions)		81.7	Human Development Index (HDI)	9/187	8/34
Population growth 2010 (%)		−0.2	GDP per capita	22/194	15/34
GDP per capita 2010 (current USD)		40 152	Emigration rate	93/203	21/34
GDP growth 2010 (%)		3.7	Emigration rate of the highly educated	96/157	16/34
Poverty rate 2010 (USD PPP 2 a day, in %)		..			

Age structure of the population 0+ (2010): "0-14": 11%; "15-24": 13%; "25-64": 55%; "65+": 20%.
Level of education of the population 15+ (2010): "Low": 10%; "Medium": 72%; "High": 18%.

Emigrant population living in OECD countries

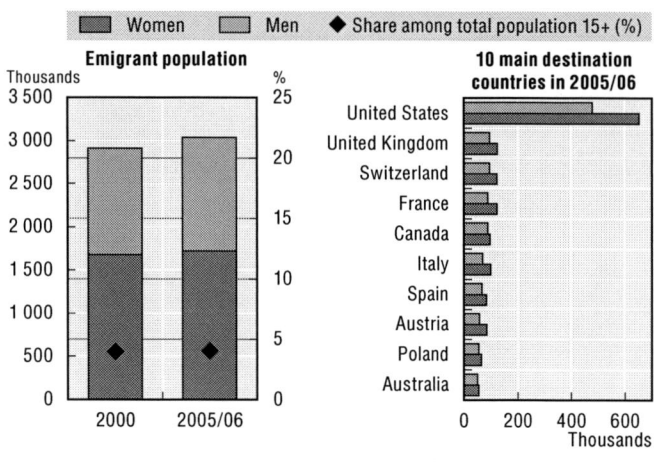

Immigrant population

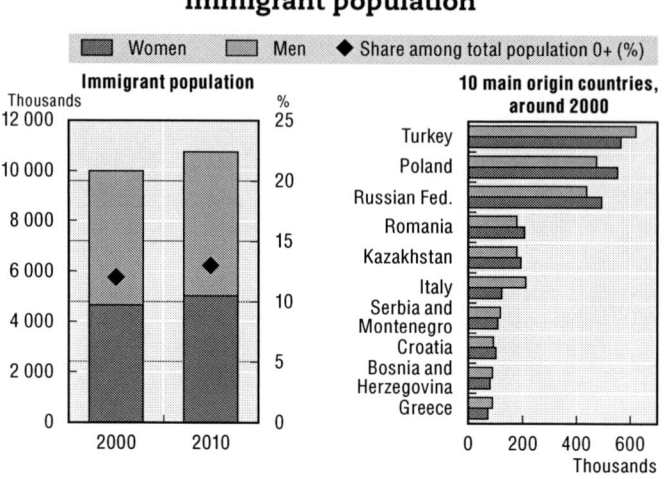

Emigrant population: persons born in Germany living abroad

	2000						2005/06		
	All destinations			OECD destinations			OECD destinations		
Population 15+	Men	Women	Total	Men	Women	Total	Men	Women	Total
Emigrant population (thousands)	1 504.8	1 953.4	3 458.2	1 236.4	1 673.7	2 910.1	1 316.0	1 722.9	3 038.8
Recent emigrants (thousands)	..	..	..	127.1	138.7	265.8	142.0	155.6	297.6
15-24 (%)	16.1	13.0	14.4	13.2	10.3	11.5	12.0	9.8	10.8
25-64 (%)	69.7	65.7	67.4	71.0	66.1	68.1	70.1	64.0	66.7
65+ (%)	14.2	21.3	18.2	15.9	23.6	20.3	17.8	26.2	22.6
Low-educated (%)	23.6	28.5	26.3	24.0	29.3	27.1	19.0	23.6	21.6
Highly educated (%)	32.8	26.5	29.2	32.6	25.8	28.7	37.6	31.0	33.8
Total emigration rates (%)	4.3	5.2	4.7	3.5	4.5	4.0	3.7	4.5	4.1
Emigration rates of the highly educated (%)	6.0	10.0	7.5	4.9	8.4	6.3	6.0	9.3	7.3

Main destinations in 2005/06

	Total		Recent emigrants	Women	Highly educated	15-24	Total in 2000
Population 15+	Thousands	%	%	%	%	%	Thousands
United States	1 129.7	37.2	6.0	57.7	36.9	14.1	1 067.7
United Kingdom	217.4	7.2	9.6	56.6	37.6	18.6	231.3
Switzerland	216.9	7.1	35.1	56.4	41.7	3.7	175.9
France	208.5	6.9	13.5	58.4	34.9	8.8	198.3
Canada	183.0	6.0	3.0	52.1	42.8	5.4	182.6
Italy	166.9	5.5	8.3	59.1	11.8	15.7	167.9
Spain	149.2	4.9	31.4	55.7	40.8	5.2	125.8
Austria	140.4	4.6	21.0	59.4	25.2	9.0	130.2
Poland	117.3	3.9	–	54.0	7.7	–	90.2
Australia	103.7	3.4	7.2	52.2	29.6	3.2	105.5

Labour market indicators of persons born in Germany living in OECD countries

Population 15-64	2000			2005/06		
	Men	Women	Total	Men	Women	Total
Employment-population ratio (%)	76.8	59.3	67.1	78.3	63.6	70.3
Unemployment rate (%)	6.6	7.7	7.1	6.1	7.3	6.7
Participation rate (%)	82.3	64.2	72.3	83.4	68.5	75.4
Total employed (thousands)	**770.5**	**731.7**	**1 502.2**	**819.3**	**782.0**	**1 601.4**
Employment rates of the highly educated (%)	88.5	73.3	80.6	92.8	80.9	86.6
Unemployment rates of the highly educated (%)	3.2	4.5	3.8	3.5	5.0	4.2
Highly educated in low- and medium-skilled jobs (%)	24.2	27.7	25.9	24.2	27.3	25.7
Highly educated employed (thousands)	**301.5**	**268.6**	**570.1**	**363.9**	**340.1**	**704.0**
Legislators, senior officials and managers	16.4	9.0	12.8	15.0	8.4	11.8
Professionals	19.7	18.1	18.9	22.9	20.9	21.9
Life science and health professionals	2.3	2.8	2.5	2.4	3.6	3.0
Teaching professionals	3.9	6.8	5.3	3.9	8.0	5.9
Technicians and associate professionals	15.0	20.6	17.7	16.6	21.9	19.2
Clerks	5.6	19.9	12.5	5.5	17.4	11.2
Service, shop and market sales workers	8.6	18.9	13.5	7.8	14.5	11.0
Skilled agricultural and fishery workers	1.8	1.2	1.5	2.3	4.2	3.2
Craft and related trades workers	16.6	2.5	9.8	14.5	4.0	9.4
Plant and machine operators and assemblers	9.0	2.3	5.8	9.2	2.6	6.1
Elementary occupations	7.4	7.6	7.5	5.8	6.0	5.9

Left margin label: Distribution of employment by occupation (%), population 15+

Persons born in Germany and their native-born children, population 15+

Living in:	Europe	United States	Australia
2008	Thousands	Thousands	Thousands
Native-born children	1 259.5	1 014.8	118.9
Foreign-born	1 017.7	608.1	106.4
Total	2 277.2	1 623.0	225.3

International students from Germany in OECD countries

Five main destinations	2004	2005	2006	2007	2008	2009
United Kingdom	12 096	12 553	13 267	14 011	13 625	14 128
Netherlands	..	6 753	8 759	10 170	12 313	14 007
United States	8 745	9 024	9 142	8 847	8 917	9 520
Switzerland	..	..	..	..	8 341	9 496
France	6 698	5 887	6 565	6 947	6 918	6 774
Total	35 973	42 658	48 224	51 224	59 589	67 443

Legal migrant flows to the OECD
Thousands

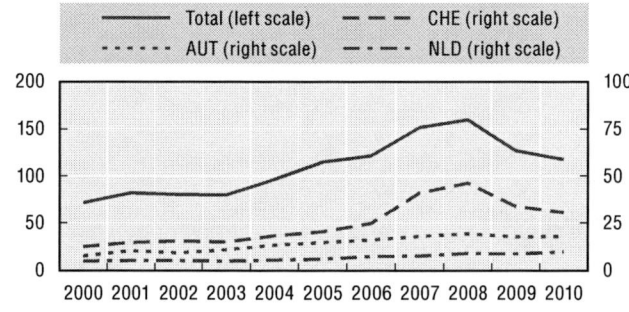

Remittance flows

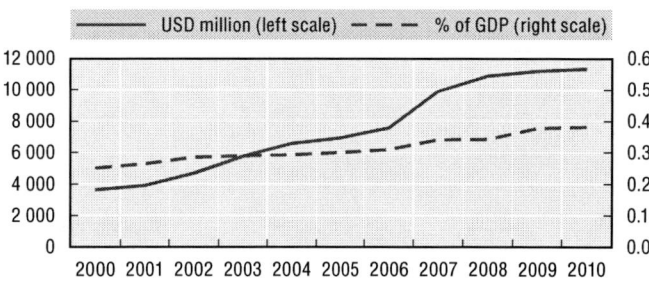

Ten main countries of destination for legal migrants in 2010 (numbers, % of total flows to the country): CHE (30745, 23.3%), AUT (17833, 18.2%), NLD (9812, 9.8%), ESP (9288, 2.2%), GBR (7000, 1.5%), USA (6888, 0.7%), JPN (4277, 3.3%), BEL (3401, 3.3%), CAN (3190, 1.1%), NOR (2678, 4.2%).

Desire to emigrate, 2008-10

	Women	15-24	Highly educated	Total	Regional total
Persons who would move permanently, if they had the opportunity to do so (%)	20	30	20	22	16
Of which: Persons who are planning to move permanently in the next 12 months (%)				5	6
Of which: Persons who have already done some preparations for this move (*e.g.* visa application) (%)					39

Three main countries of desired destination: Canada (14%), Spain (10%), United States (8%).

StatLink http://dx.doi.org/10.1787/888932673220

Total population 2010 (millions)	11.3	**Greece compared to:**	**World** **Region**
Population growth 2010 (%)	0.3	Human Development Index (HDI)	29/187 26/34
GDP per capita 2010 (current USD)	26 600	GDP per capita	34/194 23/34
GDP growth 2010 (%)	−3.5	Emigration rate	70/203 10/34
Poverty rate 2010 (USD PPP 2 a day, in %)	..	Emigration rate of the highly educated	114/157 23/34

Age structure of the population 0+ (2010): "0-14": 10%; "15-24": 15%; "25-64": 56%; "65+": 19%.
Level of education of the population 15+ (2010): "Low": 29%; "Medium": 47%; "High": 24%.

Emigrant population living in OECD countries

Immigrant population

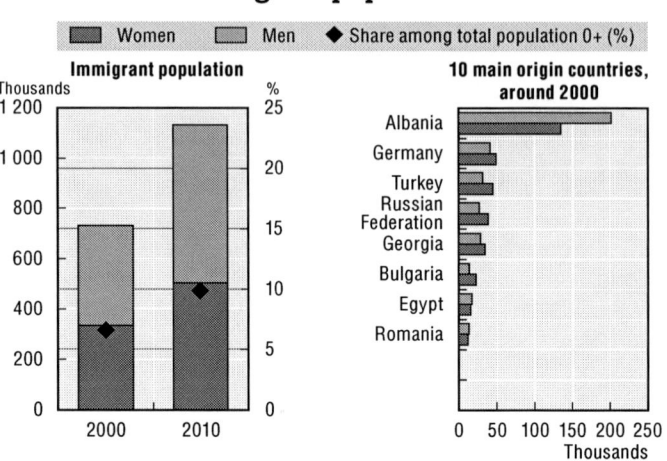

Emigrant population: persons born in Greece living abroad

	2000						2005/06		
	All destinations			OECD destinations			OECD destinations		
Population 15+	Men	Women	Total	Men	Women	Total	Men	Women	Total
Emigrant population (thousands)	374.2	338.9	713.1	334.7	295.8	630.6	359.6	311.8	671.4
Recent emigrants (thousands)	..	..	..	15.8	12.0	27.8	18.8	12.5	31.3
15-24 (%)	5.2	4.7	4.9	4.9	4.5	4.7	4.8	5.1	4.9
25-64 (%)	71.0	67.7	69.4	73.3	70.9	72.2	66.8	64.8	65.9
65+ (%)	23.8	27.6	25.6	21.8	24.6	23.1	28.4	30.1	29.2
Low-educated (%)	51.0	63.2	56.8	49.8	61.4	55.3	45.6	57.4	51.0
Highly educated (%)	18.7	12.4	15.7	19.3	13.2	16.4	20.6	15.6	18.3
Total emigration rates (%)	7.6	6.7	7.1	6.8	5.9	6.3	7.1	6.1	6.6
Emigration rates of the highly educated (%)	9.0	6.5	7.9	8.4	6.1	7.3	6.4	4.5	5.5

Main destinations in 2005/06

	Total		Recent emigrants	Women	Highly educated	15-24	Total in 2000
Population 15+	Thousands	%	%	%	%	%	Thousands
Germany	228.4	34.0	3.0	44.3	8.1	7.6	160.5
United States	161.6	24.1	3.8	46.3	27.8	2.7	173.9
Australia	109.0	16.2	1.0	50.4	8.9	1.3	115.3
Canada	73.3	10.9	1.1	48.5	17.1	1.6	75.7
United Kingdom	20.7	3.1	35.0	51.0	78.6	–	33.6
Belgium	14.1	2.1	–	47.7	–	–	14.5
Italy	13.7	2.0	9.0	51.1	26.1	–	14.4
France	11.1	1.7	17.4	52.0	46.9	11.4	11.4
Sweden	10.4	1.6	16.2	39.8	20.3	3.7	10.2
Netherlands	5.8	0.9	–	41.9	–	–	–

Labour market indicators of persons born in Greece living in OECD countries

Population 15-64	2000			2005/06		
	Men	Women	Total	Men	Women	Total
Employment-population ratio (%)	72.7	52.2	63.4	77.7	58.3	68.8
Unemployment rate (%)	7.3	4.3	6.2	9.0	8.0	8.6
Participation rate (%)	78.4	54.6	67.6	85.3	63.4	75.3
Total employed (thousands)	**186.9**	**112.5**	**299.4**	**190.4**	**121.0**	**311.4**
Employment rates of the highly educated (%)	81.7	63.4	74.7	93.1	82.5	88.8
Unemployment rates of the highly educated (%)	3.9	5.6	4.5	4.1	5.6	4.6
Highly educated in low- and medium-skilled jobs (%)	25.2	27.7	26.1	22.0	25.0	23.1
Highly educated employed (thousands)	**45.0**	**21.7**	**66.7**	**51.6**	**31.0**	**82.6**
Distribution of employment by occupation (%), population 15+ — Legislators, senior officials and managers	13.4	7.4	11.0	17.9	9.7	14.7
Professionals	10.3	10.3	10.3	11.9	9.8	11.1
Life science and health professionals	1.4	1.4	1.4	1.3	1.0	1.2
Teaching professionals	2.6	4.4	3.3	2.5	3.3	2.8
Technicians and associate professionals	8.0	9.3	8.5	5.4	7.9	6.4
Clerks	2.9	10.6	5.9	2.3	10.5	5.5
Service, shop and market sales workers	15.9	24.6	19.3	14.3	27.1	19.3
Skilled agricultural and fishery workers	0.4	0.2	0.3	0.5	0.4	0.4
Craft and related trades workers	12.9	2.8	9.0	17.5	1.5	11.3
Plant and machine operators and assemblers	18.9	5.5	13.6	16.5	8.0	13.2
Elementary occupations	17.3	29.3	22.0	13.7	25.1	18.1

Persons born in Greece and their native-born children, population 15+

Living in:	Europe	United States	Australia
2008	Thousands	Thousands	Thousands
Native-born children	192.3	214.2	71.3
Foreign-born	336.1	166.4	62.6
Total	528.4	380.7	134.0

International students from Greece in OECD countries

Five main destinations	2004	2005	2006	2007	2008	2009
United Kingdom	22 826	19 685	17 676	16 051	12 626	12 034
Italy	7 159	6 390	5 473	5 054	4 537	4 293
Germany	..	..	..	..	2 070	2 108
France	2 288	2 040	2 014	1 952	1 926	1 868
United States	2 126	2 125	2 162	2 030	1 983	1 865
Total	36 026	31 837	29 001	26 746	25 263	25 062

Legal migrant flows to the OECD
Thousands

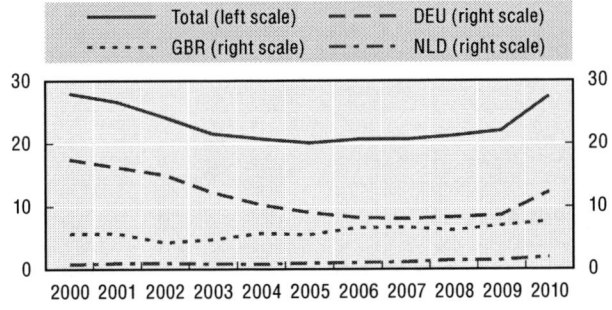

Remittance flows

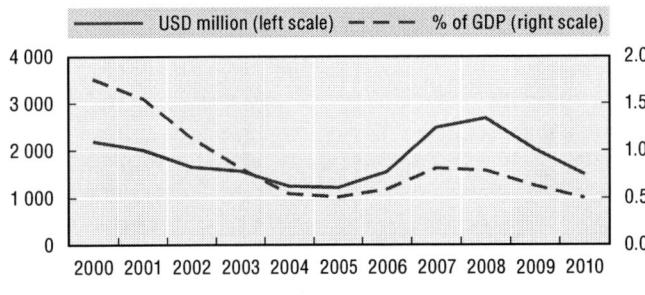

Ten main countries of destination for legal migrants in 2010 (numbers, % of total flows to the country): DEU (12256, 1.8%), GBR (7589, 1.6%), NLD (1831, 1.8%), USA (745, 0.1%), CHE (741, 0.6%), BEL (725, 0.7%), AUT (523, 1.8%), TUR (522, 1.8%), SWE (520, 0.7%), ESP (412, 0.1%).

Desire to emigrate, 2008-10

	Women	15-24	Highly educated	Total	Regional total
Persons who would move permanently, if they had the opportunity to do so (%)	16	33	26	19	16
Of which: Persons who are planning to move permanently in the next 12 months (%)				6	6
Of which: Persons who have already done some preparations for this move (e.g. visa application) (%)					39

Three main countries of desired destination: Germany (18%), United States (10%), United Kingdom (9%).

StatLink ᴍᴵᴴ http://dx.doi.org/10.1787/888932673239

			Hungary compared to:	World	Region
Total population 2010 (millions)		10.0	Human Development Index (HDI)	38/187	29/34
Population growth 2010 (%)		−0.1	GDP per capita	52/194	30/34
GDP per capita 2010 (current USD)		12 852	Emigration rate	95/203	23/34
GDP growth 2010 (%)		1.3	Emigration rate of the highly educated	80/157	10/34
Poverty rate 2007 (USD PPP 2 a day, in %)		0.4			

Age structure of the population 0+ (2010): "0-14": 12%; "15-24": 15%; "25-64": 56%; "65+": 17%.
Level of education of the population 15+ (2010): "Low": 6%; "Medium": 78%; "High": 16%.

Emigrant population living in OECD countries

Immigrant population

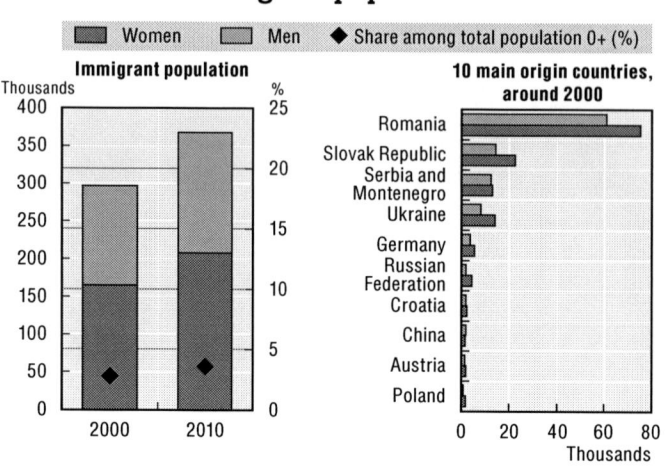

Emigrant population: persons born in Hungary living abroad

	2000						2005/06		
	All destinations			OECD destinations			OECD destinations		
Population 15+	Men	Women	Total	Men	Women	Total	Men	Women	Total
Emigrant population (thousands)	187.7	204.0	391.8	161.5	169.9	331.4	179.0	185.6	364.6
Recent emigrants (thousands)	..	..	..	7.1	10.2	17.3	17.5	24.4	41.9
15-24 (%)	7.0	7.1	7.1	4.3	5.0	4.6	3.5	5.2	4.4
25-64 (%)	61.3	58.9	60.1	62.5	61.0	61.7	56.7	60.1	58.4
65+ (%)	31.7	33.9	32.9	33.3	34.0	33.6	39.8	34.7	37.2
Low-educated (%)	22.7	29.8	26.4	22.4	27.8	25.2	16.6	22.7	19.7
Highly educated (%)	31.3	26.9	29.0	31.6	27.7	29.6	33.3	33.0	33.1
Total emigration rates (%)	4.5	4.3	4.4	3.9	3.6	3.8	4.3	4.0	4.1
Emigration rates of the highly educated (%)	11.0	10.2	10.6	9.7	8.9	9.3	9.6	9.3	9.5

Main destinations in 2005/06

	Total		Recent emigrants	Women	Highly educated	15-24	Total in 2000
Population 15+	Thousands	%	%	%	%	%	Thousands
Germany	84.9	23.3	8.2	47.6	27.2	–	44.3
United States	81.8	22.4	6.4	51.6	39.3	2.7	92.0
Canada	46.0	12.6	4.8	49.5	40.3	2.8	49.6
Austria	30.4	8.3	16.8	55.9	20.0	8.3	29.8
Australia	20.0	5.5	3.4	48.9	28.9	1.9	22.4
United Kingdom	18.9	5.2	65.9	57.1	47.7	–	12.7
Sweden	13.4	3.7	9.5	50.6	28.4	4.0	12.1
Switzerland	10.7	2.9	17.9	40.5	52.0	–	12.2
Israel	10.7	2.9	13.4	56.4	33.9	1.0	17.2
Czech Republic	10.6	2.9	..	35.3	5.1	0.4	6.2

Labour market indicators of persons born in Hungary living in OECD countries

Population 15-64	2000			2005/06		
	Men	Women	Total	Men	Women	Total
Employment-population ratio (%)	81.0	61.1	70.6	83.3	62.9	72.5
Unemployment rate (%)	5.6	7.0	6.2	6.6	8.0	7.2
Participation rate (%)	85.8	65.7	75.3	89.1	68.4	78.2
Total employed (thousands)	**71.9**	**59.2**	**131.1**	**83.2**	**70.3**	**153.6**
Employment rates of the highly educated (%)	90.7	72.1	81.3	94.0	75.5	83.4
Unemployment rates of the highly educated (%)	4.7	6.5	5.5	2.6	5.6	4.1
Highly educated in low- and medium-skilled jobs (%)	23.8	30.0	26.6	30.1	33.8	32.0
Highly educated employed (thousands)	**25.8**	**21.2**	**47.0**	**34.3**	**35.4**	**69.7**
Legislators, senior officials and managers	11.6	7.2	9.6	7.2	7.3	7.2
Professionals	19.1	17.8	18.5	19.8	18.5	19.3
Life science and health professionals	3.3	3.1	3.2	2.2	2.5	2.3
Teaching professionals	3.4	5.7	4.5	1.1	5.4	3.0
Technicians and associate professionals	12.8	18.6	15.5	12.7	18.8	15.4
Clerks	3.5	15.6	9.1	3.0	13.9	7.8
Service, shop and market sales workers	7.4	24.0	15.1	4.3	20.6	11.5
Skilled agricultural and fishery workers	1.5	0.8	1.2	1.1	4.2	2.4
Craft and related trades workers	24.0	2.6	14.0	32.1	3.7	19.5
Plant and machine operators and assemblers	11.3	3.2	7.5	10.6	3.2	7.3
Elementary occupations	8.7	10.2	9.4	9.3	9.8	9.5

Left margin label: Distribution of employment by occupation (%), population 15+

Persons born in Hungary and their native-born children, population 15+

Living in:	Europe	United States	Australia
2008	Thousands	Thousands	Thousands
Native-born children	210.8	147.3	25.6
Foreign-born	213.3	98.3	35.8
Total	424.1	245.6	61.4

International students from Hungary in OECD countries

Five main destinations	2004	2005	2006	2007	2008	2009
Germany	..	..	..	..	1 787	1 794
United Kingdom	371	584	805	1 040	1 026	1 132
United States	997	976	860	751	711	669
France	536	601	660	712	584	570
Italy	184	177	231	206	169	203
Total	2 425	2 778	3 094	3 201	5 013	5 355

Legal migrant flows to the OECD
Thousands

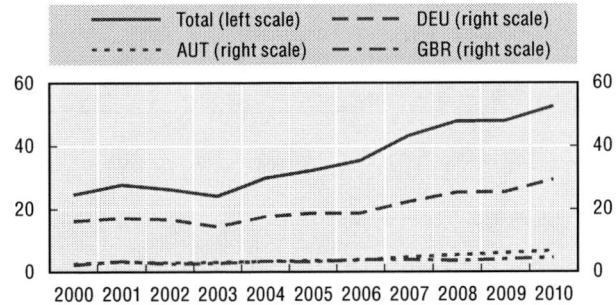

Remittance flows

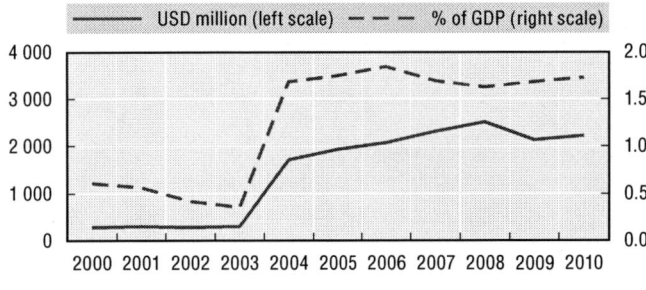

Ten main countries of destination for legal migrants in 2010 (numbers, % of total flows to the country): DEU (29286, 4.4%), AUT (6506, 6.6%), GBR (4277, 0.9%), NLD (2400, 2.4%), CHE (1160, 0.9%), SVK (1082, 8.6%), USA (1022, 0.2%), ESP (964, 0.2%), ITA (921, 0.2%), BEL (850, 0.8%).

Desire to emigrate, 2008-10

	Women	15-24	Highly educated	Total	Regional total
Persons who would move permanently, if they had the opportunity to do so (%)	17	35	13	19	16
Of which: Persons who are planning to move permanently in the next 12 months (%)				..	6
Of which: Persons who have already done some preparations for this move (*e.g.* visa application) (%)					39

StatLink http://dx.doi.org/10.1787/888932673258

Total population 2010 (millions)	0.3	**Iceland compared to:**		**World**	**Region**
Population growth 2010 (%)	−0.3	Human Development Index (HDI)		13/187	12/34
GDP per capita 2010 (current USD)	39 617	GDP per capita		24/194	16/34
GDP growth 2010 (%)	−4.0	Emigration rate		44/203	5/34
Poverty rate 2010 (USD PPP 2 a day, in %)	..	Emigration rate of the highly educated		42/157	3/34

Age structure of the population 0+ (2010): "0-14": 15%; "15-24": 21%; "25-64": 52%; "65+": 12%.
Level of education of the population 15+ (2010): "Low": 35%; "Medium": 35%; "High": 30%.

Emigrant population living in OECD countries

Immigrant population

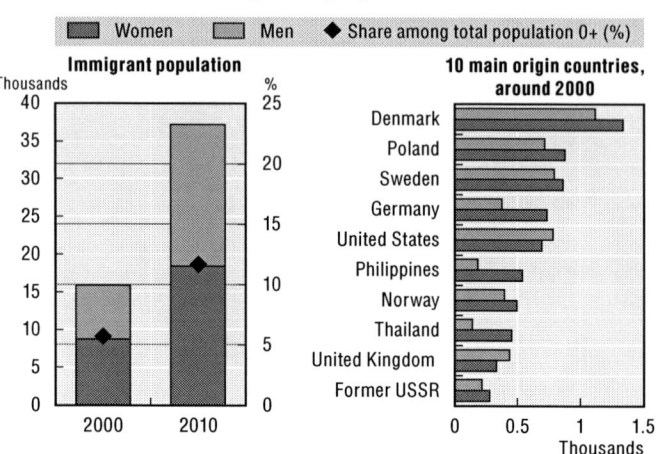

Emigrant population: persons born in Iceland living abroad

	2000						2005/06		
	All destinations			OECD destinations			OECD destinations		
Population 15+	Men	Women	Total	Men	Women	Total	Men	Women	Total
Emigrant population (thousands)	10.5	12.3	22.8	10.5	12.3	22.7	13.8	14.3	28.1
Recent emigrants (thousands)	..	..	..	2.7	2.7	5.5	3.5	3.8	7.4
15-24 (%)	16.7	17.8	17.3	16.7	17.7	17.2	13.3	13.8	13.5
25-64 (%)	77.8	72.0	74.7	77.9	72.1	74.7	80.8	76.8	78.8
65+ (%)	5.5	10.3	8.0	5.4	10.2	8.0	5.9	9.5	7.7
Low-educated (%)	17.1	17.8	17.5	17.1	17.7	17.4	13.5	15.3	14.5
Highly educated (%)	40.8	36.0	38.2	40.8	36.0	38.2	46.5	41.7	44.0
Total emigration rates (%)	8.9	10.2	9.6	8.9	10.2	9.5	10.7	11.0	10.9
Emigration rates of the highly educated (%)	15.7	16.5	16.1	15.6	16.4	16.0	16.7	16.0	16.3

Main destinations in 2005/06

	Total		Recent emigrants	Women	Highly educated	15-24	Total in 2000
Population 15+	Thousands	%	%	%	%	%	Thousands
United States	8.8	31.4	11.2	56.4	43.6	14.6	7.7
Denmark	6.3	22.5	51.0	52.9	36.9	19.1	4.8
Sweden	3.5	12.5	27.8	50.0	39.4	11.7	3.4
Norway	3.2	11.3	20.4	51.2	32.2	15.7	3.2
United Kingdom	–	–	–	–	–	–	1.3
Spain	–	–	–	–	–	–	0.2
Canada	0.6	2.2	13.0	50.0	49.2	11.5	0.5
Netherlands	–	–	–	–	–	–	–
Australia	0.5	1.7	16.1	49.5	34.5	12.2	0.3
Italy	–	–	–	–	–	–	0.1

Labour market indicators of persons born in Iceland living in OECD countries

Population 15-64	2000			2005/06		
	Men	Women	Total	Men	Women	Total
Employment-population ratio (%)	75.8	65.8	70.4	85.3	62.7	74.1
Unemployment rate (%)	4.6	4.9	4.7	2.5	10.5	6.0
Participation rate (%)	79.5	69.2	73.9	87.5	70.1	78.8
Total employed (thousands)	**5.3**	**5.5**	**10.8**	**8.4**	**6.1**	**14.5**
Employment rates of the highly educated (%)	85.5	72.8	79.0	94.9	79.5	87.6
Unemployment rates of the highly educated (%)	3.3	4.9	4.1	1.3	14.2	6.9
Highly educated in low- and medium-skilled jobs (%)	22.1	26.0	24.0	21.2	23.5	22.1
Highly educated employed (thousands)	**2.6**	**2.3**	**4.9**	**4.5**	**3.0**	**7.5**
Legislators, senior officials and managers	9.5	4.9	7.2	36.1	3.0	23.0
Professionals	25.8	21.4	23.6	24.5	24.5	24.5
Life science and health professionals	5.1	5.8	5.4	2.8	5.3	3.8
Teaching professionals	6.7	6.1	6.4	2.9	7.2	4.6
Technicians and associate professionals	15.5	22.1	18.7	8.3	19.5	12.7
Clerks	4.0	12.8	8.3	2.3	17.6	8.3
Service, shop and market sales workers	8.0	26.6	17.1	4.6	22.3	11.6
Skilled agricultural and fishery workers	0.8	0.5	0.7	3.9	0.4	2.6
Craft and related trades workers	15.9	1.2	8.7	9.1	3.7	7.0
Plant and machine operators and assemblers	10.9	2.9	7.0	6.2	2.0	4.5
Elementary occupations	9.6	7.5	8.6	5.0	6.9	5.8

Distribution of employment by occupation (%), population 15+

Persons born in Iceland and their native-born children, population 15+

Living in:	Europe	United States	Australia
2008	Thousands	Thousands	Thousands
Native-born children	2.1	..	..
Foreign-born	11.1	..	1.6
Total	13.2	..	..

International students from Iceland in OECD countries

Five main destinations	2004	2005	2006	2007	2008	2009
Denmark	721	804	922	963	844	1 009
United States	488	453	454	431	402	376
United Kingdom	317	346	346	388	340	370
Sweden	22	30	47	29	138	173
Hungary	..	..	..	..	..	81
Total	1 690	1 794	1 982	2 003	1 996	2 272

Legal migrant flows to the OECD
Thousands

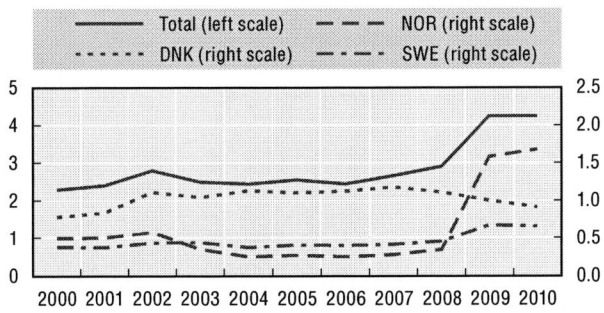

Remittance flows

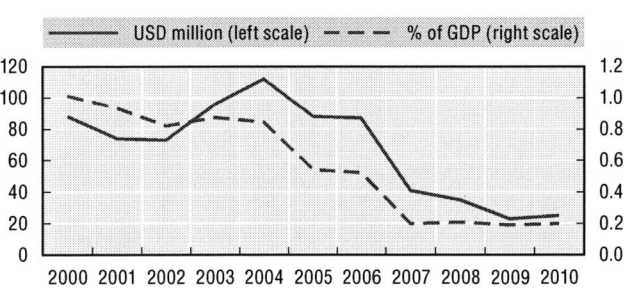

Ten main countries of destination for legal migrants in 2010 (numbers, % of total flows to the country): NOR (1678, 2.6%), DNK (911, 2.7%), SWE (661, 0.9%), DEU (270, 0%), ESP (114, 0%), USA (105, 0%), NLD (84, 0%), JPN (72, 0%), CHE (60, 0%), AUT (52, 0.1%).

Desire to emigrate, 2008-10

	Women	15-24	Highly educated	Total	Regional total
Persons who would move permanently, if they had the opportunity to do so (%)	29	40	22	26	16
Of which: Persons who are planning to move permanently in the next 12 months (%)				..	6
Of which: Persons who have already done some preparations for this move (*e.g.* visa application) (%)					39

StatLink ⧉ http://dx.doi.org/10.1787/888932673277

Total population 2010 (millions)	4.5		
Population growth 2010 (%)	0.5		
GDP per capita 2010 (current USD)	47 170		
GDP growth 2010 (%)	−0.4		
Poverty rate 2010 (USD PPP 2 a day, in %)	..		

Ireland compared to:	World	Region
Human Development Index (HDI)	5/187	5/34
GDP per capita	12/194	7/34
Emigration rate	32/203	1/34
Emigration rate of the highly educated	36/157	1/34

Age structure of the population 0+ (2010): "0-14": 13%; "15-24": 21%; "25-64": 54%; "65+": 12%.
Level of education of the population 15+ (2010): "Low": 17%; "Medium": 53%; "High": 31%.

Emigrant population living in OECD countries

Immigrant population

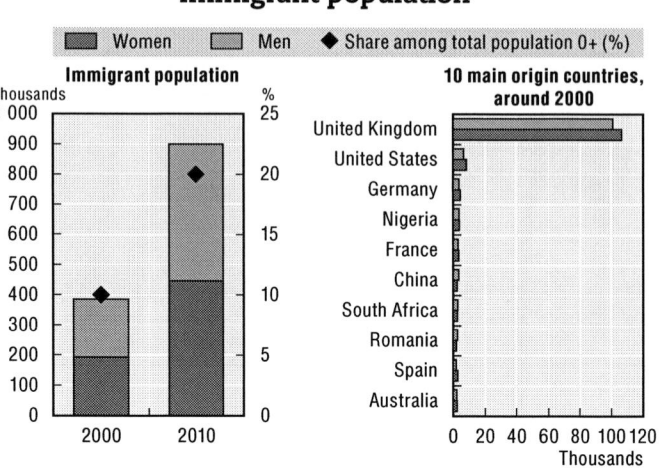

Emigrant population: persons born in Ireland living abroad

	2000						2005/06		
	All destinations			OECD destinations			OECD destinations		
Population 15+	Men	Women	Total	Men	Women	Total	Men	Women	Total
Emigrant population (thousands)	356.3	439.4	795.7	352.4	435.6	788.0	294.5	340.2	634.7
Recent emigrants (thousands)	..	..	..	25.1	26.4	51.5	24.1	23.8	47.9
15-24 (%)	5.6	5.3	5.4	5.6	5.3	5.4	3.5	4.1	3.8
25-64 (%)	65.9	60.1	62.7	65.9	60.1	62.7	67.0	56.8	61.5
65+ (%)	28.5	34.6	31.9	28.6	34.7	31.9	29.5	39.1	34.6
Low-educated (%)	44.9	43.1	43.9	45.2	43.3	44.2	22.6	23.0	22.8
Highly educated (%)	25.7	26.9	26.4	25.4	26.9	26.2	41.5	41.9	41.7
Total emigration rates (%)	19.5	22.5	21.1	19.4	22.4	20.9	15.4	17.0	16.2
Emigration rates of the highly educated (%)	19.1	21.1	20.2	18.8	20.9	19.9	19.0	17.4	18.1

Main destinations in 2005/06

	Total		Recent emigrants	Women	Highly educated	15-24	Total in 2000
Population 15+	Thousands	%	%	%	%	%	Thousands
United Kingdom	376.2	59.3	5.4	55.2	43.9	3.7	525.2
United States	139.5	22.0	7.9	53.3	35.4	3.3	161.0
Australia	48.9	7.7	12.7	48.2	36.3	5.5	49.0
Canada	22.7	3.6	2.7	51.6	46.8	2.6	26.0
Germany	9.4	1.5	..	40.9	48.4	–	–
France	7.8	1.2	36.2	57.6	59.0	13.2	5.0
New Zealand	6.6	1.0	27.1	49.2	37.5	4.7	6.5
Spain	6.1	1.0	35.6	43.7	54.5	–	3.3
Netherlands	3.7	0.6	–	58.8	–	–	–
Belgium	–	–	–	–	–	–	2.8

Labour market indicators of persons born in Ireland living in OECD countries

Population 15-64	2000			2005/06		
	Men	Women	Total	Men	Women	Total
Employment-population ratio (%)	76.9	63.4	69.7	83.2	74.0	78.8
Unemployment rate (%)	5.9	4.2	5.1	4.2	3.9	4.1
Participation rate (%)	81.7	66.2	73.4	86.8	77.0	82.1
Total employed (thousands)	**179.0**	**172.0**	**351.0**	**168.5**	**139.1**	**307.6**
Employment rates of the highly educated (%)	89.4	78.6	83.4	93.6	87.5	90.6
Unemployment rates of the highly educated (%)	3.1	2.8	2.9	2.9	2.3	2.6
Highly educated in low- and medium-skilled jobs (%)	20.8	19.8	20.3	23.1	22.0	22.6
Highly educated employed (thousands)	**60.4**	**66.4**	**126.8**	**81.0**	**75.5**	**156.5**
Legislators, senior officials and managers	18.2	11.8	15.1	21.7	13.5	17.8
Professionals	15.8	14.6	15.2	19.7	18.3	19.1
Life science and health professionals	2.1	2.8	2.4	1.5	3.5	2.5
Teaching professionals	2.9	5.7	4.3	4.5	6.8	5.6
Technicians and associate professionals	9.9	19.0	14.4	12.9	24.0	18.2
Clerks	4.8	19.7	12.2	2.2	17.4	9.4
Service, shop and market sales workers	6.0	21.7	13.8	14.2	3.6	9.2
Skilled agricultural and fishery workers	1.3	0.2	0.8	2.5	7.2	4.7
Craft and related trades workers	17.4	0.9	9.2	6.0	5.1	5.6
Plant and machine operators and assemblers	10.9	2.0	6.5	10.5	1.0	6.0
Elementary occupations	15.6	10.1	12.9	8.3	8.1	8.2

Distribution of employment by occupation (%), population 15+

Persons born in Ireland and their native-born children, population 15+

Living in:	Europe	United States	Australia
2008	Thousands	Thousands	Thousands
Native-born children	930.7	356.3	88.4
Foreign-born	358.1	153.4	104.5
Total	1 288.8	509.7	192.9

International students from Ireland in OECD countries

Five main destinations	2004	2005	2006	2007	2008	2009
United Kingdom	14 713	16 345	16 790	16 254	15 261	15 360
United States	1 020	1 019	1 139	1 105	1 019	1 042
France	522	458	498	454	392	389
Germany	..	..	..	..	285	318
Australia	159	181	172	171	193	218
Total	16 774	18 363	19 118	18 515	17 580	18 006

Legal migrant flows to the OECD
Thousands

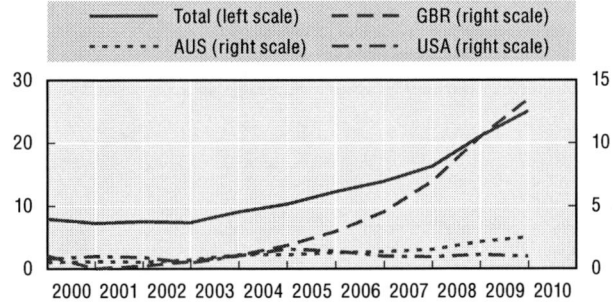

Remittance flows

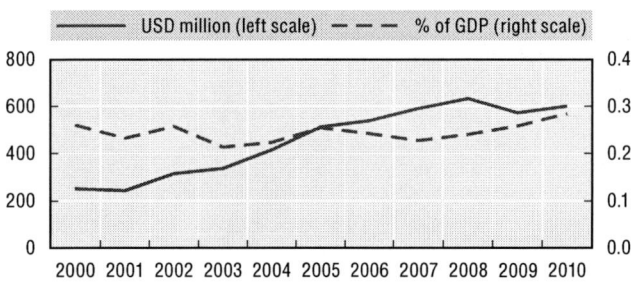

Ten main countries of destination for legal migrants in 2010 (numbers, % of total flows to the country): GBR (14000, 3%), AUS (3031, 1.5%), USA (1507, 0.1%), DEU (1426, 0.2%), ESP (1345, 0.3%), CAN (745, 0.3%), NLD (684, 0.4%), CHE (521, 0.4%), NZL (456, 1%), KOR (373, 0.1%).

Desire to emigrate, 2008-10

	Women	15-24	Highly educated	Total	Regional total
Persons who would move permanently, if they had the opportunity to do so (%)	17	32	20	19	16
Of which: Persons who are planning to move permanently in the next 12 months (%)				11	6
Of which: Persons who have already done some preparations for this move (*e.g.* visa application) (%)					39

Three main countries of desired destination: Australia (24%), United States (20%), United Kingdom (13%).

StatLink ⬛ *http://dx.doi.org/10.1787/888932673296*

Total population 2010 (millions)	7.6	Israel compared to:	World	Region
Population growth 2010 (%)	1.8	Human Development Index (HDI)	17/187	15/34
GDP per capita 2010 (current USD)	28 504	GDP per capita	32/194	22/34
GDP growth 2010 (%)	4.7	Emigration rate	92/203	20/34
Poverty rate 2010 (USD PPP 2 a day, in %)	..	Emigration rate of the highly educated	106/157	21/34

Age structure of the population 0+ (2010): "0-14": 15%; "15-24": 27%; "25-64": 47%; "65+": 10%.
Level of education of the population 15+ (2010): "Low": 26%; "Medium": 43%; "High": 31%.

Emigrant population living in OECD countries

Immigrant population

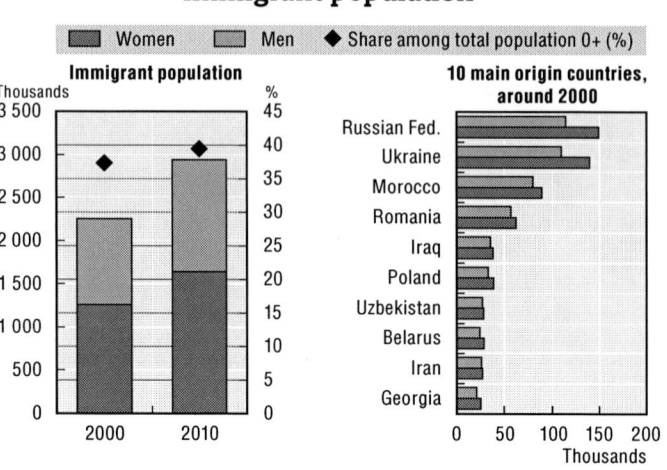

Emigrant population: persons born in Israel living abroad

	2000						2005/06		
	All destinations			OECD destinations			OECD destinations		
Population 15+	Men	Women	Total	Men	Women	Total	Men	Women	Total
Emigrant population (thousands)	97.1	76.9	174.0	88.9	71.4	160.3	116.4	90.8	207.1
Recent emigrants (thousands)	..	..	..	13.6	10.8	24.4	19.3	14.0	33.3
15-24 (%)	14.4	16.0	15.1	14.0	15.6	14.7	10.2	10.5	10.3
25-64 (%)	79.8	76.5	78.3	80.7	77.4	79.3	81.5	78.3	80.1
65+ (%)	5.8	7.5	6.5	5.3	6.9	6.0	8.3	11.2	9.6
Low-educated (%)	17.7	20.0	18.7	17.6	19.8	18.6	12.5	12.7	12.6
Highly educated (%)	44.2	41.6	43.0	44.9	42.4	43.8	48.2	50.7	49.3
Total emigration rates (%)	4.4	3.3	3.8	4.0	3.1	3.5	4.7	3.5	4.1
Emigration rates of the highly educated (%)	6.0	3.9	4.9	5.6	3.7	4.6	7.1	5.0	5.9

Main destinations in 2005/06

	Total		Recent emigrants	Women	Highly educated	15-24	Total in 2000
Population 15+	Thousands	%	%	%	%	%	Thousands
United States	141.8	68.4	16.0	45.2	49.6	9.3	107.7
Canada	19.2	9.3	14.1	47.6	57.9	13.9	14.7
United Kingdom	10.2	4.9	–	–	64.0	–	10.3
France	7.4	3.6	11.5	49.1	40.3	13.7	6.6
Australia	6.9	3.3	19.7	45.0	47.6	10.8	5.8
Italy	3.8	1.8	36.9	30.9	42.3	–	2.1
Netherlands	3.3	1.6	–	–	–	–	–
Belgium	–	–	–	–	–	–	2.3
Switzerland	2.1	1.0	64.0	–	–	–	1.8
Sweden	1.7	0.8	32.5	37.6	31.5	13.8	1.6

Information on data for Israel: http://dx.doi.org/10.1787/888932315602.

Labour market indicators of persons born in Israel living in OECD countries

Population 15-64	2000			2005/06		
	Men	Women	Total	Men	Women	Total
Employment-population ratio (%)	77.4	52.7	66.5	81.1	57.6	70.9
Unemployment rate (%)	5.2	6.9	5.8	5.1	7.8	6.0
Participation rate (%)	81.6	56.6	70.5	85.4	62.4	75.5
Total employed (thousands)	**63.4**	**34.2**	**97.6**	**83.9**	**45.3**	**129.3**
Employment rates of the highly educated (%)	86.8	67.3	78.3	93.1	73.0	83.9
Unemployment rates of the highly educated (%)	3.3	4.5	3.8	4.2	5.1	4.6
Highly educated in low- and medium-skilled jobs (%)	23.8	24.1	23.9	23.2	24.3	23.6
Highly educated employed (thousands)	**32.3**	**19.2**	**51.4**	**45.0**	**29.2**	**74.2**
Legislators, senior officials and managers	23.8	11.4	18.9	24.9	19.8	23.3
Professionals	25.5	25.3	25.4	30.3	26.1	29.0
Life science and health professionals	4.9	2.4	4.0	10.5	2.5	8.4
Teaching professionals	4.7	10.5	6.9	1.9	8.7	3.7
Technicians and associate professionals	14.3	20.2	16.6	11.6	18.0	13.6
Clerks	4.9	19.8	10.8	3.9	16.5	7.9
Service, shop and market sales workers	9.8	16.5	12.5	9.8	15.2	11.5
Skilled agricultural and fishery workers	0.7	0.2	0.5	0.8	0.1	0.6
Craft and related trades workers	9.7	1.9	6.6	9.8	1.4	7.0
Plant and machine operators and assemblers	6.3	1.4	4.4	5.6	0.6	4.0
Elementary occupations	5.0	3.4	4.4	3.4	2.5	3.1

(Left side vertical label: Distribution of employment by occupation (%), population 15+)

Persons born in Israel and their native-born children, population 15+

Living in:	Europe	United States	Australia
2008	Thousands	Thousands	Thousands
Native-born children	13.7	125.4	5.2
Foreign-born	27.3	133.5	9.6
Total	41.0	258.9	14.8

International students from Israel in OECD countries

Five main destinations	2004	2005	2006	2007	2008	2009
United States	3 474	3 471	3 540	3 341	3 007	3 010
Italy	923	1 002	1 060	1 121	1 209	1 461
Germany	..	..	..	..	1 270	1 326
Hungary	..	..	..	..	..	795
United Kingdom	1 300	1 122	937	889	616	613
Total	6 958	6 613	6 846	6 569	7 408	8 473

Legal migrant flows to the OECD
Thousands

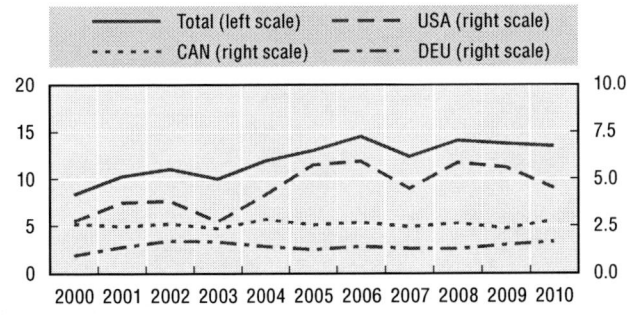

Remittance flows

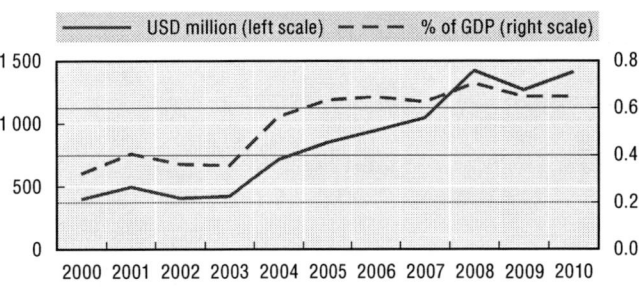

Ten main countries of destination for legal migrants in 2010 (numbers, % of total flows to the country): USA (4515, 0.4%), CAN (2795, 1%), DEU (1651, 0.2%), GBR (1461, 0.3%), AUS (523, 0.3%), HUN (311, 1.3%), JPN (283, 0.1%), ESP (234, 0.1%), ITA (211, 0%), AUT (198, 0.2%).

Desire to emigrate, 2008-10

	Women	15-24	Highly educated	Total	Regional total
Persons who would move permanently, if they had the opportunity to do so (%)	17	19	16	16	16
Of which: Persons who are planning to move permanently in the next 12 months (%)				5	6
Of which: Persons who have already done some preparations for this move (*e.g.* visa application) (%)					39

Three main countries of desired destination: United States (45%), Canada (11%), France (6%).
Information on data for Israel: *http://dx.doi.org/10.1787/888932315602.*

StatLink ⦿ *http://dx.doi.org/10.1787/888932673315*

		Italy compared to:	World	Region
Total population 2010 (millions)	60.5	Human Development Index (HDI)	24/187	22/34
Population growth 2010 (%)	0.5	GDP per capita	27/194	19/34
GDP per capita 2010 (current USD)	33 917	Emigration rate	86/203	17/34
GDP growth 2010 (%)	1.3	Emigration rate of the highly educated	98/157	17/34
Poverty rate 2010 (USD PPP 2 a day, in %)	..			

Age structure of the population 0+ (2010): "0-14": 10%; "15-24": 14%; "25-64": 56%; "65+": 20%.
Level of education of the population 15+ (2010): "Low": 24%; "Medium": 66%; "High": 10%.

Emigrant population living in OECD countries

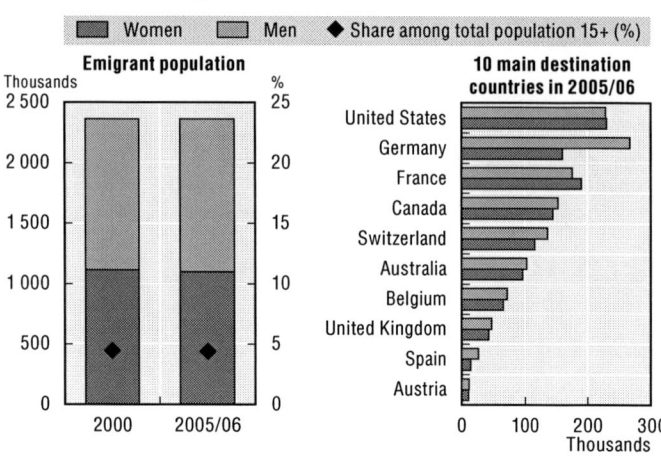

Immigrant population

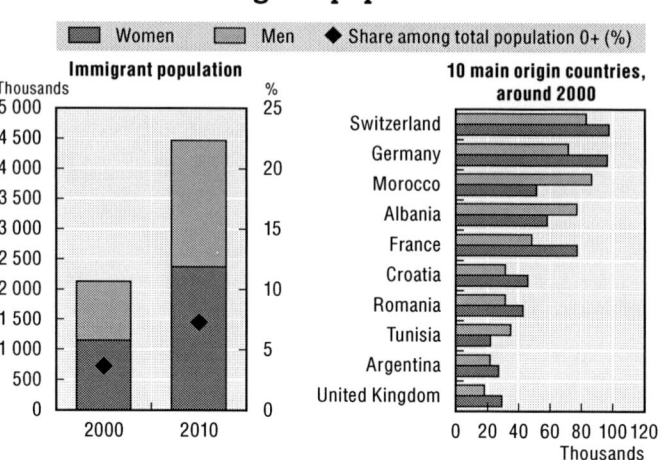

Emigrant population: persons born in Italy living abroad

	2000						2005/06		
	All destinations			OECD destinations			OECD destinations		
Population 15+	Men	Women	Total	Men	Women	Total	Men	Women	Total
Emigrant population (thousands)	1 436.4	1 288.0	2 724.4	1 251.5	1 109.0	2 360.4	1 263.9	1 097.1	2 361.0
Recent emigrants (thousands)	..	..	..	52.0	37.6	89.6	78.1	51.2	129.3
15-24 (%)	1.9	1.9	1.9	2.0	2.1	2.1	3.0	3.0	3.0
25-64 (%)	65.7	57.9	62.0	68.4	60.3	64.6	64.0	56.5	60.5
65+ (%)	32.4	40.2	36.1	29.6	37.6	33.4	33.0	40.5	36.5
Low-educated (%)	56.8	66.9	61.6	55.8	65.4	60.3	48.9	59.6	53.8
Highly educated (%)	13.3	10.3	11.9	13.2	10.8	12.1	17.1	13.9	15.6
Total emigration rates (%)	5.7	4.8	5.2	5.0	4.1	4.5	5.0	4.0	4.5
Emigration rates of the highly educated (%)	8.2	5.6	6.9	7.1	5.1	6.1	8.6	5.8	7.2

Main destinations in 2005/06

	Total		Recent emigrants	Women	Highly educated	15-24	Total in 2000
Population 15+	Thousands	%	%	%	%	%	Thousands
United States	457.7	19.4	4.6	50.2	22.7	3.4	518.2
Germany	427.1	18.1	4.6	37.6	8.2	5.0	334.5
France	365.6	15.5	4.4	51.9	10.4	1.8	403.5
Canada	298.8	12.7	0.6	48.7	15.7	0.8	317.5
Switzerland	252.9	10.7	8.5	45.9	10.8	2.8	230.8
Australia	198.2	8.4	1.2	48.3	9.0	0.6	217.7
Belgium	137.1	5.8	–	47.8	7.4	–	129.9
United Kingdom	89.7	3.8	21.2	47.4	54.5	–	103.5
Spain	40.5	1.7	45.3	34.0	43.4	4.6	23.0
Austria	22.1	0.9	16.9	48.0	23.9	10.0	25.2

Labour market indicators of persons born in Italy living in OECD countries

Population 15-64	2000			2005/06		
	Men	Women	Total	Men	Women	Total
Employment-population ratio (%)	76.7	54.3	66.9	78.1	57.7	69.2
Unemployment rate (%)	8.0	7.9	8.0	7.6	8.2	7.8
Participation rate (%)	83.4	59.0	72.6	84.5	62.9	75.1
Total employed (thousands)	**647.7**	**359.2**	**1 006.9**	**649.0**	**369.1**	**1 018.1**
Employment rates of the highly educated (%)	89.9	75.9	84.0	92.5	81.6	87.9
Unemployment rates of the highly educated (%)	3.1	4.3	3.6	4.0	5.2	4.5
Highly educated in low- and medium-skilled jobs (%)	25.7	28.5	26.8	26.3	30.4	27.9
Highly educated employed (thousands)	**123.1**	**75.5**	**198.5**	**159.8**	**101.2**	**261.0**
Legislators, senior officials and managers	11.8	7.1	10.2	13.7	6.5	11.2
Professionals	6.4	8.6	7.2	9.1	11.8	10.0
Life science and health professionals	0.5	0.7	0.6	0.9	1.2	1.0
Teaching professionals	1.2	3.5	1.9	1.2	5.6	2.7
Technicians and associate professionals	7.8	10.6	8.7	9.3	12.0	10.2
Clerks	4.0	17.2	8.3	5.0	17.0	9.1
Service, shop and market sales workers	11.7	26.8	16.7	11.4	22.5	15.2
Skilled agricultural and fishery workers	1.0	0.6	0.9	1.6	2.0	1.7
Craft and related trades workers	32.0	3.3	22.5	27.3	4.4	19.4
Plant and machine operators and assemblers	15.8	5.4	12.4	13.7	5.1	10.8
Elementary occupations	9.4	20.4	13.1	8.7	18.4	12.1

Distribution of employment by occupation (%), population 15+

Persons born in Italy and their native-born children, population 15+

Living in:	Europe	United States	Australia
2008	Thousands	Thousands	Thousands
Native-born children	1 813.5	1 244.4	202.9
Foreign-born	1 214.4	577.8	146.7
Total	3 027.9	1 822.3	349.6

International students from Italy in OECD countries

Five main destinations	2004	2005	2006	2007	2008	2009
United Kingdom	5 215	5 317	5 461	5 989	5 607	6 038
France	4 686	4 021	4 455	4 790	5 009	5 348
United States	3 308	3 406	3 338	3 416	3 539	4 205
Germany	..	..	..	..	3 275	3 470
Switzerland	..	..	..	..	2 188	2 554
Total	15 086	14 640	15 876	17 012	22 373	26 391

Legal migrant flows to the OECD
Thousands

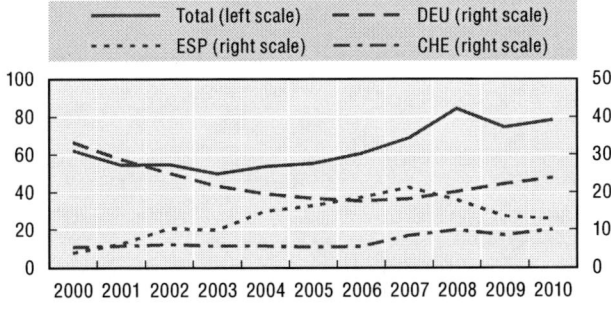

Remittance flows

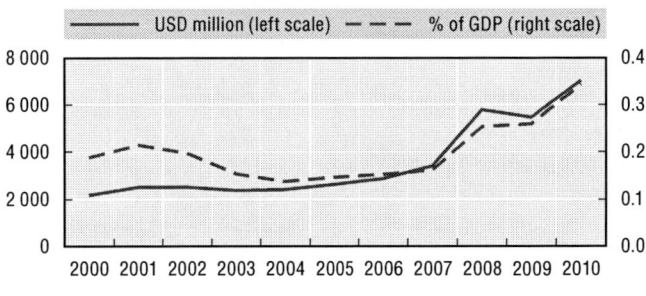

Ten main countries of destination for legal migrants in 2010 (numbers, % of total flows to the country): DEU (23894, 3.6%), ESP (12919, 3%), CHE (10098, 7.7%), GBR (9000, 1.9%), BEL (3557, 3.5%), NLD (2797, 2.8%), USA (2579, 2.2%), AUT (2191, 2.2%), JPN (2106, 0.7%), PRT (977, 3.6%).

Desire to emigrate, 2008-10

	Women	15-24	Highly educated	Total	Regional total
Persons who would move permanently, if they had the opportunity to do so (%)	15	38	33	19	16
Of which: Persons who are planning to move permanently in the next 12 months (%)				5	6
Of which: Persons who have already done some preparations for this move (*e.g.* visa application) (%)					39

Three main countries of desired destination: United Kingdom (13%), Spain (12%), France (11%).

StatLink http://dx.doi.org/10.1787/888932673334

		Japan compared to:	World	Region
Total population 2010 (millions)	127.5	Human Development Index (HDI)	12/187	11/34
Population growth 2010 (%)	–0.1	GDP per capita	18/194	13/34
GDP per capita 2010 (current USD)	42 831	Emigration rate	166/203	33/34
GDP growth 2010 (%)	4.0	Emigration rate of the highly educated	154/157	32/34
Poverty rate 2010 (USD PPP 2 a day, in %)	..			

Age structure of the population 0+ (2010): "0-14": 10%; "15-24": 13%; "25-64": 54%; "65+": 23%.
Level of education of the population 15+ (2010): "Low": 17%; "Medium": 46%; "High": 37%.

Emigrant population living in OECD countries

Immigrant population

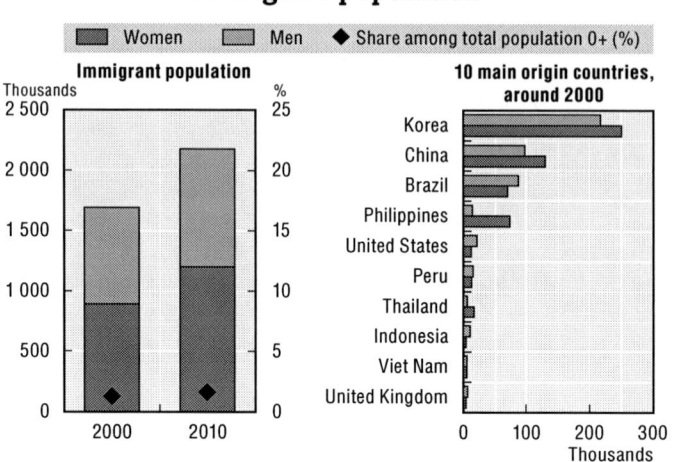

Emigrant population: persons born in Japan living abroad

	2000						2005/06		
	All destinations			OECD destinations			OECD destinations		
Population 15+	Men	Women	Total	Men	Women	Total	Men	Women	Total
Emigrant population (thousands)	288.1	410.1	698.2	215.6	348.7	564.3	229.3	376.8	606.0
Recent emigrants (thousands)	..	..	..	68.4	93.5	161.9	59.1	83.4	142.4
15-24 (%)	11.9	11.4	11.6	15.0	12.7	13.6	14.2	10.1	11.7
25-64 (%)	75.1	69.3	71.7	81.0	73.3	76.2	80.5	74.3	76.6
65+ (%)	12.9	19.3	16.7	4.0	14.0	10.2	5.3	15.6	11.7
Low-educated (%)	18.2	19.0	18.7	8.7	11.8	10.6	6.6	8.8	7.9
Highly educated (%)	50.7	42.0	45.6	56.2	45.7	49.7	57.9	52.4	54.5
Total emigration rates (%)	0.5	0.7	0.6	0.4	0.6	0.5	0.4	0.7	0.5
Emigration rates of the highly educated (%)	0.8	1.1	1.0	0.7	1.0	0.9	0.7	1.1	0.9

Main destinations in 2005/06

	Total		Recent emigrants	Women	Highly educated	15-24	Total in 2000
Population 15+	Thousands	%	%	%	%	%	Thousands
United States	463.0	76.4	20.5	61.2	51.9	11.5	437.3
Canada	28.6	4.7	24.2	67.8	66.2	12.8	25.1
Australia	27.7	4.6	41.4	68.2	54.0	17.2	22.8
United Kingdom	25.4	4.2	39.3	56.9	72.2	–	31.5
France	16.9	2.8	43.4	68.8	66.9	10.8	13.0
New Zealand	8.7	1.4	58.0	67.6	31.6	26.4	8.0
Switzerland	6.4	1.1	48.5	61.5	66.6	–	4.0
Italy	6.2	1.0	35.9	60.7	65.0	–	4.5
Spain	5.8	1.0	26.5	62.3	79.7	–	3.0
Austria	3.4	0.6	–	94.0	58.1	–	1.8

Labour market indicators of persons born in Japan living in OECD countries

Population 15-64	2000			2005/06		
	Men	Women	Total	Men	Women	Total
Employment-population ratio (%)	76.8	51.4	61.8	79.3	55.4	65.1
Unemployment rate (%)	3.4	5.1	4.2	4.1	6.1	5.1
Participation rate (%)	79.5	54.2	64.6	82.7	59.0	68.7
Total employed (thousands)	**155.9**	**150.8**	**306.7**	**168.6**	**171.9**	**340.5**
Employment rates of the highly educated (%)	84.4	54.6	67.6	89.6	61.7	72.9
Unemployment rates of the highly educated (%)	2.1	4.4	3.2	2.5	5.9	4.2
Highly educated in low- and medium-skilled jobs (%)	25.7	37.8	31.3	25.8	36.4	31.1
Highly educated employed (thousands)	**97.0**	**81.8**	**178.8**	**108.6**	**106.9**	**215.5**
Legislators, senior officials and managers	33.3	9.4	20.9	32.7	8.9	19.7
Professionals	23.3	23.1	23.2	22.5	22.4	22.4
Life science and health professionals	1.2	1.3	1.2	0.5	1.0	0.8
Teaching professionals	5.8	9.6	7.7	4.5	9.2	7.0
Technicians and associate professionals	12.5	15.8	14.3	15.7	16.9	16.3
Clerks	6.4	20.7	13.8	4.4	18.2	11.9
Service, shop and market sales workers	12.5	24.6	18.8	12.9	22.4	18.1
Skilled agricultural and fishery workers	0.9	0.5	0.7	0.5	1.9	1.3
Craft and related trades workers	5.4	1.5	3.4	3.9	4.8	4.4
Plant and machine operators and assemblers	2.7	0.7	1.7	1.5	0.6	1.0
Elementary occupations	3.0	3.6	3.3	3.6	3.5	3.5

Distribution of employment by occupation (%), population 15+

Persons born in Japan and their native-born children, population 15+

Living in:	Europe	United States	Australia
2008	Thousands	Thousands	Thousands
Native-born children	7.2	330.0	3.5
Foreign-born	67.2	282.1	20.1
Total	74.4	612.1	23.7

International students from Japan in OECD countries

Five main destinations	2004	2005	2006	2007	2008	2009
United States	40 835	44 092	40 086	36 062	34 010	28 783
United Kingdom	6 395	6 179	6 200	5 706	4 465	3 871
Australia	3 172	3 380	3 305	3 249	2 974	2 701
France	2 337	2 152	2 112	2 071	1 908	1 847
Germany	..	..	..	..	1 807	1 744
Total	56 595	58 580	56 415	51 117	49 205	43 254

Legal migrant flows to the OECD
Thousands

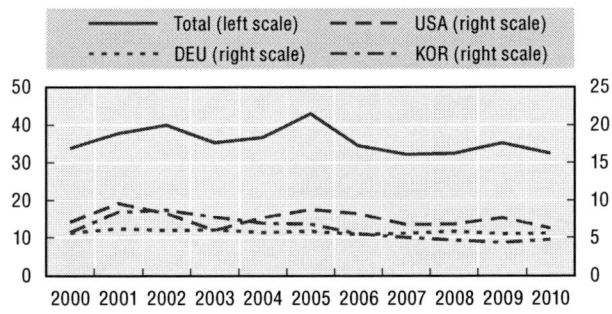

Remittance flows

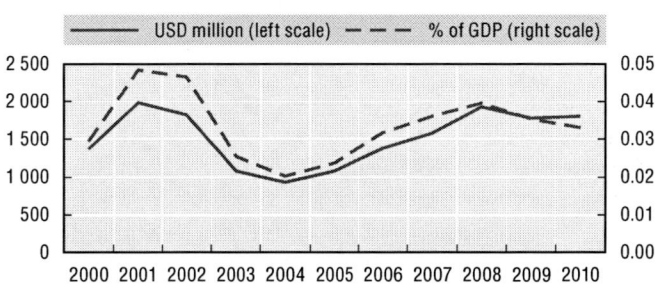

Ten main countries of destination for legal migrants in 2010 (numbers, % of total flows to the country): USA (6264, 0.6%), DEU (5567, 0.8%), KOR (4744, 1.6%), GBR (4000, 0.9%), AUS (1636, 0.8%), FRA (1464, 1.1%), CAN (1315, 1%), BEL (1063, 1%), NLD (1018, 1%), CHE (767, 0.6%).

Desire to emigrate, 2008-10

	Women	15-24	Highly educated	Total	Regional total
Persons who would move permanently, if they had the opportunity to do so (%)	16	28	22	17	16
Of which: Persons who are planning to move permanently in the next 12 months (%)				1	6
Of which: Persons who have already done some preparations for this move (*e.g.* visa application) (%)					39

Three main countries of desired destination: United States (21%), Australia (14%), Canada (9%).

StatLink ⌷⌷⌷ http://dx.doi.org/10.1787/888932673353

			Korea compared to:	World	Region
Total population 2010 (millions)	48.9		Human Development Index (HDI)	15/187	13/34
Population growth 2010 (%)	0.3		GDP per capita	38/194	26/34
GDP per capita 2010 (current USD)	20 757		Emigration rate	165/203	32/34
GDP growth 2010 (%)	6.2		Emigration rate of the highly educated	155/157	33/34
Poverty rate 2010 (USD PPP 2 a day, in %)	..				

Age structure of the population 0+ (2010): "0-14": 14%; "15-24": 16%; "25-64": 59%; "65+": 11%.
Level of education of the population 15+ (2010): "Low": 13%; "Medium": 47%; "High": 40%.

Emigrant population living in OECD countries

Immigrant population

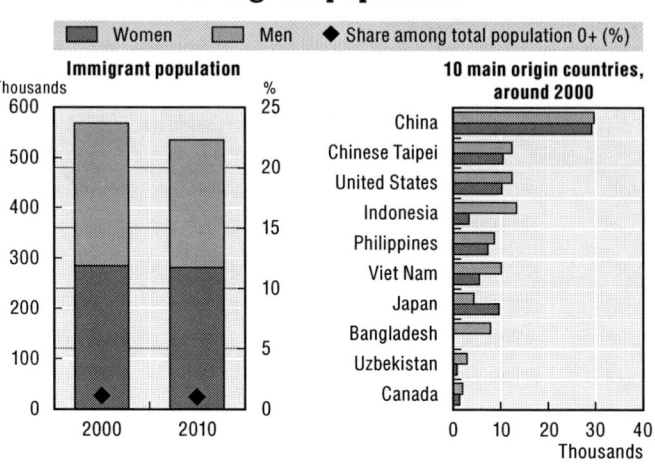

Emigrant population: persons born in Korea living abroad

	2000						2005/06		
	All destinations			OECD destinations			OECD destinations		
Population 15+	Men	Women	Total	Men	Women	Total	Men	Women	Total
Emigrant population (thousands)	652.1	837.7	1 489.8	628.9	817.2	1 446.1	717.2	935.3	1 652.5
Recent emigrants (thousands)	..	..	..	88.0	105.3	193.3	105.3	129.4	234.6
15-24 (%)	16.5	15.3	15.8	16.8	15.4	16.0	16.3	13.7	14.8
25-64 (%)	74.8	75.0	74.9	74.6	74.9	74.8	72.3	74.2	73.3
65+ (%)	8.7	9.6	9.2	8.7	9.7	9.2	11.4	12.1	11.8
Low-educated (%)	17.0	22.3	20.0	17.0	22.4	20.0	13.0	16.6	15.0
Highly educated (%)	42.2	34.6	37.9	42.3	34.6	37.9	48.7	42.3	45.1
Total emigration rates (%)	2.2	3.0	2.6	2.2	2.9	2.6	0.5	0.7	0.6
Emigration rates of the highly educated (%)	2.9	4.9	3.7	2.9	4.8	3.7	0.7	1.1	0.8

Main destinations in 2005/06

	Total		Recent emigrants	Women	Highly educated	15-24	Total in 2000
Population 15+	Thousands	%	%	%	%	%	Thousands
United States	980.3	59.3	16.7	57.4	51.6	13.3	801.7
Japan	428.5	25.9	..	55.0	23.7	12.7	467.4
Canada	104.0	6.3	31.4	53.7	61.1	22.8	72.6
Australia	46.2	2.8	39.6	55.7	47.3	25.2	33.4
New Zealand	22.8	1.4	56.1	54.7	26.5	30.5	14.0
France	16.4	1.0	23.2	62.5	57.1	31.2	13.0
United Kingdom	9.0	0.5	–	–	79.5	–	9.9
Sweden	8.2	0.5	6.9	67.6	37.6	24.5	7.9
Denmark	7.5	0.5	5.4	68.2	31.3	35.4	6.6
Norway	4.9	0.3	3.7	67.6	33.4	40.6	4.7

Labour market indicators of persons born in Korea living in OECD countries

Population 15-64	2000			2005/06		
	Men	Women	Total	Men	Women	Total
Employment-population ratio (%)	70.0	52.9	60.1	72.9	54.0	62.1
Unemployment rate (%)	5.0	6.0	5.5	5.3	6.5	5.9
Participation rate (%)	73.6	56.2	63.6	77.0	57.8	66.0
Total employed (thousands)	**265.0**	**271.8**	**536.8**	**336.5**	**331.1**	**667.6**
Employment rates of the highly educated (%)	77.2	56.0	66.0	85.7	60.8	72.1
Unemployment rates of the highly educated (%)	3.7	5.0	4.3	4.0	5.8	4.8
Highly educated in low- and medium-skilled jobs (%)	37.2	42.6	39.6	35.3	40.0	37.5
Highly educated employed (thousands)	**148.3**	**120.2**	**268.5**	**215.5**	**181.6**	**397.1**
Legislators, senior officials and managers	26.8	18.0	22.4	25.6	16.0	20.8
Professionals	18.8	15.2	17.0	18.4	17.7	18.1
Life science and health professionals	1.4	2.5	2.0	1.1	2.5	1.9
Teaching professionals	3.3	4.7	4.0	2.8	4.6	3.7
Technicians and associate professionals	12.1	13.3	12.7	12.9	15.9	14.4
Clerks	6.7	16.2	11.4	6.3	16.4	11.3
Service, shop and market sales workers	12.7	25.0	18.8	13.4	23.8	18.6
Skilled agricultural and fishery workers	0.9	0.5	0.7	0.8	0.9	0.8
Craft and related trades workers	8.7	2.6	5.6	9.5	1.9	5.7
Plant and machine operators and assemblers	5.1	2.5	3.8	5.4	2.1	3.8
Elementary occupations	8.2	6.8	7.5	7.6	5.2	6.4

Distribution of employment by occupation (%), population 15+

Persons born in Korea and their native-born children, population 15+

Living in:	Europe	United States	Australia
2008	Thousands	Thousands	Thousands
Native-born children	4.9	37.2	2.7
Foreign-born	33.4	812.1	10.2
Total	38.3	849.2	12.9

International students from Korea in OECD countries

Five main destinations	2004	2005	2006	2007	2008	2009
United States	52 484	55 731	61 117	63 772	69 198	73 832
Japan	23 280	22 571	22 344	22 109	23 290	24 850
Australia	3 915	4 222	4 491	5 430	6 270	6 796
United Kingdom	3 482	3 846	4 023	4 311	4 031	4 277
Germany	..	..	..	..	3 794	3 975
Total	87 150	88 863	95 176	98 802	109 391	118 789

Legal migrant flows to the OECD
Thousands

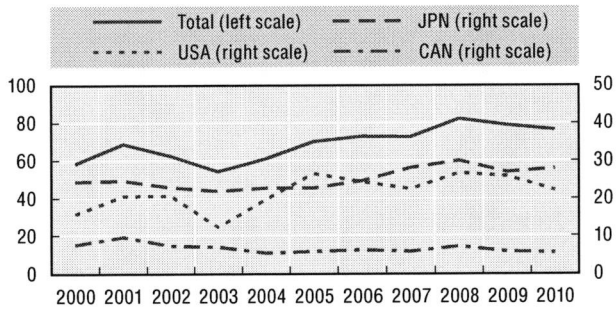

Remittance flows

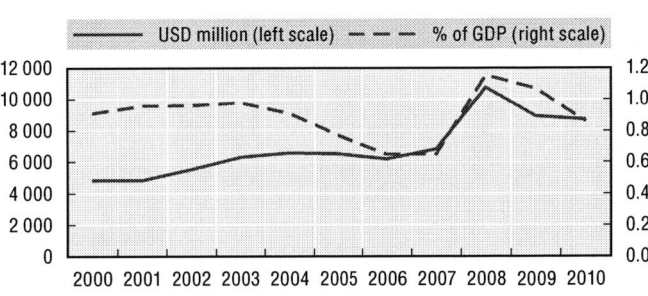

Ten main countries of destination for legal migrants in 2010 (numbers, % of total flows to the country): JPN (27868, 9.7%), USA (22227, 2.1%), CAN (5540, 2%), AUS (4327, 2.1%), DEU (4096, 0.6%), GBR (4000, 0.9%), NZL (1091, 2.6%), POL (1070, 2.6%), SVK (671, 5.3%), NLD (665, 0.7%).

Desire to emigrate, 2008-10

	Women	15-24	Highly educated	Total	Regional total
Persons who would move permanently, if they had the opportunity to do so (%)	25	36	31	25	16
Of which: Persons who are planning to move permanently in the next 12 months (%)				2	6
Of which: Persons who have already done some preparations for this move (*e.g.* visa application) (%)					39

Three main countries of desired destination: Australia (19%), Canada (18%), United States (16%).

StatLink 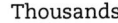 http://dx.doi.org/10.1787/888932673372

Total population 2010 (millions)	0.5	Luxembourg compared to:	World	Region
Population growth 2010 (%)	1.6	Human Development Index (HDI)	25/187	23/34
GDP per capita 2010 (current USD)	105 438	GDP per capita	3/194	1/34
GDP growth 2010 (%)	2.7	Emigration rate	50/203	6/34
Poverty rate 2010 (USD PPP 2 a day, in %)	..	Emigration rate of the highly educated	38/157	2/34

Age structure of the population 0+ (2010): "0-14": 12%; "15-24": 18%; "25-64": 57%; "65+": 14%.
Level of education of the population 15+ (2010): "Low": 29%; "Medium": 56%; "High": 15%.

Emigrant population living in OECD countries

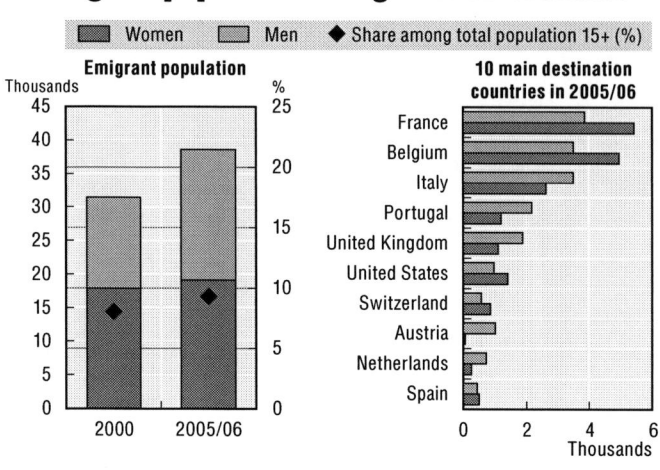

Immigrant population

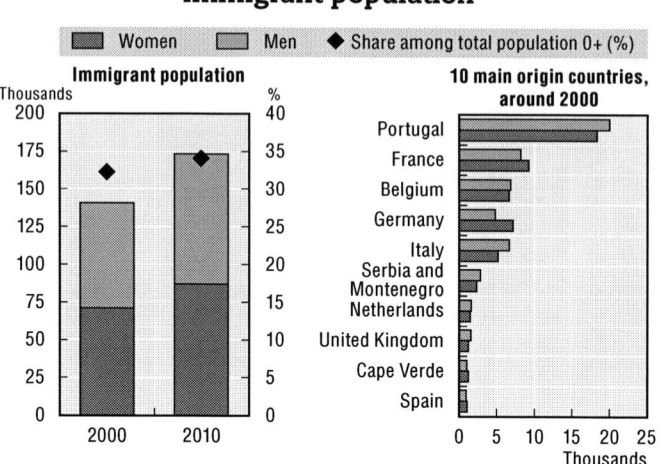

Emigrant population: persons born in Luxembourg living abroad

	2000						2005/06		
	All destinations			OECD destinations			OECD destinations		
Population 15+	Men	Women	Total	Men	Women	Total	Men	Women	Total
Emigrant population (thousands)	13.7	18.1	31.7	13.5	17.9	31.4	19.4	19.2	38.6
Recent emigrants (thousands)	..	..	..	1.8	1.4	3.2	4.3	2.3	6.7
15-24 (%)	20.2	16.0	17.8	20.2	15.9	17.8	20.6	14.3	17.5
25-64 (%)	64.0	57.2	60.1	64.0	57.4	60.2	68.9	60.4	64.7
65+ (%)	15.8	26.8	22.1	15.7	26.8	22.0	10.4	25.2	17.8
Low-educated (%)	35.9	44.5	40.8	36.0	44.5	40.8	31.4	34.4	32.9
Highly educated (%)	28.8	21.8	24.8	28.7	21.8	24.8	33.5	28.8	31.2
Total emigration rates (%)	7.3	9.0	8.2	7.3	9.0	8.1	9.6	9.2	9.4
Emigration rates of the highly educated (%)	11.4	13.6	12.4	11.2	13.5	12.3	17.4	17.7	17.6

Main destinations in 2005/06

	Total		Recent emigrants	Women	Highly educated	15-24	Total in 2000
Population 15+	Thousands	%	%	%	%	%	Thousands
France	9.3	24.1	27.3	58.5	32.2	20.7	8.9
Belgium	8.5	21.9	–	–	–	–	8.7
Italy	6.1	15.9	–	43.0	–	–	4.5
Portugal	–	–	–	–	–	–	2.2
United Kingdom	–	–	–	–	–	–	1.0
United States	2.4	6.1	4.2	59.1	44.1	7.5	2.4
Switzerland	1.4	3.6	–	–	–	–	1.3
Austria	–	–	–	–	–	–	0.5
Netherlands	–	–	–	–	–	–	–
Spain	–	–	..	–	–	–	0.8

Labour market indicators of persons born in Luxembourg living in OECD countries

Population 15-64	2000			2005/06		
	Men	Women	Total	Men	Women	Total
Employment-population ratio (%)	69.2	49.9	58.9	63.1	48.3	57.0
Unemployment rate (%)	6.3	11.7	8.8	6.0	14.2	9.1
Participation rate (%)	73.9	56.5	64.6	67.2	56.3	62.7
Total employed (thousands)	**7.6**	**6.3**	**13.9**	**12.1**	**6.5**	**18.7**
Employment rates of the highly educated (%)	79.1	65.4	72.2	90.6	73.3	82.8
Unemployment rates of the highly educated (%)	3.1	6.8	4.9	1.3	17.3	7.8
Highly educated in low- and medium-skilled jobs (%)	12.4	22.4	16.9	18.4	29.1	22.3
Highly educated employed (thousands)	**2.6**	**2.2**	**4.9**	**5.1**	**2.9**	**8.0**
Legislators, senior officials and managers	13.1	7.9	10.7	12.6	8.5	11.2
Professionals	17.2	15.4	16.4	23.3	19.1	21.8
Life science and health professionals	2.3	2.9	2.6	2.3	5.8	3.5
Teaching professionals	3.1	4.1	3.6	6.6	4.6	5.9
Technicians and associate professionals	15.1	18.4	16.7	16.6	20.2	17.9
Clerks	4.3	20.0	11.7	9.4	18.5	12.6
Service, shop and market sales workers	9.9	19.3	14.3	6.6	14.6	9.4
Skilled agricultural and fishery workers	0.8	1.0	0.9	0.7	1.3	0.9
Craft and related trades workers	19.8	4.6	12.7	17.8	9.4	14.9
Plant and machine operators and assemblers	11.7	3.5	7.9	7.2	1.4	5.2
Elementary occupations	8.0	9.7	8.8	5.8	7.0	6.2

Distribution of employment by occupation (%), population 15+

Persons born in Luxembourg and their native-born children, population 15+

Living in:	Europe	United States	Australia
2008	Thousands	Thousands	Thousands
Native-born children	19.3	..	..
Foreign-born	20.3	..	..
Total	39.6	..	..

International students from Luxembourg in OECD countries

Five main destinations	2004	2005	2006	2007	2008	2009
Germany	..	..	..	..	2 425	2 598
France	1 709	1 670	1 659	1 575	1 551	1 471
United Kingdom	833	822	838	879	834	890
Belgium	818	996	1 100	1 077	256	490
Switzerland	..	..	..	..	300	345
Total	3 566	3 715	3 894	3 830	5 629	6 092

Legal migrant flows to the OECD
Thousands

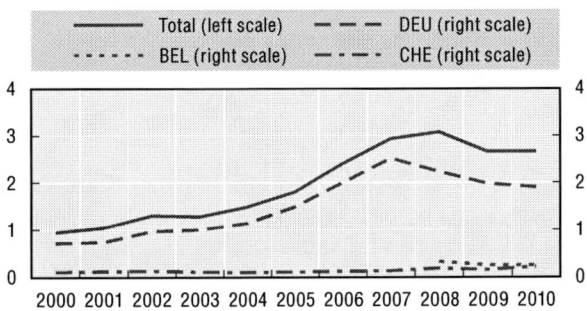

Remittance flows

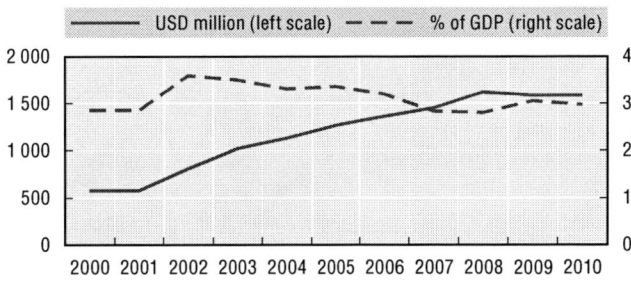

Ten main countries of destination for legal migrants in 2010 (numbers, % of total flows to the country): DEU (1903, 0.3%), BEL (242, 0.2%), CHE (209, 0.2%), AUT (80, 0.1%), ESP (56, 0%), NLD (43, 0%), JPN (37, 0%), USA (22, 0%), CAN (20, 0%), ITA (18, 0%).

Desire to emigrate, 2008-10

	Women	15-24	Highly educated	Total	Regional total
Persons who would move permanently, if they had the opportunity to do so (%)	18	28	24	20	16
Of which: Persons who are planning to move permanently in the next 12 months (%)				..	6
Of which: Persons who have already done some preparations for this move (*e.g.* visa application) (%)					39

StatLink ꜜ http://dx.doi.org/10.1787/888932673391

Total population 2010 (millions)	113.4	**Mexico compared to:**	**World**	**Region**
Population growth 2010 (%)	1.2	Human Development Index (HDI)	57/187	33/34
GDP per capita 2010 (current USD)	9 123	GDP per capita	67/194	34/34
GDP growth 2010 (%)	5.4	Emigration rate	37/203	3/34
Poverty rate 2008 (USD PPP 2 a day, in %)	8.6	Emigration rate of the highly educated	95/157	15/34

Age structure of the population 0+ (2010): "0-14": 18%; "15-24": 29%; "25-64": 46%; "65+": 6%.
Level of education of the population 15+ (2010): "Low": 32%; "Medium": 52%; "High": 17%.

Emigrant population living in OECD countries

Immigrant population

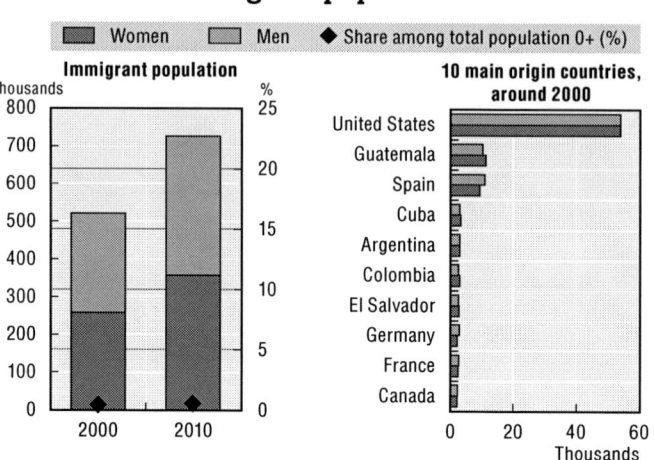

Emigrant population: persons born in Mexico living abroad

Population 15+	2000 All destinations Men	Women	Total	2000 OECD destinations Men	Women	Total	2005/06 OECD destinations Men	Women	Total
Emigrant population (thousands)	4 652.4	3 715.9	8 368.4	4 634.5	3 696.3	8 330.8	6 019.9	4 763.9	10 783.8
Recent emigrants (thousands)	..	..	..	1 229.1	829.2	2 058.3	1 177.8	776.2	1 953.9
15-24 (%)	23.7	19.7	21.9	23.7	19.6	21.9	17.3	15.7	16.6
25-64 (%)	72.7	74.5	73.5	72.7	74.5	73.5	78.0	77.2	77.6
65+ (%)	3.6	5.9	4.6	3.6	5.9	4.6	4.7	7.1	5.7
Low-educated (%)	70.6	68.2	69.5	70.6	68.3	69.6	60.4	58.7	59.6
Highly educated (%)	5.3	6.5	5.8	5.2	6.4	5.7	6.7	8.4	7.4
Total emigration rates (%)	12.5	9.8	11.1	12.5	9.7	11.1	14.8	11.3	13.0
Emigration rates of the highly educated (%)	5.6	6.9	6.2	5.5	6.8	6.1	6.8	7.8	7.2

Main destinations in 2005/06

Population 15+	Total Thousands	%	Recent emigrants %	Women %	Highly educated %	15-24 %	Total in 2000 Thousands
United States	10 668.9	98.9	18.0	44.1	7.0	16.6	8 250.9
Canada	54.6	0.5	28.0	51.6	36.2	18.7	37.5
Spain	24.3	0.2	74.2	51.1	64.9	12.3	16.6
France	8.4	0.1	43.4	60.6	60.3	27.1	5.2
United Kingdom	6.1	0.1	–	–	–	–	4.5
Switzerland	4.1	0.0	47.4	60.2	59.1	–	2.5
Italy	3.0	0.0	–	72.4	46.1	–	3.7
Netherlands	2.6	0.0	–	60.4	–	–	–
Israel	2.0	0.0	26.6	50.5	53.1	12.2	1.4
Australia	1.7	0.0	47.4	53.0	64.5	19.1	0.9

Labour market indicators of persons born in Mexico living in OECD countries

Population 15-64	2000			2005/06		
	Men	Women	Total	Men	Women	Total
Employment-population ratio (%)	69.3	41.2	57.0	84.2	49.5	69.1
Unemployment rate (%)	7.5	13.3	9.4	5.8	10.6	7.4
Participation rate (%)	75.0	47.5	63.0	89.4	55.3	74.6
Total employed (thousands)	**3 097.2**	**1 431.7**	**4 529.0**	**4 787.2**	**2 164.8**	**6 952.1**
Employment rates of the highly educated (%)	79.5	60.0	69.9	92.7	69.7	81.3
Unemployment rates of the highly educated (%)	4.2	6.6	5.2	4.2	6.4	5.1
Highly educated in low- and medium-skilled jobs (%)	56.9	48.8	53.5	63.1	51.8	58.3
Highly educated employed (thousands)	**184.5**	**136.3**	**320.8**	**344.9**	**250.1**	**594.9**
Legislators, senior officials and managers	10.9	8.0	9.6	8.6	8.0	8.3
Professionals	17.4	16.7	17.1	21.5	19.6	20.6
Life science and health professionals	3.9	3.2	3.6	6.1	0.9	3.3
Teaching professionals	6.9	8.4	7.7	6.6	14.5	10.9
Technicians and associate professionals	8.3	15.0	11.3	8.2	16.2	11.9
Clerks	4.4	15.8	9.5	3.9	16.3	9.7
Service, shop and market sales workers	7.4	20.7	13.4	11.2	15.4	13.2
Skilled agricultural and fishery workers	13.6	5.7	10.0	13.0	4.2	8.9
Craft and related trades workers	13.8	2.2	8.5	14.5	2.6	9.0
Plant and machine operators and assemblers	11.6	3.9	8.1	9.6	3.8	6.9
Elementary occupations	12.7	12.1	12.4	9.5	13.9	11.5

Distribution of employment by occupation (%), population 15+

Persons born in Mexico and their native-born children, population 15+

Living in:	Europe	United States	Australia
2008	Thousands	Thousands	Thousands
Native-born children	10.3	8 268.7	..
Foreign-born	54.4	11 860.7	..
Total	64.7	20 129.4	..

International students from Mexico in OECD countries

Five main destinations	2004	2005	2006	2007	2008	2009
United States	13 329	13 644	14 426	14 132	14 853	14 606
Spain	937	1 583	1 705	2 053	1 910	2 880
France	1 452	1 440	1 479	1 640	1 751	1 836
Germany	..	..	..	..	1 299	1 482
United Kingdom	1 973	1 843	1 738	1 663	1 303	1 327
Total	19 806	19 533	21 705	21 618	23 746	24 964

Legal migrant flows to the OECD
Thousands

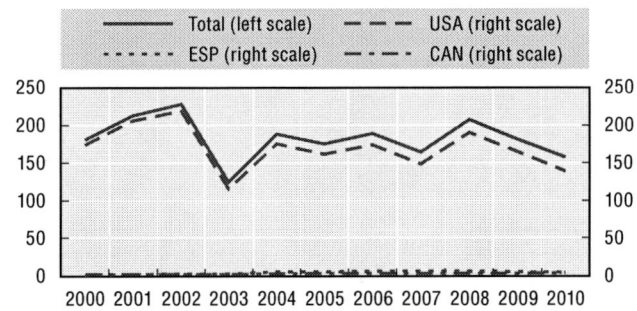

Remittance flows

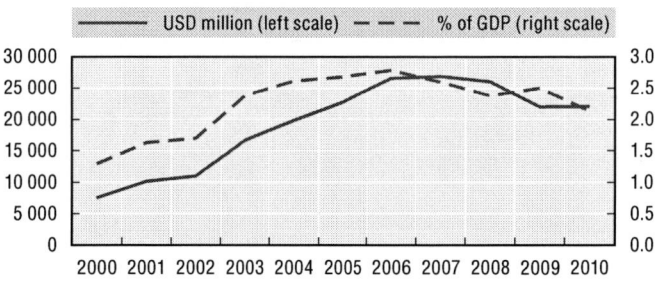

Ten main countries of destination for legal migrants in 2010 (numbers, % of total flows to the country): USA (139120, 13.4%), ESP (4789, 1.1%), CAN (3870, 1.4%), DEU (3008, 0.4%), GBR (827, 0.2%), CHL (685, 1.1%), CHE (629, 0.2%), JPN (628, 0.2%), FRA (602, 0.4%), ITA (602, 0.1%).

Desire to emigrate, 2008-10

	Women	15-24	Highly educated	Total	Regional total
Persons who would move permanently, if they had the opportunity to do so (%)	17	29	28	18	16
Of which: Persons who are planning to move permanently in the next 12 months (%)				13	6
Of which: Persons who have already done some preparations for this move (*e.g.* visa application) (%)					39

Three main countries of desired destination: United States (42%), Canada (13%), Spain (8%).

StatLink  *http://dx.doi.org/10.1787/888932673410*

		Netherlands compared to:	World	Region
Total population 2010 (millions)	16.6	Human Development Index (HDI)	3/187	3/34
Population growth 2010 (%)	0.5	GDP per capita	13/194	8/34
GDP per capita 2010 (current USD)	46 915	Emigration rate	82/203	15/34
GDP growth 2010 (%)	1.7	Emigration rate of the highly educated	91/157	14/34
Poverty rate 2010 (USD PPP 2 a day, in %)	..			

Age structure of the population 0+ (2010): "0-14": 12%; "15-24": 18%; "25-64": 55%; "65+": 15%.
Level of education of the population 15+ (2010): "Low": 12%; "Medium": 64%; "High": 23%.

Emigrant population living in OECD countries

Immigrant population

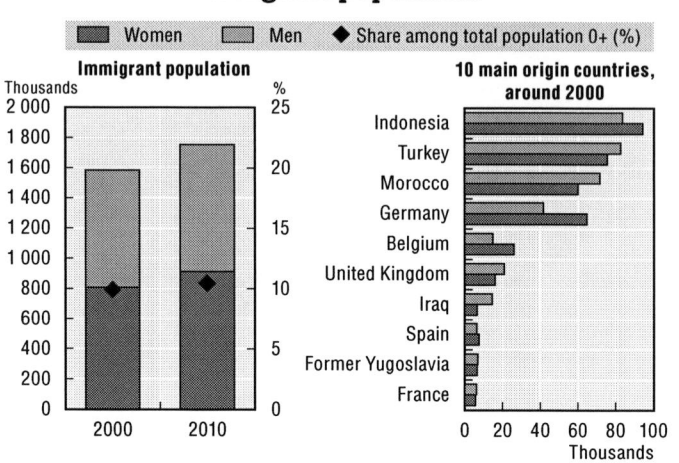

Emigrant population: persons born in the Netherlands living abroad

Population 15+	2000 All destinations Men	2000 All destinations Women	2000 All destinations Total	2000 OECD destinations Men	2000 OECD destinations Women	2000 OECD destinations Total	2005/06 OECD destinations Men	2005/06 OECD destinations Women	2005/06 OECD destinations Total
Emigrant population (thousands)	299.8	305.7	605.5	280.3	288.9	569.2	342.6	339.7	682.3
Recent emigrants (thousands)	..	..	..	33.6	28.8	62.4	58.7	49.7	108.5
15-24 (%)	5.7	5.9	5.8	4.8	4.9	4.9	5.6	4.8	5.2
25-64 (%)	69.6	67.9	68.8	70.0	68.3	69.1	68.1	66.7	67.4
65+ (%)	24.7	26.2	25.5	25.2	26.8	26.0	26.3	28.5	27.4
Low-educated (%)	21.8	32.2	27.1	21.9	32.5	27.2	17.6	26.7	22.1
Highly educated (%)	39.6	28.3	33.9	39.7	28.4	34.0	43.9	33.5	38.7
Total emigration rates (%)	4.5	4.4	4.5	4.2	4.2	4.2	5.0	4.8	4.9
Emigration rates of the highly educated (%)	6.9	6.0	6.5	6.4	5.7	6.1	8.2	7.3	7.8

Main destinations in 2005/06

Population 15+	Total Thousands	Total %	Recent emigrants %	Women %	Highly educated %	15-24 %	Total in 2000 Thousands
Canada	111.7	16.4	2.4	48.8	37.6	2.1	117.2
United States	97.2	14.2	12.0	49.1	48.1	7.2	98.8
Belgium	93.6	13.7	23.0	52.1	29.7	6.6	89.3
Germany	93.0	13.6	30.3	48.3	29.3	–	39.3
Australia	77.6	11.4	4.0	48.7	26.6	1.4	82.3
United Kingdom	43.1	6.3	27.6	47.1	63.3	18.7	35.0
Spain	35.9	5.3	39.9	53.1	53.6	7.2	–
France	34.2	5.0	28.2	53.2	47.0	6.6	26.0
New Zealand	21.3	3.1	7.9	47.0	26.6	3.5	21.7
Switzerland	20.7	3.0	24.6	50.9	47.6	–	16.1

Labour market indicators of persons born in the Netherlands living in OECD countries

Population 15-64	2000			2005/06		
	Men	Women	Total	Men	Women	Total
Employment-population ratio (%)	85.7	60.2	73.0	84.5	62.4	73.6
Unemployment rate (%)	3.4	5.1	4.1	2.9	4.9	3.8
Participation rate (%)	88.6	63.5	76.0	87.0	65.7	76.5
Total employed (thousands)	**168.5**	**118.6**	**287.1**	**207.8**	**148.5**	**356.3**
Employment rates of the highly educated (%)	91.7	71.4	82.9	93.4	76.0	85.6
Unemployment rates of the highly educated (%)	2.3	4.2	3.0	2.3	3.7	2.9
Highly educated in low- and medium-skilled jobs (%)	23.1	29.0	25.4	19.9	27.1	22.7
Highly educated employed (thousands)	**79.0**	**47.0**	**126.0**	**105.4**	**68.0**	**173.5**
Legislators, senior officials and managers	21.4	10.5	17.1	23.3	12.5	18.7
Professionals	18.4	20.2	19.1	20.5	17.7	19.3
Life science and health professionals	1.8	4.0	2.7	1.9	4.5	3.0
Teaching professionals	3.0	7.6	4.8	3.0	5.1	3.9
Technicians and associate professionals	12.8	17.7	14.8	17.1	23.9	20.0
Clerks	5.3	20.7	11.4	5.2	18.2	10.8
Service, shop and market sales workers	5.3	16.5	9.7	5.2	13.3	8.6
Skilled agricultural and fishery workers	8.0	4.9	6.7	5.5	4.3	4.9
Craft and related trades workers	14.9	1.8	9.7	11.3	2.0	7.3
Plant and machine operators and assemblers	8.6	1.9	6.0	7.4	2.2	5.2
Elementary occupations	5.3	5.8	5.5	4.4	5.9	5.0

Distribution of employment by occupation (%), population 15+

Persons born in the Netherlands and their native-born children, population 15+

Living in:	Europe	United States	Australia
2008	Thousands	Thousands	Thousands
Native-born children	186.4	106.9	118.0
Foreign-born	304.7	91.4	119.1
Total	491.0	198.2	237.0

International students from the Netherlands in OECD countries

Five main destinations	2004	2005	2006	2007	2008	2009
United Kingdom	2 473	2 432	2 680	2 811	3 024	3 201
Belgium	50	1 589	1 843	2 089	..	2 195
United States	1 505	1 540	1 623	1 622	1 682	1 839
Germany	..	..	..	..	690	712
France	616	571	603	626	652	673
Total	5 843	7 297	8 150	8 560	7 285	10 258

Legal migrant flows to the OECD
Thousands

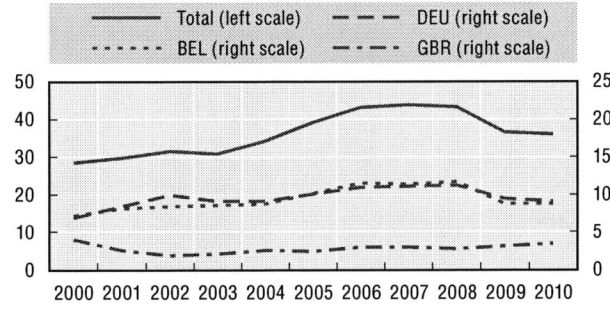

Remittance flows

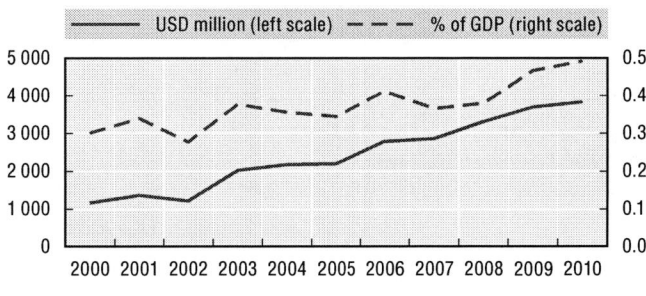

Ten main countries of destination for legal migrants in 2010 (numbers, % of total flows to the country): DEU (9143, 1.4%), BEL (8774, 8.6%), GBR (3449, 0.7%), ESP (3436, 0.8%), CHE (1607, 1.2%), USA (1321, 0.1%), AUT (859, 0.4%), AUS (832, 0.4%), JPN (805, 0.3%), CAN (800, 0.3%).

Desire to emigrate, 2008-10

	Women	15-24	Highly educated	Total	Regional total
Persons who would move permanently, if they had the opportunity to do so (%)	17	25	21	19	16
Of which: Persons who are planning to move permanently in the next 12 months (%)				3	6
Of which: Persons who have already done some preparations for this move (*e.g.* visa application) (%)					39

Two main countries of desired destination: Spain (12%), Canada (11%).

StatLink http://dx.doi.org/10.1787/888932673429

	World	Region
Total population 2010 (millions)	4.4	
Population growth 2010 (%)	1.2	
GDP per capita 2009 (current USD)	29 352	
GDP growth 2009 (%)	−0.5	
Poverty rate 2010 (USD PPP 2 a day, in %)	..	

New Zealand compared to:	World	Region
Human Development Index (HDI)	7/187	6/34
GDP per capita	30/194	21/34
Emigration rate	40/203	4/34
Emigration rate of the highly educated	84/157	12/34

Age structure of the population 0+ (2010): "0-14": 15%; "15-24": 20%; "25-64": 52%; "65+": 13%.
Level of education of the population 15+ (2010): "Low": 24%; "Medium": 24%; "High": 51%.

Emigrant population living in OECD countries

Immigrant population

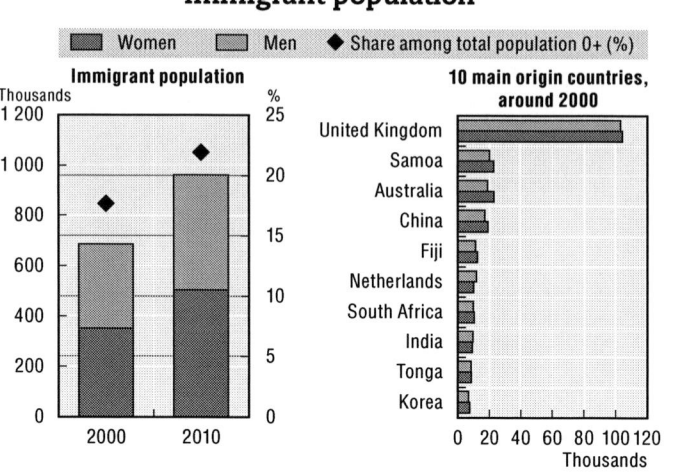

Emigrant population: persons born in New Zealand living abroad

	2000						2005/06		
	All destinations			OECD destinations			OECD destinations		
Population 15+	Men	Women	Total	Men	Women	Total	Men	Women	Total
Emigrant population (thousands)	209.8	207.6	417.4	207.9	205.6	413.5	227.3	221.0	448.3
Recent emigrants (thousands)	..	..	..	47.1	43.8	90.9	45.6	42.0	87.6
15-24 (%)	13.4	14.2	13.8	13.4	14.2	13.8	12.2	11.8	12.0
25-64 (%)	80.1	78.0	79.1	80.1	78.0	79.0	80.2	79.9	80.0
65+ (%)	6.5	7.8	7.1	6.5	7.8	7.1	7.5	8.4	7.9
Low-educated (%)	29.4	36.8	33.1	29.6	37.1	33.3	18.6	21.1	19.9
Highly educated (%)	27.3	31.0	29.1	26.9	30.8	28.8	29.0	35.6	32.2
Total emigration rates (%)	12.7	11.9	12.3	12.6	11.8	12.2	12.7	11.8	12.2
Emigration rates of the highly educated (%)	7.4	9.0	8.1	7.2	8.8	8.0	7.3	9.2	8.2

Main destinations in 2005/06

	Total		Recent emigrants	Women	Highly educated	15-24	Total in 2000
Population 15+	Thousands	%	%	%	%	%	Thousands
Australia	349.2	77.9	18.4	49.6	25.1	13.1	316.0
United Kingdom	46.9	10.5	34.6	48.5	57.9	–	54.6
United States	27.9	6.2	20.4	49.4	49.2	9.8	23.5
Canada	10.4	2.3	13.3	49.4	61.3	7.2	9.3
Netherlands	2.7	0.6	–	55.6	–	–	–
Japan	2.3	0.5	..	31.7	79.7	14.0	2.2
Ireland	2.1	0.5	62.8	46.6	60.4	11.6	2.0
France	1.5	0.3	46.4	50.9	62.1	12.0	0.9
Switzerland	–	–	–	–	–	–	1.0
Greece	–	–	–	–	–	–	0.5

Labour market indicators of persons born in New Zealand living in OECD countries

Population 15-64	2000			2005/06		
	Men	Women	Total	Men	Women	Total
Employment-population ratio (%)	83.8	69.4	76.7	88.3	72.7	80.7
Unemployment rate (%)	6.8	6.8	6.8	4.0	5.6	4.7
Participation rate (%)	89.9	74.4	82.3	92.0	77.0	84.6
Total employed (thousands)	**150.0**	**120.5**	**270.5**	**170.5**	**135.1**	**305.6**
Employment rates of the highly educated (%)	91.8	81.4	86.3	96.4	84.8	90.1
Unemployment rates of the highly educated (%)	3.7	3.8	3.7	3.3	3.4	3.3
Highly educated in low- and medium-skilled jobs (%)	19.0	24.3	21.7	20.5	24.2	22.4
Highly educated employed (thousands)	**43.5**	**44.2**	**87.7**	**51.9**	**55.1**	**107.0**
Legislators, senior officials and managers	14.7	9.2	12.2	14.1	11.1	12.7
Professionals	16.1	20.6	18.1	13.5	17.7	15.4
Life science and health professionals	1.8	5.5	3.5	1.4	4.2	2.7
Teaching professionals	2.1	5.1	3.5	2.4	5.2	3.7
Technicians and associate professionals	10.5	16.0	13.0	12.7	18.4	15.3
Clerks	4.6	23.2	13.0	6.3	22.3	13.5
Service, shop and market sales workers	8.7	17.7	12.8	9.1	17.4	12.9
Skilled agricultural and fishery workers	1.8	0.5	1.2	3.2	2.3	2.8
Craft and related trades workers	19.4	1.8	11.5	20.5	2.3	12.3
Plant and machine operators and assemblers	11.3	1.8	7.0	11.3	2.1	7.2
Elementary occupations	12.8	9.3	11.3	8.0	6.3	7.2

(left vertical label: Distribution of employment by occupation (%), population 15+)

Persons born in New Zealand and their native-born children, population 15+

Living in:	Europe	United States	Australia
2008	Thousands	Thousands	Thousands
Native-born children	28.0	3.8	105.5
Foreign-born	52.9	21.2	279.6
Total	80.9	25.0	385.1

International students from New Zealand in OECD countries

Five main destinations	2004	2005	2006	2007	2008	2009
Australia	4 524	1 762	1 998	2 008	2 085	2 393
United States	962	940	962	889	1 022	1 056
United Kingdom	546	560	560	577	508	481
Canada	110	..	105	69	76	95
Japan	85	69	76	81	88	84
Total	6 362	3 479	3 896	3 853	4 002	4 362

Legal migrant flows to the OECD
Thousands

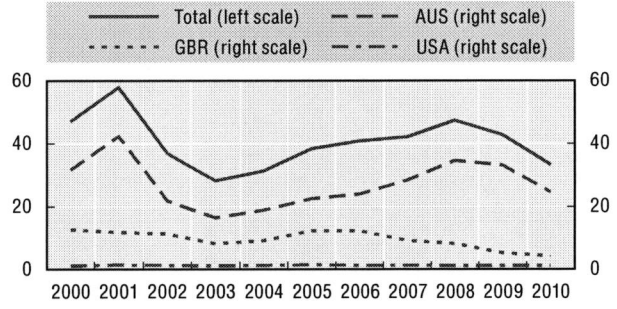

Remittance flows

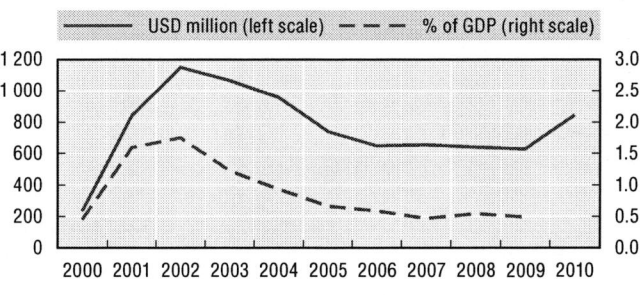

Ten main countries of destination for legal migrants in 2010 (numbers, % of total flows to the country): AUS (24447, 11.8%), GBR (4000, 0.9%), USA (919, 0.1%), KOR (756, 0.3%), JPN (739, 0.3%), DEU (598, 0.1%), CAN (565, 0.2%), NLD (232, 0.2%), FRA (124, 0.1%), CHE (117, 0.1%).

Desire to emigrate, 2008-10

	Women	15-24	Highly educated	Total	Regional total
Persons who would move permanently, if they had the opportunity to do so (%)	13	..	..	15	16
Of which: Persons who are planning to move permanently in the next 12 months (%)				..	6
Of which: Persons who have already done some preparations for this move (*e.g.* visa application) (%)					39

StatLink ⟩⟩⟩ http://dx.doi.org/10.1787/888932673448

Total population 2010 (millions)	4.9	Norway compared to:	World	Region
Population growth 2010 (%)	1.2	Human Development Index (HDI)	1/187	1/34
GDP per capita 2010 (current USD)	84 538	GDP per capita	5/194	2/34
GDP growth 2010 (%)	0.3	Emigration rate	103/203	26/34
Poverty rate 2010 (USD PPP 2 a day, in %)	..	Emigration rate of the highly educated	127/157	28/34

Age structure of the population 0+ (2010): "0-14": 13%; "15-24": 19%; "25-64": 54%; "65+": 15%.
Level of education of the population 15+ (2010): "Low": 3%; "Medium": 71%; "High": 26%.

Emigrant population living in OECD countries

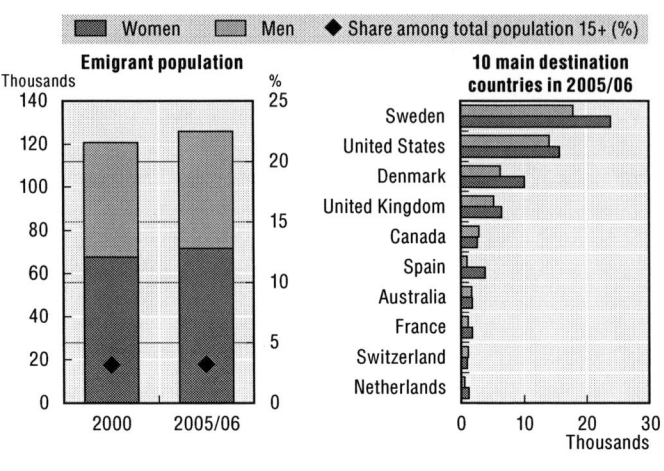

Immigrant population

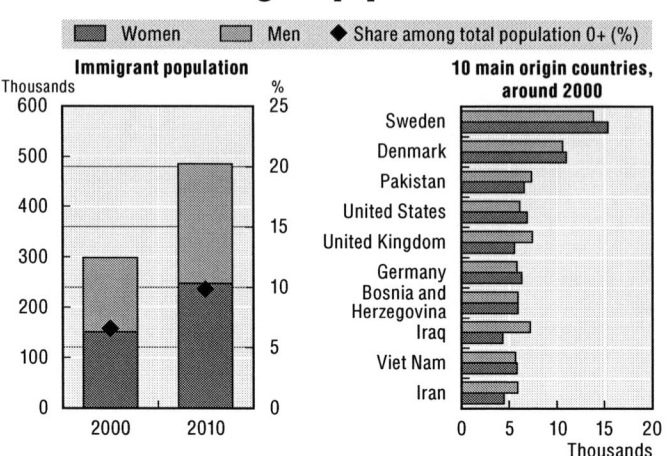

Emigrant population: persons born in Norway living abroad

	2000						2005/06		
	All destinations			OECD destinations			OECD destinations		
Population 15+	Men	Women	Total	Men	Women	Total	Men	Women	Total
Emigrant population (thousands)	56.7	70.9	127.6	53.2	67.5	120.7	54.3	71.4	125.8
Recent emigrants (thousands)	..	..	..	11.9	12.0	23.9	13.2	13.3	26.5
15-24 (%)	12.2	12.6	12.4	11.8	12.1	12.0	11.3	8.6	9.8
25-64 (%)	65.8	63.4	64.5	65.6	63.2	64.2	61.7	59.9	60.7
65+ (%)	21.9	24.0	23.1	22.6	24.7	23.8	27.0	31.4	29.5
Low-educated (%)	22.7	24.9	23.9	22.3	24.7	23.6	17.7	20.6	19.3
Highly educated (%)	39.3	30.9	34.6	39.8	31.1	34.9	45.6	35.8	40.1
Total emigration rates (%)	3.1	3.7	3.4	2.9	3.6	3.2	2.9	3.6	3.3
Emigration rates of the highly educated (%)	4.9	4.7	4.8	4.7	4.5	4.6	4.7	4.0	4.3

Main destinations in 2005/06

	Total		Recent emigrants	Women	Highly educated	15-24	Total in 2000
Population 15+	Thousands	%	%	%	%	%	Thousands
Sweden	41.8	33.2	23.9	57.3	25.7	5.8	34.1
United States	29.8	23.7	15.2	52.7	45.9	9.1	34.2
Denmark	16.3	13.0	43.9	61.9	39.2	15.4	15.0
United Kingdom	11.6	9.2	–	55.4	66.6	–	12.2
Canada	5.4	4.3	3.6	47.8	48.0	5.3	6.2
Spain	4.8	3.8	–	79.9	–	–	5.0
Australia	3.4	2.7	37.8	51.1	41.6	21.1	4.0
France	2.9	2.3	36.7	61.9	60.4	19.5	2.4
Switzerland	2.0	1.6	–	–	–	–	1.7
Netherlands	1.8	1.4	–	–	–	–	–

Labour market indicators of persons born in Norway living in OECD countries

Population 15-64	2000			2005/06		
	Men	Women	Total	Men	Women	Total
Employment-population ratio (%)	72.5	54.0	62.2	78.5	59.1	67.8
Unemployment rate (%)	5.0	6.2	5.6	4.8	5.3	5.0
Participation rate (%)	76.3	57.5	65.8	82.4	62.4	71.4
Total employed (thousands)	**18.9**	**17.7**	**36.6**	**19.6**	**18.2**	**37.8**
Employment rates of the highly educated (%)	83.2	62.7	72.9	91.5	68.9	80.1
Unemployment rates of the highly educated (%)	2.8	4.3	3.4	4.3	6.1	5.1
Highly educated in low- and medium-skilled jobs (%)	19.9	22.3	21.0	20.4	22.6	21.4
Highly educated employed (thousands)	**11.0**	**8.4**	**19.4**	**12.4**	**9.3**	**21.7**
Legislators, senior officials and managers	15.4	6.2	10.4	14.6	7.2	10.5
Professionals	22.5	17.8	20.0	28.4	17.9	22.7
Life science and health professionals	2.9	3.2	3.0	2.9	3.4	3.2
Teaching professionals	4.5	5.8	5.2	7.1	4.4	5.6
Technicians and associate professionals	18.6	20.5	19.7	16.4	23.5	20.3
Clerks	4.7	14.7	10.1	4.2	12.4	8.7
Service, shop and market sales workers	7.8	27.8	18.7	9.0	26.4	18.6
Skilled agricultural and fishery workers	1.3	0.4	0.8	0.8	0.3	0.5
Craft and related trades workers	11.9	1.7	6.4	12.6	3.8	7.8
Plant and machine operators and assemblers	11.3	3.6	7.2	9.2	3.1	5.9
Elementary occupations	6.4	7.1	6.8	4.8	5.4	5.1

Distribution of employment by occupation (%), population 15+

Persons born in Norway and their native-born children, population 15+

Living in:	Europe	United States	Australia
2008	Thousands	Thousands	Thousands
Native-born children	79.3	101.3	2.6
Foreign-born	33.6	22.9	1.6
Total	112.9	124.2	4.1

International students from Norway in OECD countries

Five main destinations	2004	2005	2006	2007	2008	2009
United Kingdom	3 653	3 343	3 059	3 017	2 797	3 028
Denmark	1 504	1 529	1 854	1 934	1 359	1 872
Australia	3 227	2 417	1 810	1 479	1 426	1 383
United States	1 471	1 477	1 343	1 217	1 265	1 327
Hungary	..	..	..	..	..	718
Total	10 993	9 743	9 417	8 918	8 950	10 552

Legal migrant flows to the OECD
Thousands

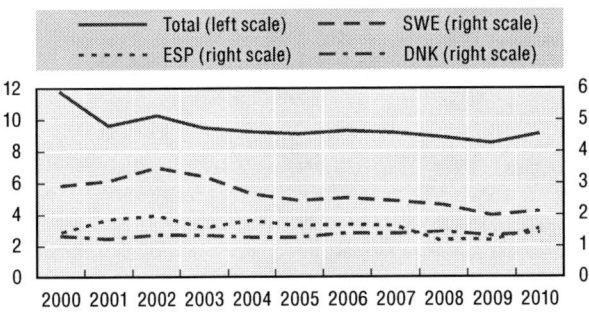

Remittance flows

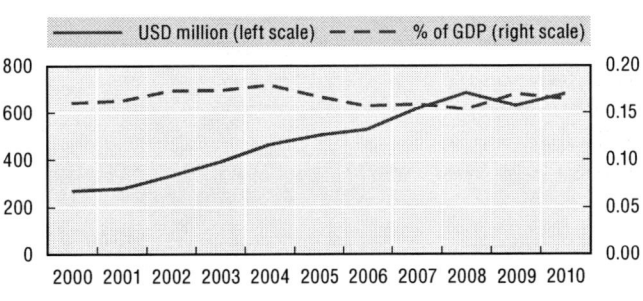

Ten main countries of destination for legal migrants in 2010 (numbers, % of total flows to the country): SWE (2070, 2.7%), ESP (1408, 0.3%), DNK (1378, 4.2%), GBR (887, 0.2%), DEU (767, 0.1%), NLD (403, 0.4%), USA (334, 0.1%), JPN (298, 0.1%), CHE (211, 0.2%), BEL (165, 0.2%).

Desire to emigrate, 2008-10

	Women	15-24	Highly educated	Total	Regional total
Persons who would move permanently, if they had the opportunity to do so (%)	19	38	24	21	16
Of which: Persons who are planning to move permanently in the next 12 months (%)				..	6
Of which: Persons who have already done some preparations for this move (*e.g.* visa application) (%)					39

StatLink http://dx.doi.org/10.1787/888932673467

Total population 2010 (millions)	38.2	Poland compared to:	World	Region
Population growth 2010 (%)	0.1	Human Development Index (HDI)	39/187	30/34
GDP per capita 2010 (current USD)	12 293	GDP per capita	55/194	32/34
GDP growth 2010 (%)	3.9	Emigration rate	58/203	7/34
Poverty rate 2008 (USD PPP 2 a day, in %)	0.3	Emigration rate of the highly educated	45/157	4/34

Age structure of the population 0+ (2010): "0-14": 14%; "15-24": 15%; "25-64": 57%; "65+": 14%.
Level of education of the population 15+ (2010): "Low": 22%; "Medium": 63%; "High": 15%.

Emigrant population living in OECD countries

Immigrant population

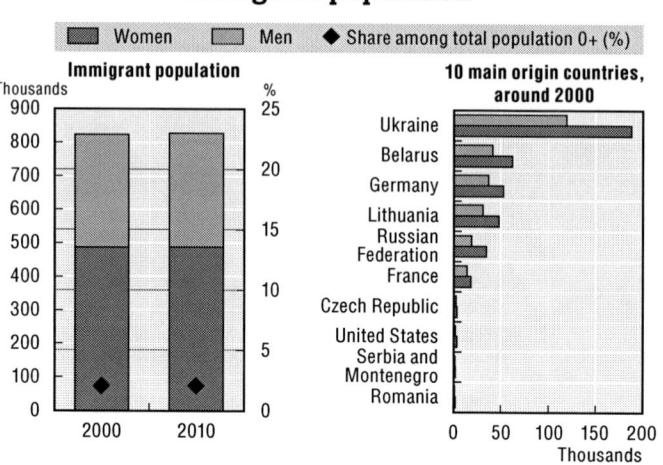

Emigrant population: persons born in Poland living abroad

	2000						2005/06		
	All destinations			OECD destinations			OECD destinations		
Population 15+	Men	Women	Total	Men	Women	Total	Men	Women	Total
Emigrant population (thousands)	1 059.2	1 334.1	2 393.3	969.0	1 206.8	2 175.8	1 301.3	1 548.1	2 849.3
Recent emigrants (thousands)	..	..	..	53.7	79.7	133.4	306.9	300.7	607.6
15-24 (%)	11.8	9.2	10.4	12.2	9.7	10.9	14.6	12.7	13.6
25-64 (%)	63.4	63.2	63.3	64.9	65.3	65.1	70.4	69.2	69.7
65+ (%)	24.8	27.6	26.4	22.9	24.9	24.0	15.0	18.1	16.7
Low-educated (%)	29.5	36.1	33.2	28.2	34.3	31.6	22.3	26.8	24.7
Highly educated (%)	23.6	20.8	22.0	23.2	20.7	21.8	26.8	26.7	26.8
Total emigration rates (%)	6.7	7.6	7.2	6.1	6.9	6.6	7.9	8.5	8.2
Emigration rates of the highly educated (%)	14.0	12.9	13.4	12.8	11.8	12.2	16.1	15.5	15.8

Main destinations in 2005/06

	Total		Recent emigrants	Women	Highly educated	15-24	Total in 2000
Population 15+	Thousands	%	%	%	%	%	Thousands
Germany	1 257.4	44.1	8.8	54.4	16.9	13.5	1 027.5
United States	468.9	16.5	12.3	54.5	36.2	8.4	452.1
United Kingdom	346.5	12.2	86.2	43.4	42.1	28.3	59.2
Canada	170.5	6.0	3.5	53.8	46.8	8.7	177.5
France	99.0	3.5	13.4	64.9	25.4	7.1	103.8
Ireland	58.6	2.1	98.0	35.4	30.9	30.2	2.0
Israel	57.4	2.0	1.4	54.4	32.0	0.1	71.8
Italy	55.1	1.9	39.1	78.4	11.3	12.8	31.4
Austria	54.5	1.9	21.0	58.6	22.1	9.8	40.1
Australia	51.8	1.8	4.6	54.8	37.7	4.5	57.1

Labour market indicators of persons born in Poland living in OECD countries

Population 15-64	2000			2005/06		
	Men	Women	Total	Men	Women	Total
Employment-population ratio (%)	76.1	61.6	68.3	81.7	63.5	72.1
Unemployment rate (%)	10.8	10.5	10.7	8.3	11.1	9.6
Participation rate (%)	85.3	68.9	76.4	89.1	71.5	79.7
Total employed (thousands)	**557.2**	**533.7**	**1 090.9**	**873.7**	**770.3**	**1 644.0**
Employment rates of the highly educated (%)	87.9	72.8	79.7	94.5	79.8	86.4
Unemployment rates of the highly educated (%)	6.5	5.5	6.0	5.0	8.1	6.6
Highly educated in low- and medium-skilled jobs (%)	35.6	31.8	33.8	53.2	48.5	50.8
Highly educated employed (thousands)	**158.1**	**154.3**	**312.4**	**265.6**	**267.1**	**532.7**
Legislators, senior officials and managers	2.8	1.9	2.3	4.0	2.7	3.4
Professionals	11.7	9.4	10.6	8.3	8.7	8.5
Life science and health professionals	0.5	0.9	0.7	0.9	1.6	1.2
Teaching professionals	0.5	0.8	0.7	0.7	1.9	1.2
Technicians and associate professionals	12.4	23.3	17.8	7.8	19.0	13.1
Clerks	2.4	12.4	7.3	3.6	11.5	7.3
Service, shop and market sales workers	3.0	24.9	13.8	9.3	21.0	14.8
Skilled agricultural and fishery workers	0.5	0.2	0.3	1.5	2.7	2.0
Craft and related trades workers	36.2	3.4	20.1	27.9	3.6	16.5
Plant and machine operators and assemblers	17.7	3.0	10.5	18.7	5.8	12.7
Elementary occupations	13.4	21.3	17.3	17.7	24.8	21.0

Distribution of employment by occupation (%), population 15+

Persons born in Poland and their native-born children, population 15+

Living in:	Europe	United States	Australia
2008	Thousands	Thousands	Thousands
Native-born children	578.1	619.0	39.9
Foreign-born	1 696.7	506.8	76.8
Total	2 274.9	1 125.8	116.7

International students from Poland in OECD countries

Five main destinations	2004	2005	2006	2007	2008	2009
United Kingdom	964	2 183	4 325	6 768	8 572	9 144
Germany	..	..	..	..	9 910	8 968
France	3 270	3 217	3 427	3 396	3 260	3 008
United States	2 913	2 988	3 127	2 872	2 734	2 726
Italy	1 002	1 151	1 332	1 478	1 430	1 462
Total	9 393	10 979	14 075	16 503	28 459	28 748

Legal migrant flows to the OECD
Thousands

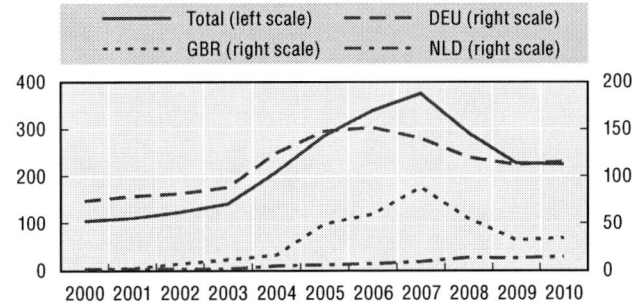

Remittance flows

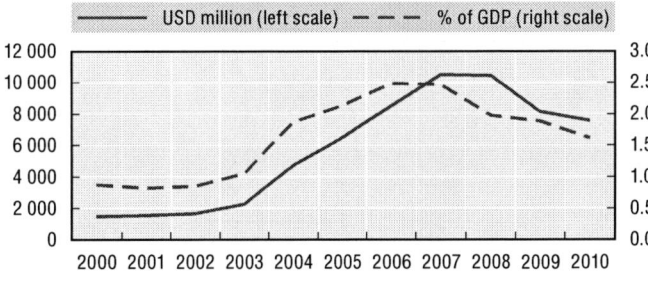

Ten main countries of destination for legal migrants in 2010 (numbers, % of total flows to the country): DEU (115587, 17.2%), GBR (34000, 7.3%), NLD (14477, 14.5%), NOR (11347, 17.7%), BEL (9911, 9.7%), USA (7643, 0.7%), ITA (7174, 5.8%), SWE (4414, 5.8%), AUT (4218, 4.3%), ESP (4197, 1%).

Desire to emigrate, 2008-10

	Women	15-24	Highly educated	Total	Regional total
Persons who would move permanently, if they had the opportunity to do so (%)	13	26	14	14	16
Of which: Persons who are planning to move permanently in the next 12 months (%)				3	6
Of which: Persons who have already done some preparations for this move (*e.g.* visa application) (%)					39

Three main countries of desired destination: Germany (17%), United Kingdom (14%), United States (8%).

StatLink  http://dx.doi.org/10.1787/888932673486

Total population 2010 (millions)	10.6	**Portugal compared to:**	**World**	**Region**
Population growth 2010 (%)	0.1	Human Development Index (HDI)	41/187	31/34
GDP per capita 2010 (current USD)	21 505	GDP per capita	37/194	25/34
GDP growth 2010 (%)	1.4	Emigration rate	34/203	2/34
Poverty rate 2010 (USD PPP 2 a day, in %)	..	Emigration rate of the highly educated	63/157	7/34

Age structure of the population 0+ (2010): "0-14": 11%; "15-24": 15%; "25-64": 56%; "65+": 18%.
Level of education of the population 15+ (2010): "Low": 55%; "Medium": 35%; "High": 11%.

Emigrant population living in OECD countries

Immigrant population

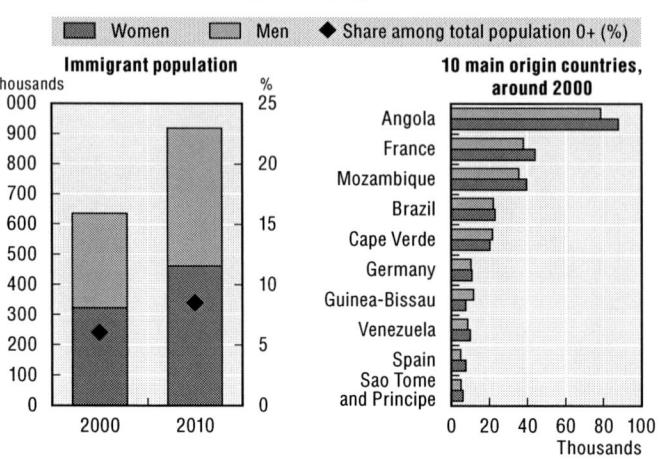

Emigrant population: persons born in Portugal living abroad

	2000						2005/06		
	All destinations			OECD destinations			OECD destinations		
Population 15+	Men	Women	Total	Men	Women	Total	Men	Women	Total
Emigrant population (thousands)	795.6	762.7	1 558.3	637.2	623.6	1 260.8	696.4	685.7	1 382.1
Recent emigrants (thousands)	..	..	..	39.2	36.6	75.8	63.7	55.4	119.2
15-24 (%)	5.5	5.6	5.5	6.5	6.5	6.5	6.4	6.5	6.5
25-64 (%)	80.0	78.2	79.1	84.7	83.2	84.0	81.9	80.2	81.0
65+ (%)	14.5	16.2	15.3	8.8	10.3	9.5	11.7	13.3	12.5
Low-educated (%)	68.6	71.9	70.2	68.2	70.7	69.4	64.4	66.9	65.6
Highly educated (%)	6.7	6.8	6.7	6.0	6.8	6.4	8.1	9.0	8.6
Total emigration rates (%)	16.3	14.5	15.4	13.5	12.2	12.8	14.1	12.9	13.5
Emigration rates of the highly educated (%)	12.0	9.0	10.3	8.8	7.4	8.0	13.4	10.4	11.6

Main destinations in 2005/06

	Total		Recent emigrants	Women	Highly educated	15-24	Total in 2000
Population 15+	Thousands	%	%	%	%	%	Thousands
France	577.6	41.8	5.1	49.2	5.9	3.9	567.7
United States	200.5	14.5	4.1	50.2	13.7	4.4	206.3
Canada	150.9	10.9	1.6	50.7	13.5	3.8	154.0
Switzerland	125.1	9.1	26.4	47.2	4.3	16.1	94.2
Germany	99.7	7.2	–	45.6	5.4	7.0	67.7
Spain	73.3	5.3	34.6	53.7	6.9	8.8	53.4
United Kingdom	55.4	4.0	40.1	54.9	21.3	16.0	32.3
Luxembourg	42.2	3.1	10.6	48.8	2.3	12.4	38.4
Belgium	21.7	1.6	–	53.7	–	–	19.9
Australia	15.0	1.1	2.9	48.7	12.7	6.6	15.0

Labour market indicators of persons born in Portugal living in OECD countries

Population 15-64	2000			2005/06		
	Men	Women	Total	Men	Women	Total
Employment-population ratio (%)	81.1	63.6	72.5	80.6	65.7	73.3
Unemployment rate (%)	7.0	8.8	7.8	6.1	8.5	7.2
Participation rate (%)	87.2	69.8	78.6	85.9	71.9	79.0
Total employed (thousands)	**450.4**	**342.8**	**793.2**	**492.3**	**387.6**	**879.9**
Employment rates of the highly educated (%)	85.6	77.4	81.3	92.6	84.4	88.3
Unemployment rates of the highly educated (%)	5.0	5.7	5.4	3.7	6.0	4.8
Highly educated in low- and medium-skilled jobs (%)	38.2	36.8	37.6	41.0	43.3	42.2
Highly educated employed (thousands)	**30.1**	**30.5**	**60.5**	**47.2**	**45.2**	**92.4**
Legislators, senior officials and managers	4.8	4.7	4.8	5.4	4.0	4.8
Professionals	2.4	4.6	2.9	3.7	3.6	3.6
Life science and health professionals	0.1	0.4	0.2	0.2	0.3	0.2
Teaching professionals	0.3	1.2	0.5	0.5	1.2	0.8
Technicians and associate professionals	5.0	8.1	5.7	5.8	7.8	6.7
Clerks	2.9	12.8	5.1	3.1	11.2	6.7
Service, shop and market sales workers	5.4	23.1	9.3	5.4	21.3	12.5
Skilled agricultural and fishery workers	3.5	1.0	2.9	3.1	2.3	2.7
Craft and related trades workers	45.0	3.8	35.9	42.5	3.9	25.4
Plant and machine operators and assemblers	19.0	7.2	16.4	17.2	6.0	12.3
Elementary occupations	12.1	34.8	17.1	13.3	39.7	25.0

Distribution of employment by occupation (%), population 15+

Persons born in Portugal and their native-born children, population 15+

Living in:	Europe	United States	Australia
2008	Thousands	Thousands	Thousands
Native-born children	624.4	158.9	4.4
Foreign-born	1 039.3	205.1	16.4
Total	1 663.6	364.0	20.8

International students from Portugal in OECD countries

Five main destinations	2004	2005	2006	2007	2008	2009
France	2 701	2 554	2 593	2 664	2 612	2 781
United Kingdom	2 649	2 785	2 885	3 010	2 828	2 754
Spain	1 377	1 651	1 655	2 272	2 026	2 584
United States	880	890	875	873	903	958
Germany	..	..	..	..	401	444
Total	7 964	8 298	8 546	9 368	9 436	10 658

Legal migrant flows to the OECD
Thousands

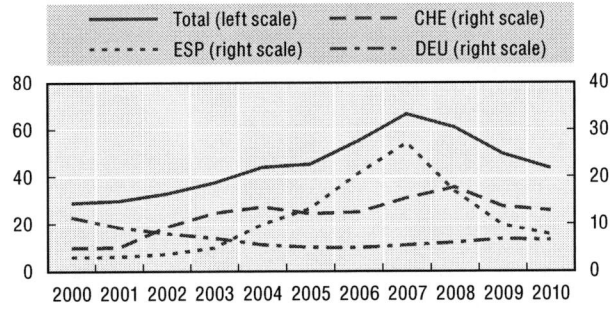

Remittance flows

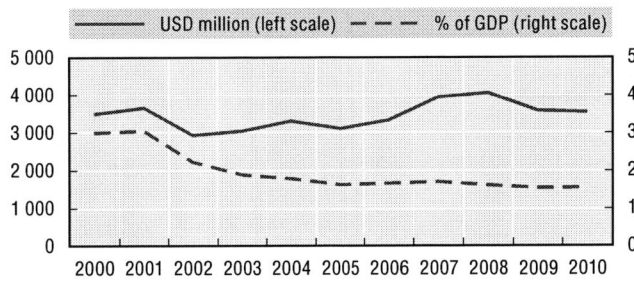

Ten main countries of destination for legal migrants in 2010 (numbers, % of total flows to the country): CHE (12826, 9.7%), ESP (7678, 1.8%), DEU (6513, 1%), GBR (4000, 0.9%), LUX (3845, 24.6%), BEL (2854, 2.8%), NLD (1958, 0.1%), USA (755, 0.1%), CAN (605, 0.2%), AUT (460, 0.5%).

Desire to emigrate, 2008-10

	Women	15-24	Highly educated	Total	Regional total
Persons who would move permanently, if they had the opportunity to do so (%)	15	31	26	17	16
Of which: Persons who are planning to move permanently in the next 12 months (%)				14	6
Of which: Persons who have already done some preparations for this move (*e.g.* visa application) (%)					39

Three main countries of desired destination: France (11%), Spain (10%), United Kingdom (10%).

StatLink  http://dx.doi.org/10.1787/888932673505

Total population 2010 (millions)	5.4	**Slovak Republic compared to:**	**World**	**Region**
Population growth 2010 (%)	0.3	Human Development Index (HDI)	35/187	28/34
GDP per capita 2010 (current USD)	16 061	GDP per capita	44/194	28/34
GDP growth 2010 (%)	4.2	Emigration rate	61/203	8/34
Poverty rate 2010 (USD PPP 2 a day, in %)	..	Emigration rate of the highly educated	65/157	9/34

Age structure of the population 0+ (2010): "0-14": 15%; "15-24": 15%; "25-64": 58%; "65+": 12%.
Level of education of the population 15+ (2010): "Low": 19%; "Medium": 69%; "High": 13%.

Emigrant population living in OECD countries

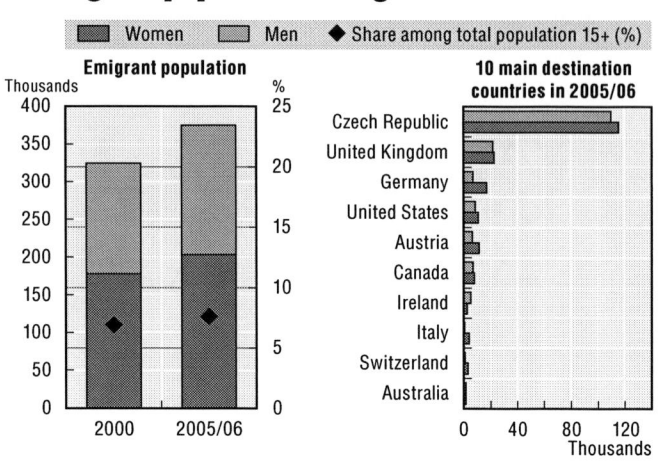

Immigrant population

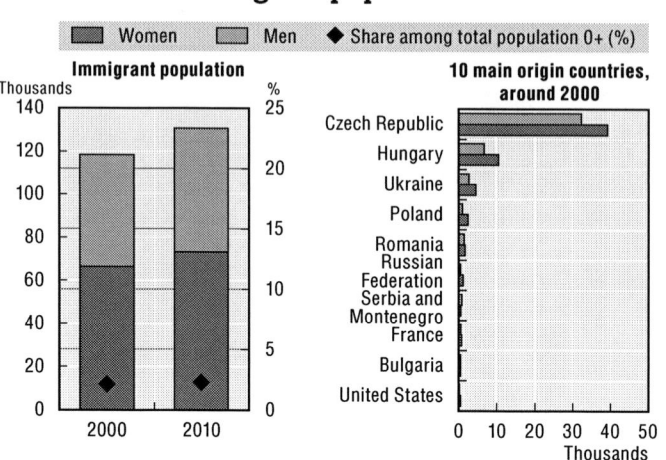

Emigrant population: persons born in the Slovak Republic living abroad

	2000						2005/06		
	All destinations			OECD destinations			OECD destinations		
Population 15+	Men	Women	Total	Men	Women	Total	Men	Women	Total
Emigrant population (thousands)	163.2	203.0	366.2	146.9	177.5	324.4	171.5	203.4	374.9
Recent emigrants (thousands)	..	..	..	3.6	9.3	12.8	28.6	37.3	65.9
15-24 (%)	6.6	7.4	7.1	6.5	7.7	7.2	9.5	11.8	10.7
25-64 (%)	69.1	61.2	64.7	71.7	63.9	67.5	70.4	65.9	68.0
65+ (%)	24.3	31.3	28.2	21.8	28.4	25.4	20.0	22.4	21.3
Low-educated (%)	30.9	49.0	40.9	29.4	47.6	39.3	22.9	35.2	29.6
Highly educated (%)	16.0	10.9	13.2	15.2	10.7	12.7	19.9	17.9	18.8
Total emigration rates (%)	7.3	8.3	7.8	6.6	7.3	7.0	7.4	8.0	7.7
Emigration rates of the highly educated (%)	10.2	10.2	10.2	8.8	8.8	8.8	11.0	12.6	11.7

Main destinations in 2005/06

	Total		Recent emigrants	Women	Highly educated	15-24	Total in 2000
Population 15+	Thousands	%	%	%	%	%	Thousands
Czech Republic	225.3	60.1	..	51.2	9.9	6.0	278.7
United Kingdom	44.1	11.8	89.0	51.1	24.5	29.7	5.1
Germany	23.8	6.3	29.6	71.6	30.3	–	–
United States	19.2	5.1	19.3	55.2	43.8	9.1	–
Austria	17.7	4.7	21.9	64.2	21.2	15.8	15.2
Canada	14.6	3.9	13.3	53.3	55.5	6.1	10.3
Ireland	7.8	2.1	97.9	34.8	23.2	32.1	0.3
Italy	4.6	1.2	64.8	83.5	–	–	2.6
Switzerland	3.8	1.0	39.2	76.5	–	–	3.6
Australia	3.2	0.9	19.7	51.4	50.5	8.4	2.7

Labour market indicators of persons born in the Slovak Republic living in OECD countries

Population 15-64	2000			2005/06		
	Men	Women	Total	Men	Women	Total
Employment-population ratio (%)	76.9	58.6	65.6	90.0	64.8	75.0
Unemployment rate (%)	8.9	10.5	9.8	4.6	8.7	6.8
Participation rate (%)	84.3	65.5	72.7	94.3	71.0	80.5
Total employed (thousands)	**10.2**	**12.6**	**22.7**	**46.3**	**49.0**	**95.3**
Employment rates of the highly educated (%)	87.3	65.8	74.4	95.0	82.3	87.3
Unemployment rates of the highly educated (%)	4.9	8.6	6.9	1.9	5.5	4.0
Highly educated in low- and medium-skilled jobs (%)	25.4	40.3	33.3	52.3	45.1	48.2
Highly educated employed (thousands)	**4.0**	**4.5**	**8.5**	**15.2**	**19.7**	**34.9**
Legislators, senior officials and managers	10.0	6.0	7.8	2.9	5.7	4.2
Professionals	19.9	12.1	15.5	9.5	11.9	10.7
Life science and health professionals	3.3	2.4	2.8	0.8	2.0	1.4
Teaching professionals	1.6	2.7	2.2	2.0	5.0	3.4
Technicians and associate professionals	13.6	19.7	17.0	6.9	15.9	11.3
Clerks	4.1	15.5	10.5	3.1	10.6	6.8
Service, shop and market sales workers	10.9	32.8	23.2	9.8	14.9	12.3
Skilled agricultural and fishery workers	1.4	0.5	0.9	2.0	5.6	3.8
Craft and related trades workers	19.6	2.2	9.9	14.8	8.6	11.7
Plant and machine operators and assemblers	9.0	2.2	5.2	17.8	4.6	11.3
Elementary occupations	11.5	9.1	10.2	32.4	19.9	26.3

Distribution of employment by occupation (%), population 15+

Persons born in the Slovak Republic and their native-born children, population 15+

Living in:	Europe	United States	Australia
2008	Thousands	Thousands	Thousands
Native-born children	244.9	41.1	3.1
Foreign-born	262.3	26.1	1.7
Total	507.2	67.1	4.8

International students from the Slovak Republic in OECD countries

Five main destinations	2004	2005	2006	2007	2008	2009
Hungary	..	..	..	..	..	2 109
United Kingdom	158	353	642	892	1 116	1 307
Germany	..	..	..	..	1 022	938
United States	585	636	722	605	537	534
France	438	420	415	380	399	424
Total	1 614	1 874	2 301	2 374	3 725	6 079

Legal migrant flows to the OECD
Thousands

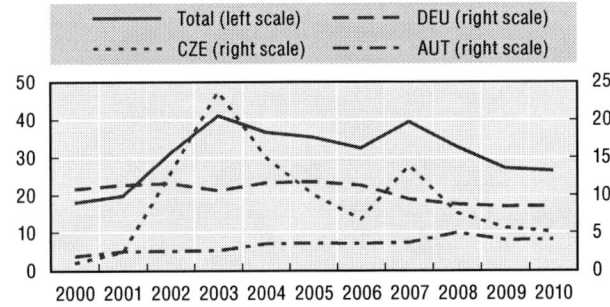

Remittance flows

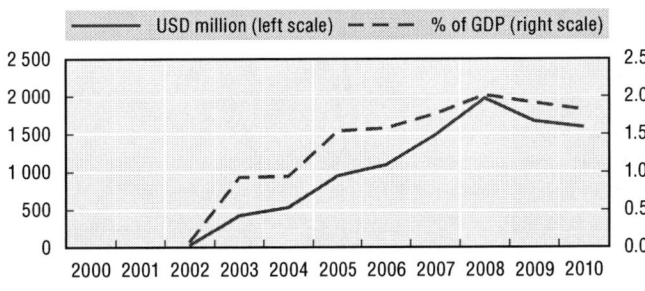

Ten main countries of destination for legal migrants in 2010 (numbers, % of total flows to the country): DEU (8590, 1.3%), CZE (5086, 20%), AUT (4099, 4.2%), HUN (1195, 5%), NLD (1079, 1.1%), CHE (981, 0.7%), ITA (895, 0.6%), BEL (599, 0.6%), NOR (594, 0.9%), ESP (591, 0.1%).

Desire to emigrate, 2008-10

	Women	15-24	Highly educated	Total	Regional total
Persons who would move permanently, if they had the opportunity to do so (%)	17	34	..	18	16
Of which: Persons who are planning to move permanently in the next 12 months (%)				..	6
Of which: Persons who have already done some preparations for this move (*e.g.* visa application) (%)					39

StatLink http://dx.doi.org/10.1787/888932673524

Total population 2010 (millions)	2.1	**Slovenia compared to:**	**World**	**Region**
Population growth 2010 (%)	0.6	Human Development Index (HDI)	21/187	18/34
GDP per capita 2010 (current USD)	22 851	GDP per capita	35/194	24/34
GDP growth 2010 (%)	1.4	Emigration rate	80/203	14/34
Poverty rate 2004 (USD PPP 2 a day, in %)	0.1	Emigration rate of the highly educated	103/157	20/34

Age structure of the population 0+ (2010): "0-14": 11%; "15-24": 14%; "25-64": 58%; "65+": 16%.
Level of education of the population 15+ (2010): "Low": 46%; "Medium": 39%; "High": 15%.

Emigrant population living in OECD countries

Immigrant population

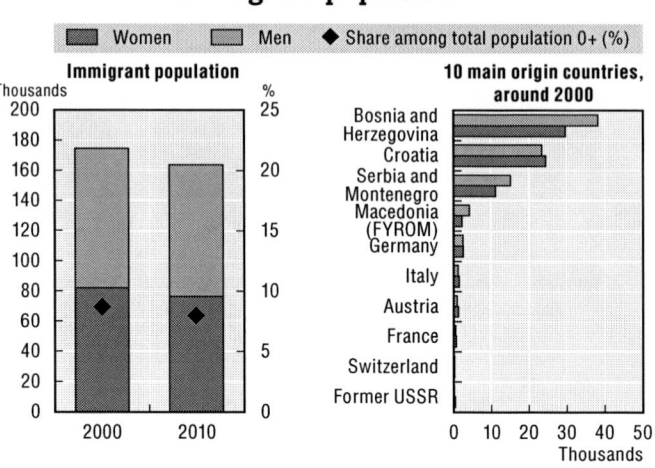

Emigrant population: persons born in Slovenia living abroad

	2000						2005/06		
	All destinations			OECD destinations			OECD destinations		
Population 15+	Men	Women	Total	Men	Women	Total	Men	Women	Total
Emigrant population (thousands)	44.5	57.2	101.7	36.1	41.8	77.9	39.7	54.6	94.3
Recent emigrants (thousands)	..	..	..	0.9	1.2	2.1	1.0	1.4	2.5
15-24 (%)	4.4	3.8	4.0	3.1	3.0	3.0	3.2	3.6	3.4
25-64 (%)	65.9	55.5	60.0	67.3	56.1	61.3	67.7	66.8	67.2
65+ (%)	29.7	40.8	35.9	29.6	40.9	35.6	29.1	29.6	29.4
Low-educated (%)	32.7	54.4	44.9	35.2	59.5	48.2	33.3	48.2	41.9
Highly educated (%)	14.8	11.7	13.1	12.8	10.8	11.7	15.1	15.2	15.2
Total emigration rates (%)	5.2	6.2	5.7	4.3	4.6	4.5	4.6	5.8	5.2
Emigration rates of the highly educated (%)	6.7	7.9	7.3	4.8	5.4	5.1	5.2	7.9	6.5

Main destinations in 2005/06

	Total		Recent emigrants	Women	Highly educated	15-24	Total in 2000
Population 15+	Thousands	%	%	%	%	%	Thousands
Germany	24.4	25.9	–	55.5	–	–	6.1
Italy	19.0	20.2	–	65.1	8.4	–	20.4
Austria	16.6	17.6	–	59.4	–	–	20.3
Canada	9.4	10.0	1.0	52.6	26.8	1.4	9.2
United States	6.3	6.7	4.1	55.9	32.5	8.5	5.9
Australia	6.2	6.6	1.9	49.1	13.7	2.1	6.4
Switzerland	4.3	4.6	–	68.6	–	–	3.8
France	2.7	2.9	9.6	58.8	17.1	3.9	2.5
Spain	1.4	1.5	–	–	85.4	–	0.2
Sweden	0.8	0.8	14.2	49.1	16.9	10.1	0.7

Labour market indicators of persons born in Slovenia living in OECD countries

Population 15-64	2000			2005/06		
	Men	Women	Total	Men	Women	Total
Employment-population ratio (%)	72.0	50.7	60.0	72.8	51.6	60.5
Unemployment rate (%)	5.8	6.7	6.2	2.8	5.5	4.2
Participation rate (%)	76.4	54.4	64.0	74.9	54.6	63.1
Total employed (thousands)	**13.4**	**12.1**	**25.5**	**19.2**	**18.8**	**38.0**
Employment rates of the highly educated (%)	87.1	69.7	78.1	86.3	80.4	82.9
Unemployment rates of the highly educated (%)	3.6	5.4	4.5	1.8	12.1	7.4
Highly educated in low- and medium-skilled jobs (%)	24.1	26.3	25.1	24.3	19.4	21.7
Highly educated employed (thousands)	**2.8**	**2.4**	**5.2**	**3.0**	**3.3**	**6.3**
Legislators, senior officials and managers	12.2	7.9	10.2	8.4	5.7	7.0
Professionals	8.0	8.4	8.2	13.5	12.9	13.2
Life science and health professionals	0.9	1.2	1.0	0.7	0.7	0.7
Teaching professionals	1.0	1.7	1.3	1.5	4.9	3.3
Technicians and associate professionals	11.6	15.4	13.3	10.3	16.1	13.4
Clerks	3.6	13.4	8.2	4.2	12.9	8.8
Service, shop and market sales workers	6.7	23.7	14.6	4.4	22.1	13.8
Skilled agricultural and fishery workers	1.5	1.3	1.4	1.1	0.6	0.8
Craft and related trades workers	29.9	5.1	18.4	33.4	3.5	17.6
Plant and machine operators and assemblers	14.5	4.6	9.9	19.3	3.2	10.8
Elementary occupations	12.0	20.2	15.8	5.3	23.0	14.7

(Left margin vertical label: Distribution of employment by occupation (%), population 15+)

Persons born in Slovenia and their native-born children, population 15+

Living in:	Europe	United States	Australia
2008	Thousands	Thousands	Thousands
Native-born children	85.9	..	5.1
Foreign-born	49.9	..	3.9
Total	135.8	..	9.0

International students from Slovenia in OECD countries

Five main destinations	2004	2005	2006	2007	2008	2009
Italy	326	305	397	387	328	335
Germany	..	..	..	..	274	272
United Kingdom	265	317	294	283	285	269
United States	209	320	227	203	210	196
France	77	83	101	87	98	83
Total	949	1 120	1 193	1 101	1 312	1 410

Legal migrant flows to the OECD
Thousands

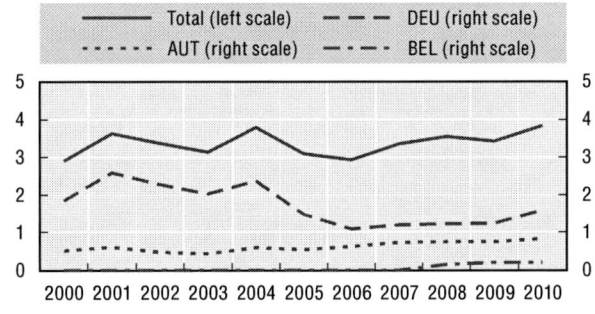

Remittance flows

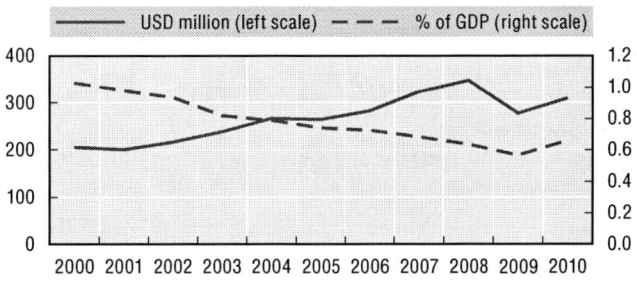

Ten main countries of destination for legal migrants in 2010 (numbers, % of total flows to the country): DEU (1591, 0.2%), AUT (833, 0.9%), BEL (193, 0.2%), ITA (191, 0%), NLD (187, 0.2%), ESP (151, 0%), CHE (144, 0%), USA (74, 0%), JPN (56, 0%), HUN (54, 0.2%).

Desire to emigrate, 2008-10

	Women	15-24	Highly educated	Total	Regional total
Persons who would move permanently, if they had the opportunity to do so (%)	11	31	..	16	16
Of which: Persons who are planning to move permanently in the next 12 months (%)				..	6
Of which: Persons who have already done some preparations for this move (*e.g.* visa application) (%)					39

StatLink ⬛🔗 *http://dx.doi.org/10.1787/888932673543*

Total population 2010 (millions)	46.1		Spain compared to:	World	Region
Population growth 2010 (%)	0.4		Human Development Index (HDI)	23/187	21/34
GDP per capita 2010 (current USD)	30 542		GDP per capita	29/194	20/34
GDP growth 2010 (%)	−0.1		Emigration rate	126/203	30/34
Poverty rate 2010 (USD PPP 2 a day, in %)	..		Emigration rate of the highly educated	144/157	31/34

Age structure of the population 0+ (2010): "0-14": 10%; "15-24": 15%; "25-64": 58%; "65+": 17%.
Level of education of the population 15+ (2010): "Low": 25%; "Medium": 51%; "High": 24%.

Emigrant population living in OECD countries

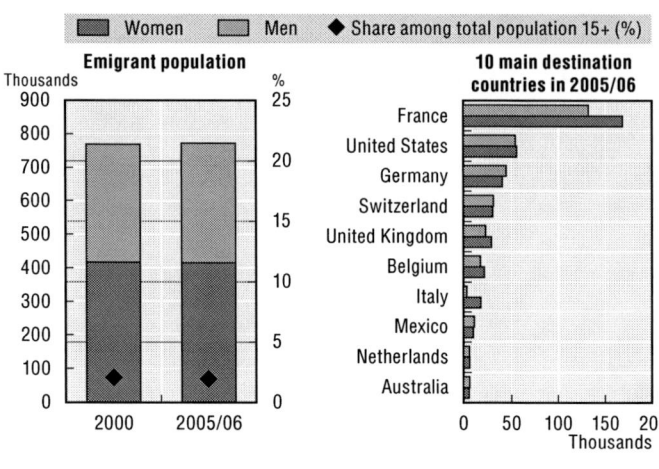

Immigrant population

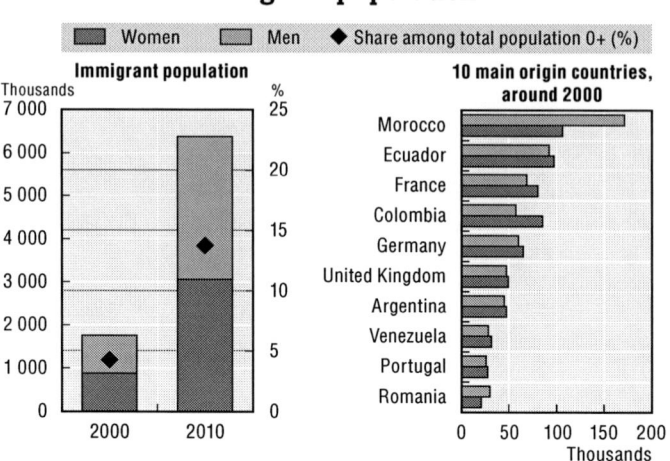

Emigrant population: persons born in Spain living abroad

Population 15+	2000						2005/06		
	All destinations			OECD destinations			OECD destinations		
	Men	Women	Total	Men	Women	Total	Men	Women	Total
Emigrant population (thousands)	499.1	575.4	1 074.6	351.1	417.2	768.3	356.9	415.4	772.3
Recent emigrants (thousands)	..	..	..	26.2	30.2	56.3	33.4	41.2	74.7
15-24 (%)	4.6	4.3	4.5	5.8	5.4	5.6	5.1	4.3	4.7
25-64 (%)	63.1	58.4	60.6	69.6	65.2	67.2	67.8	63.7	65.6
65+ (%)	32.3	37.3	35.0	24.6	29.4	27.2	27.1	31.9	29.7
Low-educated (%)	52.5	60.2	56.6	49.5	56.6	53.4	40.5	49.1	45.1
Highly educated (%)	18.7	15.9	17.2	19.1	17.7	18.4	25.7	24.3	24.9
Total emigration rates (%)	2.9	3.2	3.0	2.0	2.3	2.2	1.9	2.1	2.0
Emigration rates of the highly educated (%)	2.7	2.6	2.7	1.9	2.1	2.0	2.1	2.3	2.2

Main destinations in 2005/06

Population 15+	Total		Recent emigrants	Women	Highly educated	15-24	Total in 2000
	Thousands	%	%	%	%	%	Thousands
France	301.3	39.0	4.7	56.1	12.8	2.4	337.7
United States	110.2	14.3	13.8	50.7	44.7	10.0	104.2
Germany	85.0	11.0	13.7	47.6	20.0	–	59.6
Switzerland	61.3	7.9	8.5	49.3	14.3	5.1	60.2
United Kingdom	52.1	6.7	25.3	55.9	59.2	–	50.3
Belgium	39.0	5.0	–	55.3	16.1	–	35.5
Italy	21.3	2.8	21.0	84.2	18.0	5.1	18.8
Mexico	20.8	2.7	..	47.6	45.8	2.0	20.3
Netherlands	12.5	1.6	–	51.7	27.2	–	14.0
Australia	12.0	1.6	5.1	48.7	22.2	2.3	12.3

Labour market indicators of persons born in Spain living in OECD countries

Population 15-64	2000 Men	2000 Women	2000 Total	2005/06 Men	2005/06 Women	2005/06 Total
Employment-population ratio (%)	76.3	58.4	67.1	77.9	62.3	69.8
Unemployment rate (%)	6.1	9.2	7.5	5.0	6.6	5.8
Participation rate (%)	81.3	64.3	72.5	82.1	66.7	74.1
Total employed (thousands)	**192.3**	**157.6**	**349.9**	**200.1**	**173.2**	**373.3**
Employment rates of the highly educated (%)	86.7	72.3	79.0	89.8	78.0	83.6
Unemployment rates of the highly educated (%)	3.6	5.9	4.7	4.3	4.8	4.5
Highly educated in low- and medium-skilled jobs (%)	22.8	29.2	25.7	20.3	26.0	23.1
Highly educated employed (thousands)	**49.3**	**47.0**	**96.3**	**69.6**	**67.1**	**136.7**
Legislators, senior officials and managers	10.8	7.1	9.6	11.9	7.2	9.6
Professionals	11.5	17.6	13.4	17.8	17.9	17.8
Life science and health professionals	1.4	2.9	1.8	2.0	1.9	2.0
Teaching professionals	2.1	6.2	3.3	2.8	7.2	4.9
Technicians and associate professionals	10.9	13.0	11.5	12.6	15.2	13.9
Clerks	5.0	17.8	8.9	5.7	14.2	9.8
Service, shop and market sales workers	7.9	23.4	12.6	6.2	15.9	10.9
Skilled agricultural and fishery workers	3.1	0.3	2.3	2.2	3.1	2.7
Craft and related trades workers	29.8	2.9	21.6	23.9	4.5	14.5
Plant and machine operators and assemblers	12.9	2.3	9.7	11.5	2.8	7.3
Elementary occupations	8.1	15.5	10.4	7.5	19.1	13.1

Distribution of employment by occupation (%), population 15+

Persons born in Spain and their native-born children, population 15+

Living in:	Europe	United States	Australia
2008	Thousands	Thousands	Thousands
Native-born children	733.0	136.5	3.8
Foreign-born	476.6	187.7	14.7
Total	1 209.7	324.2	18.5

International students from Spain in OECD countries

Five main destinations	2004	2005	2006	2007	2008	2009
United Kingdom	6 105	6 001	6 224	6 352	5 739	5 689
France	3 928	3 448	3 664	3 860	3 905	3 908
United States	3 631	3 668	3 578	3 654	3 664	3 786
Germany	..	..	..	..	3 522	3 657
Italy	416	445	502	519	504	556
Total	15 480	15 168	15 927	16 431	19 398	20 143

Legal migrant flows to the OECD
Thousands

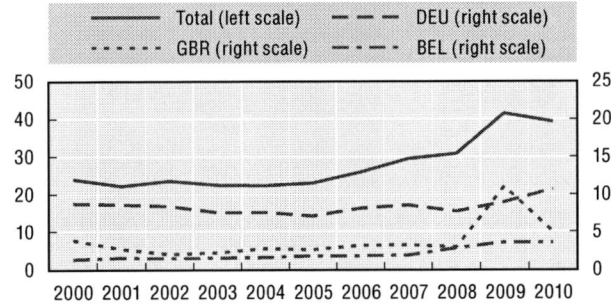

Remittance flows

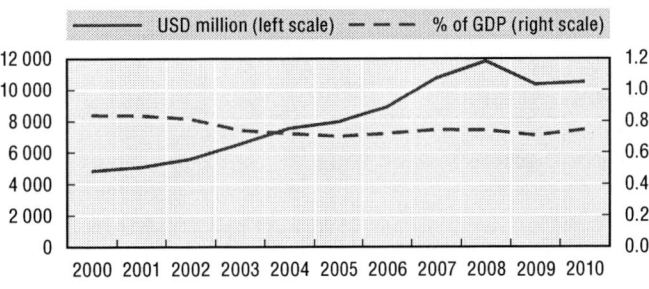

Ten main countries of destination for legal migrants in 2010 (numbers, % of total flows to the country): DEU (10657, 1.6%), GBR (5000, 1.1%), BEL (3592, 3.5%), CHE (3258, 2.5%), NLD (3149, 3.2%), USA (1684, 0.2%), PRT (1664, 0.4%), ITA (1514, 0.4%), JPN (1007, 0.4%), MEX (969, 3.7%).

Desire to emigrate, 2008-10

	Women	15-24	Highly educated	Total	Regional total
Persons who would move permanently, if they had the opportunity to do so (%)	8	17	14	9	16
Of which: Persons who are planning to move permanently in the next 12 months (%)				..	6
Of which: Persons who have already done some preparations for this move (*e.g.* visa application) (%)					39

StatLink http://dx.doi.org/10.1787/888932673562

Total population 2010 (millions)	9.4	Sweden compared to:	World	Region
Population growth 2010 (%)	0.9	Human Development Index (HDI)	10/187	9/34
GDP per capita 2010 (current USD)	48 936	GDP per capita	10/194	5/34
GDP growth 2010 (%)	5.6	Emigration rate	107/203	27/34
Poverty rate 2010 (USD PPP 2 a day, in %)	..	Emigration rate of the highly educated	118/157	24/34

Age structure of the population 0+ (2010): "0-14": 13%; "15-24": 17%; "25-64": 52%; "65+": 18%.
Level of education of the population 15+ (2010): "Low": 11%; "Medium": 66%; "High": 24%.

Emigrant population living in OECD countries

Immigrant population

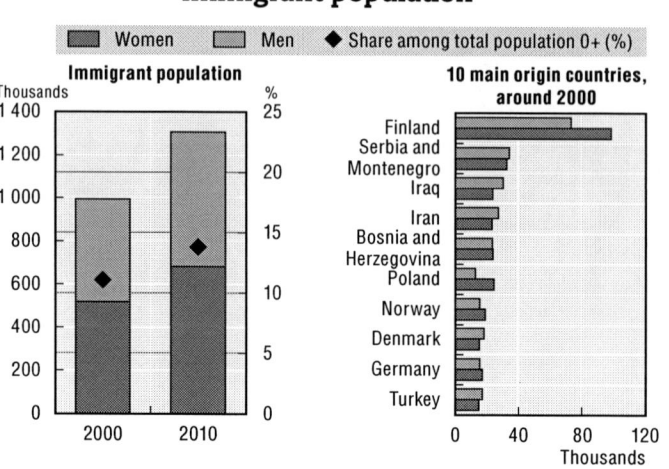

Emigrant population: persons born in Sweden living abroad

	2000						2005/06		
	All destinations			OECD destinations			OECD destinations		
Population 15+	Men	Women	Total	Men	Women	Total	Men	Women	Total
Emigrant population (thousands)	88.6	117.5	206.1	84.6	113.6	198.2	98.7	126.2	224.9
Recent emigrants (thousands)	..	..	..	17.5	23.4	41.0	18.7	21.8	40.4
15-24 (%)	17.9	17.5	17.7	17.9	17.3	17.6	11.3	11.6	11.5
25-64 (%)	71.3	69.8	70.5	71.2	69.8	70.4	79.6	74.9	77.0
65+ (%)	10.8	12.7	11.9	10.8	12.9	12.0	9.1	13.5	11.6
Low-educated (%)	20.1	18.7	19.3	20.2	18.6	19.3	15.0	14.2	14.6
Highly educated (%)	41.7	38.7	40.0	41.7	38.8	40.0	49.4	47.4	48.3
Total emigration rates (%)	2.4	3.1	2.8	2.3	3.0	2.7	2.6	3.2	2.9
Emigration rates of the highly educated (%)	4.3	4.6	4.4	4.1	4.5	4.3	5.8	5.1	5.4

Main destinations in 2005/06

	Total		Recent emigrants	Women	Highly educated	15-24	Total in 2000
Population 15+	Thousands	%	%	%	%	%	Thousands
United States	49.0	21.8	19.1	57.8	55.8	10.5	50.3
Norway	29.6	13.1	22.2	52.5	38.4	11.5	29.3
Finland	27.5	12.2	5.7	48.4	23.1	22.3	24.6
United Kingdom	20.6	9.1	–	55.2	68.7	–	20.2
Denmark	18.3	8.1	35.2	58.2	36.9	11.2	17.3
Spain	14.0	6.2	25.5	61.7	59.5	14.0	7.5
Germany	11.3	5.0	..	52.9	57.8	–	–
France	8.5	3.8	29.7	67.4	56.6	12.2	8.0
Switzerland	7.1	3.2	44.9	51.9	55.1	–	6.5
Canada	6.9	3.1	7.4	53.6	59.3	5.3	7.1

Labour market indicators of persons born in Sweden living in OECD countries

Population 15-64	2000			2005/06		
	Men	Women	Total	Men	Women	Total
Employment-population ratio (%)	73.8	60.9	66.4	81.1	69.8	74.9
Unemployment rate (%)	6.9	7.5	7.2	4.4	5.7	5.1
Participation rate (%)	79.2	65.8	71.6	84.8	74.0	78.9
Total employed (thousands)	**50.7**	**55.6**	**106.3**	**66.4**	**68.8**	**135.2**
Employment rates of the highly educated (%)	87.2	70.5	77.7	94.1	80.4	86.6
Unemployment rates of the highly educated (%)	3.2	4.6	3.9	2.3	4.6	3.5
Highly educated in low- and medium-skilled jobs (%)	18.5	27.7	23.0	15.0	32.9	23.9
Highly educated employed (thousands)	**25.5**	**26.9**	**52.4**	**37.9**	**37.9**	**75.8**
Legislators, senior officials and managers	17.5	8.7	12.8	23.3	9.3	15.9
Professionals	22.1	18.1	20.0	30.5	23.3	26.7
Life science and health professionals	2.0	2.3	2.2	3.7	2.3	2.9
Teaching professionals	4.1	5.9	5.0	2.8	7.3	5.2
Technicians and associate professionals	15.6	21.3	18.6	17.4	20.5	19.1
Clerks	5.1	16.1	10.9	3.3	22.3	13.4
Service, shop and market sales workers	8.8	23.5	16.6	7.8	13.9	11.0
Skilled agricultural and fishery workers	1.5	1.0	1.2	0.7	2.8	1.8
Craft and related trades workers	13.7	1.9	7.4	7.8	2.1	4.7
Plant and machine operators and assemblers	8.5	2.4	5.3	2.5	1.7	2.1
Elementary occupations	7.2	7.0	7.1	6.6	4.1	5.3

Distribution of employment by occupation (%), population 15+

Persons born in Sweden and their native-born children, population 15+

Living in:	Europe	United States	Australia
2008	Thousands	Thousands	Thousands
Native-born children	31.8	109.4	7.8
Foreign-born	89.8	51.7	14.8
Total	121.6	161.1	22.6

International students from Sweden in OECD countries

Five main destinations	2004	2005	2006	2007	2008	2009
United States	3 116	3 244	3 326	2 985	3 296	3 225
United Kingdom	3 379	3 431	3 327	3 382	3 194	3 183
Denmark	557	636	816	1 127	880	1 524
Australia	1 049	1 007	887	879	853	833
Germany	..	..	..	..	477	461
Total	9 564	9 531	9 801	9 650	10 199	11 204

Legal migrant flows to the OECD
Thousands

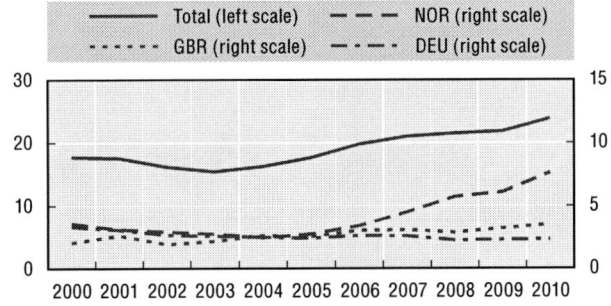

Remittance flows

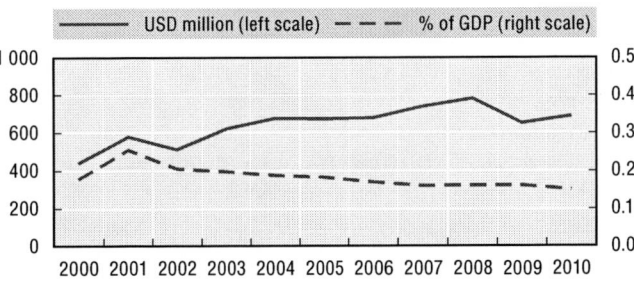

Ten main countries of destination for legal migrants in 2010 (numbers, % of total flows to the country): NOR (7595, 11.8%), GBR (3466, 0.7%), DEU (2280, 0.3%), ESP (1833, 0.4%), DNK (1125, 3.4%), USA (1097, 0.1%), JPN (1026, 0.7%), CHE (964, 0.7%), NLD (695, 0.7%), FIN (671, 3.8%).

Desire to emigrate, 2008-10

	Women	15-24	Highly educated	Total	Regional total
Persons who would move permanently, if they had the opportunity to do so (%)	14	25	12	16	16
Of which: Persons who are planning to move permanently in the next 12 months (%)				6	6
Of which: Persons who have already done some preparations for this move (*e.g.* visa application) (%)					39

Three main countries of desired destination: United States (18%), Spain (14%), United Kingdom (10%).

StatLink http://dx.doi.org/10.1787/888932673581

Total population 2010 (millions)	7.8
Population growth 2010 (%)	1.0
GDP per capita 2010 (current USD)	67 464
GDP growth 2010 (%)	2.7
Poverty rate 2010 (USD PPP 2 a day, in %)	..

Switzerland compared to:	World	Region
Human Development Index (HDI)	11/187	10/34
GDP per capita	6/194	3/34
Emigration rate	65/203	9/34
Emigration rate of the highly educated	62/157	6/34

Age structure of the population 0+ (2010): "0-14": 12%; "15-24": 15%; "25-64": 56%; "65+": 17%.
Level of education of the population 15+ (2010): "Low": 36%; "Medium": 47%; "High": 17%.

Emigrant population living in OECD countries

Immigrant population

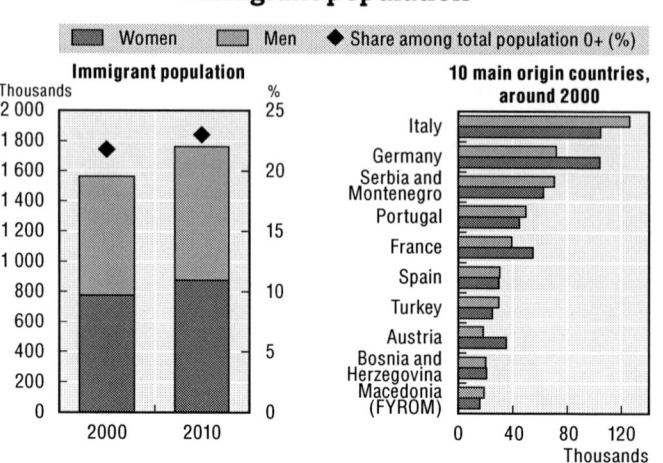

Emigrant population: persons born in Switzerland living abroad

	2000						2005/06		
	All destinations			OECD destinations			OECD destinations		
Population 15+	Men	Women	Total	Men	Women	Total	Men	Women	Total
Emigrant population (thousands)	203.1	241.2	444.4	191.9	232.2	424.0	223.2	254.6	477.8
Recent emigrants (thousands)	..	..	..	16.0	15.3	31.4	18.2	21.8	40.0
15-24 (%)	14.8	12.3	13.4	14.4	11.6	12.9	11.5	9.9	10.7
25-64 (%)	73.7	73.6	73.6	74.3	74.3	74.3	78.3	76.1	77.1
65+ (%)	11.6	14.1	12.9	11.3	14.0	12.8	10.2	14.0	12.2
Low-educated (%)	34.6	34.1	34.3	35.4	34.4	34.9	28.0	26.9	27.4
Highly educated (%)	26.1	24.3	25.1	25.1	24.0	24.5	31.0	27.6	29.2
Total emigration rates (%)	6.5	7.2	6.9	6.2	7.0	6.6	7.0	7.4	7.2
Emigration rates of the highly educated (%)	7.1	15.1	9.9	6.5	14.5	9.3	9.1	16.4	11.8

Main destinations in 2005/06

	Total		Recent emigrants	Women	Highly educated	15-24	Total in 2000
Population 15+	Thousands	%	%	%	%	%	Thousands
Italy	187.3	39.2	3.4	52.7	9.6	8.6	180.2
France	70.2	14.7	17.6	56.0	31.4	12.7	64.0
Spain	52.8	11.0	15.2	49.1	42.1	16.6	43.5
United States	45.9	9.6	15.1	50.9	58.8	9.4	44.9
Germany	32.2	6.7	18.3	67.3	38.3	–	11.9
Canada	20.6	4.3	7.7	47.6	54.8	9.5	20.1
Austria	13.8	2.9	18.8	60.2	25.2	–	10.5
Australia	10.4	2.2	12.9	47.3	42.8	7.6	9.7
United Kingdom	10.3	2.2	–	–	66.9	–	14.0
Netherlands	5.2	1.1	–	45.6	42.3	–	–

Labour market indicators of persons born in Switzerland living in OECD countries

Population 15-64	2000			2005/06		
	Men	Women	Total	Men	Women	Total
Employment-population ratio (%)	74.3	51.4	62.3	80.2	58.0	68.7
Unemployment rate (%)	8.1	12.9	10.3	5.2	8.8	6.8
Participation rate (%)	80.8	59.1	69.4	84.6	63.5	73.7
Total employed (thousands)	**124.7**	**95.1**	**219.8**	**159.9**	**124.7**	**284.6**
Employment rates of the highly educated (%)	82.5	65.3	73.6	92.6	77.9	85.1
Unemployment rates of the highly educated (%)	4.8	7.6	6.1	3.2	6.3	4.6
Highly educated in low- and medium-skilled jobs (%)	21.8	29.9	25.1	24.7	27.7	26.1
Highly educated employed (thousands)	**34.2**	**28.9**	**63.1**	**53.5**	**44.6**	**98.1**
Legislators, senior officials and managers	13.3	8.2	11.2	12.5	9.8	11.3
Professionals	11.4	10.4	11.0	12.4	11.3	11.9
Life science and health professionals	0.6	0.8	0.7	1.5	2.1	1.8
Teaching professionals	1.5	2.2	1.8	2.9	3.9	3.3
Technicians and associate professionals	15.2	20.6	17.3	16.1	24.5	19.8
Clerks	4.4	16.2	9.2	6.2	17.2	11.1
Service, shop and market sales workers	10.5	21.0	14.7	8.1	17.9	12.4
Skilled agricultural and fishery workers	3.6	2.3	3.1	2.8	2.7	2.8
Craft and related trades workers	21.8	6.9	15.8	24.3	5.1	15.8
Plant and machine operators and assemblers	10.4	3.2	7.5	10.9	4.2	7.9
Elementary occupations	9.4	11.3	10.2	6.8	7.0	6.9

Distribution of employment by occupation (%), population 15+

Persons born in Switzerland and their native-born children, population 15+

Living in:	Europe	United States	Australia
2008	Thousands	Thousands	Thousands
Native-born children	177.5	51.3	4.7
Foreign-born	130.6	38.9	7.6
Total	308.1	90.1	12.3

International students from Switzerland in OECD countries

Five main destinations	2004	2005	2006	2007	2008	2009
United Kingdom	1 467	1 501	1 679	1 896	1 892	2 087
Germany	..	..	..	..	1 637	1 808
France	1 463	1 471	1 631	1 604	1 613	1 741
United States	1 561	1 422	1 321	1 268	1 297	1 294
Italy	1 075	1 057	1 269	1 371	1 143	1 035
Total	7 144	6 441	7 251	7 556	8 713	9 432

Legal migrant flows to the OECD
Thousands

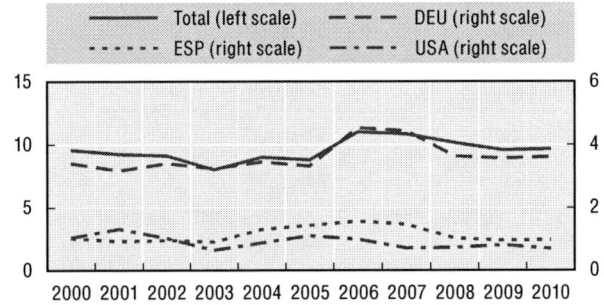

Remittance flows

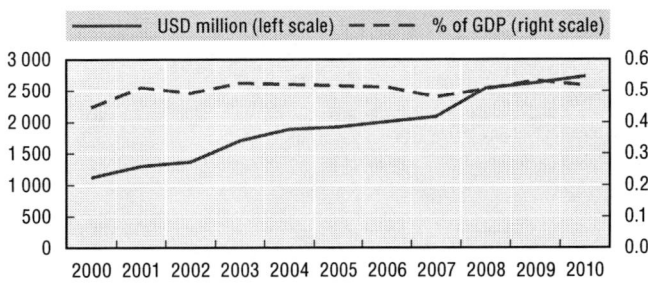

Ten main countries of destination for legal migrants in 2010 (numbers, % of total flows to the country): DEU (3614, 0.5%), ESP (956, 0.2%), USA (675, 0.1%), AUT (645, 0.7%), CAN (510, 0.2%), JPN (474, 0.2%), ITA (443, 0.4%), NLD (364, 0.4%), GBR (360, 0.1%), AUS (287, 0.1%).

Desire to emigrate, 2008-10

	Women	15-24	Highly educated	Total	Regional total
Persons who would move permanently, if they had the opportunity to do so (%)	11	..	..	13	16
Of which: Persons who are planning to move permanently in the next 12 months (%)				..	6
Of which: Persons who have already done some preparations for this move (*e.g.* visa application) (%)					39

StatLink ⧉ http://dx.doi.org/10.1787/888932673600

Total population 2010 (millions)	72.8		Turkey compared to:	World	Region
Population growth 2010 (%)	1.3		Human Development Index (HDI)	92/187	34/34
GDP per capita 2010 (current USD)	10 094		GDP per capita	62/194	33/34
GDP growth 2010 (%)	9.0		Emigration rate	83/203	16/34
Poverty rate 2005 (USD PPP 2 a day, in %)	9.1		Emigration rate of the highly educated	121/157	26/34

Age structure of the population 0+ (2010): "0-14": 18%; "15-24": 26%; "25-64": 50%; "65+": 6%.
Level of education of the population 15+ (2010): "Low": 53%; "Medium": 38%; "High": 9%.

Emigrant population living in OECD countries

Immigrant population

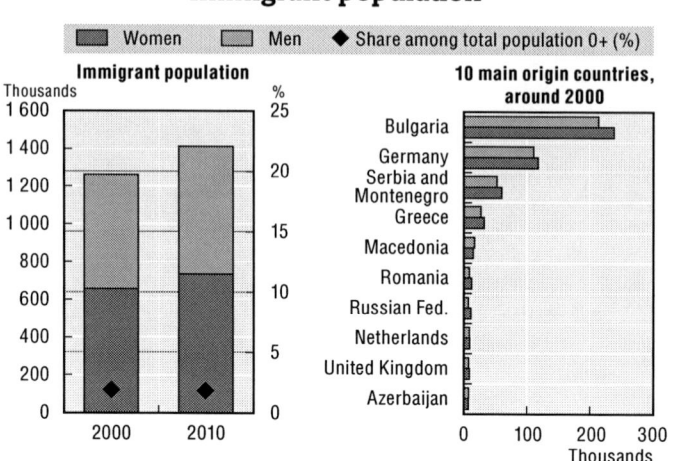

Emigrant population: persons born in Turkey living abroad

	2000						2005/06		
	All destinations			OECD destinations			OECD destinations		
Population 15+	Men	Women	Total	Men	Women	Total	Men	Women	Total
Emigrant population (thousands)	1 121.2	1 014.2	2 135.4	1 106.4	1 006.4	2 112.8	1 376.9	1 250.1	2 627.0
Recent emigrants (thousands)	..	..	..	55.7	49.6	105.3	124.7	111.2	235.9
15-24 (%)	9.2	10.8	10.0	9.2	10.8	10.0	9.4	11.3	10.3
25-64 (%)	81.7	79.2	80.5	81.9	79.5	80.7	82.1	80.8	81.4
65+ (%)	9.1	10.0	9.5	9.0	9.6	9.3	8.6	7.9	8.3
Low-educated (%)	64.2	77.3	70.4	64.7	77.5	70.8	59.9	73.5	66.4
Highly educated (%)	8.9	5.1	7.1	8.8	5.0	7.0	9.9	6.5	8.3
Total emigration rates (%)	4.5	4.1	4.3	4.4	4.1	4.3	5.0	4.6	4.8
Emigration rates of the highly educated (%)	3.5	3.0	3.3	3.4	3.0	3.2	5.2	5.0	5.2

Main destinations in 2005/06

	Total		Recent emigrants	Women	Highly educated	15-24	Total in 2000
Population 15+	Thousands	%	%	%	%	%	Thousands
Germany	1 568.7	59.7	5.5	48.1	4.5	8.9	1 188.0
France	225.6	8.6	15.0	46.4	7.6	13.9	167.3
Netherlands	179.0	6.8	9.6	46.9	8.0	9.2	158.7
Austria	142.6	5.4	16.2	47.4	3.3	17.0	113.1
United States	108.2	4.1	22.7	44.8	51.6	10.6	84.1
Belgium	89.5	3.4	16.8	49.8	–	10.2	68.1
United Kingdom	59.9	2.3	24.8	42.0	22.6	17.8	48.1
Switzerland	59.4	2.3	17.4	47.1	11.4	17.6	54.9
Sweden	36.2	1.4	17.9	46.7	11.4	10.9	31.7
Denmark	30.5	1.2	10.5	47.4	9.5	8.9	29.2

Labour market indicators of persons born in Turkey living in OECD countries

Population 15-64	2000			2005/06		
	Men	Women	Total	Men	Women	Total
Employment-population ratio (%)	66.1	35.4	51.5	66.8	35.3	51.8
Unemployment rate (%)	18.3	22.1	19.6	17.5	21.8	18.9
Participation rate (%)	81.0	45.4	64.1	81.0	45.2	63.9
Total employed (thousands)	**636.2**	**308.1**	**944.3**	**820.5**	**397.9**	**1 218.4**
Employment rates of the highly educated (%)	87.2	69.7	81.2	90.2	72.8	83.5
Unemployment rates of the highly educated (%)	4.5	6.5	5.1	9.1	12.4	10.2
Highly educated in low- and medium-skilled jobs (%)	24.3	32.5	26.5	35.9	33.1	35.0
Highly educated employed (thousands)	**70.0**	**28.8**	**98.8**	**101.4**	**49.2**	**150.7**
Legislators, senior officials and managers	2.7	0.9	2.1	6.9	2.8	5.6
Professionals	3.0	1.3	2.5	3.3	3.7	3.5
Life science and health professionals	0.1	0.1	0.1	0.5	0.3	0.4
Teaching professionals	0.3	0.3	0.3	0.4	1.3	0.7
Technicians and associate professionals	2.7	8.0	4.4	5.1	8.7	6.2
Clerks	3.6	8.1	5.1	3.7	9.9	5.7
Service, shop and market sales workers	8.7	22.2	13.0	9.0	22.7	13.3
Skilled agricultural and fishery workers	0.5	0.7	0.5	1.3	0.9	1.2
Craft and related trades workers	31.5	5.6	23.2	29.9	6.0	22.3
Plant and machine operators and assemblers	28.7	8.6	22.3	24.0	8.2	18.9
Elementary occupations	18.5	44.6	26.8	16.6	37.2	23.2

Distribution of employment by occupation (%), population 15+

Persons born in Turkey and their native-born children, population 15+

Living in:	Europe	United States	Australia
2008	Thousands	Thousands	Thousands
Native-born children	1 171.5	20.0	4.7
Foreign-born	2 126.9	168.7	18.1
Total	3 298.4	188.7	22.8

International students from Turkey in OECD countries

Five main destinations	2004	2005	2006	2007	2008	2009
United States	11 398	13 029	12 035	11 760	12 043	13 045
Germany	..	..	..	..	6 408	6 198
United Kingdom	1 960	1 913	2 084	2 233	2 370	2 683
France	2 273	2 283	2 412	2 339	2 270	2 330
Italy	182	189	288	384	465	614
Total	16 654	18 266	18 280	18 119	25 815	27 743

Legal migrant flows to the OECD
Thousands

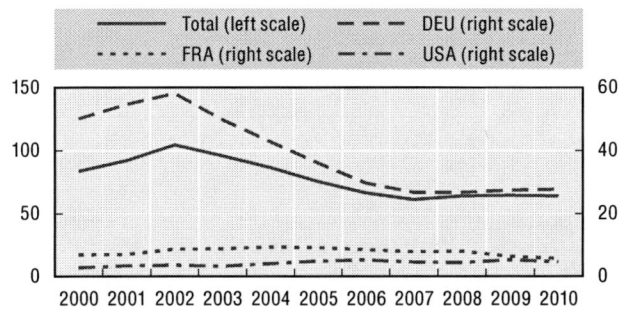

Remittance flows

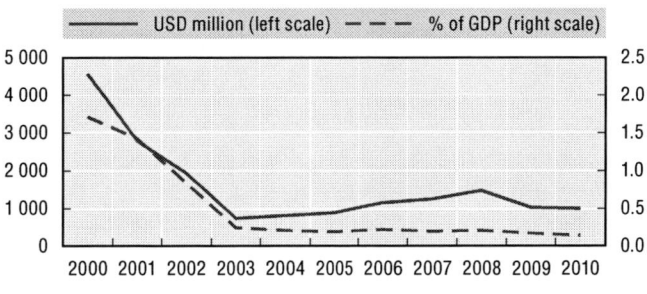

Ten main countries of destination for legal migrants in 2010 (numbers, % of total flows to the country): DEU (27564, 4.1%), FRA (5572, 4.1%), USA (4483, 0.4%), AUT (4338, 4.4%), NLD (3712, 3.7%), BEL (3118, 3.1%), SWE (2232, 1.5%), CHE (1988, 1.5%), CAN (1675, 0.6%), ITA (1483, 0.3%).

Desire to emigrate, 2008-10

	Women	15-24	Highly educated	Total	Regional total
Persons who would move permanently, if they had the opportunity to do so (%)	9	17	16	12	16
Of which: Persons who are planning to move permanently in the next 12 months (%)				5	6
Of which: Persons who have already done some preparations for this move (*e.g.* visa application) (%)					39

Three main countries of desired destination: Germany (19%), United States (12%), France (9%).

StatLink ⫸ http://dx.doi.org/10.1787/888932673619

			United Kingdom compared to:	World	Region
Total population 2010 (millions)	62.2		Human Development Index (HDI)	28/187	25/34
Population growth 2010 (%)	0.7		GDP per capita	26/194	18/34
GDP per capita 2010 (current USD)	36 144		Emigration rate	71/203	11/34
GDP growth 2010 (%)	1.4		Emigration rate of the highly educated	64/157	8/34
Poverty rate 2010 (USD PPP 2 a day, in %)	..				

Age structure of the population 0+ (2010): "0-14": 13%; "15-24": 17%; "25-64": 53%; "65+": 17%.
Level of education of the population 15+ (2010): "Low": 27%; "Medium": 49%; "High": 24%.

Emigrant population living in OECD countries

Immigrant population

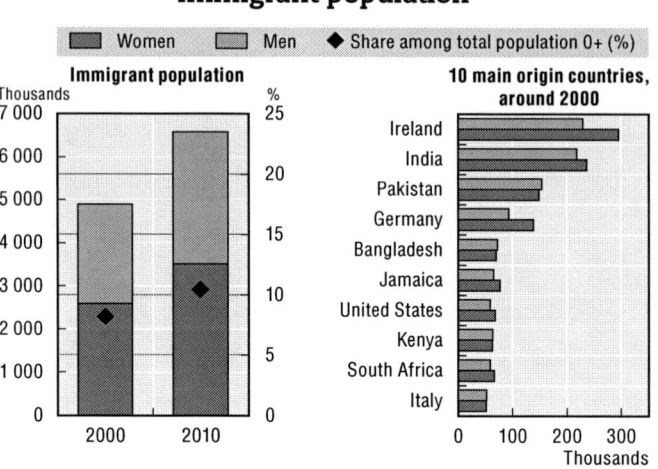

Emigrant population: persons born in the United Kingdom living abroad

	2000						2005/06		
	All destinations			OECD destinations			OECD destinations		
Population 15+	Men	Women	Total	Men	Women	Total	Men	Women	Total
Emigrant population (thousands)	1 693.3	1 815.5	3 508.8	1 556.8	1 684.7	3 241.5	1 695.7	1 753.1	3 448.8
Recent emigrants (thousands)	..	..	..	165.8	139.2	305.0	233.7	188.8	422.5
15-24 (%)	6.4	6.0	6.2	5.8	5.4	5.6	5.7	5.3	5.5
25-64 (%)	73.8	68.9	71.3	74.0	69.0	71.4	72.5	67.5	69.9
65+ (%)	19.8	25.0	22.5	20.2	25.6	23.0	21.8	27.2	24.6
Low-educated (%)	22.8	30.7	26.9	22.6	30.8	26.9	16.5	21.7	19.1
Highly educated (%)	37.1	31.0	34.0	37.8	31.9	34.7	42.7	37.8	40.2
Total emigration rates (%)	6.9	6.8	6.8	6.3	6.4	6.3	6.6	6.4	6.5
Emigration rates of the highly educated (%)	13.8	10.8	12.2	13.0	10.4	11.6	13.1	10.3	11.6

Main destinations in 2005/06

	Total		Recent emigrants	Women	Highly educated	15-24	Total in 2000
Population 15+	Thousands	%	%	%	%	%	Thousands
Australia	998.8	29.0	8.3	49.9	30.1	3.6	1 007.7
United States	796.7	23.1	10.6	53.7	46.0	7.9	757.0
Canada	587.8	17.0	3.5	52.6	49.5	2.9	612.3
Ireland	232.8	6.7	24.7	50.9	35.9	12.5	207.4
New Zealand	225.5	6.5	17.6	49.9	32.7	5.1	207.7
Spain	158.9	4.6	46.8	49.3	36.1	5.3	97.6
France	129.6	3.8	43.9	50.8	47.0	7.6	76.4
Germany	80.1	2.3	13.9	32.3	47.7	–	42.5
Italy	47.0	1.4	9.7	59.3	28.7	2.9	47.1
Netherlands	34.7	1.0	11.3	45.4	36.1	6.7	37.2

Labour market indicators of persons born in the United Kingdom living in OECD countries

Population 15-64	2000			2005/06		
	Men	Women	Total	Men	Women	Total
Employment-population ratio (%)	82.9	64.7	73.8	83.1	66.4	74.9
Unemployment rate (%)	5.4	5.2	5.3	4.9	5.0	5.0
Participation rate (%)	87.6	68.2	77.9	87.4	69.9	78.8
Total employed (thousands)	**984.2**	**772.3**	**1 756.5**	**1 056.9**	**817.4**	**1 874.3**
Employment rates of the highly educated (%)	90.6	76.2	83.7	94.2	79.6	87.1
Unemployment rates of the highly educated (%)	3.1	3.4	3.2	3.6	3.8	3.7
Highly educated in low- and medium-skilled jobs (%)	20.8	26.8	23.4	21.6	25.2	23.2
Highly educated employed (thousands)	**436.2**	**336.4**	**772.6**	**518.8**	**411.3**	**930.1**
Legislators, senior officials and managers	17.5	10.4	14.5	18.7	12.2	15.9
Professionals	22.0	22.6	22.3	23.2	24.3	23.7
Life science and health professionals	2.3	7.1	4.3	1.7	5.5	3.3
Teaching professionals	4.0	7.4	5.4	5.1	9.6	7.1
Technicians and associate professionals	12.6	16.8	14.4	12.7	18.1	15.1
Clerks	4.8	23.3	12.7	5.7	20.6	12.2
Service, shop and market sales workers	8.3	16.8	12.0	7.7	16.6	11.6
Skilled agricultural and fishery workers	1.9	0.9	1.5	2.2	1.2	1.8
Craft and related trades workers	17.2	1.5	10.5	16.6	1.3	9.9
Plant and machine operators and assemblers	8.1	1.9	5.4	7.4	1.6	4.9
Elementary occupations	7.5	5.8	6.8	5.7	4.2	5.0

Distribution of employment by occupation (%), population 15+

Persons born in the United Kingdom and their native-born children, population 15+

Living in:	Europe	United States	Australia
2008	Thousands	Thousands	Thousands
Native-born children	270.1	441.9	1 041.6
Foreign-born	663.0	466.8	1 054.5
Total	933.1	908.7	2 096.0

International students from the United Kingdom in OECD countries

Five main destinations	2004	2005	2006	2007	2008	2009
United States	8 439	8 602	8 568	8 625	8 376	8 558
France	2 611	2 299	2 570	2 595	2 519	2 580
Ireland	..	..	..	..	1 421	2 184
Australia	1 652	1 662	1 545	1 687	1 696	1 674
Germany	..	..	..	..	1 046	1 151
Total	16 719	16 134	17 709	17 383	18 523	20 154

Legal migrant flows to the OECD
Thousands

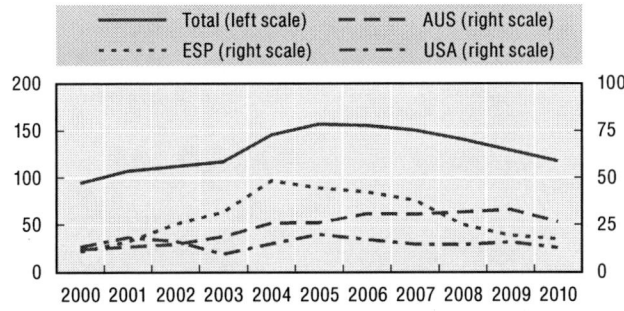

Remittance flows

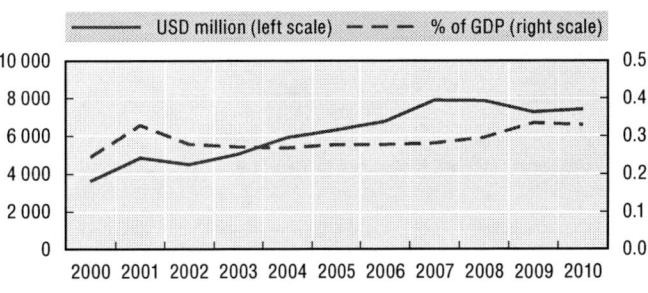

Ten main countries of destination for legal migrants in 2010 (numbers, % of total flows to the country): AUS (26699, 12.9%), ESP (17334, 4%), USA (12792, 1.2%), CAN (9500, 3.4%), DEU (9173, 1.4%), NZL (7541, 17%), JPN (5800, 4.1%), CHE (5465, 4.1%), NLD (4366, 4.4%), IRL (2400, 13.8%).

Desire to emigrate, 2008-10

	Women	15-24	Highly educated	Total	Regional total
Persons who would move permanently, if they had the opportunity to do so (%)	28	42	32	32	16
Of which: Persons who are planning to move permanently in the next 12 months (%)				4	6
Of which: Persons who have already done some preparations for this move (*e.g.* visa application) (%)					39

Three main countries of desired destination: Australia (25%), Canada (13%), United States (12%).

StatLink 🔗 *http://dx.doi.org/10.1787/888932673638*

		United States compared to:	World	Region
Total population 2010 (millions)	309.1	Human Development Index (HDI)	4/187	4/34
Population growth 2010 (%)	0.7	GDP per capita	11/194	6/34
GDP per capita 2010 (current USD)	47 199	Emigration rate	177/203	34/34
GDP growth 2010 (%)	3.0	Emigration rate of the highly educated	156/157	34/34
Poverty rate 2010 (USD PPP 2 a day, in %)	..			

Age structure of the population 0+ (2010): "0-14": 14%; "15-24": 20%; "25-64": 53%; "65+": 13%.
Level of education of the population 15+ (2010): "Low": 5%; "Medium": 63%; "High": 31%.

Emigrant population living in OECD countries

Immigrant population

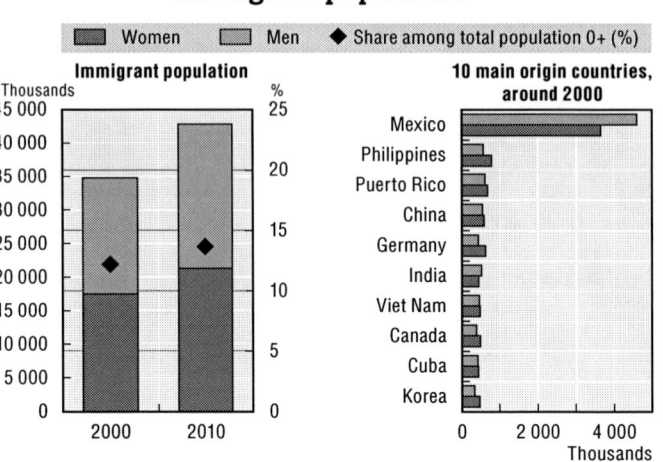

Emigrant population: persons born in the United States living abroad

	2000						2005/06		
	All destinations			OECD destinations			OECD destinations		
Population 15+	Men	Women	Total	Men	Women	Total	Men	Women	Total
Emigrant population (thousands)	590.8	640.0	1 230.8	412.5	461.7	874.3	484.9	505.7	990.5
Recent emigrants (thousands)	..	..	..	54.3	59.4	113.8	77.0	81.5	158.6
15-24 (%)	20.8	19.2	20.0	18.1	16.3	17.2	18.4	17.2	17.8
25-64 (%)	67.9	67.4	67.7	68.8	67.7	68.2	68.7	69.4	69.1
65+ (%)	11.2	13.4	12.3	13.0	16.0	14.6	12.9	13.3	13.1
Low-educated (%)	20.9	21.1	21.0	19.4	20.3	19.9	18.6	16.9	17.7
Highly educated (%)	43.4	43.5	43.4	49.4	49.0	49.2	49.4	53.2	51.4
Total emigration rates (%)	0.5	0.6	0.5	0.4	0.4	0.4	0.4	0.4	0.4
Emigration rates of the highly educated (%)	0.5	0.5	0.5	0.4	0.4	0.4	0.6	0.7	0.7

Main destinations in 2005/06

	Total		Recent emigrants	Women	Highly educated	15-24	Total in 2000
Population 15+	Thousands	%	%	%	%	%	Thousands
Canada	256.2	25.9	9.4	56.7	56.2	10.4	246.4
United Kingdom	138.9	14.0	37.1	51.8	66.4	15.2	126.5
Mexico	135.1	13.6	..	46.3	18.3	45.6	107.8
Germany	86.8	8.8	17.7	36.1	44.2	14.2	39.1
Australia	52.5	5.3	24.5	49.9	59.5	14.1	45.7
Israel	47.7	4.8	24.5	51.3	59.4	17.8	39.7
France	38.3	3.9	29.8	55.9	66.6	18.7	32.3
Italy	34.5	3.5	8.5	58.0	28.8	8.1	45.4
Japan	33.4	3.4	..	33.7	79.3	17.4	32.6
Switzerland	21.8	2.2	46.7	57.6	65.4	11.8	17.9

Labour market indicators of persons born in the United States living in OECD countries

Population 15-64	2000			2005/06		
	Men	Women	Total	Men	Women	Total
Employment-population ratio (%)	76.0	58.1	66.6	75.9	58.7	67.0
Unemployment rate (%)	5.2	6.6	5.8	5.3	6.3	5.8
Participation rate (%)	80.2	62.2	70.8	80.1	62.7	71.1
Total employed (thousands)	**240.8**	**202.9**	**443.8**	**294.6**	**244.6**	**539.2**
Employment rates of the highly educated (%)	87.9	69.7	78.0	92.2	74.5	82.4
Unemployment rates of the highly educated (%)	3.4	4.6	4.0	3.4	5.3	4.3
Highly educated in low- and medium-skilled jobs (%)	14.0	20.6	17.3	14.3	20.1	17.2
Highly educated employed (thousands)	**138.0**	**130.7**	**268.7**	**165.4**	**163.5**	**329.0**
Legislators, senior officials and managers	19.7	12.3	16.1	18.8	12.5	15.8
Professionals	34.0	33.8	33.9	35.0	32.3	33.7
Life science and health professionals	1.9	3.0	2.4	3.5	3.0	3.3
Teaching professionals	7.2	12.0	9.3	8.7	15.8	12.0
Technicians and associate professionals	13.6	17.5	15.5	15.0	21.8	18.2
Clerks	4.5	16.3	10.2	4.6	14.4	9.3
Service, shop and market sales workers	6.9	12.5	9.6	7.4	9.8	8.6
Skilled agricultural and fishery workers	2.0	1.4	1.7	1.4	2.2	1.8
Craft and related trades workers	8.5	1.4	5.1	7.2	2.2	4.8
Plant and machine operators and assemblers	5.2	1.4	3.4	4.7	1.0	2.9
Elementary occupations	5.6	3.4	4.5	5.4	3.8	4.6

Distribution of employment by occupation (%), population 15+

Persons born in the United States and their native-born children, population 15+

Living in:	Europe	United States	Australia
2008	Thousands	Thousands	Thousands
Native-born children	248.4	..	26.8
Foreign-born	300.9	..	44.7
Total	549.3	..	71.5

International students from the United States in OECD countries

Five main destinations	2004	2005	2006	2007	2008	2009
United Kingdom	13 381	14 385	14 755	15 956	13 895	14 343
Canada	7 225	..	7 851	7 935	8 310	8 485
France	2 687	2 429	2 771	3 165	3 228	3 544
Germany	..	..	..	..	2 871	3 161
Australia	3 439	3 226	2 931	3 023	3 055	2 972
Total	32 224	26 082	34 820	37 174	41 239	43 511

Legal migrant flows to the OECD
Thousands

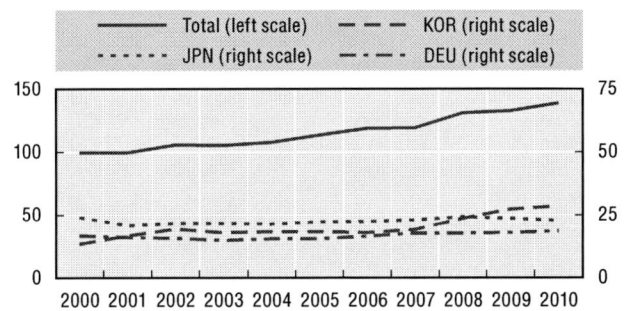

Remittance flows

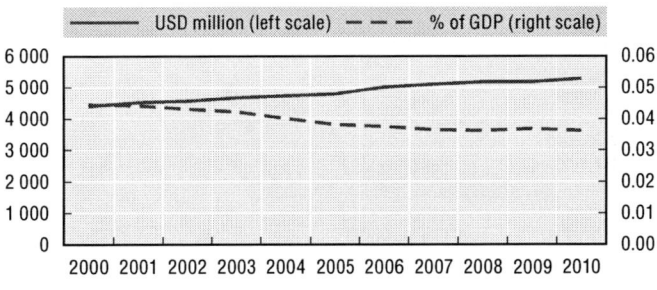

Ten main countries of destination for legal migrants in 2010 (numbers, % of total flows to the country): KOR (28328, 9.7%), JPN (22669, 7.9%), DEU (18262, 2.7%), GBR (16000, 3.5%), CAN (9240, 3.3%), ESP (4588, 1.1%), MEX (4026, 3%), CHE (3964, 3%), NLD (3325, 3.3%), AUS (3177, 1.5%).

Desire to emigrate, 2008-10

	Women	15-24	Highly educated	Total	Regional total
Persons who would move permanently, if they had the opportunity to do so (%)	10	21	9	10	16
Of which: Persons who are planning to move permanently in the next 12 months (%)				..	6
Of which: Persons who have already done some preparations for this move (*e.g.* visa application) (%)					39

StatLink ⟪⟫ http://dx.doi.org/10.1787/888932673657

Connecting with Emigrants
A Global Profile of Diasporas
© OECD 2012

Chapter 5

Non-OECD Europe and Central Asia

This chapter looks at recent migration flows and diasporas from non-OECD European and Central Asian countries to the OECD area. It shows that in 2010 about 800 000 new migrants from the region settled in OECD countries, accounting for about 15% of total immigration flows. In 2005/06 there were 11 million emigrants, 15 years old or older, from the region in OECD countries, of which 54% were women and 26% held a tertiary diploma. Total emigration rate for those over 15 years of age reached 3.9% for the region as a whole. The emigration rate for the highly educated reached 5.9%. Future challenges relate notably to the persistence of high outmigration and the need to harness the potential of the diaspora to support economic development.

This chapter also contains 14 country notes for Albania, Armenia, Bulgaria, Croatia, Kazakhstan, Kyrgyzstan, Latvia, Lithuania, Moldova, Romania, the Russian Federation, Serbia, Tajikistan and Ukraine.

1. Historical migration patterns

This chapter analyses the migratory particularities of the countries of non-OECD Europe and Central Asia. This category adopted for the study comprises countries that feature highly divergent economic characteristics. The group includes a single high-income country (Croatia), eight upper-middle-income countries (Albania, Bulgaria, Kazakhstan, Latvia, Lithuania, Romania, the Russian Federation and Serbia), three lower-middle-income countries (Armenia, Moldova and Ukraine) and two low-income countries (Kyrgyzstan and Tajikistan). Given the region's particular historical background, the countries can be divided into several categories: those of the former Yugoslavia (Croatia and Serbia), those of the former USSR (Armenia, Kazakhstan, Kyrgyzstan, Lithuania, Latvia, Moldova, the Russian Federation, Tajikistan and Ukraine) and the remaining countries, which had not formed parts of the aforementioned blocs: Albania, Bulgaria and Romania.

The migration backgrounds of countries that have belonged to the Commonwealth of Independent States (CIS) are highly similar and feature three main phases in the migratory process. Before 1991, international migration was prohibited and hence individual mobility was limited to within the Soviet sphere. The period following the system's breakup in 1991 and lasting until the regional crisis of 1998 was characterised by "ethnic" movements and family reunification of Jews heading for Israel[1] or the United States, *Aussiedler* heading for Germany, and ethnic Turks heading for Turkey. The region also experienced forced migrations triggered by conflict in the former Yugoslavia (Croatia and Serbia) in the early 1990s, which gave rise to considerable flows of refugees – primarily to Germany, Austria and Switzerland, as well as to Sweden, the Netherlands and Italy. There was also forced domestic migration in countries in the region undergoing conflict situations (Chechnya/Russian Federation and Transnistria/ Moldova). The third phase resulted from recent economic and political changes. This migratory wave has been characterised by a desire to escape unfavourable economic circumstances and to amass financial resources, so as to be able to improve the living conditions of family members who have stayed behind. Increasingly substantial flows have been recorded since 1998. Under such circumstances, migratory tendencies shifted and destination countries diversified. Unfavourable conditions have triggered mass migration not only to nearby countries, including the Russian Federation and other former Soviet republics, but also to non-traditional destinations such as Western Europe and North America.

Flows to nearby countries are essentially temporary and feature a high proportion of unskilled male construction workers. The other destination countries attract migrants with diverse socio-demographic profiles; their numbers include unskilled persons, but also (and increasingly) skilled persons and women. In all cases, the volume of undocumented migration is substantial.

For migrants from countries of the former USSR, the main destination countries remain the Russian Federation and Kazakhstan, where in many cases they work without proper documentation. In the Russian Federation, for example, it is estimated that in 2008 there were approximately 318 000 Kyrgyz workers, only 183 000 of whom had obtained work permits (OSCE, 2009).

With regard to Albania, Bulgaria and Romania, the situation has changed significantly with the cessation of the URSS. Before the 1990s, and even during the following decade, emigration levels from these countries were low. During the communist era, their participation in international migration was limited because of policies restricting immigration. After 1991, the political context – but above all the economic changes that marked the transition to a market economy – prompted many people to go abroad in search of work. As a result, labour emigration took on substantial dimensions.

The region comprises four countries that are European Union member states: Bulgaria and Romania, which became members in January 2007; and two countries of the former USSR – Lithuania and Latvia, which became members in 2004. It is important to emphasize that with regard to Croatia, the Treaty of Accession to the European Union was signed in December 2011. These non-OECD European countries that nonetheless belong to the European Union have become attractive to migrants from the region's other, less developed countries. In addition to these countries, there are others that are both immigration and emigration countries, such as the Russian Federation (with 12.3 million immigrants in 2010), Ukraine (5.3 million in 2010) and Kazakhstan (3.1 million in 2010).

2. Current profiles of emigrant populations

Flows and stocks

In the early 2000s, a number of events affected the region. Conflicts, repercussions of the 1998 Russian financial crisis and the accession of certain countries to the European Union triggered substantial migration to the OECD countries. The peak of 770 000 migrants in 2004 can be explained in great part by the accession of Lithuania and Latvia to the European Union. The number of migrants from Lithuania and Latvia in the OECD area in 2005/06 (247 000 and 93 000, respectively) represents an overall increase of 62% since 2000.

The all-time peak in migratory flows from non-OECD Europe and Central Asia was recorded in 2007: 1.1 million migrants to the OECD countries (Figure 5.1). Labour migration, in particular from Bulgaria and Romania, was influenced directly by the European Union

Figure 5.1. **Migrant flows from the non-OECD Europe and Central Asia region to OECD countries and remittance flows, 2000-10**

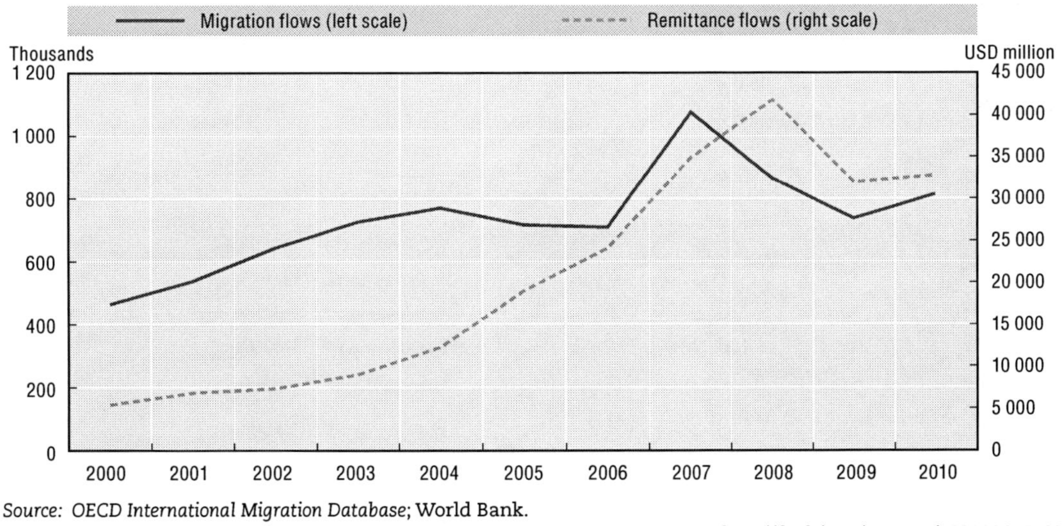

Source: OECD International Migration Database; World Bank.

StatLink ⟨⟩ http://dx.doi.org/10.1787/888932672080

accession process in January 2007, which allowed Bulgarian and Romanian migrants to work in certain EU countries and to regularise their legal standing. In the case of Romania, for instance, the number of Romanian migrants living legally in Spain totalled 393 000 in 2007 – tripling in a single year (OECD, 2008b). In Spain, Romanians constitute the largest migrant community. The same trend has been observed for Italy, with sharp growth in the number of Romanian emigrants: from approximately 40 000 in 2006 to 271 000 in 2007. Many of these emigrants had in fact left Romania well before 2007. The global financial crisis in the autumn of 2008 had direct consequences on international migration from the region. In 2009 migratory flows from non-OECD Europe to the OECD countries declined by about 127 000 persons (compared with 2008), to 737 000 migrants, a limited rebound (to 810 000) is however observed in 2010 (Figure 5.1).

The main countries of origin of legal migrant flows to the OECD area in 2009 were Romania (170 000), the Russian Federation (78 400), Bulgaria (71 700) and Ukraine (60 000). The OECD destination countries that in 2009 attracted the greatest number of migrants from non-OECD Europe and Central Asia were Germany (which took in 154 800 migrants from the region, or 26% of aggregate flows from these countries), Spain (14%), Turkey (14%) and the United States (10%).

Remittances to non-OECD Europe and Central Asia increased nearly eight-fold between 2000 and 2008 (from USD 5.4 billion in 2000 to USD 42 billion in 2008) but declined sharply in 2009 (USD 32 billion) and 2010 (USD 33 billion). The sharpest increases in remittances were recorded in Armenia, Kyrgyzstan, Moldova, Tajikistan and Ukraine as well as in Romania, which saw its transfers rise from USD 96 million in 2000 to USD 9.4 billion in 2008. The region includes three of the world's ten countries for which remittances in 2009 accounted for the greatest percentages of GDP: Tajikistan (35% of GDP), Moldova (22%) and Kyrgyzstan (21%).

The number of migrants from non-OECD Europe and Central Asia who are living in the OECD countries has been estimated at 11.1 million in 2005/06 (Figure 5.2). The main countries of origin are the Russian Federation (2.5 million), Romania (1.7 million), Ukraine (1.4 million), Albania (838 400), Serbia (740 000), Kazakhstan (701 000) and Croatia (553 000). Of these 11.1 million immigrants, 2.4 million are recent migrants who have been living in their respective destination countries for five years or less. The four main countries of origin for recent migrants are the same as for all emigrants combined, but Romania ranks first with 623 000 persons.

Figures for countries of the former USSR and former Yugoslavia are underestimated because of a non-negligible number of migrants who do not declare a specific country of birth in population censuses of destination countries. It concerns about 650 000 persons who declared former USSR as a place of birth (out of total of 6.4 million migrants originating from the region) and 430 000 persons who declared former Yugoslavia (out of a total of 2.8 million migrants). Aggregated figures are presented in Annex B.

Some countries in the region have few emigrants in the OECD countries – examples are Kyrgyzstan with 13 300 recorded emigrants, and Tajikistan with 12 300. This is attributable to the fact that the populations of these countries tend to choose other CIS countries, and the Russian Federation, Ukraine and Kazakhstan in particular, because of historical ties and ease of travel.

In 2000, only 21% of migrants from the former USSR had settled in the OECD countries. Between 2000 and 2005/06, their ranks increased from 3.6 million to 5.3 million, a rise of roughly 50% that accounts for 48% of all emigrants from the region.

Figure 5.2. **Total and highly educated emigrant population aged 15 and over from the non-OECD Europe and Central Asia region in the OECD area, 2005/06**

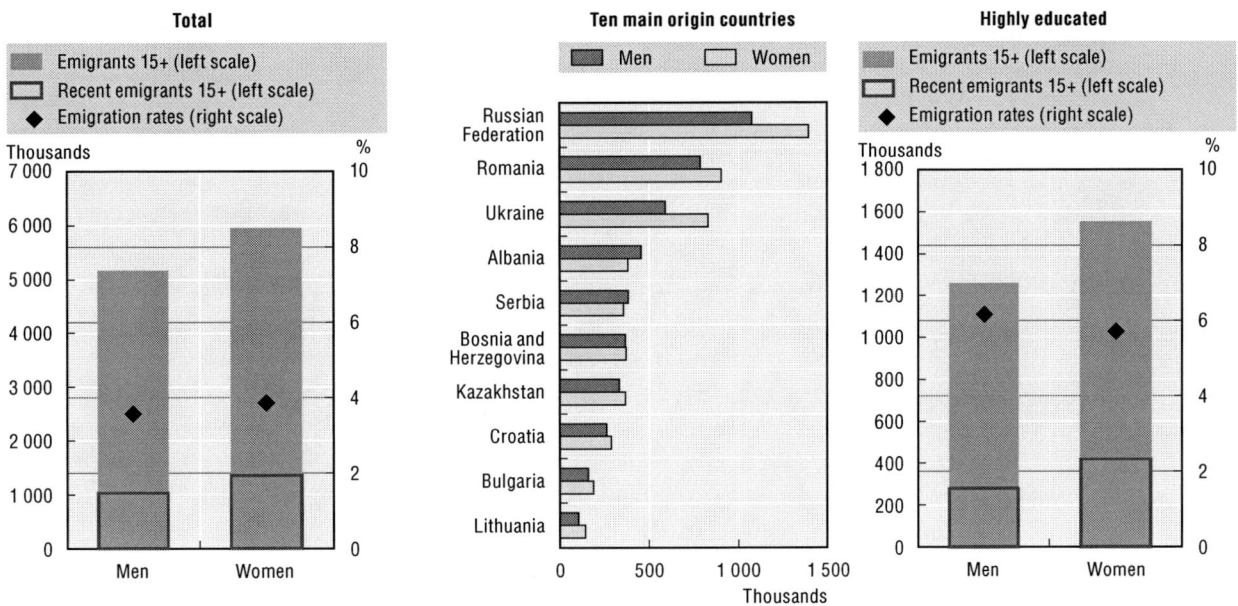

Source: Database on Immigrants in OECD Countries (DIOC 2005/06).

StatLink http://dx.doi.org/10.1787/888932672099

Germany remains the main destination of migrants from non-OECD Europe and Central Asia, with an estimated 3.6 million persons (Figure 5.3). It is followed by the United States (1.4 million), Israel (954 400), Italy (800 500) and Greece (720 000). These five countries have taken in 67% of the migrant population of non-OECD Europe and Central Asia.

Figure 5.3. **Emigrant populations and migrant flows from the non-OECD Europe and Central Asia region to the five main destinations within the OECD area, population aged 15 and over**

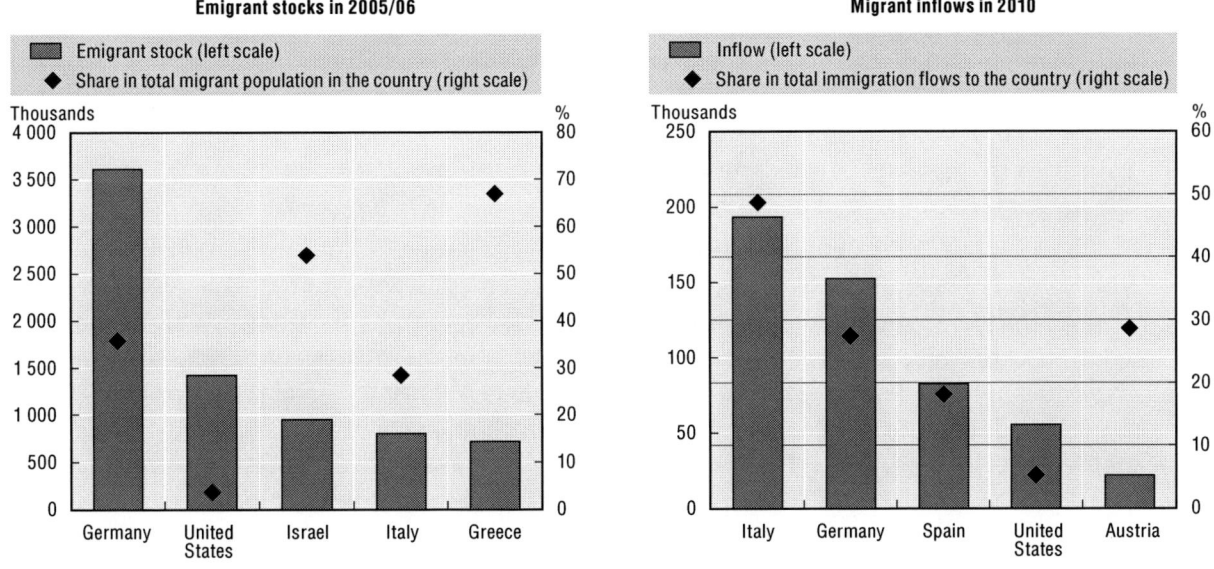

Source: Database on Immigrants in OECD Countries (DIOC 2005/06); OECD International Migration Database.

StatLink http://dx.doi.org/10.1787/888932672118

Characteristics of emigrant populations

A majority of the migrant population from non-OECD Europe and Central Asia are women. The number of women is approximately 15% greater than the number of men. Among recent migrants, the proportion of women is as high as 57%, a phenomenon reflecting the strong demand for labour in the home services sector of the OECD host countries.

A large number of emigrants from the region are between 15 and 24 years old (Table 5.1). Between 2000 and 2005/06, the proportion of young emigrants increased or remained stable in the migrant populations of non-OECD Europe and Central Asia, except in certain countries such as Albania, Armenia, Moldova and Bulgaria, where the corresponding proportions dipped slightly in 2005/06 as compared with 2000. The greatest increase in the share of young emigrants was observed for Lithuania (+8 percentage points), Latvia (+7 points), Kyrgyzstan (+6 points), Kazakhstan (+4 points) and Romania (+4 points). This increase can be attributed to the emergence of new categories of migrants, including students and young graduates.

Table 5.1. **Characteristics of migrants from the non-OECD Europe and Central Asia region in the OECD area, by gender, 2005/06**

Percentage

	Regional averages (unweighted)			Regional total (weighted)		
	Men	Women	Total	Men	Women	Total
15-24	17.6	15.6	16.5	16.5	15.0	15.7
25-64	65.6	66.2	65.9	68.9	66.8	67.8
65+	16.8	18.2	17.7	14.6	18.1	16.5
Low-educated	32.3	33.7	32.9	32.9	35.9	34.5
Highly educated	30.0	30.7	30.3	24.7	26.4	25.6
Total emigration rates	9.9	9.3	9.6	3.6	3.9	3.9
Emigration rates of the highly educated	12.4	11.8	11.9	6.2	5.7	5.9

Source: Database on Immigrants in OECD Countries (DIOC 2005/06).

StatLink ⟲ http://dx.doi.org/10.1787/888932675101

Countries recording the sharpest growth in the proportion of young people in their emigrant populations are also the ones experiencing the greatest increases in the number of foreign students. The number of students from Lithuania increased fourfold between 2004 and 2009; for Latvia the increase was threefold; and for the three other countries (Kyrgyzstan, Kazakhstan and Romania) the number doubled, as it did for the Russian Federation and Bulgaria.

In 2009, the OECD countries were hosting 159 400 students from non-OECD Europe and Central Asia, practically double the number recorded in 2004. During this reference period, the number of students leaving for the OECD countries increased in all of the countries analysed. In 2009, in absolute terms, the main origin countries were the Russian Federation (with 27 000 students), Romania (22 000), Bulgaria (20 000), Albania (15 000) and Ukraine (13 000). Regarding the main destination countries, Germany tops the list with 38 000 students from non-OECD Europe and Central Asia, followed by the United Kingdom (27 000) and Italy (24 000). These three countries account for over 55% of all students from the region who are residing in the OECD countries.

In 2005/06, on average one-third of the emigrant population from non-OECD Europe and Central Asia was low-skilled, and the proportion of highly skilled migrants was 30%

(Table 5.1). Over half of the emigrants from Albania (55%) and Serbia (54%) had a low level of education; these countries are followed by Croatia (40%) and Kazakhstan (38%). Moreover, the group includes four countries for which the proportion of persons with a high level of education exceeds 40%: Tajikistan (48%), Kyrgyzstan (48%), Moldova (44%) and Latvia (41%). The proportion of emigrants with higher education rose sharply in countries like Kyrgyzstan (a 25 percentage point increase between 2000 and 2005/06), and Tajikistan (20 percentage points). Other countries experienced smaller increases: Armenia (+7 points), Bulgaria (+7 points) and Lithuania (+5 points). Some countries even saw a decrease in the proportion of this category of emigrants between 2000 and 2005/06: Moldova and Kazakhstan (–3 points), Serbia and Romania (–2 points), and Latvia and the Russian Federation (–1 point).

One-fourth of the emigrants from non-OECD Europe and Central Asia hold skilled jobs (executives or legislators, civil servants, people working in intellectual or scientific professions) in the OECD countries. This percentage varies from country to country, ranging from 37% for Tajikistan, 32% for Kyrgyzstan to only 4% for Albania and 6% for Moldova. The percentage of persons with university diplomas but working in unskilled jobs averages approximately 47% (Table 5.2). This figure peaks to 68% for Moldovans and Lithuanians. For Albanians, Bulgarians and Kyrgyz with higher education degrees, the proportion holding unskilled jobs is close to 60%.

Table 5.2. **Labour market characteristics of migrants from the non-OECD Europe and Central Asia region in the OECD area, by gender, 2005/06**

	Regional averages (unweighted)			Regional total (weighted)		
	Men	Women	Total	Men	Women	Total
Employment rate (%)	72.2	56.2	64.2	63.7	47.1	54.8
Unemployment rate (%)	9.8	11.5	10.5	10.8	13.0	11.8
Participation rate (%)	79.5	63.0	71.2	71.4	54.1	62.2
Total employed (thousands)	**3 158**	**2 690**	**5 848**			
Employment rate of the highly educated (%)	85.1	72.5	78.4	71.4	60.1	65.2
Unemployment rate of the highly educated (%)	6.8	9.0	8.0	8.0	9.9	9.0
Participation rate of the highly educated (%)	90.6	78.7	84.3	77.6	66.7	71.6
Highly educated employed (thousands)	**871**	**906**	**1 777**			
Persons with tertiary degrees in low- or medium-skilled jobs (%)	47.1	43.9	45.9	46.1	47.1	46.6

Source: Database on Immigrants in OECD Countries (DIOC 2005/06).

StatLink ᵐˢᵖ *http://dx.doi.org/10.1787/888932675120*

Emigration rates and the "brain drain"

The countries analysed in this chapter recorded an aggregate emigration rate in 2005/06 of 3.9% (weighted average, the unweighted average being 9.6%). The highest emigration rates were observed in Albania (27%) and Croatia (13%). Albania is also the country whose emigration rate rose most sharply between 2000 and 2005/06 (+7 points), followed by Romania and Lithuania (+3 points for both). Kyrgyzstan and the Russian Federation are the countries with the smallest proportions of emigrants to the OECD countries, with 0.4% and 2% respectively.

With regard to the emigration rate of the highly skilled population, the proportion tends to be about 2 percentage points higher than the aggregate emigration rate in 2005/06. The weighted average emigration rate for highly skilled persons was 5.9% (the unweighted average being 11.9%), which in fact is somewhat low compared with most of the other regions in the world. Even so, this average masks sharp disparities across countries. The greatest emigration rates for highly skilled persons were recorded in Albania (35%), Croatia (23%) and Romania (20%), while the rates for Kyrgyzstan was very low, at 1.5%.

The sharpest increases in skilled emigration rates between 2000 and 2005/06 were observed in Albania (+9 points), Bulgaria (+6 points), Romania (+5 points) and Armenia (+4 points). On the other hand, some countries – including Serbia, Kyrgyzstan, Latvia, Moldova and Tajikistan – noted relative decreases in skilled emigration.

3. Future trends and challenges

Migratory flows from non-OECD Europe and Central Asia were shaped in great part by unfavourable economic conditions in the countries of origin. Most of this migration is linked to a search for employment in OECD area countries or nearby CIS countries. Changes taking place in the region, such as enlargement of the European Union in 2004 and 2007, contributed to shift migratory flows from new EU members states (Lithuania, Latvia, Bulgaria and Romania) to EU15 countries but it also had implication on migration movements from neighbouring countries, notably Moldova.[2]

Persons living in the European Union will continue to migrate within the free mobility area but migration flows from Croatia, as well as from Serbia will probably increase in the short term. In contrast, citizens of Central Asian countries will probably continue to aim at the Russian Federation, Ukraine and Kazakhstan because of the importance of economic and cultural ties. In the meantime, migration from Ukraine, Georgia and Moldova, will probably continue to diversify both within Europe and beyond.

Until the early 2000s the main migratory flows were mainly temporary and motivated unfavourable economic conditions but in the recent years we observed the proliferation of more permanent migratory flows to countries in Western Europe, North America and Israel. This trend has led to the emergence of new immigrant communities and initial forms of consolidation of diasporas. These migrants groups are therefore mostly recent and highly educated.

To harness the resources of a diaspora, it is necessary to institute a new form of collaboration with its members. Countries that have realised that emigrants do not constitute a net loss have developed collaborative relationships with their diasporas, by granting expatriates favourable terms for investing and creating economic activities in their countries of origin; by creating public institutions in charge of communicating with expatriates; and by encouraging circular migration. Better communication and better information would make it possible to create a strong link with the diaspora, and send a signal that would demonstrate the country of origin's interest in its population that has settled abroad.

Notes

1. The statistical data for Israel are supplied by and under the responsibility of the relevant Israeli authorities. The use of such data by the OECD is without prejudice to the status of the Golan Heights, East Jerusalem and Israeli settlements in the West Bank under the terms of international law.

2. Many Moldovans applied for Romanian citizenship taking advantage of a Romanian law adopted in 1991 which enables any person, or first or second generation descendant, having possessed Romanian nationality prior to 1940 to obtain Romanian citizenship. According to official Romanian statistics, approximately 120 000 Moldovans already have Romanian passports, over 800 000 applications for naturalisation are pending, and the number of applicants continues to increase. For many Moldovans, Romanian citizenship is synonymous with freedom of movement and an opportunity to escape poverty and seek to work legally in European Union countries, which explains the substantial number of applications.

Country Notes

Non-OECD Europe and Central Asia

		Albania compared to:	World	Region
Total population 2010 (millions)	3.2	Human Development Index (HDI)	71/187	15/26
Population growth 2010 (%)	0.4	GDP per capita	105/194	18/27
GDP per capita 2010 (current USD)	3 678	Emigration rate	21/203	3/28
GDP growth 2010 (%)	3.5	Emigration rate of the highly educated	14/157	1/19
Poverty rate 2008 (USD PPP 2 a day, in %)	4.3			

Age structure of the population 0+ (2010): "0-14": 19%; "15-24": 23%; "25-64": 49%; "65+": 10%.
Level of education of the population 15+ (2010): "Low": 11%; "Medium": 82%; "High": 7%.

Emigrant population living in OECD countries

Immigrant population

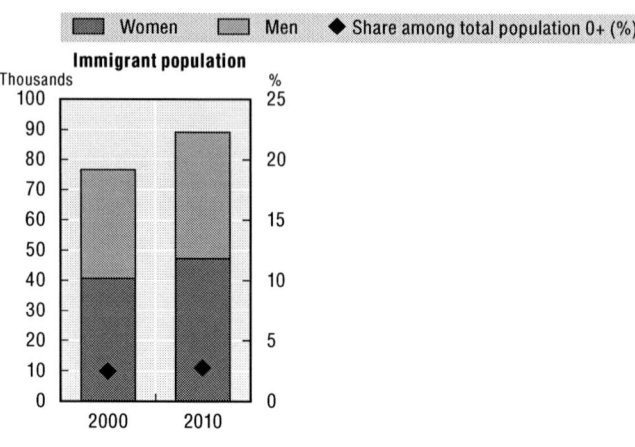

Emigrant population: persons born in Albania living abroad

	2000						2005/06		
	All destinations			OECD destinations			OECD destinations		
Population 15+	Men	Women	Total	Men	Women	Total	Men	Women	Total
Emigrant population (thousands)	309.1	219.0	528.1	305.6	215.7	521.3	457.2	381.2	838.5
Recent emigrants (thousands)	..	..	..	147.4	118.4	265.8	86.5	110.8	197.3
15-24 (%)	26.7	25.8	26.3	26.7	25.8	26.3	20.2	23.2	21.6
25-64 (%)	69.9	69.3	69.6	70.1	69.5	69.9	77.1	73.0	75.2
65+ (%)	3.4	4.9	4.0	3.2	4.6	3.8	2.7	3.9	3.2
Low-educated (%)	57.3	52.6	55.4	57.5	52.6	55.5	56.2	53.0	54.7
Highly educated (%)	8.3	10.1	9.0	8.2	10.1	9.0	9.6	10.5	10.0
Total emigration rates (%)	23.0	16.9	20.0	22.8	16.7	19.8	28.5	24.4	26.5
Emigration rates of the highly educated (%)	25.1	29.2	26.8	24.7	28.8	26.4	34.3	35.9	35.0

Main destinations in 2005/06

	Total		Recent emigrants	Women	Highly educated	15-24	Total in 2000
Population 15+	Thousands	%	%	%	%	%	Thousands
Greece	461.2	55.0	16.2	44.7	8.3	21.6	337.3
Italy	274.1	32.7	34.2	46.2	5.7	22.4	135.1
United States	62.4	7.4	27.7	48.4	30.1	17.3	32.5
Canada	9.4	1.1	53.5	48.4	59.1	19.4	4.8
United Kingdom	7.0	0.8	–	–	–	–	1.9
Austria	6.3	0.7	–	41.8	–	–	1.6
France	4.8	0.6	39.4	47.9	26.1	25.6	2.2
Switzerland	3.9	0.5	–	41.1	–	41.1	1.4
Belgium	–	–	–	–	–	–	1.3
Australia	1.9	0.2	39.3	48.5	14.6	18.0	1.2

Labour market indicators of persons born in Albania living in OECD countries

Population 15-64	2000			2005/06		
	Men	Women	Total	Men	Women	Total
Employment-population ratio (%)	82.4	39.1	64.6	84.2	43.2	65.7
Unemployment rate (%)	7.3	17.1	9.9	5.3	17.8	9.4
Participation rate (%)	88.9	47.2	71.7	89.0	52.5	72.5
Total employed (thousands)	**237.1**	**78.8**	**315.9**	**372.9**	**157.8**	**530.7**
Employment rates of the highly educated (%)	81.9	51.0	67.1	91.0	70.5	81.1
Unemployment rates of the highly educated (%)	7.5	15.3	10.5	5.2	15.5	9.6
Highly educated in low- and medium-skilled jobs (%)	39.4	50.7	43.8	74.1	53.0	65.2
Highly educated employed (thousands)	**18.6**	**10.6**	**29.2**	**35.7**	**23.3**	**59.0**
Legislators, senior officials and managers	7.7	4.5	6.9	2.0	1.5	1.9
Professionals	4.5	6.4	4.9	1.4	3.5	2.0
Life science and health professionals	0.1	0.1	0.1	0.2	1.5	0.6
Teaching professionals	0.1	0.3	0.1	0.2	0.3	0.3
Technicians and associate professionals	8.7	11.9	9.5	1.3	5.0	2.3
Clerks	1.8	10.4	3.8	2.0	4.6	2.7
Service, shop and market sales workers	6.4	20.5	9.7	7.0	20.4	10.7
Skilled agricultural and fishery workers	3.5	1.6	3.0	3.2	1.9	2.9
Craft and related trades workers	32.6	8.2	27.0	49.5	13.7	39.7
Plant and machine operators and assemblers	11.2	4.2	9.6	16.3	8.0	14.0
Elementary occupations	23.6	32.3	25.6	17.3	41.4	23.9

(left margin label: Distribution of employment by occupation (%), population 15+)

Persons born in Albania and their native-born children, population 15+

Living in:	Europe	United States	Australia
2008	Thousands	Thousands	Thousands
Native-born children	16.4	26.2	..
Foreign-born	645.1	99.2	2.6
Total	661.5	125.4	..

International students from Albania in OECD countries

Five main destinations	2004	2005	2006	2007	2008	2009
Italy	8 494	9 724	10 959	11 883	11 787	12 259
United States	916	905	936	860	690	745
Turkey	591	605	620	600	590	547
France	369	404	444	450	437	484
Germany	..	..	..	..	366	421
Total	11 721	13 199	15 929	18 440	20 287	15 081

Legal migrant flows to the OECD
Thousands

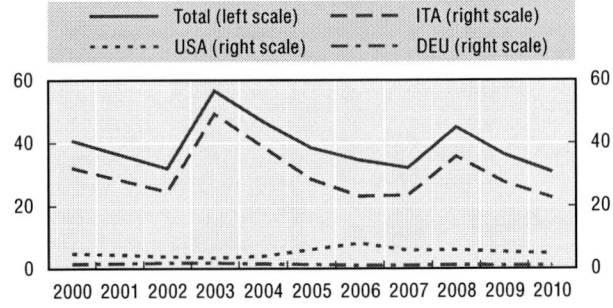

Remittance flows

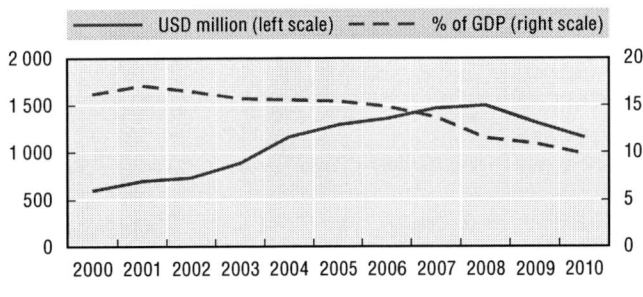

Ten main countries of destination for legal migrants in 2010 (numbers, % of total flows to the country): ITA (22591, 5.3%), USA (4711, 0.5%), DEU (913, 0.1%), CAN (520, 0.2%), BEL (351, 0.3%), FRA (267, 0.2%), ESP (218, 0.2%), SWE (164, 0.2%), AUS (160, 0.1%), POL (145, 0.4%).

Desire to emigrate, 2008-10

	Women	15-24	Highly educated	Total	Regional total
Persons who would move permanently, if they had the opportunity to do so (%)	38	56	42	40	19
Of which: Persons who are planning to move permanently in the next 12 months (%)				14	7
Of which: Persons who have already done some preparations for this move (*e.g.* visa application) (%)					..

Three main countries of desired destination: Italy (31%), United States (14%), Greece (13%).

StatLink ⟶ http://dx.doi.org/10.1787/888932673676

			World	Region
Total population 2010 (millions)	3.1	**Armenia compared to:**		
Population growth 2010 (%)	0.2	Human Development Index (HDI)	86/187	20/26
GDP per capita 2010 (current USD)	3 031	GDP per capita	112/194	19/27
GDP growth 2010 (%)	2.1	Emigration rate	81/203	16/28
Poverty rate 2008 (USD PPP 2 a day, in %)	12.4	Emigration rate of the highly educated	74/157	7/19

Age structure of the population 0+ (2010): "0-14": 19%; "15-24": 20%; "25-64": 50%; "65+": 11%.
Level of education of the population 15+ (2010): "Low": 6%; "Medium": 75%; "High": 18%.

Emigrant population living in OECD countries

Immigrant population

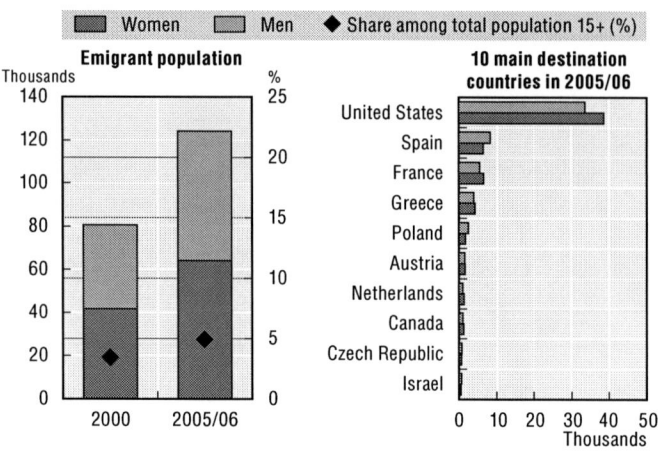

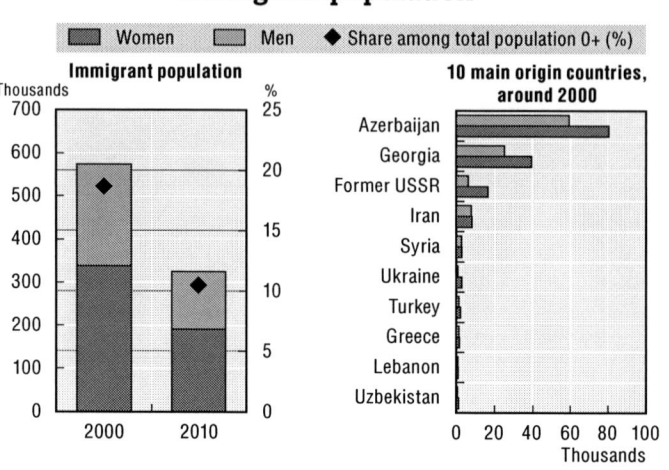

Emigrant population: persons born in Armenia living abroad

Population 15+	2000 All destinations			2000 OECD destinations			2005/06 OECD destinations		
	Men	Women	Total	Men	Women	Total	Men	Women	Total
Emigrant population (thousands)	295.3	223.7	518.9	39.0	41.8	80.7	60.1	64.1	124.2
Recent emigrants (thousands)	..	..	..	8.5	9.3	17.7	14.2	15.2	29.4
15-24 (%)	18.1	21.0	19.4	21.1	19.7	20.3	19.6	19.1	19.3
25-64 (%)	75.9	70.6	73.6	72.8	71.3	72.0	74.6	73.3	73.9
65+ (%)	6.0	8.4	7.0	6.2	9.0	7.6	5.8	7.6	6.8
Low-educated (%)	20.1	20.6	20.4	28.6	25.0	26.7	26.1	20.7	23.3
Highly educated (%)	22.5	23.2	22.8	29.5	33.1	31.3	33.7	42.1	38.0
Total emigration rates (%)	22.2	15.2	18.5	3.6	3.2	3.4	5.3	4.7	4.9
Emigration rates of the highly educated (%)	26.9	19.8	23.3	6.0	6.1	6.1	14.7	8.4	10.3

Main destinations in 2005/06

Population 15+	Total Thousands	Total %	Recent emigrants %	Women %	Highly educated %	15-24 %	Total in 2000 Thousands
United States	72.1	58.0	13.7	53.6	41.3	16.9	56.4
Spain	14.6	11.8	58.0	43.6	38.1	33.9	2.4
France	11.9	9.5	38.8	54.3	26.1	19.0	5.4
Greece	7.9	6.4	–	52.3	19.2	–	7.7
Poland	4.0	3.3	–	–	–	–	0.7
Austria	3.0	2.4	73.1	–	–	–	0.3
Netherlands	2.2	1.8	–	–	–	–	–
Canada	2.2	1.8	34.7	55.0	63.2	17.8	1.7
Czech Republic	1.3	1.0	..	45.1	38.8	24.6	0.8
Israel	1.1	0.9	49.4	42.0	87.1	7.2	2.4

Labour market indicators of persons born in Armenia living in OECD countries

Population 15-64	2000			2005/06		
	Men	Women	Total	Men	Women	Total
Employment-population ratio (%)	61.1	45.7	53.2	66.5	52.5	59.4
Unemployment rate (%)	13.8	15.3	14.4	13.8	16.5	15.0
Participation rate (%)	70.9	53.9	62.2	77.1	63.0	69.9
Total employed (thousands)	**21.9**	**17.0**	**38.9**	**36.6**	**30.1**	**66.7**
Employment rates of the highly educated (%)	70.6	58.3	63.9	86.3	72.9	78.7
Unemployment rates of the highly educated (%)	11.6	12.3	12.0	13.3	13.0	13.2
Highly educated in low- and medium-skilled jobs (%)	53.1	51.8	52.5	55.2	52.0	53.4
Highly educated employed (thousands)	**7.5**	**7.5**	**15.0**	**14.1**	**15.8**	**29.9**
Legislators, senior officials and managers	10.1	6.2	8.3	4.0	7.0	5.1
Professionals	14.8	15.1	15.0	7.4	11.2	8.8
Life science and health professionals	0.5	1.1	0.7	1.7	2.6	2.0
Teaching professionals	2.1	4.2	3.1	1.6	3.1	2.2
Technicians and associate professionals	10.1	14.3	12.0	5.1	11.0	7.3
Clerks	3.9	18.7	10.7	2.3	9.5	5.0
Service, shop and market sales workers	8.5	21.2	14.3	5.0	18.7	10.1
Skilled agricultural and fishery workers	1.1	0.9	1.0	0.5	0.3	0.4
Craft and related trades workers	29.4	3.1	17.3	33.9	5.0	23.1
Plant and machine operators and assemblers	13.3	7.8	10.8	13.7	7.5	11.4
Elementary occupations	8.9	12.7	10.7	28.3	29.8	28.8

Distribution of employment by occupation (%), population 15+

Persons born in Armenia and their native-born children, population 15+

Living in:	Europe	United States	Australia
2008	Thousands	Thousands	Thousands
Native-born children	17.0	58.8	..
Foreign-born	54.8	77.6	..
Total	71.8	136.4	..

International students from Armenia in OECD countries

Five main destinations	2004	2005	2006	2007	2008	2009
France	290	279	717	282	482	525
United States	412	428	422	436	403	394
Germany	..	..	..	..	291	284
Spain	11	12	4	11	15	69
United Kingdom	36	47	56	74	54	69
Total	864	874	1 389	1 082	1 543	1 552

Legal migrant flows to the OECD
Thousands

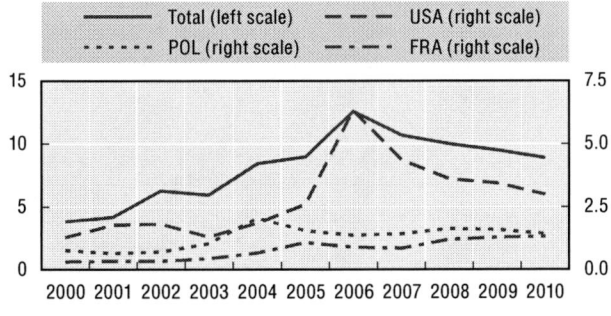

Remittance flows

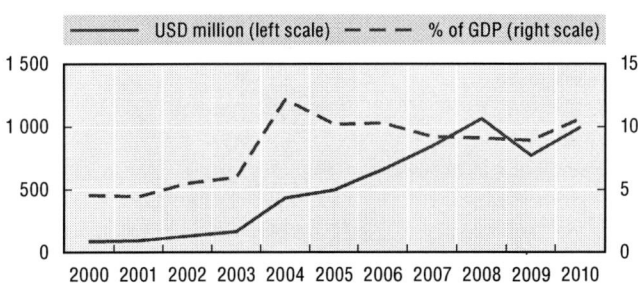

Ten main countries of destination for legal migrants in 2010 (numbers, % of total flows to the country): USA (2979, 0.3%), POL (1397, 3.4%), FRA (1308, 1%), DEU (920, 0.1%), ESP (706, 0.2%), CAN (235, 0.1%), BEL (228, 0.2%), AUT (203, 0.2%), CZE (183, 0.7%), SWE (174, 0.2%).

Desire to emigrate, 2008-10

	Women	15-24	Highly educated	Total	Regional total
Persons who would move permanently, if they had the opportunity to do so (%)	35	46	37	35	19
Of which: Persons who are planning to move permanently in the next 12 months (%)				11	7
Of which: Persons who have already done some preparations for this move (*e.g.* visa application) (%)					..

Three main countries of desired destination: Russian Federation (31%), United States (20%), France (13%).

StatLink ￼ http://dx.doi.org/10.1787/888932673695

Total population 2010 (millions)	7.5	**Bulgaria compared to:**		**World**	**Region**
Population growth 2010 (%)	−0.6	Human Development Index (HDI)		55/187	10/26
GDP per capita 2010 (current USD)	6 325	GDP per capita		81/194	11/27
GDP growth 2010 (%)	0.2	Emigration rate		84/203	17/28
Poverty rate 2007 (USD PPP 2 a day, in %)	7.3	Emigration rate of the highly educated		70/157	6/19

Age structure of the population 0+ (2010): "0-14": 12%; "15-24": 14%; "25-64": 57%; "65+": 18%.
Level of education of the population 15+ (2010): "Low": 31%; "Medium": 53%; "High": 16%.

Emigrant population living in OECD countries

Immigrant population

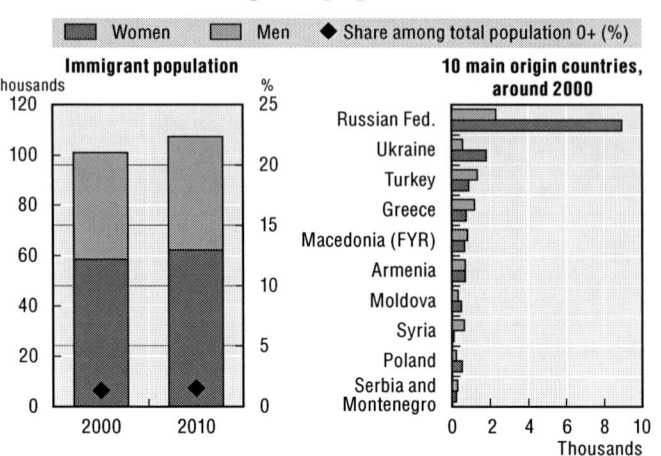

Emigrant population: persons born in Bulgaria living abroad

	2000						2005/06		
	All destinations			OECD destinations			OECD destinations		
Population 15+	Men	Women	Total	Men	Women	Total	Men	Women	Total
Emigrant population (thousands)	310.5	351.6	662.0	77.8	92.9	170.7	158.5	187.8	346.3
Recent emigrants (thousands)	..	..	..	30.9	36.3	67.1	67.3	83.2	150.5
15-24 (%)	14.5	13.6	14.0	15.0	13.9	14.4	14.0	13.2	13.6
25-64 (%)	67.4	65.7	66.5	72.6	72.6	72.6	77.9	80.3	79.2
65+ (%)	18.1	20.8	19.5	12.5	13.5	13.0	8.1	6.5	7.3
Low-educated (%)	49.0	56.1	52.8	34.2	28.6	31.2	23.4	21.8	22.5
Highly educated (%)	14.9	14.0	14.5	31.9	31.9	31.9	36.5	40.3	38.6
Total emigration rates (%)	8.7	9.2	8.9	2.3	2.6	2.5	4.7	5.1	4.9
Emigration rates of the highly educated (%)	8.9	7.0	7.8	5.1	4.4	4.7	11.7	10.8	11.2

Main destinations in 2005/06

	Total		Recent emigrants	Women	Highly educated	15-24	Total in 2000
Population 15+	Thousands	%	%	%	%	%	Thousands
Spain	94.0	27.1	85.0	49.3	34.0	12.5	23.7
United States	56.1	16.2	32.4	51.9	56.6	18.1	30.6
Greece	46.8	13.5	34.6	66.8	10.8	10.1	36.1
Germany	39.0	11.3	27.3	58.6	37.6	18.6	5.7
Israel	17.9	5.2	8.9	45.6	35.2	0.6	20.5
Canada	14.7	4.3	45.8	50.3	69.6	16.4	8.5
Italy	12.5	3.6	33.3	60.0	19.0	13.4	7.3
United Kingdom	12.4	3.6	–	55.5	73.8	–	4.9
France	11.4	3.3	36.2	60.8	52.0	22.3	6.6
Austria	9.7	2.8	32.0	53.8	37.2	19.2	6.6

Labour market indicators of persons born in Bulgaria living in OECD countries

Population 15-64	2000			2005/06		
	Men	Women	Total	Men	Women	Total
Employment-population ratio (%)	77.4	60.3	68.5	81.0	67.0	73.4
Unemployment rate (%)	9.8	11.4	10.6	6.6	9.4	8.0
Participation rate (%)	85.9	68.1	76.6	86.7	74.0	79.8
Total employed (thousands)	**49.6**	**42.3**	**91.9**	**113.5**	**113.1**	**226.5**
Employment rates of the highly educated (%)	84.1	65.5	73.8	93.0	80.5	85.9
Unemployment rates of the highly educated (%)	6.7	10.1	8.4	4.4	8.6	6.6
Highly educated in low- and medium-skilled jobs (%)	40.0	41.5	40.7	64.4	53.2	58.7
Highly educated employed (thousands)	**17.5**	**16.7**	**34.2**	**46.5**	**51.4**	**97.8**
Legislators, senior officials and managers	7.0	5.5	6.3	3.9	3.1	3.5
Professionals	13.5	17.1	15.1	6.9	10.3	8.5
Life science and health professionals	1.4	2.2	1.8	0.5	1.9	1.2
Teaching professionals	2.1	3.6	2.7	0.6	1.8	1.2
Technicians and associate professionals	7.5	13.3	10.1	4.0	8.3	6.0
Clerks	2.8	9.9	5.9	2.3	6.5	4.3
Service, shop and market sales workers	7.5	21.1	13.5	11.7	27.1	19.0
Skilled agricultural and fishery workers	3.7	0.9	2.5	2.6	1.8	2.2
Craft and related trades workers	23.0	3.3	14.3	32.1	2.8	18.3
Plant and machine operators and assemblers	12.3	3.4	8.4	13.1	3.6	8.6
Elementary occupations	22.7	25.5	23.9	23.1	36.6	29.5

Left margin label: Distribution of employment by occupation (%), population 15+

Persons born in Bulgaria and their native-born children, population 15+

Living in:	Europe	United States	Australia
2008	Thousands	Thousands	Thousands
Native-born children	29.2	19.5	0.6
Foreign-born	308.0	33.1	5.3
Total	337.2	52.6	6.0

International students from Bulgaria in OECD countries

Five main destinations	2004	2005	2006	2007	2008	2009
Germany	..	..	..	..	9 739	8 784
United States	3 734	3 806	3 762	3 555	3 208	2 842
France	2 905	2 903	2 876	2 645	2 322	2 188
United Kingdom	557	607	627	709	1 251	2 187
Turkey	1 021	1 111	1 163	1 169	1 179	1 147
Total	9 673	9 885	10 421	10 498	20 457	20 233

Legal migrant flows to the OECD
Thousands

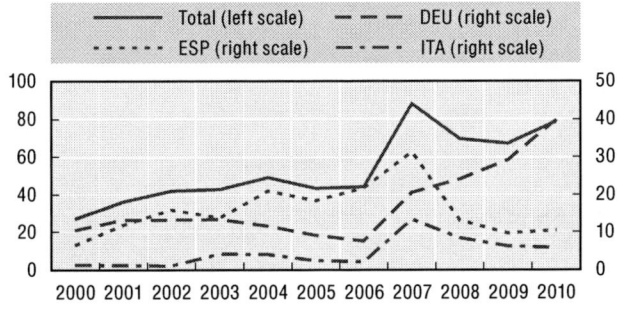

Remittance flows

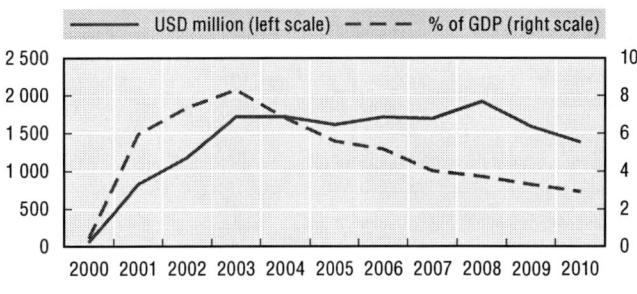

Ten main countries of destination for legal migrants in 2010 (numbers, % of total flows to the country): DEU (39844, 5.9%), ESP (10415, 2.4%), ITA (5877, 1.4%), NLD (4269, 4.3%), BEL (3277, 3.2%), AUT (3217, 3.3%), USA (2570, 5%), PRT (1367, 5%), TUR (1076, 3.6%), DNK (933, 2.8%).

Desire to emigrate, 2008-10

	Women	15-24	Highly educated	Total	Regional total
Persons who would move permanently, if they had the opportunity to do so (%)	18	40	22	18	19
Of which: Persons who are planning to move permanently in the next 12 months (%)				..	7
Of which: Persons who have already done some preparations for this move (*e.g.* visa application) (%)					..

Three main countries of desired destination: Germany (20%), United Kingdom (11%), United States (10%).

StatLink 🔗 *http://dx.doi.org/10.1787/888932673714*

Total population 2010 (millions)	4.4	**Croatia compared to:**	**World**	**Region**
Population growth 2010 (%)	–0.1	Human Development Index (HDI)	46/187	7/26
GDP per capita 2010 (current USD)	13 754	GDP per capita	49/194	5/27
GDP growth 2010 (%)	–1.2	Emigration rate	38/203	8/28
Poverty rate 2008 (USD PPP 2 a day, in %)	0.1	Emigration rate of the highly educated	29/157	3/19

Age structure of the population 0+ (2010): "0-14": 12%; "15-24": 15%; "25-64": 56%; "65+": 17%.
Level of education of the population 15+ (2010): "Low": 36%; "Medium": 55%; "High": 9%.

Emigrant population living in OECD countries

Immigrant population

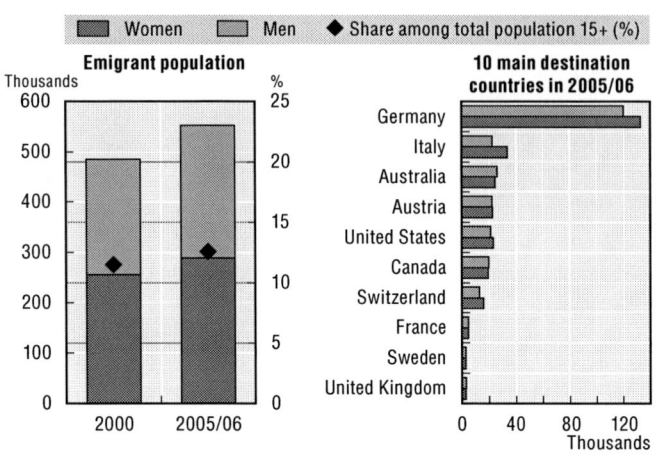

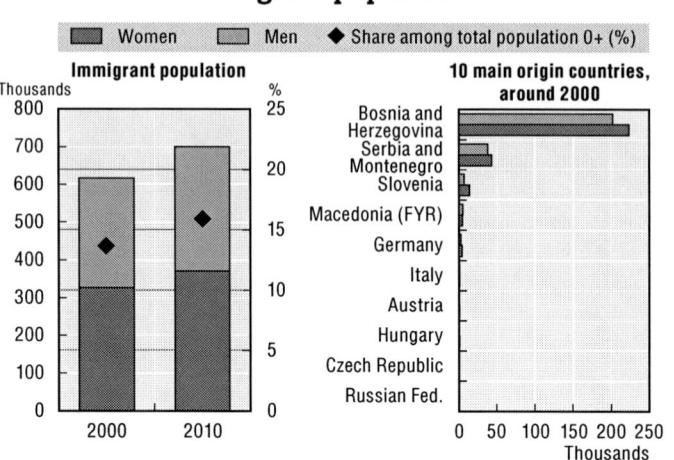

Emigrant population: persons born in Croatia living abroad

	2000						2005/06		
	All destinations			OECD destinations			OECD destinations		
Population 15+	Men	Women	Total	Men	Women	Total	Men	Women	Total
Emigrant population (thousands)	403.7	466.4	870.2	229.3	255.9	485.2	264.0	289.0	553.0
Recent emigrants (thousands)	..	..	..	11.1	13.4	24.5	11.8	16.4	28.2
15-24 (%)	7.7	6.6	7.1	4.0	3.8	3.9	7.8	7.1	7.4
25-64 (%)	73.9	69.4	71.5	80.0	76.7	78.3	74.1	75.1	74.6
65+ (%)	18.4	24.0	21.4	16.0	19.5	17.8	18.2	17.9	18.0
Low-educated (%)	33.4	52.0	43.4	37.5	54.8	46.7	32.7	46.6	40.0
Highly educated (%)	15.7	11.1	13.2	14.5	11.4	12.8	17.0	12.6	14.7
Total emigration rates (%)	18.5	19.2	18.9	11.4	11.5	11.5	12.6	12.5	12.6
Emigration rates of the highly educated (%)	37.9	30.1	34.0	24.1	19.4	21.7	28.4	18.1	22.6

Main destinations in 2005/06

	Total		Recent emigrants	Women	Highly educated	15-24	Total in 2000
Population 15+	Thousands	%	%	%	%	%	Thousands
Germany	253.0	45.7	3.0	52.5	9.1	5.5	193.8
Italy	55.4	10.0	7.9	60.1	8.0	7.3	77.1
Australia	50.3	9.1	4.9	48.6	14.1	5.7	50.3
Austria	44.3	8.0	9.6	50.5	8.1	12.1	35.7
United States	44.0	8.0	6.9	52.3	29.3	8.9	38.9
Canada	38.5	7.0	3.8	49.4	33.3	6.5	37.9
Switzerland	28.2	5.1	9.9	55.6	13.8	16.5	22.3
France	9.1	1.7	6.4	49.9	18.3	4.6	7.7
Sweden	5.7	1.0	11.3	49.9	18.0	14.1	5.1
United Kingdom	–	–	–	–	–	–	6.4

Labour market indicators of persons born in Croatia living in OECD countries

Population 15-64	2000			2005/06		
	Men	Women	Total	Men	Women	Total
Employment-population ratio (%)	69.7	57.7	63.6	72.7	60.1	66.0
Unemployment rate (%)	8.4	8.4	8.4	9.2	9.0	9.1
Participation rate (%)	76.0	63.0	69.4	80.1	66.0	72.7
Total employed (thousands)	**133.6**	**115.2**	**248.8**	**151.6**	**139.1**	**290.7**
Employment rates of the highly educated (%)	90.9	76.8	84.3	91.7	77.2	84.8
Unemployment rates of the highly educated (%)	3.0	4.3	3.5	4.4	3.8	4.2
Highly educated in low- and medium-skilled jobs (%)	31.2	34.8	32.9	30.2	38.1	33.5
Highly educated employed (thousands)	**24.4**	**18.2**	**42.6**	**31.3**	**24.0**	**55.3**
Legislators, senior officials and managers	6.5	3.7	5.2	5.6	2.3	4.0
Professionals	5.4	4.9	5.2	9.2	4.6	7.0
Life science and health professionals	0.4	0.7	0.5	0.5	0.8	0.6
Teaching professionals	0.4	0.8	0.6	0.7	0.7	0.7
Technicians and associate professionals	6.4	14.0	9.9	8.1	15.8	11.8
Clerks	2.3	7.8	4.9	3.8	8.8	6.2
Service, shop and market sales workers	4.4	35.8	19.2	6.1	32.5	18.7
Skilled agricultural and fishery workers	0.7	0.3	0.5	0.6	0.9	0.7
Craft and related trades workers	43.5	2.5	24.1	38.9	2.7	21.7
Plant and machine operators and assemblers	22.7	3.7	13.7	18.4	5.9	12.4
Elementary occupations	8.3	27.4	17.3	9.2	26.4	17.4

Distribution of employment by occupation (%), population 15+

Persons born in Croatia and their native-born children, population 15+

Living in:	Europe	United States	Australia
2008	Thousands	Thousands	Thousands
Native-born children	256.8	16.9	19.6
Foreign-born	394.0	28.1	51.0
Total	650.9	45.0	70.6

International students from Croatia in OECD countries

Five main destinations	2004	2005	2006	2007	2008	2009
Italy	1 357	1 222	1 334	1 353	1 270	1 318
Slovenia	..	532	524	597	647	711
United States	660	705	662	643	603	607
Germany	..	..	..	..	446	457
United Kingdom	226	220	215	250	215	211
Total	2 487	2 932	3 112	3 161	3 572	3 841

Legal migrant flows to the OECD
Thousands

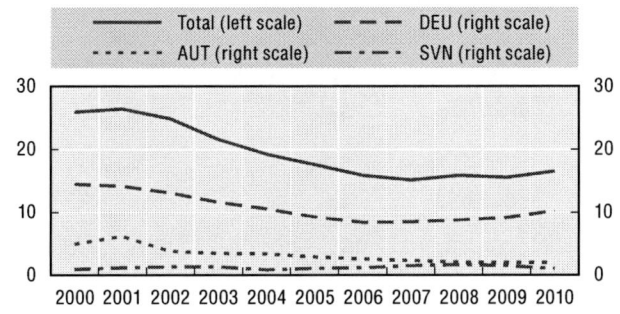

Remittance flows

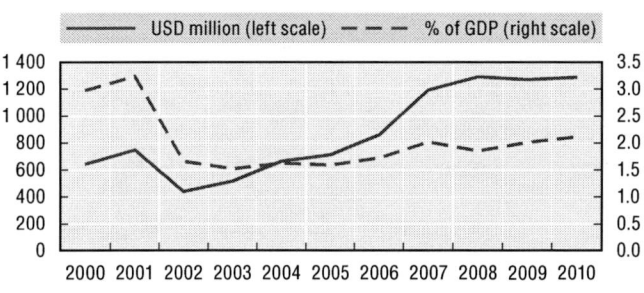

Ten main countries of destination for legal migrants in 2010 (numbers, % of total flows to the country): DEU (10198, 1.5%), AUT (1904, 1.9%), SVN (928, 9.4%), ITA (730, 0.2%), CHE (426, 0.3%), USA (357, 0%), GBR (312, 0.8%), HUN (178, 0.8%), ESP (166, 0%), SWE (142, 0.2%).

Desire to emigrate, 2008-10

	Women	15-24	Highly educated	Total	Regional total
Persons who would move permanently, if they had the opportunity to do so (%)	11	25	..	12	19
Of which: Persons who are planning to move permanently in the next 12 months (%)				..	7
Of which: Persons who have already done some preparations for this move (*e.g.* visa application) (%)					..

StatLink ᛊᛃᛋᛉ http://dx.doi.org/10.1787/888932673733

		Kazakhstan compared to:	World	Region
Total population 2010 (millions)	16.3	Human Development Index (HDI)	68/187	14/26
Population growth 2010 (%)	2.4	GDP per capita	65/194	9/27
GDP per capita 2010 (current USD)	9 136	Emigration rate	78/203	15/28
GDP growth 2010 (%)	7.3	Emigration rate of the highly educated	126/157	13/19
Poverty rate 2007 (USD PPP 2 a day, in %)	1.5			

Age structure of the population 0+ (2010): "0-14": 19%; "15-24": 24%; "25-64": 50%; "65+": 7%.
Level of education of the population 15+ (2010): "Low": 7%; "Medium": 70%; "High": 22%.

Emigrant population living in OECD countries

Immigrant population

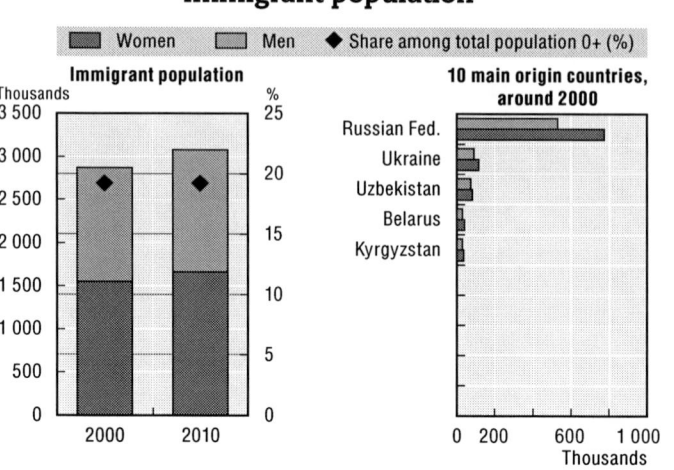

Emigrant population: persons born in Kazakhstan living abroad

	2000						2005/06		
	All destinations			OECD destinations			OECD destinations		
Population 15+	Men	Women	Total	Men	Women	Total	Men	Women	Total
Emigrant population (thousands)	1 443.1	1 647.2	3 090.3	202.9	222.4	425.3	333.3	367.9	701.2
Recent emigrants (thousands)	..	..	..	7.6	9.6	17.2	32.1	41.2	73.3
15-24 (%)	18.7	16.7	17.7	16.7	15.1	15.9	21.1	18.8	19.9
25-64 (%)	73.8	72.3	73.0	66.1	62.8	64.4	65.6	64.6	65.1
65+ (%)	7.5	11.0	9.3	17.2	22.1	19.7	13.3	16.6	15.0
Low-educated (%)	22.0	21.4	21.7	29.7	38.9	34.5	35.2	41.0	38.2
Highly educated (%)	19.6	20.9	20.3	20.2	15.9	17.9	14.9	14.5	14.7
Total emigration rates (%)	22.2	22.2	22.2	3.9	3.7	3.8	5.8	5.7	5.7
Emigration rates of the highly educated (%)	28.8	28.7	28.8	5.5	4.0	4.7	5.4	4.7	5.0

Main destinations in 2005/06

	Total		Recent emigrants	Women	Highly educated	15-24	Total in 2000
Population 15+	Thousands	%	%	%	%	%	Thousands
Germany	645.7	92.1	7.8	51.7	11.5	19.5	372.4
Israel	18.0	2.6	56.6	62.6	50.2	22.1	13.8
United States	16.0	2.3	35.0	60.7	50.8	29.2	7.1
Canada	5.8	0.8	51.3	54.8	67.0	26.3	3.1
Poland	4.8	0.7	–	–	–	–	3.0
Czech Republic	2.7	0.4	..	58.1	31.2	22.7	1.4
France	1.6	0.2	62.6	69.0	49.5	20.3	0.4
United Kingdom	–	–	–	–	–	–	0.7
Italy	1.1	0.2	–	96.0	–	–	0.4
Sweden	0.6	0.1	78.3	63.8	54.6	25.2	0.3

Labour market indicators of persons born in Kazakhstan living in OECD countries

Population 15-64	2000			2005/06		
	Men	Women	Total	Men	Women	Total
Employment-population ratio (%)	72.2	59.3	65.7	70.8	58.6	64.5
Unemployment rate (%)	12.6	12.9	12.7	14.9	14.9	14.9
Participation rate (%)	82.6	68.1	75.2	83.2	68.8	75.8
Total employed (thousands)	**120.9**	**102.2**	**223.1**	**203.8**	**178.8**	**382.7**
Employment rates of the highly educated (%)	85.6	69.0	77.6	91.4	77.3	83.8
Unemployment rates of the highly educated (%)	6.7	11.0	8.6	9.6	12.5	11.0
Highly educated in low- and medium-skilled jobs (%)	29.0	15.7	23.5	37.0	43.7	39.9
Highly educated employed (thousands)	**29.7**	**22.2**	**52.0**	**35.0**	**33.0**	**68.0**
Legislators, senior officials and managers	0.1	0.1	0.1	0.1	0.2	0.2
Professionals	11.6	8.1	9.9	4.1	2.1	3.2
Life science and health professionals	0.0	0.0	0.0	0.1	0.1	0.1
Teaching professionals	0.0	0.0	0.0	0.0	0.0	0.0
Technicians and associate professionals	12.9	25.0	18.6	8.6	19.3	13.6
Clerks	3.8	13.2	8.2	4.1	12.0	7.7
Service, shop and market sales workers	2.7	23.6	12.5	1.6	25.1	12.5
Skilled agricultural and fishery workers	0.0	0.0	0.0	0.0	0.0	0.0
Craft and related trades workers	35.4	3.4	20.4	41.3	3.2	23.6
Plant and machine operators and assemblers	21.1	4.2	13.2	24.0	5.8	15.6
Elementary occupations	12.4	22.3	17.0	16.1	32.3	23.6

Distribution of employment by occupation (%), population 15+

Persons born in Kazakhstan and their native-born children, population 15+

Living in:	Europe	United States	Australia
2008	Thousands	Thousands	Thousands
Native-born children	27.8	..	..
Foreign-born	289.8	..	..
Total	317.6	..	..

International students from Kazakhstan in OECD countries

Five main destinations	2004	2005	2006	2007	2008	2009
United States	538	498	648	1 239	1 458	1 686
United Kingdom	324	361	441	875	1 178	1 550
Turkey	742	732	738	729	709	727
Germany	..	..	..	..	668	723
France	135	132	174	184	200	232
Total	1 962	1 886	2 239	3 296	4 599	5 477

Legal migrant flows to the OECD
Thousands

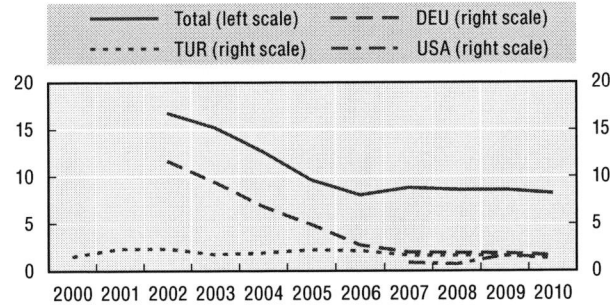

Remittance flows

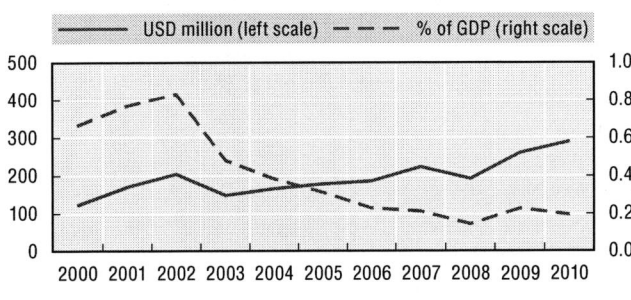

Ten main countries of destination for legal migrants in 2010 (numbers, % of total flows to the country): DEU (1637, 0.2%), TUR (1365, 4.6%), USA (1282, 0.1%), KOR (755, 0.3%), CZE (716, 2.8%), POL (398, 1%), CAN (375, 0.1%), JPN (275, 0.1%), CHE (249, 0.2%), ESP (215, 0%).

Desire to emigrate, 2008-10

	Women	15-24	Highly educated	Total	Regional total
Persons who would move permanently, if they had the opportunity to do so (%)	12	18	15	14	19
Of which: Persons who are planning to move permanently in the next 12 months (%)				6	7
Of which: Persons who have already done some preparations for this move (*e.g.* visa application) (%)					..

Three main countries of desired destination: Russian Federation (48%), United States (9%), Germany (8%).

StatLink ⟶ http://dx.doi.org/10.1787/888932673752

			Kyrgyzstan compared to:	World	Region
Total population 2010 (millions)	5.4		Human Development Index (HDI)	126/187	25/26
Population growth 2010 (%)	0.8		GDP per capita	154/194	24/27
GDP per capita 2010 (current USD)	860		Emigration rate	190/203	26/28
GDP growth 2010 (%)	−1.4		Emigration rate of the highly educated	153/157	18/19
Poverty rate 2007 (USD PPP 2 a day, in %)	29.4				

Age structure of the population 0+ (2010): "0-14": 23%; "15-24": 30%; "25-64": 43%; "65+": 4%.
Level of education of the population 15+ (2010): "Low": 26%; "Medium": 61%; "High": 13%.

Emigrant population living in OECD countries

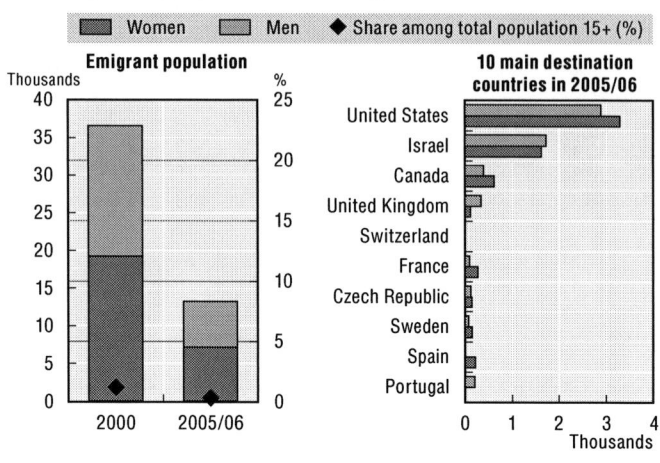

Immigrant population

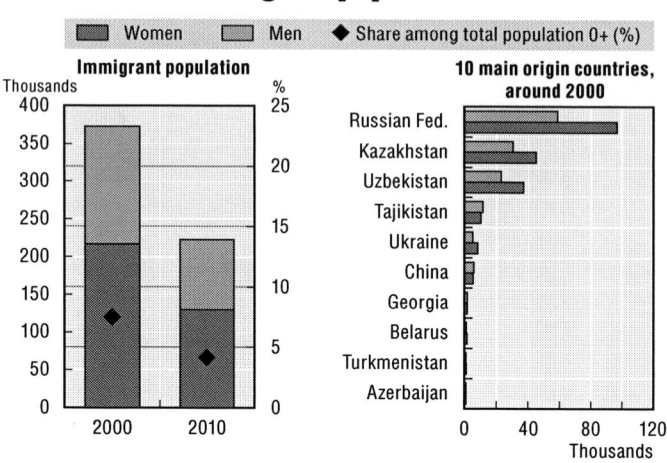

Emigrant population: persons born in Kyrgyzstan living abroad

	2000						2005/06		
	All destinations			OECD destinations			OECD destinations		
Population 15+	Men	Women	Total	Men	Women	Total	Men	Women	Total
Emigrant population (thousands)	229.9	247.6	477.5	17.3	19.3	36.6	6.1	7.1	13.3
Recent emigrants (thousands)	..	..	..	1.1	1.5	2.6	2.0	2.6	4.7
15-24 (%)	19.6	17.6	18.6	18.0	17.1	17.5	27.2	20.5	23.6
25-64 (%)	75.2	74.3	74.7	65.6	62.0	63.7	69.9	76.9	73.7
65+ (%)	5.2	8.1	6.7	16.4	20.9	18.8	2.9	2.5	2.7
Low-educated (%)	20.3	18.3	19.3	28.5	35.7	32.3	22.1	14.4	17.9
Highly educated (%)	20.1	23.7	22.0	24.8	20.5	22.5	44.4	50.4	47.7
Total emigration rates (%)	12.8	13.0	12.9	1.1	1.1	1.1	0.4	0.4	0.4
Emigration rates of the highly educated (%)	20.3	21.8	21.1	2.3	1.8	2.1	1.4	1.6	1.5

Main destinations in 2005/06

	Total		Recent emigrants	Women	Highly educated	15-24	Total in 2000
Population 15+	Thousands	%	%	%	%	%	Thousands
United States	6.2	46.6	19.4	53.3	36.7	31.4	1.7
Israel	3.4	25.3	40.6	48.4	58.9	13.2	4.0
Canada	1.0	7.6	66.8	61.2	72.1	25.9	0.5
United Kingdom	–	–	–	–	–	–	–
Switzerland	–	–	–	–	–	–	–
France	0.4	2.7	70.8	74.5	54.9	19.6	0.1
Czech Republic	–	–	–	–	–	–	0.1
Sweden	–	–	–	–	–	–	0.1
Spain	–	–	–	–	–	–	0.1

Labour market indicators of persons born in Kyrgyzstan living in OECD countries

Population 15-64	2000			2005/06		
	Men	Women	Total	Men	Women	Total
Employment-population ratio (%)	70.5	60.6	65.5	70.6	57.6	63.5
Unemployment rate (%)	13.9	11.3	12.7	7.7	11.7	9.8
Participation rate (%)	81.9	68.4	75.0	76.6	65.2	70.3
Total employed (thousands)	**10.2**	**9.2**	**19.4**	**2.3**	**2.3**	**4.6**
Employment rates of the highly educated (%)	79.4	71.9	75.7	87.6	72.5	79.0
Unemployment rates of the highly educated (%)	11.4	9.2	10.4	7.9	6.0	6.9
Highly educated in low- and medium-skilled jobs (%)	30.2	26.8	28.7	67.9	56.7	60.9
Highly educated employed (thousands)	**3.0**	**2.7**	**5.7**	**1.5**	**1.6**	**3.1**
Legislators, senior officials and managers	0.4	0.1	0.3	17.6	0.7	9.1
Professionals	11.7	8.3	10.1	8.2	38.0	23.2
Life science and health professionals	–	0.0	0.0	0.2	23.8	12.5
Teaching professionals	–	0.1	0.0	0.6	20.2	10.8
Technicians and associate professionals	12.8	24.5	18.3	3.0	6.2	4.6
Clerks	3.7	13.1	8.1	3.2	14.5	8.9
Service, shop and market sales workers	2.7	23.3	12.4	21.7	10.6	16.1
Skilled agricultural and fishery workers	0.1	–	0.1	0.3	0.5	0.4
Craft and related trades workers	34.8	3.5	20.1	35.0	19.6	27.2
Plant and machine operators and assemblers	21.0	4.5	13.2	6.2	5.6	5.9
Elementary occupations	12.8	22.7	17.4	4.7	4.4	4.6

Distribution of employment by occupation (%), population 15+

Persons born in Kyrgyzstan and their native-born children, population 15+

Living in:	Europe	United States	Australia
2008	Thousands	Thousands	Thousands
Native-born children	0.5	..	..
Foreign-born	2.3	..	..
Total	2.8	..	..

International students from Kyrgyzstan in OECD countries

Five main destinations	2004	2005	2006	2007	2008	2009
Turkey	753	718	698	643	596	563
Germany	..	..	..	..	425	498
United States	179	193	196	214	264	270
France	74	87	97	110	101	105
United Kingdom	70	67	69	77	70	82
Total	1 132	1 131	1 150	1 164	1 620	1 729

Legal migrant flows to the OECD
Thousands

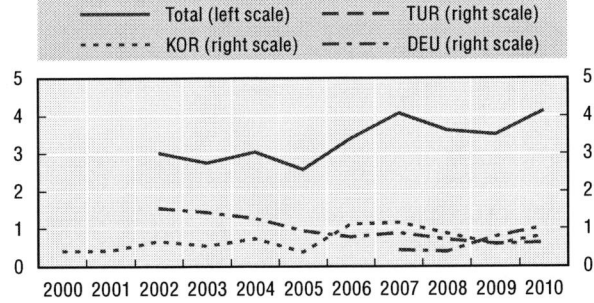

Remittance flows

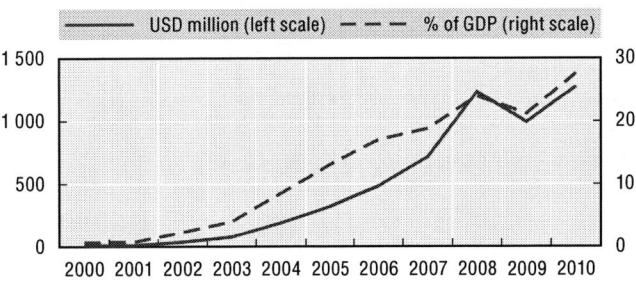

Ten main countries of destination for legal migrants in 2010 (numbers, % of total flows to the country): TUR (1046, 3.5%), KOR (817, 0.3%), DEU (620, 0.1%), USA (507, 0%), ITA (281, 0.1%), JPN (171, 0.1%), CAN (155, 0.1%), AUT (131, 0.1%), CZE (64, 0.3%), SWE (50, 0.1%).

Desire to emigrate, 2008-10

	Women	15-24	Highly educated	Total	Regional total
Persons who would move permanently, if they had the opportunity to do so (%)	19	27	23	19	19
Of which: Persons who are planning to move permanently in the next 12 months (%)				9	7
Of which: Persons who have already done some preparations for this move (*e.g.* visa application) (%)					..

Three main countries of desired destination: Russian Federation (54%), United States (10%), Kazakhstan (8%).

StatLink http://dx.doi.org/10.1787/888932673771

		Latvia compared to:	World	Region
Total population 2010 (millions)	2.2			
Population growth 2010 (%)	−0.5	Human Development Index (HDI)	44/187	6/26
GDP per capita 2010 (current USD)	10 705	GDP per capita	60/194	7/27
GDP growth 2010 (%)	−0.3	Emigration rate	97/203	18/28
Poverty rate 2004 (USD PPP 2 a day, in %)	1.0	Emigration rate of the highly educated	86/157	11/19

Age structure of the population 0+ (2010): "0-14": 14%; "15-24": 14%; "25-64": 54%; "65+": 18%.
Level of education of the population 15+ (2010): "Low": 5%; "Medium": 74%; "High": 21%.

Emigrant population living in OECD countries

Immigrant population

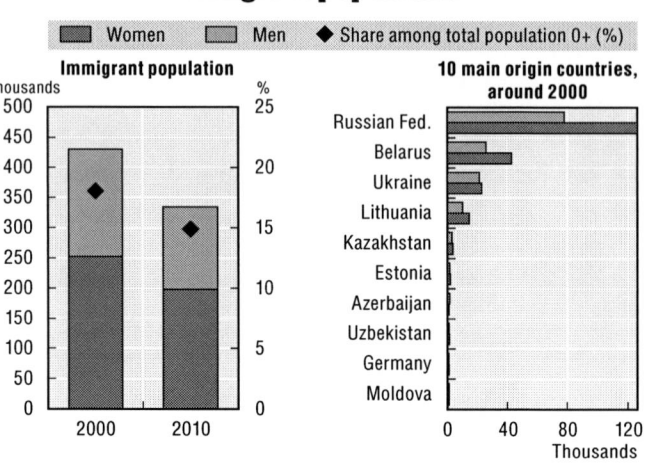

Emigrant population: persons born in Latvia living abroad

	2000						2005/06		
	All destinations			OECD destinations			OECD destinations		
Population 15+	Men	Women	Total	Men	Women	Total	Men	Women	Total
Emigrant population (thousands)	90.9	105.5	196.5	27.5	35.4	62.9	39.6	53.8	93.4
Recent emigrants (thousands)	..	..	..	2.6	4.7	7.2	11.4	14.2	25.6
15-24 (%)	18.2	16.5	17.3	8.8	9.9	9.5	18.3	14.5	16.1
25-64 (%)	64.2	63.5	63.8	46.7	46.2	46.4	48.7	52.7	51.0
65+ (%)	17.6	20.0	18.9	44.5	43.9	44.1	32.9	32.8	32.8
Low-educated (%)	19.5	17.7	18.5	19.6	21.1	20.5	20.3	18.3	19.2
Highly educated (%)	33.3	33.4	33.4	43.5	40.8	42.0	40.2	41.0	40.6
Total emigration rates (%)	9.4	8.9	9.1	3.0	3.2	3.1	4.3	4.7	4.5
Emigration rates of the highly educated (%)	23.5	18.8	20.7	10.2	8.3	9.1	10.6	9.1	9.7

Main destinations in 2005/06

	Total		Recent emigrants	Women	Highly educated	15-24	Total in 2000
Population 15+	Thousands	%	%	%	%	%	Thousands
United States	25.2	27.0	11.9	60.1	49.8	9.4	25.5
United Kingdom	14.7	15.7	71.1	55.7	44.3	–	4.1
Ireland	12.8	13.7	92.8	45.7	17.5	30.7	2.2
Israel	11.9	12.8	13.7	51.9	56.0	13.4	8.2
Canada	7.0	7.5	6.8	53.7	51.1	6.9	7.5
Australia	5.6	6.0	2.7	55.0	31.6	2.4	6.5
Poland	4.0	4.3	–	–	–	–	2.2
Germany	–	–	..	–	–	–	1.0
Sweden	2.6	2.8	45.2	65.6	49.8	18.5	1.7
Denmark	1.2	1.3	65.8	63.6	32.3	30.3	0.8

Labour market indicators of persons born in Latvia living in OECD countries

Population 15-64	2000			2005/06		
	Men	Women	Total	Men	Women	Total
Employment-population ratio (%)	80.0	64.9	71.7	85.0	64.5	73.5
Unemployment rate (%)	5.5	7.3	6.4	6.3	11.1	8.7
Participation rate (%)	84.7	70.0	76.6	90.7	72.5	80.5
Total employed (thousands)	**11.7**	**11.8**	**23.5**	**21.8**	**21.1**	**42.9**
Employment rates of the highly educated (%)	85.8	73.8	79.1	94.7	83.4	88.2
Unemployment rates of the highly educated (%)	5.4	4.4	4.9	3.3	6.6	5.1
Highly educated in low- and medium-skilled jobs (%)	28.8	35.1	31.9	48.8	58.2	54.0
Highly educated employed (thousands)	**6.6**	**7.2**	**13.8**	**10.0**	**11.4**	**21.4**
Legislators, senior officials and managers	12.3	5.8	9.1	6.3	2.8	4.6
Professionals	19.9	20.1	20.0	6.2	7.9	7.0
Life science and health professionals	2.1	4.3	3.2	0.6	1.1	0.9
Teaching professionals	4.5	5.1	4.8	0.4	2.1	1.2
Technicians and associate professionals	11.2	10.8	11.0	2.6	6.9	4.7
Clerks	3.0	14.2	8.5	5.8	15.2	10.4
Service, shop and market sales workers	6.5	22.7	14.5	10.8	20.6	15.6
Skilled agricultural and fishery workers	3.5	1.0	2.2	7.1	5.0	6.1
Craft and related trades workers	17.1	2.1	9.7	20.3	5.3	13.0
Plant and machine operators and assemblers	10.8	4.4	7.7	19.1	10.0	14.7
Elementary occupations	15.7	18.9	17.3	19.8	24.4	22.0

Distribution of employment by occupation (%), population 15+

Persons born in Latvia and their native-born children, population 15+

Living in:	Europe	United States	Australia
2008	Thousands	Thousands	Thousands
Native-born children	17.3	18.1	10.9
Foreign-born	64.5	22.8	11.9
Total	81.8	41.0	22.7

International students from Latvia in OECD countries

Five main destinations	2004	2005	2006	2007	2008	2009
United Kingdom	186	271	537	882	1 145	1 368
Germany	..	..	..	..	657	597
United States	424	426	396	440	363	315
Denmark	30	27	31	34	46	179
France	145	130	153	147	165	164
Total	958	1 250	1 528	1 839	2 851	3 100

Legal migrant flows to the OECD
Thousands

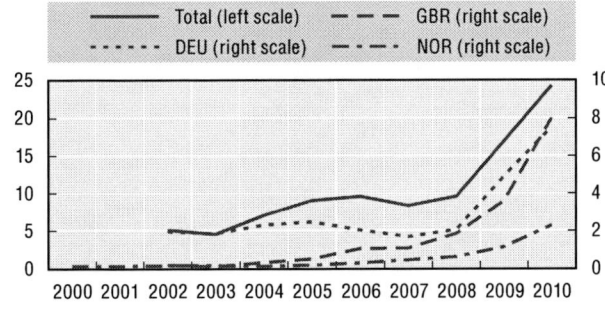

Remittance flows

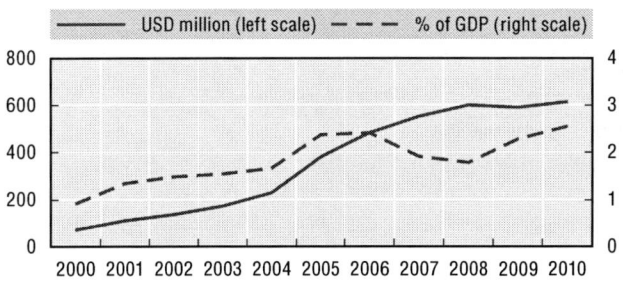

Ten main countries of destination for legal migrants in 2010 (numbers, % of total flows to the country): GBR (8000, 1.7%), DEU (7485, 1.1%), NOR (2292, 3.6%), NLD (1016, 1%), IRL (869, 5%), DNK (860, 2.6%), SWE (767, 0.1%), ESP (598, 0.1%), USA (435, 0%), ITA (330, 0.1%).

Desire to emigrate, 2008-10

	Women	15-24	Highly educated	Total	Regional total
Persons who would move permanently, if they had the opportunity to do so (%)	23	47	24	27	19
Of which: Persons who are planning to move permanently in the next 12 months (%)				..	7
Of which: Persons who have already done some preparations for this move (*e.g.* visa application) (%)					..

StatLink ⬛🔗⬛ http://dx.doi.org/10.1787/888932673790

Total population 2010 (millions)	3.3		
Population growth 2010 (%)	−0.6		
GDP per capita 2010 (current USD)	10 933		
GDP growth 2010 (%)	1.3		
Poverty rate 2008 (USD PPP 2 a day, in %)	0.4		

Lithuania compared to:	World	Region
Human Development Index (HDI)	40/187	5/26
GDP per capita	57/194	6/27
Emigration rate	62/203	14/28
Emigration rate of the highly educated	78/157	9/19

Age structure of the population 0+ (2010): "0-14": 15%; "15-24": 15%; "25-64": 54%; "65+": 16%.
Level of education of the population 15+ (2010): "Low": 9%; "Medium": 65%; "High": 26%.

Emigrant population living in OECD countries

Immigrant population

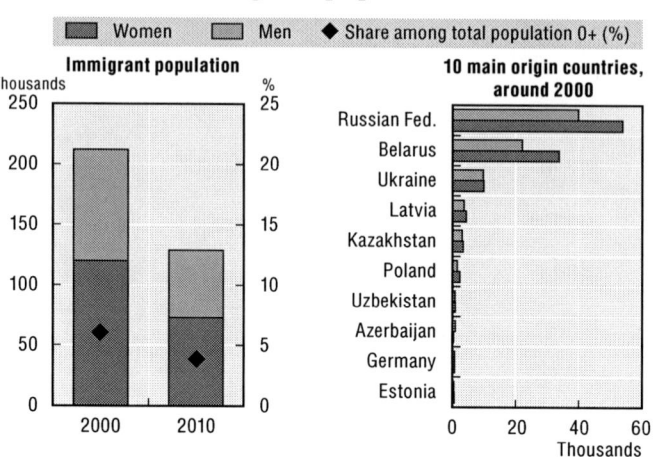

Emigrant population: persons born in Lithuania living abroad

	2000						2005/06		
	All destinations			OECD destinations			OECD destinations		
Population 15+	Men	Women	Total	Men	Women	Total	Men	Women	Total
Emigrant population (thousands)	126.9	159.1	286.0	61.1	86.0	147.1	104.5	142.8	247.3
Recent emigrants (thousands)	..	..	..	6.1	7.6	13.6	35.0	40.5	75.5
15-24 (%)	9.8	8.4	9.0	5.6	5.4	5.5	15.7	11.7	13.4
25-64 (%)	60.9	55.7	58.0	47.9	42.6	44.8	56.0	50.6	52.9
65+ (%)	29.3	35.9	33.0	46.4	52.1	49.7	28.2	37.7	33.7
Low-educated (%)	30.5	33.5	32.2	31.7	37.7	35.2	27.4	31.2	29.6
Highly educated (%)	25.9	23.7	24.7	28.0	23.3	25.2	32.4	28.9	30.3
Total emigration rates (%)	9.0	9.5	9.3	4.6	5.4	5.0	7.4	8.4	8.0
Emigration rates of the highly educated (%)	16.4	14.1	15.1	9.1	8.0	8.5	11.1	9.8	10.3

Main destinations in 2005/06

	Total		Recent emigrants	Women	Highly educated	15-24	Total in 2000
Population 15+	Thousands	%	%	%	%	%	Thousands
Poland	81.8	33.1	–	62.6	15.6	–	79.7
United Kingdom	43.5	17.6	82.9	49.7	33.4	32.5	3.8
United States	38.0	15.4	19.6	58.6	49.7	12.4	27.0
Ireland	22.2	9.0	96.4	43.2	23.0	31.2	1.9
Germany	16.5	6.7	53.9	74.2	31.0	–	0.9
Israel	12.0	4.8	3.0	57.2	61.0	4.9	12.8
Spain	10.0	4.0	91.9	43.0	22.5	29.8	4.4
Canada	6.4	2.6	9.8	57.9	42.2	4.9	6.8
Australia	3.0	1.2	4.6	54.9	29.2	2.4	3.5
Denmark	2.8	1.1	74.7	54.0	41.8	29.3	1.4

Labour market indicators of persons born in Lithuania living in OECD countries

Population 15-64	2000 Men	2000 Women	2000 Total	2005/06 Men	2005/06 Women	2005/06 Total
Employment-population ratio (%)	63.1	48.4	55.0	80.3	65.1	71.8
Unemployment rate (%)	12.3	10.0	11.2	7.6	6.7	7.2
Participation rate (%)	72.0	53.8	62.0	86.9	69.8	77.3
Total employed (thousands)	**19.9**	**18.9**	**38.8**	**54.1**	**55.8**	**109.9**
Employment rates of the highly educated (%)	87.0	69.5	77.0	91.1	82.3	86.1
Unemployment rates of the highly educated (%)	6.4	6.3	6.3	4.5	7.8	6.3
Highly educated in low- and medium-skilled jobs (%)	38.5	46.4	42.7	69.9	67.2	68.5
Highly educated employed (thousands)	**8.7**	**9.3**	**18.0**	**20.1**	**23.4**	**43.4**
Legislators, senior officials and managers	8.3	3.6	6.0	4.5	3.3	4.0
Professionals	12.4	14.7	13.5	3.3	4.9	4.0
Life science and health professionals	2.0	2.1	2.1	0.9	1.9	1.3
Teaching professionals	2.7	4.2	3.4	0.9	1.4	1.1
Technicians and associate professionals	5.7	11.2	8.3	0.9	2.8	1.8
Clerks	3.0	11.6	7.2	1.2	6.0	3.3
Service, shop and market sales workers	7.5	24.3	15.6	22.0	16.5	19.5
Skilled agricultural and fishery workers	5.0	1.2	3.2	1.2	6.9	3.7
Craft and related trades workers	17.8	3.1	10.7	16.0	3.6	10.5
Plant and machine operators and assemblers	12.2	6.8	9.6	21.6	12.1	17.4
Elementary occupations	28.1	23.5	25.8	28.0	43.3	34.8

Distribution of employment by occupation (%), population 15+

Persons born in Lithuania and their native-born children, population 15+

Living in:	Europe	United States	Australia
2008	Thousands	Thousands	Thousands
Native-born children	123.3	84.5	10.4
Foreign-born	164.0	34.2	7.9
Total	287.3	118.7	18.4

International students from Lithuania in OECD countries

Five main destinations	2004	2005	2006	2007	2008	2009
United Kingdom	210	421	969	1 487	1 968	2 411
Germany	..	..	..	..	1 234	1 116
Denmark	71	73	66	91	145	496
United States	691	663	676	548	496	413
France	229	246	235	257	237	227
Total	1 475	1 838	2 444	2 864	4 670	5 424

Legal migrant flows to the OECD
Thousands

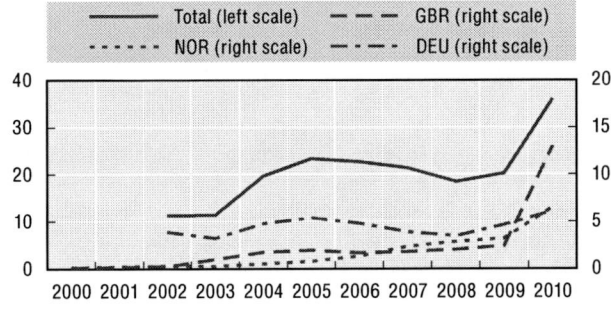

Remittance flows

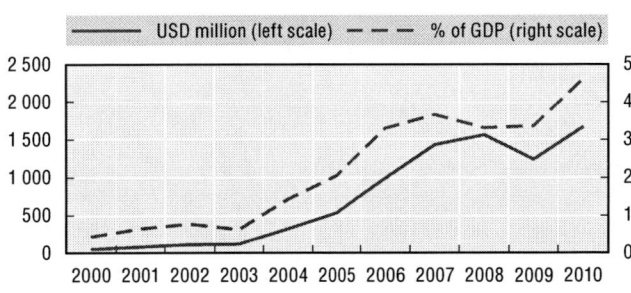

Ten main countries of destination for legal migrants in 2010 (numbers, % of total flows to the country): GBR (13000, 2.8%), NOR (6552, 10.2%), DEU (6134, 0.9%), ESP (1736, 0.4%), DNK (1486, 4.5%), SWE (1370, 1.8%), IRL (1207, 1.1%), NLD (1087, 1.1%), USA (985, 0.1%), ITA (529, 0.1%).

Desire to emigrate, 2008-10

	Women	15-24	Highly educated	Total	Regional total
Persons who would move permanently, if they had the opportunity to do so (%)	19	43	19	21	19
Of which: Persons who are planning to move permanently in the next 12 months (%)				10	7
Of which: Persons who have already done some preparations for this move (*e.g.* visa application) (%)					..

Three main countries of desired destination: United Kingdom (27%), United States (16%), Norway (9%).

StatLink http://dx.doi.org/10.1787/888932673809

Total population 2010 (millions)	3.6	Moldova compared to:	World	Region
Population growth 2010 (%)	−0.1	Human Development Index (HDI)	111/187	23/26
GDP per capita 2010 (current USD)	1 631	GDP per capita	133/194	22/27
GDP growth 2010 (%)	6.9	Emigration rate	113/203	20/28
Poverty rate 2008 (USD PPP 2 a day, in %)	12.5	Emigration rate of the highly educated	79/157	10/19

Age structure of the population 0+ (2010): "0-14": 18%; "15-24": 17%; "25-64": 54%; "65+": 11%.
Level of education of the population 15+ (2010): "Low": 11%; "Medium": 79%; "High": 11%.

Emigrant population living in OECD countries

Immigrant population

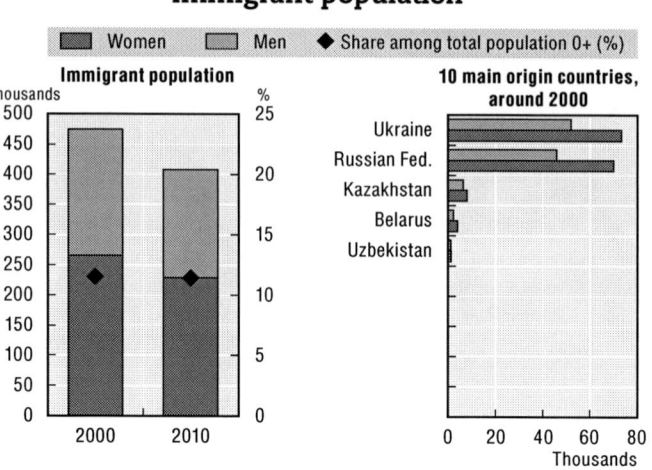

Emigrant population: persons born in Moldova living abroad

	2000						2005/06		
	All destinations			OECD destinations			OECD destinations		
Population 15+	Men	Women	Total	Men	Women	Total	Men	Women	Total
Emigrant population (thousands)	262.2	261.2	523.4	37.1	41.1	78.2	56.2	68.9	125.1
Recent emigrants (thousands)	..	..	..	6.7	10.6	17.2	22.8	29.6	52.4
15-24 (%)	16.2	15.2	15.7	19.3	15.9	17.5	17.4	16.1	16.7
25-64 (%)	73.3	72.1	72.7	64.8	63.7	64.2	73.5	71.1	72.2
65+ (%)	10.5	12.7	11.6	15.9	20.4	18.3	9.1	12.8	11.1
Low-educated (%)	23.6	24.4	24.0	22.9	21.8	22.3	21.8	21.2	21.4
Highly educated (%)	24.7	27.9	26.3	44.0	48.5	46.4	43.7	43.8	43.8
Total emigration rates (%)	15.1	13.5	14.3	2.5	2.4	2.4	3.7	4.0	3.9
Emigration rates of the highly educated (%)	35.4	27.1	30.5	12.1	9.2	10.3	19.7	12.4	14.8

Main destinations in 2005/06

	Total		Recent emigrants	Women	Highly educated	15-24	Total in 2000
Population 15+	Thousands	%	%	%	%	%	Thousands
Israel	37.2	29.7	19.5	53.4	60.2	10.8	39.1
United States	26.2	20.9	25.4	53.6	47.8	24.5	15.7
Italy	25.8	20.6	72.1	63.9	17.7	17.8	3.7
Spain	7.4	5.9	92.2	52.6	54.0	15.8	2.0
Portugal	6.9	5.5	69.6	–	–	–	3.0
Canada	4.8	3.8	53.4	51.2	69.6	17.2	2.0
Czech Republic	4.0	3.2	..	40.8	17.9	23.6	0.7
France	3.8	3.0	63.9	55.1	41.2	25.6	0.6
Greece	2.8	2.2	–	70.7	–	–	5.8
Ireland	1.9	1.5	78.5	46.0	41.7	15.6	0.9

Labour market indicators of persons born in Moldova living in OECD countries

Population 15-64	2000			2005/06		
	Men	Women	Total	Men	Women	Total
Employment-population ratio (%)	73.3	62.0	67.5	78.8	65.3	71.5
Unemployment rate (%)	8.3	10.4	9.3	8.6	8.6	8.6
Participation rate (%)	79.9	69.2	74.4	86.3	71.4	78.2
Total employed (thousands)	**22.4**	**19.8**	**42.2**	**38.1**	**37.7**	**75.8**
Employment rates of the highly educated (%)	81.8	74.0	77.6	93.7	80.0	86.1
Unemployment rates of the highly educated (%)	6.8	6.7	6.7	2.6	9.3	6.0
Highly educated in low- and medium-skilled jobs (%)	47.7	47.5	47.6	68.4	67.1	67.8
Highly educated employed (thousands)	**11.4**	**12.3**	**23.7**	**19.2**	**18.8**	**37.9**
Legislators, senior officials and managers	3.0	3.1	3.0	3.5	1.3	2.4
Professionals	7.5	10.4	8.7	3.9	2.9	3.4
Life science and health professionals	0.2	0.5	0.3	0.9	0.4	0.6
Teaching professionals	0.3	0.8	0.5	0.1	0.4	0.2
Technicians and associate professionals	6.8	13.4	9.3	1.9	5.1	3.5
Clerks	1.8	11.0	5.4	1.2	7.1	4.3
Service, shop and market sales workers	5.3	24.1	12.6	3.9	28.9	16.9
Skilled agricultural and fishery workers	1.6	1.0	1.4	0.8	0.7	0.7
Craft and related trades workers	39.6	5.8	26.5	52.4	3.3	27.0
Plant and machine operators and assemblers	10.6	4.2	8.1	18.9	3.5	10.9
Elementary occupations	23.8	26.8	25.0	13.7	47.2	31.0

Left axis label: Distribution of employment by occupation (%), population 15+

Persons born in Moldova and their native-born children, population 15+

Living in:	Europe	United States	Australia
2008	Thousands	Thousands	Thousands
Native-born children	5.4	4.7	..
Foreign-born	118.4	13.3	..
Total	123.9	17.9	..

International students from Moldova in OECD countries

Five main destinations	2004	2005	2006	2007	2008	2009
Italy	122	197	331	488	685	951
France	463	519	634	751	794	884
Germany	..	..	..	..	540	591
United States	266	298	372	373	418	477
Turkey	153	160	162	179	165	176
Total	1 179	1 339	1 754	2 112	2 954	3 561

Legal migrant flows to the OECD
Thousands

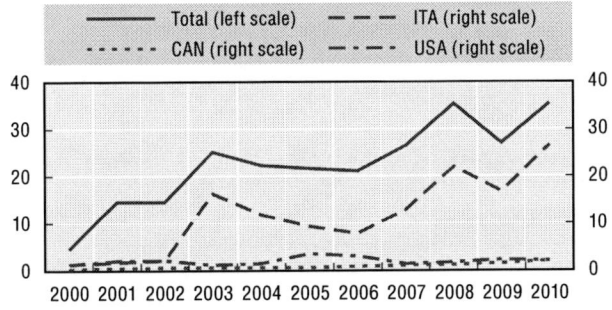

Remittance flows

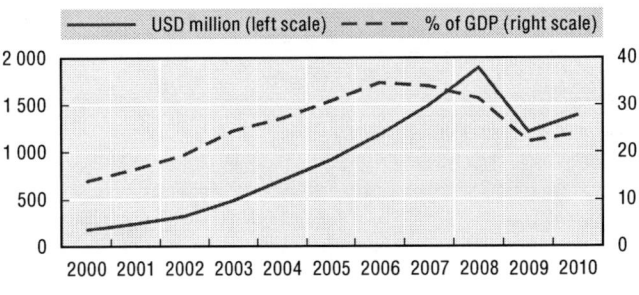

Ten main countries of destination for legal migrants in 2010 (numbers, % of total flows to the country): ITA (26591, 6.3%), CAN (1985, 0.7%), USA (1981, 0.2%), ESP (1126, 0.3%), DEU (776, 0.1%), TUR (575, 1.9%), PRT (503, 1.4%), CZE (354, 1.4%), POL (353, 0.9%), FRA (314, 0.2%).

Desire to emigrate, 2008-10

	Women	15-24	Highly educated	Total	Regional total
Persons who would move permanently, if they had the opportunity to do so (%)	35	56	37	34	19
Of which: Persons who are planning to move permanently in the next 12 months (%)				11	7
Of which: Persons who have already done some preparations for this move (_e.g._ visa application) (%)					..

Three main countries of desired destination: Russian Federation (25%), Italy (14%), United States (8%).

StatLink http://dx.doi.org/10.1787/888932673828

Total population 2010 (millions)	21.4	Romania compared to:	World	Region
Population growth 2010 (%)	−0.2	Human Development Index (HDI)	50/187	8/26
GDP per capita 2010 (current USD)	7 538	GDP per capita	74/194	10/27
GDP growth 2010 (%)	0.9	Emigration rate	59/203	12/28
Poverty rate 2008 (USD PPP 2 a day, in %)	2.0	Emigration rate of the highly educated	35/157	5/19

Age structure of the population 0+ (2010): "0-14": 13%; "15-24": 15%; "25-64": 56%; "65+": 15%.
Level of education of the population 15+ (2010): "Low": 13%; "Medium": 75%; "High": 12%.

Emigrant population living in OECD countries

Immigrant population

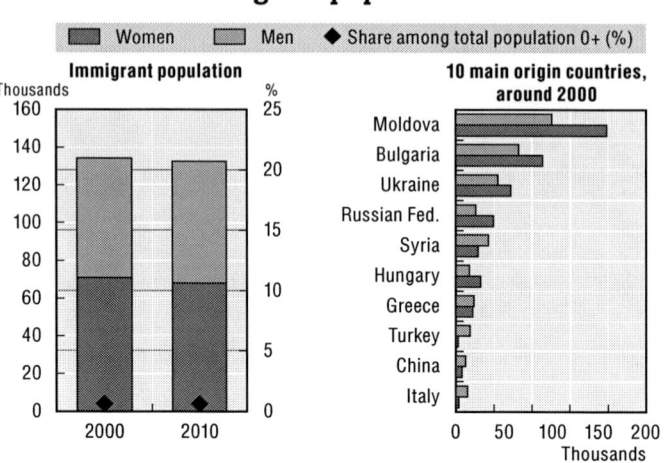

Emigrant population: persons born in Romania living abroad

	2000						2005/06		
	All destinations			OECD destinations			OECD destinations		
Population 15+	Men	Women	Total	Men	Women	Total	Men	Women	Total
Emigrant population (thousands)	537.6	610.0	1 147.6	458.0	507.5	965.5	788.4	906.0	1 694.5
Recent emigrants (thousands)	..	..	..	77.0	79.3	156.3	285.7	337.3	623.0
15-24 (%)	11.4	10.5	10.9	11.4	10.4	10.9	14.3	14.7	14.5
25-64 (%)	66.9	64.6	65.7	68.3	66.2	67.2	72.3	69.6	70.9
65+ (%)	21.7	24.9	23.4	20.3	23.4	21.9	13.4	15.7	14.6
Low-educated (%)	29.3	36.7	33.2	27.9	34.7	31.5	27.5	31.5	29.6
Highly educated (%)	26.6	22.1	24.2	27.6	23.6	25.5	24.1	23.1	23.6
Total emigration rates (%)	5.8	6.1	6.0	5.0	5.2	5.1	8.2	8.8	8.5
Emigration rates of the highly educated (%)	15.8	16.8	16.3	14.3	15.3	14.7	18.5	21.3	19.9

Main destinations in 2005/06

	Total		Recent emigrants	Women	Highly educated	15-24	Total in 2000
Population 15+	Thousands	%	%	%	%	%	Thousands
Germany	492.5	29.1	6.4	54.9	18.6	10.9	387.5
Spain	395.4	23.3	88.1	49.2	16.6	23.3	50.7
Italy	220.9	13.0	53.3	55.7	6.9	15.8	74.1
United States	163.7	9.7	17.3	54.3	45.1	11.0	123.9
Israel	107.8	6.4	4.6	55.0	37.3	1.0	120.2
Canada	76.9	4.5	30.8	51.9	63.5	11.8	54.8
Austria	47.1	2.8	24.0	56.7	12.2	13.3	36.2
France	41.2	2.4	36.2	55.0	42.9	18.7	22.0
Greece	31.0	1.8	37.7	52.7	11.1	15.8	25.3
United Kingdom	24.5	1.4	64.6	42.7	48.7	–	6.7

Labour market indicators of persons born in Romania living in OECD countries

Population 15-64	2000			2005/06		
	Men	Women	Total	Men	Women	Total
Employment-population ratio (%)	80.9	62.0	71.1	82.6	65.3	73.5
Unemployment rate (%)	7.1	10.3	8.6	8.2	11.2	9.6
Participation rate (%)	87.1	69.1	77.8	90.0	73.5	81.3
Total employed (thousands)	**285.7**	**234.5**	**520.2**	**555.0**	**490.0**	**1 045.0**
Employment rates of the highly educated (%)	88.5	72.8	80.4	95.1	81.1	87.5
Unemployment rates of the highly educated (%)	4.8	6.8	5.8	6.8	9.0	7.9
Highly educated in low- and medium-skilled jobs (%)	26.2	22.9	24.6	43.5	42.8	43.2
Highly educated employed (thousands)	**88.3**	**77.6**	**165.9**	**141.6**	**136.5**	**278.1**
Legislators, senior officials and managers	3.7	2.0	2.9	2.6	2.2	2.4
Professionals	15.5	12.8	14.2	7.7	7.5	7.6
Life science and health professionals	0.6	0.6	0.6	1.0	1.5	1.3
Teaching professionals	0.6	0.7	0.7	0.6	1.6	1.1
Technicians and associate professionals	11.2	23.6	17.0	5.4	12.1	8.5
Clerks	2.2	11.3	6.5	2.6	8.2	5.2
Service, shop and market sales workers	3.9	19.8	11.3	4.4	22.7	13.0
Skilled agricultural and fishery workers	1.2	0.4	0.8	2.6	0.8	1.7
Craft and related trades workers	34.2	2.8	19.5	40.2	4.5	23.4
Plant and machine operators and assemblers	15.9	3.1	9.9	14.3	5.0	9.9
Elementary occupations	12.1	24.1	17.7	20.3	37.1	28.2

(Left margin label: Distribution of employment by occupation (%), population 15+)

Persons born in Romania and their native-born children, population 15+

Living in:	Europe	United States	Australia
2008	Thousands	Thousands	Thousands
Native-born children	134.0	91.5	4.1
Foreign-born	1 668.8	168.9	21.2
Total	1 802.8	260.4	25.3

International students from Romania in OECD countries

Five main destinations	2004	2005	2006	2007	2008	2009
France	4 474	4 320	4 332	4 617	3 844	3 950
Italy	1 225	1 521	1 874	2 456	3 151	3 859
Germany	..	..	..	..	3 156	2 989
United States	3 320	3 360	3 339	3 203	2 905	2 569
Hungary	..	..	..	..	..	2 307
Total	11 090	10 596	11 530	13 222	16 705	21 730

Legal migrant flows to the OECD
Thousands

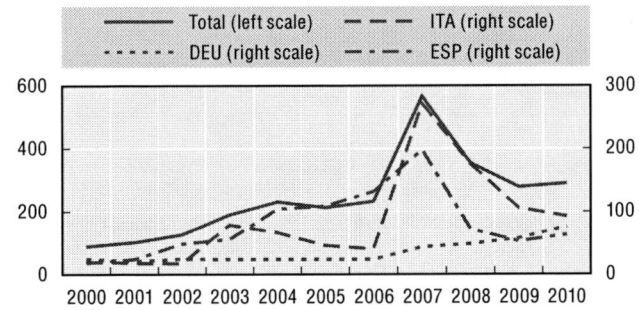

Ten main countries of destination for legal migrants in 2010 (numbers, % of total flows to the country): ITA (92116, 21.7%), DEU (75531, 11.2%), ESP (62644, 14.5%), AUT (11539, 11.8%), GBR (7000, 1.5%), HUN (6581, 27.8%), BEL (6066, 22.1%), PRT (6047, 22.1%), USA (4003, 0.4%), FRA (2715, 2%).

Remittance flows

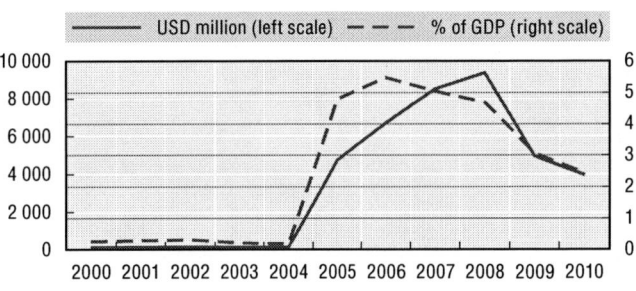

Desire to emigrate, 2008-10

	Women	15-24	Highly educated	Total	Regional total
Persons who would move permanently, if they had the opportunity to do so (%)	26	49	28	26	19
Of which: Persons who are planning to move permanently in the next 12 months (%)				10	7
Of which: Persons who have already done some preparations for this move (*e.g.* visa application) (%)					..

Three main countries of desired destination: Germany (15%), United States (12%), Italy (10%).

StatLink ⟲ http://dx.doi.org/10.1787/888932673847

		Russian Federation compared to:	World	Region
Total population 2010 (millions)	141.8	Human Development Index (HDI)	66/187	13/26
Population growth 2010 (%)	–0.1	GDP per capita	61/194	8/27
GDP per capita 2010 (current USD)	10 440	Emigration rate	132/203	22/28
GDP growth 2010 (%)	4.0	Emigration rate of the highly educated	131/157	14/19
Poverty rate 2008 (USD PPP 2 a day, in %)	0.1			

Age structure of the population 0+ (2010): "0-14": 14%; "15-24": 15%; "25-64": 58%; "65+": 13%.
Level of education of the population 15+ (2010): "Low": 7%; "Medium": 81%; "High": 12%.

Emigrant population living in OECD countries

Immigrant population

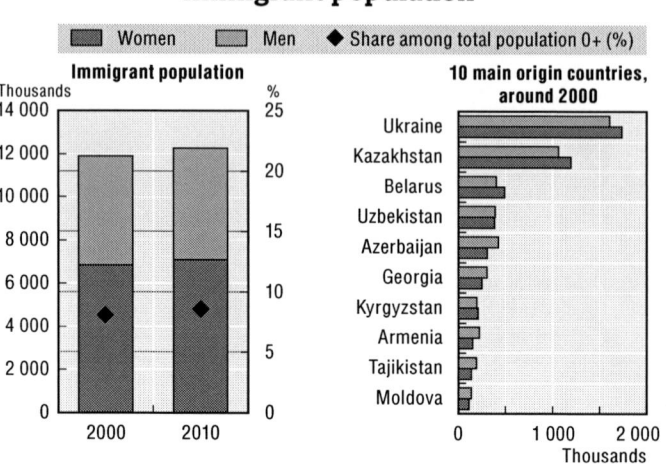

Emigrant population: persons born in the Russian Federation living abroad

	2000						2005/06		
	All destinations			OECD destinations			OECD destinations		
Population 15+	Men	Women	Total	Men	Women	Total	Men	Women	Total
Emigrant population (thousands)	2 762.4	3 830.4	6 592.8	781.5	982.2	1 763.6	1 077.4	1 394.4	2 471.8
Recent emigrants (thousands)	..	..	..	79.3	128.2	207.4	179.1	280.7	459.8
15-24 (%)	11.0	8.0	9.2	18.5	14.8	16.4	19.4	16.3	17.7
25-64 (%)	69.2	65.0	66.7	66.2	64.9	65.4	65.9	65.5	65.7
65+ (%)	19.9	27.0	24.0	15.4	20.3	18.1	14.7	18.2	16.7
Low-educated (%)	23.8	26.4	25.3	30.4	31.9	31.3	30.9	31.3	31.1
Highly educated (%)	37.0	38.7	38.0	31.4	32.8	32.2	29.1	32.8	31.2
Total emigration rates (%)	4.8	5.5	5.2	1.4	1.5	1.4	1.9	2.1	2.0
Emigration rates of the highly educated (%)	12.4	14.4	13.5	3.3	3.5	3.4	4.5	4.9	4.7

Main destinations in 2005/06

	Total		Recent emigrants	Women	Highly educated	15-24	Total in 2000
Population 15+	Thousands	%	%	%	%	%	Thousands
Germany	1 403.4	56.8	14.4	53.3	16.8	19.0	929.8
United States	348.7	14.1	16.6	58.5	58.3	17.5	287.5
Israel	268.4	10.9	30.6	57.2	57.2	15.2	264.1
Greece	96.1	3.9	15.3	59.3	18.2	17.6	65.8
Poland	71.2	2.9	4.5	60.2	11.2	–	53.7
Canada	60.7	2.5	30.7	54.9	66.2	17.3	44.6
France	29.2	1.2	45.1	68.9	52.1	19.6	15.7
Spain	28.7	1.2	79.8	71.4	51.4	19.1	12.0
United Kingdom	28.0	1.1	47.5	67.2	68.0	22.4	13.3
Czech Republic	21.4	0.9	..	64.6	48.5	11.6	12.2

Labour market indicators of persons born in the Russian Federation living in OECD countries

Population 15-64	2000			2005/06		
	Men	Women	Total	Men	Women	Total
Employment-population ratio (%)	68.3	55.2	61.2	68.7	56.1	61.8
Unemployment rate (%)	14.6	15.4	15.0	15.1	15.8	15.4
Participation rate (%)	79.9	65.2	72.0	80.9	66.6	73.0
Total employed (thousands)	**445.5**	**422.3**	**867.9**	**621.3**	**622.5**	**1 243.8**
Employment rates of the highly educated (%)	79.1	63.2	70.1	91.4	75.1	81.7
Unemployment rates of the highly educated (%)	10.6	13.1	11.9	10.5	12.4	11.5
Highly educated in low- and medium-skilled jobs (%)	34.3	37.5	35.8	35.4	40.7	38.3
Highly educated employed (thousands)	**163.3**	**169.9**	**333.2**	**213.8**	**250.8**	**464.6**
Legislators, senior officials and managers	1.4	0.9	1.1	3.4	1.8	2.6
Professionals	10.2	8.3	9.2	9.3	9.0	9.2
Life science and health professionals	0.1	0.2	0.2	1.0	1.3	1.2
Teaching professionals	0.5	0.7	0.6	0.9	2.0	1.5
Technicians and associate professionals	7.4	20.3	13.7	9.6	20.5	15.0
Clerks	1.4	9.4	5.3	4.4	11.9	8.1
Service, shop and market sales workers	1.6	24.3	12.7	2.9	23.5	13.1
Skilled agricultural and fishery workers	0.1	0.1	0.1	1.6	0.3	0.9
Craft and related trades workers	36.2	3.7	20.2	31.1	3.6	17.5
Plant and machine operators and assemblers	23.4	4.3	14.0	22.3	4.4	13.4
Elementary occupations	18.3	28.9	23.5	15.5	24.9	20.1

Distribution of employment by occupation (%), population 15+

Persons born in the Russian Federation and their native-born children, population 15+

Living in:	Europe	United States	Australia
2008	Thousands	Thousands	Thousands
Native-born children	521.2	356.7	15.6
Foreign-born	1 625.7	558.5	34.1
Total	2 147.0	915.3	49.8

International students from the Russian Federation in OECD countries

Five main destinations	2004	2005	2006	2007	2008	2009
Germany	..	..	..	..	9 135	9 346
United States	5 532	5 299	4 971	4 856	4 911	4 827
France	2 597	2 672	3 083	3 219	3 347	3 593
United Kingdom	1 878	2 027	2 187	2 580	2 646	2 953
Italy	512	600	793	930	949	1 144
Total	13 334	13 302	14 197	15 066	25 430	26 949

Legal migrant flows to the OECD
Thousands

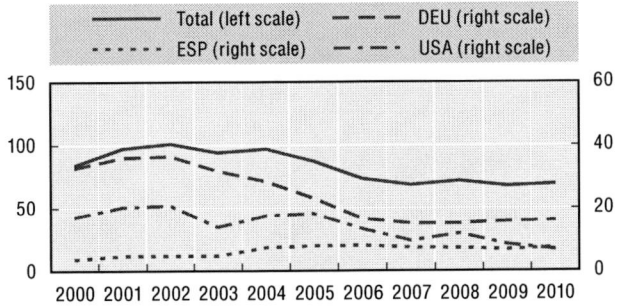

Remittance flows

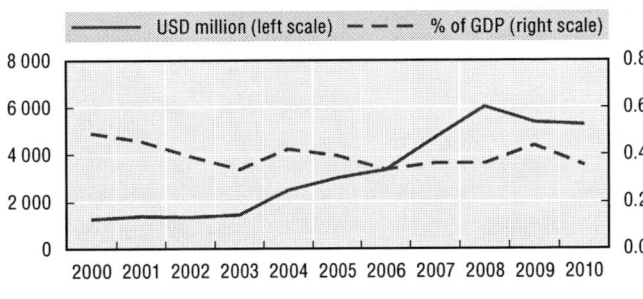

Ten main countries of destination for legal migrants in 2010 (numbers, % of total flows to the country): DEU (16063, 2.4%), ESP (7382, 1.7%), USA (6718, 0.6%), ITA (5138, 1.2%), CZE (3681, 14.5%), JPN (3462, 1.2%), FRA (3159, 0.9%), KOR (2601, 0.9%), FIN (2297, 12.9%), CAN (2215, 0.8%).

Desire to emigrate, 2008-10

	Women	15-24	Highly educated	Total	Regional total
Persons who would move permanently, if they had the opportunity to do so (%)	11	23	17	12	19
Of which: Persons who are planning to move permanently in the next 12 months (%)				2	7
Of which: Persons who have already done some preparations for this move (*e.g.* visa application) (%)					..

Three main countries of desired destination: Germany (19%), United States (12%), United Kingdom (5%).

StatLink ᵐˢᵖ http://dx.doi.org/10.1787/888932673866

Total population 2010 (millions)	7.3		Serbia compared to:	World	Region
Population growth 2010 (%)	–0.4		Human Development Index (HDI)	59/187	11/26
GDP per capita 2010 (current USD)	5 269		GDP per capita	90/194	14/27
GDP growth 2010 (%)	1.0		Emigration rate	60/203	13/28
Poverty rate 2008 (USD PPP 2 a day, in %)	0.7		Emigration rate of the highly educated	97/157	12/19

Age structure of the population 0+ (2010): "0-14": 14%; "15-24": 18%; "25-64": 54%; "65+": 14%.

Emigrant population living in OECD countries

Immigrant population

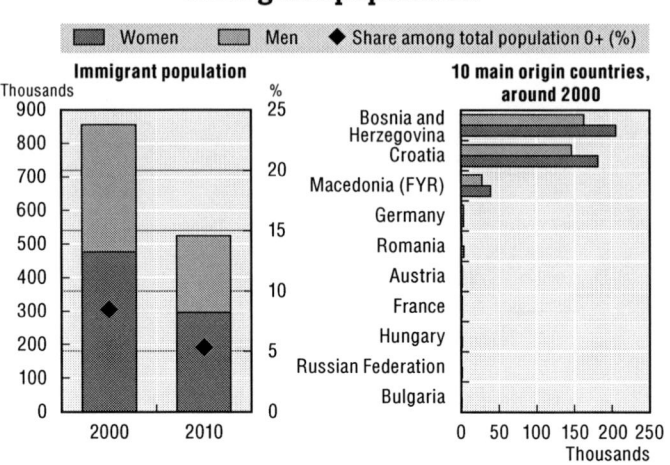

Emigrant population: persons born in Serbia living abroad

	2000						2005/06		
	All destinations			OECD destinations			OECD destinations		
Population 15+	Men	Women	Total	Men	Women	Total	Men	Women	Total
Emigrant population (thousands)	590.1	571.1	1 161.1	466.1	440.0	906.2	382.9	357.4	740.3
Recent emigrants (thousands)	..	..	..	38.7	38.7	77.4	33.5	45.0	78.5
15-24 (%)	12.9	11.4	12.1	14.7	13.1	13.9	15.5	16.0	15.7
25-64 (%)	75.2	72.3	73.8	76.3	73.9	75.1	76.7	74.7	75.8
65+ (%)	11.9	16.3	14.1	9.0	13.0	10.9	7.8	9.3	8.5
Low-educated (%)	46.5	61.5	53.9	45.1	60.2	52.4	46.0	63.1	54.3
Highly educated (%)	13.3	10.9	12.1	13.1	11.4	12.2	11.1	8.5	9.9
Total emigration rates (%)	12.2	11.5	11.9	9.9	9.1	9.5	8.4	7.6	8.0
Emigration rates of the highly educated (%)	12.6	11.5	12.1	10.0	9.4	9.7	8.1	6.3	7.2

Main destinations in 2005/06

	Total		Recent emigrants	Women	Highly educated	15-24	Total in 2000
Population 15+	Thousands	%	%	%	%	%	Thousands
Germany	339.3	45.8	6.2	48.0	7.0	13.8	225.8
Switzerland	168.4	22.8	12.8	46.8	6.7	21.2	132.8
France	63.4	8.6	14.3	50.1	13.3	9.3	2.2
Italy	58.8	7.9	24.1	52.1	4.5	14.6	45.2
Belgium	26.7	3.6	20.2	47.3	–	–	18.3
Canada	23.1	3.1	16.5	50.7	48.6	14.6	58.6
Australia	17.0	2.3	8.3	49.4	23.9	8.9	52.5
United Kingdom	16.3	2.2	–	48.5	–	–	25.9
Norway	10.5	1.4	35.6	46.4	14.3	23.8	7.1
Czech Republic	3.6	0.5	..	30.9	33.8	11.0	4.6

Labour market indicators of persons born in Serbia living in OECD countries

Population 15-64	2000			2005/06		
	Men	Women	Total	Men	Women	Total
Employment-population ratio (%)	66.7	50.4	59.2	68.1	45.1	57.1
Unemployment rate (%)	14.7	13.3	14.2	14.3	17.5	15.6
Participation rate (%)	78.2	58.1	68.9	79.5	54.6	67.6
Total employed (thousands)	**249.0**	**160.6**	**409.6**	**237.9**	**145.1**	**382.9**
Employment rates of the highly educated (%)	83.5	67.2	76.4	90.6	70.3	81.7
Unemployment rates of the highly educated (%)	6.9	10.0	8.1	10.2	7.4	9.1
Highly educated in low- and medium-skilled jobs (%)	38.9	38.1	38.5	50.3	41.6	46.6
Highly educated employed (thousands)	**37.5**	**22.9**	**60.4**	**30.0**	**18.9**	**48.9**
Legislators, senior officials and managers	4.5	3.2	4.0	2.6	2.5	2.5
Professionals	4.3	5.4	4.7	3.1	4.0	3.4
Life science and health professionals	0.2	0.6	0.3	0.2	0.5	0.3
Teaching professionals	0.2	0.5	0.3	0.2	1.0	0.5
Technicians and associate professionals	4.7	7.6	5.8	5.3	11.7	7.7
Clerks	2.2	8.6	4.6	4.2	6.0	4.9
Service, shop and market sales workers	4.5	22.4	11.2	9.4	29.6	16.9
Skilled agricultural and fishery workers	0.7	0.4	0.6	1.8	1.3	1.7
Craft and related trades workers	33.8	3.1	22.3	37.8	5.7	25.8
Plant and machine operators and assemblers	20.2	5.3	14.6	20.9	7.5	15.9
Elementary occupations	25.1	44.1	32.2	14.9	31.6	21.1

Distribution of employment by occupation (%), population 15+

Persons born in Serbia and their native-born children, population 15+

Living in:	Europe	United States	Australia
2008	Thousands	Thousands	Thousands
Native-born children	248.7	24.5	..
Foreign-born	818.4	48.4	..
Total	1 067.1	73.0	..

International students from Serbia in OECD countries

Five main destinations	2004	2005	2006	2007	2008	2009
United States	..	..	..	..	..	1 214
Hungary	..	..	..	..	..	1 171
Germany	..	..	..	..	..	707
Slovak Republic	..	..	..	..	..	311
Switzerland	..	..	..	..	..	308
Total	..	..	..	..	..	..

Legal migrant flows to the OECD
Thousands

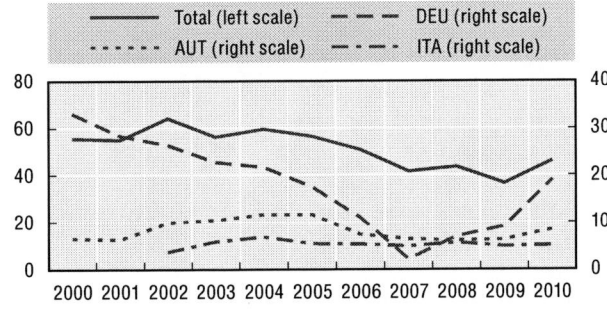

Remittance flows

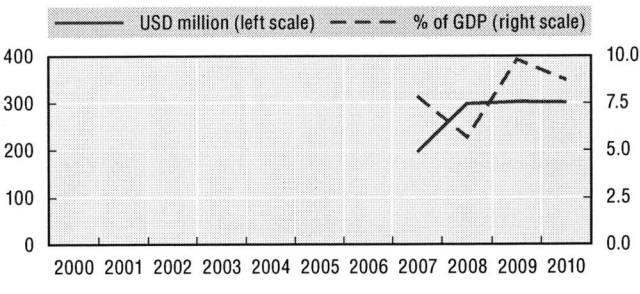

Ten main countries of destination for legal migrants in 2010 (numbers, % of total flows to the country): DEU (19058, 2.8%), AUT (8501, 8.7%), ITA (5121, 1.2%), CHE (2397, 1.8%), USA (2336, 0.2%), FRA (1822, 1.3%), SVN (1176, 4.2%), HUN (998, 4.2%), SWE (946, 1.2%), SVK (680, 5.4%).

Desire to emigrate, 2008-10

	Women	15-24	Highly educated	Total	Regional total
Persons who would move permanently, if they had the opportunity to do so (%)	20	34	20	20	19
Of which: Persons who are planning to move permanently in the next 12 months (%)				6	7
Of which: Persons who have already done some preparations for this move (*e.g.* visa application) (%)					..

Two main countries of desired destination: Germany (11%), United States (10%).

StatLink http://dx.doi.org/10.1787/888932673885

Total population 2010 (millions)	6.9	**Tajikistan compared to:**	**World**	**Region**
Population growth 2010 (%)	1.4	Human Development Index (HDI)	127/187	26/26
GDP per capita 2010 (current USD)	820	GDP per capita	155/194	25/27
GDP growth 2010 (%)	3.8	Emigration rate	198/203	27/28
Poverty rate 2004 (USD PPP 2 a day, in %)	50.9	Emigration rate of the highly educated	150/157	16/19

Age structure of the population 0+ (2010): "0-14": 23%; "15-24": 37%; "25-64": 36%; "65+": 3%.
Level of education of the population 15+ (2010): "Low": 15%; "Medium": 81%; "High": 4%.

Emigrant population living in OECD countries

Immigrant population

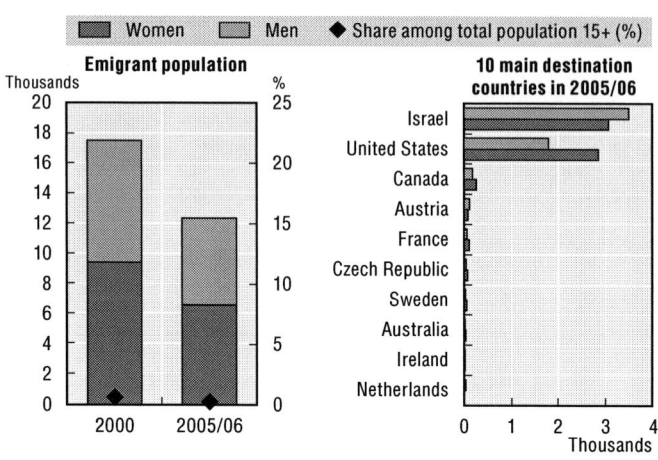

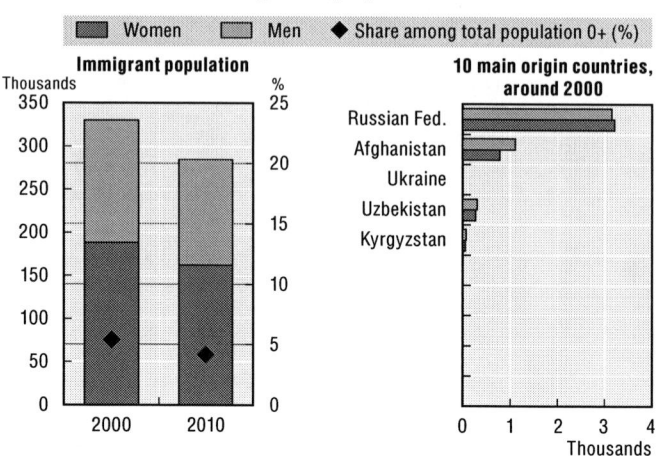

Emigrant population: persons born in Tajikistan living abroad

	2000						2005/06		
	All destinations			OECD destinations			OECD destinations		
Population 15+	Men	Women	Total	Men	Women	Total	Men	Women	Total
Emigrant population (thousands)	226.6	173.6	400.2	8.1	9.4	17.5	5.8	6.5	12.3
Recent emigrants (thousands)	..	..	..	0.5	0.7	1.2	1.0	1.4	2.3
15-24 (%)	26.2	23.7	25.1	20.1	24.2	22.3	25.8	19.5	22.5
25-64 (%)	71.5	72.2	71.8	66.3	62.1	64.0	69.4	69.1	69.3
65+ (%)	2.3	4.1	3.1	13.6	13.7	13.7	4.8	11.4	8.3
Low-educated (%)	22.5	16.6	19.9	31.5	38.1	35.0	22.7	17.7	20.0
Highly educated (%)	17.0	27.6	21.6	27.3	29.5	28.5	44.5	51.7	48.3
Total emigration rates (%)	11.4	8.8	10.1	0.5	0.5	0.5	0.3	0.3	0.3
Emigration rates of the highly educated (%)	23.1	37.0	29.1	1.7	3.3	2.3	2.2	4.1	3.0

Main destinations in 2005/06

	Total		Recent emigrants	Women	Highly educated	15-24	Total in 2000
Population 15+	Thousands	%	%	%	%	%	Thousands
Israel	6.6	53.4	16.8	46.7	49.3	23.1	8.6
United States	4.6	37.8	19.3	61.4	45.9	21.9	2.1
Canada	0.4	3.4	65.6	59.5	70.2	22.6	0.1
Austria	–	–	–	–	–	–	–
France	–	–	–	–	–	–	–
Czech Republic	–	–	–	–	–	–	0.1
Sweden	–	–	–	–	–	–	0.1

Labour market indicators of persons born in Tajikistan living in OECD countries

Population 15-64	2000			2005/06		
	Men	Women	Total	Men	Women	Total
Employment-population ratio (%)	68.2	54.5	60.9	71.0	62.4	67.1
Unemployment rate (%)	8.1	11.1	9.5	3.9	17.2	10.1
Participation rate (%)	74.2	61.3	67.3	73.9	75.4	74.6
Total employed (thousands)	**4.8**	**4.4**	**9.2**	**2.9**	**2.2**	**5.1**
Employment rates of the highly educated (%)	78.3	75.2	76.6	86.7	84.4	85.6
Unemployment rates of the highly educated (%)	3.1	8.0	5.8	1.1	17.6	9.0
Highly educated in low- and medium-skilled jobs (%)	29.9	28.6	29.3	56.3	41.6	48.4
Highly educated employed (thousands)	**1.6**	**1.9**	**3.6**	**1.6**	**1.2**	**2.9**
Legislators, senior officials and managers	0.1	–	0.0	20.4	18.8	19.6
Professionals	11.9	8.5	10.3	19.9	15.1	17.4
Life science and health professionals	–	0.4	0.2	–	1.5	0.9
Teaching professionals	–	0.4	0.2	–	3.0	1.8
Technicians and associate professionals	13.2	26.0	19.1	1.0	21.6	11.7
Clerks	3.7	12.8	8.0	8.0	14.7	11.5
Service, shop and market sales workers	3.5	23.2	12.6	1.0	17.4	9.5
Skilled agricultural and fishery workers	0.1	–	0.0	2.0	–	1.0
Craft and related trades workers	35.0	3.4	20.3	26.4	5.5	15.5
Plant and machine operators and assemblers	20.3	4.1	12.8	7.5	4.6	6.0
Elementary occupations	12.3	22.0	16.8	13.9	2.3	7.9

Distribution of employment by occupation (%), population 15+

Persons born in Tajikistan and their native-born children, population 15+

Living in:	Europe	United States	Australia
2008	Thousands	Thousands	Thousands
Native-born children	0.7	..	..
Foreign-born	1.6	..	..
Total	2.3	..	..

International students from Tajikistan in OECD countries

Five main destinations	2004	2005	2006	2007	2008	2009
United States	117	165	192	168	364	336
Turkey	262	186	189	165	162	176
Germany	..	..	..	..	67	73
United Kingdom	35	40	44	65	53	59
France	9	12	21	22	28	23
Total	452	430	484	451	717	733

Legal migrant flows to the OECD
Thousands

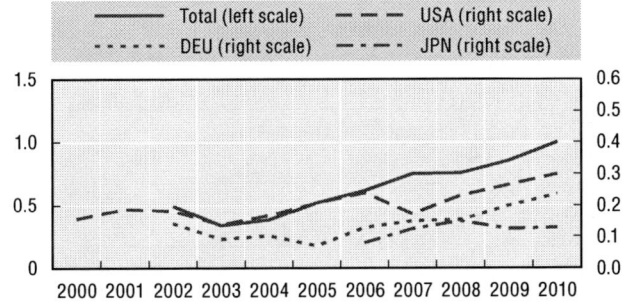

Ten main countries of destination for legal migrants in 2010 (numbers, % of total flows to the country): USA (299, 0%), DEU (235, 0%), JPN (128, 0%), TUR (83, 0.3%), KOR (71, 0%), CAN (45, 0%), AUT (41, 0%), FRA (15, 0%), POL (12, 0%), AUS (11, 0%).

Remittance flows

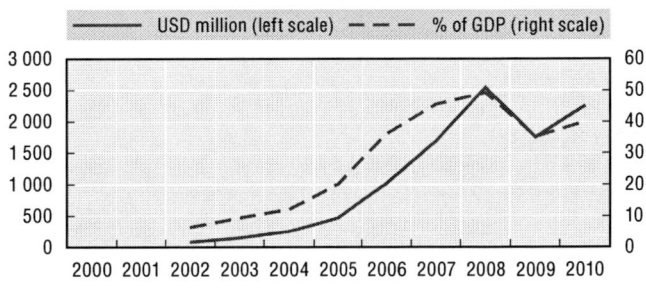

Desire to emigrate, 2008-10

	Women	15-24	Highly educated	Total	Regional total
Persons who would move permanently, if they had the opportunity to do so (%)	8	14	13	10	19
Of which: Persons who are planning to move permanently in the next 12 months (%)				10	7
Of which: Persons who have already done some preparations for this move (*e.g.* visa application) (%)					..

Two main countries of desired destination: Russian Federation (71%), United States (6%).

StatLink 🔗 *http://dx.doi.org/10.1787/888932673904*

Total population 2010 (millions)	45.9	**Ukraine compared to:**	**World**	**Region**
Population growth 2010 (%)	−0.4	Human Development Index (HDI)	76/187	18/26
GDP per capita 2010 (current USD)	3 007	GDP per capita	114/194	20/27
GDP growth 2010 (%)	4.2	Emigration rate	111/203	19/28
Poverty rate 2008 (USD PPP 2 a day, in %)	0.1	Emigration rate of the highly educated	139/157	15/19

Age structure of the population 0+ (2010): "0-14": 14%; "15-24": 14%; "25-64": 56%; "65+": 15%.
Level of education of the population 15+ (2010): "Low": 8%; "Medium": 52%; "High": 40%.

Emigrant population living in OECD countries

Immigrant population

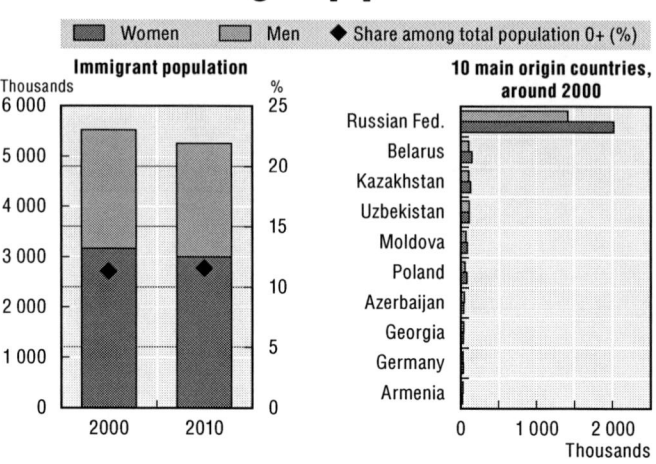

Emigrant population: persons born in Ukraine living abroad

	2000						2005/06		
	All destinations			OECD destinations			OECD destinations		
Population 15+	Men	Women	Total	Men	Women	Total	Men	Women	Total
Emigrant population (thousands)	2 216.2	2 514.7	4 730.8	426.9	562.7	989.6	592.2	830.8	1 423.0
Recent emigrants (thousands)	..	..	..	54.2	74.3	128.5	136.5	201.0	337.5
15-24 (%)	9.9	9.0	9.4	10.0	8.1	8.9	13.7	9.8	11.4
25-64 (%)	70.0	64.5	67.1	54.7	49.8	51.9	55.8	56.1	56.0
65+ (%)	20.1	26.5	23.5	35.4	42.2	39.2	30.5	34.1	32.6
Low-educated (%)	20.6	24.2	22.5	27.2	34.3	31.2	23.3	27.9	26.0
Highly educated (%)	28.2	24.5	26.2	38.5	34.7	36.3	40.8	38.9	39.7
Total emigration rates (%)	10.8	10.2	10.5	2.3	2.5	2.4	3.2	3.7	3.4
Emigration rates of the highly educated (%)	9.9	7.4	8.5	2.8	2.4	2.6	4.1	3.8	3.9

Main destinations in 2005/06

	Total		Recent emigrants	Women	Highly educated	15-24	Total in 2000
Population 15+	Thousands	%	%	%	%	%	Thousands
Poland	314.7	22.1	3.7	62.6	11.7	2.0	308.3
United States	292.6	20.6	15.2	54.6	54.6	14.9	240.7
Israel	258.5	18.2	38.4	55.2	61.2	14.5	249.7
Germany	201.7	14.2	24.9	56.5	37.7	14.6	14.5
Czech Republic	85.1	6.0	..	57.5	19.9	16.2	31.4
Spain	61.5	4.3	78.3	53.7	53.1	9.4	20.6
Canada	57.0	4.0	23.4	54.9	55.2	12.7	49.0
Italy	50.9	3.6	61.6	79.2	25.1	10.3	8.5
Greece	22.3	1.6	36.5	74.4	25.5	12.7	15.2
United Kingdom	18.5	1.3	35.9	53.7	59.4	–	11.2

Labour market indicators of persons born in Ukraine living in OECD countries

Population 15-64	2000			2005/06		
	Men	Women	Total	Men	Women	Total
Employment-population ratio (%)	69.1	52.6	60.2	70.5	60.3	64.6
Unemployment rate (%)	8.3	10.4	9.3	12.1	11.7	11.9
Participation rate (%)	75.4	58.7	66.4	80.2	68.2	73.3
Total employed (thousands)	**182.7**	**162.4**	**345.1**	**264.4**	**301.6**	**566.0**
Employment rates of the highly educated (%)	80.7	65.9	72.6	92.5	79.0	84.7
Unemployment rates of the highly educated (%)	7.2	8.8	8.0	9.1	9.3	9.2
Highly educated in low- and medium-skilled jobs (%)	43.9	45.6	44.7	52.8	56.7	54.9
Highly educated employed (thousands)	**98.3**	**96.6**	**194.9**	**146.0**	**171.4**	**317.3**
Legislators, senior officials and managers	5.3	4.6	5.0	3.3	2.4	2.7
Professionals	13.3	14.1	13.7	13.3	7.0	9.5
Life science and health professionals	0.7	1.6	1.0	0.2	0.5	0.4
Teaching professionals	1.4	2.6	1.9	1.3	1.9	1.7
Technicians and associate professionals	7.2	13.0	9.7	5.6	7.1	6.5
Clerks	2.4	12.2	6.6	3.0	8.7	6.4
Service, shop and market sales workers	5.6	23.1	13.0	7.5	24.7	17.8
Skilled agricultural and fishery workers	3.9	1.6	2.9	3.1	1.1	1.9
Craft and related trades workers	28.1	4.8	18.2	33.2	3.8	15.6
Plant and machine operators and assemblers	10.6	3.3	7.5	10.1	2.5	5.5
Elementary occupations	23.4	23.4	23.4	20.2	42.8	33.7

Distribution of employment by occupation (%), population 15+

Persons born in Ukraine and their native-born children, population 15+

Living in:	Europe	United States	Australia
2008	Thousands	Thousands	Thousands
Native-born children	518.4	115.2	7.5
Foreign-born	626.7	282.2	17.6
Total	1 145.0	397.4	25.1

International students from Ukraine in OECD countries

Five main destinations	2004	2005	2006	2007	2008	2009
Germany	..	..	..	..	6 055	5 978
United States	2 004	1 912	1 869	1 729	1 716	1 688
France	924	1 066	1 194	1 259	1 307	1 334
Hungary	..	..	..	..	..	1 033
Italy	227	303	465	615	737	920
Total	4 370	4 627	5 111	5 188	11 910	13 376

Legal migrant flows to the OECD
Thousands

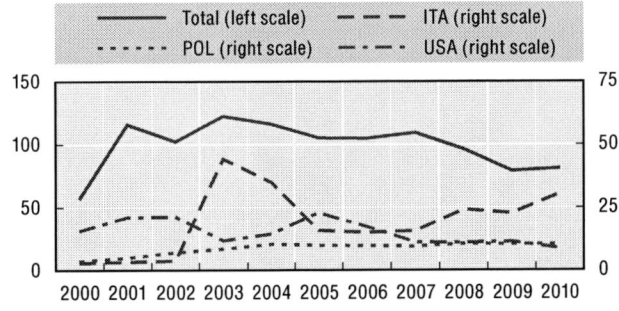

Remittance flows

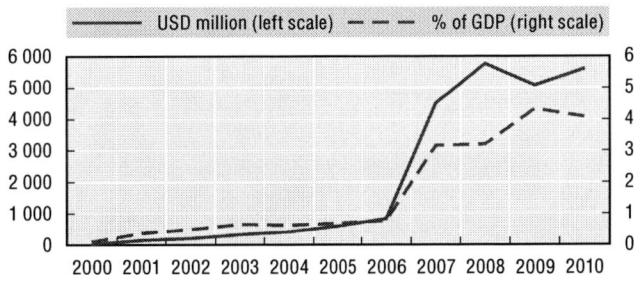

Ten main countries of destination for legal migrants in 2010 (numbers, % of total flows to the country): ITA (30416, 7.2%), POL (10250, 25%), USA (8477, 0.8%), DEU (6870, 1%), ESP (6415, 1.5%), CZE (3476, 13.7%), CAN (3095, 6.8%), HUN (1619, 6.8%), SVK (1336, 10.6%), DNK (1242, 3.7%).

Desire to emigrate, 2008-10

	Women	15-24	Highly educated	Total	Regional total
Persons who would move permanently, if they had the opportunity to do so (%)	18	32	27	19	19
Of which: Persons who are planning to move permanently in the next 12 months (%)				4	7
Of which: Persons who have already done some preparations for this move (*e.g.* visa application) (%)					..

Three main countries of desired destination: Russian Federation (20%), Germany (14%), United States (12%).

StatLink ⬛⬛ http://dx.doi.org/10.1787/888932673923

Chapter 6

Middle East and North Africa

This chapter looks at recent migration flows and diasporas from Middle East and North African countries to the OECD area. It shows that in 2010 about 380 000 new migrants from the region settled in OECD countries, accounting for about 7% of total immigration flows. In 2005/06 there were 7 million emigrants, 15 years old or older, from the region in OECD countries, of which 45% were women and 26% held a tertiary diploma. Total emigration rate for those over 15 years of age reached 2.8% for the region as a whole. The emigration rate for the highly educated reached 7.6%. Future challenges relate notably to the implication for migration of recent geopolitical changes and the need to deal with increasing cohorts of young people entering the labour market in most MENA countries.

This chapter also contains 17 country notes for Algeria, Bahrain, Egypt, Iran, Iraq, Jordan, Kuwait, Lebanon, Libya, Morocco, Qatar, Saudi Arabia, Soudan, Syria, Tunisia, United Arab Emirates and Yemen.

1. Historical migration patterns

The Middle East and North Africa is a region of widely varying national economic circumstances. The income gap is considerable between oil-producing countries with high per capita GDP (with Qatar setting a record of USD 72 000 in 2010) and a group of less-wealthy countries (Yemen being the region's poorest, with per capita GDP of USD 1 290). The oil-producing states of the Arabian peninsula (and to a lesser extent Libya) are thus in favourable economic positions – each enjoys average per capita income in excess of USD 15 000 – whereas all of the region's other countries have per capita GDP ranging between USD 2 000 and USD 5 000. This dichotomy is an old one, since Middle East oil production started up in Iran and Iraq at the very beginning of the 20th century; subsequently in Saudi Arabia, Bahrain, Kuwait and Qatar in the 1930s; and lastly, in the United Arab Emirates and Libya in the 1950s. Iran and Iraq, although rich in natural resources, nonetheless stand out today with fairly low per capita GDP (of USD 4 500 and 2 500 respectively), owing to the size of their populations but also to the conflict-ridden geopolitical circumstances that have prevailed for decades. The income gap between the two groups of countries is reflected in vastly different migration profiles, the factors driving people away being obviously far stronger in the low- and intermediate-income countries.

A second characteristic is that for over 60 years migration from the Middle East and North Africa has featured densely concentrated flows towards a limited number of destination countries. France alone takes in roughly 40% of aggregate migration from the Middle East and North Africa region to the OECD area, and the United States roughly 15%. A total of five countries – those two plus Spain, Israel and Italy – are home to roughly 5 million migrants born in the Middle East and North Africa region, accounting for 72% of the region's migrants now residing in an OECD country.

International migration from North Africa to Europe is also short-term and low-skilled. It differs fundamentally from the flows to North America that originate primarily in the Near and Middle East. Until 1974, Belgian, French and Dutch policies of admitting manual labourers from the Maghreb triggered substantial population flows, before immigration restrictions imposed after the first oil shock significantly reduced economic migration. A majority of the Maghreb-born population that had migrated to those three countries stayed there. Thus, the number of persons born in Algeria and residing in France totalled more than 1.3 million in 2005, making the Algeria/France migration corridor the largest of those originating in the Middle East and North Africa region. By way of comparison, the three next-largest migration cohorts are the 800 000 persons born in Morocco and 350 000 born in Tunisia and residing today in France, and the 500 000 Moroccan-born persons now living in Spain. Migration to Spain is more recent and stems in particular from strong economic growth in the late 1990s and early 2000s, with a low-skilled migratory profile comparable to that of France. Spain therefore became the leading destination for Moroccan migrants in 2005 – a distinction that the economic crisis triggered in 2008 may jeopardise in the short term.

It will be noted that despite the restrictions on legal economic immigration in Europe since the first oil shock, population flows into Europe have remained substantial. This is because family reunification, as governed by international law, follows economic migration with a time lag, so that when a country decides to suspend or limit economic immigration, migratory flows may in fact persist for many years in accordance with the international legislation adopted by the majority of OECD countries.

Migration to North America and the United Kingdom has stood out clearly for several decades because of its selectivity, since nearly half of the migrants from the Middle East and North Africa region living in the United States have pursued their studies into higher education, versus fewer than 20% of migrants to Mediterranean destinations. For example, the proportion of skilled migrants from Iran living in the United States exceeds 50%, which would seem to confirm the high cost of migration and the selectivity of US admission policies, and which has probably helped limit the flows of unskilled emigration.

For most of the Near East and Middle East countries, migration has therefore been "continuous", highly skilled, and aimed primarily at English-speaking countries with Australia joining the previously cited destinations as one of the main countries exerting an attraction. Historically then, it has been pull factors and the immigration policies of the OECD countries that have been the primary determinants of migration flows from the Middle East and North Africa region. Colonial ties, and the proximity between the Maghreb and France and between Morocco and Spain, are also root causes of the main population flows. The major variations from year to year depend on the political and economic circumstances of the countries on the northern shore of the Mediterranean.

2. Current profiles of emigrant populations

Flows and stocks

The data in this publication are presented in such a way as to compare recent emigration flows with older flows (towards the OECD area). As a rule, recent flows have followed the historical patterns described above, albeit with some exceptions. For example, Moroccan emigration to Spain was bolstered substantially (annual flows of nearly 100 000 persons) in 2008 (versus only 40 000 in 2000), before easing to 48 000 in 2010 as a result of the economic slowdown (Figure 6.1). This migratory corridor, the largest of

Figure 6.1. **Migrant flows from the Middle East and North Africa region to OECD countries and remittance flows, 2000-10**

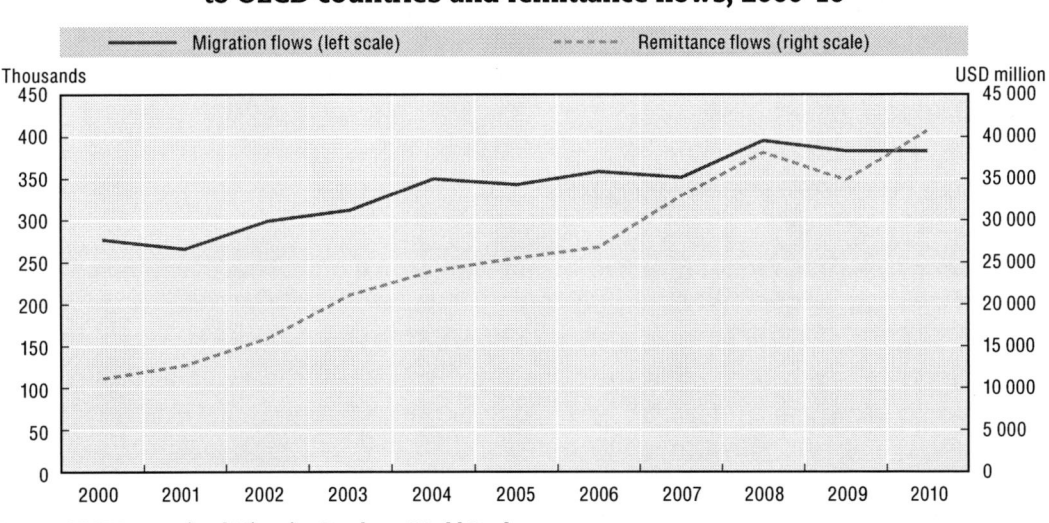

Source: OECD International Migration Database; World Bank.

StatLink ᠁ᡒᡜ *http://dx.doi.org/10.1787/888932672137*

the 2000s, was thus characterised by sharp year-on-year variations. A significant share of that immigration was recorded in 2005, when roughly 700 000 people of all nationalities combined, including nearly 65 000 Moroccans, were regularised (Khachani and Mghari, 2009). Italy also undertook massive regularisations in 2009.

Algerian emigration to France, the second-largest migratory corridor over the period, also varied sharply, from 10 000 per year in 2000 to 30 000 in 2003 and back to around 20 000 per year since then. All other bilateral migration flows remained below 20 000 per year, with Moroccan emigration to France stabilising at just below 20 000 per year and emigration from Iran to the United States rising regularly to nearly 20 000 in 2009.

In terms of flows, the United States is now the number two destination for migrants from the region (Figure 6.3). This immigration depends less on the state of the economy than flows to continental Europe, and it is more highly skilled and fast growing even if it remains at a low volume as compared with inflows from the other regions of origin. Migrants from the Middle East and North Africa in fact account for only 6% of migrants settled in the United States.

Remittances increased considerably between 2000 and 2009, tripling from USD 11 billion in 2000 to USD 38 billion in 2008, before dipping slightly in 2009 to approximately USD 35 billion as a result of the crisis (USD 41 billion in 2010). This massive influx of foreign exchange to the Southern Mediterranean is attributable to a limited number of bilateral flows, and it stems less from a rise in the number of emigrants than from substantial increases in the amount of money sent home by migrants. Egypt is the leading beneficiary of the transfers, and experienced a substantial rise in amounts received: these grew from USD 2.8 billion in 2000 to USD 8.7 billion in 2008, before dipping to USD 7.1 billion in 2009 (USD 12.5 billion in 2010).[1] Morocco experienced a similar pattern, with flows more than tripling between 2000 and 2008 before levelling off at substantial volumes, although slightly less than those of Egypt in absolute value (remittances of USD 2.2 billion in 2000 and roughly USD 6.5 billion in 2010). Throughout the Middle East and North Africa region (with the notable exception of the Gulf oil countries with low emigration rates), remittances increased significantly in percentage and showed resilience throughout the crisis, since amounts transferred decreased only very slightly in 2009 and 2010, not materially reversing the sharp growth observed between 2000 and 2008. In decreasing order of volume, the greatest increases in remittances were to Jordan (USD 1.8 billion in 2000; USD 3.6 billion in 2010); Algeria (USD 790 million in 2000;USD 2 billion in 2010); Tunisia (USD 800 million in 2000; USD 2 billion in 2010); and Syria (USD 180 million in 2000; USD 1.2 billion in 2010). In Iran, transfers remained modest in relation to the scale of the country (USD 1.2 billion in 2010) and rose primarily between 2000 and 2003, whereas in Yemen transfers were flat over the period at around USD 1.3 billion per year.

During the 2000s, remittances became a major source of income in several countries in the region, since they accounted (for example) for some 2.5% of Syrian GDP, 3.8% of Yemeni GDP, 4% of Egyptian GDP, 4.5% of Tunisian GDP, over 6% of Moroccan GDP and approximately 14% of Jordanian GDP. The rapid growth in the value and number of construction sector jobs in Morocco and Jordan in the 2000s is certainly not unrelated to the money transfers of migrants.

Figure 6.2. **Total and highly educated emigrant population aged 15 and over from the Middle East and North Africa region in the OECD area, 2005/06**

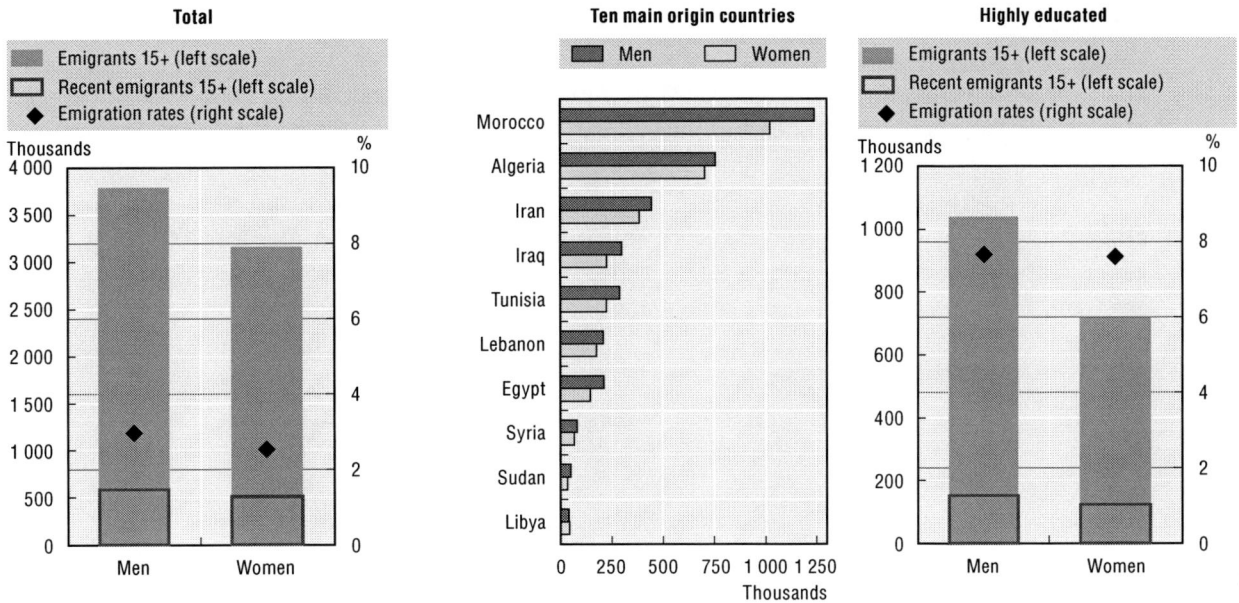

Source: Database on Immigrants in OECD Countries (DIOC 2005/06).

StatLink 🔗 http://dx.doi.org/10.1787/888932672156

In the aggregate, the number of migrants born in the Middle East and North Africa region who are living in the OECD area was estimated in 2005/06 at approximately 7 million (Figure 6.2). Morocco is the leading departure country, with an estimated diaspora of 2.3 million people in 2005/06, ahead of Algeria (1.3 million), Iran (830 000), Iraq and Tunisia (just over 500 000 each) and Egypt (360 000). This brings the region's rate of emigration to the OECD countries to 2.8%.

Figure 6.3. **Emigrant populations and migrant flows from the Middle East and North Africa region to the five main destinations within the OECD area, population aged 15 and over**

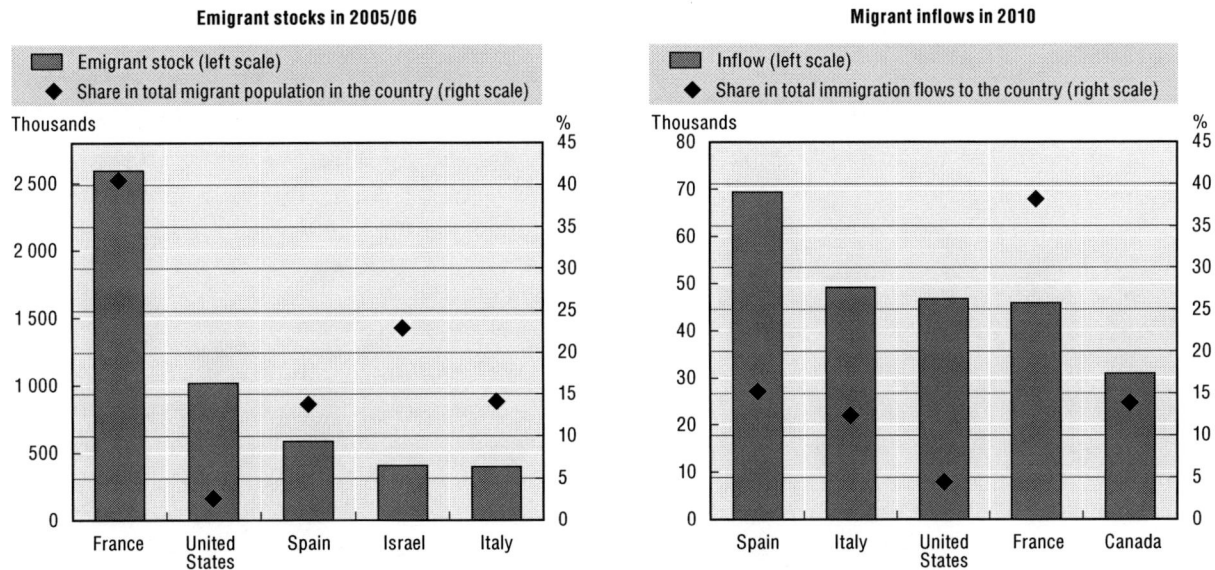

Source: Database on Immigrants in OECD Countries (DIOC 2005/06); OECD International Migration Database.

StatLink 🔗 http://dx.doi.org/10.1787/888932672175

Characteristics of emigrant populations

A majority of the migrants who have left the region are men, even if migration by women has increased and grown nearer to the volume of male migration in recent years (Table 6.1). Depending on the country, the number of men has remained between 10% and 20% greater than the number of emigrant women from the Maghreb, while the proportion of men leaving their respective countries is significantly higher notably for Egypt, Iraq, Kuwait, Qatar and Saudi Arabia. Bahrain is an exception, since it is the only country in the region from which more women than men have emigrated. The numbers of women emigrating from the Gulf are therefore fairly low, stemming from a combination of essentially economic emigration and a still fairly low women's employment rate. In contrast, in the Middle East and North Africa, the scale of family migration and greater women's participation in the workforce explain the higher proportion of migrant women.

Table 6.1. **Characteristics of migrants from the Middle East and North Africa region in the OECD area, by gender, 2005/06**

Percentage

	Regional averages (unweighted)			Regional total (weighted)		
	Men	Women	Total	Men	Women	Total
15-24	21.3	21.3	21.3	9.9	10.9	10.3
25-64	68.2	65.1	66.8	76.4	72.5	74.6
65+	10.5	13.5	11.9	13.7	16.6	15.0
Low-educated	29.1	33.6	31.3	41.8	48.5	44.8
Highly educated	37.0	34.6	35.9	27.8	23.1	25.7
Total emigration rates	3.0	2.7	2.8	3.0	2.5	2.8
Emigration rates of the highly educated	7.2	7.2	7.2	7.7	7.6	7.6

Source: Database on Immigrants in OECD Countries (DIOC 2005/06).

StatLink http://dx.doi.org/10.1787/888932675139

The data presented also yields recent and previously unpublished information on the skill level of migrants and the mobility of students. The recent period saw confirmation of the United States' attractiveness to the region's skilled migrants and students. Whichever migratory corridor is considered, the proportion of skilled migrants in flows towards the United States almost systematically equals or exceeds 40% and is never below 30%, except with respect to Yemen. This propensity to attract skilled workers and students is a feature shared with the United Kingdom and Canada, both of which took in a growing number of students between 2000 and 2009. This trend is intensifying, since in the United Kingdom the number of students admitted rose by 58% between 2004 and 2009, with corresponding increases of 51% in the United States and 11% in Canada. The United Kingdom is the destination of choice for students from the United Arab Emirates, Bahrain, Iraq, Libya and Qatar, whereas the United States ranks first for students from Saudi Arabia, Egypt, Iran, Jordan and Kuwait. In contrast, France stands out with a 7% decrease in the number of students admitted over the same period, but it remains in the top position for the absolute value of inflows. The heightened competition to attract students to English-speaking countries, where studies often cost money and are in some cases fairly onerous, is a clear departure from the situation prevailing in continental Europe, where most education remains public and free of charge, and where strategies for admitting a higher number of foreign students do not seem to lie at the core of immigration strategies.

Policies to admit students broadly overlap selective immigration policies as well as the students' interest in English-speaking universities. For example, the United Kingdom shows the highest proportion of skilled migrants from the United Arab Emirates (59%), Bahrain (over 80%), Iraq (34%), Jordan (84%), Qatar (57%) and Saudi Arabia (52%), whereas Canada is the most selective destination country for migrants from Algeria (70% of Algerian migrants in Canada being skilled), Egypt (75%), Iran (62%), Kuwait (52%), Libya (69%), Tunisia (70%) and Yemen (50%). For most of these countries, except those of the Maghreb, it is in the United States that the proportion of higher education graduates is greatest. The proportion is also high in the United Kingdom and in Canada. France ranks first only for the admission of skilled Moroccan migrants, who account for 20% of the Moroccans living in France – a proportion similar to those observed for Tunisian and Algerian migrants. Spain, Italy and Israel feature fairly low proportions of skilled migrants.

The labour market situation for migrants from the Middle East and North Africa region is hardly favourable, since their average unemployment rate in the OECD countries is 16.7%, and their average employment rate in those countries is only 47.5%, versus an unemployment rate of 7.6% and an employment rate of 58.5% for migrants originating within the OECD area (Table 6.2). This poor access to employment affects women more severely than it does for men: the employment rate differential between men and women is 25 percentage points – 58.9% for emigrant men versus 33.8% for emigrant women from the Middle East and North Africa region. While these differences in employment rates between men and women are significant, it is useful to bear in mind that they are even more so for working-age persons who have remained in their countries of origin. It would therefore be hasty to conclude that migration discourages women from working, since the exact opposite is true. Nevertheless, the over-qualification rate would seem high, since 33% of the people with a higher education degree hold low-skilled jobs. Discrimination might explain this high proportion, as would the lack of transferability of diplomas. Learning gaps between students having the same amount of schooling – as measured, for example, in the TIMSS or PISA surveys – are also likely to explain why emigrants are at a disadvantage with regard to employment.[2]

Table 6.2. **Labour market characteristics of migrants from the Middle East and North Africa region in the OECD area, by gender, 2005/06**

	Regional averages (unweighted)			Regional total (weighted)		
	Men	Women	Total	Men	Women	Total
Employment rate (%)	63.6	39.5	53.1	58.9	33.8	47.5
Unemployment rate (%)	13.0	15.7	14.0	14.8	20.6	16.7
Participation rate (%)	73.2	46.8	61.6	69.1	42.6	57.0
Total employed (thousands)	**2 129**	**1 018**	**3 146**			
Employment rate of the highly educated (%)	76.0	52.3	66.0	72.7	56.1	65.9
Unemployment rate of the highly educated (%)	8.5	12.8	9.8	9.2	11.9	10.2
Participation rate of the highly educated (%)	83.1	59.7	73.1	80.1	63.7	73.4
Highly educated employed (thousands)	**728**	**386**	**1 115**			
Persons with tertiary degrees in low- or medium-skilled jobs (%)	36.5	37.6	37.0	33.2	32.9	33.1

Source: Database on Immigrants in OECD Countries (DIOC 2005/06).

StatLink ⏩ http://dx.doi.org/10.1787/888932675158

Emigration rates and the "brain drain"

In 2005/06, the overall emigration rate from the Middle East and North Africa region to the OECD countries was 3%, and the emigration rate of highly skilled persons was 8% (Table 6.2). Lebanon (12%), Morocco (10%) and Tunisia (6%) recorded the highest overall emigration rates, whereas Morocco (16%) and Algeria, Kuwait and Syria (13% each) were the countries in the region most affected by highly skilled emigration. Since 2000, overall emigration rates have remained stable, and emigration rates for the highly skilled have dipped slightly, by 1 percentage point. This trend is attributable to an overall increase in the region's highly skilled population and not to a lesser selectiveness of emigration.

A number of countries in the region show very high emigration rates for doctors, and low rates for nurses. With regard to doctors, the Maghreb would seem to be experiencing particular difficulty, since 15% of Tunisian doctors, 23% of Algerian doctors and 28% of Moroccan doctors were practising abroad in 2000. Egypt has not been spared, since 16% of its doctors have emigrated – a proportion that is close to those of Syria (17%), Iraq (18%), Iran (13%) and Jordan (8%). Among the Gulf countries, only Kuwait has a significant emigration rate for doctors (11.5%), which can be explained by the number of doctors with at least some foreign training, which is less true of the other countries. Nurses are far less likely to leave their countries of origin, with the exception of (once again) Morocco (emigration rate of 20.5%) and Algeria (12.4%). Elsewhere in the region, emigration rates for nurses are all below 2%. The massive exodus of doctors will become even more problematic as rising average income levels and longer life expectancies in the region contribute to sharp growth in demand for medical services over the coming years. The doctor shortage already observed north of the Mediterranean may affect the other shores as well if current expatriation rates persist.

3. Future trends and challenges

The "Arab Spring", which began in Tunisia and affected a number of countries in the Middle East and North Africa, will have medium-term consequences on migratory flows from and to the region. In the very short term, political or armed conflicts will have triggered an increase in emigration – towards Europe in particular – from Tunisia, Egypt, Syria and Libya. Regional migration has also intensified, but it is not certain that these migrations are definitive or that they ultimately represent significant populations. In the medium term, the migratory consequences of the ongoing political shifts are less predictable. A deepening of democracy would likely limit the political factors driving people away and would therefore limit outflows; sustained instability could have economic – and thus migratory – consequences. It is therefore too early to advance realistic assumptions about political and economic developments in the region or their impact on the desire of the Middle East and North Africa region's populations to leave.

The importance of diasporas to the democratic movements in the Middle East and North Africa region warrants mention, due to their support in the international press, on the Internet and via social networks; their denunciation of the authoritarian excesses of certain regimes; and their subsequent support for mobilisation when the movements actually started happening. The year 2011 will therefore have shown the major impact of migration in the exchange of values and political practices. The current Tunisian president, Moncef Marzouki, who was long exiled in Europe, personifies and symbolises this decisive participation of the diasporas in the historic events of the Arab Spring.

Apart from its political dimension, the Arab Spring has also shed light on the extent of the social crisis endured by young people in North Africa and the Near East. In the coming years, unemployment, underemployment and massive underuse of young persons' skills – often in excess of 50%, even for young graduates – will obviously continue to be among the chief motivations for emigration to the OECD countries. The revolutions and political reforms of 2011 will have provided at least a partial response to the yearnings for freedom expressed by the region's youth, but social and economic dissatisfaction remains strong. Meanwhile it is clear that for today's leading destination countries (France, the United States, Spain and Italy), persistently high unemployment (roughly 9% in Italy and the United States at the beginning of 2011, 10% in France and nearly 23% in Spain) and the outlook for low growth beyond that would not suggest any outreach in migratory policies in the short term. The governments of the Middle East and North Africa region need to start by instituting employment policies likely to create jobs for the young people victimised by unemployment, before they rely on emigration as a lever of adjustment. Given the observed magnitude of the employment deficit, emigration may play only a secondary role.

Notes

1. In Egypt's case however, these flows stem from the extent of migratory movements to other countries in the region, since migration to the OECD countries is both long-standing and limited.

2. Dubai, Jordan, Tunisia and Qatar took part in the OECD PISA 2009 Survey. In mathematics, their students obtained respective scores of 453, 387, 371 and 368, versus an average of 496 for the OECD countries. Also, 8th grade students from a number of countries Lebanon, Jordan, Tunisia, Iran, Bahrain, Syria, Algeria, Oman, Kuwait, Saudi Arabia and Qatar took part in the Trends in International Mathematics and Sciences Study (TIMSS) survey of the Institute of Education Sciences in 2007, and scored 449 (Lebanon), 427 (Jordan), 420 (Tunisia), 403 (Iran), 398 (Bahrain), 395 (Syria), 391 (Egypt), 387 (Algeria), 372 (Oman), 354 (Kuwait), 329 (Saudi Arabia) and 307 (Qatar), versus 508 in the United States. The two surveys therefore revealed substantial differences in levels of learning within the region, but also substantial gaps in the levels of the students as compared to those of the OECD countries.

Country Notes

Middle East and North Africa

Total population 2010 (millions)	35.5	Algeria compared to:	World	Region
Population growth 2010 (%)	1.5	Human Development Index (HDI)	96/187	11/19
GDP per capita 2010 (current USD)	4 495	GDP per capita	95/194	11/18
GDP growth 2010 (%)	3.0	Emigration rate	74/203	4/18
Poverty rate 2010 (USD PPP 2 a day, in %)	..	Emigration rate of the highly educated	53/157	2/16

Age structure of the population 0+ (2010): "0-14": 21%; "15-24": 27%; "25-64": 48%; "65+": 5%.
Level of education of the population 15+ (2010): "Low": 50%; "Medium": 39%; "High": 11%.

Emigrant population living in OECD countries

Immigrant population

Emigrant population: persons born in Algeria living abroad

	2000						2005/06		
	All destinations			OECD destinations			OECD destinations		
Population 15+	Men	Women	Total	Men	Women	Total	Men	Women	Total
Emigrant population (thousands)	696.0	634.4	1 330.4	692.2	632.2	1 324.4	757.0	704.4	1 461.4
Recent emigrants (thousands)	..	..	..	36.7	28.6	65.3	69.1	66.6	135.7
15-24 (%)	4.2	4.3	4.3	4.1	4.2	4.2	4.9	5.2	5.0
25-64 (%)	74.6	71.8	73.3	74.6	71.9	73.3	70.9	69.6	70.3
65+ (%)	21.2	23.9	22.4	21.2	23.9	22.5	24.2	25.2	24.7
Low-educated (%)	53.4	57.7	55.5	53.5	57.8	55.5	48.8	54.7	51.7
Highly educated (%)	17.7	15.2	16.5	17.6	15.2	16.5	20.6	18.0	19.3
Total emigration rates (%)	6.5	5.9	6.2	6.4	5.9	6.2	6.1	5.8	5.9
Emigration rates of the highly educated (%)	14.2	15.7	14.8	14.1	15.6	14.7	13.2	12.5	12.9

Main destinations in 2005/06

	Total		Recent emigrants	Women	Highly educated	15-24	Total in 2000
Population 15+	Thousands	%	%	%	%	%	Thousands
France	1 305.9	89.4	8.9	49.5	17.3	4.9	1 210.6
Spain	36.6	2.5	49.4	29.8	22.0	5.7	24.8
Canada	28.9	2.0	47.1	43.7	69.9	10.8	17.4
Belgium	18.5	1.3	–	45.0	–	–	14.3
Italy	14.9	1.0	35.1	36.4	10.0	–	11.4
United States	14.4	1.0	24.4	41.8	51.8	8.8	10.5
United Kingdom	12.1	0.8	–	–	57.8	–	9.9
Israel	11.2	0.8	16.7	49.4	28.0	0.4	12.1
Switzerland	6.5	0.4	25.5	38.4	47.3	–	5.8
Netherlands	4.3	0.3	–	–	–	–	–

Labour market indicators of persons born in Algeria living in OECD countries

Population 15-64	2000 Men	2000 Women	2000 Total	2005/06 Men	2005/06 Women	2005/06 Total
Employment-population ratio (%)	62.2	43.6	53.4	61.4	43.5	52.8
Unemployment rate (%)	20.1	24.5	21.9	18.3	24.0	20.6
Participation rate (%)	77.8	57.7	68.4	75.1	57.3	66.5
Total employed (thousands)	**336.0**	**208.5**	**544.5**	**350.5**	**228.9**	**579.4**
Employment rates of the highly educated (%)	78.1	67.5	73.4	87.4	74.0	81.3
Unemployment rates of the highly educated (%)	11.3	12.2	11.6	11.5	14.2	12.6
Highly educated in low- and medium-skilled jobs (%)	17.9	19.1	18.4	27.8	27.1	27.5
Highly educated employed (thousands)	**85.2**	**59.0**	**144.2**	**106.0**	**72.7**	**178.7**
Legislators, senior officials and managers	11.0	6.2	9.2	10.2	6.2	8.6
Professionals	14.4	11.9	13.4	14.9	13.2	14.2
Life science and health professionals	3.3	2.5	3.0	3.2	2.5	2.9
Teaching professionals	2.7	4.7	3.5	3.1	5.5	4.1
Technicians and associate professionals	13.9	20.3	16.4	13.2	18.2	15.2
Clerks	5.4	20.7	11.4	5.4	17.0	10.1
Service, shop and market sales workers	7.6	20.9	12.8	8.3	20.2	13.1
Skilled agricultural and fishery workers	1.9	0.7	1.4	1.5	0.6	1.1
Craft and related trades workers	19.3	2.1	12.6	19.5	2.3	12.6
Plant and machine operators and assemblers	15.4	2.9	10.6	15.2	2.4	10.0
Elementary occupations	11.0	14.3	12.3	11.7	19.8	14.9

Distribution of employment by occupation (%), population 15+

Persons born in Algeria and their native-born children, population 15+

Living in:	Europe	United States	Australia
2008	Thousands	Thousands	Thousands
Native-born children	1 423.5	..	..
Foreign-born	1 133.2	12.1	3.4
Total	2 556.8	..	..

International students from Algeria in OECD countries

Five main destinations	2004	2005	2006	2007	2008	2009
France	22 250	22 228	21 641	20 125	18 780	19 171
Canada	1 161	..	180	1 197	796	1 109
United Kingdom	452	544	466	477	335	261
United States	148	149	137	148	179	169
Germany	..	..	..	..	146	144
Total	24 151	23 087	22 577	22 157	20 595	21 351

Legal migrant flows to the OECD
Thousands

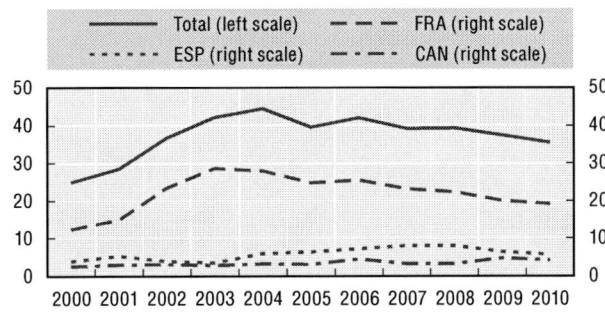

Remittance flows

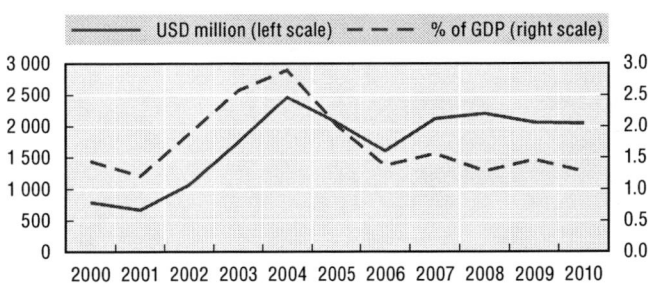

Ten main countries of destination for legal migrants in 2010 (numbers, % of total flows to the country): FRA (19135, 14.1%), ESP (5720, 1.3%), CAN (4120, 1.5%), DEU (1539, 0.2%), USA (1305, 0.1%), ITA (1199, 0.3%), BEL (1074, 0.2%), CHE (296, 0.2%), AUT (236, 0.2%), POL (149, 0.4%).

Desire to emigrate, 2008-10

	Women	15-24	Highly educated	Total	Regional total
Persons who would move permanently, if they had the opportunity to do so (%)	23	42	24	29	21
Of which: Persons who are planning to move permanently in the next 12 months (%)				26	16
Of which: Persons who have already done some preparations for this move (*e.g.* visa application) (%)					46

Three main countries of desired destination: France (42%), Canada (12%), United Kingdom (11%).

StatLink http://dx.doi.org/10.1787/888932673942

	World	Region
Total population 2010 (millions)	1.3	
Population growth 2010 (%)	7.6	
GDP per capita 2009 (current USD)	17 609	
GDP growth 2008 (%)	6.3	
Poverty rate 2010 (USD PPP 2 a day, in %)	..	

Bahrain compared to:	World	Region
Human Development Index (HDI)	42/187	3/19
GDP per capita	42/194	4/18
Emigration rate	146/203	11/18
Emigration rate of the highly educated	117/157	10/16

Age structure of the population 0+ (2010): "0-14": 15%; "15-24": 20%; "25-64": 63%; "65+": 2%.
Level of education of the population 15+ (2010): "Low": 21%; "Medium": 67%; "High": 12%.

Emigrant population living in OECD countries

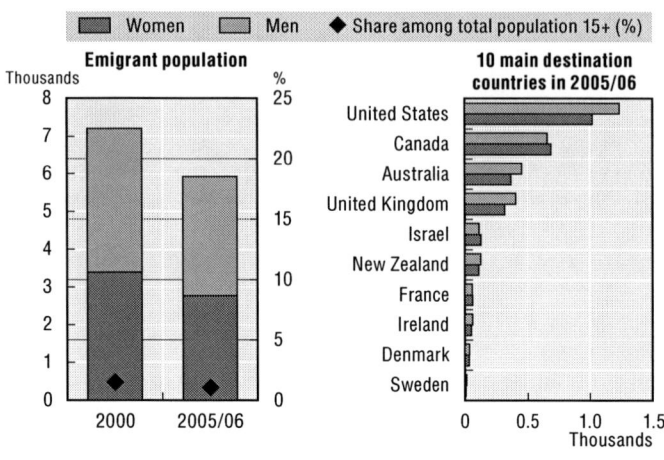

Immigrant population

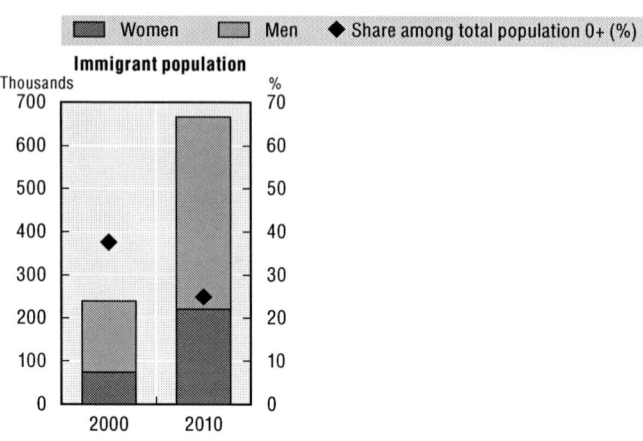

Emigrant population: persons born in Bahrain living abroad

	2000						2005/06		
	All destinations			OECD destinations			OECD destinations		
Population 15+	Men	Women	Total	Men	Women	Total	Men	Women	Total
Emigrant population (thousands)	39.9	40.9	80.9	3.8	3.4	7.2	3.2	2.8	5.9
Recent emigrants (thousands)	..	..	..	0.8	0.5	1.3	0.6	0.4	1.0
15-24 (%)	30.9	31.1	31.0	39.1	37.2	38.2	37.6	31.0	34.5
25-64 (%)	64.4	62.5	63.5	59.6	61.2	60.3	60.5	67.7	63.9
65+ (%)	4.7	6.4	5.6	1.4	1.6	1.5	1.9	1.3	1.6
Low-educated (%)	45.1	43.8	44.4	15.2	17.6	16.4	7.1	14.5	10.6
Highly educated (%)	15.0	16.2	15.6	43.9	39.2	41.6	57.8	58.2	58.0
Total emigration rates (%)	12.5	17.9	14.7	1.3	1.8	1.5	1.0	1.3	1.1
Emigration rates of the highly educated (%)	18.0	26.5	21.7	6.0	7.0	6.4	4.6	6.6	5.4

Main destinations in 2005/06

	Total		Recent emigrants	Women	Highly educated	15-24	Total in 2000
Population 15+	Thousands	%	%	%	%	%	Thousands
United States	2.3	38.1	12.7	45.1	59.3	27.2	1.8
Canada	1.4	22.8	18.9	51.1	59.3	49.3	0.9
Australia	0.8	13.8	31.0	44.8	50.1	43.4	0.4
United Kingdom	–	–	–	–	–	–	3.5
Israel	–	–	–	–	–	–	–
New Zealand	–	–	–	–	–	–	0.1
France	–	–	–	–	–	–	0.1
Ireland	–	–	–	–	–	–	0.1
Denmark	–	–	–	–	–	–	0.1

Labour market indicators of persons born in Bahrain living in OECD countries

Population 15-64	2000			2005/06		
	Men	Women	Total	Men	Women	Total
Employment-population ratio (%)	62.7	53.2	58.2	65.8	62.4	64.1
Unemployment rate (%)	8.5	7.1	7.9	5.0	7.9	6.4
Participation rate (%)	68.6	57.2	63.2	69.2	67.7	68.5
Total employed (thousands)	**2.3**	**1.7**	**4.0**	**1.3**	**1.2**	**2.5**
Employment rates of the highly educated (%)	70.4	63.2	67.2	85.1	74.3	79.9
Unemployment rates of the highly educated (%)	8.1	4.8	6.7	2.8	3.9	3.3
Highly educated in low- and medium-skilled jobs (%)	19.3	27.4	22.8	22.2	18.9	20.6
Highly educated employed (thousands)	**1.1**	**0.8**	**2.0**	**1.0**	**0.8**	**1.8**
Legislators, senior officials and managers	20.3	12.9	16.7	33.6	2.9	19.1
Professionals	24.0	20.7	22.4	19.1	27.2	22.9
Life science and health professionals	3.0	3.0	3.0	3.1	1.9	2.5
Teaching professionals	2.8	7.7	5.2	2.1	20.0	11.0
Technicians and associate professionals	14.1	16.2	15.1	14.3	36.7	24.9
Clerks	9.2	24.9	16.7	7.4	19.4	13.1
Service, shop and market sales workers	13.7	17.2	15.4	11.4	9.5	10.5
Skilled agricultural and fishery workers	0.6	0.2	0.4	0.1	0.1	0.1
Craft and related trades workers	8.2	2.6	5.5	2.6	2.2	2.4
Plant and machine operators and assemblers	4.0	0.9	2.5	4.6	0.1	2.5
Elementary occupations	6.0	4.4	5.2	7.0	1.8	4.5

Left side label: Distribution of employment by occupation (%), population 15+

Persons born in Bahrain and their native-born children, population 15+

Living in:	Europe	United States	Australia
2008	Thousands	Thousands	Thousands
Native-born children	1.5	..	..
Foreign-born	1.9	..	0.9
Total	3.3	..	..

International students from Bahrain in OECD countries

Five main destinations	2004	2005	2006	2007	2008	2009
United Kingdom	871	964	988	953	980	989
United States	444	394	386	401	394	424
Australia	122	183	210	256	253	234
Canada	101	..	99	105	99	99
New Zealand	16	16	18	29	51	74
Total	1 609	1 597	1 733	1 785	1 861	1 964

Legal migrant flows to the OECD
Thousands

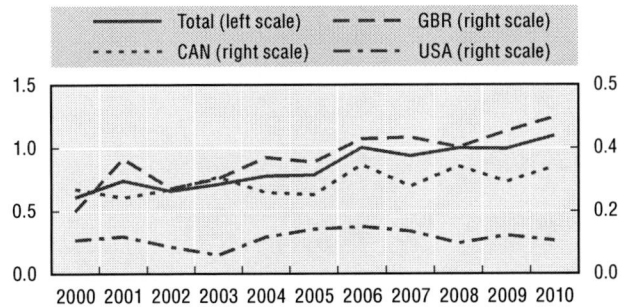

Ten main countries of destination for legal migrants in 2010 (numbers, % of total flows to the country): GBR (498, 0.1%), CAN (340, 0.1%), USA (104, 0%), DEU (89, 0%), JPN (27, 0%), CHE (8, 0%), AUS (7, 0%), FRA (5, 0%), KOR (3, 0%), IRL (2, 0%).

Desire to emigrate, 2008-10

	Women	15-24	Highly educated	Total	Regional total
Persons who would move permanently, if they had the opportunity to do so (%)	4	6	8	5	21
Of which: Persons who are planning to move permanently in the next 12 months (%)				..	16
Of which: Persons who have already done some preparations for this move (*e.g.* visa application) (%)					46

StatLink http://dx.doi.org/10.1787/888932673961

Total population 2010 (millions)	81.1	Egypt compared to:	World	Region
Population growth 2010 (%)	1.7	Human Development Index (HDI)	112/187	13/19
GDP per capita 2010 (current USD)	2 698	GDP per capita	123/194	15/18
GDP growth 2010 (%)	5.1	Emigration rate	160/203	13/18
Poverty rate 2005 (USD PPP 2 a day, in %)	18.5	Emigration rate of the highly educated	136/157	11/16

Age structure of the population 0+ (2010): "0-14": 20%; "15-24": 32%; "25-64": 44%; "65+": 5%.
Level of education of the population 15+ (2010): "Low": 40%; "Medium": 49%; "High": 11%.

Emigrant population living in OECD countries

Immigrant population

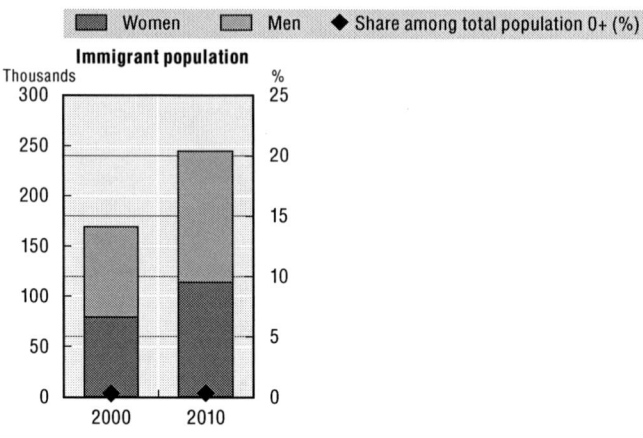

Emigrant population: persons born in Egypt living abroad

	2000						2005/06		
	All destinations			OECD destinations			OECD destinations		
Population 15+	Men	Women	Total	Men	Women	Total	Men	Women	Total
Emigrant population (thousands)	203.2	145.7	348.9	187.6	139.6	327.2	212.3	146.5	358.8
Recent emigrants (thousands)	..	..	..	27.9	17.3	45.2	28.8	20.8	49.6
15-24 (%)	5.4	6.2	5.7	5.5	6.0	5.7	6.0	7.8	6.8
25-64 (%)	79.3	68.9	74.9	78.6	69.0	74.5	77.6	68.5	73.9
65+ (%)	15.3	24.9	19.3	15.9	25.0	19.8	16.4	23.7	19.4
Low-educated (%)	18.2	26.2	21.5	16.1	25.7	20.2	14.8	18.8	16.5
Highly educated (%)	50.6	39.0	45.8	53.0	39.7	47.4	54.3	47.1	51.3
Total emigration rates (%)	1.0	0.7	0.8	0.9	0.6	0.8	0.9	0.6	0.7
Emigration rates of the highly educated (%)	4.7	5.9	5.1	4.6	5.7	4.9	3.3	3.8	3.5

Main destinations in 2005/06

	Total		Recent emigrants	Women	Highly educated	15-24	Total in 2000
Population 15+	Thousands	%	%	%	%	%	Thousands
United States	125.0	34.8	16.0	42.0	64.6	9.1	107.6
Italy	41.1	11.5	18.3	34.1	25.8	5.8	32.3
Canada	38.7	10.8	14.1	46.8	73.8	8.9	34.2
Australia	31.8	8.8	6.3	49.0	43.0	5.7	32.2
France	26.2	7.3	12.0	35.1	42.2	5.2	21.1
Israel	21.0	5.9	0.2	54.9	24.8	0.5	19.2
Greece	18.8	5.2	12.4	38.1	28.2	–	32.4
United Kingdom	18.7	5.2	–	34.8	63.2	–	23.2
Netherlands	12.4	3.5	20.0	32.8	35.5	–	2.1
Austria	9.2	2.6	–	30.8	45.1	–	8.4

Labour market indicators of persons born in Egypt living in OECD countries

Population 15-64	2000			2005/06		
	Men	Women	Total	Men	Women	Total
Employment-population ratio (%)	79.7	48.6	67.3	80.7	47.8	68.1
Unemployment rate (%)	7.6	9.2	8.1	8.2	11.9	9.2
Participation rate (%)	86.2	53.5	73.2	87.9	54.3	75.0
Total employed (thousands)	**122.1**	**49.5**	**171.6**	**140.0**	**51.7**	**191.7**
Employment rates of the highly educated (%)	84.6	57.7	74.8	92.0	65.4	81.8
Unemployment rates of the highly educated (%)	5.8	7.8	6.4	6.1	10.4	7.4
Highly educated in low- and medium-skilled jobs (%)	31.3	33.8	32.0	37.6	35.6	37.1
Highly educated employed (thousands)	**71.6**	**28.0**	**99.6**	**82.3**	**34.5**	**116.8**
Legislators, senior officials and managers	19.1	11.2	17.0	17.4	9.5	15.5
Professionals	23.2	23.1	23.2	17.8	26.2	19.8
Life science and health professionals	5.9	5.1	5.7	4.5	12.2	6.0
Teaching professionals	2.7	6.7	3.6	1.7	5.6	2.5
Technicians and associate professionals	11.5	16.1	12.7	10.1	15.6	11.4
Clerks	4.8	23.1	9.5	4.0	21.0	8.1
Service, shop and market sales workers	12.7	15.6	13.4	15.7	13.9	15.2
Skilled agricultural and fishery workers	0.6	0.3	0.5	0.8	0.6	0.7
Craft and related trades workers	11.6	1.4	9.0	17.8	2.5	14.1
Plant and machine operators and assemblers	6.6	1.6	5.3	6.7	1.2	5.4
Elementary occupations	10.0	7.7	9.4	9.8	9.6	9.7

Distribution of employment by occupation (%), population 15+

Persons born in Egypt and their native-born children, population 15+

Living in:	Europe	United States	Australia
2008	Thousands	Thousands	Thousands
Native-born children	63.7	85.3	11.3
Foreign-born	139.8	169.8	40.7
Total	203.5	255.1	52.0

International students from Egypt in OECD countries

Five main destinations	2004	2005	2006	2007	2008	2009
United States	1 822	1 644	1 563	1 701	1 768	1 884
United Kingdom	799	804	962	1 204	1 395	1 439
France	849	886	926	862	1 032	1 190
Germany	..	..	..	..	1 017	1 139
Canada	452	..	420	498	711	1 036
Total	4 510	3 978	4 653	5 225	7 162	8 015

Legal migrant flows to the OECD
Thousands

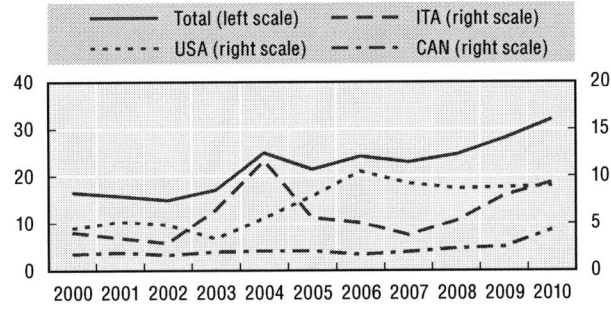

Remittance flows

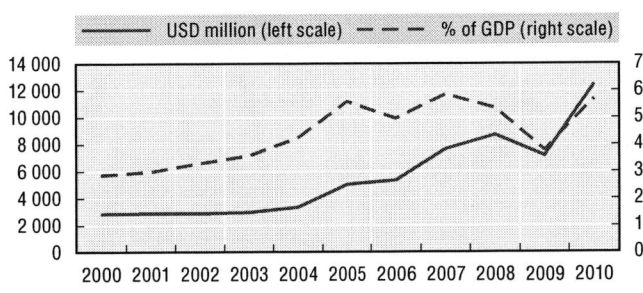

Ten main countries of destination for legal migrants in 2010 (numbers, % of total flows to the country): ITA (9345, 2.2%), USA (8978, 0.9%), CAN (4305, 1.5%), DEU (2057, 0.3%), GBR (1149, 0.2%), AUS (1035, 0.5%), FRA (960, 0.2%), JPN (635, 0.2%), POL (441, 1.1%), NLD (425, 0.4%).

Desire to emigrate, 2008-10

	Women	15-24	Highly educated	Total	Regional total
Persons who would move permanently, if they had the opportunity to do so (%)	12	27	22	19	21
Of which: Persons who are planning to move permanently in the next 12 months (%)				15	16
Of which: Persons who have already done some preparations for this move (*e.g.* visa application) (%)					46

Three main countries of desired destination: Saudi Arabia (34%), Kuwait (11%), United States (10%).

StatLink http://dx.doi.org/10.1787/888932673980

			Iran compared to:	World	Region
Total population 2010 (millions)		74.0	Human Development Index (HDI)	88/187	8/19
Population growth 2010 (%)		1.1	GDP per capita	94/194	10/18
GDP per capita 2009 (current USD)		4 526	Emigration rate	136/203	9/18
GDP growth 2009 (%)		1.8	Emigration rate of the highly educated	101/157	7/16
Poverty rate 2005 (USD PPP 2 a day, in %)		8.0			

Age structure of the population 0+ (2010): "0-14": 22%; "15-24": 23%; "25-64": 50%; "65+": 5%.
Level of education of the population 15+ (2010): "Low": 43%; "Medium": 43%; "High": 14%.

Emigrant population living in OECD countries

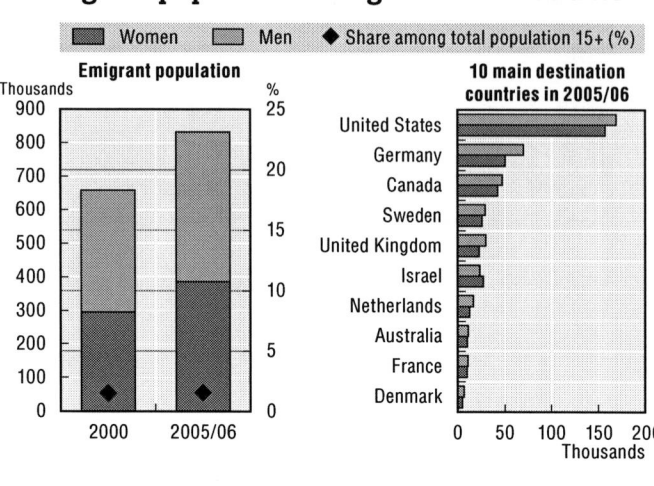

Immigrant population

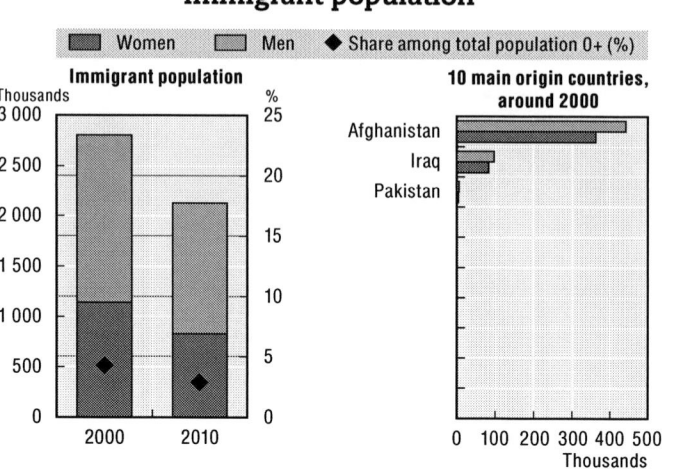

Emigrant population: persons born in Iran living abroad

	2000						2005/06		
	All destinations			OECD destinations			OECD destinations		
Population 15+	Men	Women	Total	Men	Women	Total	Men	Women	Total
Emigrant population (thousands)	389.5	317.6	707.1	361.9	295.8	657.8	445.8	387.0	832.9
Recent emigrants (thousands)	..	..	..	39.5	42.5	82.0	59.7	62.5	122.2
15-24 (%)	10.1	11.4	10.7	9.7	11.1	10.4	10.6	10.5	10.6
25-64 (%)	80.2	76.8	78.7	81.1	77.5	79.5	77.5	75.2	76.4
65+ (%)	9.7	11.8	10.6	9.2	11.3	10.2	11.9	14.3	13.0
Low-educated (%)	19.3	25.8	22.2	17.0	23.5	19.9	15.7	20.6	18.0
Highly educated (%)	47.0	37.2	42.6	49.2	39.1	44.7	50.5	42.5	46.8
Total emigration rates (%)	1.8	1.5	1.6	1.6	1.4	1.5	1.8	1.6	1.7
Emigration rates of the highly educated (%)	9.1	7.9	8.6	8.9	7.8	8.4	7.2	6.6	6.9

Main destinations in 2005/06

	Total		Recent emigrants	Women	Highly educated	15-24	Total in 2000
Population 15+	Thousands	%	%	%	%	%	Thousands
United States	326.7	39.2	12.4	48.2	57.4	6.7	281.1
Germany	120.0	14.4	9.1	41.8	29.6	12.3	69.2
Canada	89.7	10.8	27.6	47.3	61.4	17.5	68.5
Sweden	54.6	6.6	14.8	46.9	34.1	14.6	50.3
United Kingdom	52.0	6.2	30.0	43.2	50.8	17.3	39.6
Israel	50.0	6.0	5.0	53.9	17.6	1.7	53.2
Netherlands	28.9	3.5	5.9	43.1	26.4	18.0	–
Australia	20.8	2.5	22.2	47.6	45.3	15.4	17.2
France	20.3	2.4	12.4	47.0	63.6	6.2	17.9
Denmark	11.4	1.4	12.6	41.8	35.9	12.4	10.8

Labour market indicators of persons born in Iran living in OECD countries

Population 15-64	2000			2005/06		
	Men	Women	Total	Men	Women	Total
Employment-population ratio (%)	77.6	50.1	65.2	72.7	53.7	64.0
Unemployment rate (%)	6.8	9.7	7.8	11.6	11.7	11.7
Participation rate (%)	83.3	55.5	70.8	82.3	60.8	72.4
Total employed (thousands)	**214.5**	**113.5**	**328.0**	**260.6**	**162.5**	**423.2**
Employment rates of the highly educated (%)	85.4	63.1	76.9	90.8	70.0	81.8
Unemployment rates of the highly educated (%)	4.9	8.3	6.0	7.8	8.1	7.9
Highly educated in low- and medium-skilled jobs (%)	28.8	34.1	30.5	29.0	33.8	30.8
Highly educated employed (thousands)	**129.1**	**59.4**	**188.5**	**156.7**	**92.3**	**248.9**
Legislators, senior officials and managers	17.0	8.8	14.1	17.5	6.8	13.5
Professionals	29.4	20.7	26.4	24.6	21.7	23.5
Life science and health professionals	4.7	6.3	5.3	7.0	6.8	6.9
Teaching professionals	3.7	5.3	4.2	2.6	4.2	3.2
Technicians and associate professionals	11.9	17.9	14.0	11.2	17.3	13.5
Clerks	4.5	14.5	8.0	4.5	14.5	8.2
Service, shop and market sales workers	12.2	28.6	18.0	10.9	27.9	17.2
Skilled agricultural and fishery workers	0.3	0.1	0.2	0.3	1.6	0.8
Craft and related trades workers	8.2	2.0	6.0	11.6	2.7	8.3
Plant and machine operators and assemblers	10.3	2.0	7.4	13.3	1.7	9.0
Elementary occupations	6.2	5.3	5.9	5.7	5.3	5.5

Distribution of employment by occupation (%), population 15+

Persons born in Iran and their native-born children, population 15+

Living in:	Europe	United States	Australia
2008	Thousands	Thousands	Thousands
Native-born children	58.9	102.5	..
Foreign-born	313.3	375.5	14.2
Total	372.2	478.0	..

International students from Iran in OECD countries

Five main destinations	2004	2005	2006	2007	2008	2009
United States	2 321	2 351	2 506	2 857	3 063	3 475
United Kingdom	1 436	1 752	2 016	2 454	2 400	2 849
Germany	..	..	..	..	2 080	2 352
Canada	708	..	1 515	1 716	2 086	2 047
France	1 441	1 491	1 607	1 690	1 728	1 772
Total	8 021	8 229	10 730	12 314	16 479	20 172

Legal migrant flows to the OECD
Thousands

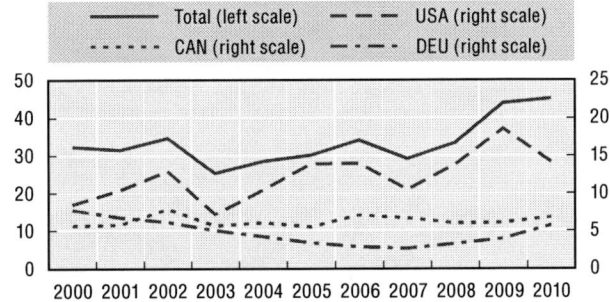

Remittance flows

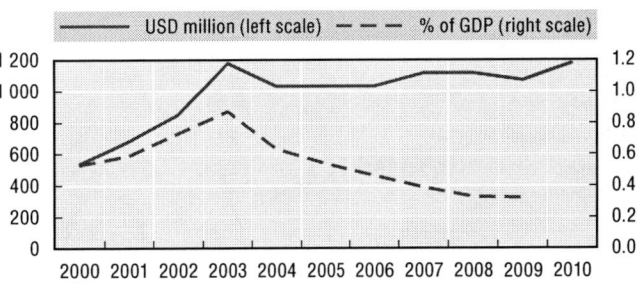

Ten main countries of destination for legal migrants in 2010 (numbers, % of total flows to the country): USA (14182, 1.4%), CAN (6815, 2.4%), DEU (5695, 0.8%), GBR (4401, 0.9%), SWE (2820, 3.7%), AUS (2107, 1%), AUT (1631, 5.2%), TUR (1539, 5.2%), ITA (744, 0.2%), NLD (689, 0.7%).

Desire to emigrate, 2008-10

	Women	15-24	Highly educated	Total	Regional total
Persons who would move permanently, if they had the opportunity to do so (%)	15	31	33	21	21
Of which: Persons who are planning to move permanently in the next 12 months (%)				..	16
Of which: Persons who have already done some preparations for this move (*e.g.* visa application) (%)					46

StatLink ᴍᴤᴾ *http://dx.doi.org/10.1787/888932673999*

Total population 2010 (millions)	32.0	**Iraq compared to:**	**World**	**Region**
Population growth 2010 (%)	3.0	Human Development Index (HDI)	132/187	17/19
GDP per capita 2010 (current USD)	2 565	GDP per capita	126/194	16/18
GDP growth 2010 (%)	0.8	Emigration rate	114/203	5/18
Poverty rate 2007 (USD PPP 2 a day, in %)	25.3	Emigration rate of the highly educated	92/157	6/16

Age structure of the population 0+ (2010): "0-14": 20%; "15-24": 43%; "25-64": 34%; "65+": 3%.
Level of education of the population 15+ (2010): "Low": 64%; "Medium": 26%; "High": 10%.

Emigrant population living in OECD countries

Immigrant population

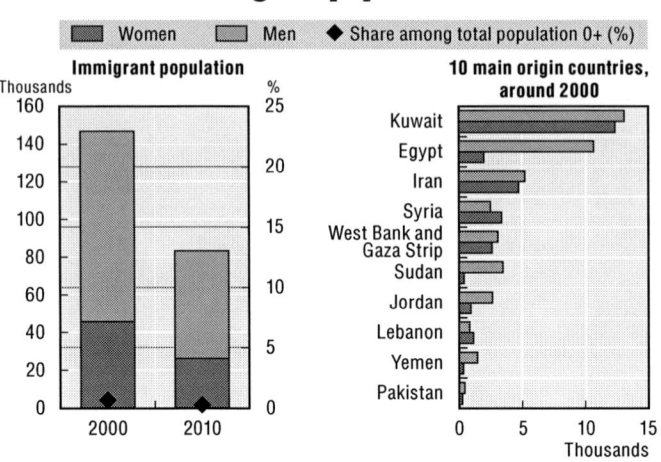

Emigrant population: persons born in Iraq living abroad

	2000						2005/06		
	All destinations			OECD destinations			OECD destinations		
Population 15+	Men	Women	Total	Men	Women	Total	Men	Women	Total
Emigrant population (thousands)	246.6	166.2	412.8	239.4	162.5	401.9	300.7	225.4	526.1
Recent emigrants (thousands)	..	..	..	61.5	37.5	99.0	61.7	53.0	114.7
15-24 (%)	14.7	13.1	14.0	14.7	12.9	13.9	17.2	17.5	17.3
25-64 (%)	76.2	72.8	74.8	76.1	72.8	74.8	71.7	68.1	70.2
65+ (%)	9.1	14.2	11.1	9.3	14.3	11.3	11.1	14.3	12.5
Low-educated (%)	40.6	51.4	44.9	41.0	51.6	45.3	41.4	47.9	44.2
Highly educated (%)	29.5	21.0	26.1	29.0	20.8	25.7	27.6	23.0	25.6
Total emigration rates (%)	3.3	2.3	2.8	3.2	2.2	2.7	3.5	2.7	3.1
Emigration rates of the highly educated (%)	9.0	6.9	8.2	8.6	6.7	7.9	8.7	7.6	8.3

Main destinations in 2005/06

	Total		Recent emigrants	Women	Highly educated	15-24	Total in 2000
Population 15+	Thousands	%	%	%	%	%	Thousands
United States	105.1	20.0	18.3	47.7	30.9	13.5	82.5
Germany	74.5	14.2	14.8	34.5	17.9	21.3	47.8
Israel	72.2	13.7	0.2	49.9	12.5	0.1	73.8
Sweden	72.1	13.7	40.2	44.0	28.5	24.9	53.6
United Kingdom	46.5	8.8	31.6	34.5	39.2	20.7	29.1
Netherlands	32.1	6.1	12.6	38.1	21.7	20.4	20.9
Canada	31.5	6.0	27.0	46.8	42.4	18.7	23.0
Australia	29.2	5.5	31.6	47.4	25.1	20.5	21.2
Denmark	17.6	3.3	16.0	43.9	21.6	25.3	13.4
Norway	12.2	2.3	66.8	39.4	17.3	28.2	11.6

Labour market indicators of persons born in Iraq living in OECD countries

Population 15-64	2000			2005/06		
	Men	Women	Total	Men	Women	Total
Employment-population ratio (%)	61.5	34.3	50.6	59.1	29.9	47.1
Unemployment rate (%)	15.3	13.4	14.8	20.3	21.2	20.6
Participation rate (%)	72.6	39.6	59.4	74.2	37.9	59.3
Total employed (thousands)	**100.7**	**37.4**	**138.1**	**130.3**	**45.6**	**175.9**
Employment rates of the highly educated (%)	76.9	53.6	68.6	84.0	52.0	72.0
Unemployment rates of the highly educated (%)	9.7	11.8	10.3	15.0	13.0	14.5
Highly educated in low- and medium-skilled jobs (%)	38.8	42.9	40.0	41.4	42.0	41.6
Highly educated employed (thousands)	**32.4**	**12.4**	**44.7**	**44.2**	**16.8**	**61.0**
Legislators, senior officials and managers	11.4	6.3	9.9	10.0	3.6	8.4
Professionals	19.8	17.7	19.2	13.9	18.1	15.0
Life science and health professionals	7.5	6.3	7.2	6.6	8.2	6.9
Teaching professionals	4.2	6.5	4.9	1.9	5.4	2.7
Technicians and associate professionals	7.7	9.8	8.3	7.8	10.9	8.6
Clerks	6.4	14.5	8.8	4.8	13.7	7.0
Service, shop and market sales workers	12.9	30.8	18.2	15.9	33.7	20.4
Skilled agricultural and fishery workers	0.3	0.2	0.2	0.3	0.2	0.3
Craft and related trades workers	11.8	2.3	9.0	12.0	1.8	9.4
Plant and machine operators and assemblers	15.5	5.1	12.4	16.2	3.9	13.1
Elementary occupations	14.2	13.4	14.0	18.2	14.2	17.2

Distribution of employment by occupation (%), population 15+

Persons born in Iraq and their native-born children, population 15+

Living in:	Europe	United States	Australia
2008	Thousands	Thousands	Thousands
Native-born children	17.7	31.0	..
Foreign-born	261.3	121.2	18.5
Total	279.0	152.2	..

International students from Iraq in OECD countries

Five main destinations	2004	2005	2006	2007	2008	2009
United Kingdom	126	176	244	332	557	652
United States	120	148	197	268	307	353
Germany	..	..	..	..	324	337
Turkey	182	209	236	246	267	293
France	188	199	192	202	197	200
Total	780	909	1 116	1 379	2 080	2 322

Legal migrant flows to the OECD
Thousands

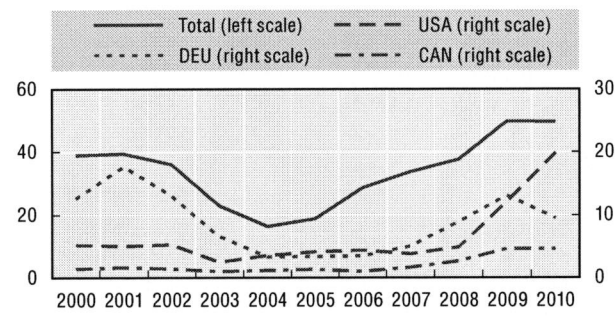

Remittance flows

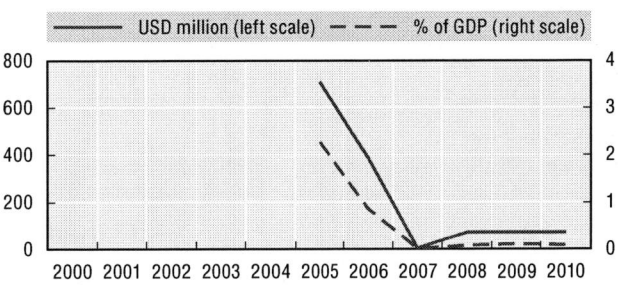

Ten main countries of destination for legal migrants in 2010 (numbers, % of total flows to the country): USA (19855, 1.9%), DEU (9496, 1.4%), CAN (4545, 1.6%), SWE (4534, 5.9%), AUS (2852, 1.4%), TUR (1165, 3.9%), FIN (1057, 0.9%), NLD (923, 0.9%), GBR (916, 0.2%), NOR (875, 1.4%).

Desire to emigrate, 2008-10

	Women	15-24	Highly educated	Total	Regional total
Persons who would move permanently, if they had the opportunity to do so (%)	12	23	22	17	21
Of which: Persons who are planning to move permanently in the next 12 months (%)				21	16
Of which: Persons who have already done some preparations for this move (*e.g.* visa application) (%)					46

Three main countries of desired destination: Sweden (12%), United Kingdom (8%), United States (7%).

StatLink  http://dx.doi.org/10.1787/888932674018

			World	Region
Total population 2010 (millions)	6.0	**Jordan compared to:**		
Population growth 2010 (%)	2.2	Human Development Index (HDI)	94/187	12/19
GDP per capita 2010 (current USD)	4 560	GDP per capita	93/194	9/18
GDP growth 2010 (%)	3.1	Emigration rate	118/203	6/18
Poverty rate 2006 (USD PPP 2 a day, in %)	3.5	Emigration rate of the highly educated	108/157	8/16

Age structure of the population 0+ (2010): "0-14": 22%; "15-24": 38%; "25-64": 37%; "65+": 4%.
Level of education of the population 15+ (2010): "Low": 29%; "Medium": 52%; "High": 19%.

Emigrant population living in OECD countries

Immigrant population

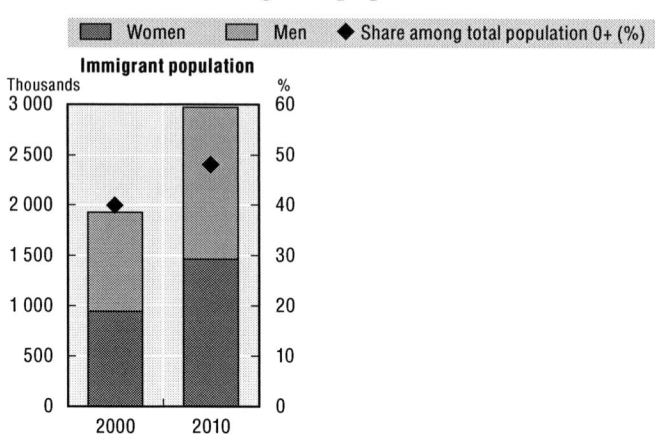

Emigrant population: persons born in Jordan living abroad

	2000						2005/06		
	All destinations			OECD destinations			OECD destinations		
Population 15+	Men	Women	Total	Men	Women	Total	Men	Women	Total
Emigrant population (thousands)	45.8	26.7	72.5	38.9	24.3	63.3	47.0	34.9	81.8
Recent emigrants (thousands)	..	..	..	6.7	5.1	11.8	8.3	7.6	15.8
15-24 (%)	15.6	16.5	16.0	11.1	15.7	12.8	10.4	15.5	12.6
25-64 (%)	80.3	77.1	79.1	84.7	77.9	82.1	82.2	76.4	79.7
65+ (%)	4.0	6.5	4.9	4.2	6.4	5.1	7.4	8.1	7.7
Low-educated (%)	17.2	28.3	21.3	16.9	25.8	20.4	16.2	19.2	17.4
Highly educated (%)	44.2	31.9	39.7	45.9	33.9	41.3	46.5	38.9	43.3
Total emigration rates (%)	3.0	1.9	2.5	2.5	1.7	2.2	2.5	2.0	2.3
Emigration rates of the highly educated (%)	8.3	4.7	6.8	7.4	4.6	6.2	6.4	5.1	5.8

Main destinations in 2005/06

	Total		Recent emigrants	Women	Highly educated	15-24	Total in 2000
Population 15+	Thousands	%	%	%	%	%	Thousands
United States	60.5	73.9	15.9	43.4	41.7	11.1	45.2
Canada	6.3	7.7	32.5	48.6	58.3	27.2	4.2
Australia	3.2	3.9	20.6	43.3	43.7	14.6	2.7
United Kingdom	–	–	–	–	–	–	2.6
Italy	1.8	2.2	–	–	–	–	1.9
Sweden	1.4	1.8	40.7	42.6	31.1	17.6	1.2
France	1.1	1.3	19.4	40.3	62.4	17.1	0.8
Denmark	1.0	1.2	12.4	42.3	23.1	13.4	0.9
Spain	–	–	–	–	–	–	1.1
Austria	–	–	–	–	–	–	0.4

Labour market indicators of persons born in Jordan living in OECD countries

Population 15-64	2000			2005/06		
	Men	Women	Total	Men	Women	Total
Employment-population ratio (%)	76.5	34.3	60.6	79.1	36.6	61.1
Unemployment rate (%)	6.7	11.4	7.8	5.8	11.3	7.2
Participation rate (%)	82.0	38.6	65.7	84.0	41.2	65.8
Total employed (thousands)	**27.8**	**7.5**	**35.3**	**33.1**	**11.3**	**44.4**
Employment rates of the highly educated (%)	83.3	41.4	70.1	91.2	53.4	76.6
Unemployment rates of the highly educated (%)	5.1	10.3	6.1	4.7	11.0	6.4
Highly educated in low- and medium-skilled jobs (%)	41.1	36.4	40.2	43.4	39.7	42.5
Highly educated employed (thousands)	**14.3**	**3.3**	**17.6**	**17.8**	**6.1**	**23.9**
Legislators, senior officials and managers	15.6	8.9	14.1	17.8	7.6	15.2
Professionals	30.2	17.7	27.4	30.2	14.5	26.2
Life science and health professionals	12.3	4.9	10.9	14.2	2.3	11.7
Teaching professionals	3.3	6.7	4.0	13.2	3.7	11.2
Technicians and associate professionals	10.9	16.3	12.1	10.6	23.3	13.9
Clerks	5.8	21.2	9.3	4.0	14.5	6.7
Service, shop and market sales workers	12.6	24.0	15.1	10.1	25.7	14.1
Skilled agricultural and fishery workers	0.3	0.1	0.3	0.8	–	0.6
Craft and related trades workers	8.1	1.6	6.7	7.0	0.7	5.4
Plant and machine operators and assemblers	8.6	3.7	7.5	7.9	1.7	6.3
Elementary occupations	7.8	6.5	7.5	11.6	11.9	11.7

(Left side label: Distribution of employment by occupation (%), population 15+)

Persons born in Jordan and their native-born children, population 15+

Living in:	Europe	United States	Australia
2008	Thousands	Thousands	Thousands
Native-born children	7.2	43.0	0.8
Foreign-born	9.9	83.4	..
Total	17.2	126.4	..

International students from Jordan in OECD countries

Five main destinations	2004	2005	2006	2007	2008	2009
United States	1 853	1 832	1 795	1 764	1 801	2 188
United Kingdom	1 151	1 296	1 351	1 503	1 286	1 329
Germany	..	..	..	..	453	524
Canada	384	..	318	405	333	357
Australia	247	240	233	269	271	322
Total	4 322	4 058	4 537	4 835	4 924	5 430

Legal migrant flows to the OECD
Thousands

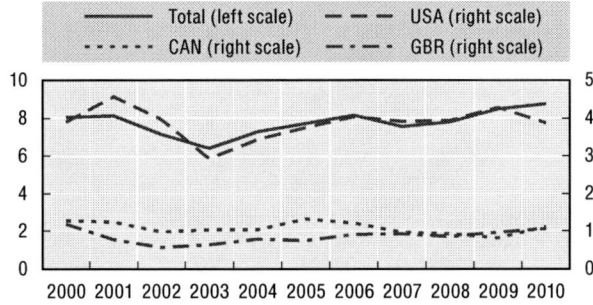

Remittance flows

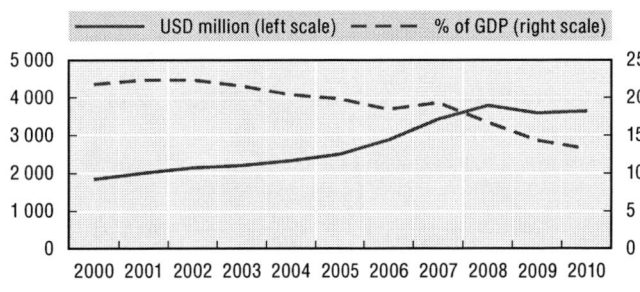

Ten main countries of destination for legal migrants in 2010 (numbers, % of total flows to the country): USA (3868, 0.4%), CAN (1115, 0.4%), GBR (1055, 0.2%), DEU (879, 0.1%), AUS (308, 0.1%), JPN (275, 0.1%), SWE (249, 0%), ESP (187, 0%), KOR (147, 0.1%), ITA (124, 0%).

Desire to emigrate, 2008-10

	Women	15-24	Highly educated	Total	Regional total
Persons who would move permanently, if they had the opportunity to do so (%)	25	37	36	30	21
Of which: Persons who are planning to move permanently in the next 12 months (%)				13	16
Of which: Persons who have already done some preparations for this move (*e.g.* visa application) (%)					46

Three main countries of desired destination: United Arab Emirates (27%), Saudi Arabia (18%), United States (15%).

StatLink ⟨⟨⟨ http://dx.doi.org/10.1787/888932674037

Total population 2010 (millions)	2.7	**Kuwait compared to:**	**World**	**Region**
Population growth 2010 (%)	3.4	Human Development Index (HDI)	63/187	5/19
GDP per capita 2009 (current USD)	41 365	GDP per capita	20/194	2/18
GDP growth 2007 (%)	4.4	Emigration rate	119/203	7/18
Poverty rate 2010 (USD PPP 2 a day, in %)	..	Emigration rate of the highly educated	54/157	3/16

Age structure of the population 0+ (2010): "0-14": 15%; "15-24": 27%; "25-64": 55%; "65+": 3%.
Level of education of the population 15+ (2010): "Low": 50%; "Medium": 44%; "High": 6%.

Emigrant population living in OECD countries

Immigrant population

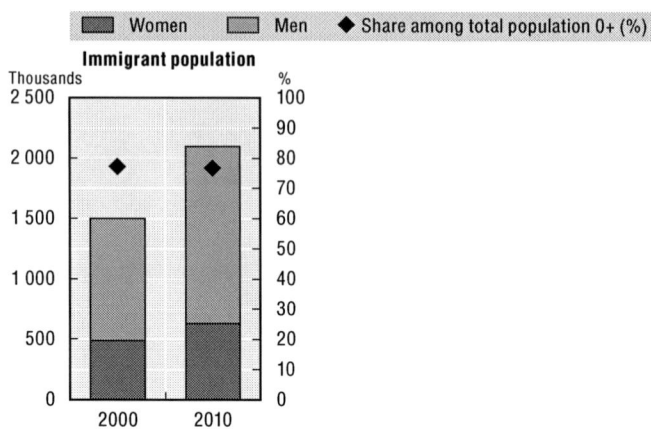

Emigrant population: persons born in Kuwait living abroad

	2000						2005/06		
	All destinations			OECD destinations			OECD destinations		
Population 15+	Men	Women	Total	Men	Women	Total	Men	Women	Total
Emigrant population (thousands)	39.3	31.1	70.4	21.8	15.2	37.0	26.7	20.0	46.7
Recent emigrants (thousands)	..	..	..	6.5	4.4	10.9	6.5	4.5	10.9
15-24 (%)	39.5	44.3	41.6	34.5	37.3	35.7	32.5	27.8	30.5
25-64 (%)	59.9	54.8	57.6	65.1	62.3	63.9	67.3	71.8	69.2
65+ (%)	0.6	0.9	0.7	0.3	0.4	0.4	0.2	0.4	0.3
Low-educated (%)	36.1	45.0	40.0	14.8	20.3	17.0	14.1	20.7	16.9
Highly educated (%)	28.6	23.6	26.4	47.2	42.4	45.2	47.5	43.7	45.8
Total emigration rates (%)	3.6	5.0	4.1	2.0	2.5	2.2	2.0	2.6	2.2
Emigration rates of the highly educated (%)	11.4	10.5	11.0	10.4	9.2	9.9	14.4	10.8	12.7

Main destinations in 2005/06

	Total		Recent emigrants	Women	Highly educated	15-24	Total in 2000
Population 15+	Thousands	%	%	%	%	%	Thousands
United States	22.3	47.8	22.2	43.3	52.9	23.0	18.6
Canada	9.9	21.3	22.3	42.8	53.1	45.4	7.4
United Kingdom	–	–	–	–	–	–	4.9
Australia	2.6	5.6	26.4	45.7	41.2	34.4	1.9
Denmark	1.2	2.6	12.3	42.6	12.9	32.5	0.9
Netherlands	–	–	–	–	–	–	–
Sweden	1.0	2.2	35.9	41.8	27.1	30.3	0.8
Austria	–	–	–	–	–	–	–
France	0.6	1.3	39.8	47.0	53.4	30.6	0.6
New Zealand	0.5	1.1	..	40.8	37.7	50.0	0.3

Labour market indicators of persons born in Kuwait living in OECD countries

Population 15-64	2000			2005/06		
	Men	Women	Total	Men	Women	Total
Employment-population ratio (%)	58.1	37.8	49.8	62.6	33.6	50.0
Unemployment rate (%)	8.3	11.3	9.3	10.0	23.3	14.3
Participation rate (%)	63.4	42.7	54.9	69.5	43.9	58.4
Total employed (thousands)	**12.1**	**5.5**	**17.6**	**15.8**	**6.5**	**22.2**
Employment rates of the highly educated (%)	72.9	50.3	64.1	83.3	52.1	70.5
Unemployment rates of the highly educated (%)	4.8	9.1	6.1	6.4	15.5	9.1
Highly educated in low- and medium-skilled jobs (%)	32.7	34.4	33.2	32.8	39.8	34.8
Highly educated employed (thousands)	**7.3**	**3.2**	**10.4**	**9.5**	**3.7**	**13.2**
Legislators, senior officials and managers	15.5	9.0	13.0	11.5	10.4	11.2
Professionals	23.4	19.7	22.0	20.0	19.8	19.9
Life science and health professionals	6.3	4.3	5.5	2.6	4.7	3.1
Teaching professionals	2.8	6.4	4.2	0.8	5.8	2.0
Technicians and associate professionals	12.5	17.2	14.4	14.5	11.1	13.4
Clerks	10.5	25.2	16.2	9.3	29.7	15.7
Service, shop and market sales workers	15.9	23.0	18.7	13.1	22.4	16.0
Skilled agricultural and fishery workers	0.1	0.0	0.1	0.2	0.1	0.2
Craft and related trades workers	8.5	0.2	5.3	10.8	1.4	7.8
Plant and machine operators and assemblers	6.9	1.9	4.9	7.5	1.9	5.7
Elementary occupations	6.6	3.7	5.5	13.1	3.3	10.0

Distribution of employment by occupation (%), population 15+

Persons born in Kuwait and their native-born children, population 15+

Living in:	Europe	United States	Australia
2008	Thousands	Thousands	Thousands
Native-born children	0.3	9.0	..
Foreign-born	0.4	11.9	..
Total	0.8	20.9	..

International students from Kuwait in OECD countries

Five main destinations	2004	2005	2006	2007	2008	2009
United States	1 846	1 796	1 763	1 669	1 825	1 998
United Kingdom	805	885	976	1 163	1 265	1 546
Australia	136	147	191	232	240	264
Slovak Republic	57	22	24	43	413	254
Canada	191	..	159	192	228	215
Total	3 142	2 952	3 217	3 400	4 259	4 592

Legal migrant flows to the OECD
Thousands

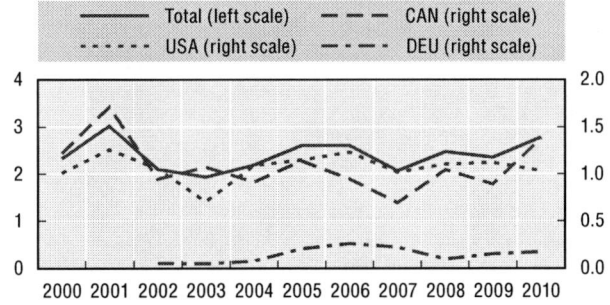

Ten main countries of destination for legal migrants in 2010 (numbers, % of total flows to the country): CAN (1380, 0.5%), USA (1037, 0.1%), DEU (174, 0%), JPN (92, 0%), ESP (15, 0%), FRA (12, 0%), SVK (12, 0.1%), IRL (10, 0.1%), AUS (9, 0%), TUR (9, 0%).

Desire to emigrate, 2008-10

	Women	15-24	Highly educated	Total	Regional total
Persons who would move permanently, if they had the opportunity to do so (%)	7	6	13	8	21
Of which: Persons who are planning to move permanently in the next 12 months (%)				..	16
Of which: Persons who have already done some preparations for this move (*e.g.* visa application) (%)					46

StatLink 🖳 http://dx.doi.org/10.1787/888932674056

			Lebanon compared to:	World	Region
Total population 2010 (millions)	4.2		Human Development Index (HDI)	70/187	7/19
Population growth 2010 (%)	0.7		GDP per capita	64/194	8/18
GDP per capita 2010 (current USD)	9 227		Emigration rate	42/203	1/18
GDP growth 2010 (%)	7.0		Emigration rate of the highly educated	..	..
Poverty rate 2010 (USD PPP 2 a day, in %)	..				

Age structure of the population 0+ (2010): "0-14": 18%; "15-24": 25%; "25-64": 50%; "65+": 7%.

Emigrant population living in OECD countries

Immigrant population

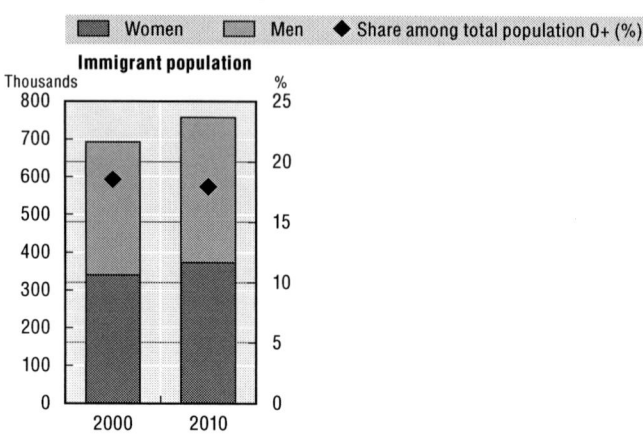

Emigrant population: persons born in Lebanon living abroad

	2000						2005/06		
	All destinations			OECD destinations			OECD destinations		
Population 15+	Men	Women	Total	Men	Women	Total	Men	Women	Total
Emigrant population (thousands)	211.8	168.0	379.8	187.1	152.5	339.6	207.6	176.3	383.9
Recent emigrants (thousands)	..	..	..	18.5	17.0	35.5	22.6	21.5	44.1
15-24 (%)	10.9	12.2	11.4	10.9	12.4	11.6	8.7	9.7	9.1
25-64 (%)	79.6	75.2	77.7	81.1	76.4	79.0	81.4	77.4	79.6
65+ (%)	9.5	12.6	10.9	8.0	11.2	9.4	9.9	12.9	11.3
Low-educated (%)	32.3	41.3	36.3	31.2	40.2	35.2	24.3	29.5	26.7
Highly educated (%)	34.4	25.0	30.2	36.1	26.4	31.8	42.6	35.3	39.3
Total emigration rates (%)	14.4	11.0	12.7	12.9	10.1	11.5	13.1	10.6	11.8
Emigration rates of the highly educated (%)	–	–	–	–	–	–	–	–	–

Main destinations in 2005/06

	Total		Recent emigrants	Women	Highly educated	15-24	Total in 2000
Population 15+	Thousands	%	%	%	%	%	Thousands
United States	118.6	30.9	11.1	45.8	46.4	5.8	106.2
Canada	74.0	19.3	12.8	46.8	45.1	11.7	65.0
Australia	72.9	19.0	8.4	48.2	15.1	7.0	69.3
France	40.7	10.6	16.1	42.8	54.7	11.3	33.4
Sweden	22.1	5.7	16.2	44.8	14.0	16.5	19.9
Denmark	12.0	3.1	3.7	45.6	16.3	18.6	11.4
United Kingdom	10.7	2.8	–	63.1	56.3	–	9.8
Switzerland	5.9	1.5	26.4	39.5	48.9	–	3.8
Italy	4.5	1.2	–	32.5	33.8	–	3.5
Israel	3.9	1.0	39.4	51.9	14.9	11.3	5.0

Labour market indicators of persons born in Lebanon living in OECD countries

Population 15-64	2000			2005/06		
	Men	Women	Total	Men	Women	Total
Employment-population ratio (%)	71.6	39.7	57.6	76.6	45.7	62.7
Unemployment rate (%)	9.2	12.0	10.1	7.9	11.5	9.1
Participation rate (%)	78.9	45.1	64.0	83.1	51.6	69.0
Total employed (thousands)	**111.6**	**48.5**	**160.1**	**128.5**	**62.4**	**190.9**
Employment rates of the highly educated (%)	83.9	59.3	74.7	91.3	67.3	81.5
Unemployment rates of the highly educated (%)	5.8	9.1	6.8	5.1	9.4	6.6
Highly educated in low- and medium-skilled jobs (%)	26.4	31.3	27.8	27.9	29.8	28.5
Highly educated employed (thousands)	**51.4**	**21.6**	**73.0**	**67.6**	**33.2**	**100.7**
Legislators, senior officials and managers	17.5	10.8	15.4	18.0	12.1	16.0
Professionals	17.5	15.7	16.9	19.5	17.8	18.9
Life science and health professionals	5.4	3.7	4.9	5.9	3.5	5.1
Teaching professionals	2.2	4.6	2.9	2.2	3.8	2.7
Technicians and associate professionals	11.5	16.6	13.1	9.6	17.6	12.3
Clerks	4.8	20.9	9.8	5.0	19.9	10.0
Service, shop and market sales workers	12.3	22.8	15.6	12.8	21.4	15.7
Skilled agricultural and fishery workers	0.5	0.2	0.4	0.8	1.8	1.1
Craft and related trades workers	14.8	2.2	10.9	14.7	1.6	10.2
Plant and machine operators and assemblers	12.2	3.0	9.3	12.1	2.6	8.9
Elementary occupations	8.9	7.8	8.6	7.6	5.3	6.9

Distribution of employment by occupation (%), population 15+

Persons born in Lebanon and their native-born children, population 15+

Living in:	Europe	United States	Australia
2008	Thousands	Thousands	Thousands
Native-born children	34.8	105.4	8.0
Foreign-born	73.2	143.9	44.9
Total	108.0	249.2	52.9

International students from Lebanon in OECD countries

Five main destinations	2004	2005	2006	2007	2008	2009
France	4 671	4 695	5 083	5 391	5 609	5 254
United States	2 179	2 131	2 019	1 893	1 809	1 793
Italy	577	590	626	649	702	783
Canada	1 049	..	921	1 056	651	686
Germany	..	..	..	..	639	648
Total	9 414	8 395	9 710	10 105	10 628	10 309

Legal migrant flows to the OECD
Thousands

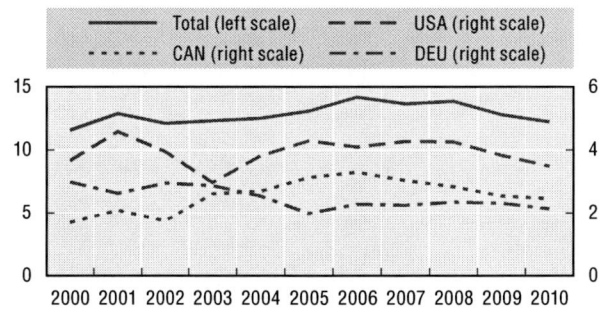

Remittance flows

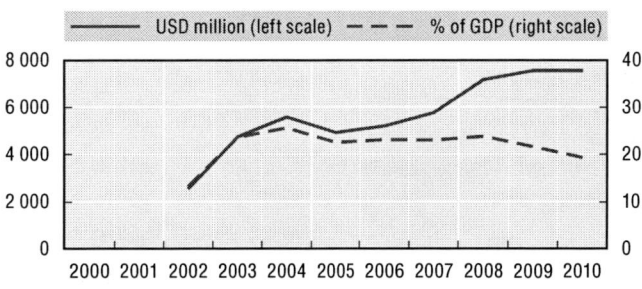

Ten main countries of destination for legal migrants in 2010 (numbers, % of total flows to the country): USA (3487, 0.3%), CAN (2450, 0.9%), DEU (2118, 0.3%), AUS (1177, 0.6%), FRA (935, 0.7%), SWE (421, 0.5%), ITA (314, 0.3%), BEL (262, 0.3%), GBR (243, 0.1%), CHE (209, 0.2%).

Desire to emigrate, 2008-10

	Women	15-24	Highly educated	Total	Regional total
Persons who would move permanently, if they had the opportunity to do so (%)	..	..	..	..	21
Of which: Persons who are planning to move permanently in the next 12 months (%)				..	16
Of which: Persons who have already done some preparations for this move (*e.g.* visa application) (%)					46

StatLink http://dx.doi.org/10.1787/888932674075

Total population 2010 (millions)	6.4		Libya compared to:	World	Region
Population growth 2010 (%)	1.5		Human Development Index (HDI)	64/187	6/19
GDP per capita 2009 (current USD)	9 957		GDP per capita	63/194	7/18
GDP growth 2009 (%)	2.1		Emigration rate	135/203	8/18
Poverty rate 2010 (USD PPP 2 a day, in %)	..		Emigration rate of the highly educated	143/157	12/16

Age structure of the population 0+ (2010): "0-14": 18%; "15-24": 30%; "25-64": 48%; "65+": 4%.
Level of education of the population 15+ (2010): "Low": 46%; "Medium": 31%; "High": 23%.

Emigrant population living in OECD countries

Immigrant population

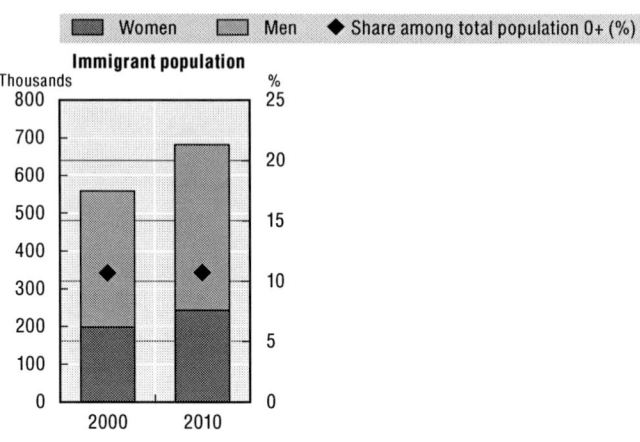

Emigrant population: persons born in Libya living abroad

	2000						2005/06		
	All destinations			OECD destinations			OECD destinations		
Population 15+	Men	Women	Total	Men	Women	Total	Men	Women	Total
Emigrant population (thousands)	43.0	40.0	82.9	40.7	38.5	79.2	39.9	43.3	83.2
Recent emigrants (thousands)	..	..	..	1.6	1.2	2.9	2.2	1.4	3.6
15-24 (%)	7.3	6.7	7.0	4.2	4.0	4.1	2.1	2.4	2.3
25-64 (%)	74.7	69.1	72.0	76.9	71.1	74.1	69.4	63.1	66.1
65+ (%)	18.0	24.1	21.0	18.9	24.9	21.8	28.5	34.5	31.6
Low-educated (%)	43.3	57.2	50.1	43.5	57.6	50.4	40.3	55.5	48.2
Highly educated (%)	25.4	16.9	21.3	25.8	17.1	21.6	29.0	17.3	22.9
Total emigration rates (%)	2.2	2.3	2.2	2.1	2.2	2.1	1.8	2.1	2.0
Emigration rates of the highly educated (%)	6.0	3.3	4.5	5.8	3.2	4.4	3.4	2.0	2.7

Main destinations in 2005/06

	Total		Recent emigrants	Women	Highly educated	15-24	Total in 2000
Population 15+	Thousands	%	%	%	%	%	Thousands
Italy	40.0	48.1	–	57.9	8.8	–	37.4
Israel	17.5	21.0	0.0	52.7	10.7	0.0	17.2
United States	8.7	10.4	8.3	42.5	59.1	3.7	8.4
United Kingdom	6.6	8.0	–	–	–	–	7.7
Canada	2.8	3.4	32.6	40.6	69.4	19.5	2.1
France	1.6	2.0	29.8	44.4	41.7	10.8	1.3
Australia	1.4	1.7	11.6	46.7	32.1	7.6	1.2
Ireland	0.6	0.8	34.6	38.9	65.7	12.9	0.6
Poland	–	–	–	–	–	–	0.2
Sweden	0.6	0.7	55.0	25.4	35.0	19.7	0.4

Labour market indicators of persons born in Libya living in OECD countries

Population 15-64	2000			2005/06		
	Men	Women	Total	Men	Women	Total
Employment-population ratio (%)	68.2	44.5	57.1	70.6	41.2	55.9
Unemployment rate (%)	8.6	7.1	8.1	7.9	6.8	7.5
Participation rate (%)	74.7	47.9	62.1	76.6	44.2	60.4
Total employed (thousands)	**22.1**	**12.7**	**34.8**	**17.8**	**10.4**	**28.2**
Employment rates of the highly educated (%)	75.8	56.3	68.2	82.9	58.1	75.0
Unemployment rates of the highly educated (%)	7.4	7.0	7.3	9.9	5.8	8.9
Highly educated in low- and medium-skilled jobs (%)	22.5	26.0	23.6	19.6	32.7	22.8
Highly educated employed (thousands)	**7.0**	**3.3**	**10.3**	**6.5**	**2.2**	**8.7**
Legislators, senior officials and managers	17.8	9.2	14.5	11.2	5.7	9.1
Professionals	17.2	10.6	14.7	18.8	12.0	16.2
Life science and health professionals	3.1	1.0	2.3	3.7	4.9	4.2
Teaching professionals	1.2	2.1	1.5	1.2	2.4	1.7
Technicians and associate professionals	15.3	20.8	17.4	18.9	23.7	20.8
Clerks	7.4	24.4	13.9	9.6	27.2	16.4
Service, shop and market sales workers	9.3	14.8	11.3	6.6	7.6	7.0
Skilled agricultural and fishery workers	0.8	0.8	0.8	0.6	7.1	3.1
Craft and related trades workers	14.7	3.7	10.6	17.6	1.2	11.2
Plant and machine operators and assemblers	8.1	2.3	5.9	7.0	0.9	4.6
Elementary occupations	9.4	13.3	10.9	4.5	14.7	8.4

(Left margin label: Distribution of employment by occupation (%), population 15+)

Persons born in Libya and their native-born children, population 15+

Living in:	Europe	United States	Australia
2008	Thousands	Thousands	Thousands
Native-born children	32.8	..	..
Foreign-born	20.6	..	..
Total	53.4	..	..

International students from Libya in OECD countries

Five main destinations	2004	2005	2006	2007	2008	2009
United Kingdom	1 221	1 306	1 243	1 686	1 623	2 112
United States	39	41	39	95	155	656
Canada	116	..	183	132	300	251
France	247	246	223	228	235	245
Germany	..	..	..	..	195	189
Total	1 859	1 845	1 892	2 360	2 775	3 738

Legal migrant flows to the OECD
Thousands

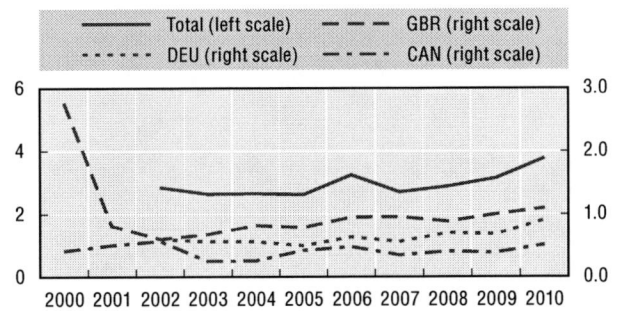

Remittance flows

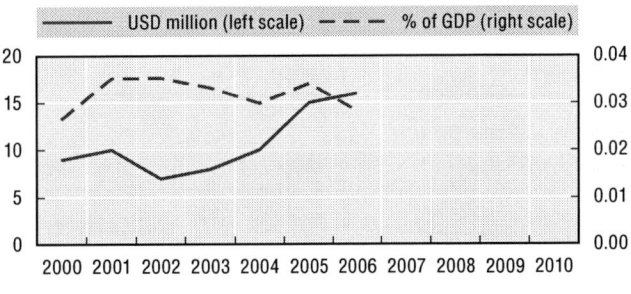

Ten main countries of destination for legal migrants in 2010 (numbers, % of total flows to the country): GBR (1097, 0.2%), DEU (902, 0.1%), CAN (505, 0.2%), USA (355, 0%), SWE (126, 0.2%), ITA (108, 0%), SVK (103, 0.1%), FRA (95, 0.1%), ESP (84, 0%), AUT (70, 0.1%).

Desire to emigrate, 2008-10

	Women	15-24	Highly educated	Total	Regional total
Persons who would move permanently, if they had the opportunity to do so (%)	26	32	31	29	21
Of which: Persons who are planning to move permanently in the next 12 months (%)				..	16
Of which: Persons who have already done some preparations for this move (*e.g.* visa application) (%)					46

Three main countries of desired destination: United Arab Emirates (29%), Saudi Arabia (21%), Kuwait (11%).

StatLink http://dx.doi.org/10.1787/888932674094

Total population 2010 (millions)	32.0	**Morocco compared to:**	**World**	**Region**
Population growth 2010 (%)	1.0	Human Development Index (HDI)	130/187	16/19
GDP per capita 2010 (current USD)	2 796	GDP per capita	122/194	14/18
GDP growth 2010 (%)	3.7	Emigration rate	54/203	2/18
Poverty rate 2007 (USD PPP 2 a day, in %)	14.0	Emigration rate of the highly educated	48/157	1/16

Age structure of the population 0+ (2010): "0-14": 20%; "15-24": 28%; "25-64": 47%; "65+": 5%.
Level of education of the population 15+ (2010): "Low": 67%; "Medium": 23%; "High": 10%.

Emigrant population living in OECD countries

Immigrant population

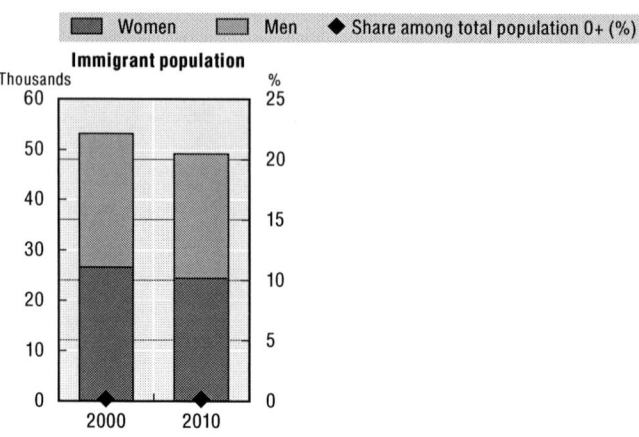

Emigrant population: persons born in Morocco living abroad

	2000						2005/06		
	All destinations			OECD destinations			OECD destinations		
Population 15+	Men	Women	Total	Men	Women	Total	Men	Women	Total
Emigrant population (thousands)	926.8	753.3	1 680.1	923.5	751.3	1 674.8	1 241.5	1 021.0	2 262.6
Recent emigrants (thousands)	..	..	..	140.2	102.2	242.3	240.6	214.7	455.3
15-24 (%)	11.9	12.7	12.3	11.9	12.6	12.2	10.2	13.2	11.5
25-64 (%)	80.6	77.7	79.3	80.6	77.7	79.3	81.0	76.9	79.1
65+ (%)	7.5	9.6	8.5	7.5	9.6	8.5	8.8	9.9	9.3
Low-educated (%)	59.1	63.2	60.9	59.2	63.3	61.1	56.5	63.3	59.5
Highly educated (%)	15.3	12.9	14.2	15.3	12.9	14.2	16.7	13.6	15.3
Total emigration rates (%)	9.0	7.1	8.1	9.0	7.1	8.1	10.7	8.5	9.6
Emigration rates of the highly educated (%)	13.1	16.7	14.3	13.0	16.7	14.3	15.5	18.1	16.4

Main destinations in 2005/06

	Total		Recent emigrants	Women	Highly educated	15-24	Total in 2000
Population 15+	Thousands	%	%	%	%	%	Thousands
France	820.0	36.2	11.3	48.2	20.0	9.9	686.3
Spain	539.0	23.8	50.1	40.5	7.8	17.5	278.5
Italy	204.2	9.0	28.3	40.6	4.5	17.7	137.7
Israel	156.2	6.9	0.9	52.5	18.0	0.2	169.8
Netherlands	155.9	6.9	11.9	45.2	9.7	9.8	132.0
Belgium	152.6	6.7	21.6	47.3	10.6	8.7	113.7
Germany	91.4	4.0	14.2	38.9	6.7	9.8	52.8
United States	61.0	2.7	26.3	43.0	44.9	7.1	38.7
Canada	37.4	1.7	35.2	45.7	62.7	9.0	24.4
United Kingdom	12.3	0.5	–	–	54.6	–	11.9

Labour market indicators of persons born in Morocco living in OECD countries

Population 15-64	2000			2005/06		
	Men	Women	Total	Men	Women	Total
Employment-population ratio (%)	66.5	35.8	53.0	69.9	35.5	54.5
Unemployment rate (%)	16.6	24.2	19.0	16.0	25.6	19.0
Participation rate (%)	79.7	47.2	65.4	83.2	47.7	67.3
Total employed (thousands)	**555.6**	**234.1**	**789.6**	**782.0**	**324.2**	**1 106.2**
Employment rates of the highly educated (%)	77.0	64.4	71.8	87.8	74.0	82.2
Unemployment rates of the highly educated (%)	10.9	12.4	11.5	10.9	14.3	12.1
Highly educated in low- and medium-skilled jobs (%)	24.9	26.1	25.4	39.4	34.4	37.6
Highly educated employed (thousands)	**101.4**	**58.4**	**159.8**	**150.1**	**83.4**	**233.5**
Legislators, senior officials and managers	7.7	5.6	7.1	6.4	5.5	6.2
Professionals	8.1	9.9	8.6	6.9	9.8	7.7
Life science and health professionals	1.4	1.9	1.5	1.0	1.8	1.3
Teaching professionals	1.8	4.1	2.5	1.6	3.8	2.2
Technicians and associate professionals	7.7	14.2	9.6	6.5	11.9	8.0
Clerks	3.3	14.1	6.4	3.4	11.5	5.7
Service, shop and market sales workers	8.8	20.8	12.2	8.8	20.9	12.2
Skilled agricultural and fishery workers	5.3	1.4	4.2	3.2	0.9	2.6
Craft and related trades workers	22.3	3.8	17.0	24.4	3.3	18.4
Plant and machine operators and assemblers	14.4	4.0	11.4	15.3	3.7	12.0
Elementary occupations	22.5	26.3	23.5	25.0	32.4	27.1

Distribution of employment by occupation (%), population 15+

Persons born in Morocco and their native-born children, population 15+

Living in:	Europe	United States	Australia
2008	Thousands	Thousands	Thousands
Native-born children	845.2	58.1	1.1
Foreign-born	1 963.7	98.7	0.7
Total	2 808.9	156.8	1.8

International students from Morocco in OECD countries

Five main destinations	2004	2005	2006	2007	2008	2009
France	32 802	29 859	29 299	27 684	26 998	27 051
Germany	..	..	..	..	3 553	3 535
Spain	1 450	1 517	1 613	1 782	1 803	3 165
Canada	2 696	..	1 026	2 652	1 587	1 770
Italy	664	776	813	1 017	1 207	1 398
Total	39 760	34 506	34 946	34 958	37 226	39 139

Legal migrant flows to the OECD
Thousands

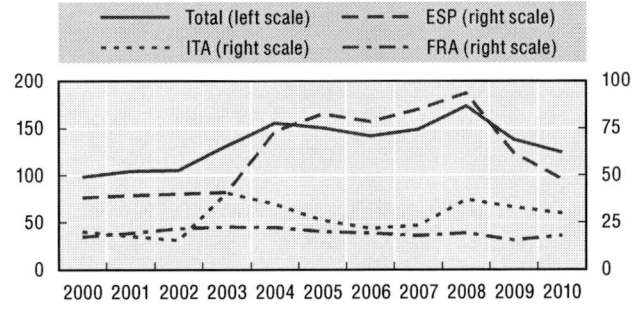

Remittance flows

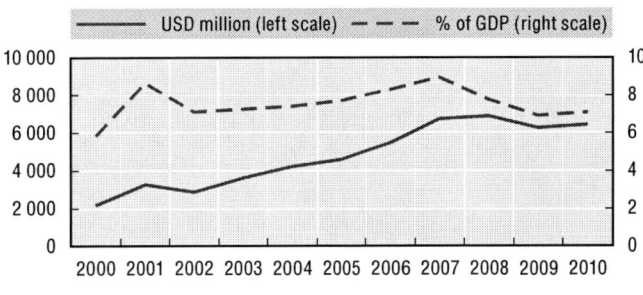

Ten main countries of destination for legal migrants in 2010 (numbers, % of total flows to the country): ESP (47938, 11.1%), ITA (29960, 7.1%), FRA (17976, 13.2%), BEL (9093, 8.9%), CAN (5945, 2.1%), USA (5013, 0.5%), DEU (3762, 1.6%), NLD (1632, 1.6%), CHE (730, 0.6%), SWE (421, 0.5%).

Desire to emigrate, 2008-10

	Women	15-24	Highly educated	Total	Regional total
Persons who would move permanently, if they had the opportunity to do so (%)	17	42	18	24	21
Of which: Persons who are planning to move permanently in the next 12 months (%)				25	16
Of which: Persons who have already done some preparations for this move (*e.g.* visa application) (%)					46

Three main countries of desired destination: France (26%), Spain (20%), Italy (16%).

StatLink http://dx.doi.org/10.1787/888932674113

			Qatar compared to:	World	Region
Total population 2010 (millions)		1.8			
Population growth 2010 (%)		9.6	Human Development Index (HDI)	37/187	2/19
GDP per capita 2009 (current USD)		61 532	GDP per capita	7/194	1/18
GDP growth 2009 (%)		8.6	Emigration rate	158/203	12/18
Poverty rate 2010 (USD PPP 2 a day, in %)		..	Emigration rate of the highly educated	145/157	13/16

Age structure of the population 0+ (2010): "0-14": 15%; "15-24": 14%; "25-64": 71%; "65+": 1%.
Level of education of the population 15+ (2010): "Low": 40%; "Medium": 44%; "High": 16%.

Emigrant population living in OECD countries

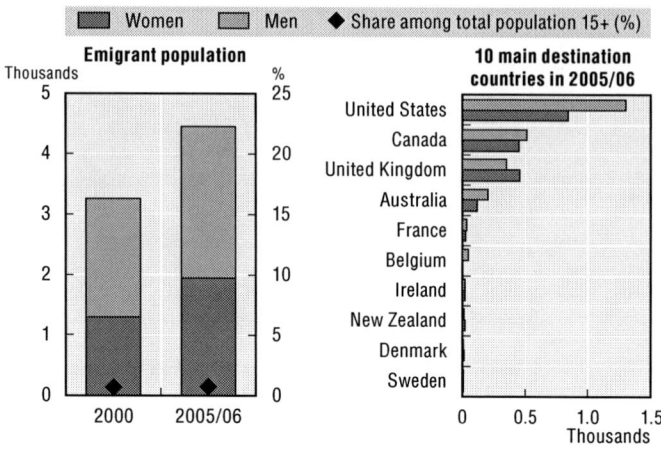

Immigrant population

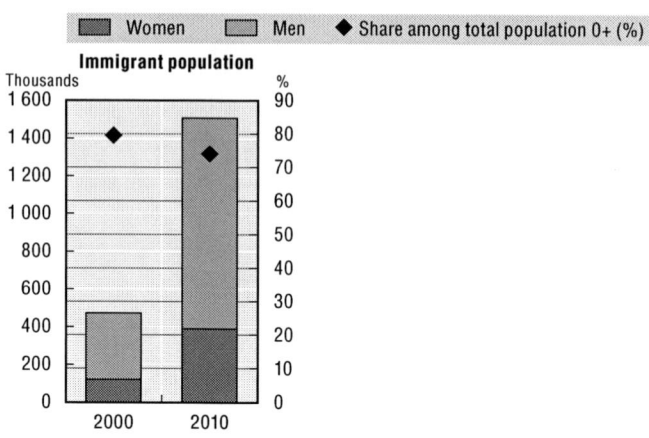

Emigrant population: persons born in Qatar living abroad

	2000						2005/06		
	All destinations			OECD destinations			OECD destinations		
Population 15+	Men	Women	Total	Men	Women	Total	Men	Women	Total
Emigrant population (thousands)	2.0	1.3	3.4	2.0	1.3	3.3	2.5	1.9	4.5
Recent emigrants (thousands)	..	..	..	0.6	0.4	1.0	0.5	0.3	0.7
15-24 (%)	47.2	43.1	45.5	47.7	43.6	46.1	–	–	–
25-64 (%)	51.8	54.3	52.8	51.3	54.0	52.4	–	–	–
65+ (%)	1.1	2.6	1.7	1.0	2.4	1.5	–	–	–
Low-educated (%)	15.2	19.0	16.7	15.2	18.7	16.6	23.6	13.4	19.1
Highly educated (%)	44.9	44.3	44.6	45.4	45.1	45.3	41.4	63.8	51.3
Total emigration rates (%)	0.6	1.0	0.7	0.6	0.9	0.7	0.6	1.1	0.7
Emigration rates of the highly educated (%)	2.1	2.0	2.0	2.1	1.9	2.0	1.5	3.0	2.0

Main destinations in 2005/06

	Total		Recent emigrants	Women	Highly educated	15-24	Total in 2000
Population 15+	Thousands	%	%	%	%	%	Thousands
United States	2.2	48.3	13.1	39.1	55.2	34.0	1.4
Canada	1.0	21.7	27.0	46.6	42.5	52.3	0.6
United Kingdom	–	–	–	–	–	–	0.8
Australia	0.3	7.0	39.9	36.4	45.4	43.8	0.1
France	–	–	–	–	–	–	0.1

Labour market indicators of persons born in Qatar living in OECD countries

Population 15-64	2000			2005/06		
	Men	Women	Total	Men	Women	Total
Employment-population ratio (%)	45.8	34.9	41.5	46.4	27.6	37.8
Unemployment rate (%)	10.1	10.4	10.2	39.1	12.1	32.1
Participation rate (%)	50.9	38.9	46.2	76.2	31.3	55.6
Total employed (thousands)	**0.9**	**0.4**	**1.3**	**0.7**	**0.3**	**1.0**
Employment rates of the highly educated (%)	64.3	41.6	55.3	80.2	31.4	49.7
Unemployment rates of the highly educated (%)	6.4	8.4	7.0	13.2	12.1	12.8
Highly educated in low- and medium-skilled jobs (%)	15.8	24.4	18.3	36.8	49.4	42.8
Highly educated employed (thousands)	**0.5**	**0.2**	**0.8**	**0.4**	**0.2**	**0.6**
Legislators, senior officials and managers	18.8	3.3	12.2	10.5	1.9	7.4
Professionals	21.9	20.9	21.5	15.2	16.3	15.6
Life science and health professionals	10.3	2.3	7.4	6.1	3.5	5.4
Teaching professionals	–	3.1	1.1	2.0	–	1.5
Technicians and associate professionals	8.5	17.6	12.4	20.3	15.6	18.6
Clerks	9.1	28.7	17.5	8.0	21.0	12.8
Service, shop and market sales workers	24.9	23.8	24.4	25.0	33.5	28.1
Skilled agricultural and fishery workers	0.9	0.4	0.7	–	1.6	0.6
Craft and related trades workers	5.8	0.4	3.5	6.7	6.2	6.5
Plant and machine operators and assemblers	4.0	1.2	2.8	8.7	–	5.5
Elementary occupations	6.1	3.7	5.1	5.6	3.9	5.0

Distribution of employment by occupation (%), population 15+

Persons born in Qatar and their native-born children, population 15+

Living in:	Europe	United States	Australia
2008	Thousands	Thousands	Thousands
Native-born children	..	..	..
Foreign-born	0.2	..	..
Total	..	..	..

International students from Qatar in OECD countries

Five main destinations	2004	2005	2006	2007	2008	2009
United Kingdom	420	509	514	599	704	951
United States	354	303	263	303	345	455
Australia	61	149	169	167	122	117
Canada	31	..	63	75	55	52
France	30	39	41	55	50	24
Total	915	1 006	1 056	1 209	1 321	1 636

Legal migrant flows to the OECD
Thousands

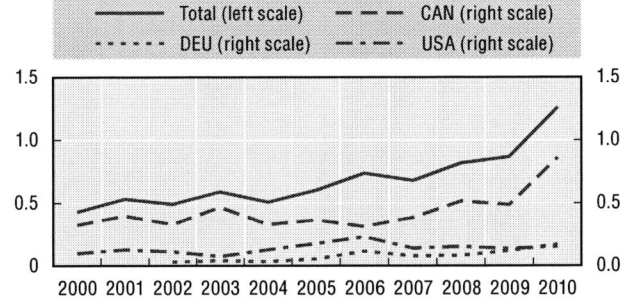

Ten main countries of destination for legal migrants in 2010 (numbers, % of total flows to the country): CAN (860, 0.3%), DEU (167, 0%), USA (148, 0%), JPN (30, 0%), FRA (27, 0%), HUN (7, 0%), ESP (4, 0%), DNK (3, 0%), NLD (3, 0%), KOR (3, 0%).

Desire to emigrate, 2008-10

	Women	15-24	Highly educated	Total	Regional total
Persons who would move permanently, if they had the opportunity to do so (%)	10	10	18	13	21
Of which: Persons who are planning to move permanently in the next 12 months (%)				..	16
Of which: Persons who have already done some preparations for this move (*e.g.* visa application) (%)					46

StatLink ⬛ http://dx.doi.org/10.1787/888932674132

		Saudi Arabia compared to:	World	Region
Total population 2010 (millions)	27.4	Human Development Index (HDI)	56/187	4/19
Population growth 2010 (%)	2.4	GDP per capita	45/194	6/18
GDP per capita 2010 (current USD)	15 836	Emigration rate	182/203	16/18
GDP growth 2010 (%)	3.8	Emigration rate of the highly educated	149/157	16/16
Poverty rate 2010 (USD PPP 2 a day, in %)	..			

Age structure of the population 0+ (2010): "0-14": 18%; "15-24": 30%; "25-64": 49%; "65+": 3%.
Level of education of the population 15+ (2010): "Low": 36%; "Medium": 52%; "High": 12%.

Emigrant population living in OECD countries

Immigrant population

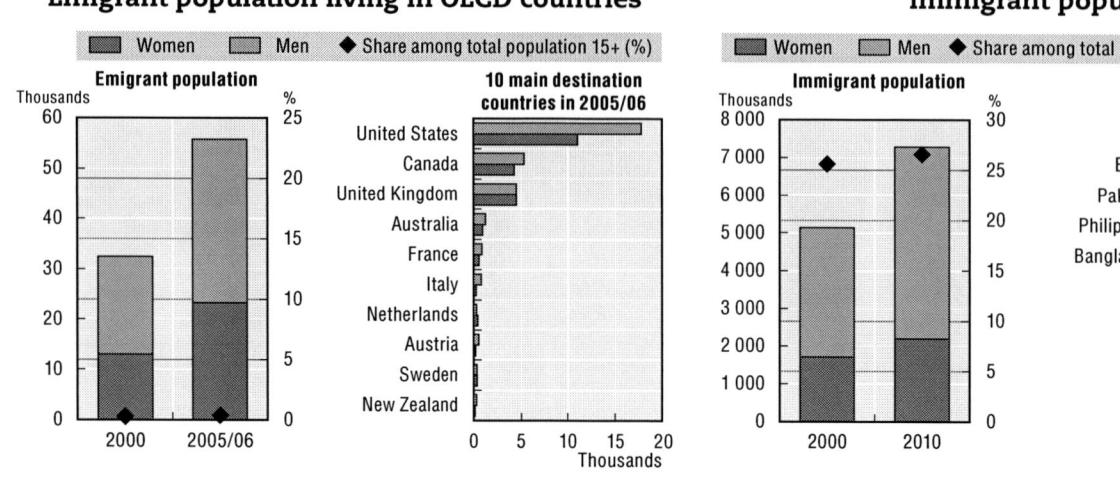

Emigrant population: persons born in Saudi Arabia living abroad

	2000						2005/06		
	All destinations			OECD destinations			OECD destinations		
Population 15+	Men	Women	Total	Men	Women	Total	Men	Women	Total
Emigrant population (thousands)	25.3	17.0	42.4	19.4	13.0	32.4	32.6	23.2	55.8
Recent emigrants (thousands)	..	..	..	7.3	3.9	11.2	13.6	8.2	21.8
15-24 (%)	40.9	46.2	43.0	46.1	49.6	47.5	50.0	46.4	48.5
25-64 (%)	57.3	51.8	55.1	52.9	49.0	51.3	49.6	53.2	51.1
65+ (%)	1.8	2.0	1.9	1.0	1.3	1.1	0.4	0.5	0.4
Low-educated (%)	23.6	28.6	25.6	18.9	25.7	21.6	13.7	15.7	14.5
Highly educated (%)	33.8	28.4	31.6	40.9	33.9	38.1	47.0	46.7	46.9
Total emigration rates (%)	0.3	0.3	0.3	0.3	0.2	0.3	0.4	0.4	0.4
Emigration rates of the highly educated (%)	0.8	0.8	0.8	0.8	0.7	0.7	1.4	1.4	1.4

Main destinations in 2005/06

	Total		Recent emigrants	Women	Highly educated	15-24	Total in 2000
Population 15+	Thousands	%	%	%	%	%	Thousands
United States	28.9	51.7	44.9	38.3	48.2	48.1	18.2
Canada	9.6	17.1	27.3	44.6	46.4	63.8	5.0
United Kingdom	9.0	16.1	–	–	–	–	5.1
Australia	2.1	3.8	56.8	42.7	50.9	45.6	0.7
France	1.4	2.5	47.9	39.9	36.8	45.4	0.8
Italy	1.0	1.9	–	–	–	–	0.4
Netherlands	–	–	–	–	–	–	–
Austria	–	–	–	–	–	–	0.2
Sweden	0.6	1.1	47.2	52.0	25.5	47.2	0.4
New Zealand	0.4	0.7	..	29.2	22.8	70.8	0.1

Labour market indicators of persons born in Saudi Arabia living in OECD countries

Population 15-64	2000 Men	2000 Women	2000 Total	2005/06 Men	2005/06 Women	2005/06 Total
Employment-population ratio (%)	44.3	32.4	39.6	39.4	34.1	37.2
Unemployment rate (%)	11.4	11.5	11.5	11.4	11.6	11.5
Participation rate (%)	50.0	36.6	44.7	44.5	38.6	42.0
Total employed (thousands)	**8.3**	**4.0**	**12.3**	**12.4**	**7.6**	**20.0**
Employment rates of the highly educated (%)	55.0	39.3	49.5	57.3	41.5	50.7
Unemployment rates of the highly educated (%)	7.5	9.0	7.9	8.3	11.8	9.5
Highly educated in low- and medium-skilled jobs (%)	26.6	33.6	28.5	32.3	36.0	33.5
Highly educated employed (thousands)	**4.2**	**1.7**	**5.9**	**7.9**	**3.9**	**11.8**
Legislators, senior officials and managers	15.0	7.8	12.4	8.2	4.1	6.5
Professionals	29.2	17.8	25.1	36.5	12.3	26.6
Life science and health professionals	4.7	3.7	4.3	2.3	1.5	1.9
Teaching professionals	3.6	6.4	4.7	7.1	2.5	5.1
Technicians and associate professionals	11.7	13.8	12.5	7.0	26.7	15.1
Clerks	8.8	21.6	13.4	11.4	25.6	17.2
Service, shop and market sales workers	14.6	29.2	19.9	18.0	19.2	18.5
Skilled agricultural and fishery workers	0.3	0.1	0.2	0.1	–	0.1
Craft and related trades workers	5.5	0.9	3.8	8.8	1.0	5.6
Plant and machine operators and assemblers	6.1	1.7	4.5	3.6	0.7	2.4
Elementary occupations	8.9	7.2	8.3	6.3	10.3	7.9

Distribution of employment by occupation (%), population 15+

Persons born in Saudi Arabia and their native-born children, population 15+

Living in:	Europe	United States	Australia
2008	Thousands	Thousands	Thousands
Native-born children	4.8	8.9	..
Foreign-born	12.0	40.2	..
Total	16.9	49.1	..

International students from Saudi Arabia in OECD countries

Five main destinations	2004	2005	2006	2007	2008	2009
United States	3 521	3 170	3 570	8 060	9 884	12 453
United Kingdom	2 192	2 438	2 753	3 249	3 535	5 203
Australia	243	439	782	1 244	1 929	3 676
Canada	484	..	837	654	1 017	1 266
France	100	127	100	208	263	403
Total	6 692	6 331	8 239	13 632	17 082	23 873

Legal migrant flows to the OECD
Thousands

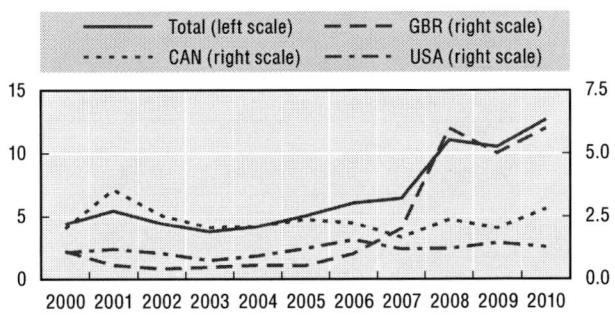

Remittance flows

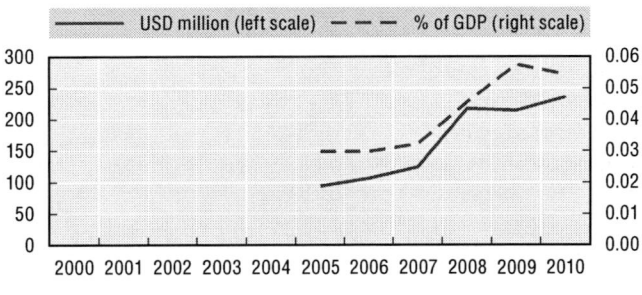

Ten main countries of destination for legal migrants in 2010 (numbers, % of total flows to the country): GBR (6000, 1.3%), CAN (2800, 1%), USA (1263, 0.1%), DEU (782, 0.1%), NLD (337, 0.3%), JPN (317, 0.1%), KOR (291, 0.4%), POL (169, 0.4%), ESP (136, 0%), CHE (106, 0.1%).

Desire to emigrate, 2008-10

	Women	15-24	Highly educated	Total	Regional total
Persons who would move permanently, if they had the opportunity to do so (%)	8	8	9	8	21
Of which: Persons who are planning to move permanently in the next 12 months (%)				..	16
Of which: Persons who have already done some preparations for this move (*e.g.* visa application) (%)					46

StatLink http://dx.doi.org/10.1787/888932674151

		Sudan compared to:	World	Region
Total population 2010 (millions)	43.6	Human Development Index (HDI)	169/187	19/19
Population growth 2010 (%)	2.5	GDP per capita	136/194	17/18
GDP per capita 2010 (current USD)	1 425	Emigration rate	178/203	15/18
GDP growth 2010 (%)	4.5	Emigration rate of the highly educated	115/157	9/16
Poverty rate 2010 (USD PPP 2 a day, in %)	..			

Age structure of the population 0+ (2010): "0-14": 20%; "15-24": 40%; "25-64": 37%; "65+": 4%.
Level of education of the population 15+ (2010): "Low": 86%; "Medium": 10%; "High": 4%.

Emigrant population living in OECD countries

Immigrant population

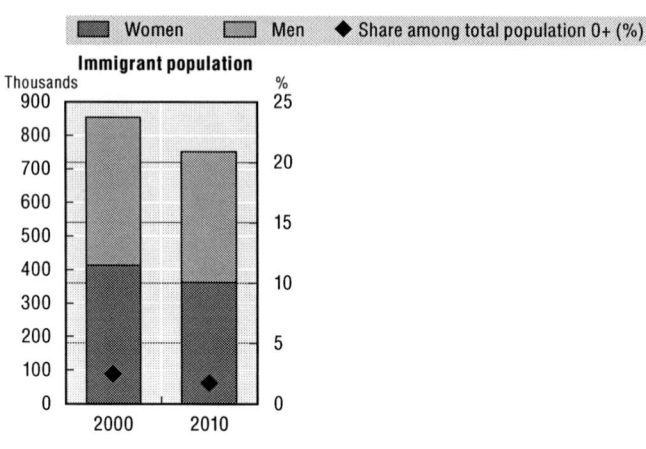

Emigrant population: persons born in Sudan living abroad

	2000						2005/06		
	All destinations			OECD destinations			OECD destinations		
Population 15+	Men	Women	Total	Men	Women	Total	Men	Women	Total
Emigrant population (thousands)	105.4	91.3	196.7	25.3	16.8	42.1	50.4	34.5	84.8
Recent emigrants (thousands)	..	..	..	9.3	6.0	15.3	18.0	13.3	31.3
15-24 (%)	38.4	39.0	38.7	18.0	21.0	19.2	21.4	26.5	23.5
25-64 (%)	57.3	56.1	56.7	77.8	72.3	75.6	75.3	69.6	73.0
65+ (%)	4.3	4.9	4.6	4.2	6.7	5.2	3.3	3.9	3.6
Low-educated (%)	71.3	81.8	76.2	20.4	30.1	24.2	22.8	33.9	27.2
Highly educated (%)	15.9	9.7	13.0	45.4	35.0	41.3	38.2	34.1	36.6
Total emigration rates (%)	1.1	0.9	1.0	0.3	0.2	0.2	0.5	0.3	0.4
Emigration rates of the highly educated (%)	9.6	5.9	7.9	6.6	3.9	5.3	7.2	3.9	5.4

Main destinations in 2005/06

	Total		Recent emigrants	Women	Highly educated	15-24	Total in 2000
Population 15+	Thousands	%	%	%	%	%	Thousands
United States	35.2	41.6	28.9	38.4	33.3	22.7	16.0
Australia	14.0	16.5	72.5	45.5	21.1	33.2	3.7
United Kingdom	12.1	14.2	–	–	58.2	–	9.1
Canada	11.3	13.4	47.4	42.0	40.7	25.0	6.3
Netherlands	4.4	5.1	–	–	–	–	–
France	2.2	2.6	30.9	31.3	30.6	9.3	1.3
Sweden	1.0	1.1	43.1	43.0	41.4	22.3	0.7
Ireland	0.9	1.1	67.8	31.3	71.3	11.5	0.5
Italy	–	–	–	–	–	–	0.7
Finland	0.6	0.7	89.0	41.2	10.8	23.2	0.1

Labour market indicators of persons born in Sudan living in OECD countries

Population 15-64	2000			2005/06		
	Men	Women	Total	Men	Women	Total
Employment-population ratio (%)	63.7	37.4	53.4	63.8	38.1	53.7
Unemployment rate (%)	13.9	20.7	15.9	17.1	23.4	19.0
Participation rate (%)	74.0	47.2	63.5	77.0	49.7	66.3
Total employed (thousands)	**14.7**	**5.5**	**20.2**	**29.2**	**11.3**	**40.5**
Employment rates of the highly educated (%)	74.3	46.6	64.9	90.7	66.9	81.8
Unemployment rates of the highly educated (%)	11.8	19.5	13.8	11.3	24.2	15.3
Highly educated in low- and medium-skilled jobs (%)	43.1	44.6	43.4	45.6	39.7	44.0
Highly educated employed (thousands)	**7.8**	**2.5**	**10.4**	**14.0**	**5.3**	**19.3**
Legislators, senior officials and managers	11.6	8.1	10.6	6.6	14.1	8.8
Professionals	27.2	21.9	25.6	20.6	15.3	19.0
Life science and health professionals	16.2	8.8	14.1	13.2	9.1	12.0
Teaching professionals	3.7	7.4	4.8	0.9	2.2	1.3
Technicians and associate professionals	10.4	11.5	10.8	9.3	15.7	11.2
Clerks	6.7	20.5	10.7	5.6	19.9	9.8
Service, shop and market sales workers	10.9	22.5	14.4	9.2	17.5	11.7
Skilled agricultural and fishery workers	0.2	0.5	0.3	1.2	0.9	1.1
Craft and related trades workers	6.5	1.4	5.0	8.7	1.9	6.7
Plant and machine operators and assemblers	12.7	3.1	9.9	17.7	4.0	13.7
Elementary occupations	13.7	10.4	12.8	21.1	10.7	18.0

Distribution of employment by occupation (%), population 15+

Persons born in Sudan and their native-born children, population 15+

Living in:	Europe	United States	Australia
2008	Thousands	Thousands	Thousands
Native-born children	4.9	12.9	..
Foreign-born	26.3	41.1	6.1
Total	31.2	54.0	..

International students from Sudan in OECD countries

Five main destinations	2004	2005	2006	2007	2008	2009
United Kingdom	354	339	302	343	347	352
United States	279	303	320	328	224	213
Germany	..	..	..	..	209	203
Sweden	1	0	1	0	41	66
Canada	38	..	51	36	61	64
Total	860	884	944	994	1 164	1 159

Legal migrant flows to the OECD
Thousands

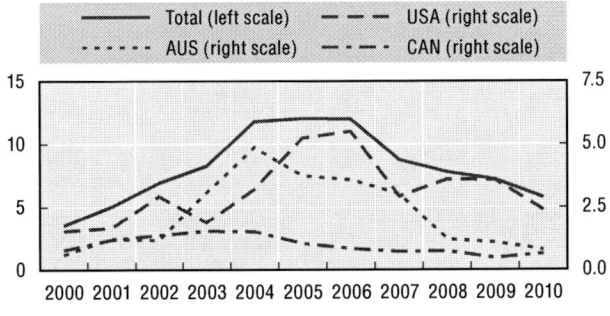

Remittance flows

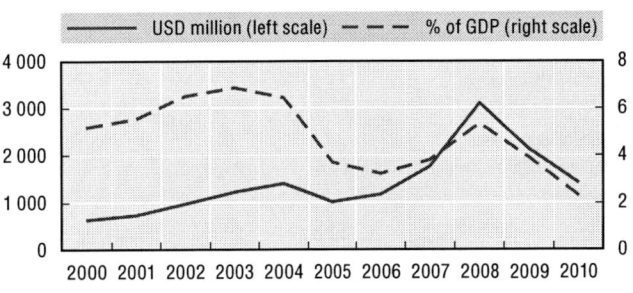

Ten main countries of destination for legal migrants in 2010 (numbers, % of total flows to the country): USA (2397, 0.2%), AUS (798, 0.4%), CAN (620, 0.2%), DEU (381, 0.1%), FRA (298, 0.2%), GBR (292, 0.1%), NOR (173, 0.2%), SWE (132, 0.2%), ITA (128, 0%), KOR (104, 0%).

Desire to emigrate, 2008-10

	Women	15-24	Highly educated	Total	Regional total
Persons who would move permanently, if they had the opportunity to do so (%)	27	39	38	30	21
Of which: Persons who are planning to move permanently in the next 12 months (%)				34	16
Of which: Persons who have already done some preparations for this move (*e.g.* visa application) (%)					46

Three main countries of desired destination: United States (24%), Saudi Arabia (18%), United Arab Emirates (12%).

StatLink ᴴᴵᴸ http://dx.doi.org/10.1787/888932674797

Total population 2010 (millions)	20.4	**Syria compared to:**	**World**	**Region**
Population growth 2010 (%)	2.0	Human Development Index (HDI)	119/187	15/19
GDP per capita 2010 (current USD)	2 893	GDP per capita	119/194	13/18
GDP growth 2010 (%)	3.2	Emigration rate	142/203	10/18
Poverty rate 2004 (USD PPP 2 a day, in %)	16.9	Emigration rate of the highly educated	55/157	4/16

Age structure of the population 0+ (2010): "0-14": 20%; "15-24": 37%; "25-64": 39%; "65+": 4%.
Level of education of the population 15+ (2010): "Low": 71%; "Medium": 27%; "High": 3%.

Emigrant population living in OECD countries

Immigrant population

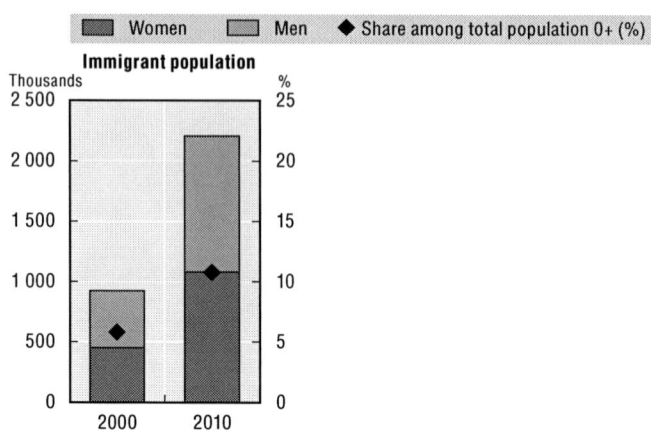

Emigrant population: persons born in Syria living abroad

	2000						2005/06		
	All destinations			OECD destinations			OECD destinations		
Population 15+	Men	Women	Total	Men	Women	Total	Men	Women	Total
Emigrant population (thousands)	103.1	79.0	182.1	73.8	58.5	132.3	80.7	67.2	147.9
Recent emigrants (thousands)	..	..	..	11.4	9.2	20.6	11.2	10.1	21.4
15-24 (%)	10.1	11.2	10.6	8.9	11.3	9.9	8.1	10.7	9.3
25-64 (%)	77.8	71.0	74.9	80.1	73.0	77.0	78.5	70.1	74.6
65+ (%)	12.0	17.8	14.5	11.0	15.7	13.1	13.4	19.3	16.1
Low-educated (%)	33.3	47.6	39.5	30.0	41.0	34.8	26.0	37.0	30.9
Highly educated (%)	34.6	20.9	28.7	39.8	25.7	33.6	42.7	28.8	36.5
Total emigration rates (%)	2.1	1.6	1.8	1.5	1.2	1.3	1.3	1.1	1.2
Emigration rates of the highly educated (%)	11.8	14.2	12.5	9.9	13.1	10.8	12.0	15.2	12.9

Main destinations in 2005/06

	Total		Recent emigrants	Women	Highly educated	15-24	Total in 2000
Population 15+	Thousands	%	%	%	%	%	Thousands
United States	55.3	37.4	11.2	45.2	36.9	7.9	52.7
Canada	17.9	12.1	20.1	49.2	50.9	10.9	14.7
Sweden	17.1	11.6	20.3	50.2	18.1	13.6	14.6
France	14.4	9.7	17.4	42.5	53.4	5.5	12.2
Israel	8.9	6.0	0.0	54.6	11.6	3.9	7.4
Netherlands	6.6	4.5	–	46.7	22.7	–	–
Australia	6.6	4.5	12.2	51.7	22.0	8.2	6.2
United Kingdom	–	–	–	–	–	–	3.8
Italy	3.3	2.3	–	37.1	33.0	–	2.6
Belgium	–	–	–	–	–	–	2.1

Labour market indicators of persons born in Syria living in OECD countries

Population 15-64	2000			2005/06		
	Men	Women	Total	Men	Women	Total
Employment-population ratio (%)	75.7	37.5	59.7	74.0	36.2	57.9
Unemployment rate (%)	8.1	12.6	9.4	10.4	17.6	12.5
Participation rate (%)	82.4	42.9	65.9	82.6	43.9	66.1
Total employed (thousands)	**43.6**	**15.5**	**59.1**	**44.8**	**16.3**	**61.0**
Employment rates of the highly educated (%)	80.7	47.0	69.5	88.5	56.9	77.3
Unemployment rates of the highly educated (%)	7.0	12.4	8.3	8.7	15.6	10.5
Highly educated in low- and medium-skilled jobs (%)	26.1	39.5	28.9	27.4	39.2	30.6
Highly educated employed (thousands)	**20.5**	**6.0**	**26.5**	**23.5**	**7.7**	**31.2**
Legislators, senior officials and managers	17.0	7.5	14.5	14.1	7.2	11.9
Professionals	25.9	13.2	22.6	28.5	19.0	25.5
Life science and health professionals	16.5	2.0	13.2	16.8	4.8	13.4
Teaching professionals	3.4	6.9	4.2	6.3	5.3	6.0
Technicians and associate professionals	10.2	11.9	10.6	7.5	12.6	9.1
Clerks	4.1	15.8	7.2	4.1	14.3	7.3
Service, shop and market sales workers	10.8	30.3	15.9	11.4	32.5	18.0
Skilled agricultural and fishery workers	0.2	0.0	0.2	0.6	0.2	0.5
Craft and related trades workers	14.5	2.7	11.4	16.2	1.6	11.7
Plant and machine operators and assemblers	9.4	4.8	8.2	8.7	2.9	6.9
Elementary occupations	7.9	13.8	9.5	8.8	9.7	9.1

Distribution of employment by occupation (%), population 15+

Persons born in Syria and their native-born children, population 15+

Living in:	Europe	United States	Australia
2008	Thousands	Thousands	Thousands
Native-born children	20.5	33.5	0.8
Foreign-born	64.6	50.7	5.6
Total	85.1	84.2	6.4

International students from Syria in OECD countries

Five main destinations	2004	2005	2006	2007	2008	2009
France	2 237	2 323	2 517	2 618	2 334	2 252
Germany	..	..	..	..	1 648	1 825
United Kingdom	450	497	479	571	527	533
United States	556	520	462	472	518	447
Turkey	2	291	279	264	260	291
Total	3 818	3 981	4 345	4 661	6 009	5 891

Legal migrant flows to the OECD
Thousands

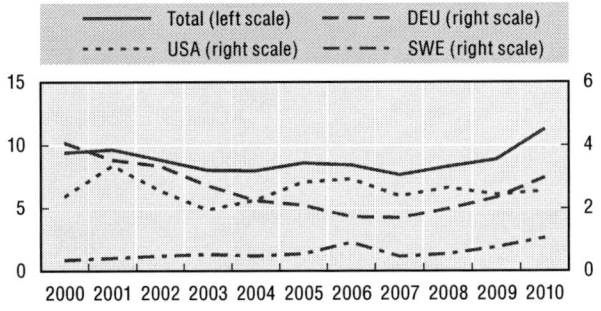

Remittance flows

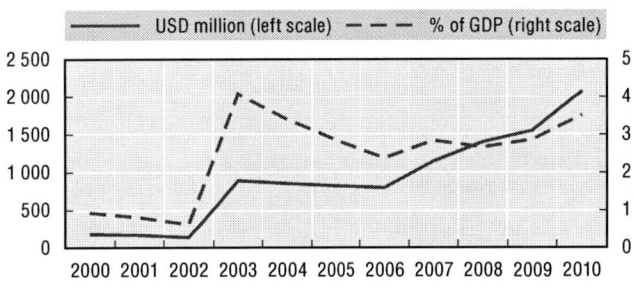

Ten main countries of destination for legal migrants in 2010 (numbers, % of total flows to the country): DEU (2983, 0.4%), USA (2555, 0.2%), SWE (1047, 1.4%), TUR (881, 3%), CAN (795, 0.3%), DNK (400, 1.2%), FRA (359, 0.1%), ITA (350, 0.1%), ESP (307, 0.1%), AUT (231, 0.2%).

Desire to emigrate, 2008-10

	Women	15-24	Highly educated	Total	Regional total
Persons who would move permanently, if they had the opportunity to do so (%)	22	25	23	24	21
Of which: Persons who are planning to move permanently in the next 12 months (%)				25	16
Of which: Persons who have already done some preparations for this move (*e.g.* visa application) (%)					46

Three main countries of desired destination: United Arab Emirates (20%), United States (6%), Saudi Arabia (6%).

StatLink ⟐ *http://dx.doi.org/10.1787/888932674170*

Total population 2010 (millions)	10.5	Tunisia compared to:	World	Region
Population growth 2010 (%)	1.0	Human Development Index (HDI)	95/187	10/19
GDP per capita 2010 (current USD)	4 199	GDP per capita	100/194	12/18
GDP growth 2010 (%)	3.7	Emigration rate	73/203	3/18
Poverty rate 2000 (USD PPP 2 a day, in %)	12.8	Emigration rate of the highly educated	59/157	5/16

Age structure of the population 0+ (2010): "0-14": 19%; "15-24": 23%; "25-64": 51%; "65+": 7%.
Level of education of the population 15+ (2010): "Low": 51%; "Medium": 37%; "High": 12%.

Emigrant population living in OECD countries

Immigrant population

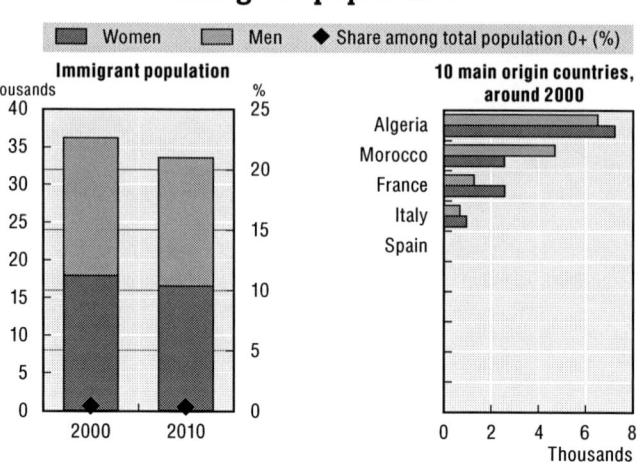

Emigrant population: persons born in Tunisia living abroad

	2000						2005/06		
	All destinations			OECD destinations			OECD destinations		
Population 15+	Men	Women	Total	Men	Women	Total	Men	Women	Total
Emigrant population (thousands)	255.0	207.9	462.9	253.5	207.2	460.7	288.6	224.3	513.0
Recent emigrants (thousands)	..	..	..	15.6	11.0	26.6	30.2	21.0	51.2
15-24 (%)	4.2	4.6	4.4	4.1	4.6	4.3	5.6	5.2	5.4
25-64 (%)	80.0	71.6	76.3	80.1	71.7	76.3	77.3	69.8	74.0
65+ (%)	15.7	23.7	19.3	15.8	23.8	19.4	17.1	25.0	20.6
Low-educated (%)	52.6	59.5	55.7	52.8	59.6	55.9	49.2	56.3	52.3
Highly educated (%)	17.9	13.8	16.0	17.8	13.8	16.0	19.4	16.4	18.1
Total emigration rates (%)	7.1	5.9	6.5	7.1	5.9	6.5	7.2	5.7	6.4
Emigration rates of the highly educated (%)	15.4	16.7	15.9	15.2	16.7	15.8	13.2	11.9	12.6

Main destinations in 2005/06

	Total		Recent emigrants	Women	Highly educated	15-24	Total in 2000
Population 15+	Thousands	%	%	%	%	%	Thousands
France	356.6	69.5	8.4	45.8	18.8	5.1	333.9
Italy	74.2	14.5	23.7	35.8	2.2	7.3	56.6
Israel	31.6	6.2	3.1	58.5	20.7	0.0	33.8
Belgium	9.2	1.8	–	–	–	–	7.7
Canada	7.7	1.5	43.7	35.5	70.4	10.3	5.2
United States	7.6	1.5	8.3	36.6	60.0	4.5	6.5
Switzerland	6.6	1.3	42.9	27.1	29.1	–	5.4
Netherlands	5.6	1.1	–	37.8	–	–	–
Austria	3.7	0.7	–	–	–	–	2.0
Sweden	3.3	0.6	26.3	32.5	18.4	6.7	2.8

Labour market indicators of persons born in Tunisia living in OECD countries

Population 15-64	2000			2005/06		
	Men	Women	Total	Men	Women	Total
Employment-population ratio (%)	66.4	41.5	55.7	67.0	41.3	56.4
Unemployment rate (%)	18.3	23.1	19.9	15.7	21.2	17.5
Participation rate (%)	81.2	53.9	69.6	79.6	52.4	68.3
Total employed (thousands)	**139.0**	**64.8**	**203.8**	**156.3**	**68.1**	**224.4**
Employment rates of the highly educated (%)	79.2	65.7	73.9	83.7	72.3	79.1
Unemployment rates of the highly educated (%)	9.2	10.7	9.7	10.2	12.1	10.9
Highly educated in low- and medium-skilled jobs (%)	16.3	24.2	16.8	25.3	24.3	25.0
Highly educated employed (thousands)	**31.6**	**16.9**	**48.5**	**35.1**	**19.7**	**54.8**
Distribution of employment by occupation (%), population 15+ — Legislators, senior officials and managers	12.1	7.0	11.8	9.1	7.1	8.5
Professionals	12.8	10.1	12.6	11.9	14.3	12.6
Life science and health professionals	3.0	0.3	2.8	2.3	2.8	2.4
Teaching professionals	2.3	2.1	2.3	2.1	5.2	3.1
Technicians and associate professionals	11.1	13.3	11.2	9.5	15.7	11.3
Clerks	4.4	15.6	5.0	4.3	14.8	7.4
Service, shop and market sales workers	8.5	19.9	9.1	8.8	19.8	12.0
Skilled agricultural and fishery workers	2.8	1.2	2.8	2.0	0.6	1.6
Craft and related trades workers	23.5	5.1	22.5	27.6	3.2	20.4
Plant and machine operators and assemblers	12.6	3.2	12.1	13.3	2.3	10.1
Elementary occupations	12.1	24.8	12.8	13.5	22.1	16.0

Persons born in Tunisia and their native-born children, population 15+

Living in:	Europe	United States	Australia
2008	Thousands	Thousands	Thousands
Native-born children	382.6	..	1.0
Foreign-born	378.5	..	..
Total	761.1	..	..

International students from Tunisia in OECD countries

Five main destinations	2004	2005	2006	2007	2008	2009
France	9 748	9 750	10 386	10 533	10 812	11 177
Germany	..	..	..	..	2 461	2 623
Italy	202	252	302	493	611	834
Canada	1 136	..	711	1 137	583	734
Switzerland	..	..	..	..	308	337
Total	11 570	10 436	11 861	12 654	15 398	16 332

Legal migrant flows to the OECD
Thousands

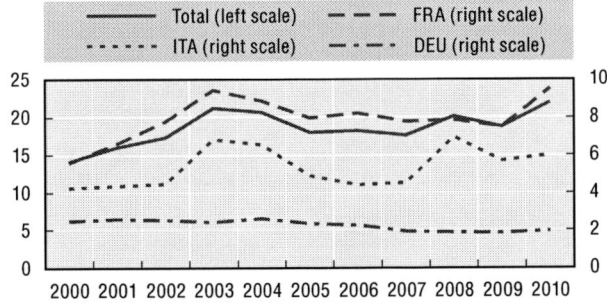

Remittance flows

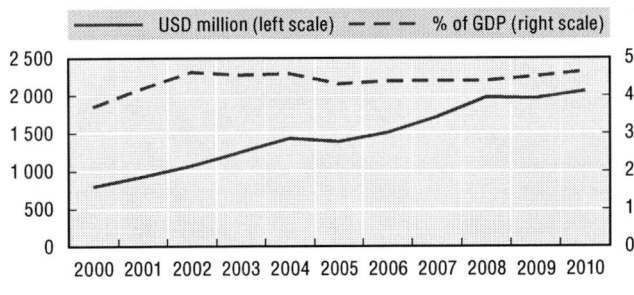

Ten main countries of destination for legal migrants in 2010 (numbers, % of total flows to the country): FRA (9520, 7%), ITA (6007, 1.4%), DEU (1955, 0.3%), CAN (1225, 0.4%), BEL (607, 0.6%), CHE (569, 0.4%), POL (498, 0%), USA (418, 0%), SWE (250, 0.3%), ESP (205, 0%).

Desire to emigrate, 2008-10

	Women	15-24	Highly educated	Total	Regional total
Persons who would move permanently, if they had the opportunity to do so (%)	22	44	31	28	21
Of which: Persons who are planning to move permanently in the next 12 months (%)				22	16
Of which: Persons who have already done some preparations for this move (*e.g.* visa application) (%)					46

Three main countries of desired destination: France (42%), Italy (16%), Germany (9%).

StatLink http://dx.doi.org/10.1787/888932674189

			United Arab Emirates compared to:	World	Region
Total population 2010 (millions)		7.5			
Population growth 2010 (%)		7.9	Human Development Index (HDI)	30/187	1/19
GDP per capita 2010 (current USD)		39 625	GDP per capita	23/194	3/18
GDP growth 2010 (%)		1.4	Emigration rate	161/203	14/18
Poverty rate 2010 (USD PPP 2 a day, in %)		..	Emigration rate of the highly educated	148/157	15/16

Age structure of the population 0+ (2010): "0-14": 16%; "15-24": 17%; "25-64": 66%; "65+": 0%.
Level of education of the population 15+ (2010): "Low": 20%; "Medium": 59%; "High": 21%.

Emigrant population living in OECD countries

Immigrant population

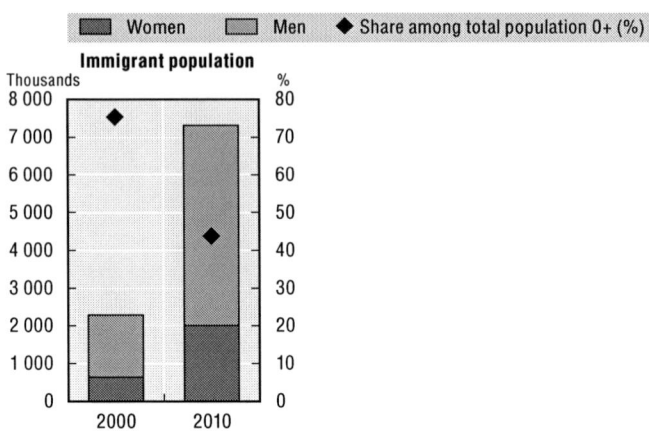

Emigrant population: persons born in United Arab Emirates living abroad

	2000						2005/06		
	All destinations			OECD destinations			OECD destinations		
Population 15+	Men	Women	Total	Men	Women	Total	Men	Women	Total
Emigrant population (thousands)	16.3	11.5	27.8	8.8	5.6	14.4	12.3	10.0	22.3
Recent emigrants (thousands)	..	..	..	3.4	1.5	4.9	3.3	1.6	4.9
15-24 (%)	48.8	48.2	48.6	81.7	76.6	79.7	59.9	64.6	62.0
25-64 (%)	50.6	51.2	50.8	18.0	22.7	19.8	40.0	35.3	37.9
65+ (%)	0.6	0.5	0.6	0.4	0.7	0.5	0.1	0.1	0.1
Low-educated (%)	25.8	23.5	24.9	19.9	25.3	22.0	20.3	19.2	19.8
Highly educated (%)	15.1	18.7	16.6	24.1	27.2	25.3	34.9	45.1	39.5
Total emigration rates (%)	0.9	1.7	1.1	0.5	0.8	0.6	0.5	1.1	0.7
Emigration rates of the highly educated (%)	0.9	2.3	1.3	0.8	1.6	1.0	0.9	2.9	1.4

Main destinations in 2005/06

	Total		Recent emigrants	Women	Highly educated	15-24	Total in 2000
Population 15+	Thousands	%	%	%	%	%	Thousands
United States	8.2	36.7	13.2	36.8	32.8	52.0	5.1
Canada	6.3	28.3	25.1	44.6	38.0	76.6	3.2
United Kingdom	–	–	–	–	–	–	3.6
Australia	1.8	7.9	49.6	38.8	39.5	66.7	0.7
Sweden	0.4	1.8	35.4	48.1	19.7	63.0	0.3
New Zealand	0.4	1.8	48.1	43.9	33.3	81.8	0.2
France	0.4	1.7	27.0	55.9	49.2	56.4	0.3
Netherlands	–	–	–	–	–	–	–
Italy	–	–	–	–	–	–	0.1
Ireland	–	–	–	–	–	–	0.1

Labour market indicators of persons born in United Arab Emirates living in OECD countries

Population 15-64	2000			2005/06		
	Men	Women	Total	Men	Women	Total
Employment-population ratio (%)	35.5	36.4	35.9	58.1	45.6	52.1
Unemployment rate (%)	13.9	16.8	15.0	9.9	10.3	10.1
Participation rate (%)	41.2	43.8	42.2	64.5	50.9	58.0
Total employed (thousands)	**2.9**	**1.9**	**4.8**	**4.4**	**3.2**	**7.6**
Employment rates of the highly educated (%)	54.8	55.8	55.2	82.2	67.1	74.0
Unemployment rates of the highly educated (%)	9.0	13.1	10.8	6.5	7.9	7.2
Highly educated in low- and medium-skilled jobs (%)	26.5	26.3	26.4	52.8	66.5	59.8
Highly educated employed (thousands)	**1.1**	**0.8**	**1.9**	**2.3**	**2.2**	**4.6**
Legislators, senior officials and managers	7.2	3.8	5.7	12.6	2.5	8.1
Professionals	17.1	15.4	16.4	16.1	15.3	15.7
Life science and health professionals	2.7	1.4	2.1	0.6	3.5	1.9
Teaching professionals	1.3	6.0	3.4	2.0	3.4	2.6
Technicians and associate professionals	15.5	17.5	16.4	15.1	10.4	13.0
Clerks	10.2	24.7	16.6	8.4	25.8	16.1
Service, shop and market sales workers	26.8	31.8	29.0	15.4	14.8	15.2
Skilled agricultural and fishery workers	0.1	1.2	0.5	0.2	21.6	9.7
Craft and related trades workers	6.2	0.5	3.7	20.1	2.8	12.4
Plant and machine operators and assemblers	7.2	2.3	5.0	2.8	0.9	1.9
Elementary occupations	9.8	2.8	6.7	9.3	5.9	7.8

Distribution of employment by occupation (%), population 15+

Persons born in United Arab Emirates and their native-born children, population 15+

Living in:	Europe	United States	Australia
2008	Thousands	Thousands	Thousands
Native-born children	1.4	..	..
Foreign-born	1.2	..	..
Total	2.7	..	..

International students from United Arab Emirates in OECD countries

Five main destinations	2004	2005	2006	2007	2008	2009
United Kingdom	1 633	1 803	2 074	2 218	2 309	2 696
Australia	859	944	1 002	1 120	1 184	1 342
United States	1 248	1 209	1 013	905	984	1 198
Canada	368	..	219	573	227	222
France	29	40	70	78	166	194
Total	4 192	4 063	4 446	4 970	5 114	5 952

Legal migrant flows to the OECD
Thousands

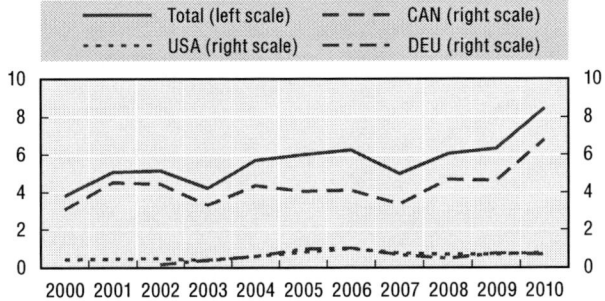

Ten main countries of destination for legal migrants in 2010 (numbers, % of total flows to the country): CAN (6795, 2.4%), USA (779, 0.1%), DEU (688, 0.1%), GBR (77, 0%), AUT (30, 0%), JPN (28, 0%), FRA (12, 0%), CHE (11, 0%), ITA (8, 0%), KOR (8, 0%).

Desire to emigrate, 2008-10

	Women	15-24	Highly educated	Total	Regional total
Persons who would move permanently, if they had the opportunity to do so (%)	6	7	10	7	21
Of which: Persons who are planning to move permanently in the next 12 months (%)				..	16
Of which: Persons who have already done some preparations for this move (*e.g.* visa application) (%)					46

StatLink http://dx.doi.org/10.1787/888932674208

Total population 2010 (millions)	24.1		Yemen compared to:	World	Region
Population growth 2010 (%)	3.1		Human Development Index (HDI)	154/187	18/19
GDP per capita 2009 (current USD)	1 130		GDP per capita	149/194	18/18
GDP growth 2009 (%)	3.8		Emigration rate	184/203	17/18
Poverty rate 2010 (USD PPP 2 a day, in %)	..		Emigration rate of the highly educated	146/157	14/16

Age structure of the population 0+ (2010): "0-14": 22%; "15-24": 44%; "25-64": 31%; "65+": 3%.
Level of education of the population 15+ (2010): "Low": 74%; "Medium": 23%; "High": 3%.

Emigrant population living in OECD countries

Immigrant population

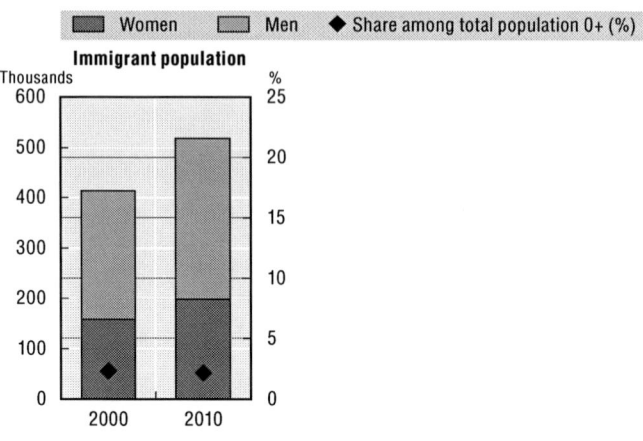

Emigrant population: persons born in Yemen living abroad

	2000						2005/06		
	All destinations			OECD destinations			OECD destinations		
Population 15+	Men	Women	Total	Men	Women	Total	Men	Women	Total
Emigrant population (thousands)	41.4	32.6	74.0	39.0	31.8	70.8	38.0	34.1	72.1
Recent emigrants (thousands)	..	..	..	3.7	2.0	5.6	4.0	4.7	8.6
15-24 (%)	12.1	7.2	10.0	9.7	6.6	8.3	13.6	11.9	12.8
25-64 (%)	60.7	56.1	58.7	61.6	56.0	59.1	62.8	51.9	57.6
65+ (%)	27.2	36.7	31.3	28.8	37.4	32.6	23.6	36.2	29.6
Low-educated (%)	55.2	70.9	62.1	57.8	71.8	64.1	50.3	69.0	59.1
Highly educated (%)	16.8	12.1	14.7	15.0	11.5	13.4	11.7	11.4	11.6
Total emigration rates (%)	0.9	0.7	0.8	0.8	0.7	0.7	0.7	0.6	0.6
Emigration rates of the highly educated (%)	5.8	6.6	6.0	4.9	6.2	5.3	2.7	3.4	3.0

Main destinations in 2005/06

	Total		Recent emigrants	Women	Highly educated	15-24	Total in 2000
Population 15+	Thousands	%	%	%	%	%	Thousands
Israel	32.6	45.3	0.4	58.0	9.6	0.1	39.1
United States	31.5	43.7	21.0	35.1	11.6	23.0	17.0
United Kingdom	–	–	–	–	–	–	11.1
Canada	1.2	1.7	28.2	47.8	49.8	23.1	0.9
Australia	0.4	0.5	14.9	44.1	51.4	6.7	0.2
France	0.3	0.5	43.4	38.9	46.5	22.8	1.6
Netherlands	–	–	–	–	–	–	–
Sweden	–	–	–	–	–	–	0.2
Czech Republic	–	–	–	–	–	–	0.1
Denmark	–	–	–	–	–	–	0.1

Labour market indicators of persons born in Yemen living in OECD countries

Population 15-64	2000			2005/06		
	Men	Women	Total	Men	Women	Total
Employment-population ratio (%)	68.0	39.5	56.1	73.2	28.2	53.9
Unemployment rate (%)	6.7	6.8	6.7	10.1	12.5	10.7
Participation rate (%)	72.8	42.5	60.2	81.4	32.2	60.3
Total employed (thousands)	**18.6**	**7.7**	**26.3**	**20.6**	**6.0**	**26.5**
Employment rates of the highly educated (%)	76.8	60.1	70.3	86.7	54.4	71.4
Unemployment rates of the highly educated (%)	5.5	5.3	5.4	9.7	12.2	10.6
Highly educated in low- and medium-skilled jobs (%)	40.9	36.1	39.7	63.2	35.8	55.4
Highly educated employed (thousands)	**4.2**	**2.1**	**6.4**	**3.0**	**1.7**	**4.7**
Legislators, senior officials and managers	20.1	13.1	17.9	19.7	2.0	11.0
Professionals	15.4	14.8	15.2	11.8	21.7	16.7
Life science and health professionals	2.9	2.3	2.7	1.6	0.8	1.2
Teaching professionals	2.0	7.1	3.5	1.6	18.3	10.2
Technicians and associate professionals	11.7	13.7	12.3	4.1	37.6	20.7
Clerks	8.4	23.6	13.1	5.0	4.7	4.8
Service, shop and market sales workers	10.1	23.6	14.3	21.8	4.4	13.2
Skilled agricultural and fishery workers	0.4	0.5	0.4	1.6	0.1	0.9
Craft and related trades workers	9.5	0.5	6.7	22.5	27.7	25.1
Plant and machine operators and assemblers	12.3	3.6	9.6	7.3	1.0	4.2
Elementary occupations	12.1	6.8	10.4	6.1	0.7	3.4

(Left margin label for occupation rows: Distribution of employment by occupation (%), population 15+)

Persons born in Yemen and their native-born children, population 15+

Living in:	Europe	United States	Australia
2008	Thousands	Thousands	Thousands
Native-born children	5.4	1.9	..
Foreign-born	10.4	53.8	1.0
Total	15.9	55.8	..

International students from Yemen in OECD countries

Five main destinations	2004	2005	2006	2007	2008	2009
Germany	..	..	..	..	299	362
United States	284	249	255	253	233	245
United Kingdom	464	238	166	195	166	139
Canada	38	..	90	63	114	112
France	49	55	59	55	73	69
Total	887	611	650	637	973	1 056

Legal migrant flows to the OECD
Thousands

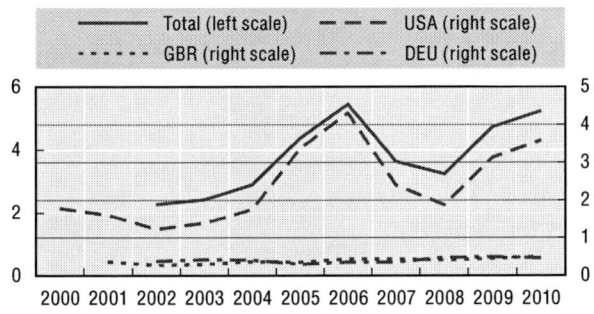

Remittance flows

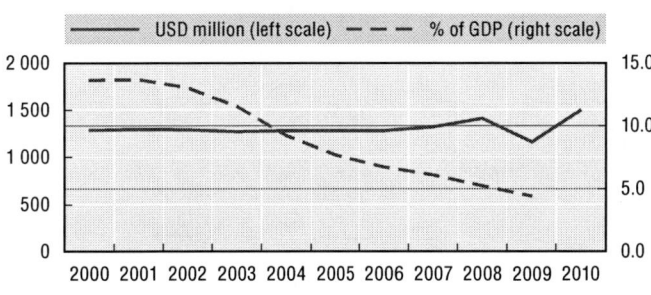

Ten main countries of destination for legal migrants in 2010 (numbers, % of total flows to the country): USA (3591, 0.3%), GBR (496, 0.1%), DEU (465, 0.1%), CAN (180, 0.1%), JPN (96, 0%), SWE (92, 0.1%), NOR (46, 0.2%), TUR (46, 0.2%), POL (37, 0.1%), CHE (34, 0%).

Desire to emigrate, 2008-10

	Women	15-24	Highly educated	Total	Regional total
Persons who would move permanently, if they had the opportunity to do so (%)	18	34	42	27	21
Of which: Persons who are planning to move permanently in the next 12 months (%)				24	16
Of which: Persons who have already done some preparations for this move (*e.g.* visa application) (%)					46

Three main countries of desired destination: Saudi Arabia (56%), United Arab Emirates (13%), United States (6%).

StatLink http://dx.doi.org/10.1787/888932674227

Chapter 7

Sub-Saharan Africa

This chapter looks at recent migration flows and diasporas from the Sub-Saharan African countries to the OECD area. It shows that in 2010 about 330 000 new migrants from the region settled in OECD countries, accounting for about 6% of total immigration flows. In 2005/06 there were 4 million emigrants, 15 years old or older, from the region in OECD countries, of which 49% were women and 36% held a tertiary diploma. Total emigration rate for those over 15 years of age was only 1% for the region as a whole but the emigration rate for the highly educated was the highest recorded at 13.3%. Future challenges relate notably to the persistence of significant highly skilled outmigration and the need to find new and more effective forms of international co-operation to minimise the cost and maximise the development impact of migration.

This chapter also contains 34 country notes for Benin, Botswana, Burkina Faso, Burundi, Cameroon, Chad, Congo, Côte d'Ivoire, Democratic Republic of the Congo, Eritrea, Ethiopia, Gabon, Gambia, Ghana, Guinea, Kenya, Liberia, Madagascar, Malawi, Mali, Mauritius, Mozambique, Namibia, Niger, Nigeria, Rwanda, Senegal, Sierra Leone, South Africa, Togo, Uganda, Tanzania, Zambia and Zimbabawe.

1. Historical migration patterns

In 2010 the Sub-Saharan Africa region, consisting of 40 countries, registered an average GDP per capita (in purchasing power parities) of USD 1 300. The very low standard of living of Sub-Saharan Africa countries, coupled with a high average poverty rate of 70.1% (poverty headcount ratio at USD 2 a day, purchasing power parity), is one of the major push factors for migration, not only from the region but also within the region due to great disparities among countries. Moreover, the rapid population growth (+2.5% in 2010), a nearly two-thirds population share that is under the age of 24, and improved access to education jointly lead to increased demographic and labour market pressure to emigrate, and so shape migration patterns in the region.

The features mentioned above, as well as unstable politics, escalating ethnic conflicts, persistent economic decline, poverty and environmental deterioration, have established Sub-Saharan Africa as a region of high population mobility. Whereas migration in Sub-Saharan Africa has received increasing attention from the research and policy communities over recent decades, little is known about migration flows and stocks to, from, and within the region. This is mainly due to deficient population registration systems and the lack of suitable data, but also to nomadic traditions, cross-border ethnic groups and porous borders that somehow make the notion of migration dubious in its common acceptation and difficult to measure.

Although there is no consensus over the number of people born in a Sub-Saharan African country and living abroad, the United Nations[1] estimated that the overall number of Sub-Saharan migrants in the world amounted to about 16 million in 2005. This stock has steadily increased since 1960, but showed numerous fluctuations resulting from geopolitical and socioeconomic contexts. It increased significantly after the independence movements, reached a peak over the 1975-80 period (+5%), and then slowed down during the 1980s and early 1990s; a decrease followed between 1995 and 2000 (–1% per year); and finally the 2000-05 period saw stabilisation at 1% per year. Three main features emerge from analysis of Sub-Saharan migration:

- Sub-Saharan migrants account for a marginal and decreasing share of the world migrant population, from 10% in 1990 to 8% in 2005.

- Population growth rates in Sub-Saharan Africa being much greater than growth in the number of international migrants from the region, overall emigration rates in the region have steadily decreased since 1990 and remain relatively low, amounting to 2.2% on average in 2005.

- It is now acknowledged that the bulk of migration takes place within the region.

In 2005 the United Nations estimated that migration within the region involved between 7 million and 10 million people, accounting for more than 60% of the total Sub-Saharan migrant population and therefore putting forward a picture of Africa as a vast region of migration. These intra-regional population flows predated the colonial era, due to ancestral traditions such as nomadism but also agricultural seasonality that implied short-term and circular migrations. However, they were reinforced and encouraged during the colonial period to meet labour needs in booming employment areas, so that those patterns kept shaping persistent cross-border migrations after independences. One major feature is that intra-regional migration flows remain extremely focused: from landlocked Sahelian countries to coastal countries in West Africa, to large plantations in Kenya, Tanzania and Uganda in East Africa, to mining and oil-producing countries such as Gabon and Democratic Republic of the Congo (DRC) in Central Africa. Intra-regional migration is fostered by rapid urbanisation and rural depopulation; the establishment of regional economic and monetary areas such as ECOWAS (1975) and ECCAS (1994); and the emergence of Northern African countries and new African "Eldorados" such as Nigeria, Gabon, South Africa and Botswana. However, the configuration of intra-regional migration is constantly changing due to the extreme instability and precariousness of the continent.

Migrations outside the continent are predominantly directed to OECD countries, which in 2005 hosted between 30% and 40% of the total international Sub-Saharan migrant population. Migrations were encouraged after the Second World War through guest worker agreements – mainly in Europe – but flows really intensified after independence over the 1975-80 period, following the economic boom and labour shortages, especially in low-skilled occupations. Subsequently their growth slowed; they were mainly driven by family and humanitarian factors until the late 1990s and again labour factors since 2000, although constrained by more and more restrictive immigration laws. Migration patterns remain strongly determined by former historical and colonial links and linguistic proximity. However, the implementation of selective migration policies in traditional host countries and the economic boom in Southern and Eastern Europe contributed to strengthening migrations to North America and reshaping flows over the past decade towards new European destination countries such as Spain, Italy, Portugal and Greece. The 2008 economic crisis put an end to these recent evolutions. Overall, Sub-Saharan migrants in OECD countries remain highly concentrated, with ten countries (*e.g.* the United States, the United Kingdom, France and Portugal) hosting the vast majority (more than 90%) of their total population.

Apart from those voluntary (family and labour) migrations, one additional feature that cannot be neglected in the Sub-Saharan context is the importance of "forced" migration. Indeed, political instability, conflicts and civil wars were a major cause of migration within the continent over the past three decades. In 2005, according to UNHCR data Sub-Saharan Africa was the region in the world with the highest number of refugees (2.7 million), accounting for more than 15% of the total Sub-Saharan migrant population. Moreover, climate change and desertification keep increasing the number of "environmental refugees", estimated at about 7 million people in the late 1990s.

2. Current profile of emigrant populations

Flows and stocks

In 2010, about 328 000 legal migrants originating from Sub-Saharan Africa moved to an OECD country (Figure 7.1). Migration flows from Sub-Saharan Africa slightly decreased (by 4%) between 2009 and 2010: the 2008 financial crisis strongly impacted low-skilled labour-intensive sectors in which Sub-Saharan Africa migrants are overrepresented (construction, wholesale, etc.). However, this is only a slight drop compared with the over 100% increase in migration flows from Sub-Saharan Africa to the OECD area over the past decade.

Remittance flows to Sub-Saharan Africa rose sharply and steadily over the 2000-09 period, from less than USD 4 billion in 2000 to USD 19 billion in 2010. This increase can be explained by the increasing number of Sub-Saharan migrants, but also reflects the

Figure 7.1. **Migrant flows from Sub-Saharan Africa to OECD countries and remittance flows, 2000-10**

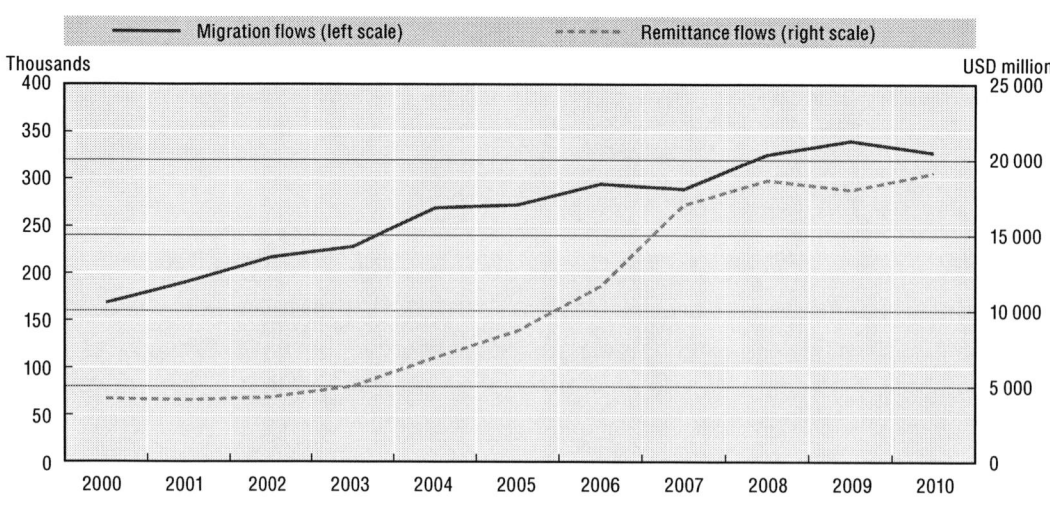

Source: OECD International Migration Database; World Bank.

StatLink ⫴⫴⫴ http://dx.doi.org/10.1787/888932672194

decreasing share of transfers sent via informal channels and previously not recorded. Several countries received at least USD 1 billion in remittances in 2010 (Nigeria 10; Kenya 1.8; Senegal 1.4; Sudan 1.4; South Africa 1.1). Remittances represented about 3.7% of GDP on average in the region – 23.0% in Lesotho, 10.7% in Togo, 10.4% in Senegal, 10.2% in Gambia and a substantial share in small island countries (*e.g.* Cape Verde).

Regarding migrant stocks, the population of people (over age 15) born in Sub-Saharan Africa and living in OECD countries amounted to about 4.1 million in 2005/06, of which 948 000 persons were recent migrants (*i.e.* persons having a residency of five years or less in the destination country) (Figure 7.2). While the number of migrants from Sub-Saharan Africa increased by 1.1 million over the 2000-05/06 period, their share in the total stock of migrants in the OECD area remains rather low (4.8%).

Not surprisingly, among the main sending countries of the African continent, most of the biggest in terms of population size (Democratic Republic of Congo, Ethiopia, Ghana, Kenya, Nigeria and South Africa) are at the top of the list, in both flows and stocks. There are exceptions, however: big countries such as Tanzania do not send many migrants to the OECD area while the reverse holds true for very small ones, such as Cape Verde and Mauritius. Cape Verde is a unique country when it comes to migration. According to some sources, the Cape Verdean diaspora would actually outnumber the current population residing in the country, estimated by the population census at 492 000 in 2010. Of these emigrants, a significant share resides in Portugal and the United States. Within Africa, the biggest Cape Verdean communities can be found in other Portuguese-speaking countries such as Angola and Sao Tome and Principe, but also Senegal.

Returning to the top of the list, South Africa ranks first, with about 474 000 migrants in the OECD area; it is followed by Nigeria (380 000), Ghana (249 000), Ethiopia (248 000) and Kenya (231 000) (Figure 7.2). The main destination countries for South African migrants are the United Kingdom (160 000), Australia (90 000), the United States (80 000) and, to a lesser extent, Canada and New Zealand. For Nigerians and Ghanaians, the two main destination countries are the United States and the United Kingdom, with respective shares of about 48% and 33% for Nigerians and 39% and 31% for Ghanaians.

Figure 7.2. **Total and highly educated emigrant population aged 15 and over from Sub-Saharan Africa in the OECD area, 2005/06**

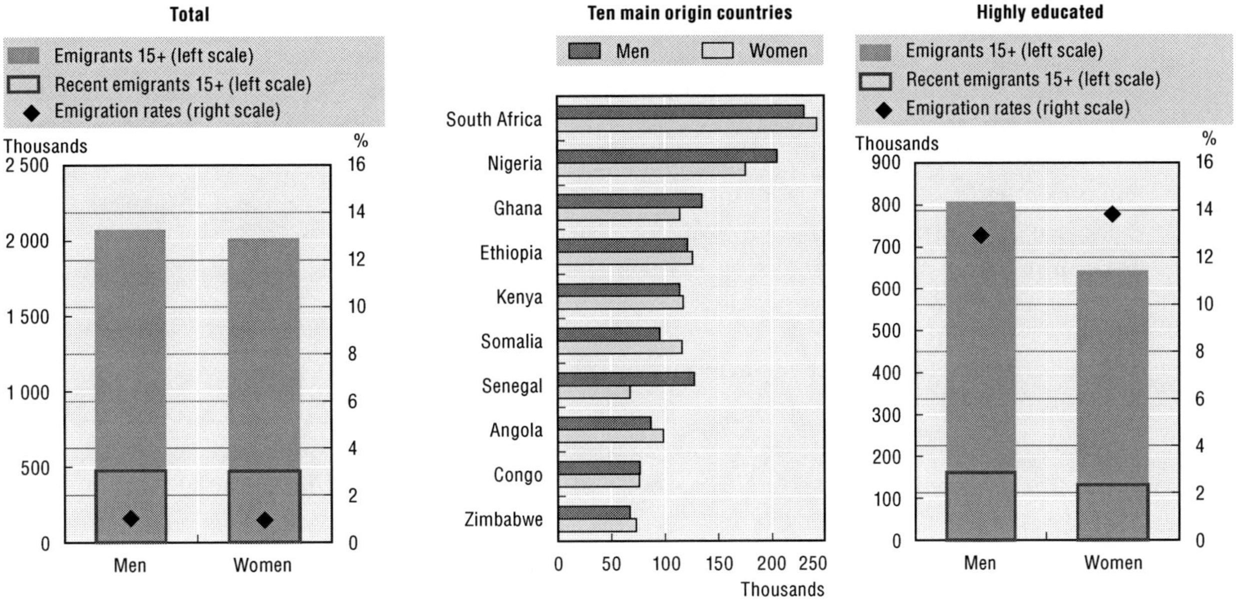

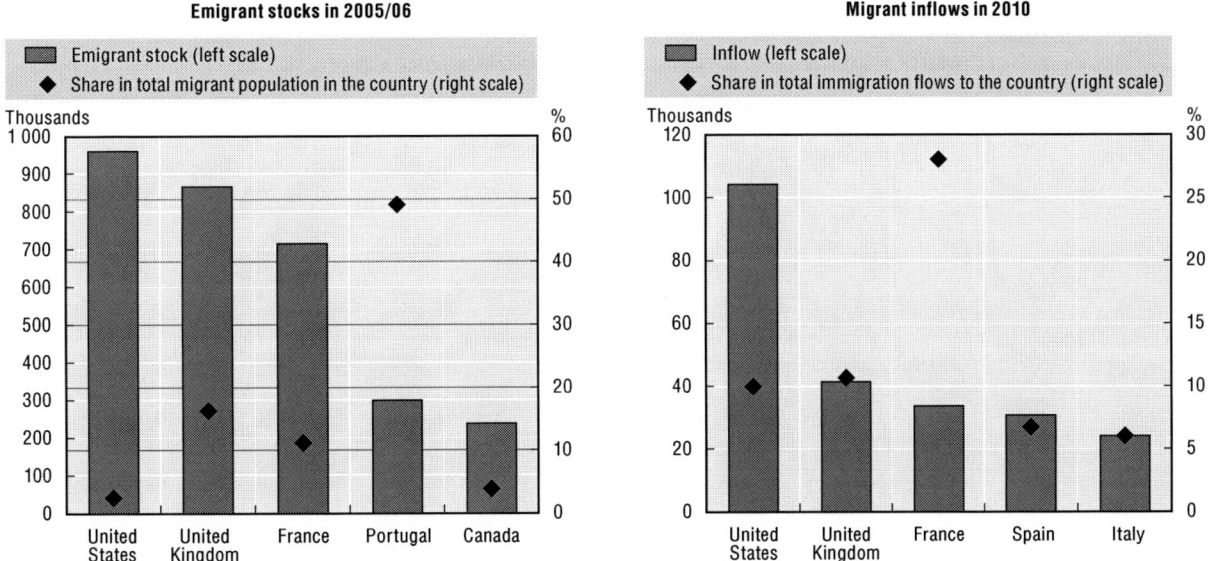

Source: Database on Immigrants in OECD Countries (DIOC 2005/06).

StatLink http://dx.doi.org/10.1787/888932672213

Overall, even though the number of destinations has expanded over the recent years for most African migrants, historical links between populations – a common colonial past in particular – and a common language still strongly determine the direction of migration (Figure 7.3). For example, Portugal still attracts most of the Angolans (75%) and the Mozambicans (85%) residing in the OECD area; France draws migrants from Madagascar

Figure 7.3. **Emigrant populations and migrant flows from Sub-Saharan Africa to the five main destinations within the OECD area, population aged 15 and over**

Source: Database on Immigrants in OECD Countries (DIOC 2005/06); OECD International Migration Database.

StatLink http://dx.doi.org/10.1787/888932672232

(91%), Côte d'Ivoire (66%) and Senegal (50%); and the United Kingdom attracts migrants from Kenya (51%) and Uganda (56%). All together, these three countries host about three-quarters (1.8 million) of the Sub-Saharan migrants residing in the European Union.

As suggested by recent migration flows, Italy and Spain have been attracting a growing number of Sub-Saharan migrants in the past 20 years (Figure 7.3). As a result, Italy now stands as the second main destination country for Senegalese and the third one for Ivoirians, Ghanaians and Nigerians. Turning to Spain, the rise in the number of Sub-Saharan migrants is also quite pronounced, with significant inflows from Western Africa (Mali, Nigeria, Senegal and the Gambia in particular) in the past ten years. The 2008 economic crisis and the massive layoffs that followed, especially in the Spanish construction sector, have however led to a sharp decrease in migration to this country.

Characteristics of emigrant populations in OECD countries

With regard to gender and age, in 2005/06 the number of Sub-Saharan migrant women in the OECD area was very close to the number of Sub-Saharan migrant men (Table 7.1). Such parity is recent, as migration flows both within the African continent and from Sub-Saharan Africa to the OECD have historically been male-dominated. The improved access of women to education and the expansion of the services sector have enhanced women's employability locally and across national borders, while the increase in female migration networks has lowered the cost of migrating and improved access to information about opportunities abroad. As a result, a significant proportion of women are now moving independently to fulfil their own economic needs; they are no longer simply joining a husband or other family members. Within the Sub-Saharan continent, however, Western African countries stand apart, with only 89 women for every 100 men. The share of women is particularly low for countries such as Mauritania (41 women for every 100 men), Guinea-Bissau (47), Senegal (53) and, to a lesser extent, Mali (61), even if the gap between men and women has been narrowing over the past 20 years. At the other extreme are countries such as Botswana and Namibia in Southern Africa; Madagascar, Zambia, Djibouti and the Seychelles in Eastern Africa; and Gabon and Equatorial Guinea in Central Africa, for which the share of women in migrant stocks varies between 55% and 65%.

Table 7.1. **Characteristics of migrants from Sub-Saharan Africa in the OECD area, by gender, 2005/06**

Percentage

	Regional averages (unweighted)			Regional total (weighted)		
	Men	Women	Total	Men	Women	Total
15-24	17.0	17.4	17.0	14.8	15.8	15.3
25-64	78.8	77.5	78.3	80.3	78.3	79.3
65+	4.2	5.1	4.7	4.9	6.0	5.4
Low-educated	30.1	38.9	34.7	28.7	34.8	31.7
Highly educated	37.2	29.7	33.4	39.7	33.0	36.4
Total emigration rates	3.1	3.1	3.1	1.0	1.0	1.0
Emigration rates of the highly educated	15.7	21.5	17.3	13.0	13.8	13.3

Source: Database on Immigrants in OECD Countries (DIOC 2005/06).

StatLink ᴍⓈᴾ http://dx.doi.org/10.1787/888932675177

Analysis of the age structure of the emigrant population from Sub-Saharan Africa countries reveals that Sub-Saharan migrants are on average younger than those from other parts of the world (Table 7.1). Seventeen per cent of Sub-Saharan Africa migrants are aged between 15 and 24, against 10% of migrants born in an OECD country, 12% of migrants born in South, East or Central Asia and 10% for migrants born in the MENA region. However, there are huge variations in the age distribution of migrants depending on which region of Sub-Saharan Africa they come from. The share of young emigrants is the highest for migrants born in Southern African countries (19%) and the lowest for migrants born in Eastern African countries (13%). The higher share of young migrants from Sub-Saharan Africa as compared with other regions may be partly explained by the age distribution of the African population as a whole. Youth currently represents more than 20% of the African population, compared to 18% for other developing regions (Asia and Latin America) and 13% in Europe. In addition, while the share of young people in the total population has started to decrease since the mid-1980s, noticeably in major developing regions and in the world as a whole, this has not been the case in Sub-Saharan Africa, where the share of the youth has remained very stable. The high share of young emigrants from Sub-Saharan Africa may also be explained by the large number of international students from the region studying in OECD countries. Nigeria and Cameroon are the main Sub-Saharan Africa countries of origin of international students in the OECD area, followed by Senegal and Kenya.

On average, the share of highly educated individuals among the emigrant population from Sub-Saharan Africa countries is rather high, and increased between 2000 and 2005/06. It reached 37% in 2005/06, against 32% in 2000. Migrant women have on average lower educational attainment levels than migrant men, but the share of highly educated Sub-Saharan African migrant women in the OECD area also increased over the period, from 28% to 32%. There are, however, strong disparities in education levels among Sub-Saharan migrants depending on which OECD country they reside in. The share of highly educated migrants in the total stock of migrants from Sub-Saharan African countries exceeds 40% in English-speaking countries (Australia, Canada, Ireland, New Zealand, the United Kingdom and the United States, plus Japan) and is close to 50% in former socialist countries,[2] compared with 16% in Southern and Northern European countries, with a share of 26%; continental Europe stands in between. While migration to Europe has long been dominated by low-educated individuals, it now concerns an increasing number of medium or highly educated individuals, so that the share of highly educated migrants observed today is much higher than the one observed twenty or even ten years ago. This marked evolution is due to both the adoption of more selective migration policies biased towards the highly educated, and to the increasing proportion of educated individuals in sending countries.

In terms of labour market outcomes, however, overqualification of Sub-Saharan migrants is an issue, with about a third of employed immigrants with a tertiary degree working in low-skilled jobs (Table 7.2). This phenomenon has substantially increased since 2000, except for migrants coming from a few countries (Congo, Ethiopia, Lesotho, Namibia, South Africa and Mauritania) for whom it has either stagnated or slightly declined.

Table 7.2. **Labour market characteristics of migrants from Sub-Saharan Africa in the OECD area, by gender, 2005/06**

	Regional averages (unweighted)			Regional total (weighted)		
	Men	Women	Total	Men	Women	Total
Employment rate (%)	70.7	57.2	64.4	72.4	57.9	65.3
Unemployment rate (%)	12.2	18.2	14.7	10.4	14.0	12.0
Participation rate (%)	80.2	69.1	75.1	80.7	67.3	74.1
Total employed (thousands)	**1 408**	**1 086**	**2 494**			
Employment rate of the highly educated (%)	78.7	69.7	75.0	81.6	73.8	78.1
Unemployment rate of the highly educated (%)	9.9	12.8	11.0	7.2	8.0	7.5
Participation rate of the highly educated (%)	87.2	79.5	83.9	87.9	80.2	84.5
Highly educated employed (thousands)	**635**	**462**	**1 097**			
Persons with tertiary degrees in low- or medium-skilled jobs (%)	35.8	38.6	37.3	34.0	33.5	33.8

Source: Database on Immigrants in OECD Countries (DIOC 2005/06).

StatLink ⬛ http://dx.doi.org/10.1787/888932675196

Emigration rates and "brain drain"

Since emigration flows are rather low on average, the expatriation rates from Sub-Saharan Africa to OECD countries are very low. (These rates are calculated by dividing the expatriate population aged 15 and over from a given country by the native-born population aged 15 and over of the same country.) Taking Sub-Saharan Africa as a whole, the expatriation rate to the OECD was around 0.8% in 2000 and around 1% in 2005/06. The highest expatriation rates are observed for small island developing states such as Cape Verde, where 28% of the total population aged 15 and over lives abroad; Sao Tome and Principe (20%); the Seychelles (13%); and Mauritius (10%).

Turning to the emigration rates of the highly educated, several interesting features emerge. First, Sub-Saharan Africa's highly educated individuals are much more likely to emigrate than less educated ones: in 2005/06, the emigration rates for tertiary-educated people (13.3%) far exceeded total emigration rates (1%).[3] Second, available data on the size of the "brain drain" in Sub-Saharan African countries exhibit strong disparities. The departure of highly educated individuals in West Africa particularly affects Sierra Leone (with one-third of the highly educated living in an OECD country), Ghana (30%) and Gambia (26%). In East Africa, Mauritius, Malawi and Zimbabwe are strongly affected by the "brain drain" (with expatriation rates higher than a third in all cases), followed by Mozambique, Zambia and Tanzania. In contrast, the "brain drain" is relatively low in French-speaking Western African countries such as Burkina Faso (4.1%), Guinea (5.4%), Niger (5.9%), Benin (7.8%) and Gabon (8.1%).

Between 2000 and 2005/06, emigration rates of the highly educated increased the most in Congo (+25 percentage points), Zimbabwe (+20 percentage points), Malawi (+19 percentage points), Zambia (+9 percentage points) and, to a lesser extent, Gambia and Côte d'Ivoire (+7 percentage points). Over the same period, they significantly decreased in some countries, among which are Mozambique (–8 percentage points), Sierra Leone and Liberia (–4 percentage points), all of which are in post-war regimes.

In 28 of the 33 Sub-Saharan Africa countries for which data on "brain drain" are available, highly educated women are more likely to emigrate to the OECD area than highly educated men. The differences are largest for persons born in Malawi (with a gender gap of 22 percentage points), Zimbabwe (20 percentage points), Zambia (14 percentage points) and Chad (12 percentage points).

3. Future trends and challenges

In recent years, most OECD countries' migration management policies have been influenced by increasing needs for highly educated workers due to labour shortages and population ageing. This partly explains observed trends in migration flows from Sub-Saharan Africa to the OECD area, which have been composed of increasing numbers of individuals with medium or high levels of education.

Such a trend is likely to persist and even increase in the future, not only because of demand-driven factors but also because of push effects. Given the age structure of their population, most Sub-Saharan Africa countries will be subject to heavy pressure on their labour markets for several years, especially as the expansion of their working-age population is being coupled with rising labour force participation rate among young workers. This is likely to be so for Western African countries such as Nigeria, Niger, Mali, Burkina Faso and Liberia, and for Eastern African countries such as Uganda, Rwanda and Kenya. Their populations are indeed expected to grow at an annual rate of at least 2% until 2040, with the share of young people (0-14 years) remaining higher than 40%. This suggests that the number of potential migrants from these countries is expected to be on the rise in the next two or three decades, especially among those with medium or high levels of education, who suffer from higher unemployment levels than the lower-skilled (DIAL, 2007).

However, the recent world crisis – combined with OECD countries' tightening immigration policies, especially in Europe – may deter prospective migrants. This may well result in a substantial increase in migration flows within the African continent, or at least in their persistence at sustained levels, as well as in the establishment of new destinations. Migration patterns to some parts of the continent are also expected to change, with some fast-growing countries such as Botswana, Namibia, South Africa and Gabon attracting an ever larger influx of immigrants. Skilled professionals in particular, pressured by uncertain economic conditions in their home countries, could well consider these booming economies as realistic alternatives to Europe, the United States and the Gulf States. Migration from the rest of Africa to some *Southern African Development Community (SADC)* countries has already increased dramatically since the early 1990s: South Africa has received a growing influx of migrants from various parts of the Sub-Saharan region, including Congo, Mali, Ghana, Nigeria, Senegal, Sierra Leone, Zaire, Kenya and Uganda; Botswana has been hosting increasing numbers of undocumented Zimbabweans, etc. In some cases these unprecedented volumes of new immigrants have given rise to high levels of xenophobia among the population, as illustrated for example by the events of May 2008 in South Africa.[4] One of the upcoming challenges for these newly attractive African countries is thus to better comprehend and manage those increasing flows, in order to make them an additional driving force for their sustained growth.

The likely heightened pressure to emigrate from Sub-Saharan Africa also calls for new and more effective forms of international co-operation to minimise the costs and maximise the development impact of migration, and in the longer term to reduce the pressure to emigrate. Part of the solution is at the level of African sending countries themselves. Strong support for development of the agricultural sector (which still stands out as the main absorption sector), together with sound macroeconomic policies and good governance to attract foreign direct investments and promote job creation in urban labour markets, is critical. So far, most African countries have demonstrated limited capacity to achieve these goals or, more generally, to deal with issues relating to migration. As an illustration, while the volume of migrant remittances and the potential for African diasporas to contribute to development are generally acknowledged, efforts to move migration returns towards development remain far too lacking. However, some progress has been made in recent years. In Senegal for example, the Ministry of Foreign Affairs and Senegalese Abroad was restructured in 1993 to enhance the welfare of nationals abroad and to encourage emigrants to be involved in the socioeconomic development of their home communities. Overall, more than ten African countries (Ethiopia, Ghana, Mali, Nigeria, Rwanda and Sierra Leone among them) have now set up diaspora-related institutions and ministries in order to co-ordinate diaspora-led development issues (Adepoju, 2010). These structures are still new and weak, but with adequate training and additional resources, officials in these institutions could design feasible strategic interventions.

On the whole, the Sub-Saharan African diaspora undoubtedly constitutes an international social capital and a social organisation, made of "networks, norms and trust that could facilitate co-ordination and co-operation of mutual benefit" (Putnam, 1993) and help achieve ends such as economic development and socio-political stabilisation. Yet, whether the diaspora would be willing to participate in the home country's development remains an open question. That jointly depends on the context in the home country and the circumstances that sometimes lead members to curtail links with their origin community in the long run.

Notes

1. Unless otherwise specified, all figures in this section come from the UN's *International Migration Report 2009: A Global Assessment* (United Nations, ST/ESA//SER.A/316), United Nations, Department of Economic and Social Affairs/Population Division (2011).

2. These countries are also those in which the number of Sub-Saharan migrants is very low.

3. These figures refer to weighted averages. The unweighted total emigration rate of Sub-Saharan Africa is 3% and the unweighted average of the emigration rates of the highly educated 17%.

4. On 12 May 2008, a series of riots broke out in the township of Alexandra (in the north-eastern part of Johannesburg) when locals attacked migrants from Mozambique, Malawi and Zimbabwe, killing two people and injuring 40 others.

Country Notes

Sub-Saharan Africa

		Benin compared to:	World	Region
Total population 2010 (millions)	8.8	Human Development Index (HDI)	167/187	28/46
Population growth 2010 (%)	2.8	GDP per capita	158/194	22/46
GDP per capita 2010 (current USD)	750	Emigration rate	174/203	37/47
GDP growth 2010 (%)	3.0	Emigration rate of the highly educated	90/157	30/39
Poverty rate 2003 (USD PPP 2 a day, in %)	75.3			

Age structure of the population 0+ (2010): "0-14": 20%; "15-24": 44%; "25-64": 34%; "65+": 3%.
Level of education of the population 15+ (2010): "Low": 74%; "Medium": 22%; "High": 4%.

Emigrant population living in OECD countries

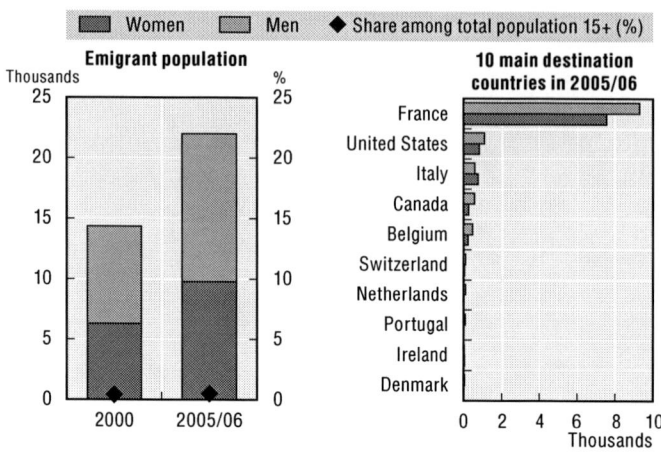

Immigrant population

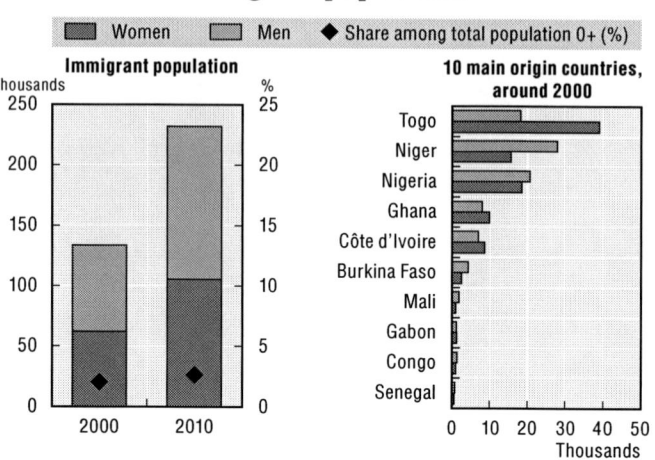

Emigrant population: persons born in Benin living abroad

	2000						2005/06		
	All destinations			OECD destinations			OECD destinations		
Population 15+	Men	Women	Total	Men	Women	Total	Men	Women	Total
Emigrant population (thousands)	15.0	14.4	29.4	8.0	6.3	14.3	12.3	9.7	22.0
Recent emigrants (thousands)	..	..	..	1.4	1.0	2.4	2.4	2.0	4.4
15-24 (%)	17.9	25.3	21.5	14.2	17.9	15.8	14.7	15.3	15.0
25-64 (%)	78.0	71.4	74.7	81.8	78.0	80.1	80.0	80.1	80.0
65+ (%)	4.1	3.3	3.7	4.1	4.1	4.1	5.2	4.7	5.0
Low-educated (%)	33.4	57.9	45.4	20.1	34.0	26.2	16.1	32.4	23.3
Highly educated (%)	36.8	17.0	27.1	51.8	31.3	42.8	54.5	34.1	45.5
Total emigration rates (%)	0.8	0.7	0.7	0.4	0.3	0.4	0.5	0.4	0.5
Emigration rates of the highly educated (%)	8.6	13.4	9.7	6.6	11.0	7.6	6.5	13.6	7.8

Main destinations in 2005/06

	Total		Recent emigrants	Women	Highly educated	15-24	Total in 2000
Population 15+	Thousands	%	%	%	%	%	Thousands
France	16.8	76.5	20.8	44.8	45.8	14.7	11.2
United States	1.9	8.6	17.4	43.3	60.9	13.6	0.9
Italy	1.3	6.0	–	–	–	–	0.7
Canada	0.8	3.8	62.0	31.9	84.3	23.5	0.4
Belgium	–	–	–	–	–	–	0.4
Switzerland	–	–	–	–	–	–	0.2

Labour market indicators of persons born in Benin living in OECD countries

Population 15-64	2000			2005/06		
	Men	Women	Total	Men	Women	Total
Employment-population ratio (%)	66.0	51.2	59.5	65.9	60.6	63.6
Unemployment rate (%)	16.1	25.0	19.7	15.2	20.3	17.4
Participation rate (%)	78.7	68.3	74.1	77.7	76.1	77.0
Total employed (thousands)	**5.0**	**3.0**	**8.0**	**7.1**	**5.2**	**12.3**
Employment rates of the highly educated (%)	73.3	61.2	69.3	82.7	79.6	81.6
Unemployment rates of the highly educated (%)	13.6	16.3	14.4	12.3	15.0	13.2
Highly educated in low- and medium-skilled jobs (%)	24.0	30.6	26.0	29.0	35.4	31.1
Highly educated employed (thousands)	**2.9**	**1.2**	**4.0**	**4.1**	**2.0**	**6.1**
Legislators, senior officials and managers	10.1	5.0	8.1	9.4	5.0	7.6
Professionals	26.1	12.0	20.6	24.1	11.6	18.8
Life science and health professionals	4.5	3.3	4.0	4.9	1.5	3.4
Teaching professionals	8.7	3.5	6.6	5.0	4.1	4.6
Technicians and associate professionals	20.3	19.5	20.0	16.2	18.2	17.1
Clerks	9.3	21.4	14.0	7.2	16.0	11.0
Service, shop and market sales workers	7.6	27.0	15.2	8.6	20.7	13.7
Skilled agricultural and fishery workers	0.4	0.0	0.3	0.4	0.3	0.4
Craft and related trades workers	10.4	1.4	6.9	11.4	1.3	7.1
Plant and machine operators and assemblers	6.2	1.0	4.2	9.4	2.0	6.3
Elementary occupations	9.6	12.6	10.8	13.2	24.8	18.1

Distribution of employment by occupation (%), population 15+

Persons born in Benin and their native-born children, population 15+

Living in:	Europe	United States	Australia
2008	Thousands	Thousands	Thousands
Native-born children	7.0	..	..
Foreign-born	22.8	..	..
Total	29.8	..	..

International students from Benin in OECD countries

Five main destinations	2004	2005	2006	2007	2008	2009
France	2 250	2 340	2 492	2 413	2 258	2 027
United States	168	188	225	259	319	323
Canada	202	..	177	225	167	222
Germany	..	..	..	..	117	127
Italy	13	10	18	28	34	40
Total	2 649	2 565	2 951	2 959	2 965	2 840

Legal migrant flows to the OECD
Thousands

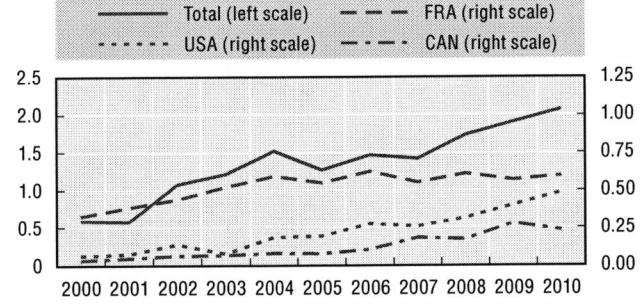

Remittance flows

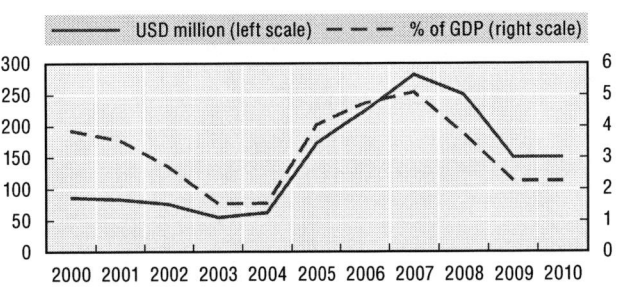

Ten main countries of destination for legal migrants in 2010 (numbers, % of total flows to the country): FRA (596, 0.4%), USA (486, 0%), CAN (235, 0.1%), DEU (233, 0%), ITA (231, 0.1%), BEL (110, 0.1%), JPN (59, 0%), ESP (36, 0%), CHE (31, 0%), NLD (17, 0%).

Desire to emigrate, 2008-10

	Women	15-24	Highly educated	Total	Regional total
Persons who would move permanently, if they had the opportunity to do so (%)	..	..	..	..	33
Of which: Persons who are planning to move permanently in the next 12 months (%)				..	12
Of which: Persons who have already done some preparations for this move (*e.g.* visa application) (%)					33

StatLink ⟶ http://dx.doi.org/10.1787/888932674246

			Botswana compared to:	World	Region
Total population 2010 (millions)		2.0	Human Development Index (HDI)	118/187	4/46
Population growth 2010 (%)		1.3	GDP per capita	75/194	5/46
GDP per capita 2010 (current USD)		7 403	Emigration rate	170/203	34/47
GDP growth 2010 (%)		7.2	Emigration rate of the highly educated	112/157	34/39
Poverty rate 2010 (USD PPP 2 a day, in %)		..			

Age structure of the population 0+ (2010): "0-14": 22%; "15-24": 33%; "25-64": 41%; "65+": 4%.
Level of education of the population 15+ (2010): "Low": 16%; "Medium": 80%; "High": 4%.

Emigrant population living in OECD countries

Immigrant population

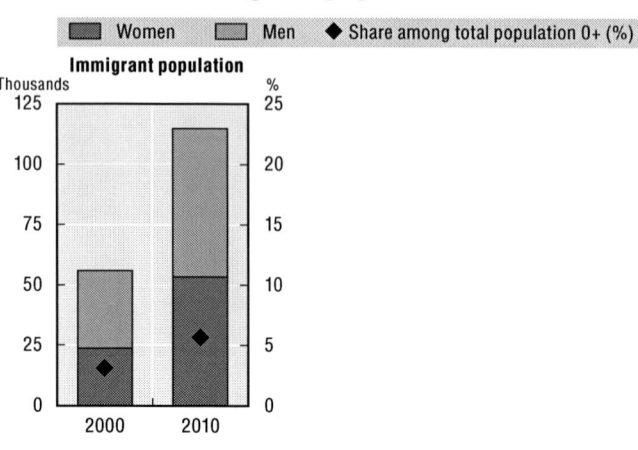

Emigrant population: persons born in Botswana living abroad

	2000						2005/06		
	All destinations			OECD destinations			OECD destinations		
Population 15+	Men	Women	Total	Men	Women	Total	Men	Women	Total
Emigrant population (thousands)	13.0	7.9	20.9	2.1	2.0	4.1	2.3	3.5	5.9
Recent emigrants (thousands)	..	..	..	0.7	0.8	1.5	0.5	1.2	1.7
15-24 (%)	30.6	31.2	30.8	43.8	38.9	41.3	38.3	21.5	28.2
25-64 (%)	62.7	58.3	61.1	54.6	60.0	57.3	61.0	78.1	71.3
65+ (%)	6.7	10.5	8.1	1.6	1.2	1.4	0.7	0.4	0.5
Low-educated (%)	58.0	46.6	53.7	13.6	12.2	12.9	4.3	19.1	13.2
Highly educated (%)	9.8	13.6	11.2	37.5	40.0	38.8	47.1	38.6	42.0
Total emigration rates (%)	2.4	1.4	1.9	0.4	0.4	0.4	0.4	0.6	0.5
Emigration rates of the highly educated (%)	5.5	6.7	6.0	3.3	5.0	4.0	4.3	7.3	5.6

Main destinations in 2005/06

	Total		Recent emigrants	Women	Highly educated	15-24	Total in 2000
Population 15+	Thousands	%	%	%	%	%	Thousands
United Kingdom	–	–	–	–	–	–	1.6
United States	1.7	28.2	17.0	50.5	34.3	16.6	1.3
Australia	0.7	11.6	70.2	39.0	41.8	42.6	0.5
Canada	0.4	6.2	36.1	38.4	43.8	60.3	0.1
Ireland	–	–	–	–	–	–	0.1
Netherlands	–	–	–	–	–	–	–
New Zealand	–	–	–	–	–	–	–
Denmark	–	–	–	–	–	–	–
France	–	–	–	–	–	–	0.2
Sweden	–	–	–	–	–	–	0.1

Labour market indicators of persons born in Botswana living in OECD countries

Population 15-64	2000			2005/06		
	Men	Women	Total	Men	Women	Total
Employment-population ratio (%)	34.9	44.2	39.5	59.0	67.9	64.6
Unemployment rate (%)	17.1	11.4	14.0	18.7	15.0	16.3
Participation rate (%)	42.0	49.9	46.0	72.6	79.8	77.2
Total employed (thousands)	**0.7**	**0.9**	**1.5**	**1.0**	**1.9**	**2.9**
Employment rates of the highly educated (%)	39.7	50.9	45.4	90.2	72.3	80.4
Unemployment rates of the highly educated (%)	12.2	9.4	10.6	19.6	3.7	11.8
Highly educated in low- and medium-skilled jobs (%)	28.3	32.8	31.0	32.3	69.0	52.4
Highly educated employed (thousands)	**0.3**	**0.4**	**0.7**	**0.6**	**0.7**	**1.4**
Legislators, senior officials and managers	11.5	9.9	10.6	2.0	0.3	0.8
Professionals	24.2	18.6	21.1	45.9	11.1	22.0
Life science and health professionals	5.0	3.9	4.4	3.2	1.1	1.8
Teaching professionals	6.0	8.9	7.6	0.8	7.3	5.3
Technicians and associate professionals	11.2	17.1	14.5	2.9	6.5	5.4
Clerks	5.7	15.0	10.9	0.9	41.6	28.8
Service, shop and market sales workers	18.7	24.5	21.9	5.3	4.5	4.8
Skilled agricultural and fishery workers	2.5	–	1.1	0.4	33.2	22.9
Craft and related trades workers	6.7	0.6	3.3	17.4	–	5.5
Plant and machine operators and assemblers	5.2	1.9	3.4	2.0	0.2	0.8
Elementary occupations	14.2	12.4	13.2	23.3	2.6	9.1

Distribution of employment by occupation (%), population 15+

Persons born in Botswana and their native-born children, population 15+

Living in:	Europe	United States	Australia
2008	Thousands	Thousands	Thousands
Native-born children	..	..	..
Foreign-born	1.0	..	..
Total	..	..	..

International students from Botswana in OECD countries

Five main destinations	2004	2005	2006	2007	2008	2009
United Kingdom	700	688	652	629	591	710
Australia	792	761	665	537	511	468
United States	488	353	294	232	236	293
Canada	107	..	159	123	190	222
Ireland	..	..	..	..	54	59
Total	2 105	1 819	1 790	1 554	1 625	1 843

Legal migrant flows to the OECD
Thousands

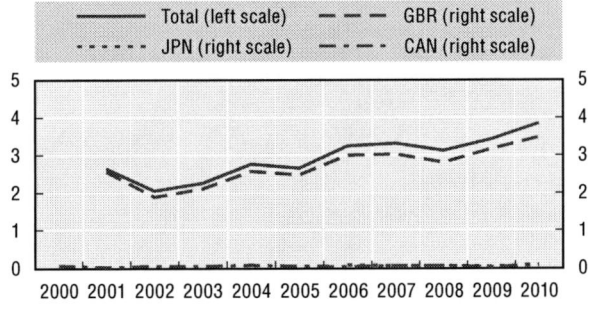

Remittance flows

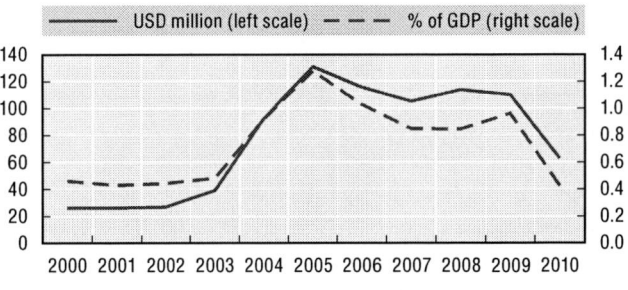

Ten main countries of destination for legal migrants in 2010 (numbers, % of total flows to the country): GBR (3481, 0.8%), JPN (91, 0%), CAN (70, 0%), USA (66, 0%), AUS (60, 0%), IRL (17, 0.1%), DEU (15, 0%), NZL (14, 0%), NLD (6, 0%), FRA (5, 0%).

Desire to emigrate, 2008-10

	Women	15-24	Highly educated	Total	Regional total
Persons who would move permanently, if they had the opportunity to do so (%)	..	..	..	..	33
Of which: Persons who are planning to move permanently in the next 12 months (%)				..	12
Of which: Persons who have already done some preparations for this move (*e.g.* visa application) (%)					33

StatLink ⟪⟫ http://dx.doi.org/10.1787/888932674265

BURKINA FASO – Country Notes

		Burkina Faso compared to:	World	Region
Total population 2010 (millions)	16.5	Human Development Index (HDI)	181/187	40/46
Population growth 2010 (%)	3.0	GDP per capita	167/194	28/46
GDP per capita 2010 (current USD)	536	Emigration rate	195/203	44/47
GDP growth 2010 (%)	9.2	Emigration rate of the highly educated	130/157	37/39
Poverty rate 2003 (USD PPP 2 a day, in %)	81.2			

Age structure of the population 0+ (2010): "0-14": 20%; "15-24": 45%; "25-64": 32%; "65+": 2%.

Emigrant population living in OECD countries

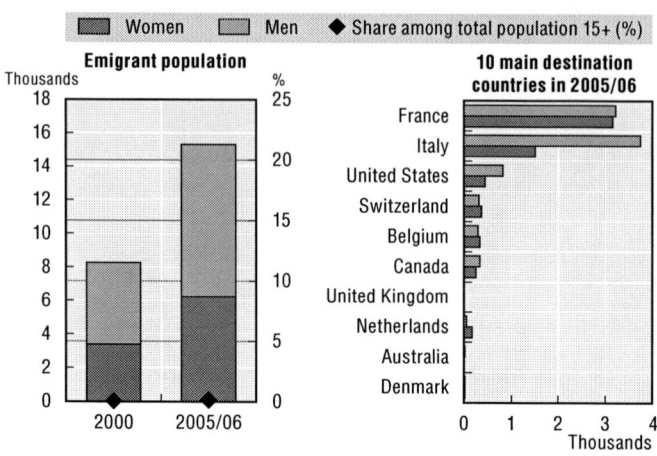

Immigrant population

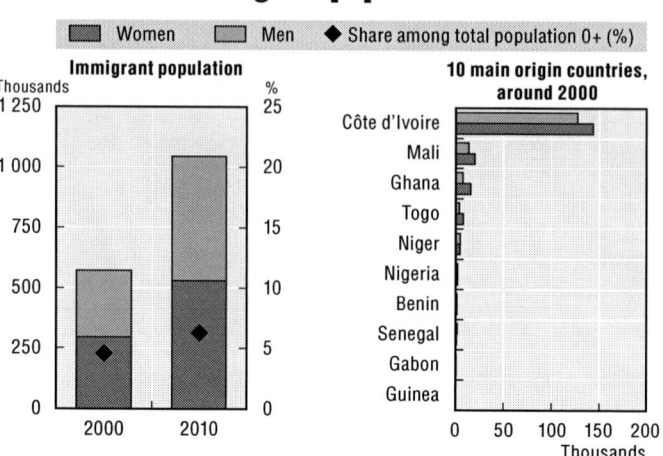

Emigrant population: persons born in Burkina Faso living abroad

	2000						2005/06		
	All destinations			OECD destinations			OECD destinations		
Population 15+	Men	Women	Total	Men	Women	Total	Men	Women	Total
Emigrant population (thousands)	498.3	405.0	903.3	4.9	3.4	8.3	9.1	6.3	15.3
Recent emigrants (thousands)	..	..	..	1.2	1.2	2.4	2.8	1.9	4.8
15-24 (%)	29.0	41.6	34.7	10.4	19.6	14.2	12.0	22.0	16.0
25-64 (%)	67.3	57.0	62.7	87.8	78.7	84.1	85.9	75.4	81.6
65+ (%)	3.6	1.4	2.6	1.7	1.7	1.7	2.1	2.6	2.3
Low-educated (%)	96.1	97.3	96.7	47.5	48.3	47.9	46.5	51.6	48.6
Highly educated (%)	0.9	0.4	0.7	32.9	23.5	29.1	28.1	25.4	27.0
Total emigration rates (%)	14.0	11.2	12.6	0.2	0.1	0.1	0.2	0.2	0.2
Emigration rates of the highly educated (%)	7.4	10.2	8.0	2.8	4.9	3.2	3.2	7.3	4.1

Main destinations in 2005/06

	Total		Recent emigrants	Women	Highly educated	15-24	Total in 2000
Population 15+	Thousands	%	%	%	%	%	Thousands
France	6.4	41.7	26.9	49.5	37.9	15.1	4.3
Italy	5.3	34.4	39.4	28.8	–	19.8	2.2
United States	1.3	8.2	18.1	34.5	50.1	11.7	0.6
Switzerland	–	–	–	–	–	–	0.2
Belgium	–	–	–	–	–	–	0.4
Canada	0.6	3.7	62.7	43.0	62.3	29.8	0.3

Labour market indicators of persons born in Burkina Faso living in OECD countries

Population 15-64	2000			2005/06		
	Men	Women	Total	Men	Women	Total
Employment-population ratio (%)	75.0	45.0	62.6	74.1	48.9	63.8
Unemployment rate (%)	12.5	20.9	15.2	9.3	19.5	12.8
Participation rate (%)	85.6	56.9	73.7	81.7	60.8	73.2
Total employed (thousands)	**3.5**	**1.5**	**5.0**	**6.1**	**2.8**	**8.9**
Employment rates of the highly educated (%)	76.4	56.2	69.7	80.4	79.7	80.2
Unemployment rates of the highly educated (%)	11.8	18.2	13.6	6.9	12.7	9.1
Highly educated in low- and medium-skilled jobs (%)	25.7	33.0	26.2	22.3	25.5	23.6
Highly educated employed (thousands)	**1.2**	**0.4**	**1.6**	**1.6**	**1.0**	**2.6**
Legislators, senior officials and managers	6.6	1.1	6.0	3.6	3.4	3.5
Professionals	15.7	7.6	14.9	16.0	14.6	15.5
Life science and health professionals	2.8	–	2.6	1.2	2.3	1.6
Teaching professionals	3.0	0.4	2.8	6.6	6.3	6.5
Technicians and associate professionals	10.6	11.8	10.7	7.4	16.8	10.4
Clerks	3.4	16.3	4.8	2.9	11.6	5.7
Service, shop and market sales workers	4.9	16.9	6.2	4.9	20.2	9.8
Skilled agricultural and fishery workers	1.7	1.1	1.6	0.7	0.6	0.7
Craft and related trades workers	19.3	8.7	18.2	6.1	12.9	8.3
Plant and machine operators and assemblers	12.7	3.7	11.8	20.3	5.3	15.5
Elementary occupations	25.1	32.9	25.9	38.1	14.5	30.6

Distribution of employment by occupation (%), population 15+

Persons born in Burkina Faso and their native-born children, population 15+

Living in:	Europe	United States	Australia
2008	Thousands	Thousands	Thousands
Native-born children	6.5	..	..
Foreign-born	14.8	..	..
Total	21.3	..	..

International students from Burkina Faso in OECD countries

Five main destinations	2004	2005	2006	2007	2008	2009
France	703	853	1 004	1 140	1 127	1 114
United States	191	289	351	432	515	559
Canada	160	..	174	177	188	199
Germany	..	..	..	..	83	83
Italy	34	29	37	38	46	51
Total	1 098	1 184	1 576	1 805	2 059	2 105

Legal migrant flows to the OECD
Thousands

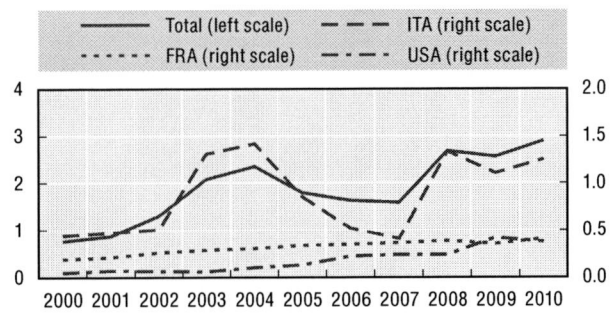

Remittance flows

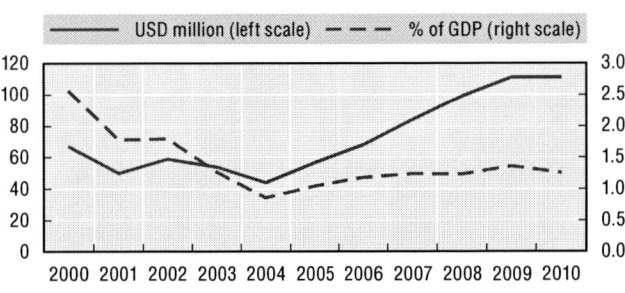

Ten main countries of destination for legal migrants in 2010 (numbers, % of total flows to the country): ITA (1255, 0.3%), FRA (409, 0.3%), USA (377, 0%), DEU (191, 0%), JPN (170, 0.1%), CAN (165, 0.1%), ESP (128, 0.1%), BEL (75, 0.1%), CHE (44, 0%), AUT (22, 0%).

Desire to emigrate, 2008-10

	Women	15-24	Highly educated	Total	Regional total
Persons who would move permanently, if they had the opportunity to do so (%)	22	40	..	28	33
Of which: Persons who are planning to move permanently in the next 12 months (%)				20	12
Of which: Persons who have already done some preparations for this move (*e.g.* visa application) (%)					33

Three main countries of desired destination: Côte d'Ivoire (24%), United States (20%), France (8%).

StatLink http://dx.doi.org/10.1787/888932674284

Total population 2010 (millions)	8.4	Burundi compared to:	World	Region
Population growth 2010 (%)	2.6	Human Development Index (HDI)	185/187	44/46
GDP per capita 2010 (current USD)	192	GDP per capita	186/194	45/46
GDP growth 2010 (%)	3.9	Emigration rate	179/203	39/47
Poverty rate 2006 (USD PPP 2 a day, in %)	93.5	Emigration rate of the highly educated	34/157	12/39

Age structure of the population 0+ (2010): "0-14": 23%; "15-24": 38%; "25-64": 37%; "65+": 3%.
Level of education of the population 15+ (2010): "Low": 91%; "Medium": 8%; "High": 1%.

Emigrant population living in OECD countries

Immigrant population

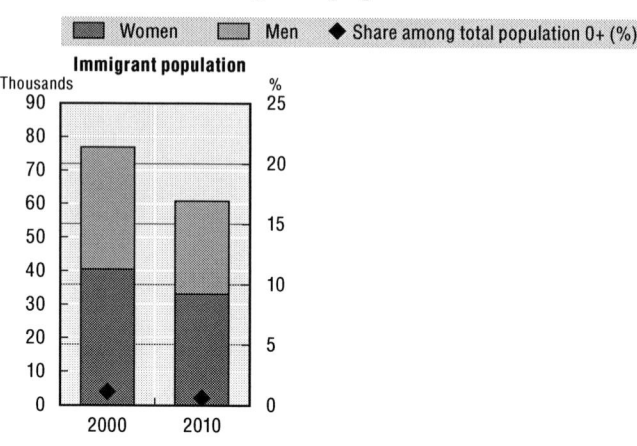

Emigrant population: persons born in Burundi living abroad

	2000						2005/06		
	All destinations			OECD destinations			OECD destinations		
Population 15+	Men	Women	Total	Men	Women	Total	Men	Women	Total
Emigrant population (thousands)	66.9	65.3	132.1	5.2	5.5	10.7	7.6	9.2	16.7
Recent emigrants (thousands)	..	..	..	1.6	1.7	3.3	2.7	3.6	6.3
15-24 (%)	20.5	20.9	20.7	18.7	23.0	21.0	27.5	21.1	24.0
25-64 (%)	66.0	69.9	67.9	79.6	75.6	77.5	70.8	76.7	74.0
65+ (%)	13.6	9.2	11.4	1.7	1.3	1.5	1.8	2.3	2.0
Low-educated (%)	87.0	88.7	87.8	21.3	31.2	26.4	26.3	33.5	30.2
Highly educated (%)	5.7	4.1	4.9	50.1	35.2	42.4	47.4	39.4	43.1
Total emigration rates (%)	3.9	3.4	3.7	0.3	0.3	0.3	0.4	0.4	0.4
Emigration rates of the highly educated (%)	27.8	31.1	29.1	19.4	23.3	20.9	15.4	26.0	19.3

Main destinations in 2005/06

	Total		Recent emigrants	Women	Highly educated	15-24	Total in 2000
Population 15+	Thousands	%	%	%	%	%	Thousands
Canada	4.0	23.6	50.1	48.0	54.2	26.6	2.1
Belgium	–	–	–	–	–	–	3.2
United States	2.3	14.0	14.3	39.9	41.7	30.2	0.8
United Kingdom	–	–	–	–	–	–	1.7
Sweden	1.3	8.0	96.3	54.7	36.0	33.3	0.3
France	1.3	7.7	27.6	56.8	46.2	23.3	1.1
Netherlands	–	–	–	–	–	–	–
Australia	0.6	3.4	95.6	47.6	15.5	34.4	–
Denmark	0.4	2.1	34.3	57.1	23.6	25.2	0.2
Switzerland	–	–	–	–	–	–	0.3

Labour market indicators of persons born in Burundi living in OECD countries

Population 15-64	2000			2005/06		
	Men	Women	Total	Men	Women	Total
Employment-population ratio (%)	58.3	41.2	49.4	57.8	39.9	47.8
Unemployment rate (%)	19.8	27.9	23.5	18.0	22.4	20.1
Participation rate (%)	72.6	57.1	64.6	70.5	51.4	59.9
Total employed (thousands)	**2.6**	**2.0**	**4.6**	**3.3**	**2.8**	**6.1**
Employment rates of the highly educated (%)	70.5	60.4	66.2	87.3	73.4	80.2
Unemployment rates of the highly educated (%)	16.4	18.9	17.4	13.9	18.8	16.1
Highly educated in low- and medium-skilled jobs (%)	35.4	38.6	36.6	34.2	39.6	36.7
Highly educated employed (thousands)	**1.6**	**1.0**	**2.6**	**2.1**	**1.7**	**3.8**
Legislators, senior officials and managers	7.6	3.9	5.9	13.4	2.5	8.2
Professionals	25.4	15.2	20.9	19.1	25.0	21.9
Life science and health professionals	8.6	0.8	5.0	3.5	11.6	7.5
Teaching professionals	3.5	2.9	3.2	2.8	12.0	7.4
Technicians and associate professionals	13.7	18.6	15.9	19.1	13.8	16.5
Clerks	13.0	24.0	17.9	12.7	22.6	17.4
Service, shop and market sales workers	9.5	25.8	16.7	8.9	19.2	13.8
Skilled agricultural and fishery workers	1.4	0.2	0.9	0.9	0.7	0.8
Craft and related trades workers	9.1	2.2	6.1	8.5	0.4	4.6
Plant and machine operators and assemblers	8.0	1.9	5.3	5.5	2.5	4.1
Elementary occupations	12.4	8.1	10.5	12.1	13.2	12.6

Distribution of employment by occupation (%), population 15+

Persons born in Burundi and their native-born children, population 15+

Living in:	Europe	United States	Australia
2008	Thousands	Thousands	Thousands
Native-born children	2.6	..	..
Foreign-born	8.8	..	..
Total	11.4	..	..

International students from Burundi in OECD countries

Five main destinations	2004	2005	2006	2007	2008	2009
France	186	193	214	281	300	334
Canada	131	..	84	159	159	193
United States	80	86	81	87	87	84
Italy	99	31	41	40	53	43
United Kingdom	25	25	40	45	40	26
Total	535	378	496	669	717	767

Legal migrant flows to the OECD
Thousands

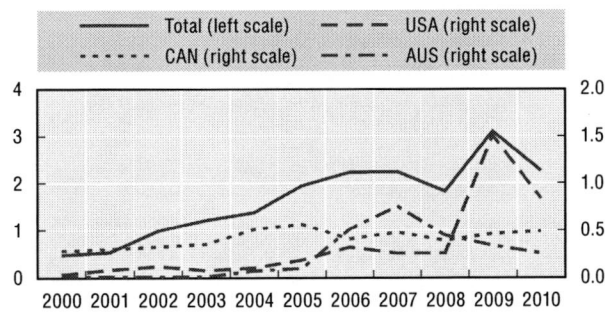

Remittance flows

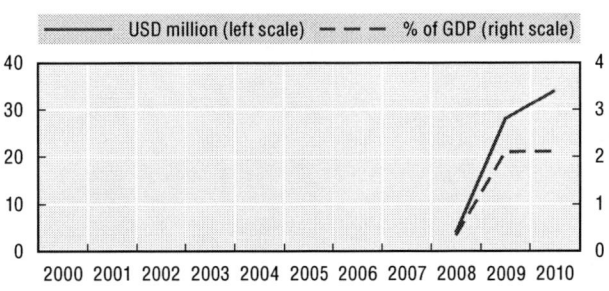

Ten main countries of destination for legal migrants in 2010 (numbers, % of total flows to the country): USA (841, 0.1%), CAN (490, 0.2%), AUS (253, 0.1%), BEL (212, 0.2%), SWE (107, 0.1%), JPN (99, 0%), FRA (77, 0%), ITA (37, 0%), NOR (34, 0.1%), NLD (29, 0%).

Desire to emigrate, 2008-10

	Women	15-24	Highly educated	Total	Regional total
Persons who would move permanently, if they had the opportunity to do so (%)	14	22	..	14	33
Of which: Persons who are planning to move permanently in the next 12 months (%)				29	12
Of which: Persons who have already done some preparations for this move (*e.g.* visa application) (%)					33

Three main countries of desired destination: United States (21%), Canada (14%), Tanzania (13%).

StatLink ⟶ http://dx.doi.org/10.1787/888932674303

Total population 2010 (millions)	19.6		Cameroon compared to:	World	Region
Population growth 2010 (%)	2.2		Human Development Index (HDI)	150/187	15/46
GDP per capita 2010 (current USD)	1 143		GDP per capita	147/194	17/46
GDP growth 2010 (%)	2.6		Emigration rate	145/203	22/47
Poverty rate 2007 (USD PPP 2 a day, in %)	30.4		Emigration rate of the highly educated	39/157	13/39

Age structure of the population 0+ (2010): "0-14": 21%; "15-24": 41%; "25-64": 35%; "65+": 4%.
Level of education of the population 15+ (2010): "Low": 70%; "Medium": 27%; "High": 3%.

Emigrant population living in OECD countries

Immigrant population

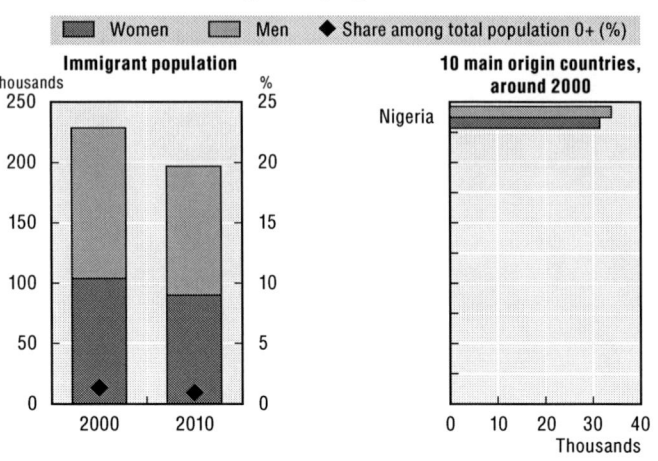

Emigrant population: persons born in Cameroon living abroad

	2000						2005/06		
	All destinations			OECD destinations			OECD destinations		
Population 15+	Men	Women	Total	Men	Women	Total	Men	Women	Total
Emigrant population (thousands)	31.8	31.3	63.1	29.0	29.6	58.6	51.3	59.8	111.0
Recent emigrants (thousands)	..	..	..	6.1	9.2	15.3	16.5	19.6	36.1
15-24 (%)	19.1	22.1	20.6	17.8	21.1	19.5	17.0	17.4	17.2
25-64 (%)	79.4	75.9	77.7	80.7	77.0	78.8	80.9	79.7	80.3
65+ (%)	1.5	1.9	1.7	1.5	1.9	1.7	2.1	2.9	2.5
Low-educated (%)	18.0	30.2	24.1	17.6	29.9	23.8	15.8	29.8	23.3
Highly educated (%)	50.2	34.5	42.4	51.3	35.0	43.1	53.0	33.9	42.7
Total emigration rates (%)	0.7	0.7	0.7	0.6	0.6	0.6	1.0	1.1	1.1
Emigration rates of the highly educated (%)	13.0	22.6	15.8	12.4	22.1	15.1	15.7	20.4	17.4

Main destinations in 2005/06

	Total		Recent emigrants	Women	Highly educated	15-24	Total in 2000
Population 15+	Thousands	%	%	%	%	%	Thousands
France	58.8	53.0	27.8	58.4	35.9	19.7	33.1
United States	25.1	22.6	41.0	49.7	58.2	16.6	11.1
Switzerland	6.1	5.5	64.9	70.0	25.7	–	2.2
United Kingdom	–	–	–	–	–	–	2.9
Italy	4.3	3.8	47.9	45.5	26.1	–	2.1
Belgium	–	–	–	–	–	–	2.2
Canada	3.5	3.2	52.0	44.6	77.1	16.0	2.2
Netherlands	–	–	–	–	–	–	–
Sweden	0.6	0.5	88.5	27.3	71.6	11.6	0.2
Ireland	0.5	0.5	85.3	55.6	45.9	17.2	0.2

Labour market indicators of persons born in Cameroon living in OECD countries

Population 15-64	2000			2005/06		
	Men	Women	Total	Men	Women	Total
Employment-population ratio (%)	61.2	49.3	55.2	64.3	53.5	58.5
Unemployment rate (%)	18.6	25.3	21.7	16.4	25.6	21.2
Participation rate (%)	75.2	66.0	70.5	76.9	71.9	74.2
Total employed (thousands)	**17.0**	**13.9**	**30.9**	**31.9**	**30.8**	**62.7**
Employment rates of the highly educated (%)	71.9	62.8	68.1	85.0	79.0	82.4
Unemployment rates of the highly educated (%)	15.1	17.2	15.9	13.1	15.1	13.9
Highly educated in low- and medium-skilled jobs (%)	27.6	33.6	29.9	35.2	36.9	35.9
Highly educated employed (thousands)	**10.2**	**6.3**	**16.5**	**19.4**	**13.3**	**32.7**
Legislators, senior officials and managers	11.5	5.6	8.8	9.4	5.1	7.3
Professionals	25.3	10.6	18.5	25.0	11.5	18.3
Life science and health professionals	3.4	1.9	2.7	5.0	2.7	3.9
Teaching professionals	5.7	3.1	4.5	5.5	2.8	4.1
Technicians and associate professionals	19.6	21.0	20.2	13.8	16.5	15.1
Clerks	6.7	16.9	11.4	6.3	13.7	10.0
Service, shop and market sales workers	7.1	28.3	16.9	7.4	26.2	16.7
Skilled agricultural and fishery workers	0.8	0.4	0.6	1.2	1.6	1.4
Craft and related trades workers	10.5	2.3	6.7	10.1	2.6	6.4
Plant and machine operators and assemblers	7.8	2.0	5.2	10.4	2.1	6.2
Elementary occupations	10.7	12.9	11.7	16.5	20.7	18.6

Distribution of employment by occupation (%), population 15+

Persons born in Cameroon and their native-born children, population 15+

Living in:	Europe	United States	Australia
2008	Thousands	Thousands	Thousands
Native-born children	26.0	9.7	..
Foreign-born	100.8	17.2	..
Total	126.8	26.9	..

International students from Cameroon in OECD countries

Five main destinations	2004	2005	2006	2007	2008	2009
France	4 963	5 043	5 387	5 570	5 655	5 826
Germany	..	..	..	..	5 000	5 038
Italy	1 041	1 364	1 405	1 614	1 915	2 155
United States	1 216	1 425	1 638	1 839	1 893	1 796
Canada	491	..	402	522	469	563
Total	8 100	8 543	9 578	10 338	16 466	17 454

Legal migrant flows to the OECD
Thousands

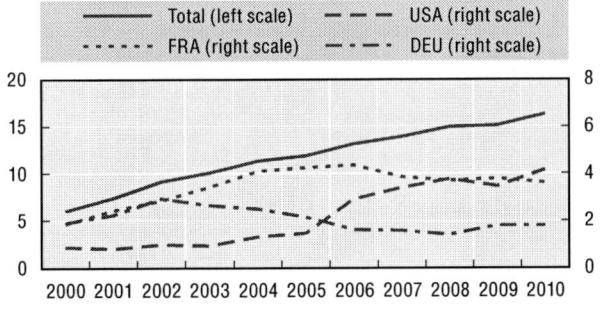

Remittance flows

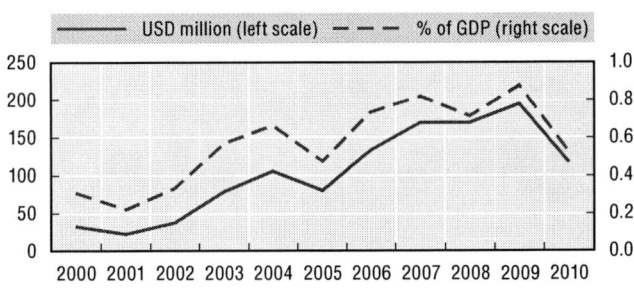

Ten main countries of destination for legal migrants in 2010 (numbers, % of total flows to the country): USA (4161, 0.4%), FRA (3607, 2.7%), DEU (1786, 0.3%), ITA (1226, 0.3%), CAN (1225, 0.4%), BEL (1176, 1.2%), GBR (912, 0.2%), ESP (723, 0.2%), CHE (396, 0.3%), JPN (145, 0.1%).

Desire to emigrate, 2008-10

	Women	15-24	Highly educated	Total	Regional total
Persons who would move permanently, if they had the opportunity to do so (%)	..	..	..	..	33
Of which: Persons who are planning to move permanently in the next 12 months (%)				..	12
Of which: Persons who have already done some preparations for this move (*e.g.* visa application) (%)					33

StatLink 🔣 http://dx.doi.org/10.1787/888932674322

Total population 2010 (millions)	11.2		Chad compared to:	World	Region
Population growth 2010 (%)	2.6		Human Development Index (HDI)	183/187	42/46
GDP per capita 2010 (current USD)	676		GDP per capita	160/194	24/46
GDP growth 2010 (%)	4.3		Emigration rate	196/203	45/47
Poverty rate 2003 (USD PPP 2 a day, in %)	83.3		Emigration rate of the highly educated	94/157	32/39

Age structure of the population 0+ (2010): "0-14": 20%; "15-24": 45%; "25-64": 32%; "65+": 3%.

Emigrant population living in OECD countries

Immigrant population

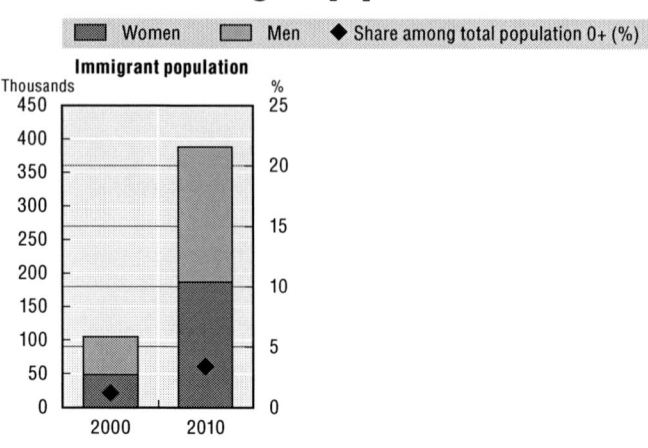

Emigrant population: persons born in Chad living abroad

	2000						2005/06		
	All destinations			OECD destinations			OECD destinations		
Population 15+	Men	Women	Total	Men	Women	Total	Men	Women	Total
Emigrant population (thousands)	6.1	4.0	10.1	3.4	2.4	5.8	4.8	3.6	8.4
Recent emigrants (thousands)	..	..	..	0.4	0.2	0.7	0.9	0.6	1.5
15-24 (%)	23.1	24.4	23.6	14.0	15.3	14.6	11.4	13.8	12.4
25-64 (%)	75.1	73.2	74.4	85.3	83.4	84.5	85.5	79.3	82.9
65+ (%)	1.8	2.4	2.0	0.7	1.2	0.9	3.1	6.9	4.7
Low-educated (%)	33.7	47.2	39.2	18.4	30.3	23.3	17.5	32.6	24.0
Highly educated (%)	40.9	27.7	35.6	47.6	36.7	43.0	46.1	34.1	40.9
Total emigration rates (%)	0.3	0.2	0.2	0.2	0.1	0.1	0.2	0.1	0.2
Emigration rates of the highly educated (%)	7.6	22.6	9.6	5.2	19.1	7.0	5.6	17.3	7.4

Main destinations in 2005/06

	Total		Recent emigrants	Women	Highly educated	15-24	Total in 2000
Population 15+	Thousands	%	%	%	%	%	Thousands
France	5.7	67.3	19.2	46.5	41.6	10.5	4.2
Canada	0.9	10.4	55.6	35.2	59.1	21.6	0.6
United States	0.6	7.3	17.0	20.7	35.5	24.6	0.3
Austria	–	–	–	–	–	–	–
Belgium	–	–	–	–	–	–	0.2
Switzerland	–	–	–	–	–	–	0.1
United Kingdom	–	–	–	–	–	–	0.2

Labour market indicators of persons born in Chad living in OECD countries

Population 15-64	2000			2005/06		
	Men	Women	Total	Men	Women	Total
Employment-population ratio (%)	64.6	51.7	59.2	70.8	53.5	63.3
Unemployment rate (%)	18.8	22.9	20.3	12.7	23.2	16.9
Participation rate (%)	79.5	67.1	74.3	81.1	69.6	76.1
Total employed (thousands)	**2.1**	**1.2**	**3.3**	**3.0**	**1.8**	**4.8**
Employment rates of the highly educated (%)	71.1	66.6	69.5	83.7	85.6	84.4
Unemployment rates of the highly educated (%)	17.6	14.5	16.5	12.2	13.6	12.7
Highly educated in low- and medium-skilled jobs (%)	25.0	23.4	24.4	28.3	24.7	26.9
Highly educated employed (thousands)	**1.1**	**0.6**	**1.7**	**1.5**	**0.9**	**2.4**
Legislators, senior officials and managers	12.4	7.5	10.4	10.1	5.7	8.5
Professionals	24.2	14.6	20.4	20.3	20.1	20.2
Life science and health professionals	4.1	3.5	3.8	4.0	3.2	3.7
Teaching professionals	5.1	5.3	5.2	4.7	8.5	6.2
Technicians and associate professionals	20.3	29.9	24.2	16.7	21.5	18.5
Clerks	7.7	18.9	12.2	7.3	16.8	10.9
Service, shop and market sales workers	5.3	17.6	10.2	11.0	19.4	14.1
Skilled agricultural and fishery workers	1.0	0.1	0.6	1.0	0.6	0.9
Craft and related trades workers	9.6	2.0	6.6	9.2	2.2	6.6
Plant and machine operators and assemblers	7.8	3.0	5.9	9.1	2.4	6.6
Elementary occupations	11.6	6.3	9.5	15.3	11.2	13.8

(Left margin label: Distribution of employment by occupation (%), population 15+)

Persons born in Chad and their native-born children, population 15+

Living in:	Europe	United States	Australia
2008	Thousands	Thousands	Thousands
Native-born children	4.6	..	..
Foreign-born	14.6	..	..
Total	19.2	..	..

International students from Chad in OECD countries

Five main destinations	2004	2005	2006	2007	2008	2009
France	421	439	497	465	465	453
United States	95	78	76	123	127	136
Canada	89	..	27	54	26	34
Belgium	0	1	1	0	13	21
Germany	..	..	..	..	20	21
Total	623	544	636	668	695	708

Legal migrant flows to the OECD
Thousands

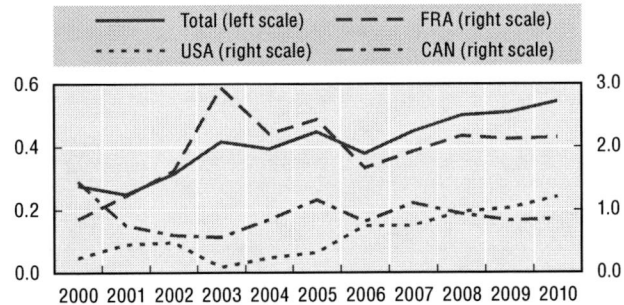

Ten main countries of destination for legal migrants in 2010 (numbers, % of total flows to the country): FRA (214, 0.2%), USA (120, 0%), CAN (85, 0%), DEU (36, 0%), ESP (20, 0%), ITA (13, 0%), BEL (11, 0%), JPN (11, 0%), CHE (7, 0%), TUR (6, 0%).

Desire to emigrate, 2008-10

	Women	15-24	Highly educated	Total	Regional total
Persons who would move permanently, if they had the opportunity to do so (%)	16	21	..	18	33
Of which: Persons who are planning to move permanently in the next 12 months (%)				29	12
Of which: Persons who have already done some preparations for this move (*e.g.* visa application) (%)					33

Three main countries of desired destination: Nigeria (10%), United States (10%), Cameroon (8%).

StatLink http://dx.doi.org/10.1787/888932674341

Total population 2010 (millions)	4.0	Congo compared to:	World	Region
Population growth 2010 (%)	2.5	Human Development Index (HDI)	137/187	10/46
GDP per capita 2010 (current USD)	2 943	GDP per capita	117/194	11/46
GDP growth 2010 (%)	8.8	Emigration rate	69/203	7/47
Poverty rate 2005 (USD PPP 2 a day, in %)	74.4	Emigration rate of the highly educated	5/157	1/39

Age structure of the population 0+ (2010): "0-14": 19%; "15-24": 41%; "25-64": 36%; "65+": 4%.
Level of education of the population 15+ (2010): "Low": 53%; "Medium": 46%; "High": 1%.

Emigrant population living in OECD countries

Immigrant population

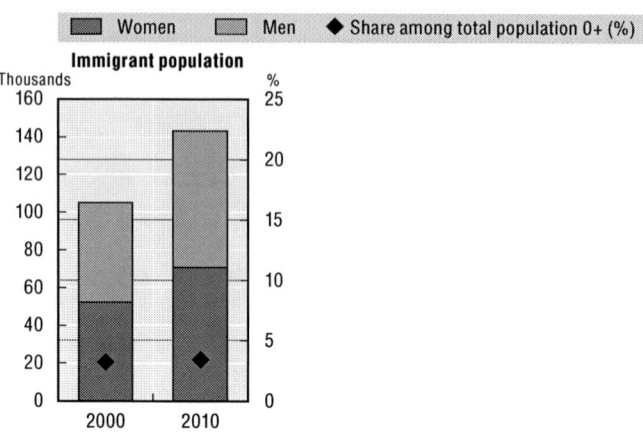

Emigrant population: persons born in Congo living abroad

	2000						2005/06		
	All destinations			OECD destinations			OECD destinations		
Population 15+	Men	Women	Total	Men	Women	Total	Men	Women	Total
Emigrant population (thousands)	42.6	37.1	79.7	35.8	33.0	68.8	76.6	76.0	152.6
Recent emigrants (thousands)	..	..	..	5.2	5.2	10.4	9.1	11.9	21.1
15-24 (%)	14.4	18.1	16.1	11.9	15.5	13.6	11.9	13.8	12.8
25-64 (%)	84.3	79.7	82.2	86.7	82.3	84.6	82.7	81.5	82.1
65+ (%)	1.3	2.2	1.7	1.4	2.2	1.8	5.5	4.7	5.1
Low-educated (%)	22.1	34.9	28.1	22.2	34.5	28.1	22.3	33.2	27.7
Highly educated (%)	40.5	26.6	34.0	43.8	28.4	36.4	46.7	31.6	39.2
Total emigration rates (%)	4.5	3.8	4.1	3.8	3.4	3.6	6.9	6.7	6.8
Emigration rates of the highly educated (%)	35.8	43.6	38.3	33.9	42.6	36.7	59.0	65.5	61.5

Main destinations in 2005/06

	Total		Recent emigrants	Women	Highly educated	15-24	Total in 2000
Population 15+	Thousands	%	%	%	%	%	Thousands
Belgium	67.2	44.0	–	50.7	44.2	8.6	14.6
France	54.7	35.8	22.0	50.1	34.2	14.6	39.5
United States	10.8	7.1	17.0	44.2	40.0	23.7	4.4
United Kingdom	6.8	4.5	–	–	–	–	2.5
Switzerland	3.7	2.4	–	43.4	31.4	–	0.8
Italy	3.1	2.0	38.3	39.7	44.0	–	1.9
Ireland	1.6	1.0	63.4	47.3	34.5	22.4	0.8
Netherlands	1.6	1.0	–	–	–	–	–
Canada	0.6	0.4	46.3	40.4	70.2	12.3	0.3
Portugal	–	–	–	–	–	–	1.7

Labour market indicators of persons born in Congo living in OECD countries

Population 15-64	2000			2005/06		
	Men	Women	Total	Men	Women	Total
Employment-population ratio (%)	61.8	46.5	54.5	66.1	47.5	56.7
Unemployment rate (%)	22.7	31.2	26.4	17.1	24.6	20.4
Participation rate (%)	80.0	67.5	74.0	79.7	62.9	71.3
Total employed (thousands)	**20.9**	**14.3**	**35.2**	**44.4**	**32.3**	**76.7**
Employment rates of the highly educated (%)	71.7	63.6	68.7	88.6	76.9	83.8
Unemployment rates of the highly educated (%)	18.2	19.7	18.7	13.3	14.1	13.6
Highly educated in low- and medium-skilled jobs (%)	41.0	41.1	41.1	30.1	31.8	30.7
Highly educated employed (thousands)	**10.6**	**5.6**	**16.2**	**24.4**	**14.5**	**38.9**
Legislators, senior officials and managers	6.5	3.7	5.4	12.7	5.2	9.5
Professionals	18.4	9.3	14.8	22.2	22.7	22.4
Life science and health professionals	3.5	2.3	3.0	4.2	9.7	6.5
Teaching professionals	5.2	3.4	4.5	4.4	6.9	5.4
Technicians and associate professionals	14.0	16.0	14.8	14.8	13.7	14.3
Clerks	8.1	16.1	11.3	9.3	19.1	13.4
Service, shop and market sales workers	9.0	28.5	16.7	7.9	19.4	12.8
Skilled agricultural and fishery workers	0.7	0.4	0.6	0.9	0.6	0.8
Craft and related trades workers	14.9	1.5	9.6	9.9	1.8	6.5
Plant and machine operators and assemblers	11.0	2.3	7.6	9.0	1.6	5.9
Elementary occupations	17.5	22.1	19.3	13.3	15.9	14.4

Distribution of employment by occupation (%), population 15+

Persons born in Congo and their native-born children, population 15+

Living in:	Europe	United States	Australia
2008	Thousands	Thousands	Thousands
Native-born children	38.8	..	..
Foreign-born	91.9	..	1.1
Total	130.7	..	..

International students from Congo in OECD countries

Five main destinations	2004	2005	2006	2007	2008	2009
France	3 176	3 066	3 048	2 906	2 704	2 712
Italy	146	169	203	222	299	423
United States	9	24	89	146	150	205
Canada	276	..	108	171	184	161
Belgium	3	44	28	39	12	54
Total	3 706	3 420	3 619	3 638	3 618	3 729

Legal migrant flows to the OECD
Thousands

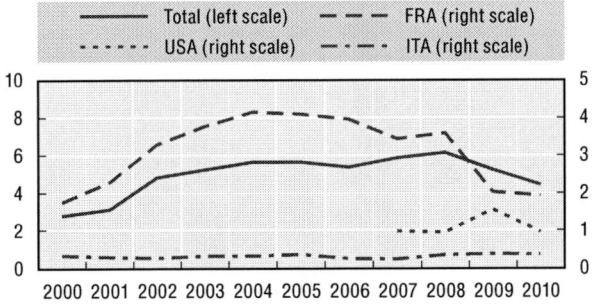

Remittance flows

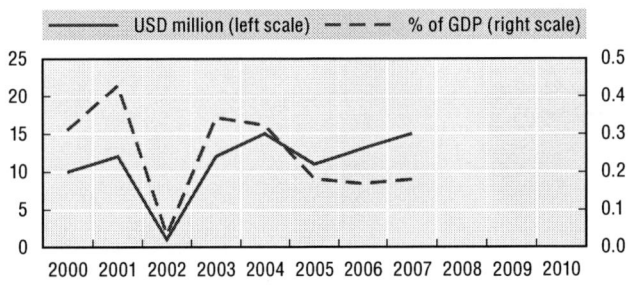

Ten main countries of destination for legal migrants in 2010 (numbers, % of total flows to the country): FRA (1934, 1.4%), USA (968, 0.1%), ITA (367, 0.1%), DEU (289, 0%), AUS (141, 0.1%), ESP (136, 0%), NOR (99, 0.1%), BEL (79, 0.1%), POL (63, 0.2%), DNK (61, 0.2%).

Desire to emigrate, 2008-10

	Women	15-24	Highly educated	Total	Regional total
Persons who would move permanently, if they had the opportunity to do so (%)	42	54	..	46	33
Of which: Persons who are planning to move permanently in the next 12 months (%)				61	12
Of which: Persons who have already done some preparations for this move (*e.g.* visa application) (%)					33

Three main countries of desired destination: France (28%), Canada (19%), United States (16%).

StatLink 🔗 *http://dx.doi.org/10.1787/888932674360*

CÔTE D'IVOIRE – Country Notes

Total population 2010 (millions)	19.7		
Population growth 2010 (%)	2.0		
GDP per capita 2010 (current USD)	1 154		
GDP growth 2010 (%)	3.0		
Poverty rate 2008 (USD PPP 2 a day, in %)	46.3		

Côte d'Ivoire compared to:	World	Region
Human Development Index (HDI)	170/187	31/46
GDP per capita	146/194	16/46
Emigration rate	150/203	26/47
Emigration rate of the highly educated	43/157	15/39

Age structure of the population 0+ (2010): "0-14": 20%; "15-24": 41%; "25-64": 35%; "65+": 4%.
Level of education of the population 15+ (2010): "Low": 79%; "Medium": 20%; "High": 1%.

Emigrant population living in OECD countries

Immigrant population

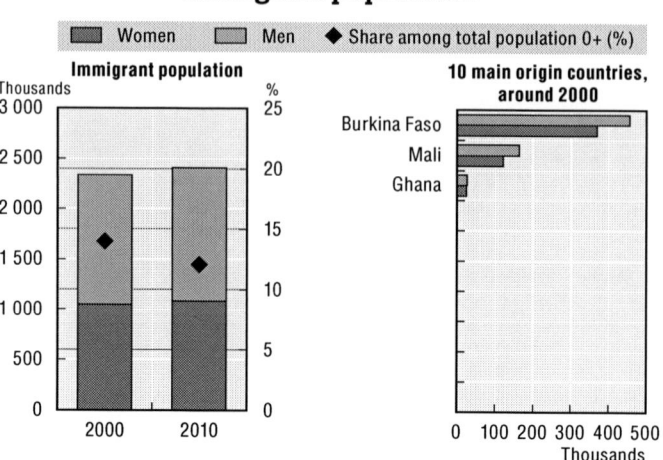

Emigrant population: persons born in Côte d'Ivoire living abroad

	2000						2005/06		
	All destinations			OECD destinations			OECD destinations		
Population 15+	Men	Women	Total	Men	Women	Total	Men	Women	Total
Emigrant population (thousands)	198.0	215.4	413.4	32.6	30.2	62.8	51.3	55.7	107.0
Recent emigrants (thousands)	..	..	..	5.0	6.3	11.4	10.1	12.9	23.0
15-24 (%)	50.3	52.5	51.5	19.0	24.9	21.9	18.2	19.2	18.7
25-64 (%)	49.1	46.4	47.7	79.9	74.0	77.0	80.4	79.5	79.9
65+ (%)	0.5	1.1	0.8	1.1	1.1	1.1	1.4	1.3	1.3
Low-educated (%)	56.4	74.4	65.8	31.3	46.6	38.7	31.2	43.3	37.5
Highly educated (%)	12.4	4.9	8.5	32.8	20.0	26.7	33.9	25.7	29.6
Total emigration rates (%)	3.8	4.4	4.1	0.6	0.6	0.6	0.9	1.0	1.0
Emigration rates of the highly educated (%)	16.3	18.8	17.0	7.9	11.8	9.0	15.0	16.8	15.8

Main destinations in 2005/06

	Total		Recent emigrants	Women	Highly educated	15-24	Total in 2000
Population 15+	Thousands	%	%	%	%	%	Thousands
France	70.5	65.9	22.8	53.8	28.7	18.4	41.9
United States	13.1	12.2	17.2	45.6	39.8	18.0	6.8
Italy	10.4	9.8	34.6	47.3	–	22.2	6.4
United Kingdom	–	–	–	–	–	–	2.4
Canada	2.6	2.4	56.5	45.5	69.0	23.9	1.6
Belgium	–	–	–	–	–	–	1.2
Switzerland	1.2	1.1	–	–	–	–	1.0
Sweden	0.4	0.4	40.0	41.7	38.7	19.0	0.3
Denmark	0.4	0.3	22.4	40.3	24.4	25.7	0.3

Labour market indicators of persons born in Côte d'Ivoire living in OECD countries

Population 15-64	2000 Men	2000 Women	2000 Total	2005/06 Men	2005/06 Women	2005/06 Total
Employment-population ratio (%)	63.3	46.9	55.4	66.7	55.5	60.8
Unemployment rate (%)	18.7	27.9	22.7	15.8	23.6	19.7
Participation rate (%)	77.8	65.0	71.6	79.1	72.7	75.7
Total employed (thousands)	**20.1**	**13.7**	**33.8**	**29.7**	**27.6**	**57.3**
Employment rates of the highly educated (%)	71.5	57.8	66.6	80.4	76.4	78.5
Unemployment rates of the highly educated (%)	14.7	19.0	16.1	12.7	16.1	14.3
Highly educated in low- and medium-skilled jobs (%)	36.6	37.6	36.9	40.4	48.7	44.3
Highly educated employed (thousands)	**7.4**	**3.4**	**10.8**	**10.1**	**8.1**	**18.2**
Legislators, senior officials and managers	8.5	4.5	6.8	7.0	4.4	5.7
Professionals	13.1	6.7	10.4	10.7	6.4	8.6
Life science and health professionals	1.8	1.1	1.5	1.2	0.8	1.0
Teaching professionals	2.5	2.3	2.4	2.2	2.3	2.2
Technicians and associate professionals	15.9	14.8	15.4	13.9	14.5	14.2
Clerks	6.3	13.9	9.6	9.1	11.9	10.5
Service, shop and market sales workers	9.3	28.5	17.5	8.1	27.3	17.6
Skilled agricultural and fishery workers	0.9	0.3	0.7	0.7	0.3	0.5
Craft and related trades workers	13.3	2.6	8.7	13.0	6.9	10.0
Plant and machine operators and assemblers	13.3	2.4	8.6	16.3	3.0	9.7
Elementary occupations	19.3	26.4	22.3	21.2	25.3	23.3

Distribution of employment by occupation (%), population 15+

Persons born in Côte d'Ivoire and their native-born children, population 15+

Living in:	Europe	United States	Australia
2008	Thousands	Thousands	Thousands
Native-born children	35.3	..	..
Foreign-born	72.8	..	..
Total	108.1	..	..

International students from Côte d'Ivoire in OECD countries

Five main destinations	2004	2005	2006	2007	2008	2009
France	3 904	3 816	3 796	3 692	3 526	3 444
United States	636	650	679	672	712	793
Canada	483	..	309	315	263	364
Germany	..	..	..	..	219	203
Italy	56	61	68	104	107	113
Total	5 215	4 673	5 014	4 940	5 051	5 152

Legal migrant flows to the OECD
Thousands

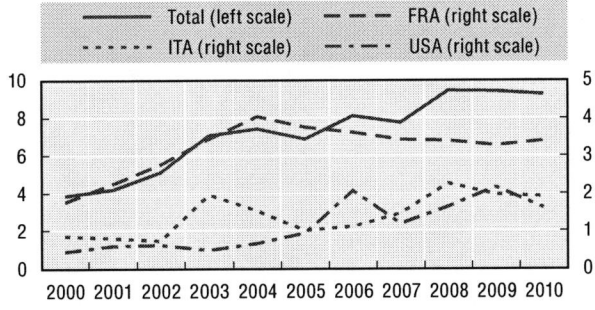

Remittance flows

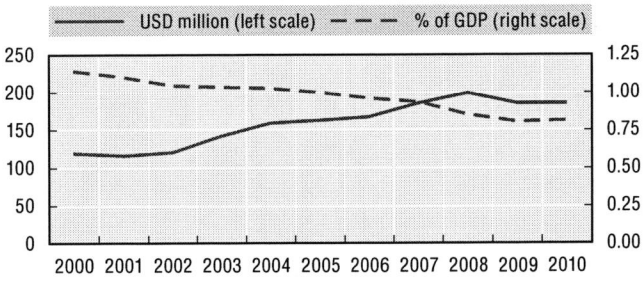

Ten main countries of destination for legal migrants in 2010 (numbers, % of total flows to the country): FRA (3392, 2.5%), ITA (1915, 0.5%), USA (1621, 0.2%), CAN (1025, 0.4%), ESP (351, 0.1%), BEL (240, 0.2%), DEU (234, 0.1%), CHE (166, 0.1%), JPN (83, 0%), SWE (50, 0.1%).

Desire to emigrate, 2008-10

	Women	15-24	Highly educated	Total	Regional total
Persons who would move permanently, if they had the opportunity to do so (%)	..	..	..	..	33
Of which: Persons who are planning to move permanently in the next 12 months (%)				..	12
Of which: Persons who have already done some preparations for this move (*e.g.* visa application) (%)					33

StatLink 🔗 http://dx.doi.org/10.1787/888932674379

			Democratic Republic of the Congo compared to:	World	Region
Total population 2010 (millions)		66.0			
Population growth 2010 (%)		2.7	Human Development Index (HDI)	187/187	46/46
GDP per capita 2010 (current USD)		199	GDP per capita	185/194	44/46
GDP growth 2010 (%)		7.2	Emigration rate	185/203	41/47
Poverty rate 2006 (USD PPP 2 a day, in %)		79.6	Emigration rate of the highly educated	76/157	26/39

Age structure of the population 0+ (2010): "0-14": 20%; "15-24": 46%; "25-64": 31%; "65+": 3%.
Level of education of the population 15+ (2010): "Low": 76%; "Medium": 23%; "High": 1%.

Emigrant population living in OECD countries

Immigrant population

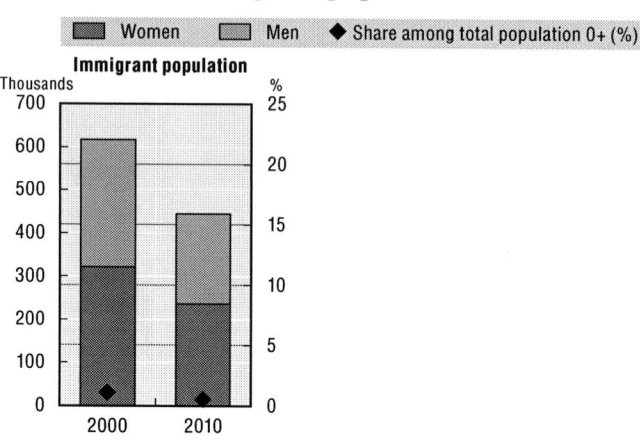

Emigrant population: persons born in the Democratic Republic of the Congo living abroad

	2000						2005/06		
	All destinations			OECD destinations			OECD destinations		
Population 15+	Men	Women	Total	Men	Women	Total	Men	Women	Total
Emigrant population (thousands)	140.1	144.0	284.1	50.9	50.2	101.2	52.3	52.8	105.2
Recent emigrants (thousands)	..	..	..	6.6	7.7	14.3	11.2	14.1	25.3
15-24 (%)	28.6	33.9	31.3	16.1	18.6	17.3	19.7	23.2	21.5
25-64 (%)	67.9	62.3	65.1	80.6	76.9	78.8	78.3	74.0	76.2
65+ (%)	3.5	3.8	3.6	3.3	4.5	3.9	2.0	2.8	2.4
Low-educated (%)	61.0	71.9	66.5	22.4	31.4	26.8	23.9	36.2	30.1
Highly educated (%)	19.5	12.1	15.8	43.2	32.8	38.0	37.2	21.6	29.3
Total emigration rates (%)	1.1	1.0	1.0	0.4	0.4	0.4	0.3	0.3	0.3
Emigration rates of the highly educated (%)	10.0	21.5	12.6	7.9	19.8	10.6	9.7	10.3	9.9

Main destinations in 2005/06

	Total		Recent emigrants	Women	Highly educated	15-24	Total in 2000
Population 15+	Thousands	%	%	%	%	%	Thousands
France	46.7	44.4	20.0	52.2	22.5	21.9	23.0
United Kingdom	13.7	13.1	–	–	–	–	6.8
Canada	13.6	12.9	44.1	51.4	50.1	24.3	8.2
United States	8.9	8.5	17.0	47.2	45.4	20.4	5.2
Belgium	7.8	7.4	–	–	–	–	46.6
Italy	3.9	3.7	–	58.2	–	–	2.0
Netherlands	3.8	3.6	–	41.1	–	–	–
Portugal	–	–	–	–	–	–	1.5
Sweden	1.3	1.2	36.7	46.1	25.1	31.4	1.0
Switzerland	1.3	1.2	–	–	–	–	3.2

Labour market indicators of persons born in the Democratic Republic of the Congo living in OECD countries

	2000			2005/06		
Population 15-64	Men	Women	Total	Men	Women	Total
Employment-population ratio (%)	63.2	46.7	55.0	58.6	41.9	50.2
Unemployment rate (%)	18.8	25.1	21.6	19.4	29.9	24.2
Participation rate (%)	77.9	62.3	70.2	72.8	59.7	66.2
Total employed (thousands)	**28.6**	**20.7**	**49.3**	**27.3**	**19.7**	**47.1**
Employment rates of the highly educated (%)	73.9	65.6	70.4	80.4	74.9	78.4
Unemployment rates of the highly educated (%)	15.3	14.8	15.1	16.5	19.2	17.4
Highly educated in low- and medium-skilled jobs (%)	39.6	41.3	40.2	51.5	51.3	51.4
Highly educated employed (thousands)	**14.5**	**9.7**	**24.2**	**11.4**	**6.0**	**17.3**
Legislators, senior officials and managers	7.3	4.2	6.1	7.5	2.4	5.3
Professionals	14.9	10.8	13.3	12.9	8.8	11.2
Life science and health professionals	2.1	2.5	2.3	0.9	1.9	1.3
Teaching professionals	2.0	3.2	2.5	1.3	2.2	1.7
Technicians and associate professionals	13.8	12.7	13.3	11.9	13.3	12.5
Clerks	8.6	16.1	11.7	7.9	13.7	10.4
Service, shop and market sales workers	10.4	26.9	17.1	9.1	26.7	16.5
Skilled agricultural and fishery workers	0.5	0.3	0.4	2.8	0.9	2.0
Craft and related trades workers	14.1	2.5	9.4	14.4	2.9	9.6
Plant and machine operators and assemblers	11.7	2.6	8.0	15.6	1.8	9.8
Elementary occupations	18.6	23.9	20.7	18.0	29.6	22.8

Distribution of employment by occupation (%), population 15+

Persons born in the Democratic Republic of the Congo and their native-born children, population 15+

Living in:	Europe	United States	Australia
2008	Thousands	Thousands	Thousands
Native-born children	29.6	..	..
Foreign-born	57.2	..	..
Total	86.8	..	..

International students from the Democratic Republic of the Congo in OECD countries

Five main destinations	2004	2005	2006	2007	2008	2009
France	816	807	797	729	741	751
United States	340	337	319	277	282	243
Canada	152	..	72	150	158	183
Italy	90	88	97	97	133	174
United Kingdom	58	39	44	63	85	106
Total	1 480	1 326	1 380	1 409	1 667	1 708

Legal migrant flows to the OECD
Thousands

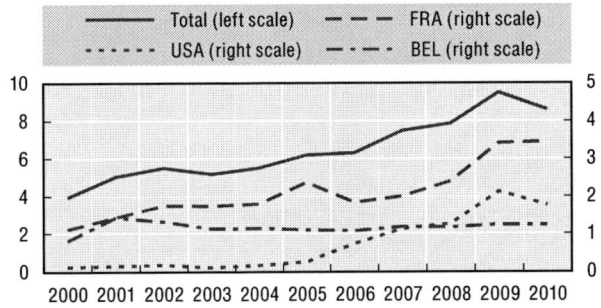

Ten main countries of destination for legal migrants in 2010 (numbers, % of total flows to the country): FRA (3453, 2.5%), USA (1764, 0.2%), BEL (1231, 1.2%), AUS (409, 0.2%), CHE (362, 0.3%), DEU (258, 0%), ITA (236, 1.1%), FIN (194, 1.1%), SWE (186, 0.2%), JPN (111, 0%).

Desire to emigrate, 2008-10

	Women	15-24	Highly educated	Total	Regional total
Persons who would move permanently, if they had the opportunity to do so (%)	36	46	44	40	33
Of which: Persons who are planning to move permanently in the next 12 months (%)				53	12
Of which: Persons who have already done some preparations for this move (*e.g.* visa application) (%)					33

StatLink ᴍ⎗ᴱ᙮ http://dx.doi.org/10.1787/888932674398

Total population 2010 (millions)	5.3	**Eritrea compared to:**	**World**	**Region**
Population growth 2010 (%)	3.0	Human Development Index (HDI)	177/187	36/46
GDP per capita 2010 (current USD)	403	GDP per capita	179/194	38/46
GDP growth 2010 (%)	2.2	Emigration rate	125/203	15/47
Poverty rate 2010 (USD PPP 2 a day, in %)	..	Emigration rate of the highly educated	61/157	22/39

Age structure of the population 0+ (2010): "0-14": 20%; "15-24": 42%; "25-64": 36%; "65+": 2%.

Emigrant population living in OECD countries

Immigrant population

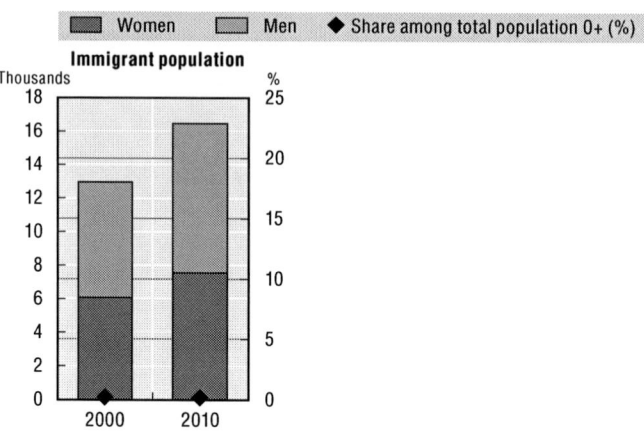

Emigrant population: persons born in Eritrea living abroad

	2000						2005/06		
	All destinations			OECD destinations			OECD destinations		
Population 15+	Men	Women	Total	Men	Women	Total	Men	Women	Total
Emigrant population (thousands)	23.0	25.4	48.4	22.8	25.2	48.0	25.8	27.4	53.2
Recent emigrants (thousands)	..	..	..	2.9	3.9	6.8	5.1	5.5	10.5
15-24 (%)	11.8	13.0	12.5	11.7	13.0	12.4	10.0	9.8	9.9
25-64 (%)	85.0	82.3	83.6	85.1	82.4	83.7	82.0	82.7	82.4
65+ (%)	3.2	4.7	4.0	3.1	4.6	3.9	7.9	7.5	7.7
Low-educated (%)	27.9	46.2	37.4	28.0	46.2	37.5	24.2	40.1	32.3
Highly educated (%)	28.3	15.5	21.6	28.3	15.5	21.6	33.2	19.8	26.3
Total emigration rates (%)	2.3	2.4	2.3	2.3	2.3	2.3	2.0	2.0	2.0
Emigration rates of the highly educated (%)	9.5	21.4	12.0	9.4	21.3	11.9	9.2	20.4	11.7

Main destinations in 2005/06

	Total		Recent emigrants	Women	Highly educated	15-24	Total in 2000
Population 15+	Thousands	%	%	%	%	%	Thousands
United States	20.0	37.5	20.0	52.4	29.9	7.7	16.8
Italy	9.9	18.5	9.8	59.7	18.7	–	12.3
Canada	6.2	11.7	22.2	50.1	35.4	8.9	4.7
Sweden	5.7	10.7	29.1	50.5	11.6	13.3	4.2
United Kingdom	–	–	–	–	–	–	5.8
Netherlands	3.3	6.2	–	54.1	–	–	–
Australia	1.9	3.6	26.2	50.7	30.2	11.9	1.3
Switzerland	–	–	–	–	–	–	1.0
Norway	0.8	1.5	41.6	53.6	16.1	16.6	1.6
France	–	–	–	–	–	–	0.1

Labour market indicators of persons born in Eritrea living in OECD countries

Population 15-64	2000			2005/06		
	Men	Women	Total	Men	Women	Total
Employment-population ratio (%)	70.4	52.7	61.0	77.0	56.5	66.6
Unemployment rate (%)	9.8	12.9	11.2	7.0	16.0	11.1
Participation rate (%)	78.0	60.5	68.8	82.8	67.2	74.9
Total employed (thousands)	**13.3**	**11.1**	**24.3**	**16.3**	**12.4**	**28.7**
Employment rates of the highly educated (%)	81.1	69.2	76.5	88.9	83.9	87.0
Unemployment rates of the highly educated (%)	7.2	8.4	7.6	6.1	15.1	9.3
Highly educated in low- and medium-skilled jobs (%)	40.5	40.0	40.3	53.5	34.9	47.2
Highly educated employed (thousands)	**4.6**	**2.4**	**7.0**	**6.5**	**3.3**	**9.8**
Legislators, senior officials and managers	11.3	3.8	7.8	8.4	9.1	8.7
Professionals	12.6	7.4	10.2	10.2	6.6	8.7
Life science and health professionals	0.6	0.5	0.6	0.7	0.4	0.6
Teaching professionals	1.4	0.6	1.0	4.7	1.1	3.2
Technicians and associate professionals	11.8	11.2	11.5	9.1	11.2	10.0
Clerks	7.7	13.3	10.3	8.6	6.9	7.9
Service, shop and market sales workers	15.3	28.9	21.7	11.0	35.1	20.8
Skilled agricultural and fishery workers	0.5	0.2	0.3	0.4	0.1	0.3
Craft and related trades workers	9.8	2.2	6.2	16.3	1.2	10.2
Plant and machine operators and assemblers	15.9	2.2	9.4	16.2	1.7	10.4
Elementary occupations	15.2	30.8	22.5	17.1	28.0	21.5

Distribution of employment by occupation (%), population 15+

Persons born in Eritrea and their native-born children, population 15+

Living in:	Europe	United States	Australia
2008	Thousands	Thousands	Thousands
Native-born children	10.6	1.9	..
Foreign-born	41.9	18.3	1.8
Total	52.5	20.2	..

International students from Eritrea in OECD countries

Five main destinations	2004	2005	2006	2007	2008	2009
United States	127	203	206	188	163	165
Italy	105	91	103	97	105	98
United Kingdom	20	63	57	115	87	60
Germany	..	..	..	..	33	29
Canada	7	..	12	12	19	19
Total	270	374	397	434	430	409

Legal migrant flows to the OECD
Thousands

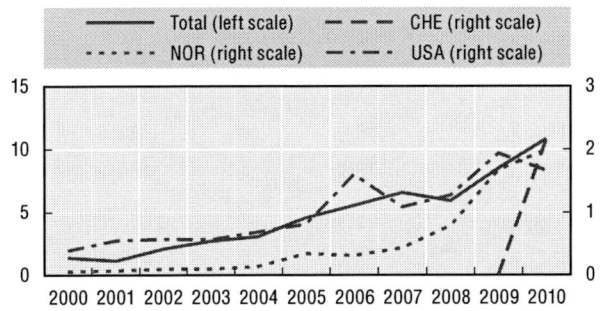

Ten main countries of destination for legal migrants in 2010 (numbers, % of total flows to the country): CHE (2147, 1.6%), NOR (1987, 3.1%), USA (1656, 0.2%), SWE (1604, 2.1%), ITA (1106, 0.3%), DEU (868, 0.1%), CAN (740, 0.2%), FRA (312, 0.2%), AUS (207, 0.1%), NLD (43, 0%).

Desire to emigrate, 2008-10

	Women	15-24	Highly educated	Total	Regional total
Persons who would move permanently, if they had the opportunity to do so (%)	..	..	..	..	33
Of which: Persons who are planning to move permanently in the next 12 months (%)				..	12
Of which: Persons who have already done some preparations for this move (*e.g.* visa application) (%)					33

StatLink 🖉 *http://dx.doi.org/10.1787/888932674417*

		Ethiopia compared to:	World	Region
Total population 2010 (millions)	82.9			
Population growth 2010 (%)	2.1	Human Development Index (HDI)	174/187	33/46
GDP per capita 2010 (current USD)	358	GDP per capita	180/194	39/46
GDP growth 2010 (%)	10.1	Emigration rate	175/203	38/47
Poverty rate 2005 (USD PPP 2 a day, in %)	77.6	Emigration rate of the highly educated	52/157	19/39

Age structure of the population 0+ (2010): "0-14": 21%; "15-24": 41%; "25-64": 34%; "65+": 3%.

Emigrant population living in OECD countries

Immigrant population

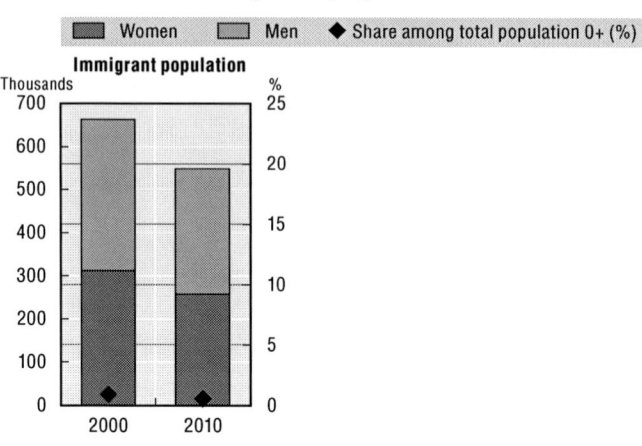

Emigrant population: persons born in Ethiopia living abroad

	2000						2005/06		
	All destinations			OECD destinations			OECD destinations		
Population 15+	Men	Women	Total	Men	Women	Total	Men	Women	Total
Emigrant population (thousands)	91.4	90.2	181.6	82.3	83.5	165.8	121.5	126.1	247.5
Recent emigrants (thousands)	..	..	..	15.4	17.4	32.8	33.4	34.4	67.8
15-24 (%)	20.6	20.9	20.8	18.7	19.4	19.1	18.4	18.4	18.4
25-64 (%)	75.1	74.0	74.6	77.3	75.5	76.4	77.4	76.3	76.9
65+ (%)	4.2	5.1	4.6	4.0	5.0	4.5	4.1	5.2	4.7
Low-educated (%)	35.9	44.9	40.4	30.8	41.4	36.1	26.7	34.7	30.8
Highly educated (%)	26.6	17.1	21.9	28.8	18.2	23.5	32.0	22.4	27.1
Total emigration rates (%)	0.5	0.5	0.5	0.4	0.4	0.4	0.6	0.6	0.6
Emigration rates of the highly educated (%)	8.6	15.7	10.5	8.4	15.5	10.2	11.2	21.1	14.0

Main destinations in 2005/06

	Total		Recent emigrants	Women	Highly educated	15-24	Total in 2000
Population 15+	Thousands	%	%	%	%	%	Thousands
United States	123.0	49.7	31.4	50.1	34.9	14.8	66.1
Israel	50.3	20.3	27.9	51.5	6.1	32.8	41.4
Canada	19.3	7.8	30.8	50.2	38.6	12.8	13.5
Italy	13.9	5.6	12.7	63.3	13.0	6.4	12.7
Sweden	10.7	4.3	14.4	47.9	19.6	13.7	10.6
United Kingdom	8.6	3.5	–	–	–	–	7.2
Australia	4.8	1.9	38.7	49.9	27.1	17.9	2.9
France	4.1	1.7	21.1	67.5	18.8	20.2	2.2
Netherlands	3.9	1.6	–	–	–	–	–
Norway	3.2	1.3	40.3	43.9	27.0	21.6	2.1

Labour market indicators of persons born in Ethiopia living in OECD countries

Population 15-64	2000			2005/06		
	Men	Women	Total	Men	Women	Total
Employment-population ratio (%)	64.9	51.8	58.3	71.4	59.5	65.4
Unemployment rate (%)	10.1	11.6	10.8	9.4	12.6	10.9
Participation rate (%)	72.2	58.6	65.4	78.8	68.1	73.4
Total employed (thousands)	**47.2**	**37.9**	**85.1**	**77.9**	**66.9**	**144.8**
Employment rates of the highly educated (%)	80.3	73.8	77.8	91.1	83.7	88.0
Unemployment rates of the highly educated (%)	7.0	6.1	6.7	7.6	8.9	8.1
Highly educated in low- and medium-skilled jobs (%)	45.3	47.6	46.2	42.7	45.0	43.6
Highly educated employed (thousands)	**17.6**	**10.4**	**28.0**	**30.6**	**20.2**	**50.8**
Legislators, senior officials and managers	8.9	4.4	6.8	9.7	2.0	6.1
Professionals	13.6	8.4	11.3	12.6	10.7	11.7
Life science and health professionals	1.7	1.3	1.5	0.9	3.2	2.0
Teaching professionals	2.4	1.3	1.9	4.7	4.7	4.7
Technicians and associate professionals	10.5	11.5	11.0	8.9	8.4	8.7
Clerks	9.1	15.6	12.1	8.2	10.4	9.2
Service, shop and market sales workers	13.9	32.8	22.5	12.3	37.6	23.9
Skilled agricultural and fishery workers	0.3	0.4	0.3	0.3	1.2	0.7
Craft and related trades workers	9.8	2.2	6.3	7.7	4.1	6.0
Plant and machine operators and assemblers	18.3	3.9	11.7	22.8	3.9	14.1
Elementary occupations	15.5	20.9	18.0	17.4	21.8	19.5

Left margin label: Distribution of employment by occupation (%), population 15+

Persons born in Ethiopia and their native-born children, population 15+

Living in:	Europe	United States	Australia
2008	Thousands	Thousands	Thousands
Native-born children	10.8	41.9	..
Foreign-born	32.0	123.4	3.4
Total	42.7	165.2	..

International students from Ethiopia in OECD countries

Five main destinations	2004	2005	2006	2007	2008	2009
United States	1 060	1 179	1 311	1 357	1 317	1 557
Germany	..	..	..	..	273	319
France	123	126	173	217	258	260
United Kingdom	263	235	235	230	219	220
Sweden	0	0	2	0	88	186
Total	1 802	1 922	2 230	2 336	2 735	3 250

Legal migrant flows to the OECD
Thousands

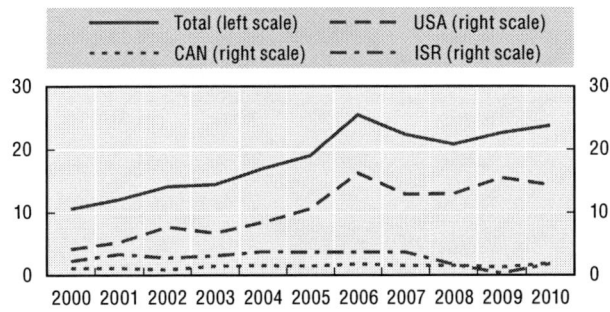

Remittance flows

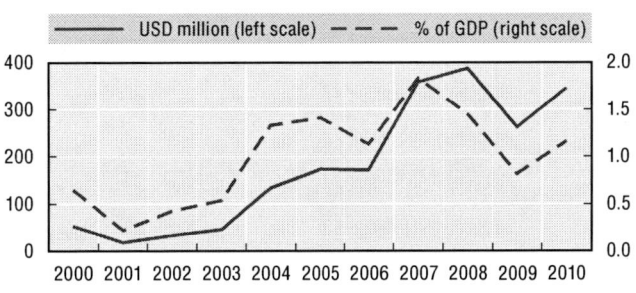

Ten main countries of destination for legal migrants in 2010 (numbers, % of total flows to the country): USA (14266, 1.4%), CAN (1750, 0.6%), ISR (1655, 10%), SWE (958, 1.2%), DEU (931, 0.1%), ITA (830, 0.2%), AUS (825, 0.7%), NOR (479, 0.7%), CHE (322, 0.2%), NLD (281, 0.3%).

Desire to emigrate, 2008-10

	Women	15-24	Highly educated	Total	Regional total
Persons who would move permanently, if they had the opportunity to do so (%)	..	..	..	..	33
Of which: Persons who are planning to move permanently in the next 12 months (%)				..	12
Of which: Persons who have already done some preparations for this move (*e.g.* visa application) (%)					33

StatLink ⌘ http://dx.doi.org/10.1787/888932674436

Total population 2010 (millions)	1.5	Gabon compared to:	World	Region
Population growth 2010 (%)	1.9	Human Development Index (HDI)	106/187	3/46
GDP per capita 2010 (current USD)	8 643	GDP per capita	68/194	3/46
GDP growth 2010 (%)	5.7	Emigration rate	123/203	14/47
Poverty rate 2005 (USD PPP 2 a day, in %)	19.6	Emigration rate of the highly educated	85/157	29/39

Age structure of the population 0+ (2010): "0-14": 21%; "15-24": 35%; "25-64": 39%; "65+": 4%.
Level of education of the population 15+ (2010): "Low": 46%; "Medium": 43%; "High": 11%.

Emigrant population living in OECD countries

Immigrant population

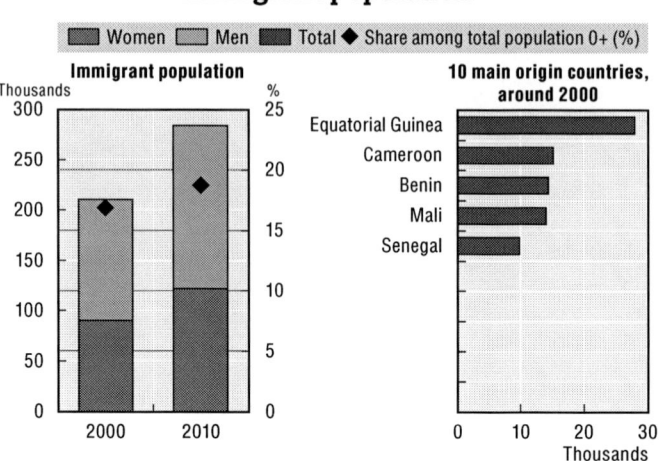

Emigrant population: persons born in Gabon living abroad

	2000						2005/06		
	All destinations			OECD destinations			OECD destinations		
Population 15+	Men	Women	Total	Men	Women	Total	Men	Women	Total
Emigrant population (thousands)	8.5	8.6	17.1	5.2	5.7	10.9	7.9	9.7	17.6
Recent emigrants (thousands)	..	..	..	1.1	1.2	2.3	1.7	2.4	4.1
15-24 (%)	43.1	40.0	41.5	33.8	30.8	32.2	31.4	30.9	31.1
25-64 (%)	55.3	57.4	56.4	64.6	66.1	65.4	66.4	65.1	65.7
65+ (%)	1.5	2.6	2.1	1.6	3.1	2.4	2.2	4.0	3.2
Low-educated (%)	29.0	37.5	33.3	26.3	33.4	30.0	17.0	24.5	21.1
Highly educated (%)	38.7	28.8	33.7	41.6	31.7	36.4	48.5	40.0	43.8
Total emigration rates (%)	2.3	2.3	2.3	1.4	1.5	1.5	1.9	2.3	2.1
Emigration rates of the highly educated (%)	11.9	4.2	6.7	8.8	3.3	5.0	14.0	5.7	8.1

Main destinations in 2005/06

	Total		Recent emigrants	Women	Highly educated	15-24	Total in 2000
Population 15+	Thousands	%	%	%	%	%	Thousands
France	15.5	88.1	31.4	55.5	42.6	31.2	9.4
United States	0.9	5.3	17.0	52.7	31.6	24.5	0.4
Canada	0.6	3.6	38.4	51.2	72.8	40.8	0.4
Belgium	–	–	–	–	–	–	0.3

Labour market indicators of persons born in Gabon living in OECD countries

Population 15-64	2000			2005/06		
	Men	Women	Total	Men	Women	Total
Employment-population ratio (%)	44.1	33.8	38.8	47.7	40.4	43.7
Unemployment rate (%)	18.6	28.1	23.1	19.8	28.5	24.5
Participation rate (%)	54.2	47.0	50.5	59.5	56.5	57.8
Total employed (thousands)	**2.3**	**1.9**	**4.1**	**3.5**	**3.6**	**7.1**
Employment rates of the highly educated (%)	50.5	45.4	48.2	65.7	60.1	62.9
Unemployment rates of the highly educated (%)	15.2	19.8	17.2	17.4	21.3	19.3
Highly educated in low- and medium-skilled jobs (%)	22.2	33.7	27.1	25.7	35.0	29.9
Highly educated employed (thousands)	**1.1**	**0.8**	**1.9**	**2.0**	**1.8**	**3.7**
Legislators, senior officials and managers	11.5	7.0	9.4	10.7	7.8	9.3
Professionals	19.4	12.0	16.0	23.8	13.6	18.6
Life science and health professionals	3.4	1.3	2.5	2.8	2.6	2.7
Teaching professionals	4.4	4.9	4.6	4.8	4.5	4.7
Technicians and associate professionals	23.3	25.0	24.1	20.4	20.2	20.3
Clerks	5.4	25.6	14.7	6.3	18.6	12.6
Service, shop and market sales workers	9.7	18.0	13.5	10.0	21.2	15.8
Skilled agricultural and fishery workers	1.2	0.9	1.1	1.2	0.6	0.9
Craft and related trades workers	12.1	1.5	7.3	8.2	1.5	4.8
Plant and machine operators and assemblers	7.6	1.7	4.9	9.5	2.2	5.8
Elementary occupations	9.8	8.1	9.0	9.7	14.2	12.0

Distribution of employment by occupation (%), population 15+

Persons born in Gabon and their native-born children, population 15+

Living in:	Europe	United States	Australia
2008	Thousands	Thousands	Thousands
Native-born children	0.9	..	..
Foreign-born	11.4	..	..
Total	12.3	..	..

International students from Gabon in OECD countries

Five main destinations	2004	2005	2006	2007	2008	2009
France	2 866	2 998	3 263	3 401	3 585	3 870
Canada	260	..	261	237	257	260
United States	105	151	167	235	303	258
Germany	..	..	..	..	177	184
Italy	14	10	11	14	20	25
Total	3 284	3 204	3 764	3 933	4 387	4 662

Legal migrant flows to the OECD
Thousands

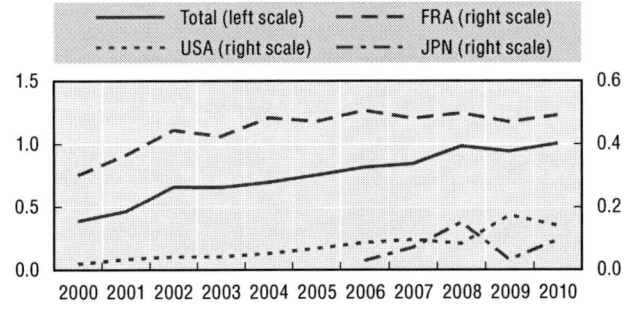

Remittance flows

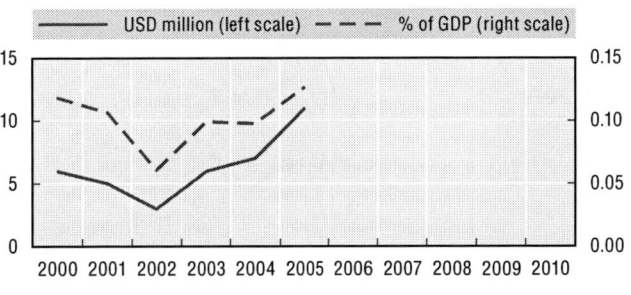

Ten main countries of destination for legal migrants in 2010 (numbers, % of total flows to the country): FRA (490, 0.4%), USA (138, 0%), JPN (93, 0%), CAN (65, 0%), ESP (55, 0%), BEL (38, 0%), DEU (38, 0%), ITA (28, 0%), KOR (19, 0%), NLD (13, 0%).

Desire to emigrate, 2008-10

	Women	15-24	Highly educated	Total	Regional total
Persons who would move permanently, if they had the opportunity to do so (%)	..	..	..	..	33
Of which: Persons who are planning to move permanently in the next 12 months (%)				..	12
Of which: Persons who have already done some preparations for this move (*e.g.* visa application) (%)					33

StatLink http://dx.doi.org/10.1787/888932674455

Total population 2010 (millions)	1.7	**Gambia compared to:**		**World**	**Region**
Population growth 2010 (%)	2.7	Human Development Index (HDI)		168/187	29/46
GDP per capita 2010 (current USD)	467	GDP per capita		173/194	33/46
GDP growth 2010 (%)	5.0	Emigration rate		89/203	10/47
Poverty rate 2003 (USD PPP 2 a day, in %)	56.7	Emigration rate of the highly educated		21/157	8/39

Age structure of the population 0+ (2010): "0-14": 20%; "15-24": 44%; "25-64": 33%; "65+": 2%.
Level of education of the population 15+ (2010): "Low": 68%; "Medium": 31%; "High": 2%.

Emigrant population living in OECD countries

Immigrant population

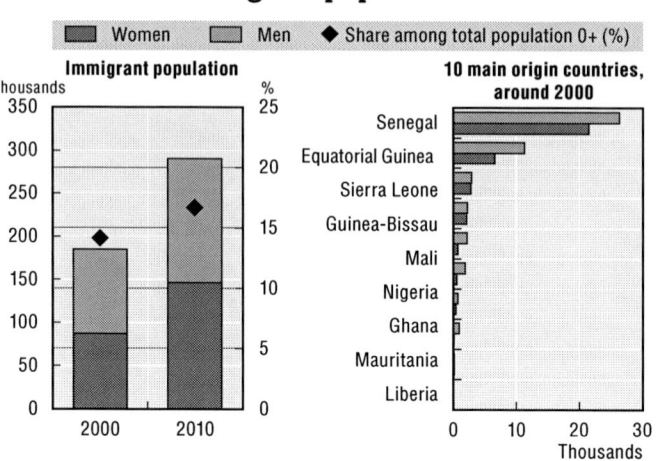

Emigrant population: persons born in Gambia living abroad

	2000						2005/06		
	All destinations			OECD destinations			OECD destinations		
Population 15+	Men	Women	Total	Men	Women	Total	Men	Women	Total
Emigrant population (thousands)	16.1	8.7	24.8	13.6	7.3	20.9	27.7	15.9	43.6
Recent emigrants (thousands)	..	..	..	3.4	1.8	5.2	5.4	5.3	10.7
15-24 (%)	15.1	25.3	18.7	14.0	23.0	17.2	10.2	22.3	14.6
25-64 (%)	83.0	72.7	79.4	85.0	75.7	81.7	89.5	76.9	84.9
65+ (%)	1.9	2.0	1.9	1.0	1.3	1.1	0.3	0.8	0.5
Low-educated (%)	54.5	58.5	55.9	49.1	52.4	50.3	60.7	64.8	62.2
Highly educated (%)	16.9	12.5	15.4	19.0	14.2	17.3	14.5	11.0	13.2
Total emigration rates (%)	3.9	2.1	3.0	3.3	1.8	2.5	5.5	3.2	4.4
Emigration rates of the highly educated (%)	20.6	18.9	20.2	20.0	18.2	19.6	26.6	25.9	26.4

Main destinations in 2005/06

	Total		Recent emigrants	Women	Highly educated	15-24	Total in 2000
Population 15+	Thousands	%	%	%	%	%	Thousands
Spain	19.5	44.7	19.9	33.0	–	15.0	5.8
United States	9.6	21.9	17.6	41.1	31.3	17.2	5.6
United Kingdom	–	–	–	–	–	–	3.6
Sweden	2.8	6.4	25.0	40.9	12.8	18.0	2.6
France	1.6	3.6	16.2	43.9	8.5	7.6	1.0
Norway	0.8	1.9	21.4	36.0	16.0	12.8	0.8
Netherlands	–	–	–	–	–	–	–
Italy	–	–	–	–	–	–	0.3
Denmark	0.5	1.1	12.0	42.3	14.0	16.4	0.5
Canada	0.4	0.9	8.3	38.8	38.8	7.5	0.2

Labour market indicators of persons born in Gambia living in OECD countries

Population 15-64	2000			2005/06		
	Men	Women	Total	Men	Women	Total
Employment-population ratio (%)	69.4	42.9	60.4	79.4	36.3	64.6
Unemployment rate (%)	14.1	18.5	15.2	11.7	34.4	17.2
Participation rate (%)	80.8	52.7	71.3	90.0	55.3	78.0
Total employed (thousands)	**8.0**	**2.5**	**10.5**	**17.0**	**4.1**	**21.0**
Employment rates of the highly educated (%)	77.8	67.4	74.8	81.2	91.1	84.0
Unemployment rates of the highly educated (%)	6.1	9.8	7.1	3.3	1.6	2.8
Highly educated in low- and medium-skilled jobs (%)	54.3	51.4	53.6	90.2	51.8	76.9
Highly educated employed (thousands)	**1.8**	**0.6**	**2.4**	**1.7**	**0.7**	**2.4**
Legislators, senior officials and managers	3.9	2.4	3.5	1.0	0.6	0.9
Professionals	2.8	5.1	3.4	0.5	1.1	0.7
Life science and health professionals	0.3	0.5	0.4	0.1	0.1	0.1
Teaching professionals	0.6	1.9	0.9	0.1	0.3	0.1
Technicians and associate professionals	4.1	5.8	4.5	0.6	7.7	2.0
Clerks	5.6	8.2	6.2	0.9	4.7	1.7
Service, shop and market sales workers	9.5	34.2	15.9	4.6	14.2	6.5
Skilled agricultural and fishery workers	4.3	1.1	3.5	9.4	2.7	8.1
Craft and related trades workers	18.6	5.9	15.4	20.6	0.6	16.6
Plant and machine operators and assemblers	13.0	4.6	10.9	19.7	10.9	17.9
Elementary occupations	38.1	32.7	36.7	42.8	57.5	45.8

Distribution of employment by occupation (%), population 15+

Persons born in Gambia and their native-born children, population 15+

Living in:	Europe	United States	Australia
2008	Thousands	Thousands	Thousands
Native-born children	0.8	..	..
Foreign-born	19.1	..	..
Total	19.9	..	..

International students from Gambia in OECD countries

Five main destinations	2004	2005	2006	2007	2008	2009
United Kingdom	306	339	373	356	332	349
United States	523	465	417	380	330	323
Canada	17	..	27	18	35	39
France	22	13	28	26	25	14
Turkey	2	0	0	1	5	10
Total	880	835	860	791	751	761

Legal migrant flows to the OECD
Thousands

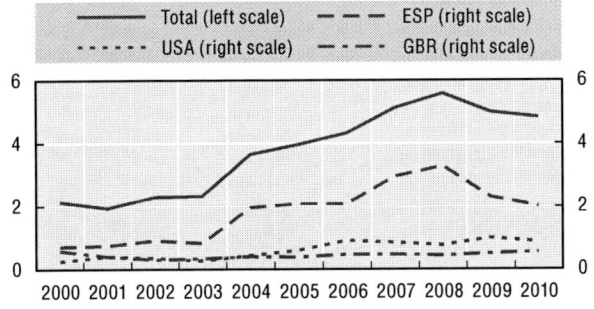

Remittance flows

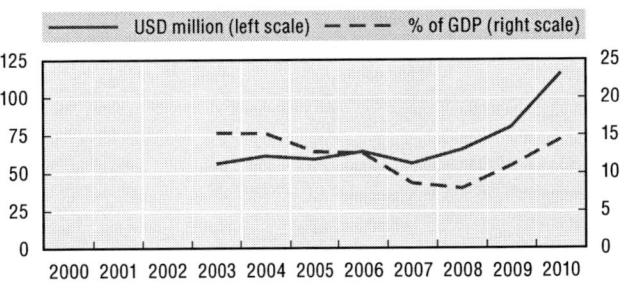

Ten main countries of destination for legal migrants in 2010 (numbers, % of total flows to the country): ESP (2013, 0.5%), USA (859, 0.1%), GBR (527, 0.1%), DEU (387, 0.1%), SWE (290, 0.4%), ITA (153, 0%), AUT (123, 0.1%), FRA (99, 0.1%), NLD (54, 0.1%), CHE (54, 0%).

Desire to emigrate, 2008-10

	Women	15-24	Highly educated	Total	Regional total
Persons who would move permanently, if they had the opportunity to do so (%)	..	..	..	..	33
Of which: Persons who are planning to move permanently in the next 12 months (%)				..	12
Of which: Persons who have already done some preparations for this move (*e.g.* visa application) (%)					33

StatLink ⟶ http://dx.doi.org/10.1787/888932674474

Total population 2010 (millions)	24.4	**Ghana compared to:**	**World**	**Region**
Population growth 2010 (%)	2.4	Human Development Index (HDI)	135/187	8/46
GDP per capita 2010 (current USD)	1 283	GDP per capita	139/194	12/46
GDP growth 2010 (%)	6.6	Emigration rate	131/203	16/47
Poverty rate 2006 (USD PPP 2 a day, in %)	53.6	Emigration rate of the highly educated	19/157	7/39

Age structure of the population 0+ (2010): "0-14": 20%; "15-24": 39%; "25-64": 38%; "65+": 4%.
Level of education of the population 15+ (2010): "Low": 34%; "Medium": 64%; "High": 3%.

Emigrant population living in OECD countries

Immigrant population

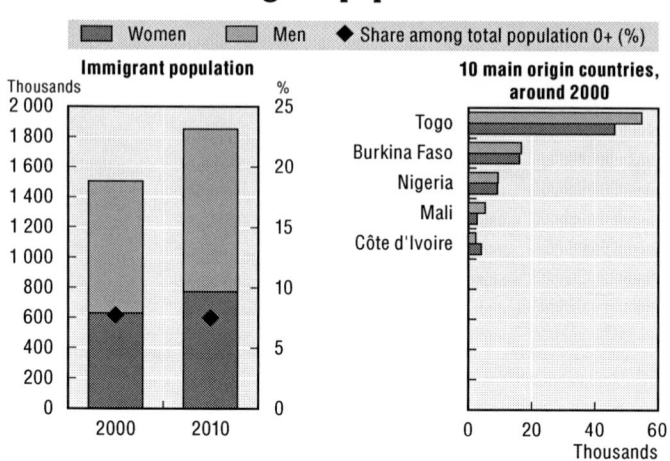

Emigrant population: persons born in Ghana living abroad

	2000						2005/06		
	All destinations			OECD destinations			OECD destinations		
Population 15+	Men	Women	Total	Men	Women	Total	Men	Women	Total
Emigrant population (thousands)	138.6	131.3	269.9	90.1	75.7	165.8	135.0	114.1	249.0
Recent emigrants (thousands)	..	..	..	20.3	17.5	37.9	35.7	30.1	65.8
15-24 (%)	15.9	19.1	17.5	12.5	15.4	13.8	13.1	16.9	14.9
25-64 (%)	81.6	78.4	80.0	85.3	82.7	84.1	83.2	80.5	82.0
65+ (%)	2.5	2.5	2.5	2.2	1.9	2.1	3.6	2.6	3.1
Low-educated (%)	44.0	59.2	51.4	23.2	32.9	27.6	23.6	32.4	27.6
Highly educated (%)	26.1	15.6	21.0	37.7	26.5	32.6	39.7	32.6	36.4
Total emigration rates (%)	2.3	2.2	2.2	1.5	1.3	1.4	1.9	1.6	1.8
Emigration rates of the highly educated (%)	28.6	50.2	33.9	27.3	49.5	32.8	26.3	36.7	29.7

Main destinations in 2005/06

	Total		Recent emigrants	Women	Highly educated	15-24	Total in 2000
Population 15+	Thousands	%	%	%	%	%	Thousands
United States	97.5	39.2	27.4	43.5	41.9	14.0	62.0
United Kingdom	75.1	30.1	29.6	48.3	46.6	12.1	53.3
Italy	27.4	11.0	22.3	45.2	–	16.7	16.4
Canada	18.6	7.5	17.4	49.4	48.3	20.1	15.8
Belgium	6.0	2.4	–	–	–	–	2.5
France	5.3	2.1	17.0	52.3	15.1	17.7	4.2
Netherlands	4.6	1.8	–	56.1	–	–	–
Austria	3.2	1.3	–	–	–	–	–
Australia	2.5	1.0	28.2	45.9	44.1	19.3	1.7
Switzerland	2.3	0.9	–	–	–	–	1.5

Labour market indicators of persons born in Ghana living in OECD countries

	2000			2005/06		
Population 15-64	Men	Women	Total	Men	Women	Total
Employment-population ratio (%)	77.4	61.3	70.0	83.6	67.2	76.1
Unemployment rate (%)	7.9	12.0	9.6	7.1	10.8	8.7
Participation rate (%)	84.0	69.7	77.4	90.0	75.4	83.3
Total employed (thousands)	**64.9**	**43.5**	**108.4**	**106.0**	**72.2**	**178.2**
Employment rates of the highly educated (%)	83.3	73.5	79.6	93.0	86.3	90.3
Unemployment rates of the highly educated (%)	6.0	7.2	6.4	5.6	8.2	6.6
Highly educated in low- and medium-skilled jobs (%)	39.1	37.5	38.5	48.2	48.8	48.4
Highly educated employed (thousands)	**26.1**	**13.9**	**40.0**	**44.2**	**28.0**	**72.2**
Legislators, senior officials and managers	8.6	5.4	7.3	6.5	5.2	6.0
Professionals	13.2	7.9	11.0	8.5	8.2	8.4
Life science and health professionals	1.9	1.0	1.5	0.8	1.4	1.1
Teaching professionals	3.0	2.5	2.8	1.9	0.3	1.2
Technicians and associate professionals	10.5	13.5	11.7	9.8	8.4	9.2
Clerks	7.3	14.6	10.3	5.2	7.8	6.2
Service, shop and market sales workers	8.2	25.8	15.6	4.5	7.5	5.7
Skilled agricultural and fishery workers	0.5	0.2	0.4	2.7	13.3	7.1
Craft and related trades workers	14.9	3.3	10.1	13.5	11.3	12.6
Plant and machine operators and assemblers	14.2	5.9	10.7	21.4	6.9	15.4
Elementary occupations	22.6	23.5	23.0	28.0	27.2	27.7

Left vertical label: Distribution of employment by occupation (%), population 15+

Persons born in Ghana and their native-born children, population 15+

Living in:	Europe	United States	Australia
2008	Thousands	Thousands	Thousands
Native-born children	20.8	39.5	1.2
Foreign-born	151.0	112.0	3.5
Total	171.9	151.4	4.7

International students from Ghana in OECD countries

Five main destinations	2004	2005	2006	2007	2008	2009
United States	3 288	3 252	3 272	3 026	2 898	2 939
United Kingdom	2 798	3 035	2 894	2 675	2 237	2 033
Canada	274	..	321	216	323	323
Germany	..	..	..	..	241	243
Italy	17	30	50	83	114	161
Total	6 678	6 704	6 927	6 401	6 334	6 335

Legal migrant flows to the OECD
Thousands

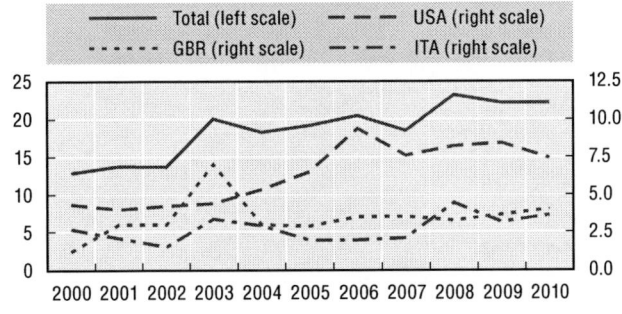

Remittance flows

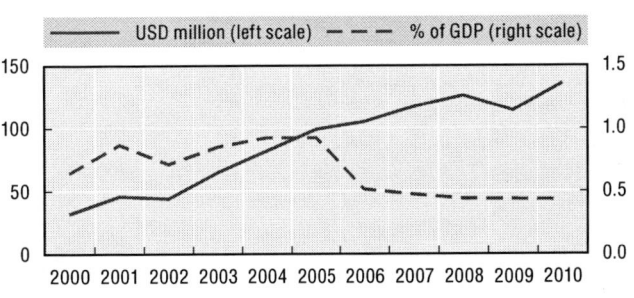

Ten main countries of destination for legal migrants in 2010 (numbers, % of total flows to the country): USA (7429, 0.7%), GBR (4052, 0.9%), ITA (3627, 0.9%), ESP (1968, 0.5%), DEU (1521, 0.2%), CAN (745, 0.3%), NLD (607, 0.4%), BEL (454, 0.4%), JPN (309, 0.1%), AUS (268, 0.1%).

Desire to emigrate, 2008-10

	Women	15-24	Highly educated	Total	Regional total
Persons who would move permanently, if they had the opportunity to do so (%)	40	55	36	41	33
Of which: Persons who are planning to move permanently in the next 12 months (%)				17	12
Of which: Persons who have already done some preparations for this move (*e.g.* visa application) (%)					33

Three main countries of desired destination: United States (46%), United Kingdom (16%), Germany (8%).

StatLink http://dx.doi.org/10.1787/888932674493

		Guinea compared to:	World	Region
Total population 2010 (millions)	10.0			
Population growth 2010 (%)	2.2	Human Development Index (HDI)	178/187	37/46
GDP per capita 2010 (current USD)	452	GDP per capita	175/194	35/46
GDP growth 2010 (%)	1.9	Emigration rate	153/203	28/47
Poverty rate 2007 (USD PPP 2 a day, in %)	69.6	Emigration rate of the highly educated	116/157	35/39

Age structure of the population 0+ (2010): "0-14": 20%; "15-24": 43%; "25-64": 34%; "65+": 3%.

Emigrant population living in OECD countries

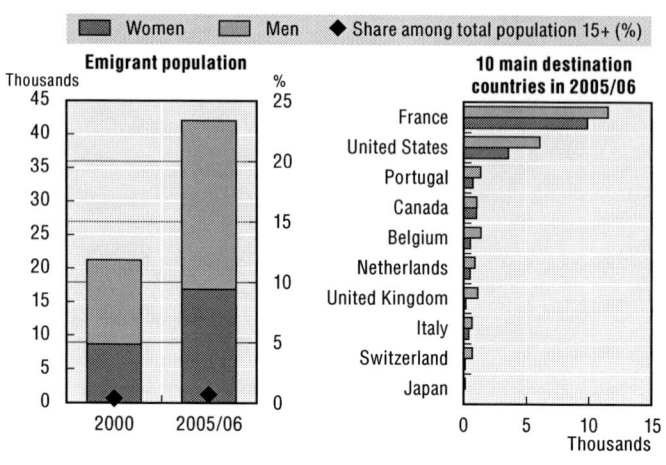

Immigrant population

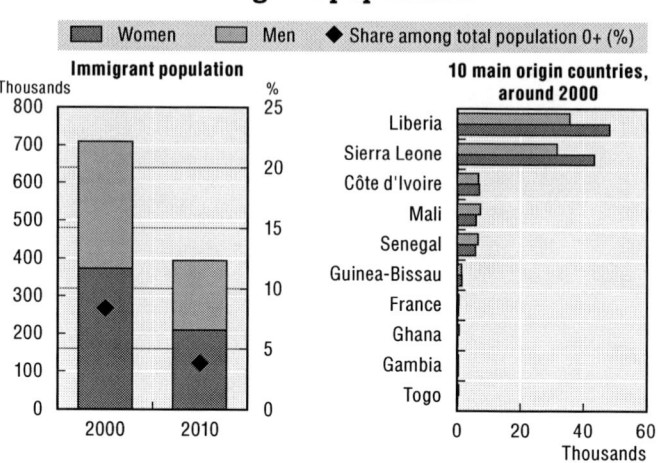

Emigrant population: persons born in Guinea living abroad

	2000						2005/06		
	All destinations			OECD destinations			OECD destinations		
Population 15+	Men	Women	Total	Men	Women	Total	Men	Women	Total
Emigrant population (thousands)	48.9	33.5	82.3	12.6	8.7	21.3	25.1	17.0	42.0
Recent emigrants (thousands)	..	..	..	3.7	2.8	6.6	6.2	4.8	11.1
15-24 (%)	19.6	28.3	23.1	12.1	18.5	14.7	20.4	22.3	21.1
25-64 (%)	74.1	67.5	71.4	85.1	78.9	82.5	75.7	73.5	74.8
65+ (%)	6.3	4.2	5.4	2.8	2.7	2.8	3.9	4.3	4.1
Low-educated (%)	79.9	82.3	80.9	51.2	50.6	51.0	47.2	55.9	50.7
Highly educated (%)	8.3	6.3	7.5	24.4	20.9	23.0	25.7	17.6	22.5
Total emigration rates (%)	2.1	1.4	1.8	0.5	0.4	0.5	1.0	0.7	0.8
Emigration rates of the highly educated (%)	3.3	5.5	3.8	2.5	4.8	3.1	4.9	6.9	5.4

Main destinations in 2005/06

	Total		Recent emigrants	Women	Highly educated	15-24	Total in 2000
Population 15+	Thousands	%	%	%	%	%	Thousands
France	21.4	51.0	23.9	46.1	22.1	16.7	7.4
United States	9.6	22.9	31.8	36.8	26.5	16.4	4.8
Portugal	–	–	–	–	–	–	0.3
Canada	2.0	4.8	51.0	49.0	56.4	20.7	1.2
Belgium	–	–	–	–	–	–	0.7
Netherlands	–	–	–	–	–	–	–
United Kingdom	–	–	–	–	–	–	0.2
Italy	1.1	2.5	–	–	–	–	0.7
Switzerland	–	–	–	–	–	–	0.4

Labour market indicators of persons born in Guinea living in OECD countries

Population 15-64	2000			2005/06		
	Men	Women	Total	Men	Women	Total
Employment-population ratio (%)	60.8	42.9	53.4	60.6	41.9	53.0
Unemployment rate (%)	22.3	28.6	24.5	21.9	29.7	24.6
Participation rate (%)	78.3	60.0	70.7	77.5	59.6	70.3
Total employed (thousands)	**7.1**	**3.5**	**10.7**	**14.4**	**6.8**	**21.1**
Employment rates of the highly educated (%)	70.1	63.8	67.7	82.8	72.9	79.6
Unemployment rates of the highly educated (%)	15.6	15.3	15.5	16.2	19.0	17.0
Highly educated in low- and medium-skilled jobs (%)	46.0	52.9	48.5	54.9	53.5	54.5
Highly educated employed (thousands)	**2.0**	**1.1**	**3.1**	**4.3**	**1.7**	**5.9**
Legislators, senior officials and managers	5.9	5.3	5.7	4.1	5.2	4.5
Professionals	11.1	7.9	10.0	11.4	6.3	9.7
Life science and health professionals	1.9	3.3	2.4	1.6	1.2	1.5
Teaching professionals	1.5	0.9	1.3	1.5	2.2	1.7
Technicians and associate professionals	8.8	12.4	10.0	8.5	14.0	10.3
Clerks	5.8	11.1	7.6	4.8	13.3	7.7
Service, shop and market sales workers	8.3	26.8	14.5	9.9	25.8	15.2
Skilled agricultural and fishery workers	3.2	0.2	2.2	0.8	0.5	0.7
Craft and related trades workers	22.1	7.9	17.3	17.2	1.9	12.1
Plant and machine operators and assemblers	7.9	4.0	6.6	14.8	1.8	10.4
Elementary occupations	27.0	24.4	26.2	28.5	31.3	29.4

Distribution of employment by occupation (%), population 15+

Persons born in Guinea and their native-born children, population 15+

Living in:	Europe	United States	Australia
2008	Thousands	Thousands	Thousands
Native-born children	10.0	..	..
Foreign-born	36.5	..	1.1
Total	46.5	..	..

International students from Guinea in OECD countries

Five main destinations	2004	2005	2006	2007	2008	2009
France	1 263	1 499	2 099	2 563	2 751	3 020
United States	250	235	226	185	167	187
Canada	207	..	162	144	154	173
Spain	4	3	1	5	4	156
Germany	..	..	..	..	101	100
Total	1 770	1 796	2 553	2 969	3 381	3 773

Legal migrant flows to the OECD
Thousands

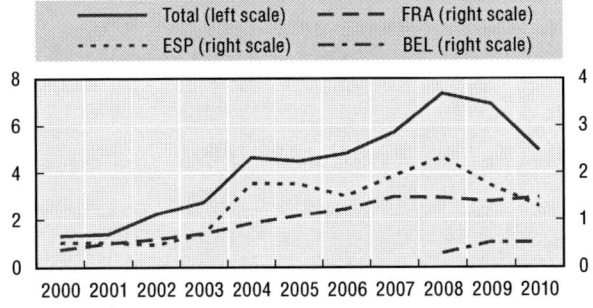

Remittance flows

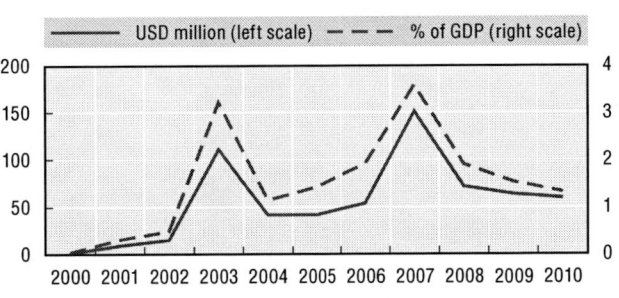

Ten main countries of destination for legal migrants in 2010 (numbers, % of total flows to the country): FRA (1485, 1.1%), ESP (1300, 0.3%), BEL (518, 0.5%), DEU (494, 0.1%), ITA (391, 0.1%), CAN (250, 0.1%), PRT (139, 0.1%), CHE (73, 0.1%), AUS (54, 0%), AUT (51, 0.1%).

Desire to emigrate, 2008-10

	Women	15-24	Highly educated	Total	Regional total
Persons who would move permanently, if they had the opportunity to do so (%)	..	..	..	..	33
Of which: Persons who are planning to move permanently in the next 12 months (%)				..	12
Of which: Persons who have already done some preparations for this move (*e.g.* visa application) (%)					33

StatLink http://dx.doi.org/10.1787/888932674512

Total population 2010 (millions)	40.5	**Kenya compared to:**	**World**	**Region**
Population growth 2010 (%)	2.6	Human Development Index (HDI)	144/187	13/46
GDP per capita 2010 (current USD)	775	GDP per capita	157/194	21/46
GDP growth 2010 (%)	5.3	Emigration rate	144/203	21/47
Poverty rate 2005 (USD PPP 2 a day, in %)	39.9	Emigration rate of the highly educated	44/157	16/39

Age structure of the population 0+ (2010): "0-14": 21%; "15-24": 42%; "25-64": 34%; "65+": 3%.
Level of education of the population 15+ (2010): "Low": 64%; "Medium": 33%; "High": 3%.

Emigrant population living in OECD countries

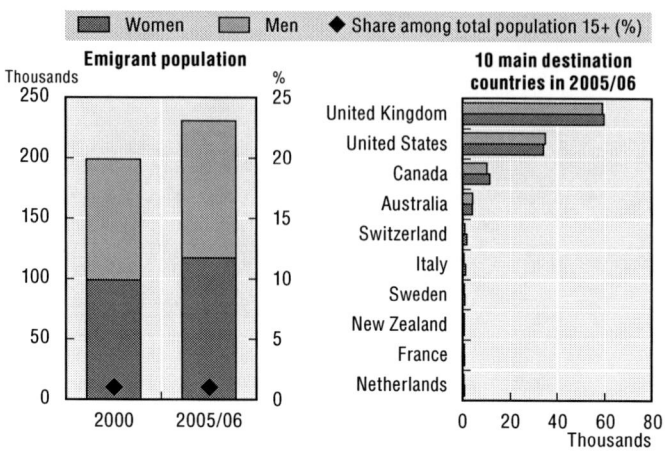

Immigrant population

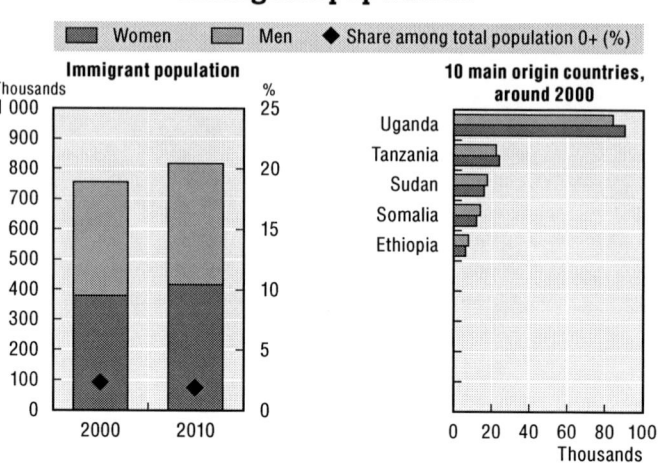

Emigrant population: persons born in Kenya living abroad

	2000						2005/06		
	All destinations			OECD destinations			OECD destinations		
Population 15+	Men	Women	Total	Men	Women	Total	Men	Women	Total
Emigrant population (thousands)	126.8	138.1	264.8	99.9	98.8	198.7	113.8	117.0	230.8
Recent emigrants (thousands)	..	..	..	10.9	10.4	21.3	19.4	19.5	38.9
15-24 (%)	15.1	16.8	16.0	11.1	11.4	11.2	10.7	11.1	10.9
25-64 (%)	79.2	76.8	77.9	83.9	83.1	83.5	82.6	80.9	81.7
65+ (%)	5.7	6.4	6.1	5.0	5.5	5.2	6.7	8.1	7.4
Low-educated (%)	34.5	44.7	39.8	24.4	29.8	27.1	16.1	27.0	21.5
Highly educated (%)	35.5	25.6	30.3	43.0	34.3	38.7	53.1	40.0	46.6
Total emigration rates (%)	1.4	1.5	1.5	1.1	1.1	1.1	1.1	1.1	1.1
Emigration rates of the highly educated (%)	13.3	21.4	16.0	12.7	20.5	15.3	13.6	20.1	15.8

Main destinations in 2005/06

	Total		Recent emigrants	Women	Highly educated	15-24	Total in 2000
Population 15+	Thousands	%	%	%	%	%	Thousands
United Kingdom	118.8	51.5	6.0	50.3	41.2	5.4	125.5
United States	69.3	30.0	33.3	49.4	51.1	18.4	37.5
Canada	21.4	9.3	13.5	52.7	61.6	11.3	19.1
Australia	8.1	3.5	31.0	48.8	59.9	15.4	6.1
Switzerland	2.5	1.1	50.8	64.9	–	–	1.5
Italy	1.6	0.7	–	69.8	–	–	1.5
Sweden	1.4	0.6	31.2	59.6	35.2	18.1	1.2
New Zealand	1.3	0.6	19.6	51.2	48.3	6.6	1.0
France	1.2	0.5	42.5	57.6	49.3	19.7	0.7

Labour market indicators of persons born in Kenya living in OECD countries

Population 15-64	2000			2005/06		
	Men	Women	Total	Men	Women	Total
Employment-population ratio (%)	79.6	66.1	72.8	82.6	69.6	76.1
Unemployment rate (%)	5.8	6.1	6.0	4.8	6.3	5.5
Participation rate (%)	84.5	70.3	77.4	86.7	74.3	80.6
Total employed (thousands)	**72.0**	**59.4**	**131.4**	**86.0**	**71.6**	**157.6**
Employment rates of the highly educated (%)	87.9	77.6	83.3	93.0	82.1	88.3
Unemployment rates of the highly educated (%)	3.8	4.5	4.1	4.7	4.0	4.4
Highly educated in low- and medium-skilled jobs (%)	22.5	30.1	25.7	31.6	34.7	32.9
Highly educated employed (thousands)	**34.8**	**24.7**	**59.5**	**49.3**	**33.0**	**82.3**
Legislators, senior officials and managers	25.2	11.9	19.2	20.7	10.7	16.2
Professionals	20.1	15.6	18.1	20.2	15.5	18.1
Life science and health professionals	4.0	3.1	3.6	4.4	3.4	4.0
Teaching professionals	2.2	4.9	3.4	3.2	5.6	4.3
Technicians and associate professionals	11.5	14.2	12.8	11.9	16.8	14.1
Clerks	9.2	28.5	17.9	6.7	23.3	14.2
Service, shop and market sales workers	7.1	17.3	11.7	10.8	4.7	8.1
Skilled agricultural and fishery workers	0.5	0.3	0.4	4.9	7.0	5.8
Craft and related trades workers	11.0	1.0	6.5	4.0	5.5	4.7
Plant and machine operators and assemblers	7.5	4.4	6.1	7.4	4.1	5.9
Elementary occupations	7.9	6.9	7.5	10.5	10.9	10.7

Distribution of employment by occupation (%), population 15+

Persons born in Kenya and their native-born children, population 15+

Living in:	Europe	United States	Australia
2008	Thousands	Thousands	Thousands
Native-born children	96.6	26.0	1.5
Foreign-born	70.2	67.0	0.5
Total	166.7	92.9	2.0

International students from Kenya in OECD countries

Five main destinations	2004	2005	2006	2007	2008	2009
United States	7 381	7 027	6 792	6 489	5 844	5 780
United Kingdom	3 083	2 977	2 889	2 759	2 428	2 394
Australia	1 115	1 085	1 116	1 278	1 417	1 426
Canada	396	..	447	297	400	359
Germany	..	..	..	..	289	297
Total	12 416	11 631	11 880	11 493	11 056	11 050

Legal migrant flows to the OECD
Thousands

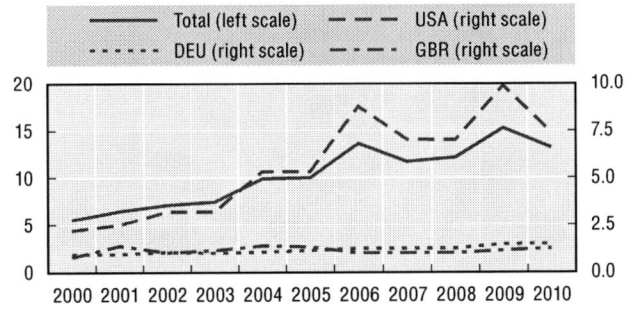

Remittance flows

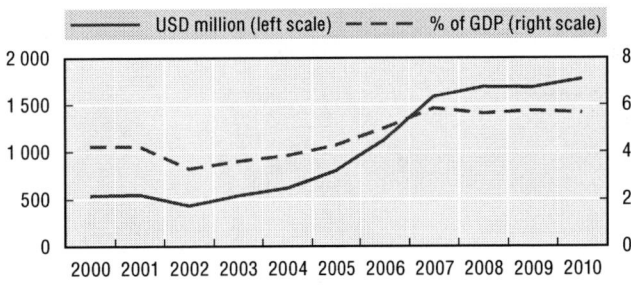

Ten main countries of destination for legal migrants in 2010 (numbers, % of total flows to the country): USA (7421, 0.7%), DEU (1502, 0.2%), GBR (1240, 0.3%), CAN (590, 0.2%), AUS (422, 0.2%), JPN (348, 0.1%), ITA (270, 0.2%), NLD (180, 0.2%), SWE (161, 0.2%), ESP (155, 0%).

Desire to emigrate, 2008-10

	Women	15-24	Highly educated	Total	Regional total
Persons who would move permanently, if they had the opportunity to do so (%)	30	42	30	31	33
Of which: Persons who are planning to move permanently in the next 12 months (%)				8	12
Of which: Persons who have already done some preparations for this move (*e.g.* visa application) (%)					33

Three main countries of desired destination: United States (43%), United Kingdom (12%), Canada (6%).

StatLink ᴍᴸᵉ *http://dx.doi.org/10.1787/888932674531*

		Liberia compared to:	World	Region
Total population 2010 (millions)	4.0	Human Development Index (HDI)	182/187	41/46
Population growth 2010 (%)	4.0	GDP per capita	184/194	43/46
GDP per capita 2010 (current USD)	247	Emigration rate	98/203	11/47
GDP growth 2010 (%)	5.5	Emigration rate of the highly educated	66/157	23/39
Poverty rate 2007 (USD PPP 2 a day, in %)	94.8			

Age structure of the population 0+ (2010): "0-14": 19%; "15-24": 44%; "25-64": 34%; "65+": 3%.
Level of education of the population 15+ (2010): "Low": 60%; "Medium": 25%; "High": 15%.

Emigrant population living in OECD countries

Immigrant population

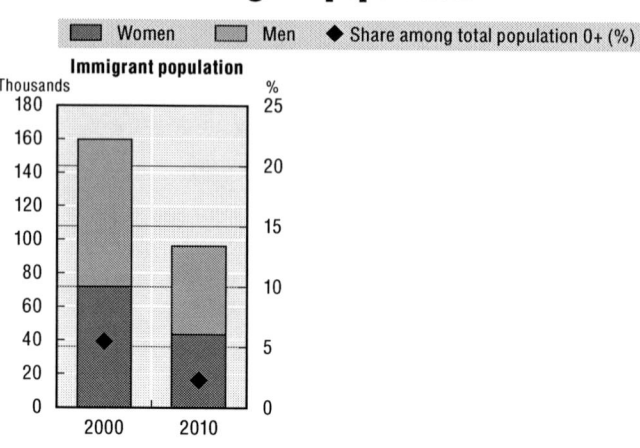

Emigrant population: persons born in Liberia living abroad

	2000						2005/06		
	All destinations			OECD destinations			OECD destinations		
Population 15+	Men	Women	Total	Men	Women	Total	Men	Women	Total
Emigrant population (thousands)	61.2	76.2	137.5	20.2	20.9	41.1	35.3	34.7	69.9
Recent emigrants (thousands)	..	..	..	5.8	6.1	12.0	10.5	12.0	22.5
15-24 (%)	36.4	36.0	36.2	20.3	20.7	20.5	27.0	25.9	26.4
25-64 (%)	57.8	57.7	57.8	77.0	72.9	74.9	69.5	69.2	69.4
65+ (%)	5.8	6.2	6.0	2.7	6.4	4.6	3.5	4.9	4.2
Low-educated (%)	68.5	77.4	73.4	17.9	23.5	20.7	19.2	25.0	22.1
Highly educated (%)	14.7	8.1	11.1	39.9	27.9	33.8	33.9	27.4	30.6
Total emigration rates (%)	7.0	8.5	7.7	2.4	2.5	2.5	3.7	3.6	3.7
Emigration rates of the highly educated (%)	14.9	18.0	16.0	13.8	17.4	15.1	10.8	12.3	11.4

Main destinations in 2005/06

	Total		Recent emigrants	Women	Highly educated	15-24	Total in 2000
Population 15+	Thousands	%	%	%	%	%	Thousands
United States	62.3	89.1	30.4	49.7	30.4	27.1	35.5
Netherlands	–	–	–	–	–	–	–
Canada	1.3	1.9	62.5	53.7	32.8	26.6	0.6
Australia	1.3	1.8	92.3	54.0	14.0	43.6	–
Sweden	0.7	1.0	31.9	51.1	26.0	18.4	0.7
United Kingdom	–	–	–	–	–	–	1.4
France	0.6	0.9	24.7	41.2	20.5	16.5	0.7
Belgium	–	–	–	–	–	–	0.3
Austria	–	–	–	–	–	–	–
Italy	–	–	–	–	–	–	0.2

Labour market indicators of persons born in Liberia living in OECD countries

Population 15-64	2000			2005/06		
	Men	Women	Total	Men	Women	Total
Employment-population ratio (%)	74.1	67.6	70.8	74.8	70.5	72.7
Unemployment rate (%)	9.5	8.7	9.1	10.2	10.9	10.5
Participation rate (%)	81.8	74.1	77.9	83.3	79.1	81.2
Total employed (thousands)	**14.1**	**13.0**	**27.1**	**24.4**	**22.4**	**46.8**
Employment rates of the highly educated (%)	86.1	80.7	83.8	93.7	91.8	92.8
Unemployment rates of the highly educated (%)	5.0	5.0	5.0	8.9	6.6	7.9
Highly educated in low- and medium-skilled jobs (%)	48.5	41.9	45.8	50.7	49.1	50.0
Highly educated employed (thousands)	**6.6**	**4.5**	**11.1**	**9.7**	**7.7**	**17.3**
Legislators, senior officials and managers	6.3	4.2	5.6	2.9	1.1	2.1
Professionals	11.8	11.6	11.7	7.4	8.3	7.8
Life science and health professionals	1.1	1.5	1.3	0.2	1.3	0.7
Teaching professionals	2.5	6.2	3.9	0.7	5.1	2.7
Technicians and associate professionals	9.8	16.3	12.1	8.4	18.7	13.1
Clerks	6.1	12.9	8.5	4.4	15.7	9.5
Service, shop and market sales workers	12.9	31.1	19.4	13.1	23.4	17.8
Skilled agricultural and fishery workers	0.6	0.6	0.6	0.2	21.6	9.9
Craft and related trades workers	12.7	0.6	8.4	19.6	1.3	11.3
Plant and machine operators and assemblers	12.5	1.3	8.5	24.3	1.3	13.9
Elementary occupations	27.3	21.3	25.2	19.8	8.7	14.7

Distribution of employment by occupation (%), population 15+

Persons born in Liberia and their native-born children, population 15+

Living in:	Europe	United States	Australia
2008	Thousands	Thousands	Thousands
Native-born children	0.2	21.4	..
Foreign-born	7.0	60.6	..
Total	7.2	82.0	..

International students from Liberia in OECD countries

Five main destinations	2004	2005	2006	2007	2008	2009
United States	411	358	377	343	298	257
United Kingdom	25	23	18	21	18	25
France	13	14	10	12	19	14
Italy	1	1	1	1	3	9
Canada	7	..	3	3	6	6
Total	463	414	423	392	374	336

Legal migrant flows to the OECD
Thousands

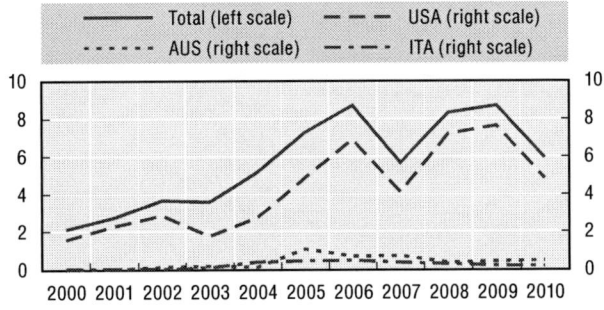

Remittance flows

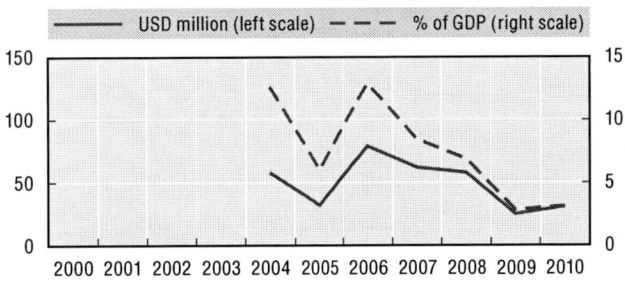

Ten main countries of destination for legal migrants in 2010 (numbers, % of total flows to the country): USA (4837, 0.5%), AUS (475, 0.2%), ITA (170, 0%), DEU (77, 0%), JPN (49, 0%), GBR (42, 0%), SWE (41, 0%), ESP (37, 0%), AUT (36, 0%), CAN (25, 0%).

Desire to emigrate, 2008-10

	Women	15-24	Highly educated	Total	Regional total
Persons who would move permanently, if they had the opportunity to do so (%)	49	55	..	47	33
Of which: Persons who are planning to move permanently in the next 12 months (%)				22	12
Of which: Persons who have already done some preparations for this move (_e.g._ visa application) (%)					33

Three main countries of desired destination: United States (62%), United Kingdom (5%), Canada (5%).

StatLink 🔗 http://dx.doi.org/10.1787/888932674550

		Madagascar compared to:	World	Region
Total population 2010 (millions)	20.7	Human Development Index (HDI)	151/187	16/46
Population growth 2010 (%)	2.9	GDP per capita	177/194	36/46
GDP per capita 2010 (current USD)	421	Emigration rate	151/203	27/47
GDP growth 2010 (%)	1.6	Emigration rate of the highly educated	71/157	24/39
Poverty rate 2005 (USD PPP 2 a day, in %)	89.6			

Age structure of the population 0+ (2010): "0-14": 20%; "15-24": 43%; "25-64": 34%; "65+": 3%.

Emigrant population living in OECD countries

Immigrant population

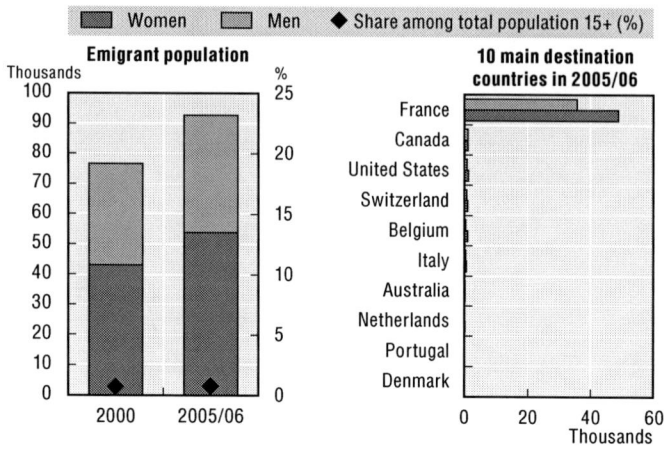

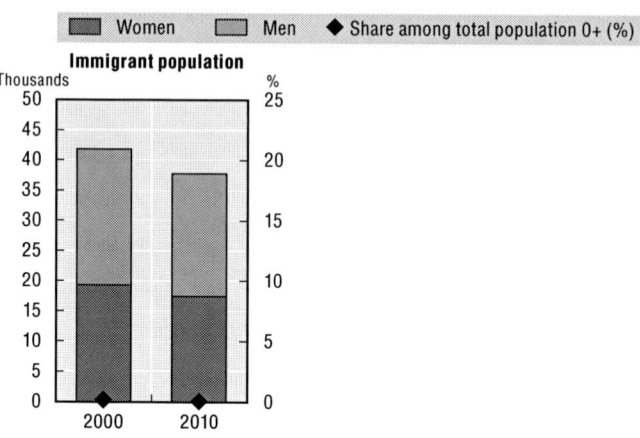

Emigrant population: persons born in Madagascar living abroad

	2000						2005/06		
	All destinations			OECD destinations			OECD destinations		
Population 15+	Men	Women	Total	Men	Women	Total	Men	Women	Total
Emigrant population (thousands)	34.4	44.2	78.6	33.5	43.1	76.6	38.9	53.8	92.7
Recent emigrants (thousands)	..	..	..	2.6	5.3	7.9	3.8	7.3	11.0
15-24 (%)	9.7	9.7	9.7	9.4	9.4	9.4	11.0	10.1	10.5
25-64 (%)	82.3	79.4	80.7	82.5	79.5	80.8	79.1	78.3	78.7
65+ (%)	8.0	10.9	9.6	8.1	11.0	9.8	9.8	11.6	10.9
Low-educated (%)	26.6	39.5	33.8	26.1	39.2	33.4	25.4	36.3	31.7
Highly educated (%)	36.3	27.6	31.4	36.7	28.1	31.9	38.3	30.7	33.9
Total emigration rates (%)	0.8	1.0	0.9	0.8	0.9	0.8	0.7	1.0	0.9
Emigration rates of the highly educated (%)	8.6	11.2	9.7	8.5	11.1	9.6	9.2	12.4	10.6

Main destinations in 2005/06

	Total		Recent emigrants	Women	Highly educated	15-24	Total in 2000
Population 15+	Thousands	%	%	%	%	%	Thousands
France	84.5	91.1	14.9	57.8	32.2	9.9	69.4
Canada	2.1	2.3	16.6	49.4	70.2	9.0	1.9
United States	1.9	2.0	14.7	60.0	66.6	11.4	1.1
Switzerland	1.5	1.7	–	–	–	–	0.8
Belgium	–	–	–	–	–	–	0.9
Italy	0.9	1.0	–	–	–	–	1.0

Labour market indicators of persons born in Madagascar living in OECD countries

Population 15-64	2000			2005/06		
	Men	Women	Total	Men	Women	Total
Employment-population ratio (%)	71.5	53.1	61.3	72.0	56.2	63.0
Unemployment rate (%)	13.6	21.7	17.7	12.1	21.1	17.0
Participation rate (%)	82.8	67.9	74.5	82.0	71.3	75.8
Total employed (thousands)	**22.0**	**20.2**	**42.2**	**24.9**	**26.3**	**51.2**
Employment rates of the highly educated (%)	78.4	66.0	72.2	88.6	80.2	84.2
Unemployment rates of the highly educated (%)	10.3	13.8	11.9	8.9	13.8	11.4
Highly educated in low- and medium-skilled jobs (%)	19.4	27.1	23.0	22.4	32.6	27.5
Highly educated employed (thousands)	**9.0**	**7.6**	**16.6**	**10.9**	**10.4**	**21.3**
Legislators, senior officials and managers	9.9	5.9	7.9	9.5	6.3	7.8
Professionals	21.0	11.4	16.3	21.7	12.5	16.9
Life science and health professionals	4.0	3.0	3.5	4.2	2.6	3.4
Teaching professionals	3.7	3.7	3.7	3.5	4.1	3.8
Technicians and associate professionals	18.4	21.3	19.8	17.6	19.2	18.5
Clerks	7.6	22.2	14.8	7.6	17.9	13.0
Service, shop and market sales workers	6.8	20.6	13.6	7.3	19.7	13.8
Skilled agricultural and fishery workers	1.1	0.9	1.0	1.2	1.3	1.2
Craft and related trades workers	15.4	2.3	8.9	13.5	2.2	7.6
Plant and machine operators and assemblers	12.8	3.3	8.1	14.6	3.1	8.6
Elementary occupations	7.0	12.2	9.6	7.0	17.8	12.7

Distribution of employment by occupation (%), population 15+

Persons born in Madagascar and their native-born children, population 15+

Living in:	Europe	United States	Australia
2008	Thousands	Thousands	Thousands
Native-born children	42.3	..	..
Foreign-born	67.1	..	0.9
Total	109.4	..	..

International students from Madagascar in OECD countries

Five main destinations	2004	2005	2006	2007	2008	2009
France	3 487	3 626	3 667	3 550	3 456	3 484
United States	109	133	116	139	130	121
Canada	79	..	72	87	71	76
Switzerland	..	..	..	..	59	51
Germany	..	..	..	..	52	50
Total	3 736	3 833	3 932	3 872	3 877	3 890

Legal migrant flows to the OECD
Thousands

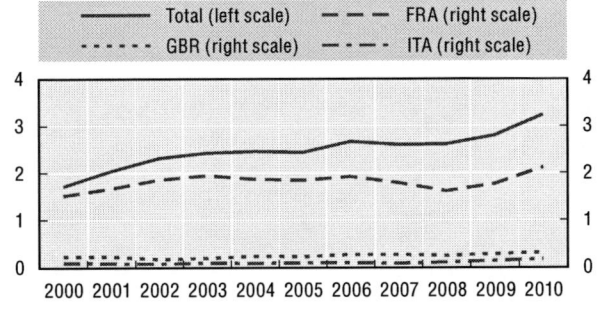

Remittance flows

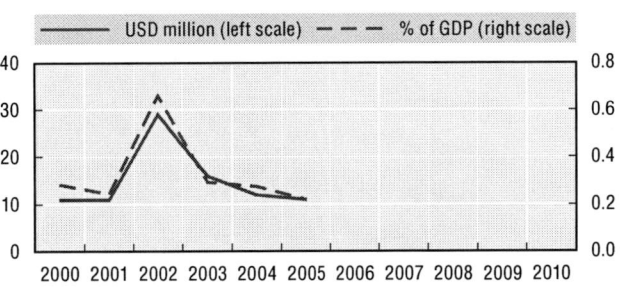

Ten main countries of destination for legal migrants in 2010 (numbers, % of total flows to the country): FRA (2125, 1.6%), GBR (312, 0.1%), ITA (167, 0%), CAN (150, 0.1%), DEU (124, 0%), BEL (100, 0.1%), USA (80, 0.1%), CHE (69, 0.1%), JPN (31, 0%), NOR (21, 0%).

Desire to emigrate, 2008-10

	Women	15-24	Highly educated	Total	Regional total
Persons who would move permanently, if they had the opportunity to do so (%)	..	..	..	..	33
Of which: Persons who are planning to move permanently in the next 12 months (%)				..	12
Of which: Persons who have already done some preparations for this move (*e.g.* visa application) (%)					33

StatLink http://dx.doi.org/10.1787/888932674569

			Malawi compared to:	World	Region
Total population 2010 (millions)	14.9		Human Development Index (HDI)	171/187	30/46
Population growth 2010 (%)	3.1		GDP per capita	182/194	41/46
GDP per capita 2010 (current USD)	343		Emigration rate	186/203	42/47
GDP growth 2010 (%)	7.1		Emigration rate of the highly educated	13/157	4/39
Poverty rate 2004 (USD PPP 2 a day, in %)	90.5				

Age structure of the population 0+ (2010): "0-14": 20%; "15-24": 46%; "25-64": 31%; "65+": 3%.
Level of education of the population 15+ (2010): "Low": 84%; "Medium": 16%; "High": 0%.

Emigrant population living in OECD countries

Immigrant population

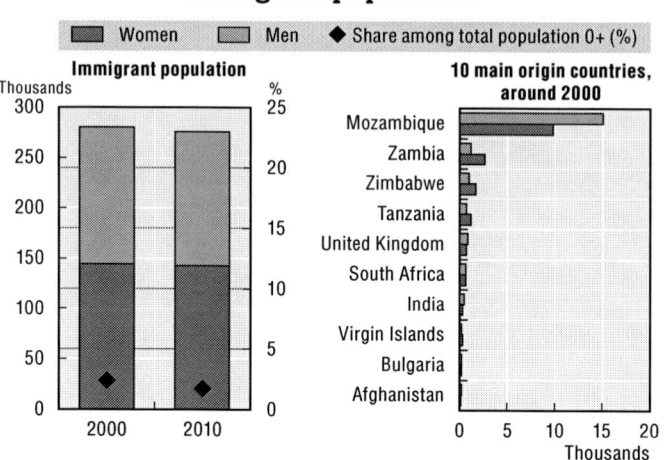

Emigrant population: persons born in Malawi living abroad

	2000						2005/06		
	All destinations			OECD destinations			OECD destinations		
Population 15+	Men	Women	Total	Men	Women	Total	Men	Women	Total
Emigrant population (thousands)	31.0	15.0	46.0	7.6	7.4	14.9	10.7	11.9	22.6
Recent emigrants (thousands)	..	..	..	0.5	0.4	0.8	2.7	2.7	5.4
15-24 (%)	12.1	21.3	15.1	13.3	13.8	13.5	12.4	9.8	11.0
25-64 (%)	72.9	74.1	73.3	84.2	83.5	83.8	87.1	88.7	87.9
65+ (%)	15.0	4.6	11.6	2.5	2.7	2.6	0.5	1.6	1.0
Low-educated (%)	64.7	58.9	62.8	28.5	39.4	33.9	15.6	29.1	22.6
Highly educated (%)	12.3	16.2	13.6	42.5	30.1	36.4	54.1	49.3	51.6
Total emigration rates (%)	1.0	0.5	0.7	0.2	0.2	0.2	0.3	0.3	0.3
Emigration rates of the highly educated (%)	19.7	29.1	22.5	16.6	26.8	19.7	30.5	52.7	38.7

Main destinations in 2005/06

	Total		Recent emigrants	Women	Highly educated	15-24	Total in 2000
Population 15+	Thousands	%	%	%	%	%	Thousands
United Kingdom	17.8	78.8	–	53.3	51.7	–	11.7
United States	2.7	12.1	14.3	42.5	50.7	17.8	1.7
Australia	0.6	2.7	31.2	51.1	61.4	14.4	0.3
Canada	0.5	2.2	19.5	51.5	75.2	14.9	0.4
Netherlands	–	–	–	–	–	–	–
New Zealand	–	–	–	–	–	–	0.1
Ireland	–	–	–	–	–	–	0.1
France	–	–	–	–	–	–	0.1

Labour market indicators of persons born in Malawi living in OECD countries

Population 15-64	2000			2005/06		
	Men	Women	Total	Men	Women	Total
Employment-population ratio (%)	77.6	55.5	66.7	70.2	64.1	66.9
Unemployment rate (%)	6.5	7.8	7.0	13.1	5.3	9.3
Participation rate (%)	82.9	60.2	71.8	80.7	67.7	73.8
Total employed (thousands)	**5.6**	**3.9**	**9.4**	**6.4**	**6.7**	**13.1**
Employment rates of the highly educated (%)	86.1	75.4	81.7	90.8	76.6	83.6
Unemployment rates of the highly educated (%)	4.6	5.1	4.7	20.4	8.9	15.1
Highly educated in low- and medium-skilled jobs (%)	18.0	25.4	20.8	20.7	48.7	34.8
Highly educated employed (thousands)	**2.6**	**1.6**	**4.2**	**3.7**	**3.6**	**7.3**
Legislators, senior officials and managers	25.5	12.6	20.1	18.0	5.4	11.5
Professionals	21.6	15.9	19.3	28.1	2.4	14.9
Life science and health professionals	3.3	2.6	3.0	4.2	0.5	2.3
Teaching professionals	3.0	6.2	4.3	0.2	0.3	0.3
Technicians and associate professionals	12.6	15.5	13.8	13.3	18.5	15.9
Clerks	9.5	23.5	15.3	0.4	14.5	7.6
Service, shop and market sales workers	8.6	19.6	13.2	10.5	3.3	6.8
Skilled agricultural and fishery workers	0.3	0.1	0.2	3.7	21.6	12.9
Craft and related trades workers	6.3	0.8	4.0	8.6	11.9	10.3
Plant and machine operators and assemblers	8.4	4.9	7.0	2.3	5.1	3.7
Elementary occupations	7.1	7.1	7.1	15.1	9.9	12.4

Distribution of employment by occupation (%), population 15+

Persons born in Malawi and their native-born children, population 15+

Living in:	Europe	United States	Australia
2008	Thousands	Thousands	Thousands
Native-born children	8.9	..	..
Foreign-born	11.6	..	..
Total	20.5	..	..

International students from Malawi in OECD countries

Five main destinations	2004	2005	2006	2007	2008	2009
United Kingdom	404	440	454	581	533	494
United States	399	392	359	328	297	310
Australia	77	75	74	85	83	87
Canada	12	..	24	18	19	25
Germany	..	..	..	..	18	20
Total	913	948	953	1 057	1 008	1 022

Legal migrant flows to the OECD
Thousands

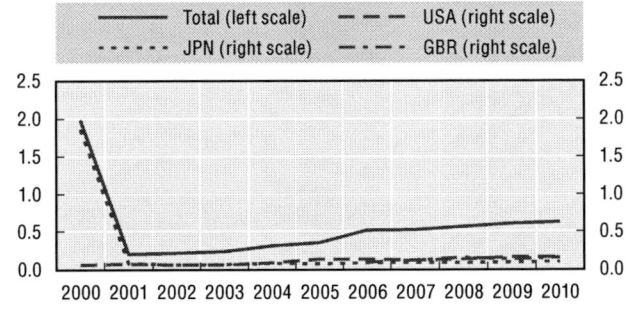

Remittance flows

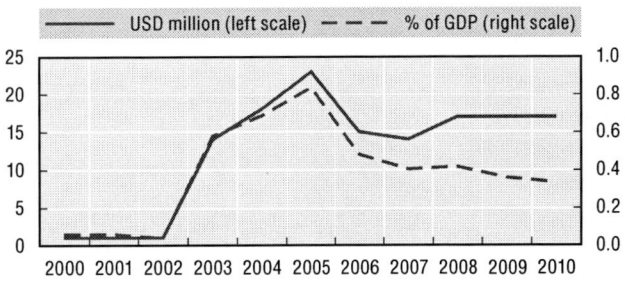

Ten main countries of destination for legal migrants in 2010 (numbers, % of total flows to the country): USA (164, 0%), JPN (155, 0.1%), GBR (103, 0%), CAN (40, 0%), DEU (39, 0%), IRL (31, 0.2%), AUS (19, 0%), NLD (15, 0%), NOR (15, 0%), TUR (8, 0%).

Desire to emigrate, 2008-10

	Women	15-24	Highly educated	Total	Regional total
Persons who would move permanently, if they had the opportunity to do so (%)	37	53	..	40	33
Of which: Persons who are planning to move permanently in the next 12 months (%)				30	12
Of which: Persons who have already done some preparations for this move (*e.g.* visa application) (%)					33

Three main countries of desired destination: South Africa (50%), United Kingdom (19%), United States (13%).

StatLink http://dx.doi.org/10.1787/888932674588

Total population 2010 (millions)	15.4	Mali compared to:	World	Region
Population growth 2010 (%)	3.0	Human Development Index (HDI)	175/187	34/46
GDP per capita 2010 (current USD)	602	GDP per capita	164/194	25/46
GDP growth 2010 (%)	4.5	Emigration rate	148/203	24/47
Poverty rate 2006 (USD PPP 2 a day, in %)	77.1	Emigration rate of the highly educated	72/157	25/39

Age structure of the population 0+ (2010): "0-14": 20%; "15-24": 47%; "25-64": 31%; "65+": 2%.
Level of education of the population 15+ (2010): "Low": 93%; "Medium": 5%; "High": 2%.

Emigrant population living in OECD countries

Immigrant population

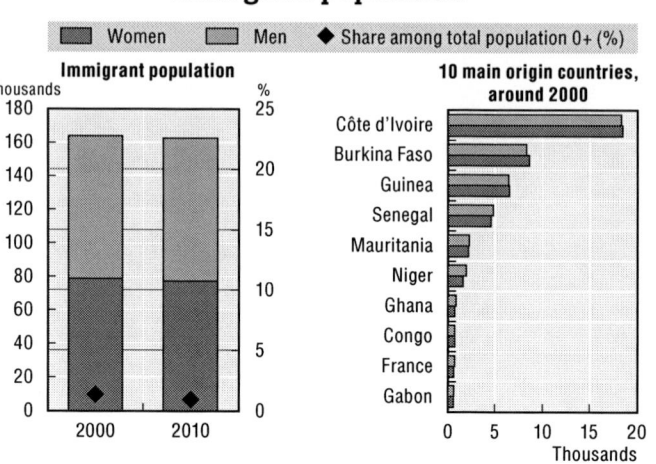

Emigrant population: persons born in Mali living abroad

Population 15+	2000						2005/06		
	All destinations			OECD destinations			OECD destinations		
	Men	Women	Total	Men	Women	Total	Men	Women	Total
Emigrant population (thousands)	239.4	179.0	418.3	30.0	15.4	45.3	39.7	24.2	63.8
Recent emigrants (thousands)	..	..	..	4.2	2.0	6.3	4.8	3.6	8.4
15-24 (%)	25.9	38.5	31.3	8.8	15.1	10.9	7.8	15.6	10.7
25-64 (%)	69.5	59.5	65.2	88.6	82.9	86.7	86.9	81.9	85.0
65+ (%)	4.6	2.1	3.5	2.6	2.0	2.4	5.3	2.5	4.2
Low-educated (%)	91.2	94.8	92.7	70.5	64.9	68.6	65.7	63.9	65.0
Highly educated (%)	2.3	1.6	2.0	12.4	12.9	12.6	15.2	13.6	14.6
Total emigration rates (%)	8.9	6.2	7.5	1.2	0.6	0.9	1.4	0.7	1.0
Emigration rates of the highly educated (%)	14.0	21.9	15.7	9.8	16.8	11.3	9.7	13.1	10.7

Main destinations in 2005/06

Population 15+	Total		Recent emigrants	Women	Highly educated	15-24	Total in 2000
	Thousands	%	%	%	%	%	Thousands
France	56.1	87.9	17.3	37.7	12.0	10.5	37.6
United States	4.5	7.1	17.2	45.8	32.1	11.9	2.7
Canada	0.9	1.5	42.5	47.8	64.5	23.1	0.8
Italy	0.9	1.4	–	–	–	–	0.3
Switzerland	–	–	–	–	–	–	0.2
Belgium	–	–	–	–	–	–	0.3

Labour market indicators of persons born in Mali living in OECD countries

Population 15-64	2000			2005/06		
	Men	Women	Total	Men	Women	Total
Employment-population ratio (%)	67.3	39.1	57.7	65.8	46.0	58.3
Unemployment rate (%)	22.6	31.6	24.9	14.7	27.3	18.9
Participation rate (%)	87.0	57.2	76.8	77.2	63.3	71.9
Total employed (thousands)	**19.6**	**5.9**	**25.5**	**23.4**	**10.1**	**33.5**
Employment rates of the highly educated (%)	76.2	58.2	69.8	81.5	70.9	77.8
Unemployment rates of the highly educated (%)	12.2	19.5	14.5	10.9	18.9	13.5
Highly educated in low- and medium-skilled jobs (%)	39.0	43.9	40.5	49.8	51.1	50.2
Highly educated employed (thousands)	**2.8**	**1.2**	**3.9**	**3.8**	**1.6**	**5.3**
Legislators, senior officials and managers	4.5	2.2	4.0	2.7	2.3	2.6
Professionals	6.7	5.8	6.5	6.3	4.9	5.9
Life science and health professionals	0.9	0.7	0.9	0.8	1.1	0.9
Teaching professionals	1.3	2.0	1.5	0.9	1.7	1.2
Technicians and associate professionals	6.7	10.9	7.7	6.8	8.9	7.4
Clerks	3.4	9.9	4.9	5.0	11.2	6.9
Service, shop and market sales workers	10.8	19.8	12.9	13.6	17.5	14.8
Skilled agricultural and fishery workers	1.6	0.2	1.3	1.4	0.3	1.0
Craft and related trades workers	15.7	2.2	12.6	19.0	1.9	13.8
Plant and machine operators and assemblers	16.6	2.5	13.4	17.4	2.1	12.7
Elementary occupations	33.9	46.5	36.8	28.0	50.9	35.0

Distribution of employment by occupation (%), population 15+

Persons born in Mali and their native-born children, population 15+

Living in:	Europe	United States	Australia
2008	Thousands	Thousands	Thousands
Native-born children	39.8	..	..
Foreign-born	53.0	..	..
Total	92.8	..	..

International students from Mali in OECD countries

Five main destinations	2004	2005	2006	2007	2008	2009
France	1 523	1 559	1 678	1 686	1 766	1 896
United States	378	360	416	465	435	471
Canada	211	..	204	132	197	216
Germany	..	..	..	..	47	45
United Kingdom	22	19	21	14	12	18
Total	2 147	1 954	2 342	2 329	2 513	2 709

Legal migrant flows to the OECD
Thousands

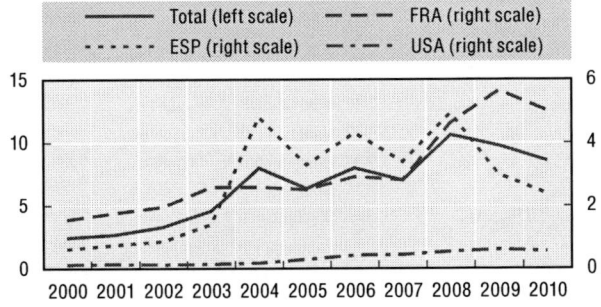

Ten main countries of destination for legal migrants in 2010 (numbers, % of total flows to the country): FRA (5006, 3.7%), ESP (2365, 0.5%), USA (528, 0.1%), ITA (193, 0%), CAN (135, 0%), DEU (118, 0%), BEL (81, 0%), JPN (42, 0%), AUT (23, 0%), CHE (19, 0%).

Remittance flows

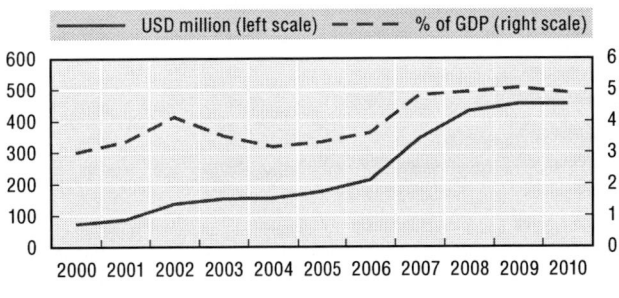

Desire to emigrate, 2008-10

	Women	15-24	Highly educated	Total	Regional total
Persons who would move permanently, if they had the opportunity to do so (%)	19	37	..	25	33
Of which: Persons who are planning to move permanently in the next 12 months (%)				39	12
Of which: Persons who have already done some preparations for this move (*e.g.* visa application) (%)					33

Three main countries of desired destination: France (27%), Spain (19%), United States (15%).

StatLink ⌐⌐ *http://dx.doi.org/10.1787/888932674607*

Total population 2010 (millions)	1.3
Population growth 2010 (%)	0.5
GDP per capita 2010 (current USD)	7 593
GDP growth 2010 (%)	4.0
Poverty rate 2010 (USD PPP 2 a day, in %)	..

Mauritius compared to:	World	Region
Human Development Index (HDI)	78/187	2/46
GDP per capita	72/194	4/46
Emigration rate	47/203	4/47
Emigration rate of the highly educated	8/157	2/39

Age structure of the population 0+ (2010): "0-14": 17%; "15-24": 22%; "25-64": 55%; "65+": 7%.
Level of education of the population 15+ (2010): "Low": 43%; "Medium": 51%; "High": 5%.

Emigrant population living in OECD countries

Immigrant population

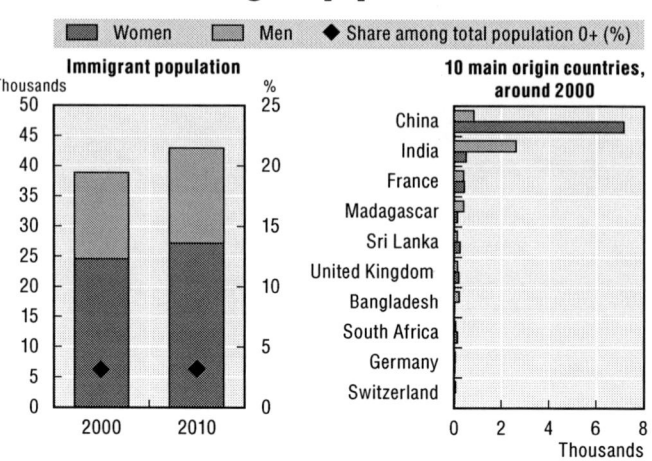

Emigrant population: persons born in Mauritius living abroad

	2000						2005/06		
	All destinations			OECD destinations			OECD destinations		
Population 15+	Men	Women	Total	Men	Women	Total	Men	Women	Total
Emigrant population (thousands)	43.2	52.7	95.9	40.8	50.7	91.5	50.4	58.9	109.3
Recent emigrants (thousands)	..	..	..	2.6	3.7	6.4	6.7	8.2	14.9
15-24 (%)	10.4	9.0	9.7	10.2	8.8	9.5	10.7	9.6	10.1
25-64 (%)	81.0	82.0	81.5	81.8	82.7	82.3	81.6	81.1	81.3
65+ (%)	8.6	9.0	8.8	8.0	8.5	8.3	7.7	9.3	8.5
Low-educated (%)	35.9	51.1	44.2	36.9	51.6	45.0	32.9	44.3	39.0
Highly educated (%)	32.2	19.3	25.1	33.1	19.7	25.7	37.2	23.2	29.7
Total emigration rates (%)	9.0	10.6	9.8	8.6	10.2	9.4	9.8	11.0	10.4
Emigration rates of the highly educated (%)	49.4	60.7	53.7	48.7	60.3	53.1	48.8	51.3	49.8

Main destinations in 2005/06

	Total		Recent emigrants	Women	Highly educated	15-24	Total in 2000
Population 15+	Thousands	%	%	%	%	%	Thousands
France	33.9	31.0	10.0	59.9	17.3	8.8	29.7
United Kingdom	26.6	24.4	–	44.9	49.9	–	26.5
Australia	17.8	16.3	12.4	51.5	29.3	10.0	16.6
Italy	11.3	10.3	14.4	53.5	–	22.3	5.5
Canada	9.1	8.3	23.7	50.5	60.9	10.4	6.5
Belgium	–	–	–	–	–	–	2.6
United States	2.6	2.4	14.6	58.7	54.6	16.5	1.5
Switzerland	2.6	2.4	46.3	62.5	–	–	1.9
Ireland	0.7	0.6	78.6	39.9	31.4	32.4	0.1
New Zealand	–	–	–	–	–	–	0.2

Labour market indicators of persons born in Mauritius living in OECD countries

Population 15-64	2000			2005/06		
	Men	Women	Total	Men	Women	Total
Employment-population ratio (%)	75.0	59.1	66.2	76.4	62.5	69.0
Unemployment rate (%)	10.3	13.3	11.8	8.8	10.6	9.7
Participation rate (%)	83.7	68.1	75.1	83.7	69.9	76.4
Total employed (thousands)	**27.3**	**26.3**	**53.5**	**34.1**	**31.4**	**65.5**
Employment rates of the highly educated (%)	83.1	74.3	79.4	84.3	82.7	83.7
Unemployment rates of the highly educated (%)	4.4	5.5	4.8	6.6	4.4	5.7
Highly educated in low- and medium-skilled jobs (%)	17.1	29.4	21.9	23.1	33.9	27.7
Highly educated employed (thousands)	**10.2**	**6.8**	**17.0**	**13.2**	**9.4**	**22.5**
Legislators, senior officials and managers	11.1	5.0	8.1	10.8	7.6	9.2
Professionals	13.8	7.7	10.8	14.9	8.0	11.6
Life science and health professionals	2.9	1.3	2.1	2.3	0.8	1.6
Teaching professionals	2.1	2.2	2.1	2.9	2.0	2.5
Technicians and associate professionals	17.9	15.1	16.6	13.5	16.6	15.0
Clerks	9.4	21.8	15.4	10.2	16.5	13.3
Service, shop and market sales workers	10.8	23.0	16.8	11.9	15.0	13.4
Skilled agricultural and fishery workers	0.4	0.6	0.5	3.3	4.3	3.8
Craft and related trades workers	12.3	1.7	7.2	11.1	2.1	6.8
Plant and machine operators and assemblers	8.9	2.5	5.8	6.4	1.8	4.2
Elementary occupations	15.4	22.5	18.9	17.0	28.1	22.4

Distribution of employment by occupation (%), population 15+

Persons born in Mauritius and their native-born children, population 15+

Living in:	Europe	United States	Australia
2008	Thousands	Thousands	Thousands
Native-born children	57.9	..	4.9
Foreign-born	98.5	..	19.6
Total	156.4	..	24.5

International students from Mauritius in OECD countries

Five main destinations	2004	2005	2006	2007	2008	2009
France	1 893	1 940	1 987	1 909	1 826	1 703
United Kingdom	1 646	1 660	1 772	1 886	1 702	1 656
Australia	860	873	963	1 087	1 273	1 529
Canada	188	..	198	216	207	233
United States	209	196	217	210	218	217
Total	4 828	4 711	5 192	5 360	5 343	5 568

Legal migrant flows to the OECD
Thousands

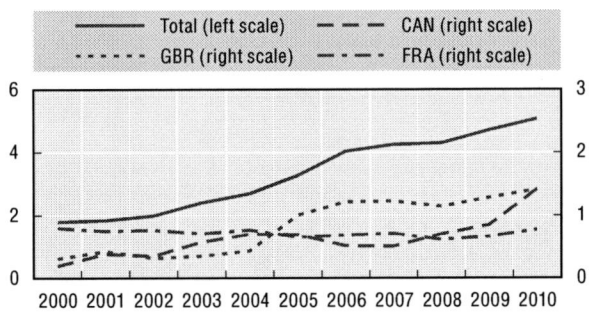

Remittance flows

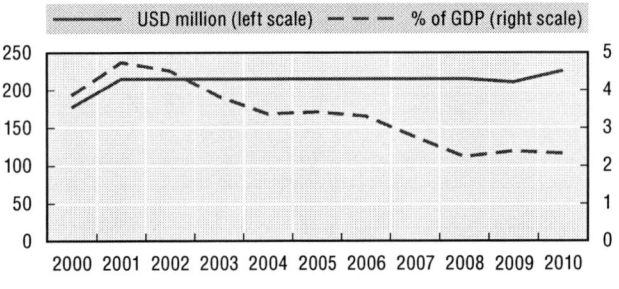

Ten main countries of destination for legal migrants in 2010 (numbers, % of total flows to the country): CAN (1405, 0.5%), GBR (1403, 0.3%), FRA (769, 0.6%), AUS (568, 0.3%), ITA (397, 0.1%), BEL (99, 0.1%), USA (84, 0.1%), CHE (73, 0.1%), DEU (70, 0%), NZL (44, 0.1%).

Desire to emigrate, 2008-10

	Women	15-24	Highly educated	Total	Regional total
Persons who would move permanently, if they had the opportunity to do so (%)	..	..	..	..	33
Of which: Persons who are planning to move permanently in the next 12 months (%)				..	12
Of which: Persons who have already done some preparations for this move (*e.g.* visa application) (%)					33

StatLink ᓕᔭᔃᐤ *http://dx.doi.org/10.1787/888932674626*

Total population 2010 (millions)	23.4		Mozambique compared to:	World	Region
Population growth 2010 (%)	2.3		Human Development Index (HDI)	184/187	43/46
GDP per capita 2010 (current USD)	410		GDP per capita	178/194	37/46
GDP growth 2010 (%)	7.2		Emigration rate	163/203	31/47
Poverty rate 2008 (USD PPP 2 a day, in %)	81.8		Emigration rate of the highly educated	18/157	6/39

Age structure of the population 0+ (2010): "0-14": 20%; "15-24": 44%; "25-64": 33%; "65+": 3%.
Level of education of the population 15+ (2010): "Low": 94%; "Medium": 5%; "High": 1%.

Emigrant population living in OECD countries

Immigrant population

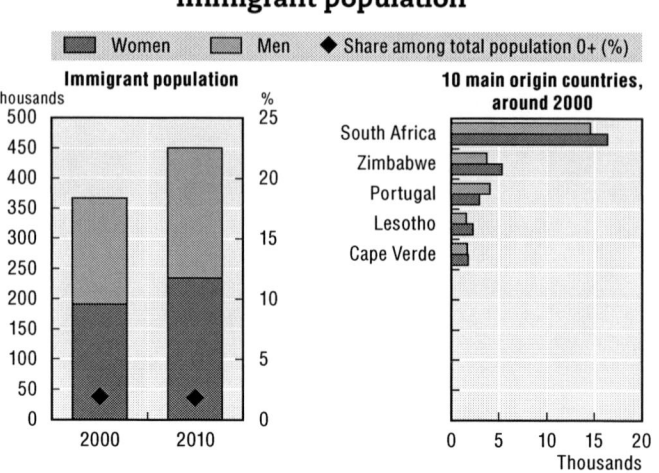

Emigrant population: persons born in Mozambique living abroad

	2000						2005/06		
	All destinations			OECD destinations			OECD destinations		
Population 15+	Men	Women	Total	Men	Women	Total	Men	Women	Total
Emigrant population (thousands)	260.3	144.2	404.5	40.6	45.1	85.7	32.9	39.8	72.7
Recent emigrants (thousands)	..	..	..	0.6	0.7	1.3	2.1	1.7	3.8
15-24 (%)	20.5	20.0	20.3	7.0	6.6	6.8	2.7	2.9	2.8
25-64 (%)	73.7	70.1	72.5	87.0	84.8	85.8	92.9	89.8	91.2
65+ (%)	5.7	9.9	7.2	6.1	8.5	7.4	4.5	7.2	6.0
Low-educated (%)	86.4	79.5	83.9	44.8	44.1	44.4	38.4	39.2	38.8
Highly educated (%)	4.4	9.0	6.0	25.1	27.8	26.5	30.6	29.6	30.1
Total emigration rates (%)	5.2	2.6	3.8	0.8	0.8	0.8	0.6	0.7	0.6
Emigration rates of the highly educated (%)	29.8	59.4	40.6	27.5	58.5	38.9	24.6	40.3	31.1

Main destinations in 2005/06

	Total		Recent emigrants	Women	Highly educated	15-24	Total in 2000
Population 15+	Thousands	%	%	%	%	%	Thousands
Portugal	61.9	85.1	–	55.8	28.8	–	75.4
United States	2.8	3.9	14.4	50.1	45.9	9.3	2.0
United Kingdom	–	–	–	–	–	–	3.2
Canada	1.1	1.5	8.5	54.2	52.3	0.9	0.9
France	1.0	1.4	17.2	50.5	27.9	6.1	0.9
Switzerland	–	–	–	–	–	–	0.8
Italy	–	–	–	–	–	–	0.4
Australia	0.6	0.8	28.4	49.0	42.2	7.0	0.4
Netherlands	–	–	–	–	–	–	–
Belgium	–	–	–	–	–	–	0.3

Labour market indicators of persons born in Mozambique living in OECD countries

Population 15-64	2000			2005/06		
	Men	Women	Total	Men	Women	Total
Employment-population ratio (%)	84.8	72.8	78.6	83.4	77.5	80.2
Unemployment rate (%)	5.4	8.2	6.7	5.8	5.8	5.8
Participation rate (%)	89.6	79.3	84.2	88.6	82.3	85.2
Total employed (thousands)	**32.1**	**29.9**	**61.9**	**25.1**	**27.5**	**52.6**
Employment rates of the highly educated (%)	92.6	89.0	90.6	95.7	93.5	94.5
Unemployment rates of the highly educated (%)	3.0	4.0	3.6	0.9	4.9	3.1
Highly educated in low- and medium-skilled jobs (%)	11.7	12.2	12.0	8.7	16.1	12.6
Highly educated employed (thousands)	**8.8**	**10.7**	**19.4**	**8.7**	**9.7**	**18.5**
Legislators, senior officials and managers	12.6	5.8	9.3	11.5	4.6	7.9
Professionals	17.1	23.3	20.1	22.4	24.9	23.7
Life science and health professionals	2.6	5.5	4.0	1.0	8.1	4.7
Teaching professionals	4.2	9.4	6.7	6.8	6.6	6.7
Technicians and associate professionals	16.8	17.6	17.2	15.0	15.4	15.2
Clerks	11.8	23.5	17.6	9.2	26.9	18.4
Service, shop and market sales workers	12.6	14.8	13.7	9.6	17.5	13.7
Skilled agricultural and fishery workers	0.9	0.3	0.6	2.9	1.0	1.9
Craft and related trades workers	14.4	2.0	8.4	14.2	2.1	7.9
Plant and machine operators and assemblers	6.5	1.5	4.1	13.2	1.2	6.9
Elementary occupations	7.1	11.2	9.1	2.0	6.5	4.3

Distribution of employment by occupation (%), population 15+

Persons born in Mozambique and their native-born children, population 15+

Living in:	Europe	United States	Australia
2008	Thousands	Thousands	Thousands
Native-born children	17.0	..	1.6
Foreign-born	35.6	..	2.5
Total	52.6	..	4.1

International students from Mozambique in OECD countries

Five main destinations	2004	2005	2006	2007	2008	2009
Portugal	..	..	..	..	297	516
United States	93	111	101	82	78	88
Australia	67	77	75	62	54	55
United Kingdom	71	87	84	61	56	54
Italy	21	27	35	33	49	49
Total	331	373	417	326	641	936

Legal migrant flows to the OECD
Thousands

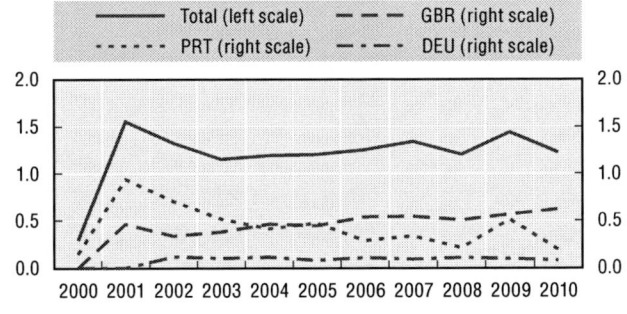

Remittance flows

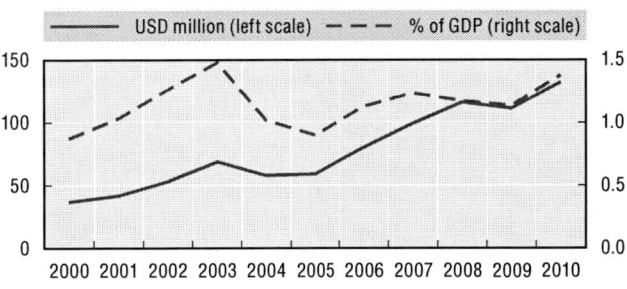

Ten main countries of destination for legal migrants in 2010 (numbers, % of total flows to the country): GBR (625, 0.1%), PRT (193, 0.7%), DEU (81, 0%), ESP (68, 0%), JPN (53, 0%), USA (53, 0%), ITA (32, 0%), AUS (21, 0%), SWE (15, 0%), NLD (12, 0%).

Desire to emigrate, 2008-10

	Women	15-24	Highly educated	Total	Regional total
Persons who would move permanently, if they had the opportunity to do so (%)	25	33	..	26	33
Of which: Persons who are planning to move permanently in the next 12 months (%)				..	12
Of which: Persons who have already done some preparations for this move (*e.g.* visa application) (%)					33

StatLink ⬛⬛ http://dx.doi.org/10.1787/888932674645

		Namibia compared to:	World	Region
Total population 2010 (millions)	2.3	Human Development Index (HDI)	121/187	5/46
Population growth 2010 (%)	1.8	GDP per capita	88/194	7/46
GDP per capita 2010 (current USD)	5 330	Emigration rate	168/203	33/47
GDP growth 2010 (%)	4.8	Emigration rate of the highly educated	83/157	28/39
Poverty rate 2010 (USD PPP 2 a day, in %)	..			

Age structure of the population 0+ (2010): "0-14": 21%; "15-24": 36%; "25-64": 39%; "65+": 4%.
Level of education of the population 15+ (2010): "Low": 49%; "Medium": 48%; "High": 3%.

Emigrant population living in OECD countries

Immigrant population

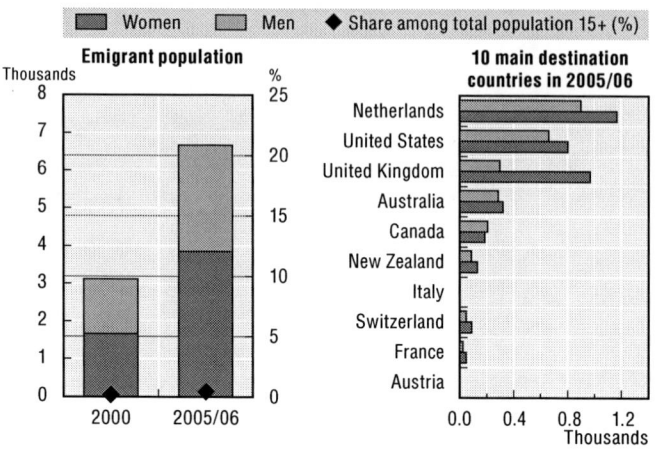

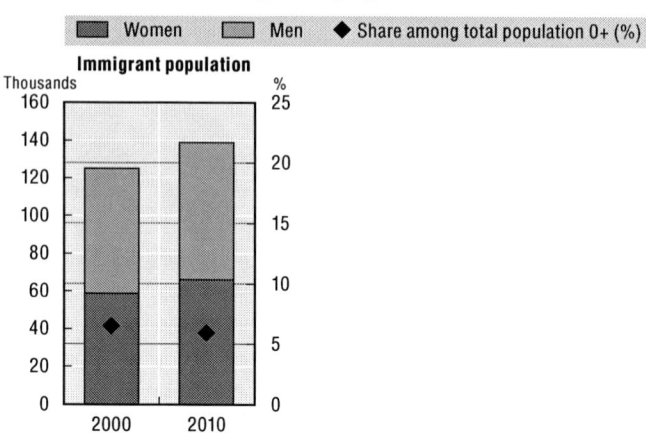

Emigrant population: persons born in Namibia living abroad

	2000						2005/06		
	All destinations			OECD destinations			OECD destinations		
Population 15+	Men	Women	Total	Men	Women	Total	Men	Women	Total
Emigrant population (thousands)	22.1	22.5	44.7	1.5	1.7	3.1	2.8	3.8	6.7
Recent emigrants (thousands)	..	..	..	0.3	0.5	0.8	0.9	1.6	2.5
15-24 (%)	21.4	19.7	20.5	25.3	22.2	23.7	18.9	26.8	23.5
25-64 (%)	70.6	71.7	71.2	70.4	71.4	70.9	78.5	70.5	73.9
65+ (%)	8.0	8.6	8.3	4.3	6.4	5.4	2.6	2.7	2.7
Low-educated (%)	34.8	34.2	34.5	15.6	16.4	16.0	17.3	9.5	12.7
Highly educated (%)	17.8	13.7	15.7	52.2	43.7	47.7	51.1	60.5	56.6
Total emigration rates (%)	4.1	3.9	4.0	0.3	0.3	0.3	0.5	0.6	0.5
Emigration rates of the highly educated (%)	17.9	15.9	17.0	3.9	4.1	4.0	6.0	11.3	8.4

Main destinations in 2005/06

	Total		Recent emigrants	Women	Highly educated	15-24	Total in 2000
Population 15+	Thousands	%	%	%	%	%	Thousands
Netherlands	2.1	31.0	–	–	–	–	–
United States	1.5	21.9	17.0	54.7	40.2	28.7	0.8
United Kingdom	–	–	–	–	–	–	1.1
Australia	0.6	9.1	36.9	52.8	57.8	13.6	0.2
Canada	0.4	5.8	29.2	47.4	65.4	10.3	0.2
New Zealand	–	–	–	–	–	–	0.2
Italy	–	–	–	–	–	–	0.1
Switzerland	–	–	–	–	–	–	0.1
France	–	–	–	–	–	–	0.1

Labour market indicators of persons born in Namibia living in OECD countries

Population 15-64	2000			2005/06		
	Men	Women	Total	Men	Women	Total
Employment-population ratio (%)	78.9	61.1	69.2	88.4	79.7	83.3
Unemployment rate (%)	4.9	7.1	6.0	3.1	4.7	4.0
Participation rate (%)	82.9	65.8	73.6	91.3	83.7	86.8
Total employed (thousands)	**1.0**	**1.0**	**2.0**	**1.9**	**2.4**	**4.3**
Employment rates of the highly educated (%)	89.4	69.0	79.1	97.3	89.0	91.8
Unemployment rates of the highly educated (%)	2.5	7.7	4.9	0.8	2.8	2.1
Highly educated in low- and medium-skilled jobs (%)	18.9	23.9	21.1	6.4	5.8	6.0
Highly educated employed (thousands)	**0.6**	**0.5**	**1.1**	**1.0**	**1.8**	**2.9**
Legislators, senior officials and managers	17.2	6.7	12.2	6.5	4.5	5.4
Professionals	34.4	28.3	31.5	36.4	24.2	29.5
Life science and health professionals	6.0	5.8	5.9	5.4	1.4	3.1
Teaching professionals	2.8	10.7	6.6	0.5	3.4	2.2
Technicians and associate professionals	12.5	17.8	15.0	21.1	49.1	36.9
Clerks	6.2	22.5	14.0	3.8	8.4	6.4
Service, shop and market sales workers	5.4	18.4	11.6	2.8	9.9	6.8
Skilled agricultural and fishery workers	0.1	–	0.1	0.3	0.3	0.3
Craft and related trades workers	9.8	0.8	5.5	8.2	0.3	3.7
Plant and machine operators and assemblers	5.7	0.5	3.2	1.5	0.0	0.7
Elementary occupations	8.6	5.2	7.0	19.3	3.2	10.3

Distribution of employment by occupation (%), population 15+

Persons born in Namibia and their native-born children, population 15+

Living in:	Europe	United States	Australia
2008	Thousands	Thousands	Thousands
Native-born children	0.6	..	..
Foreign-born	3.9	..	..
Total	4.5	..	..

International students from Namibia in OECD countries

Five main destinations	2004	2005	2006	2007	2008	2009
United Kingdom	74	71	108	105	91	76
United States	95	69	92	62	66	59
Germany	..	..	..	..	26	27
Australia	24	21	25	17	22	18
France	7	6	8	9	9	10
Total	218	185	250	206	237	226

Legal migrant flows to the OECD
Thousands

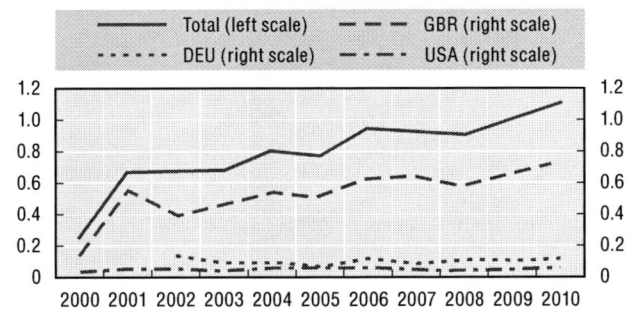

Remittance flows

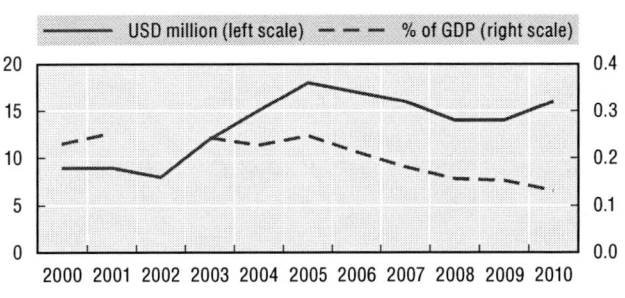

Ten main countries of destination for legal migrants in 2010 (numbers, % of total flows to the country): GBR (730, 0.2%), DEU (124, 0%), USA (60, 0%), JPN (54, 0%), AUS (42, 0%), CAN (25, 0%), NLD (13, 0%), AUT (9, 0%), SWE (9, 0%), NOR (7, 0%).

Desire to emigrate, 2008-10

	Women	15-24	Highly educated	Total	Regional total
Persons who would move permanently, if they had the opportunity to do so (%)	..	..	..	..	33
Of which: Persons who are planning to move permanently in the next 12 months (%)				..	12
Of which: Persons who have already done some preparations for this move (*e.g.* visa application) (%)					33

StatLink ⟶ http://dx.doi.org/10.1787/888932674664

NIGER – Country Notes

			Niger compared to:	World	Region
Total population 2010 (millions)		15.5			
Population growth 2010 (%)		3.5	Human Development Index (HDI)	186/187	45/46
GDP per capita 2010 (current USD)		358	GDP per capita	181/194	40/46
GDP growth 2010 (%)		8.8	Emigration rate	199/203	47/47
Poverty rate 2007 (USD PPP 2 a day, in %)		75.9	Emigration rate of the highly educated	109/157	33/39

Age structure of the population 0+ (2010): "0-14": 18%; "15-24": 49%; "25-64": 31%; "65+": 2%.
Level of education of the population 15+ (2010): "Low": 93%; "Medium": 6%; "High": 1%.

Emigrant population living in OECD countries

Immigrant population

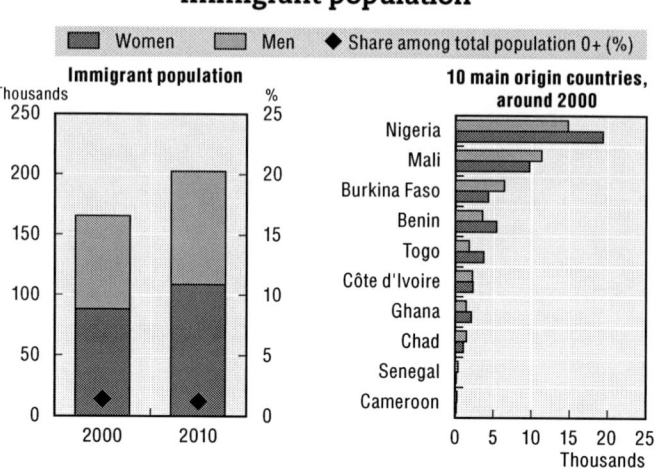

Emigrant population: persons born in Niger living abroad

	2000						2005/06		
	All destinations			OECD destinations			OECD destinations		
Population 15+	Men	Women	Total	Men	Women	Total	Men	Women	Total
Emigrant population (thousands)	38.2	24.2	62.4	2.8	2.1	4.8	5.4	4.1	9.5
Recent emigrants (thousands)	..	..	..	0.8	0.4	1.3	1.2	0.7	1.9
15-24 (%)	27.4	33.2	29.7	15.6	18.9	17.1	23.0	20.6	22.0
25-64 (%)	69.4	63.7	67.2	83.3	78.3	81.1	75.1	73.0	74.2
65+ (%)	3.2	3.1	3.2	1.1	2.7	1.8	1.9	6.5	3.9
Low-educated (%)	85.0	84.9	84.9	23.9	31.2	27.1	21.1	27.5	23.8
Highly educated (%)	5.8	5.3	5.6	39.7	36.0	38.1	40.3	41.5	40.8
Total emigration rates (%)	1.3	0.8	1.1	0.1	0.1	0.1	0.2	0.1	0.1
Emigration rates of the highly educated (%)	5.1	10.4	6.3	2.9	6.7	3.7	4.6	8.9	5.9

Main destinations in 2005/06

	Total		Recent emigrants	Women	Highly educated	15-24	Total in 2000
Population 15+	Thousands	%	%	%	%	%	Thousands
France	4.4	46.8	25.8	50.5	46.2	18.6	3.2
United States	3.2	33.2	18.2	32.9	38.2	22.1	0.9
Italy	–	–	–	–	–	–	0.1
Belgium	–	–	–	–	–	–	0.2
Canada	–	–	–	–	–	–	0.2
Switzerland	–	–	–	–	–	–	0.1

Labour market indicators of persons born in Niger living in OECD countries

Population 15-64	2000 Men	2000 Women	2000 Total	2005/06 Men	2005/06 Women	2005/06 Total
Employment-population ratio (%)	64.7	46.4	56.7	65.4	53.8	60.2
Unemployment rate (%)	14.8	24.5	18.5	14.1	17.9	15.7
Participation rate (%)	75.9	61.4	69.6	76.2	65.5	71.4
Total employed (thousands)	**1.7**	**1.0**	**2.7**	**2.4**	**1.6**	**4.0**
Employment rates of the highly educated (%)	71.3	58.0	65.8	78.1	72.3	75.6
Unemployment rates of the highly educated (%)	11.1	19.2	14.2	7.8	15.0	10.8
Highly educated in low- and medium-skilled jobs (%)	23.7	40.0	25.1	20.6	32.2	25.6
Highly educated employed (thousands)	**0.8**	**0.4**	**1.2**	**1.2**	**0.7**	**1.9**
Legislators, senior officials and managers	12.1	26.8	12.7	9.7	8.4	9.1
Professionals	20.6	9.8	20.2	24.7	16.5	21.1
Life science and health professionals	2.5	3.2	2.5	2.9	4.6	3.6
Teaching professionals	3.5	–	3.4	3.7	5.8	4.6
Technicians and associate professionals	19.7	9.8	19.3	27.5	16.3	22.6
Clerks	7.8	9.8	7.9	4.5	28.7	15.1
Service, shop and market sales workers	5.8	14.6	6.2	6.7	16.4	10.9
Skilled agricultural and fishery workers	1.6	2.4	1.6	1.4	0.8	1.1
Craft and related trades workers	14.2	9.8	14.1	6.3	0.3	3.7
Plant and machine operators and assemblers	10.1	2.4	9.8	9.9	2.4	6.6
Elementary occupations	8.0	14.6	8.2	9.4	10.3	9.8

Distribution of employment by occupation (%), population 15+

Persons born in Niger and their native-born children, population 15+

Living in:	Europe	United States	Australia
2008	Thousands	Thousands	Thousands
Native-born children	8.5	..	..
Foreign-born	5.5	..	..
Total	14.0	..	..

International students from Niger in OECD countries

Five main destinations	2004	2005	2006	2007	2008	2009
France	478	630	790	866	777	741
United States	169	244	372	264	289	245
Canada	75	..	81	78	94	101
Germany	..	..	..	..	19	26
United Kingdom	13	15	19	17	19	22
Total	746	902	1 289	1 414	1 259	1 177

Legal migrant flows to the OECD
Thousands

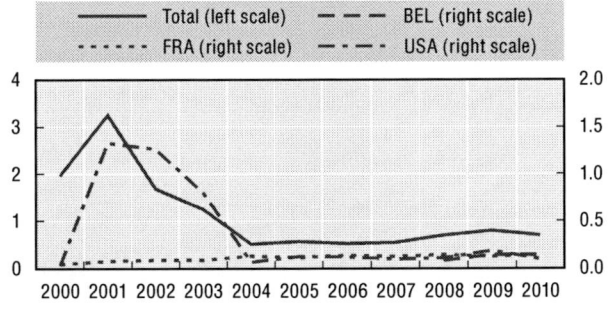

Remittance flows

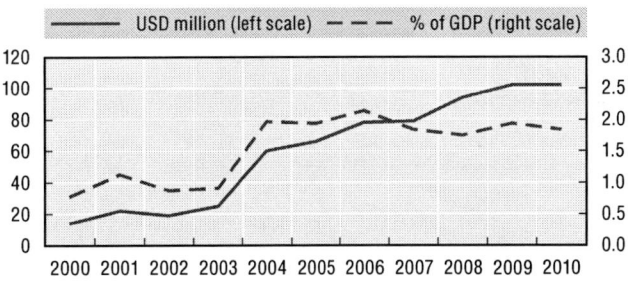

Ten main countries of destination for legal migrants in 2010 (numbers, % of total flows to the country): BEL (139, 0.1%), FRA (138, 0.1%), USA (96, 0%), ITA (80, 0%), DEU (77, 0%), CAN (55, 0%), ESP (32, 0%), JPN (22, 0%), NLD (15, 0%), CHE (11, 0%).

Desire to emigrate, 2008-10

	Women	15-24	Highly educated	Total	Regional total
Persons who would move permanently, if they had the opportunity to do so (%)	7	21	..	15	33
Of which: Persons who are planning to move permanently in the next 12 months (%)				36	12
Of which: Persons who have already done some preparations for this move (*e.g.* visa application) (%)					33

Three main countries of desired destination: Nigeria (28%), Côte d'Ivoire (11%), Libya (11%).

StatLink ⫘ http://dx.doi.org/10.1787/888932674683

Total population 2010 (millions)	158.4	**Nigeria compared to:** **World**	**Region**
Population growth 2010 (%)	2.5	Human Development Index (HDI) 155/187	19/46
GDP per capita 2010 (current USD)	1 222	GDP per capita 143/194	14/46
GDP growth 2010 (%)	7.9	Emigration rate 171/203	35/47
Poverty rate 2004 (USD PPP 2 a day, in %)	83.9	Emigration rate of the highly educated 134/157	38/39

Age structure of the population 0+ (2010): "0-14": 20%; "15-24": 43%; "25-64": 34%; "65+": 3%.

Emigrant population living in OECD countries

Immigrant population

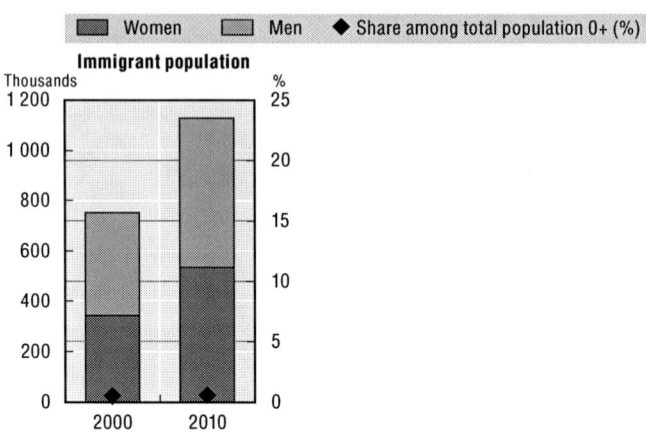

Emigrant population: persons born in Nigeria living abroad

	2000						2005/06		
	All destinations			OECD destinations			OECD destinations		
Population 15+	Men	Women	Total	Men	Women	Total	Men	Women	Total
Emigrant population (thousands)	235.9	202.6	438.4	142.9	118.2	261.1	205.0	175.4	380.5
Recent emigrants (thousands)	..	..	..	30.3	29.4	59.7	59.6	50.9	110.6
15-24 (%)	17.1	20.0	18.4	12.2	15.6	13.8	12.7	12.9	12.8
25-64 (%)	79.8	76.3	78.2	85.9	81.9	84.1	84.5	82.7	83.6
65+ (%)	3.1	3.7	3.4	1.9	2.5	2.2	2.8	4.4	3.5
Low-educated (%)	38.1	48.2	42.8	12.4	20.3	16.0	9.3	15.8	12.3
Highly educated (%)	39.5	28.7	34.5	61.1	47.1	54.8	65.0	55.2	60.5
Total emigration rates (%)	0.7	0.6	0.6	0.4	0.3	0.4	0.5	0.4	0.5
Emigration rates of the highly educated (%)	2.5	3.4	2.8	2.4	3.2	2.7	3.2	4.6	3.7

Main destinations in 2005/06

	Total		Recent emigrants	Women	Highly educated	15-24	Total in 2000
Population 15+	Thousands	%	%	%	%	%	Thousands
United States	179.2	47.1	26.0	43.3	63.4	13.6	126.6
United Kingdom	127.2	33.4	31.8	49.7	69.2	11.4	79.9
Italy	23.1	6.1	32.9	56.9	10.6	10.3	14.8
Canada	14.9	3.9	44.5	44.6	70.7	20.2	9.2
Ireland	12.8	3.4	73.2	55.6	55.9	13.1	7.4
Netherlands	4.0	1.1	–	–	–	–	–
Austria	3.9	1.0	47.3	–	–	–	2.7
France	3.9	1.0	38.4	50.4	37.0	13.5	2.5
Australia	2.2	0.6	36.5	39.7	67.6	13.4	1.4
Belgium	–	–	–	–	–	–	1.5

Labour market indicators of persons born in Nigeria living in OECD countries

	2000			2005/06		
Population 15-64	Men	Women	Total	Men	Women	Total
Employment-population ratio (%)	75.0	60.9	68.7	80.5	66.5	74.1
Unemployment rate (%)	9.8	12.8	11.1	9.3	11.5	10.2
Participation rate (%)	83.2	69.9	77.2	88.7	75.1	82.5
Total employed (thousands)	**101.7**	**67.8**	**169.5**	**156.2**	**108.8**	**265.0**
Employment rates of the highly educated (%)	82.5	71.9	78.4	93.5	83.7	89.3
Unemployment rates of the highly educated (%)	7.2	8.9	7.8	7.5	8.5	7.9
Highly educated in low- and medium-skilled jobs (%)	37.4	33.8	36.1	43.8	35.0	40.4
Highly educated employed (thousands)	**68.5**	**38.3**	**106.8**	**109.5**	**71.1**	**180.6**
Legislators, senior officials and managers	12.3	7.5	10.2	9.6	7.0	8.5
Professionals	21.1	13.3	17.7	19.8	17.5	18.8
Life science and health professionals	4.5	2.5	3.6	4.5	3.8	4.2
Teaching professionals	2.9	3.8	3.3	2.6	2.9	2.7
Technicians and associate professionals	12.4	17.8	14.7	9.2	17.7	12.8
Clerks	8.6	16.2	11.9	8.2	13.5	10.5
Service, shop and market sales workers	9.7	25.4	16.5	4.8	7.4	5.9
Skilled agricultural and fishery workers	0.5	0.3	0.4	7.1	13.5	9.9
Craft and related trades workers	8.1	2.4	5.6	8.1	8.5	8.2
Plant and machine operators and assemblers	8.2	2.3	5.7	6.8	1.8	4.6
Elementary occupations	19.2	14.9	17.3	26.0	11.1	19.6

Distribution of employment by occupation (%), population 15+

Persons born in Nigeria and their native-born children, population 15+

Living in:	Europe	United States	Australia
2008	Thousands	Thousands	Thousands
Native-born children	40.9	117.1	..
Foreign-born	179.5	194.4	4.0
Total	220.4	311.5	..

International students from Nigeria in OECD countries

Five main destinations	2004	2005	2006	2007	2008	2009
United Kingdom	5 942	8 147	9 604	11 136	11 783	14 380
United States	6 140	6 617	6 412	6 074	6 229	6 153
Canada	252	..	687	405	985	1 098
Germany	..	..	..	..	430	444
Sweden	2	1	5	12	329	380
Total	12 778	15 443	17 604	18 481	20 859	23 907

Legal migrant flows to the OECD
Thousands

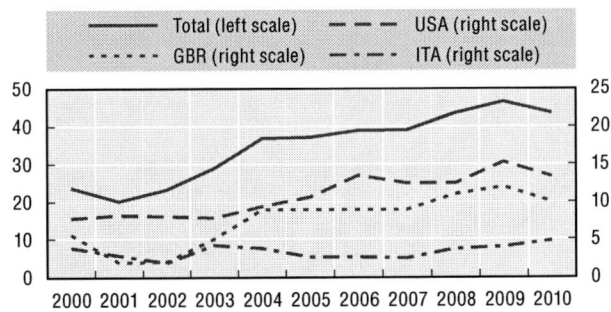

Remittance flows

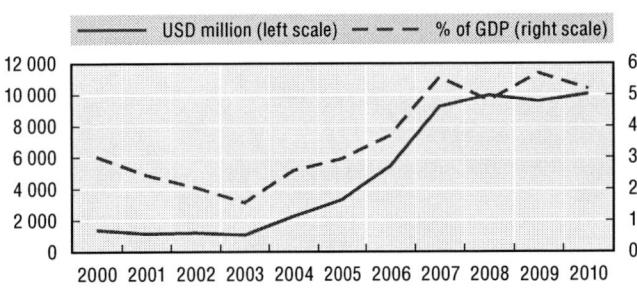

Ten main countries of destination for legal migrants in 2010 (numbers, % of total flows to the country): USA (13376, 1.3%), GBR (10000, 2.2%), ITA (4842, 1.1%), ESP (3993, 0.9%), CAN (3270, 1.2%), DEU (2351, 0.3%), AUT (807, 1.5%), POL (624, 1.5%), FRA (605, 0.4%), NLD (467, 0.5%).

Desire to emigrate, 2008-10

	Women	15-24	Highly educated	Total	Regional total
Persons who would move permanently, if they had the opportunity to do so (%)	42	53	43	44	33
Of which: Persons who are planning to move permanently in the next 12 months (%)				14	12
Of which: Persons who have already done some preparations for this move (*e.g.* visa application) (%)					33

Three main countries of desired destination: United States (40%), United Kingdom (20%), Saudi Arabia (8%).

StatLink *http://dx.doi.org/10.1787/888932674702*

Total population 2010 (millions)	10.6	Rwanda compared to:	World	Region
Population growth 2010 (%)	3.0	Human Development Index (HDI)	166/187	27/46
GDP per capita 2010 (current USD)	530	GDP per capita	168/194	29/46
GDP growth 2010 (%)	7.5	Emigration rate	172/203	36/47
Poverty rate 2005 (USD PPP 2 a day, in %)	89.6	Emigration rate of the highly educated	49/157	17/39

Age structure of the population 0+ (2010): "0-14": 21%; "15-24": 43%; "25-64": 34%; "65+": 3%.
Level of education of the population 15+ (2010): "Low": 91%; "Medium": 7%; "High": 2%.

Emigrant population living in OECD countries

Immigrant population

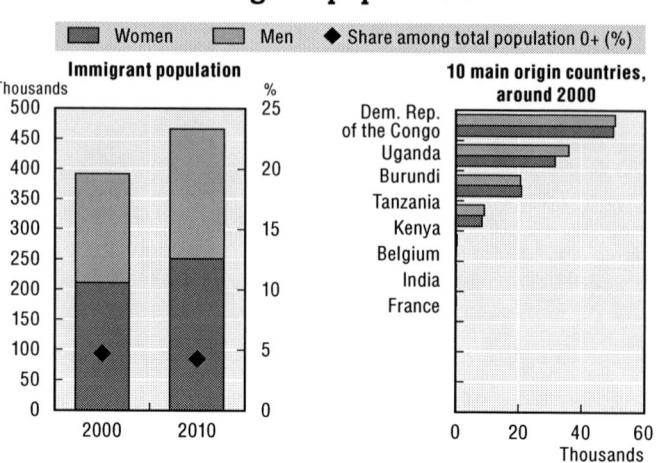

Emigrant population: persons born in Rwanda living abroad

	2000						2005/06		
	All destinations			OECD destinations			OECD destinations		
Population 15+	Men	Women	Total	Men	Women	Total	Men	Women	Total
Emigrant population (thousands)	44.2	42.9	87.1	7.0	7.9	14.9	11.5	13.6	25.1
Recent emigrants (thousands)	..	..	..	2.4	3.0	5.4	2.5	3.0	5.5
15-24 (%)	17.6	21.7	19.6	25.3	25.2	25.2	33.8	24.9	29.0
25-64 (%)	63.7	63.1	63.4	73.8	71.9	72.8	64.6	73.1	69.2
65+ (%)	18.7	15.2	16.9	0.9	2.9	2.0	1.6	2.0	1.8
Low-educated (%)	86.0	85.6	85.8	24.5	29.4	27.1	27.6	24.4	25.9
Highly educated (%)	7.5	6.0	6.7	45.0	31.9	38.0	42.5	35.2	38.6
Total emigration rates (%)	2.2	1.8	2.0	0.3	0.3	0.3	0.5	0.5	0.5
Emigration rates of the highly educated (%)	13.5	29.3	17.5	12.2	27.9	16.2	11.1	23.0	14.9

Main destinations in 2005/06

	Total		Recent emigrants	Women	Highly educated	15-24	Total in 2000
Population 15+	Thousands	%	%	%	%	%	Thousands
Belgium	8.2	32.5	–	–	–	–	5.5
France	4.2	16.8	35.3	54.7	33.3	35.6	1.7
United States	4.1	16.4	14.4	50.3	36.9	23.2	1.7
Canada	3.3	13.0	38.1	54.2	50.8	23.3	2.1
United Kingdom	–	–	–	–	–	–	1.9
Netherlands	1.7	6.7	–	–	–	–	–
Switzerland	–	–	–	–	–	–	0.6
Denmark	–	–	–	–	–	–	0.1
Sweden	–	–	–	–	–	–	0.2

Labour market indicators of persons born in Rwanda living in OECD countries

Population 15-64	2000			2005/06		
	Men	Women	Total	Men	Women	Total
Employment-population ratio (%)	50.9	39.5	44.8	48.8	44.9	46.7
Unemployment rate (%)	23.9	28.6	26.2	29.6	24.8	27.1
Participation rate (%)	66.9	55.3	60.7	69.3	59.7	64.1
Total employed (thousands)	**3.2**	**2.8**	**6.0**	**4.7**	**5.2**	**9.8**
Employment rates of the highly educated (%)	64.3	60.2	62.5	91.4	75.9	83.5
Unemployment rates of the highly educated (%)	22.1	20.7	21.5	31.5	18.7	25.6
Highly educated in low- and medium-skilled jobs (%)	29.0	36.1	31.7	36.9	26.1	31.4
Highly educated employed (thousands)	**1.8**	**1.4**	**3.2**	**2.5**	**2.6**	**5.2**
Legislators, senior officials and managers	6.3	6.2	6.3	6.4	12.5	9.6
Professionals	25.6	12.4	20.3	24.6	21.6	23.1
Life science and health professionals	2.3	1.2	1.9	3.3	11.2	7.6
Teaching professionals	4.9	3.9	4.6	5.6	1.2	3.2
Technicians and associate professionals	15.5	18.8	16.8	11.2	13.9	12.6
Clerks	8.4	18.6	12.5	11.6	15.3	13.5
Service, shop and market sales workers	9.5	29.7	17.6	10.2	24.6	17.8
Skilled agricultural and fishery workers	1.1	0.2	0.8	1.0	0.5	0.8
Craft and related trades workers	8.8	0.7	5.6	5.0	1.5	3.1
Plant and machine operators and assemblers	9.2	1.5	6.1	12.9	1.0	6.6
Elementary occupations	15.6	11.8	14.1	17.0	9.1	12.9

Distribution of employment by occupation (%), population 15+

Persons born in Rwanda and their native-born children, population 15+

Living in:	Europe	United States	Australia
2008	Thousands	Thousands	Thousands
Native-born children	3.7	..	..
Foreign-born	15.0	..	..
Total	18.7	..	..

International students from Rwanda in OECD countries

Five main destinations	2004	2005	2006	2007	2008	2009
France	482	504	588	599	561	556
United States	275	199	223	215	270	360
United Kingdom	82	75	82	88	91	112
Canada	207	..	69	210	132	90
Belgium	1	9	11	8	50	76
Total	1 101	854	1 037	1 173	1 290	1 411

Legal migrant flows to the OECD
Thousands

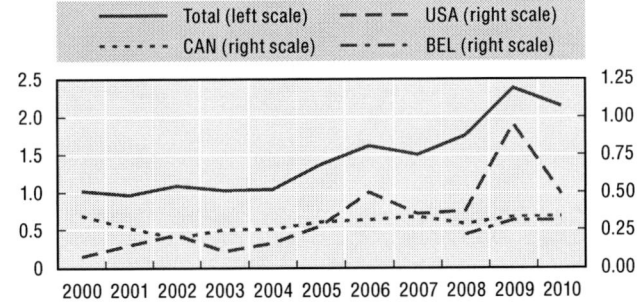

Remittance flows

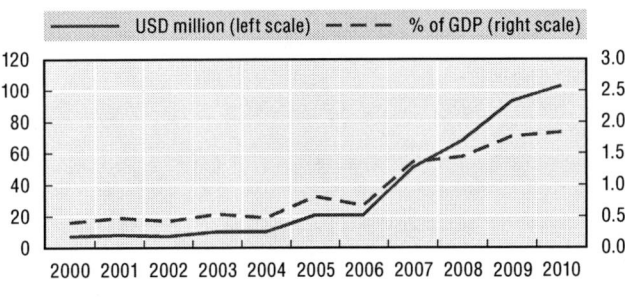

Ten main countries of destination for legal migrants in 2010 (numbers, % of total flows to the country): USA (489, 0%), CAN (340, 0.1%), BEL (313, 0.3%), FRA (254, 0.2%), AUS (145, 0.1%), DEU (86, 0%), NLD (84, 0%), GBR (76, 0%), JPN (75, 0%), SWE (46, 0.1%).

Desire to emigrate, 2008-10

	Women	15-24	Highly educated	Total	Regional total
Persons who would move permanently, if they had the opportunity to do so (%)	11	19	..	13	33
Of which: Persons who are planning to move permanently in the next 12 months (%)				..	12
Of which: Persons who have already done some preparations for this move (*e.g.* visa application) (%)					33

StatLink http://dx.doi.org/10.1787/888932674721

Total population 2010 (millions)	12.4	Senegal compared to:	World	Region
Population growth 2010 (%)	2.7	Human Development Index (HDI)	156/187	18/46
GDP per capita 2010 (current USD)	1 042	GDP per capita	151/194	19/46
GDP growth 2010 (%)	4.2	Emigration rate	112/203	12/47
Poverty rate 2005 (USD PPP 2 a day, in %)	60.4	Emigration rate of the highly educated	41/157	14/39

Age structure of the population 0+ (2010): "0-14": 21%; "15-24": 44%; "25-64": 33%; "65+": 2%.
Level of education of the population 15+ (2010): "Low": 81%; "Medium": 15%; "High": 4%.

Emigrant population living in OECD countries

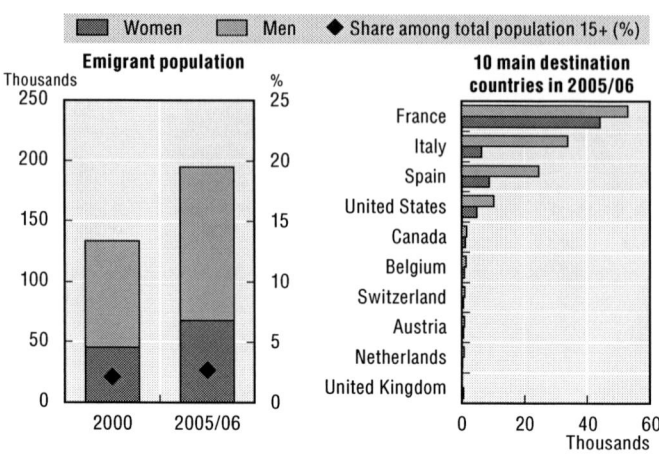

Immigrant population

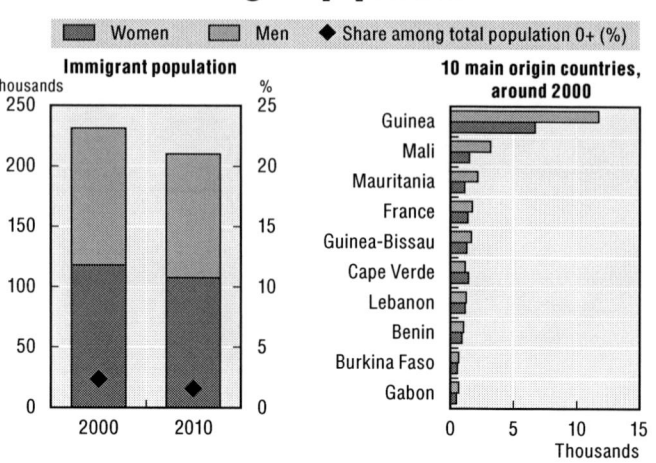

Emigrant population: persons born in Senegal living abroad

	2000						2005/06		
	All destinations			OECD destinations			OECD destinations		
Population 15+	Men	Women	Total	Men	Women	Total	Men	Women	Total
Emigrant population (thousands)	130.0	79.4	209.4	88.0	45.3	133.2	127.4	67.5	194.9
Recent emigrants (thousands)	..	..	..	17.2	8.3	25.5	32.9	17.7	50.6
15-24 (%)	14.6	23.3	17.9	9.5	15.0	11.4	11.2	16.0	12.9
25-64 (%)	82.2	72.8	78.7	87.8	81.4	85.6	85.3	80.1	83.5
65+ (%)	3.2	3.9	3.4	2.7	3.6	3.0	3.6	3.9	3.7
Low-educated (%)	64.1	63.8	64.0	60.5	50.3	57.0	57.3	52.7	55.7
Highly educated (%)	14.6	14.0	14.3	18.0	21.5	19.2	18.5	22.9	20.0
Total emigration rates (%)	4.3	2.6	3.5	2.9	1.5	2.2	3.7	1.9	2.8
Emigration rates of the highly educated (%)	16.4	22.3	18.4	14.9	21.0	16.9	14.0	24.0	16.8

Main destinations in 2005/06

	Total		Recent emigrants	Women	Highly educated	15-24	Total in 2000
Population 15+	Thousands	%	%	%	%	%	Thousands
France	97.3	49.9	17.5	45.4	27.0	13.0	78.0
Italy	40.1	20.6	30.8	15.7	2.3	7.3	28.5
Spain	33.3	17.1	59.1	25.9	8.7	18.3	10.9
United States	14.8	7.6	23.5	31.8	37.9	13.6	10.0
Canada	2.4	1.3	47.1	41.2	72.1	19.1	1.7
Belgium	–	–	–	–	–	–	1.3
Switzerland	1.2	0.6	–	–	–	–	0.9
Austria	–	–	–	–	–	–	–
Netherlands	–	–	–	–	–	–	–
United Kingdom	–	–	–	–	–	–	0.7

Labour market indicators of persons born in Senegal living in OECD countries

Population 15-64	2000			2005/06		
	Men	Women	Total	Men	Women	Total
Employment-population ratio (%)	71.7	46.1	63.0	73.8	49.3	65.4
Unemployment rate (%)	15.8	26.0	18.5	12.6	25.1	16.2
Participation rate (%)	85.1	62.2	77.4	84.5	65.8	78.1
Total employed (thousands)	**60.8**	**19.9**	**80.8**	**90.5**	**31.8**	**122.2**
Employment rates of the highly educated (%)	74.2	62.6	69.7	84.4	73.5	80.1
Unemployment rates of the highly educated (%)	11.6	13.7	12.3	9.7	12.1	10.6
Highly educated in low- and medium-skilled jobs (%)	30.5	40.2	31.5	43.8	43.5	43.7
Highly educated employed (thousands)	**11.4**	**5.9**	**17.3**	**17.4**	**9.7**	**27.1**
Legislators, senior officials and managers	7.8	5.6	7.7	4.7	5.1	4.8
Professionals	7.3	7.5	7.3	6.4	9.1	7.1
Life science and health professionals	1.0	0.3	1.0	0.9	1.2	1.0
Teaching professionals	1.3	1.4	1.3	1.2	3.3	1.8
Technicians and associate professionals	9.2	10.4	9.3	6.5	13.6	8.4
Clerks	3.8	9.1	4.0	5.0	13.1	7.2
Service, shop and market sales workers	8.3	17.2	8.7	6.6	23.1	11.1
Skilled agricultural and fishery workers	1.7	1.7	1.7	2.8	0.5	2.2
Craft and related trades workers	20.7	6.6	20.0	21.3	3.2	16.4
Plant and machine operators and assemblers	14.9	9.0	14.6	16.8	1.6	12.7
Elementary occupations	26.3	32.9	26.7	30.0	30.7	30.2

Distribution of employment by occupation (%), population 15+

Persons born in Senegal and their native-born children, population 15+

Living in:	Europe	United States	Australia
2008	Thousands	Thousands	Thousands
Native-born children	63.3	0.9	..
Foreign-born	158.0	18.5	..
Total	221.3	19.4	..

International students from Senegal in OECD countries

Five main destinations	2004	2005	2006	2007	2008	2009
France	8 329	8 766	9 399	9 302	9 298	8 948
United States	805	757	690	696	659	631
Canada	319	..	339	420	419	615
Germany	..	..	..	..	188	173
Switzerland	..	..	..	..	158	137
Total	9 584	9 661	10 588	10 615	10 957	10 835

Legal migrant flows to the OECD
Thousands

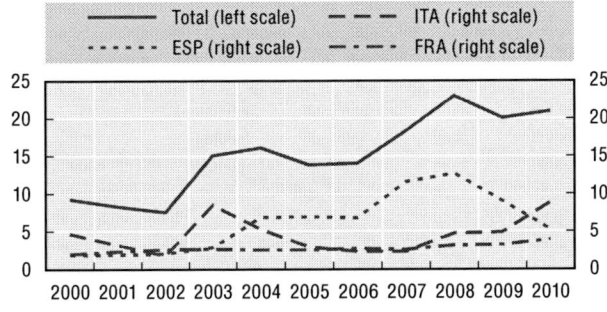

Remittance flows

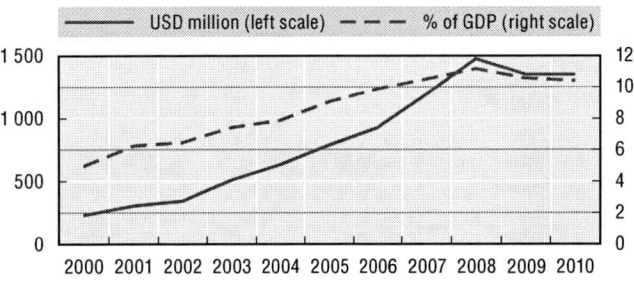

Ten main countries of destination for legal migrants in 2010 (numbers, % of total flows to the country): ITA (8851, 2.1%), ESP (5299, 1.2%), FRA (3842, 2.8%), USA (1285, 0.1%), CAN (540, 0.2%), BEL (300, 0.3%), DEU (265, 0.1%), JPN (145, 0.1%), CHE (121, 0.1%), AUT (52, 0.1%).

Desire to emigrate, 2008-10

	Women	15-24	Highly educated	Total	Regional total
Persons who would move permanently, if they had the opportunity to do so (%)	31	57	..	40	33
Of which: Persons who are planning to move permanently in the next 12 months (%)				46	12
Of which: Persons who have already done some preparations for this move (*e.g.* visa application) (%)					33

Three main countries of desired destination: Spain (25%), Italy (18%), France (18%).

StatLink ᴹˢᴾ *http://dx.doi.org/10.1787/888932674740*

Total population 2010 (millions)	5.9	**Sierra Leone compared to:**	**World**	**Region**
Population growth 2010 (%)	2.2	Human Development Index (HDI)	180/187	39/46
GDP per capita 2010 (current USD)	325	GDP per capita	183/194	42/46
GDP growth 2010 (%)	4.9	Emigration rate	134/203	18/47
Poverty rate 2003 (USD PPP 2 a day, in %)	76.1	Emigration rate of the highly educated	16/157	5/39

Age structure of the population 0+ (2010): "0-14": 19%; "15-24": 43%; "25-64": 36%; "65+": 2%.
Level of education of the population 15+ (2010): "Low": 77%; "Medium": 21%; "High": 2%.

Emigrant population living in OECD countries

Immigrant population

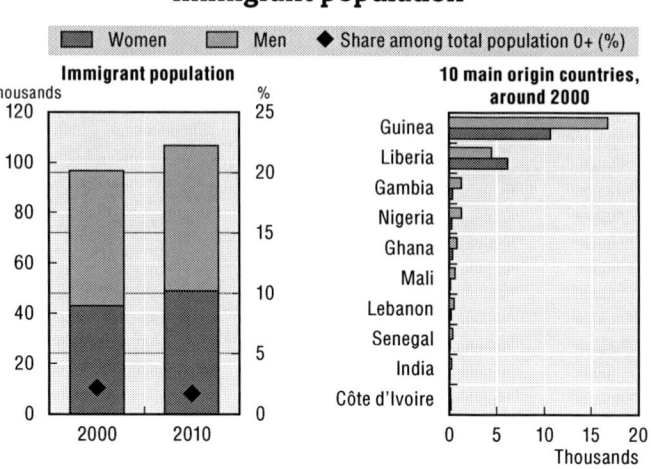

Emigrant population: persons born in Sierra Leone living abroad

	2000						2005/06		
	All destinations			OECD destinations			OECD destinations		
Population 15+	Men	Women	Total	Men	Women	Total	Men	Women	Total
Emigrant population (thousands)	55.4	67.0	122.3	20.1	20.1	40.2	28.4	26.9	55.3
Recent emigrants (thousands)	..	..	..	4.3	4.0	8.3	8.8	7.4	16.1
15-24 (%)	28.0	29.8	29.0	17.6	16.1	16.8	24.7	19.9	22.3
25-64 (%)	66.5	64.3	65.3	78.7	77.5	78.1	71.1	72.8	71.9
65+ (%)	5.5	5.9	5.7	3.7	6.4	5.1	4.2	7.3	5.7
Low-educated (%)	64.6	74.2	69.9	22.2	27.5	24.8	24.1	31.3	27.6
Highly educated (%)	16.4	10.4	13.2	39.7	31.6	35.6	35.2	29.3	32.4
Total emigration rates (%)	4.2	4.8	4.5	1.6	1.5	1.5	1.8	1.6	1.7
Emigration rates of the highly educated (%)	31.4	57.8	39.1	28.4	55.3	36.2	26.1	46.5	32.3

Main destinations in 2005/06

	Total		Recent emigrants	Women	Highly educated	15-24	Total in 2000
Population 15+	Thousands	%	%	%	%	%	Thousands
United States	30.6	55.4	21.1	51.8	39.4	15.3	19.2
United Kingdom	13.1	23.6	–	53.4	–	–	15.6
Netherlands	4.3	7.8	52.7	–	–	60.6	–
Canada	2.5	4.5	67.2	51.2	40.4	23.5	0.9
Australia	1.4	2.6	83.5	48.7	21.0	35.6	0.2
France	0.9	1.6	45.4	42.7	20.6	27.4	0.6
Austria	–	–	–	–	–	–	–
Belgium	–	–	–	–	–	–	0.4
Sweden	0.4	0.8	67.4	49.4	20.3	37.1	0.3
Ireland	0.3	0.6	45.3	36.5	33.6	22.5	0.3

Labour market indicators of persons born in Sierra Leone living in OECD countries

Population 15-64	2000 Men	2000 Women	2000 Total	2005/06 Men	2005/06 Women	2005/06 Total
Employment-population ratio (%)	71.3	64.8	68.1	75.2	65.7	70.6
Unemployment rate (%)	11.3	9.5	10.5	9.8	9.3	9.6
Participation rate (%)	80.4	71.6	76.1	83.4	72.5	78.1
Total employed (thousands)	**13.1**	**11.6**	**24.7**	**19.8**	**16.1**	**35.9**
Employment rates of the highly educated (%)	82.0	78.7	80.6	91.2	87.4	89.5
Unemployment rates of the highly educated (%)	7.8	4.8	6.5	3.8	7.4	5.3
Highly educated in low- and medium-skilled jobs (%)	40.6	35.2	38.3	46.7	30.7	39.8
Highly educated employed (thousands)	**6.0**	**4.5**	**10.6**	**8.2**	**6.0**	**14.3**
Legislators, senior officials and managers	11.8	6.1	9.1	3.2	13.2	6.9
Professionals	14.5	10.3	12.5	3.4	4.4	3.8
Life science and health professionals	2.2	0.8	1.5	0.2	0.8	0.4
Teaching professionals	3.9	4.1	4.0	0.2	0.6	0.4
Technicians and associate professionals	11.7	17.6	14.5	13.7	23.0	17.1
Clerks	10.1	19.8	14.8	9.1	9.5	9.2
Service, shop and market sales workers	14.8	30.8	22.5	5.4	17.1	9.7
Skilled agricultural and fishery workers	0.7	0.1	0.4	2.5	3.2	2.8
Craft and related trades workers	7.0	0.5	3.8	13.5	14.3	13.8
Plant and machine operators and assemblers	6.5	1.7	4.2	7.6	6.1	7.1
Elementary occupations	23.0	13.0	18.2	37.1	9.2	26.8

Distribution of employment by occupation (%), population 15+

Persons born in Sierra Leone and their native-born children, population 15+

Living in:	Europe	United States	Australia
2008	Thousands	Thousands	Thousands
Native-born children	4.5	0.2	..
Foreign-born	18.3	4.3	..
Total	22.8	4.5	..

International students from Sierra Leone in OECD countries

Five main destinations	2004	2005	2006	2007	2008	2009
United Kingdom	229	282	253	265	243	221
United States	306	322	308	306	230	170
Germany	..	..	..	..	31	33
Canada	17	..	24	15	16	19
France	19	20	24	18	16	14
Total	598	687	673	680	605	500

Legal migrant flows to the OECD
Thousands

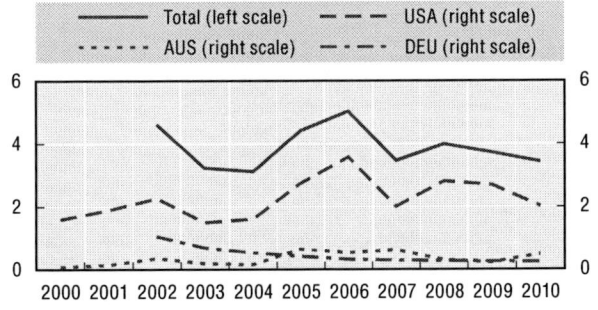

Remittance flows

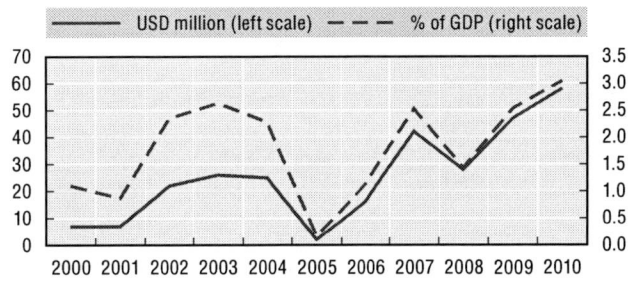

Ten main countries of destination for legal migrants in 2010 (numbers, % of total flows to the country): USA (2011, 0.2%), AUS (472, 0.2%), DEU (219, 0%), CAN (150, 0.1%), ITA (106, 0%), FRA (95, 0.1%), NLD (67, 0%), ESP (67, 0%), BEL (52, 0.1%), SWE (44, 0.1%).

Desire to emigrate, 2008-10

	Women	15-24	Highly educated	Total	Regional total
Persons who would move permanently, if they had the opportunity to do so (%)	52	67	62	52	33
Of which: Persons who are planning to move permanently in the next 12 months (%)				18	12
Of which: Persons who have already done some preparations for this move (*e.g.* visa application) (%)					33

Three main countries of desired destination: United States (56%), United Kingdom (17%), Canada (5%).

StatLink 🔗 http://dx.doi.org/10.1787/888932674759

			South Africa compared to:	World	Region
Total population 2010 (millions)		50.0			
Population growth 2010 (%)		1.4	Human Development Index (HDI)	123/187	6/46
GDP per capita 2010 (current USD)		7 275	GDP per capita	77/194	6/46
GDP growth 2010 (%)		2.8	Emigration rate	138/203	19/47
Poverty rate 2006 (USD PPP 2 a day, in %)		35.7	Emigration rate of the highly educated	77/157	27/39

Age structure of the population 0+ (2010): "0-14": 20%; "15-24": 30%; "25-64": 45%; "65+": 5%.
Level of education of the population 15+ (2010): "Low": 28%; "Medium": 65%; "High": 7%.

Emigrant population living in OECD countries

Immigrant population

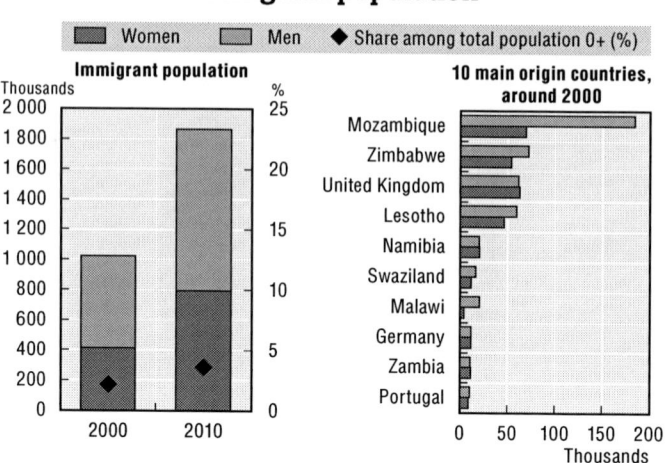

Emigrant population: persons born in South Africa living abroad

	2000						2005/06		
	All destinations			OECD destinations			OECD destinations		
Population 15+	Men	Women	Total	Men	Women	Total	Men	Women	Total
Emigrant population (thousands)	175.9	188.3	364.2	174.1	186.9	360.9	230.8	243.1	473.9
Recent emigrants (thousands)	..	..	..	46.9	47.2	94.0	61.3	61.8	123.1
15-24 (%)	19.5	18.4	19.0	19.6	18.5	19.0	16.2	16.2	16.2
25-64 (%)	73.4	71.9	72.6	73.3	71.9	72.6	75.2	74.0	74.5
65+ (%)	7.1	9.6	8.4	7.1	9.6	8.4	8.6	9.8	9.2
Low-educated (%)	13.9	17.0	15.5	13.7	16.8	15.3	10.3	12.3	11.3
Highly educated (%)	50.3	45.1	47.6	50.5	45.3	47.8	55.6	52.5	54.1
Total emigration rates (%)	1.2	1.2	1.2	1.2	1.2	1.2	1.4	1.4	1.4
Emigration rates of the highly educated (%)	7.2	6.7	7.0	7.1	6.7	6.9	10.6	9.3	9.9

Main destinations in 2005/06

	Total		Recent emigrants	Women	Highly educated	15-24	Total in 2000
Population 15+	Thousands	%	%	%	%	%	Thousands
United Kingdom	161.3	34.0	27.7	53.4	59.4	15.4	124.7
Australia	90.8	19.2	27.7	51.3	51.2	15.8	68.9
United States	82.3	17.4	20.6	49.3	59.1	13.9	60.1
Canada	37.7	8.0	14.5	51.1	65.5	14.4	33.6
New Zealand	34.3	7.2	48.6	51.2	41.9	23.5	19.9
Netherlands	13.8	2.9	24.9	46.3	41.9	14.8	5.4
Israel	9.2	1.9	20.6	51.4	64.1	9.9	9.1
Portugal	8.7	1.8	–	–	–	–	9.1
Ireland	6.4	1.3	64.3	50.3	53.3	19.0	5.0
Switzerland	6.3	1.3	51.9	46.2	44.8	22.8	4.1

Labour market indicators of persons born in South Africa living in OECD countries

Population 15-64	2000			2005/06		
	Men	Women	Total	Men	Women	Total
Employment-population ratio (%)	83.4	67.4	75.3	88.3	72.8	80.4
Unemployment rate (%)	4.9	6.1	5.4	2.9	5.2	3.9
Participation rate (%)	87.7	71.8	79.6	90.9	76.8	83.7
Total employed (thousands)	**128.8**	**107.2**	**236.0**	**181.8**	**154.9**	**336.7**
Employment rates of the highly educated (%)	92.0	76.4	84.4	97.3	83.7	90.5
Unemployment rates of the highly educated (%)	3.1	4.5	3.7	2.0	3.1	2.5
Highly educated in low- and medium-skilled jobs (%)	16.1	23.2	19.3	15.8	23.9	19.5
Highly educated employed (thousands)	**71.9**	**57.4**	**129.3**	**109.7**	**93.2**	**202.9**
Legislators, senior officials and managers	19.7	10.4	15.3	19.3	10.7	15.3
Professionals	28.8	25.6	27.3	28.2	25.7	27.0
Life science and health professionals	5.2	5.4	5.3	4.3	4.1	4.2
Teaching professionals	3.8	9.2	6.4	3.8	9.7	6.5
Technicians and associate professionals	14.9	19.1	16.9	18.5	22.2	20.2
Clerks	6.0	23.5	14.3	4.4	19.4	11.4
Service, shop and market sales workers	8.4	15.2	11.6	7.1	8.5	7.7
Skilled agricultural and fishery workers	0.8	0.3	0.6	1.0	5.6	3.1
Craft and related trades workers	11.0	1.1	6.3	10.2	3.7	7.2
Plant and machine operators and assemblers	4.0	1.0	2.6	4.2	1.0	2.7
Elementary occupations	6.3	3.8	5.1	6.6	3.0	5.0

Distribution of employment by occupation (%), population 15+

Persons born in South Africa and their native-born children, population 15+

Living in:	Europe	United States	Australia
2008	Thousands	Thousands	Thousands
Native-born children	64.4	12.5	12.9
Foreign-born	164.8	79.8	69.4
Total	229.1	92.3	82.3

International students from South Africa in OECD countries

Five main destinations	2004	2005	2006	2007	2008	2009
United States	1 971	1 775	1 770	1 702	1 622	1 675
United Kingdom	1 408	1 531	1 559	1 699	1 539	1 582
Australia	643	633	644	707	763	875
Ireland	..	..	..	..	42	161
Germany	..	..	..	..	157	138
Total	4 427	4 268	4 454	4 626	4 710	5 064

Legal migrant flows to the OECD
Thousands

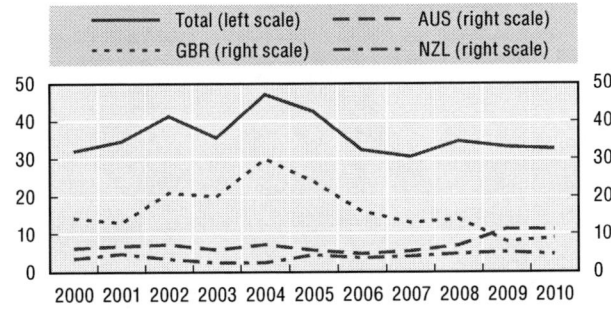

Remittance flows

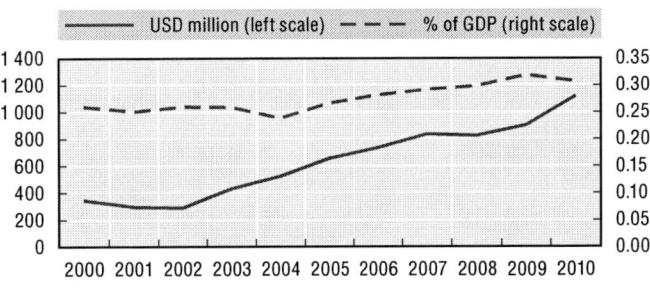

Ten main countries of destination for legal migrants in 2010 (numbers, % of total flows to the country): AUS (11105, 5.4%), GBR (8802, 1.9%), NZL (4591, 10.4%), USA (2758, 0.3%), CAN (1350, 0.5%), KOR (765, 0.3%), DEU (698, 0.6%), NLD (586, 0.6%), JPN (371, 0.1%), CHE (253, 0.2%).

Desire to emigrate, 2008-10

	Women	15-24	Highly educated	Total	Regional total
Persons who would move permanently, if they had the opportunity to do so (%)	16	26	20	17	33
Of which: Persons who are planning to move permanently in the next 12 months (%)				12	12
Of which: Persons who have already done some preparations for this move (*e.g.* visa application) (%)					33

Three main countries of desired destination: United States (41%), United Kingdom (22%), Australia (6%).

StatLink ⬛🔗 http://dx.doi.org/10.1787/888932674778

Total population 2010 (millions)	6.0
Population growth 2010 (%)	2.1
GDP per capita 2010 (current USD)	523
GDP growth 2010 (%)	3.4
Poverty rate 2006 (USD PPP 2 a day, in %)	69.3

Togo compared to:	World	Region
Human Development Index (HDI)	162/187	23/46
GDP per capita	170/194	31/46
Emigration rate	149/203	25/47
Emigration rate of the highly educated	51/157	18/39

Age structure of the population 0+ (2010): "0-14": 21%; "15-24": 40%; "25-64": 36%; "65+": 3%.
Level of education of the population 15+ (2010): "Low": 65%; "Medium": 33%; "High": 2%.

Emigrant population living in OECD countries

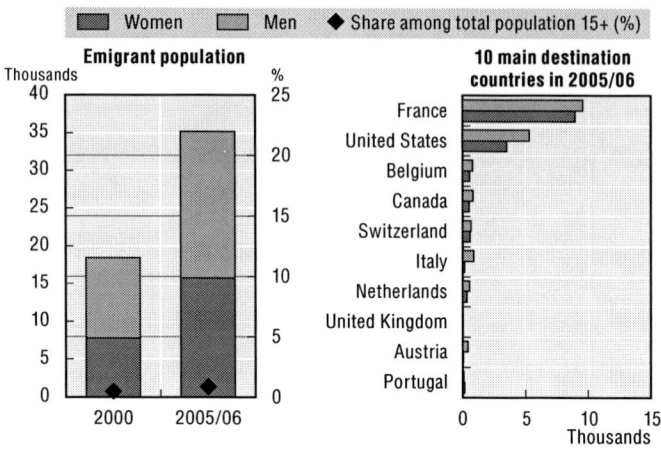

Immigrant population

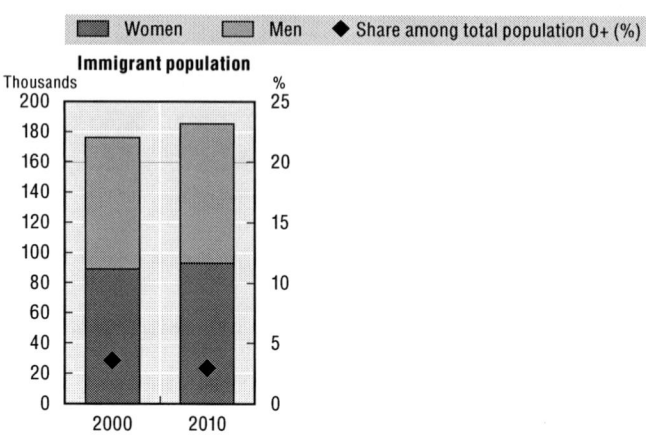

Emigrant population: persons born in Togo living abroad

	2000						2005/06		
	All destinations			OECD destinations			OECD destinations		
Population 15+	Men	Women	Total	Men	Women	Total	Men	Women	Total
Emigrant population (thousands)	90.9	105.4	196.3	10.7	7.8	18.4	19.4	15.8	35.2
Recent emigrants (thousands)	..	..	..	2.4	1.8	4.3	4.4	3.5	7.8
15-24 (%)	37.8	31.8	34.6	12.3	17.8	14.6	16.2	19.7	17.7
25-64 (%)	57.6	65.4	61.8	86.4	79.8	83.6	81.9	77.7	80.0
65+ (%)	4.5	2.7	3.6	1.3	2.4	1.8	1.9	2.6	2.2
Low-educated (%)	73.0	87.9	81.0	20.3	39.9	28.6	22.5	40.8	30.7
Highly educated (%)	7.2	2.4	4.6	45.4	24.6	36.6	41.4	24.4	33.8
Total emigration rates (%)	5.8	6.4	6.1	0.7	0.5	0.6	1.1	0.9	1.0
Emigration rates of the highly educated (%)	11.9	15.7	12.7	9.5	13.2	10.3	12.6	19.6	14.3

Main destinations in 2005/06

	Total		Recent emigrants	Women	Highly educated	15-24	Total in 2000
Population 15+	Thousands	%	%	%	%	%	Thousands
France	18.5	52.7	22.3	48.3	37.3	13.5	12.0
United States	8.8	25.0	17.7	39.8	33.7	25.3	2.6
Belgium	–	–	–	–	–	–	0.9
Canada	1.3	3.7	58.2	37.8	68.3	18.5	0.8
Switzerland	1.2	3.5	–	–	–	–	0.4
Italy	1.0	2.9	–	–	–	–	0.7
Netherlands	–	–	–	–	–	–	–
United Kingdom	–	–	–	–	–	–	0.5

Labour market indicators of persons born in Togo living in OECD countries

Population 15-64	2000			2005/06		
	Men	Women	Total	Men	Women	Total
Employment-population ratio (%)	64.9	48.4	58.0	69.4	56.5	63.6
Unemployment rate (%)	18.2	26.3	21.2	15.3	23.7	18.9
Participation rate (%)	79.3	65.7	73.6	81.9	74.1	78.4
Total employed (thousands)	**6.6**	**3.5**	**10.1**	**10.2**	**6.9**	**17.1**
Employment rates of the highly educated (%)	72.5	57.6	68.3	87.9	82.0	85.8
Unemployment rates of the highly educated (%)	14.7	20.9	16.2	11.9	15.6	13.2
Highly educated in low- and medium-skilled jobs (%)	37.3	35.3	37.1	32.2	40.6	35.1
Highly educated employed (thousands)	**3.3**	**1.0**	**4.4**	**4.6**	**2.2**	**6.9**
Legislators, senior officials and managers	6.5	4.2	6.3	8.0	5.5	6.9
Professionals	18.3	12.0	17.8	17.7	7.2	13.2
Life science and health professionals	3.2	–	3.0	2.7	1.0	2.0
Teaching professionals	5.6	0.9	5.3	3.4	1.6	2.6
Technicians and associate professionals	20.1	14.0	19.6	15.4	14.0	14.8
Clerks	9.7	13.8	10.0	6.1	15.1	9.9
Service, shop and market sales workers	8.6	25.8	10.0	9.0	23.9	15.3
Skilled agricultural and fishery workers	0.7	0.2	0.7	0.6	7.4	3.5
Craft and related trades workers	11.9	3.3	11.2	21.0	1.8	12.8
Plant and machine operators and assemblers	10.5	3.6	10.0	11.4	1.9	7.3
Elementary occupations	13.6	22.9	14.4	10.9	23.4	16.2

Distribution of employment by occupation (%), population 15+

Persons born in Togo and their native-born children, population 15+

Living in:	Europe	United States	Australia
2008	Thousands	Thousands	Thousands
Native-born children	7.8	..	..
Foreign-born	22.2	..	..
Total	30.0	..	..

International students from Togo in OECD countries

Five main destinations	2004	2005	2006	2007	2008	2009
France	1 584	1 733	1 737	1 667	1 584	1 399
United States	413	537	464	374	439	375
Germany	..	..	..	..	335	310
Italy	33	48	81	107	130	143
Canada	130	..	90	123	93	125
Total	2 181	2 345	2 398	2 301	2 674	2 464

Legal migrant flows to the OECD
Thousands

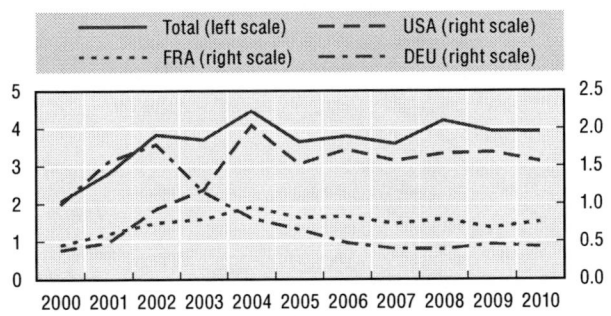

Remittance flows

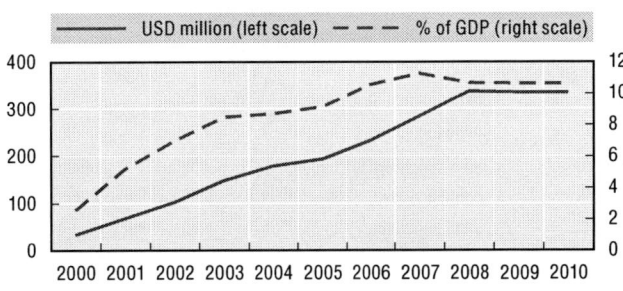

Ten main countries of destination for legal migrants in 2010 (numbers, % of total flows to the country): USA (1563, 0.2%), FRA (764, 0.6%), DEU (426, 0.1%), ITA (407, 0.1%), BEL (225, 0.2%), CAN (210, 0.1%), CHE (83, 0%), AUS (68, 0%), ESP (49, 0%), JPN (26, 0%).

Desire to emigrate, 2008-10

	Women	15-24	Highly educated	Total	Regional total
Persons who would move permanently, if they had the opportunity to do so (%)	..	..	..	..	33
Of which: Persons who are planning to move permanently in the next 12 months (%)				..	12
Of which: Persons who have already done some preparations for this move (e.g. visa application) (%)					33

StatLink ⟨⟩ http://dx.doi.org/10.1787/888932674835

Total population 2010 (millions)	33.4	Uganda compared to:	World	Region
Population growth 2010 (%)	3.2	Human Development Index (HDI)	161/187	22/46
GDP per capita 2010 (current USD)	509	GDP per capita	171/194	32/46
GDP growth 2010 (%)	5.2	Emigration rate	167/203	32/47
Poverty rate 2009 (USD PPP 2 a day, in %)	64.5	Emigration rate of the highly educated	93/157	31/39

Age structure of the population 0+ (2010): "0-14": 20%; "15-24": 48%; "25-64": 29%; "65+": 3%.
Level of education of the population 15+ (2010): "Low": 85%; "Medium": 12%; "High": 3%.

Emigrant population living in OECD countries

Immigrant population

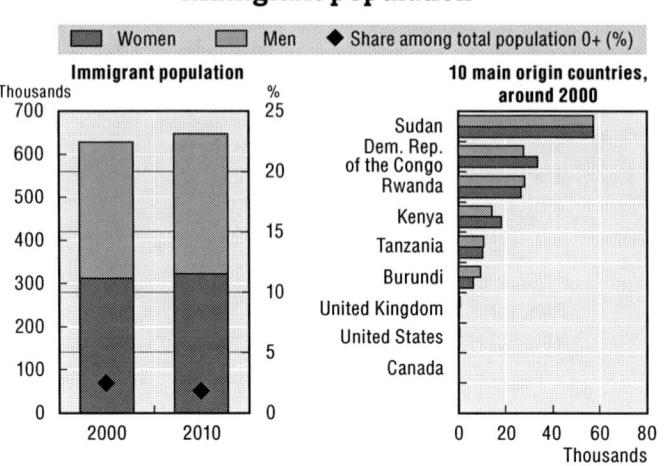

Emigrant population: persons born in Uganda living abroad

	2000						2005/06		
	All destinations			OECD destinations			OECD destinations		
Population 15+	Men	Women	Total	Men	Women	Total	Men	Women	Total
Emigrant population (thousands)	167.7	168.9	336.6	41.6	40.7	82.3	42.1	37.6	79.7
Recent emigrants (thousands)	..	..	..	2.2	2.5	4.7	5.2	4.9	10.1
15-24 (%)	31.1	31.4	31.3	6.5	8.0	7.2	7.4	7.2	7.3
25-64 (%)	64.7	63.6	64.2	88.8	87.1	88.0	81.6	84.6	83.0
65+ (%)	4.2	4.9	4.6	4.7	4.9	4.8	11.0	8.2	9.7
Low-educated (%)	76.6	80.8	78.7	26.2	31.3	28.7	18.6	16.5	17.6
Highly educated (%)	13.0	9.5	11.2	44.7	37.1	40.9	52.7	48.7	50.8
Total emigration rates (%)	2.7	2.6	2.6	0.7	0.6	0.7	0.6	0.5	0.5
Emigration rates of the highly educated (%)	7.3	9.5	8.1	6.1	8.7	7.1	7.1	8.3	7.6

Main destinations in 2005/06

	Total		Recent emigrants	Women	Highly educated	15-24	Total in 2000
Population 15+	Thousands	%	%	%	%	%	Thousands
United Kingdom	44.6	55.9	–	44.9	45.1	–	53.1
United States	15.8	19.8	21.6	47.6	61.5	10.2	11.5
Canada	11.0	13.8	6.5	50.6	62.4	4.8	10.9
Sweden	2.4	3.0	15.9	50.8	27.8	19.6	2.2
Australia	1.4	1.7	21.1	48.5	69.7	7.3	1.0
Denmark	1.1	1.3	19.6	63.6	17.6	29.1	0.8
Netherlands	–	–	–	–	–	–	–
Italy	–	–	–	–	–	–	0.5
France	0.4	0.5	16.6	60.9	52.2	7.6	0.4
Switzerland	–	–	–	–	–	–	0.4

Labour market indicators of persons born in Uganda living in OECD countries

Population 15-64	2000			2005/06		
	Men	Women	Total	Men	Women	Total
Employment-population ratio (%)	79.4	63.7	71.7	82.3	69.9	76.5
Unemployment rate (%)	6.3	7.8	7.0	7.6	5.6	6.8
Participation rate (%)	84.8	69.1	77.0	89.2	74.0	82.0
Total employed (thousands)	**29.4**	**23.0**	**52.5**	**29.6**	**22.4**	**52.0**
Employment rates of the highly educated (%)	87.5	76.0	82.3	93.0	81.6	87.8
Unemployment rates of the highly educated (%)	4.5	5.6	5.0	4.2	3.8	4.1
Highly educated in low- and medium-skilled jobs (%)	23.0	32.5	27.0	31.3	33.0	32.0
Highly educated employed (thousands)	**15.0**	**10.6**	**25.5**	**17.3**	**12.7**	**30.0**
Legislators, senior officials and managers	26.6	13.1	20.7	25.6	11.5	19.6
Professionals	20.6	15.2	18.2	20.3	21.4	20.8
Life science and health professionals	4.4	2.7	3.6	0.4	6.3	2.9
Teaching professionals	2.0	4.3	3.0	4.4	8.3	6.0
Technicians and associate professionals	11.4	14.8	12.9	10.7	13.8	12.1
Clerks	8.9	25.3	16.1	9.7	19.6	13.9
Service, shop and market sales workers	7.5	19.8	12.9	5.2	7.2	6.0
Skilled agricultural and fishery workers	0.3	0.2	0.2	3.3	5.7	4.3
Craft and related trades workers	7.7	0.6	4.6	4.6	3.6	4.2
Plant and machine operators and assemblers	8.3	4.7	6.7	7.4	1.9	5.1
Elementary occupations	8.7	6.3	7.7	12.5	15.3	13.7

Distribution of employment by occupation (%), population 15+

Persons born in Uganda and their native-born children, population 15+

Living in:	Europe	United States	Australia
2008	Thousands	Thousands	Thousands
Native-born children	26.4	16.2	..
Foreign-born	45.0	9.3	..
Total	71.4	25.5	..

International students from Uganda in OECD countries

Five main destinations	2004	2005	2006	2007	2008	2009
United Kingdom	885	890	880	910	921	1 038
United States	696	660	709	759	770	822
Germany	..	..	..	..	107	126
Canada	72	..	114	75	112	115
Australia	75	67	69	86	99	113
Total	1 824	1 747	1 936	1 988	2 233	2 483

Legal migrant flows to the OECD
Thousands

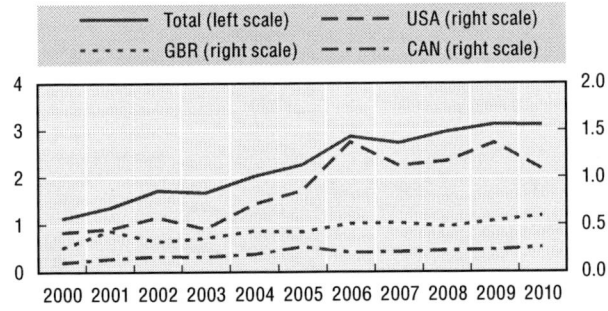

Remittance flows

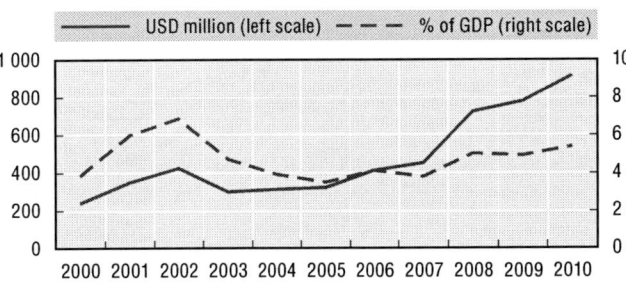

Ten main countries of destination for legal migrants in 2010 (numbers, % of total flows to the country): USA (1085, 0.1%), GBR (591, 0.1%), CAN (255, 0.1%), DEU (217, 0%), SWE (191, 0.2%), JPN (167, 0.1%), NLD (98, 0.1%), NOR (82, 0.1%), AUS (65, 0%), DNK (65, 0.2%).

Desire to emigrate, 2008-10

	Women	15-24	Highly educated	Total	Regional total
Persons who would move permanently, if they had the opportunity to do so (%)	36	48	..	38	33
Of which: Persons who are planning to move permanently in the next 12 months (%)				8	12
Of which: Persons who have already done some preparations for this move (*e.g.* visa application) (%)					33

Three main countries of desired destination: United States (35%), United Kingdom (18%), Kenya (6%).

StatLink http://dx.doi.org/10.1787/888932674854

Total population 2010 (millions)	44.8	**Tanzania compared to:**	**World** / **Region**
Population growth 2010 (%)	3.0	Human Development Index (HDI)	152/187 / 17/46
GDP per capita 2010 (current USD)	527	GDP per capita	169/194 / 30/46
GDP growth 2010 (%)	7.0	Emigration rate	187/203 / 43/47
Poverty rate 2007 (USD PPP 2 a day, in %)	87.9	Emigration rate of the highly educated	32/157 / 10/39

Age structure of the population 0+ (2010): "0-14": 20%; "15-24": 45%; "25-64": 32%; "65+": 3%.
Level of education of the population 15+ (2010): "Low": 92%; "Medium": 7%; "High": 1%.

Emigrant population living in OECD countries

Immigrant population

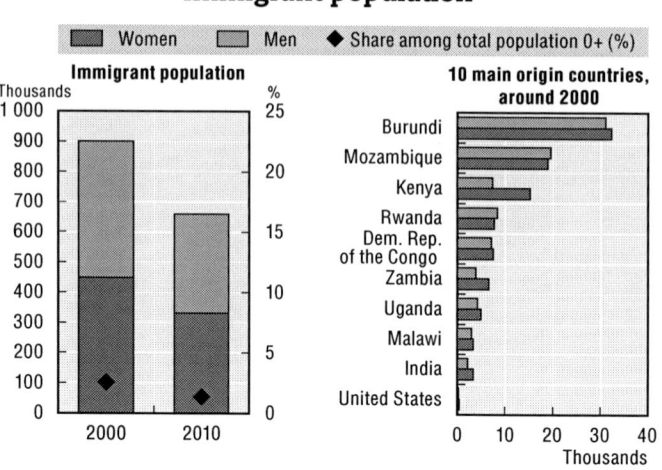

Emigrant population: persons born in Tanzania living abroad

	2000						2005/06		
	All destinations			OECD destinations			OECD destinations		
Population 15+	Men	Women	Total	Men	Women	Total	Men	Women	Total
Emigrant population (thousands)	81.1	79.9	161.0	35.5	34.8	70.2	33.5	35.0	68.5
Recent emigrants (thousands)	..	..	..	3.2	3.0	6.2	3.9	3.0	6.9
15-24 (%)	21.6	24.2	22.9	7.8	7.8	7.8	6.6	5.7	6.2
25-64 (%)	70.1	68.0	69.1	84.0	82.6	83.3	80.6	79.3	80.0
65+ (%)	8.3	7.8	8.1	8.2	9.6	8.9	12.8	14.9	13.9
Low-educated (%)	61.9	67.3	64.6	22.4	29.8	26.1	12.7	23.3	18.0
Highly educated (%)	21.7	16.9	19.3	46.5	37.9	42.3	57.5	47.5	52.5
Total emigration rates (%)	0.9	0.8	0.8	0.4	0.4	0.4	0.3	0.3	0.3
Emigration rates of the highly educated (%)	17.5	21.8	19.1	16.3	21.0	18.1	22.8	18.9	20.8

Main destinations in 2005/06

	Total		Recent emigrants	Women	Highly educated	15-24	Total in 2000
Population 15+	Thousands	%	%	%	%	%	Thousands
United Kingdom	23.4	34.1	–	60.5	51.7	–	31.9
Canada	19.4	28.3	7.0	51.6	53.9	4.7	19.5
United States	17.5	25.5	20.2	40.8	54.0	10.4	11.7
Australia	1.8	2.7	17.1	43.7	63.1	6.2	1.5
Switzerland	1.3	1.9	–	–	–	–	0.5
Sweden	1.0	1.4	30.4	52.9	29.9	17.3	0.9
Netherlands	–	–	–	–	–	–	–
Denmark	0.8	1.2	16.2	58.2	33.7	15.2	0.7
Italy	–	–	–	–	–	–	0.9
France	0.5	0.7	23.8	62.3	57.4	4.1	0.5

Labour market indicators of persons born in Tanzania living in OECD countries

Population 15-64	2000			2005/06		
	Men	Women	Total	Men	Women	Total
Employment-population ratio (%)	80.6	63.6	72.2	86.0	71.6	78.8
Unemployment rate (%)	5.5	6.4	5.9	3.8	8.0	5.7
Participation rate (%)	85.2	67.9	76.7	89.4	77.8	83.6
Total employed (thousands)	**25.1**	**19.2**	**44.3**	**24.6**	**20.2**	**44.9**
Employment rates of the highly educated (%)	87.8	74.9	82.0	94.0	89.1	91.8
Unemployment rates of the highly educated (%)	3.6	4.9	4.2	3.6	5.1	4.2
Highly educated in low- and medium-skilled jobs (%)	22.4	31.5	26.2	27.2	27.1	27.2
Highly educated employed (thousands)	**13.2**	**9.2**	**22.4**	**15.5**	**12.1**	**27.7**
Legislators, senior officials and managers	23.9	11.8	18.6	21.5	17.8	19.7
Professionals	21.9	17.0	19.7	24.1	21.3	22.7
Life science and health professionals	4.6	3.4	4.1	1.0	7.8	4.4
Teaching professionals	2.8	5.5	3.9	1.0	4.2	2.6
Technicians and associate professionals	12.1	16.3	14.0	10.0	16.0	12.9
Clerks	10.1	27.8	17.9	14.7	19.6	17.1
Service, shop and market sales workers	7.1	16.2	11.1	4.7	7.2	5.9
Skilled agricultural and fishery workers	0.3	0.3	0.3	0.3	2.5	1.3
Craft and related trades workers	9.2	1.1	5.6	8.4	4.7	6.6
Plant and machine operators and assemblers	7.6	3.9	6.0	7.3	3.3	5.3
Elementary occupations	7.7	5.5	6.8	4.8	7.7	6.2

Distribution of employment by occupation (%), population 15+

Persons born in Tanzania and their native-born children, population 15+

Living in:	Europe	United States	Australia
2008	Thousands	Thousands	Thousands
Native-born children	14.6	2.0	1.0
Foreign-born	23.8	11.4	2.3
Total	38.5	13.4	3.4

International students from Tanzania in OECD countries

Five main destinations	2004	2005	2006	2007	2008	2009
United States	1 471	1 391	1 283	1 222	1 193	1 197
United Kingdom	1 053	986	1 005	1 049	989	1 116
Canada	113	..	183	138	218	191
Australia	119	113	123	142	155	161
Germany	..	..	..	..	102	96
Total	2 992	2 795	2 906	2 877	2 976	3 163

Legal migrant flows to the OECD
Thousands

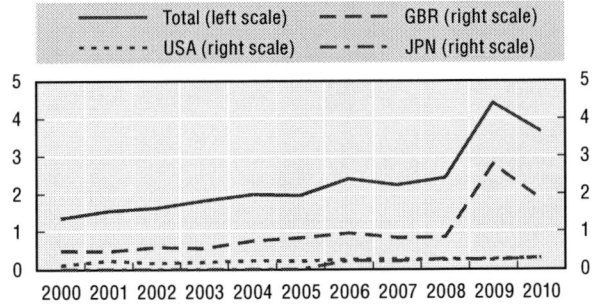

Remittance flows

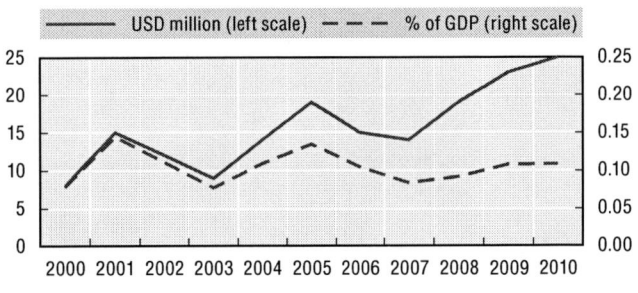

Ten main countries of destination for legal migrants in 2010 (numbers, % of total flows to the country): USA (1850, 0.2%), GBR (301, 0.1%), JPN (292, 0.1%), CAN (205, 0.1%), DEU (182, 0%), SWE (104, 0.1%), NLD (103, 0%), ITA (89, 0%), NOR (89, 0.1%), BEL (73, 0.1%).

Desire to emigrate, 2008-10

	Women	15-24	Highly educated	Total	Regional total
Persons who would move permanently, if they had the opportunity to do so (%)	29	42	..	32	33
Of which: Persons who are planning to move permanently in the next 12 months (%)				12	12
Of which: Persons who have already done some preparations for this move (*e.g.* visa application) (%)					33

Three main countries of desired destination: United States (24%), United Kingdom (13%), South Africa (9%).

StatLink http://dx.doi.org/10.1787/888932674816

			Zambia compared to:	World	Region
Total population 2010 (millions)	12.9				
Population growth 2010 (%)	1.6		Human Development Index (HDI)	164/187	26/46
GDP per capita 2010 (current USD)	1 253		GDP per capita	141/194	13/46
GDP growth 2010 (%)	7.6		Emigration rate	157/203	30/47
Poverty rate 2010 (USD PPP 2 a day, in %)	..		Emigration rate of the highly educated	24/157	9/39

Age structure of the population 0+ (2010): "0-14": 20%; "15-24": 46%; "25-64": 31%; "65+": 3%.
Level of education of the population 15+ (2010): "Low": 63%; "Medium": 36%; "High": 1%.

Emigrant population living in OECD countries

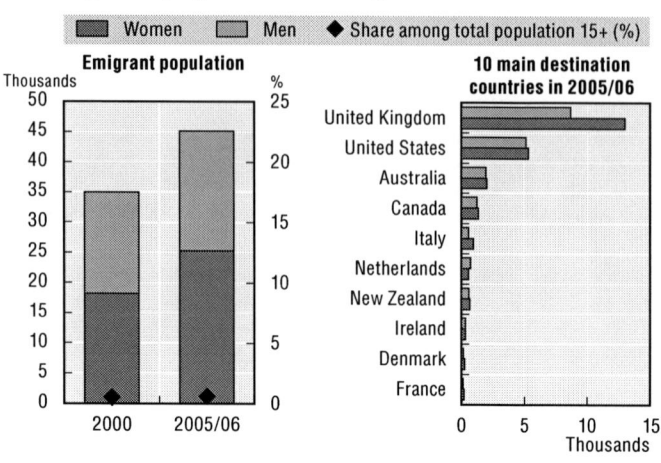

Immigrant population

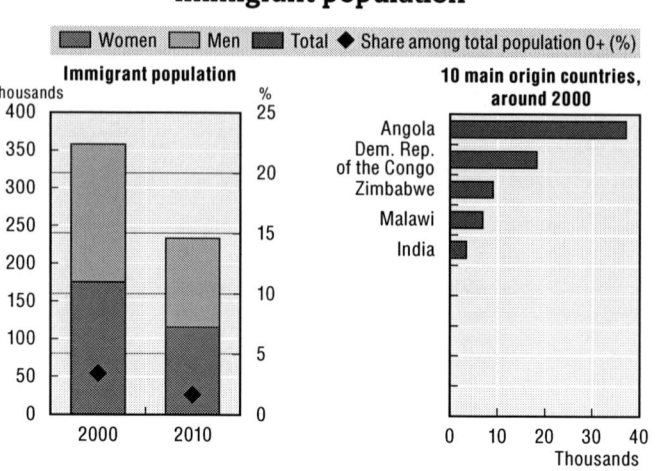

Emigrant population: persons born in Zambia living abroad

	2000						2005/06		
	All destinations			OECD destinations			OECD destinations		
Population 15+	Men	Women	Total	Men	Women	Total	Men	Women	Total
Emigrant population (thousands)	33.1	39.4	72.5	16.7	18.2	35.0	19.8	25.2	45.1
Recent emigrants (thousands)	..	..	..	1.8	1.8	3.6	4.7	6.0	10.6
15-24 (%)	16.9	19.5	18.4	15.9	16.8	16.4	8.9	15.7	12.7
25-64 (%)	79.4	77.5	78.3	82.7	81.2	81.9	90.0	80.9	84.9
65+ (%)	3.7	3.0	3.3	1.4	1.9	1.7	1.1	3.4	2.4
Low-educated (%)	26.0	36.1	31.5	12.5	16.7	14.7	7.5	17.5	13.0
Highly educated (%)	33.7	25.2	29.1	53.1	46.3	49.5	63.8	53.5	58.1
Total emigration rates (%)	1.2	1.3	1.3	0.6	0.6	0.6	0.6	0.8	0.7
Emigration rates of the highly educated (%)	16.3	26.0	19.7	13.2	22.7	16.5	20.3	33.9	25.6

Main destinations in 2005/06

	Total		Recent emigrants	Women	Highly educated	15-24	Total in 2000
Population 15+	Thousands	%	%	%	%	%	Thousands
United Kingdom	21.7	48.2	28.6	60.0	64.3	–	20.4
United States	10.5	23.2	14.5	51.0	50.2	20.1	5.7
Australia	3.9	8.7	31.5	50.9	60.0	12.6	2.8
Canada	2.5	5.5	16.9	52.4	70.4	19.8	2.1
Italy	1.5	3.3	–	63.1	–	–	0.6
Netherlands	–	–	–	–	–	–	–
New Zealand	1.2	2.7	40.6	53.2	53.4	10.4	0.9
Ireland	0.6	1.3	38.1	49.1	66.7	12.1	0.5
Denmark	0.4	0.8	21.8	63.9	25.4	27.2	0.3
France	–	–	–	–	–	–	0.2

Labour market indicators of persons born in Zambia living in OECD countries

Population 15-64	2000			2005/06		
	Men	Women	Total	Men	Women	Total
Employment-population ratio (%)	80.3	67.4	73.6	80.4	70.6	74.9
Unemployment rate (%)	6.2	6.4	6.3	5.3	6.0	5.6
Participation rate (%)	85.6	72.1	78.6	84.9	75.1	79.4
Total employed (thousands)	**12.8**	**11.6**	**24.4**	**12.4**	**13.7**	**26.1**
Employment rates of the highly educated (%)	88.3	77.9	83.2	85.8	80.1	82.9
Unemployment rates of the highly educated (%)	4.0	4.3	4.1	1.4	4.1	2.7
Highly educated in low- and medium-skilled jobs (%)	19.0	24.7	21.6	15.7	21.8	18.7
Highly educated employed (thousands)	**7.5**	**6.3**	**13.7**	**8.7**	**8.4**	**17.2**
Legislators, senior officials and managers	22.0	11.4	16.8	32.1	17.5	24.4
Professionals	28.3	21.7	25.0	22.7	15.9	19.1
Life science and health professionals	4.1	4.5	4.3	3.0	6.4	4.9
Teaching professionals	4.1	7.5	5.7	4.5	4.7	4.6
Technicians and associate professionals	14.3	20.8	17.5	17.7	26.1	22.2
Clerks	7.3	22.1	14.6	4.7	10.2	7.6
Service, shop and market sales workers	7.7	17.4	12.5	3.2	6.8	5.1
Skilled agricultural and fishery workers	0.5	0.3	0.4	1.2	12.9	7.4
Craft and related trades workers	8.8	0.7	4.8	3.2	1.0	2.0
Plant and machine operators and assemblers	4.7	1.2	3.0	3.4	0.2	1.7
Elementary occupations	6.4	4.5	5.5	11.9	9.4	10.6

(Left margin label: Distribution of employment by occupation (%), population 15+)

Persons born in Zambia and their native-born children, population 15+

Living in:	Europe	United States	Australia
2008	Thousands	Thousands	Thousands
Native-born children	3.7	..	..
Foreign-born	12.1	..	1.9
Total	15.8	..	..

International students from Zambia in OECD countries

Five main destinations	2004	2005	2006	2007	2008	2009
United States	859	829	845	895	788	731
United Kingdom	541	547	611	604	629	643
Australia	317	396	442	552	551	514
Canada	34	..	57	45	134	139
Ireland	..	..	..	..	23	28
Total	1 815	1 848	2 097	2 194	2 250	2 197

Legal migrant flows to the OECD
Thousands

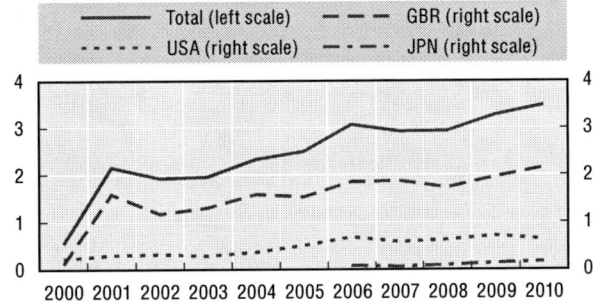

Remittance flows

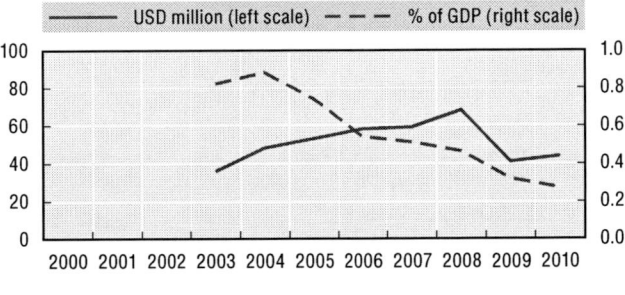

Ten main countries of destination for legal migrants in 2010 (numbers, % of total flows to the country): GBR (2153, 0.5%), USA (628, 0.1%), JPN (162, 0.1%), AUS (131, 0.1%), CAN (115, 0%), NLD (53, 0.1%), NOR (47, 0%), DEU (37, 0%), BEL (24, 0%), DNK (19, 0.1%).

Desire to emigrate, 2008-10

	Women	15-24	Highly educated	Total	Regional total
Persons who would move permanently, if they had the opportunity to do so (%)	21	25	26	21	33
Of which: Persons who are planning to move permanently in the next 12 months (%)				16	12
Of which: Persons who have already done some preparations for this move (*e.g.* visa application) (%)					33

Three main countries of desired destination: United States (28%), South Africa (15%), United Kingdom (13%).

StatLink ᔖᔏ http://dx.doi.org/10.1787/888932674873

Total population 2010 (millions)	12.6	Zimbabwe compared to:	World	Region
Population growth 2010 (%)	0.8	Human Development Index (HDI)	173/187	32/46
GDP per capita 2010 (current USD)	595	GDP per capita	165/194	26/46
GDP growth 2010 (%)	9.0	Emigration rate	133/203	17/47
Poverty rate 2010 (USD PPP 2 a day, in %)	..	Emigration rate of the highly educated	10/157	3/39

Age structure of the population 0+ (2010): "0-14": 25%; "15-24": 39%; "25-64": 32%; "65+": 4%.
Level of education of the population 15+ (2010): "Low": 43%; "Medium": 56%; "High": 1%.

Emigrant population living in OECD countries

Immigrant population

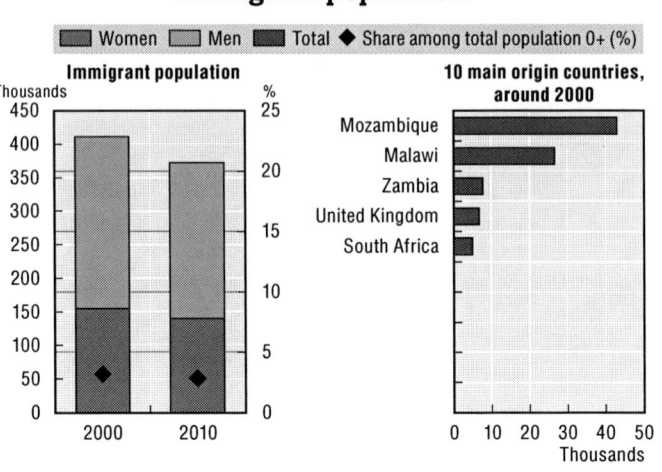

Emigrant population: persons born in Zimbabwe living abroad

Population 15+	2000						2005/06		
	All destinations			OECD destinations			OECD destinations		
	Men	Women	Total	Men	Women	Total	Men	Women	Total
Emigrant population (thousands)	111.2	98.0	209.2	36.8	41.0	77.8	67.2	72.9	140.1
Recent emigrants (thousands)	..	..	..	4.9	4.8	9.7	28.2	30.8	59.0
15-24 (%)	21.1	20.2	20.7	19.7	20.8	20.3	17.5	17.1	17.3
25-64 (%)	74.8	74.9	74.9	77.6	75.9	76.7	80.2	77.4	78.7
65+ (%)	4.1	4.9	4.5	2.7	3.3	3.0	2.4	5.5	4.0
Low-educated (%)	41.1	32.1	36.9	13.7	17.1	15.5	15.7	17.6	16.7
Highly educated (%)	21.1	22.5	21.8	44.5	41.0	42.7	49.8	48.3	49.0
Total emigration rates (%)	3.0	2.5	2.8	1.0	1.1	1.0	1.7	1.8	1.7
Emigration rates of the highly educated (%)	30.6	48.8	37.4	23.0	41.4	29.7	41.4	61.3	49.6

Main destinations in 2005/06

Population 15+	Total		Recent emigrants	Women	Highly educated	15-24	Total in 2000
	Thousands	%	%	%	%	%	Thousands
United Kingdom	84.9	60.6	43.8	53.4	47.8	17.6	44.5
Australia	17.8	12.7	43.8	50.4	50.8	18.3	10.7
United States	16.3	11.6	30.2	48.9	58.8	16.8	10.6
Canada	7.3	5.2	49.7	51.3	62.9	18.3	3.8
New Zealand	6.6	4.7	75.5	50.9	37.1	18.1	2.5
Ireland	1.9	1.4	66.3	52.0	50.2	19.9	1.2
Portugal	–	–	–	–	–	–	1.3
Netherlands	–	–	–	–	–	–	–
Switzerland	–	–	–	–	–	–	0.5
France	0.5	0.3	34.8	52.5	49.5	15.1	0.3

Labour market indicators of persons born in Zimbabwe living in OECD countries

Population 15-64	2000			2005/06		
	Men	Women	Total	Men	Women	Total
Employment-population ratio (%)	76.2	65.1	70.3	82.5	72.1	77.2
Unemployment rate (%)	6.8	6.9	6.9	6.1	7.0	6.5
Participation rate (%)	81.8	69.9	75.5	87.8	77.5	82.5
Total employed (thousands)	**26.1**	**24.8**	**50.9**	**52.6**	**48.0**	**100.5**
Employment rates of the highly educated (%)	85.0	75.7	80.3	94.6	85.2	89.9
Unemployment rates of the highly educated (%)	4.3	4.5	4.4	3.5	4.1	3.8
Highly educated in low- and medium-skilled jobs (%)	20.0	25.1	22.5	28.2	32.6	30.3
Highly educated employed (thousands)	**13.0**	**11.9**	**24.9**	**29.3**	**26.5**	**55.9**
Legislators, senior officials and managers	19.4	9.0	14.3	16.6	8.0	12.5
Professionals	23.1	17.6	20.4	24.0	15.4	19.9
Life science and health professionals	3.1	3.5	3.3	7.2	3.8	5.5
Teaching professionals	3.4	6.4	4.9	4.5	4.7	4.6
Technicians and associate professionals	15.8	23.4	19.6	13.3	24.6	18.7
Clerks	6.6	24.3	15.4	6.1	18.8	12.2
Service, shop and market sales workers	9.1	18.7	13.9	7.6	5.4	6.5
Skilled agricultural and fishery workers	0.8	0.3	0.6	6.3	16.6	11.3
Craft and related trades workers	12.0	0.6	6.3	9.2	4.2	6.8
Plant and machine operators and assemblers	4.7	1.1	2.9	9.6	1.5	5.7
Elementary occupations	8.5	5.0	6.7	7.0	5.2	6.1

Distribution of employment by occupation (%), population 15+

Persons born in Zimbabwe and their native-born children, population 15+

Living in:	Europe	United States	Australia
2008	Thousands	Thousands	Thousands
Native-born children	14.6	6.4	2.5
Foreign-born	75.8	6.5	7.7
Total	90.5	12.9	10.3

International students from Zimbabwe in OECD countries

Five main destinations	2004	2005	2006	2007	2008	2009
United Kingdom	2 741	2 658	2 655	2 475	2 027	1 740
Australia	892	983	1 075	1 361	1 464	1 373
United States	1 999	1 770	1 764	1 552	1 423	1 248
Canada	58	..	129	129	176	203
Germany	..	..	..	..	72	68
Total	5 771	5 490	5 714	5 601	5 289	4 816

Legal migrant flows to the OECD
Thousands

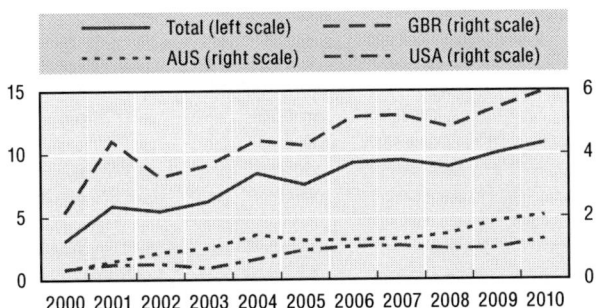

Ten main countries of destination for legal migrants in 2010 (numbers, % of total flows to the country): GBR (5974, 1.3%), AUS (2018, 1%), USA (1274, 0.1%), CAN (475, 0.2%), NZL (301, 0.7%), DEU (181, 0%), JPN (113, 0.1%), NLD (100, 0.1%), CHE (53, 0%), AUT (42, 0%).

Desire to emigrate, 2008-10

	Women	15-24	Highly educated	Total	Regional total
Persons who would move permanently, if they had the opportunity to do so (%)	36	52	50	40	33
Of which: Persons who are planning to move permanently in the next 12 months (%)				23	12
Of which: Persons who have already done some preparations for this move (*e.g.* visa application) (%)					33

Three main countries of desired destination: South Africa (35%), United Kingdom (18%), United States (14%).

StatLink ▐▬▐ http://dx.doi.org/10.1787/888932674892

ANNEX A

Data sources and definitions

1. Data sources

Background information

World Development Indicators, World Bank (Total population; Population by age; GDP; Poverty rate).

Barro and Lee (2010), Education dataset, Total population 15+ by educational attainment.

United Nations Development Programme (Human Development Index).

OECD Database on Immigrants in OECD Countries (DIOC 2005/06), Emigration rates.

Emigration and immigration

OECD Database on Immigrants in OECD Countries (DIOC-E 2000, DIOC 2005/06).

Immigration by origin country for the following countries are extracted from the United Nations Global Migration Database (UNPD): Gabon, Iran, Kazakhstan, Moldova, Mozambique, Myanmar, Saudi Arabia, Tajikistan, Tunisia, Zambia, Zimbabwe.

Labour market indicators

OECD Database on Immigrants in OECD Countries (DIOC-E 2000, DIOC 2005/06).

Native-born children of immigrants

European Union Labour Force Survey, 2008 *ad hoc* module (Eurostat); US Current Population Survey 2008; Household, Income and Labour Dynamics in Australia (HILDA) Survey 2009.

International students

UNESCO-OECD-Eurostat (UOE) data collection on education statistics, compiled on the basis of national administrative sources, reported by Ministries of Education or National Statistical Offices.

Legal migrant flows to the OECD

OECD Database on International Migration.

Remittance flows

World Bank remittances data.

Desire to emigrate

Gallup World Poll Survey 2008-10.

2. Description of data sources

OECD Database on Immigrants in OECD Countries (DIOC-E 2000)

DIOC-E (release 3.0) contains data on 100 countries of residence and covers all individuals aged 15 and over living in these countries, by educational attainment level, age, sex, labour force status and occupation. For most countries the place of birth is used to identify migrants, although in some few cases (Japan, Korea) the criteria of nationality had to be used. The database identifies about 200 countries or regions of origin. The share of persons with unknown place of birth is less than 1% for the whole database.

Census data was used for 89 countries, population register data for four countries (Denmark, Finland, Norway and Sweden) and national labour force survey data (LFS) for Germany, the Netherlands and Israel. For India the National Sample Survey calibrated on census data 2001 was used.

In many African destinations, including large receiving countries, such as Nigeria, only aggregated data by main regions of origin are available.

OECD Database on Immigrants in OECD Countries (DIOC 2005/06)

The Database on Immigrants in OECD Countries (DIOC 2005/06) is an update of DIOC 2000. DIOC 2005/06 contains information on about 200 countries or regions of origin, by educational attainment level, age, sex, labour force status and occupation for 27 OECD destination countries (excluding Estonia, Hungary, Iceland, Korea, Slovak Republic, Slovenia and Turkey). Data are based on population register and census data around 2005/06, and on labour force survey data for 14 OECD countries. The latter data are averaged over a three-year period to improve the reliability of population estimates.

Data on occupation presented in the country notes do not include migrants living in the United States and Mexico, since it was not possible to map the national classification to the international ISCO classification at 1-digit. No data are available for Poland, Norway, Israel and Greece. For Canada the 2-digit categories "Life science and health professionals" and "Teaching professionals" are not available.

The percentage of highly educated in low-skilled jobs is not shown when numbers are below 200 highly educated.

Data on emigrant population by main destination under specific thresholds have been omitted for destination countries where the data source is a labour force survey: Austria (1 732); Belgium (5 000); Germany (2 887); Greece (1 443); Italy (866); Luxembourg (289); Netherlands (1 500); Poland (2 887); Portugal (4 500); Spain (1 155); Switzerland (1 155); United Kingdom (6 000). All figures corresponding to a total number of emigrants below 300 have also been omitted from this table.

Legal migrant flows (OECD International Migration Database)

International migration flows to the OECD countries are not harmonised across countries and should therefore be interpreted with caution. For example Australian and US data include only permanent migrants while German ones include many temporary migrants (temporary and seasonal workers, asylum seekers, students, etc.). For France no data on intra-European migrant flows are available. Data for Ireland are adjusted based on the structure of the PPS number allocations by nationality and for the United Kingdom the International Passenger Survey is taken into account.

Data sources by country, DIOC 2005/06

	Source
Australia	Census 2006
Austria	Microcensus 2004/2005/2006
Belgium	Labour Force Survey 2004/2005/2006
Canada	Census 2006
Chile	CASEN 2006
Czech Republic	Register data 2005, Census 2001, European Labour Force Survey 2005
Denmark	Population Register 2005
Finland	Population Register 2005
France	Census 2006
Germany	Microcensus 2005/2006/2007
Greece	Labour Force Survey 2004/2005/2006
Ireland	Census 2006
Israel	Labour Force Survey 2005
Italy	Labour Force Survey 2004/2005/2006
Japan	Census 2005, DIOC 2000
Luxembourg	Labour Force Survey 2004/2005/2006
Mexico	Labour Force Survey 2005/2006/2007
Netherlands	Labour Force Survey 2004/2005/2006
New Zealand	Census 2006
Norway	Population Register 2005
Poland	Labour Force Survey 2004/2005/2006
Portugal	Labour Force Survey 2005/2006
Spain	Labour Force Survey 2004/2005/2006
Sweden	Population Register 2005
Switzerland	Labour Force Survey 2004/2005/2006
United Kingdom	Labour Force Survey 2007
United States	American Community Survey (ACS) 2005-2009

Remittances data (World Bank)

Migrant remittances are defined as the sum of workers' remittances, compensation of employees, and migrants' transfers. Workers' remittances are private transfers from migrant workers who are considered residents of the host country to recipients in the workers' country of origin.

Informal flows are the most difficult aspect of remittance data to estimate. Some countries do not report data on remittances in the IMF Balance of Payments statistics, several developing countries (such as Afghanistan, Cuba, Turkmenistan, Uzbekistan, and Zimbabwe) do not report remittance inflows data to the IMF, and some high-income countries (for example Canada, Qatar, Singapore, and the United Arab Emirates) do not report data on remittance outflows (World Bank, 2011).

International students (UOE data collection)

International students are defined as students with permanent residence outside the reporting country. However, data on international students are only available from 2004 onwards. Prior to 2004, data on foreign (non-citizen) students are used instead. In order to capture student mobility, a distinction is therefore made between resident foreign students, that is to say foreign students who are resident in the country because of a prior migration by themselves or their parents, and non-resident foreign students who came to the country expressly for pursuing their education. The definition of foreign students is used in this publication for the following countries: France, Greece, Italy, Japan, Korea and Turkey.

Gallup World Poll Survey

The Gallup World Poll Survey covers a large range of behavioural and economic topics and is conducted in approximately 140 countries around the world based on a common questionnaire, translated into the predominant languages of each country. Since 2006, more than 100 questions are asked each year to a representative sample of around 1 000 persons aged 15 and over. Gallup collects oversamples in major cities or regions of special interest in some countries. In large countries, such as China, India and the Russian Federation, sample sizes for each survey administration include up to 4 000 adults. Results may however be affected by sampling and non-sampling errors.

UN Migrant Stock data (2008 revision)

For three Gulf countries, namely United Arab Emirates, Bahrain and Qatar, national statistics were used for total and foreign population figures.

3. Definitions

Emigration rates

The emigration rate of a given origin country i in a given year is defined as the share of the native population of country i residing abroad at this time:

$m_i = M_i/(M_i + N_i)$

where M_i is the emigrant population from country i living abroad, and N_i is the native-born population of country i. Similarly, the emigration rate of the high educated is the same calculation, limited to the highly educated.

Highly educated

Tertiary educational attainment level according to the International Standard Classification of Education (ISCED 5/6).

Highly educated in low- and medium-skilled jobs

Percentage of highly educated employed persons who are in occupations other than those defined as highly skilled. Managers, professionals, technicians and associate professionals are classified as highly skilled occupations.

Low-educated

Lower secondary educational attainment level according to the International Standard Classification of Education (ISCED 0/1/2).

Native-born children of immigrants

Native-born children aged 15 years and over with at least one parent foreign-born living in an OECD country. Therefore, those with both parents born abroad in different countries are counted twice.

Recent emigrant

Foreign-born persons with a residence of less than five years in the current country of residence.

Country codes (ISO)

AFG	Afghanistan	GMB	Gambia	NOR	Norway
AGO	Angola	GNB	Guinea-Bissau	NPL	Nepal
ALB	Albania	GNQ	Equatorial Guinea	NRU	Nauru
AND	Andorra	GRC	Greece	NZL	New Zealand
ARE	United Arab Emirates	GRD	Grenada	OMN	Oman
ARG	Argentina	GTM	Guatemala	PAK	Pakistan
ARM	Armenia	GUM	Guam	PAN	Panama
ATG	Antigua and Barbuda	GUY	Guyana	PER	Peru
AUS	Australia	HKG	Hong Kong, China	PHL	Philippines
AUT	Austria	HND	Honduras	PLW	Palau
AZE	Azerbaijan	HRV	Croatia	PNG	Papua New Guinea
BDI	Burundi	HTI	Haiti	POL	Poland
BEL	Belgium	HUN	Hungary	PRI	Puerto Rico
BEN	Benin	IDN	Indonesia	PRK	Dem. People's Rep. of Korea
BFA	Burkina Faso	IND	India	PRT	Portugal
BGD	Bangladesh	IRL	Ireland	PRY	Paraguay
BGR	Bulgaria	IRN	Iran	PSE	West Bank and Gaza Strip
BHR	Bahrain	IRQ	Iraq	QAT	Qatar
BHS	Bahamas	ISL	Iceland	ROU	Romania
BIH	Bosnia and Herzegovina	ISR	Israel	RUS	Russian Federation
BLR	Belarus	ITA	Italy	RWA	Rwanda
BLZ	Belize	JAM	Jamaica	SAU	Saudi Arabia
BMU	Bermuda	JOR	Jordan	SDN	Sudan
BOL	Bolivia	JPN	Japan	SEN	Senegal
BRA	Brazil	KAZ	Kazakhstan	SGP	Singapore
BRB	Barbados	KEN	Kenya	SLB	Solomon Islands
BRN	Brunei Darussalam	KGZ	Kyrgyzstan	SLE	Sierra Leone
BTN	Bhutan	KHM	Cambodia	SLV	El Salvador
BWA	Botswana	KIR	Kiribati	SMR	San Marino
CAF	Central African Republic	KNA	Saint Kitts and Nevis	SOM	Somalia
CAN	Canada	KOR	Korea	SRB	Serbia
CHE	Switzerland	KWT	Kuwait	STP	Sao Tome and Principe
CHL	Chile	LAO	Laos	SUN	Former USSR
CHN	China	LBN	Lebanon	SUR	Suriname
CIV	Côte d'Ivoire	LBR	Liberia	SVK	Slovak Republic
CMR	Cameroon	LBY	Libya	SWE	Sweden
COD	Dem. Rep. of the Congo	LCA	Saint Lucia	SWZ	Swaziland
COG	Congo	LIE	Liechtenstein	SYR	Syria
COK	Cook Islands	LKA	Sri Lanka	TCD	Chad
COL	Colombia	LSO	Lesotho	TGO	Togo
COM	Comoros	LTU	Lithuania	THA	Thailand
CPV	Cape Verde	LVA	Latvia	TJK	Tajikistan
CRI	Costa Rica	MAC	Macao, China	TKL	Tokelau
CSK	Former Czechoslovakia	MAR	Morocco	TKM	Turkmenistan
CUB	Cuba	MCO	Monaco	TLS	Timor-Leste
CZE	Czech Republic	MDA	Moldova	TON	Tonga
DEU	Germany	MDG	Madagascar	TTO	Trinidad and Tobago
DJI	Djibouti	MDV	Maldives	TUN	Tunisia
DMA	Dominica	MEX	Mexico	TUR	Turkey
DNK	Denmark	MHL	Marshall Islands	TUV	Tuvalu
DOM	Dominican Republic	MKD	Macedonia, FYR of	TWN	Chinese Taipei
DZA	Algeria	MLI	Mali	UGA	Uganda
ECU	Ecuador	MLT	Malta	UKR	Ukraine
EGY	Egypt	MMR	Myanmar	URY	Uruguay
ERI	Eritrea	MNE	Montenegro	USA	United States
ESP	Spain	MNG	Mongolia	UZB	Uzbekistan
EST	Estonia	MOZ	Mozambique	VCT	Saint Vincent and the Grenadines
ETH	Ethiopia	MRT	Mauritania	VEN	Venezuela
FIN	Finland	MUS	Mauritius	VUT	Vanuatu
FJI	Fiji	MWI	Malawi	WSM	Samoa
FRA	France	MYS	Malaysia	YEM	Yemen
FSM	Micronesia	NAM	Namibia	YUCS	Former Yugoslavia
GAB	Gabon	NER	Niger	ZAF	South Africa
GBR	United Kingdom	NGA	Nigeria	ZMB	Zambia
GEO	Georgia	NIC	Nicaragua	ZWE	Zimbabwe
GHA	Ghana	NIU	Niue		
GIN	Guinea	NLD	Netherlands		

ANNEX B

Emigrant population: Persons born in the former USSR and in the former Yugoslavia

Emigrant population: persons born in the former USSR living abroad

Population 15+	2000						2005/06		
	All destinations			OECD destinations			OECD destinations		
	Men	Women	Total	Men	Women	Total	Men	Women	Total
Emigrant population (thousands)	10 073.7	11 695.0	21 768.7	1 864.5	2 337.0	4 201.5	2 829.3	3 590.3	6 419.6
Recent emigrants (thousands)	..	..	..	198.1	288.7	486.7	502.9	720.5	1 223.3
15-24 (%)	13.7	11.5	12.5	15.4	12.6	13.8	18.0	14.6	16.1
25-64 (%)	71.4	67.2	69.1	62.3	59.4	60.7	63.0	61.9	62.4
65+ (%)	15.0	21.3	18.4	22.3	28.0	25.5	19.1	23.5	21.6
Low-educated (%)	22.1	23.9	23.1	29.0	32.8	31.1	29.0	31.0	30.1
Highly educated (%)	28.1	29.3	28.7	32.7	32.1	32.4	30.3	32.1	31.3
Total emigration rates (%)	10.0	9.2	9.6	1.9	1.8	1.8	2.8	2.7	2.7
Emigration rates of the highly educated (%)	15.1	15.5	15.3	3.2	3.4	3.3	5.0	2.8	4.8

2000				2005/06	
All destinations		OECD destinations		OECD destinations	
Country	%	Country	%	Country	%
Russian Federation	19.3	Germany	27.2	Germany	30.3
Ukraine	15.8	Israel	13.9	United States	13.2
Germany	13.6	United States	10.8	Israel	11.1
Belarus	8.1	Poland	10.2	Poland	10.5
Israel	6.3	Estonia	8.2	Canada	7.4
United States	5.9	Greece	7.7	Greece	5.2
Poland	4.5	Canada	7.5	Spain	5.0
Latvia	4.4	Czech Republic	5.9	Czech Republic	4.9
Kyrgyzstan	3.8	Spain	5.4	United Kingdom	3.2
Estonia	3.7	Australia	3.3	Italy	1.9

Emigrant population: persons born in the former Yugoslavia living abroad

Population 15+	2000						2005/06		
	All destinations			OECD destinations			OECD destinations		
	Men	Women	Total	Men	Women	Total	Men	Women	Total
Emigrant population (thousands)	1 923.9	2 016.0	3 939.9	1 153.5	1 133.9	2 287.4	1 377.2	1 380.0	2 757.1
Recent emigrants (thousands)	..	..	..	134.9	133.9	268.7	117.4	141.8	259.2
15-24 (%)	11.3	10.1	10.7	12.5	11.5	12.0	13.9	13.5	13.7
25-64 (%)	75.2	72.0	73.6	78.0	75.3	76.6	75.2	74.2	74.7
65+ (%)	13.5	17.9	15.8	9.5	13.2	11.4	10.9	12.2	11.6
Low-educated (%)	39.5	56.1	48.0	42.4	57.1	49.7	37.8	51.6	44.7
Highly educated (%)	14.1	10.3	12.2	12.9	10.5	11.7	14.2	12.1	13.1
Total emigration rates (%)	18.9	18.7	18.8	11.3	10.5	10.9	13.0	12.4	12.7
Emigration rates of the highly educated (%)	24.4	20.6	22.6	13.1	11.7	12.5	16.9	14.7	15.8

2000				2005/06	
All destinations		OECD destinations		OECD destinations	
Country	%	Country	%	Country	%
Serbia	19.3	Germany	27.2	Germany	30.3
Germany	15.8	Austria	13.9	Austria	13.2
Croatia	13.6	United States	10.8	Switzerland	11.1
Austria	8.1	Switzerland	10.2	United States	10.5
United States	6.3	Italy	7.7	Italy	7.4
Switzerland	5.9	Australia	7.5	Canada	5.2
Italy	4.5	Slovenia	6.5	Australia	5.0
Australia	4.4	Canada	5.9	Sweden	4.9
Slovenia	3.8	Sweden	5.4	France	3.2
Turkey	3.7	France	3.3	Netherlands	1.9

ANNEX C

Expatriation rates for nurses and doctors, circa 2000

Nurses

Country of birth	ISO codes	Number of persons working in OECD countries	Expatriation rate
Albania	ALB	415	3.5
Algeria	DZA	8 796	12.4
Angola	AGO	1 703	11.5
Antigua and Barbuda	ATG	678	74.4
Argentina	ARG	1 288	4.3
Australia	AUS	4 620	2.6
Austria	AUT	2 914	3.7
Bahamas	BHS	560	29.7
Bahrain	BHR	77	2.5
Bangladesh	BGD	651	3.1
Barbados	BRB	3 496	78.0
Belgium	BEL	4 125	6.4
Belize	BLZ	1 365	81.8
Benin	BEN	166	3.2
Bolivia	BOL	358	1.3
Botswana	BWA	47	1.0
Brazil	BRA	2 258	0.3
Brunei Darussalam	BRN	129	12.6
Bulgaria	BGR	789	2.6
Burkina Faso	BFA	16	0.3
Burundi	BDI	57	4.1
Cambodia	KHM	1 119	12.2
Cameroon	CMR	1 338	4.9
Canada	CAN	24 620	7.4
Cape Verde	CPV	261	38.9
Central African Republic	CAF	92	8.4
Chad	TCD	117	5.2
Chile	CHL	1 965	16.4
China	CHN	12 249	0.9
Colombia	COL	2 625	9.9
Comoros	COM	64	11.7
Congo	COG	452	12.3
Congo, Democratic Republic of	COD	404	1.4
Costa Rica	CRI	562	13.4
Côte d'Ivoire	CIV	337	4.2
Cuba	CUB	4 209	4.8
Cyprus	CYP	706	19.1
Denmark	DNK	2 641	4.5
Dominica	DMA	620	66.2
Dominican Republic	DOM	1 857	10.8

Nurses *(cont.)*

Country of birth	ISO codes	Number of persons working in OECD countries	Expatriation rate
Ecuador	ECU	1 126	5.4
Egypt	EGY	1 128	0.8
El Salvador	SLV	2 398	32.0
Equatorial Guinea	GNQ	98	31.0
Eritrea	ERI	548	18.8
Ethiopia	ETH	1 421	9.1
Fiji	FJI	2 025	56.2
Finland	FIN	5 870	7.3
Former Czechoslovakia	CSFR	2 835	
Former USSR	F-USSR	10 034	
Former Yugoslavia	F-YUG	12 948	
France	FRA	8 589	1.9
Gabon	GAB	106	1.6
Gambia	GMB	62	3.7
Germany	DEU	31 623	3.8
Ghana	GHA	5 230	24.9
Greece	GRC	1 367	3.1
Grenada	GRD	2 131	87.6
Guatemala	GTM	1 204	2.6
Guinea	GIN	94	2.1
Guinea-Bissau	GNB	227	18.0
Guyana	GUY	7 450	81.1
Haiti	HTI	13 001	94.0
Honduras	HND	917	9.9
Hungary	HUN	2 117	2.4
Iceland	ISL	287	6.8
India	IND	22 786	2.6
Indonesia	IDN	3 449	2.7
Iran	IRN	4 234	4.8
Iraq	IRQ	415	1.3
Ireland	IRL	20 166	24.9
Israel	ISR	980	2.4
Italy	ITA	6 945	2.2
Jamaica	JAM	31 186	87.7
Japan	JPN	4 711	0.5
Jordan	JOR	363	2.0
Kenya	KEN	2 523	6.4
Kiribati	KIR	19	9.0
Kuwait	KWT	152	1.6
Laos	LAO	867	15.0
Lebanon	LBN	1 400	25.2
Liberia	LBR	1 240	66.9
Libya	LBY	100	0.6
Luxembourg	LUX	104	2.4
Madagascar	MDG	1 157	24.4
Malawi	MWI	200	2.7
Malaysia	MYS	7 569	19.6
Mali	MLI	227	3.7
Malta	MLT	649	22.0
Mauritania	MRT	96	5.5
Mauritius	MUS	4 502	50.4
Mexico	MEX	12 357	12.2
Morocco	MAR	5 730	20.5
Mozambique	MOZ	779	16.5
Myanmar	MMR	418	4.1
Namibia	NAM	30	0.5

Nurses (cont.)

Country of birth	ISO codes	Number of persons working in OECD countries	Expatriation rate
Nepal	NPL	205	3.5
Netherlands	NLD	6 798	3.0
New Zealand	NZL	7 564	19.5
Nicaragua	NIC	1 155	16.5
Niger	NER	19	0.8
Nigeria	NGA	13 398	9.5
Norway	NOR	1 700	2.5
Oman	OMN	18	0.2
Pakistan	PAK	1 803	3.6
Panama	PAN	1 902	29.5
Papua New Guinea	PNG	455	13.8
Paraguay	PRY	130	1.3
Peru	PER	2 807	14.1
Philippines	PHL	110 774	46.5
Poland	POL	9 153	4.6
Portugal	PRT	2 655	5.7
Romania	ROU	4 440	4.9
Rwanda	RWA	54	1.5
Saint Kitts and Nevis	KNA	711	76.7
Saint Lucia	LCA	369	52.7
Saint Vincent and the Grenadines	VCT	1 228	81.6
Samoa	WSM	566	62.1
Sao Tome and Principe	STP	138	35.0
Saudi Arabia	SAU	151	0.2
Senegal	SEN	256	8.9
Seychelles	SYC	151	19.2
Sierra Leone	SLE	2 057	56.3
Singapore	SGP	1 913	9.9
Solomon Islands	SLB	38	10.1
Somalia	SOM	250	14.4
South Africa	ZAF	6 016	3.2
Spain	ESP	3 527	1.1
Sri Lanka	LKA	2 032	8.1
Sudan	SDN	183	1.0
Suriname	SUR	18	2.5
Swaziland	SWZ	37	0.8
Sweden	SWE	3 028	3.2
Switzerland	CHE	1 839	2.3
Syria	SYR	319	1.0
Thailand	THA	3 050	1.7
Timor-Leste	TLS	61	4.0
Togo	TGO	78	4.0
Tonga	TON	449	58.2
Trinidad and Tobago	TTO	9 808	72.9
Tunisia	TUN	410	1.6
Turkey	TUR	3 565	2.9
United Arab Emirates	ARE	11	0.1
United Kingdom	GBR	45 638	6.1
United Republic of Tanzania	TZA	970	6.8
United States	USA	6 022	0.2
Unganda	UGA	1 210	7.4
Uruguay	URY	506	14.9
Vanuatu	VUT	20	4.5
Viet Nam	VNM	5 778	11.5
Yemen	YEM	231	1.7
Zambia	ZMB	820	4.6
Zimbabwe	ZWE	3 619	27.9

Doctors

Country of birth	ISO codes	Number of persons working in OECD countries	Expatriation rate
Afghanistan	AFG	613	13.0
Albania	ALB	271	6.2
Algeria	DZA	10 793	23.4
Angola	AGO	1 512	63.2
Antigua and Barbuda	ATG	100	89.3
Argentina	ARG	4 143	3.7
Australia	AUS	2 067	4.1
Austria	AUT	1 599	5.5
Bahamas	BHS	178	36.3
Bahrain	BHR	74	8.4
Bangladesh	BGD	2 127	5.2
Barbados	BRB	275	46.1
Belgium	BEL	2 438	5.0
Belize	BLZ	76	23.2
Benin	BEN	215	40.9
Bolivia	BOL	717	6.5
Botswana	BWA	33	4.4
Brazil	BRA	2 288	1.1
Brunei Darussalam	BRN	94	21.9
Bulgaria	BGR	1 856	6.2
Burkina Faso	BFA	65	7.6
Burundi	BDI	71	26.2
Cambodia	KHM	669	24.6
Cameroon	CMR	572	15.5
Canada	CAN	9 946	13.0
Cape Verde	CPV	165	41.7
Central African Republic	CAF	83	20.0
Chad	TCD	69	16.7
Chile	CHL	863	4.8
China	CHN	13 391	1.0
Colombia	COL	3 885	6.2
Comoros	COM	20	14.8
Congo	COG	539	41.6
Congo, Democratic Republic of	COD	350	5.7
Cook Islands	COK	16	53.3
Costa Rica	CRI	340	6.1
Côte d'Ivoire	CIV	261	11.1
Cuba	CUB	5 911	8.2
Cyprus	CYP	627	25.2
Denmark	DNK	1 629	9.4
Djibouti	DJI	25	16.2
Dominica	DMA	58	60.4
Dominican Republic	DOM	1 602	9.3
Ecuador	ECU	970	5.0
Egypt	EGY	7 243	15.8
El Salvador	SLV	833	9.5
Equatorial Guinea	GNQ	78	33.8
Eritrea	ERI	104	32.6
Ethiopia	ETH	633	24.6
Fiji	FJI	382	58.5
Finland	FIN	1 018	5.8
Former Czechoslovakia	CSFR	2 509	
Former USSR	F-USSR	11 360	
Former Yugoslavia	F-YUG	3 772	

Doctors (cont.)

Country of birth	ISO codes	Number of persons working in OECD countries	Expatriation rate
France	FRA	4 131	2.0
Gabon	GAB	57	12.6
Gambia	GMB	46	22.8
Germany	DEU	17 214	5.8
Ghana	GHA	1 469	31.2
Greece	GRC	2 830	5.6
Grenada	GRD	109	72.7
Guatemala	GTM	486	4.7
Guinea	GIN	99	9.1
Guinea-Bissau	GNB	182	49.2
Guyana	GUY	949	72.2
Haiti	HTI	2 209	53.1
Honduras	HND	329	8.2
Hungary	HUN	2 538	7.2
Iceland	ISL	435	29.2
India	IND	55 794	8.0
Indonesia	IDN	2 773	8.6
Iran	IRN	8 991	12.9
Iraq	IRQ	3 730	18.0
Ireland	IRL	4 029	26.6
Israel	ISR	2 436	9.0
Italy	ITA	4 386	1.8
Jamaica	JAM	2 114	48.4
Japan	JPN	2 674	1.1
Jordan	JOR	1 014	8.2
Kenya	KEN	2 385	34.6
Kuwait	KWT	465	11.5
Laos	LAO	331	10.5
Lebanon	LBN	4 552	28.3
Lesotho	LSO	7	7.3
Liberia	LBR	122	54.2
Libya	LBY	592	8.5
Luxembourg	LUX	549	31.3
Madagascar	MDG	889	14.6
Malawi	MWI	162	37.9
Malaysia	MYS	4 679	22.5
Maldives	MDV	6	1.9
Mali	MLI	160	13.2
Malta	MLT	458	26.8
Mauritania	MRT	38	10.8
Mauritius	MUS	725	35.7
Mexico	MEX	4 234	2.1
Mongolia	MNG	39	0.6
Morocco	MAR	6 221	28.0
Mozambique	MOZ	935	64.5
Myanmar	MMR	1 725	8.8
Namibia	NAM	75	11.1
Nepal	NPL	288	5.1
Netherlands	NLD	2 412	4.5
New Zealand	NZL	1 904	17.4
Nicaragua	NIC	722	26.1
Niger	NER	26	6.5
Nigeria	NGA	4 611	11.7
Norway	NOR	712	4.8

Doctors (cont.)

Country of birth	ISO codes	Number of persons working in OECD countries	Expatriation rate
Oman	OMN	23	0.6
Pakistan	PAK	10 505	8.3
Panama	PAN	1 026	18.8
Papua New Guinea	PNG	136	33.1
Paraguay	PRY	283	4.3
Peru	PER	2 546	7.9
Philippines	PHL	15 859	26.4
Poland	POL	5 821	5.8
Portugal	PRT	792	2.2
Qatar	QAT	45	3.3
Romania	ROU	5 182	10.9
Rwanda	RWA	45	10.1
Saint Kitts and Nevis	KNA	15	22.7
Saint Lucia	LCA	39	4.9
Saint Vincent and the Grenadines	VCT	115	53.2
Samoa	WSM	46	27.7
Sao Tome and Principe	STP	71	46.7
Saudi Arabia	SAU	421	1.2
Senegal	SEN	449	43.0
Seychelles	SYC	36	22.9
Sierra Leone	SLE	236	58.4
Singapore	SGP	1 356	19.1
Solomon Islands	SLB	11	16.9
Somalia	SOM	155	33.3
South Africa	ZAF	7 355	17.4
Spain	ESP	2 687	1.9
Sri Lanka	LKA	4 668	30.8
Sudan	SDN	778	9.3
Suriname	SUR	39	17.0
Swaziland	SWZ	9	5.0
Sweden	SWE	1 532	5.0
Switzerland	CHE	1 125	4.2
Syria	SYR	4 721	16.6
Thailand	THA	1 390	5.8
Timor-Leste	TLS	35	30.7
Togo	TGO	153	40.5
Tonga	TON	23	39.7
Trinidad and Tobago	TTO	1 206	54.6
Tunisia	TUN	2 415	15.3
Turkey	TUR	2 311	2.4
United Arab Emirates	ARE	44	0.7
United Kingdom	GBR	17 006	11.3
United Republic of Tanzania	TZA	1 018	55.3
United States	USA	4 354	0.6
Uganda	UGA	1 084	32.9
Uruguay	URY	493	3.8
Vanuatu	VUT	5	20.0
Venezuela	VEN	1 710	3.4
Viet Nam	VNM	7 591	15.2
Yemen	YEM	248	3.5
Zambia	ZMB	567	31.0
Zimbabwe	ZWE	828	28.4

Note: Expatriation rates are computed as follows: X_i number of foreign-born doctors (nurses) working in OECD countries born in country i; Y_i = number of doctors (nurses) working in country i (source WHO Global Health Atlas 1995-2004 average); emigration rate= $X_i/(X_i + Y_i)$.

Connecting with Emigrants
A Global Profile of Diasporas
© OECD 2012

References

Adams, Jr., H. Richard and J. Page (2005), "Do International Migration and Remittances Reduce Poverty in Developing Countries?", *World Development*, Vol. 33, No. 10, pp. 1645-1669.

Adepoju, A. (2010), "The Future of Migration Policies in Africa", Background Paper WMR 2010, International Organization for Migration (IOM), Geneva.

Agunias, D.R. and K. Newland (2012), "Developing a Road Map for Engaging Diasporas in Development. A Handbook for Policymakers and Practitioners in Home and Host Countries", IOM/MPI.

Barro, R. and J.-W. Lee (2010), "A New Data Set of Educational Attainment in the World, 1950-2010", NBER Working Paper No. 15902, Cambridge, MA.

Chaloff, J. (2011), "International Migration to Israel and its Impact", *International Migration Outlook*, OECD Publishing, Paris.

Chaloff, J. (2012), "The Changing Role of Asia in International Migration", *International Migration Outlook*, OECD Publishing, Paris.

Cohen, R. (1997), *Global Diasporas: An Introduction*, University of Washington Press, Seattle, WA.

De Haas, H. (2006), "Engaging Diasporas: How Governments and Development Agencies Can Support Diaspora Involvement in the Development of Origin Countries. A Study for Oxfam", Novib, International Migration Institute, Oxford.

DIAL (2007), "Youth and Labour Markets in Africa: A Literature Review", DT DIAL 2007-02, *www.dial.prd.fr/dial_publications/PDF/Doc_travail/2007-02.pdf*.

Dumont, J.C., J.P. Martin and G. Spielvogel (2007). "Women on the Move: The Neglected Gender Dimension of the Brain Drain", IZA Discussion Paper No. 2920, Bonn.

Dumont, J.C., G. Spielvogel and S. Widmaier (2010), "International Migrants in Developed, Emerging and Developing Countries: An Extended Profile", OECD Social, Employment and Migration Working Paper No. 114, OECD Publishing, Paris.

Ellerman, D. (2006), "The Dynamics of Migration of the Highly Skilled: A Survey of the Literature", in Y. Kuznetsov (ed.), *Diaspora Networks and the International Migration of Skills*, World Bank, Washington, DC.

Escobar Latapi, A. (2010), "The Future of Migration Policies in the Americas", World Migration Report, Background Paper, International Organization for Migration (IOM), Geneva.

European Commission (2005), "Migration and Development: Some Concrete Orientations", COM(2005) 390 final, Communication from the Commission and the Committee of the Regions, Brussels, available at *http://eur-lex.europa.eu/LexUriServ/site/en/com/2005/com2005_0390en01.pdf*, consulted 1 September 2005.

Fajnzylber, P. and J.H. López (2007), *Close to Home, The Development Impact of Remittances in Latin America*, World Bank, Washington, DC.

Hernandez, V., C. Mera, J.-B. Meyer and E. Oteiza (2011), *Circulacion de saberes y movilidades internacionales : perspectivas latinoamericanas*, Editorial Biblos, Buenos Aires.

Khachani, M. and M. Mghari (2009), *L'immigration marocaine en Espagne*, CARIM Project, Analytical & Synthetic Notes, Demographic and Economic Module.

Khadria, B. and J.-B. Meyer (2011), "The Role of Migration in the Restructuring of Innovation Systems/ El papel de la migracion en la reestructuracion de los sistemas de innovacion", *Migration and Development/Migracion y desarrollo*, Vol. 9, No. 16, pp. 81-120.

Koolhaas, M., N. Fiori and A. Pellegrino (2010), "International Skilled Migration Recent Trends and Characteristics: The Case of Latinamericans in Spain and the Unites States", IMDS Working Paper, New Delhi.

Kuznetsov, Y. (ed.) (2006), *Diaspora Networks and the International Migration of Skills*, World Bank, Washington, DC.

Kuznetsov, Y. and F. Torres (2006), "Mexico: Leveraging Migrants' Capital to Develop Hometown Communities", in Y. Kuznetsov (ed.), *Diaspora Networks and the International Migration of Skills*, World Bank, Washington, DC.

Lozano, G. and L. Gandini (2009), "La emigracion de recursos humanos calificados desde paises de America Latina y el Caribe", Latin America and Caribbean Economic System (SELA), International Organization for Migration (IOM), Geneva.

Luchilo, L. (ed.) (2011), *Mas alla de la fuga de cerebros; movilidad, migracion y diasporas de argentinos calificados*, Eudeba, Buenos Aires.

MacRae, M. and M. Wight (2006), "A Model Diaspora Network: The Origin and Evolution of Globalscot", in Y. Kuznetsov (ed.), *Diaspora Networks and the International Migration of Skills*, World Bank, Washington, DC.

Marks, J. (2004), "Expatriate Professionals as an Entry Point into Global Knowledge-Intensive Value Chains: South Africa", Report prepared for the Knowledge Development Program, World Bank Institute, Washington, DC, available at *http://siteresources.worldbank.org/EDUCATION/Resources/278200-1126210664195/1636971-1126210694253/South_Africa_Diasporas.pdf*.

McKenzie, D. and H. Rapoport (2007), "*Self-selection Patterns in Mexico-U.S. Migration: The Role of Migration Networks*", Policy Research Working Paper Series No. 4118, World Bank, Washington, DC.

Meyer, J.-B. (2010), "Human Resource Flows from and between Developing Countries: Implications for Social and Public Policies", in K. Hujo and N. Piper (eds.), *South-South Migration: Implications for Social Policy and Development*, Palgrave/Mac Millan, Basingstoke.

Newland, K. (2010), *Diasporas. New Partners in Global Development Policy*, USAId-MPI, Washington, DC.

Newland, K. and H. Tanaka (2010), *Mobilizing Diaspora Entrepreneurship for Development*, Migration Policy Institute, Washington, DC.

OECD (2005), *Migration, Remittances and Development*, OECD Publishing, Paris.

OECD (2008a), *The Looming Crisis in the Health Workforce. How Can OECD Countries Respond?*, OECD Publishing, Paris.

OECD (2008b), *International Migration Outlook*, OECD Publishing, Paris.

OECD (2010), *Latin American Economic Outlook 2010*, OECD, Development Centre, OECD Publishing, Paris.

OECD (2011), *International Migration Outlook*, OECD Publishing, Paris.

OECD (2012), *International Migration Outlook*, OECD Publishing, Paris.

OSCE (2009), *Impact of the Global Financial Crisis on Labour Migration from Kyrgyzstan to Russia*, Bishkek.

Plaza, S. and D. Ratha (2011), *Diaspora for Development in Africa*, World Bank, New York.

Putnam, R.D. (1993), "The Prosperous Community: Social Capital and Public Life", *The American Prospect*, Vol. 13, pp. 35-42.

Ratha, D. (2007), "Leveraging Remittances for Development", MPI Policy Brief, Washington DC, June.

Sander, C. (2003), "Capturing a Market Share? Migrant Remittances and Money Transfers as a Microfinance Service in Sub-Sahara Africa", *Small Enterprise Development*, Vol. 15, Bath University, United Kingdom, pp. 20-34.

Sheffer, G. (ed.) (1986), *Modern Diasporas in International Politics*, Croom Helm, Sydney.

Terrazas, A. (2010), *Connected Through Service: Diaspora Volunteers and Global Development*, Migration Policy Institute, Washington, DC.

United Nations, Department of Economic and Social Affairs, Population Division (2009), "Trends in International Migrant Stock: The 2008 Revision", Retrieved 10 January 2011, available online: *http://esa.un.org/migration/index.asp?panel=4*.

Wickramasekara, P. (2009), "Diasporas and Development: Perspectives on Definitions and Contributions", *Perspectives on Labour Migration*, No. 9, International Labour Office, Social Protection Sector, International Migration Programme, ILO, Geneva.

Widmaier, S. and J.C. Dumont (2011), "Are Recent Immigrants Different? A New Profile of Immigrants in the OECD (DIOC 2005/06)", OECD Social, Employment and Migration Working Paper No. 126, OECD Publishing, Paris.

World Bank (2009), *A Long-Term Perspective of People and Job Mobility for the Middle East and North Africa*, Washington, DC.

World Bank (2011), *Migration and Remittances Factbook*, Washington, DC.

ORGANISATION FOR ECONOMIC CO-OPERATION AND DEVELOPMENT

The OECD is a unique forum where governments work together to address the economic, social and environmental challenges of globalisation. The OECD is also at the forefront of efforts to understand and to help governments respond to new developments and concerns, such as corporate governance, the information economy and the challenges of an ageing population. The Organisation provides a setting where governments can compare policy experiences, seek answers to common problems, identify good practice and work to co-ordinate domestic and international policies.

The OECD member countries are: Australia, Austria, Belgium, Canada, Chile, the Czech Republic, Denmark, Estonia, Finland, France, Germany, Greece, Hungary, Iceland, Ireland, Israel, Italy, Japan, Korea, Luxembourg, Mexico, the Netherlands, New Zealand, Norway, Poland, Portugal, the Slovak Republic, Slovenia, Spain, Sweden, Switzerland, Turkey, the United Kingdom and the United States. The European Union takes part in the work of the OECD.

OECD Publishing disseminates widely the results of the Organisation's statistics gathering and research on economic, social and environmental issues, as well as the conventions, guidelines and standards agreed by its members.

OECD PUBLISHING, 2, rue André-Pascal, 75775 PARIS CEDEX 16
(81 2012 08 1 P) ISBN 978-92-64-17793-2 – No. 60227 2012